FAIRWA

Schott's Miscellany

2008

LIBER PRAETERITORUM ET POSTERITATIS CARMEN

An Almanac

Everyone spoke of information overload,
but what there was, in fact, was a non-information overload.
— RICHARD SAUL WURMAN, *What-If, Could-Be*, 1976

Published by Bloomsbury USA, New York
175 Fifth Avenue, New York, NY 10010, USA
Distributed to the trade by Holtzbrinck Publishers

www.benschott.com

First US Edition 2007

1 2 3 4 5 6 7 8 9 10

NOTE · Information included within is believed to be correct at
the time of going to press. Neither the author nor the publisher
can accept any responsibility for any error or subsequent changes.

ISBN-10 1-59691-382-7 · ISBN-13 978-1-59691-382-0

Library of Congress Cataloging-in-Publication Data have been applied for.

All papers used by Bloomsbury USA are natural, recyclable products made from
wood grown in well-managed forests. The manufacturing processes conform to
the environmental regulations of the country of origin.

Designed and typeset by BEN SCHOTT
Printed in the USA by QUEBECOR WORLD FAIRFIELD

* * * *

Also by BEN SCHOTT

Schott's Original Miscellany
Schott's Food & Drink Miscellany
Schott's Sporting, Gaming, & Idling Miscellany
Schott's Miscellany Diary (with Smythson of Bond St, London)
Schott's Almanac Page-A-Day® Calendar (Workman Publishing Co.)
British and German Editions of *Schott's Miscellany* are also available.

Schott's Miscellany

2008

An Almanac

LIBER PRAETERITORUM ET POSTERITATIS CARMEN

· *The book of things past and the song of the future* ·

Conceived, edited, and designed by

BEN SCHOTT

US Editor · Bess Lovejoy

UK & Series Editor · Claire Cock-Starkey
German Editor · Alexander Weber
Researcher · James Matthews

BLOOMSBURY

Preface

A calendar, a calendar! look in the almanack;
find out moonshine, find out moonshine.
— A Midsummer Night's Dream, III, i

Completely revised and updated (and slightly renamed), *Schott's Miscellany* 2008 picks up from where the 2007 *Schott's Almanac* left off, to create a seamless biography of the year. ❦ The journalist and screenwriter Ben Hecht (1894–1964) once said that 'trying to determine what is going on in the world by reading newspapers is like trying to tell the time by watching the second hand of a clock'. *Schott's Miscellany* aspires to follow the minute hand of world events – stepping back from the barrage of rolling news to offer an informative, selective, and entertaining analysis of the year. ❦ The C21st almanac is necessarily different from its distinguished predecessors [see p.6], which were published in times when the year was defined by matters astronomical, ecclesiastical, or aristocratic. By exploring high art and pop culture, geopolitics and gossip, scientific discovery and sporting achievement, *Schott's Miscellany* endeavors to describe the year as it is lived, in all its complexity.

— *Schott's Miscellany* is an almanac written to be read.

─────────────── THE MISCELLANY'S YEAR ───────────────

In order to be as inclusive as possible, the *Schott's Miscellany* year runs until late August.

Data cited in *Schott's Miscellany* are taken from the latest sources available at the time of writing.

─────────────── CHERISH TRUTH, PARDON ERROR ───────────────

Every effort has been taken to ensure that the information contained within *Schott's Miscellany* is both accurate and up-to-date, and grateful acknowledgment is made to the various sources used. However, as Goethe once said: 'Error is to truth as sleep is to waking'. Consequently, the author would be pleased to be informed of any errors, inaccuracies, or omissions that might help improve future editions.

Please send all comments or suggestions to the author, care of:

Bloomsbury USA, 175 Fifth Avenue, New York, NY 10010, USA
or email *editor@schottsalmanac.com*

In keeping with most newspapers and journals, *Schott's Miscellany* will publish any significant corrections and clarifications each year in its Errata section [see p.368].

Contents

—————————— EARLY ALMANACS OF NOTE ——————————

Solomon Jarchi.................. *c.*1150	Zainer (at Ulm) 1478
Peter de Dacia................... *c.*1300	Francis Moore's Almanack.1698–1713
John Somers (Oxford) 1380	Poor Richard's Almanack 1732
Nicholas de Lynna 1386	Almanach de Gotha............... 1764
Purbach..................... 1150–1461	The Old Farmer's Almanac 1792
After the invention of printing	Whitaker's Almanack 1868
Gutenberg (at Mainz)............. 1457	The World Almanac 1868
Regiomontanus (at Nuremberg) .1474	Information Please Almanac...... 1947

————— 'MISCELLANY' & 'ALMANAC' vs 'ALMANACK' —————

The *Oxford English Dictionary* (*OED*) defines 'miscellany' as 'a mixture, medley, or assortment; (a collection of) miscellaneous objects or items' – noting the word is now commonly used to describe 'separate articles, treatises, or other studies on a subject collected into one volume; literary compositions of various kinds brought together to form a book'. [The word derives from the Latin 'miscellanea'.] The *OED* credits Ben Jonson with an early use of the term in *The Fountaine of Selfe-Love* (1601), in which he wrote, 'As a miscellany madame [I would] inuent new tyres, and goe visite courtiers'. The American pronunciation of 'miscellany' – stressing the first syllable [*mis*–el–any] – may be the most authentic. According to the *OED*, the modern British pronunciation which stresses the second syllable [mi–*sel*–any] might reflect a later trend in the pronunciation of four-syllable words like 'accompany', 'epiphany', and 'mahogany'. ❦ The spelling and etymology of 'almanac' are disputed. The *OED* cites an early use of 'almanac' by Roger Bacon in 1267, though Chaucer used 'almenak' in *c.*1391; and Shakespeare, 'almanack' in 1590. Variations include almanach(e), amminick, almanacke, &c. A number of etymologies for *almanac* have been suggested: that it comes from the Arabic *al* [the] *mana(h)* [reckoning or diary]; that it comes from the Anglo-Saxon *al-moan-heed* ['to wit, the regard or observations of all the moons'], or from the Anglo-Saxon *al-monath* [all the months]; or that it is linked to the Latin *manachus* [sundial]. In 1838, *Murphy's Almanac* made the prediction that January 20, 1838, would be 'Fair, prob. lowest deg. of winter temp'. When, on the day, this actually turned out to be true, *Murphy's Almanac* became a best seller.

——————— SYMBOLS & ABBREVIATIONS ———————

> ....greater than	≈ .... approximately equal to
≥ .... greater than or equal to	km............................ kilometer
< .... less than	m .... meter
≤ .... less than or equal to	mi.................................mile
♂ ....male/men	'/" .... feet (ft)/inches (in)
♀........................ female/women	C................... century (e.g. C20th)
c...... *circa*, meaning around or roughly	m/bn .... million/billion

Throughout the *Miscellany*, figures may not add to totals because of rounding.

Chronicle

So the little minutes, Humble though they be,
Make the mighty ages Of eternity.
— JULIA CARNEY, *Little Things*, 1845

──────── SOME AWARDS OF NOTE ────────

TIME Magazine Person of the Year [2006]
'YOU'
'for seizing the reins of the global media, for founding and framing the new digital
democracy, for working for nothing and beating the pros at their own game'

Scripps National Spelling Bee . . . . Evan O'Dorney (13 years old), CA
Librarian of the Year . . . . Mary Baykan, Maryland
Miss Universe . . . . Riyo Mori, Japan
World's Sexiest Vegetarian [PETA] . . . . Carrie Underwood
Eclipse Award for Horse of the Year [2006] . . . . Invasor
Bachelor of the Year [*People*] . . . . Matthew McConaughey
Intel Science Talent Search . . . . Mary Masterman (17 years old), OK
Reuben Award for Outstanding Cartoonist of the Year . . . . Bill Amend, *FoxTrot*
UNESCO Prize for Peace Education [2006] . . . . . Christopher Gregory Weeramantry
Wine of the Year [2006] . . . . .Casanova di Neri, Brunello di Montalcino, 2001
Australian of the Year . . . . Professor Tim Flannery (environmentalist)
Car of the Year [caroftheyear.org] . . . . Ford S-Max
Airline of the Year [Skytrax] . . . . Singapore Airlines
Best Cat [The Cat Fanciers' Association] . . . . Melositos White Owl of D'Eden Lover
Most Anticipated Gadget of 2007, Reader's Choice [Engadget] . . . . Apple iPhone
World Barista Champion . . . . James Hoffman, UK
Bookseller of the Year [*Publishers Weekly*] . . . . .Changing Hands Bookstore, Tempe, AZ
National Teacher of the Year . . . . Andrea Peterson, Washington
Entertainers of the Year [*Entertainment Weekly* · 2006] . . . . cast of *Grey's Anatomy*
ISAF World Sailor of the Year [2006] . . . . Paige Railey, USA · Mike Sanderson, NZ
Eagle Scout of the Year . . . . Welland Dane Burnside, South Carolina

──────── DOUBLESPEAK AWARD ────────

The National Council of Teachers of English annually bestows its Doublespeak
Award upon an American public figure who has 'perpetuated language that is grossly
deceptive, evasive, euphemistic, confusing, or self-contradictory'. The Council gave
its 2006 Award to President Bush, for a September 15, 2005, speech on Hurricane
Katrina in which Bush pledged to 'confront poverty' – one week after issuing an
executive order that allowed federal contractors to pay area workers lower wages.

——————MISC. LISTS OF 2007—————— · —2008 WORDS—

MADAME TUSSAUDS
New wax figures at Madame Tussauds, New York

———

David Wright
Rachael Ray
Bullseye the Target dog†
David & Victoria Beckham‡ [see p.251]
Aishwarya Rai‡
Justin Timberlake‡
Christina Aguilera‡
Princes William & Harry‡

———

† The Target mascot; a wax figure launched Oct 2006
‡ On temporary loan from Madame Tussauds, London

WORDS TO BANISH
Each year since 1976, Lake Superior State University has produced a list of words to be stricken from the language, based on suggestions from around the globe

———

'ask your doctor'
'awesome' · 'boasts'
(used as replacement for 'possesses') · chipotle combined celeb names
(i.e. TomKat) · 'Gitmo'
'gone/went missing'
(is missing a place one can visit?) · 'healthy' food
'i-'anything
'now playing in theaters'
'pwn' or 'pwned' (gaming speak for 'own') · 'search'
(might as well say 'Google')
'undocumented alien'
'we're pregnant'

BEST MEN
AskMen.com's list of the 'best representatives of the male gender'

———

1	George Clooney
2	Jay-Z
3	Richard Branson
4	Lance Armstrong
5	Tom Ford
6	Jerry Bruckheimer
7	Johnny Depp
8	David Beckham
9	Jorge Perez
10	Bill Clinton

THE MOST EXPENSIVE CITIES *according to CNNMoney.com*

———

1	Moscow
2	London
3	Seoul
4	Tokyo
5	Hong Kong
6	Copenhagen
7	Geneva
8	Osaka
9	Zurich
10	Oslo

'DREAM' SCHOOLS
The top choices for college applicants, according to the Princeton Review

———

1	NYU
2	Harvard
3	Stanford
4	Princeton
5	Columbia
6	Yale
7	UCLA
8	Brown
9	Georgetown
10	U. Pennsylvania

The following words celebrate anniversaries in 2008, based upon the earliest cited use traced by the venerable *Oxford English Dictionary*:

{1508} *voluptuousness* (being voluptuous)
{1608} *monarchizer* (one who advocates monarchy) · *sugar-plum* (something given as a sop) · *wenchless* (lacking wenches)
{1708} *auctioneer* (one who conducts auctions) · *dendrology* (the study of trees) · *stakeholder* (one who keeps stake money secure) {1808} *barium* (the element) · *Falstaffian* (resembling Shakespeare's Falstaff) · *gas-light* (the light of a gas lamp) · *hoax* (a naughty deception) · *koala* (the marsupial) · *piano-player* (a pianist) · {1908} *bejesus* (an Anglo-Irish oath) · *dead man's handle* (the control of an electric train) · *strap-hang* (to hold on to train or bus straps) {1958} *Afro-Caribbean* · *bootstrap* (computer initiation) · *doner kebab* (the Turkish dish) · *Gedankenexperiment* (a thought experiment) · *nanosecond* (one thousand-millionth of a second) · *sheepshagger* (one who …) {1998} *Bluetooth* (radio technology) · *chav* (disparaging term for disaffected young member of the British urban underclass)

SOME SURVEY RESULTS OF 2006–07

%	result *(of American adults, unless otherwise stated)*	source & month
92	want 'country of origin' labels on food packaging [see pp.220–21]	[Consumer Reports; Jul]
87	believe an innocent person has been executed in the previous 15 years	[DPIC; Jun]
85	of women would rather reveal their age than their weight	[GfK Roper; Mar]
84	of workers do not have their dream job	[CareerBuilder.com; Jan]
81	of adults think smoking in films encourages children [see p.139]	[AMA; Feb]
73	of men choose a luxury label when buying a handbag	[Luxury Institute; May]
72	think bad service is the greatest irritant when dining in restaurants	[Zagat; Nov 06]
71	believe Congress must do more to 'deal with' illegal immigrants	[Quinnipiac; Nov 06]
71	think the US is not respected around the world today [see p.31]	[CBS News; Jun]
68	of fathers have talked to their sons about violence-free relationships	[Hart Rsrch; Jun]
68	predict a civil war in Iraq if the US withdraws in 2008	[*USA Today*/Gallup; May]
68	think circumstances exist where a patient should be allowed to die	[AP/Ipsos; May]
67	consider full-fat ice cream to be 'worth the guilt'	[Harris Interactive; Jul]
67	admit using a wireless device to contact work when on vacation	[Yahoo!/HotJobs; Apr]
65	spend more time with their home computer than their spouse	[Kelton Research; Jan]
62	fly the Stars and Stripes at home, in the office, or in their car	[Pew Research Center; Jul]
60	believe smokers should pay higher health insurance premiums	[Health Affairs; Nov 06]
58	have no homosexual friends or relatives	[Pew Research Center; May]
57	drink coffee every day	[National Coffee Association; Mar]
57	oppose allowing cell phones to be used during flights	[Maritz Research; Jul]
56	of bosses give their employees holiday season presents	[CareerBuilder.com; Dec 06]
56	believe homosexuals cannot change their sexual orientation	[CNN; Jul]
51	of global CEOs have made a conference call wearing a bathrobe, or less	[Avaya; Jul]
49	of women would want to know the sex of their unborn baby (45% of men)	[Gallup; Jul]
47	believe that 'nearly everything causes cancer'	[AACR/National Cancer Institute; May]
47	of *Harry Potter* fans predicted he would survive the final book [see p.166]	[Zogby; Jul]
45	of female executives think playing golf improves a child's self-confidence	[HSBC; Jul]
44	of adults plan to make a New Year's resolution	[WNBC; Dec 06]
34	had encountered/overheard improper sexual remarks at work	[Novations Group; Mar]
34	of college graduates accept as fact the Biblical story of creation	[*Newsweek*; Mar]
33	changed summer vacation plans because of gas prices [see p.30]	[Quinnipiac Uni; Jun]
32	of large US companies employ people to read employee emails	[Proofpoint; Jul]
31	of Southern state residents would not evacuate if a hurricane struck	[Harvard; Jul]
30	of extramarital affairs last a week or less (47% are finished within a month)	[MSNBC; Apr]
24	of home improvers would make environmentally friendly changes	[Wells Fargo; Oct 06]
22	of high school students say they have considered dropping out	[Indiana University; Feb]
21	of women are unable to resist peeking at their Christmas presents	[Harris Int.; Dec 06]
17	of women have felt sexually harassed at work	[Harris Interactive; Jun]
16	of Hurricane Katrina survivors report mental health problems	[Kaiser; May]
15	have neither an internet connection nor a cell phone	[Pew Research Center; May]
15	abstained from sex until they were at least 21	[NCHS; Jun]
13	of US Muslims said that suicide attacks might be justified	[Pew Research Center; May]
11	know the recommended number of calories to consume daily	[IFIC; May]
7	are prepared for a disaster or emergency	[American Red Cross/Harris Interactive; Apr]
5	have been diagnosed with a food allergy	[FDA; Jun]

—————————————— SIGNIFICA · 2007 ——————————————

Some (in)significa(nt) footnotes to the year. ❦ Former US Secretary of State Lawrence S. Eagleburger has three sons: Lawrence S. Eagleburger II, Lawrence A. Eagleburger, and Lawrence J. Eagleburger. ❦ The Human Genome Organization announced that genes given unusual names, such as 'lunatic fringe', 'faint sausage', and 'mothers against decapentaplegia (MAD)', would be renamed in order to avoid awkward doctor–patient conversations, should the genes be linked to defects. ❦ A

Tennessee man running for Senate legally changed his middle name to 'None of the Above', in a bid to appeal to disenchanted voters. ❦ According to *New Scientist*, all of the gold mined in history (193,000 tons) would fit inside a cube with sides 22 meters long. ❦ A *60 Minutes* investigation discovered that Saddam Hussein, Zacarias Moussaoui, and 14 of the (dead) 9/11 hijackers were still barred from travel by the federal 'No Fly' list. ❦ Press reports revealed that Clint Eastwood's *In the Line of Fire* and Whitney Houston's *The Bodyguard* are some of North Korean leader Kim Jong-il's favorite films; he was said also to enjoy James Bond and Godzilla movies [see p.76]. ❦ Mitch Daniels, George W. Bush's first budget director, tried (and failed) to get the Office of Management and Budget to use *You Can't Always Get What You Want* by the Rolling Stones as its hold music. ❦ Barbie's full name is Barbara Millicent Roberts, and she apparently owns 38 pets, including cats, dogs, horses, a panda, a lion cub, and a zebra. ❦ A pearl earring lost by Marlene Dietrich 73 years ago was found by workmen when they drained a lake under the Big Dipper ride at Britain's Blackpool Pleasure Beach. The workmen also recovered three sets of false teeth, a glass eye, a toupée, a bra, and *c.*$170 in (very) loose change. ❦ According to the US Census Bureau, more people are injured each year by wheelchairs than lawn mowers. ❦ A Portuguese aristocrat bequeathed his entire fortune to 70 strangers picked at random from a telephone directory. A close friend suggested he wanted to 'create confusion'. ❦ A couple from Michigan received packages in the mail containing a liver and a human ear, instead of the table legs they had bid for on eBay. ❦ Research by Bosch indicated that the average British woman will vacuum a distance of 7,300 miles over the course of her lifetime; men will vacuum only 850 miles. ❦ Marvel Comics killed off Captain America in the last installment of the comic; the 'pinnacle of human perfection' was shot three times by a sniper. ❦ Three schoolgirls were suspended from John Jay High School, New York, for saying the word 'vagina' during a reading of Eve Ensler's *The Vagina Monologues*. ❦ Beijing announced plans to replace poorly translated English road signs in advance of the 2008 Summer Olympics, depriving the city of such classics as: '*To take notice of safe: the slippery are very crafty*', and '*Show mercy to the slender grass*'. ❦ The US Postal Service removed clocks in 37,000 post offices nationwide, in an effort to persuade 'people to focus on the postal service and not the clock'. ❦ 171 Swiss soldiers accidentally invaded Liechtenstein during a night-training exercise; the government of Liechtenstein admitted it had not noticed. ❦ At 30,000 square feet, the red carpet at the Golden Globes was the longest red carpet of any Hollywood awards ceremony. ❦ Colonel Muammar Gaddafi called for every Italian (all 59m of them) to undergo DNA testing, to ascertain if any were descendents of the 3,500 Libyans deported to Italy in 1911.

—————————— SIGNIFICA · 2007 cont. ——————————

Gaddafi promised full Libyan citizenship to all descendents. ❧ James Doohan (Scotty from *Star Trek*) had his last wish fulfilled when his cremated remains were blasted into orbit in a capsule with the ashes of 200 other Earthlings. The capsule eventually fell to Earth, and was found three weeks later in New Mexico. ❧ The cocktail of choice for Princes William and Harry was reported to be the 'Treasure Chest' – half a liter of vodka and a bottle of champagne poured into a wooden box filled with juice, ice cubes, and chopped fruit. ❧ Hyperinflation in Zimbabwe became so rampant [see pp.26–27] that golfers habitually paid for their drinks before they set off on a round because, by the time they reached the 19th hole, the prices had gone up. ❧ The Japanese island of Iwo Jima reverted to its original name, Iwo To. Both names are written using the same two Japanese characters – and both mean Sulphur Island – but they are pronounced differently. ❧ According to Halifax Home Insurance, the number of windows broken in the UK rises by 20% during the Wimbledon fortnight, as youngsters around the country attempt to emulate their tennis heroes. ❧ Mika Brzezinski, a news anchor on MSNBC's *Morning Joe*, repeatedly refused to read a story about Paris Hilton's release from jail. Ms Brzezinski crumpled her script into a ball, tried to burn it, and eventually put it through a paper shredder. ❧ To fill a shortfall in recruitment, US Army personnel who identify a prospective recruit (other than an immediate family member) were promised a $2,000 bounty [see p.269]. ❧ A German performance-art student dressed as one of China's 2,000-year-old terracotta warriors, and posed among the statues for several minutes before being discovered by police. ❧ According to political strategists in the 2006 book *Applebee's America*, Republicans prefer to drink Coors beer, shop at Target, and read *US News and World Report*; Democrats are more likely to enjoy Starbucks, read *TV Guide*, and drive Saabs. ❧ President Bush invited incoming House Speaker Nancy Pelosi for lunch at the White House. They dined on pasta salad as a tribute to Pelosi's Italian heritage, and ate a dessert ominously called 'chocolate freedom'. ❧ In an effort to improve civic order, Beijing began celebrating 'Queuing Day' on the 11th of each month. Those who waited patiently in line were rewarded with long-stemmed roses. ❧  Former Roswell Airbase press officer Lieutenant Walter Haut, who spent much of his career denying conspiracy theories, left a sworn affidavit to be opened after his death. In the statement, Haut asserted that the 'weather balloon claim' was a cover story for a crashed UFO and 'small humanoid extraterrestrials'. ❧ Belgian TV channel RTBF hoaxed people into believing that, following a unilateral declaration of independence by Flanders, Belgium had split. The station interrupted its programming with the spoof newsflash at 8·21pm, but was forced to broadcast the message '*This is fiction*' at 8·50pm, following widespread viewer panic. ❧ Nancy Pelosi's spokesperson revealed the House Speaker is a 'huge Grateful Dead fan'. ❧ A Moscow exhibition of gifts presented to Russian leaders 1921–90 featured a 1930s portrait of Lenin made entirely from human hair. ❧ Waltzing was added to the national curriculum in China, in an effort to combat child obesity. ❧ In an attempt to break the world record, Brazilian Claudio Paulo Pinto stretched his eyeballs 0·3" out of their sockets (sadly, he failed; the world record is 0·43").

————————————— WORDS OF THE YEAR —————————————

STOP · the final word of the final episode of *The Sopranos* – from Journey's *Don't Stop Believin'* – which could be heard on a jukebox as the screen faded to black.

SURGE · term used to describe Bush's deployment of an extra 21,500 troops to Iraq, part of the NEW WAY FORWARD.

PANSURGENCY · global terror threat, defined by the US National War College as a strategy to 'incite worldwide insurgencies to overthrow Western ideals and replace them with a new world order under radical views of Islam'.

MASSTIGE · retail marriage of mass and prestige (e.g. *Viktor & Rolf* for H&M).

PHILANTHROPRENEURS · sponsors of nonprofit ventures; often young tech billionaires. *Also* FILMANTHROPISTS · philanthropists who finance socially aware films. *Also* MINIGARCH · not quite an oligarch (annual income ≤$50m).

DEEP SHALLOW · description by Rep. Congressman Rob Bishop of the nonbinding resolution on the Iraq war. [The term comes from the musical *Wicked*.]

TORTURE PORN · misogynist (horror) films that frequently depict sexualized violence against women. *Also* GORNO · excessively violent films (e.g. *Hostel*).

CHRISTIANISM · analogue of Islamism.

A THUMPING · Bush's description of the GOP's 2006 midterm [see p.16].

PRETEXTING · use of false pretenses to obtain information. The term gained currency in 2006, after investigators for Hewlett-Packard allegedly used pretexting to get private phone records.

SARKONAUTES · supporters of French President Nicolas Sarkozy.

ONESICKMANSHIP · game played by hypochondriacal men during a woman's menstrual cycle. *Also* BEERIODS · male periods (caused by alcoholic excess). *Also* MOOBS · man boobs. *Also* MITS · man tits. *Also* THE MALE MENOPAUNCH · the dreaded beer-gut of middle age. *Also* MANCATION · an all-male holiday. *Also* BROMANCE · platonic male-only relationships. *Also* MANBAND · an older, more mature, or reformed, boyband.

ZOEBOTS · followers of stylist Rachel Zoe – including Nicole Richie, Lindsay Lohan, and Mischa Barton.

FED-EX · nickname for Kevin Federline after his divorce from Britney Spears.

PEERENTS · parents who aspire to be like their children's peers.

5 S's · graduated escalation of force, said to be part of the US military's Iraq rules of engagement: *Shout; Show weapon; Shove; Shoot to warn; Shoot to kill.*

NASHI ['*Ours*' in Russian] · a jingoistic pro-Putin Russian youth group. Nashi claims to be anti-Fascist, though its thuggish track record has led some to warn of the threat from NASHISM.

BURQINI · full-length swimsuit for Muslim women [see p.338]. MANKINI · male swimsuit, à la Borat [see p.150].

PITCH BEAST · animals used in advertising: usually cute, like penguins.

9818783 · Paris Hilton's inmate number at the Century Regional Detention Facility in Lynwood, CA.

———— WORDS OF THE YEAR cont. ————

VULTURE FUNDS · companies that buy cheap the debt of poor countries, and then sue for the full sum, plus interest.

TREATED AS: TOP SECRET · an apparently new security designation that the secrecy-minded Dick Cheney devised, and places on even routine paperwork, according to the *Washington Post*.

SHOCK & JAW · the Imus affair over his slur, 'NAPPY-HEADED HOs' [See p.20].

PIED PIPERS OF PERFORMANCE · Warren Buffett's caustic description of hedge fund (and other) managers who demand ever-greater commissions and fees in an attempt to increase returns. *Also* HEDGE HOGS · wealthy hedge fund managers.

CHILD DECOYS · children (and sometimes women) used by insurgents in Iraq to deflect the attention of the security forces away from car bombs.

THE ELDERS · a group of senior statesmen, funded by Richard Branson, who will act as international troubleshooters: Nelson Mandela, Jimmy Carter, Mary Robinson, Desmond Tutu, and Mohammed Yunus [see p.66].

NINJA LOANS · Unsafe loans made to those with '*No Income, No Job, and No Assets*' – see SUBPRIME on p.30.

SCROTUM · a word that caused a storm when it appeared on the first page of Susan Patron's children's book *The Higher Power of Lucky*. Bizarrely, some libraries banned the book – even though the reference was to canine genitalia.

MOREGEOISIE · consumers who strive to attain more than others.

GUT FEELING · Homeland Security chief Michael Chertoff's basis for believing the US would face a heightened security threat in summer 2007.

BECLOWN · to embarrass oneself by pontificating out of ignorance.

BULLY TV · shows that glorify bullies: *The Apprentice, The Weakest Link*, &c.

GLAMPING · glamorous camping.

GHOST FLIGHTS · empty aircraft flown to secure key airport 'runway slots'.

NEWPEAT · a TV episode edited to include previously unseen material.

SLURB · suburban area with poor housing (a mixture of SLum and subURB).

GO HANG! · Mugabe's defiant imprecation to those who criticized his violent crackdown on the opposition [see p.26].

GLOCAL *and* GLOCALIZATION · when global companies aspire to respect local customs and sensitivities.

THE ANTI-RUMSFELD · new Defense Sec. Robert Gates, whose character and style are said to differ markedly from his abrasive predecessor, Donald Rumsfeld.

RED CELL TEAMS · security analysts who imagine novel forms of terrorism.

GORACLE · fan nickname for Al Gore. *Conversely* AL BORE · derisive reference to Gore's ECO-VANGELISM.

FREDO · The weakest and dumbest of the Corleone brothers in *The Godfather*. Bush's nickname for (now ex-) Attorney General Alberto Gonzales [see p.27].

─────────── WORDS OF THE YEAR cont. ───────────

GIFT · Iranian President's description of his release of British sailors [see p.27].

MULTIMEDIA MANIFESTO · See p.24.

THE MOTHER OF ALL TARGETS · Prince Harry, who was said to have been targeted by insurgents as he planned to join his regiment in Iraq.

POVERTARIAN · one who works in the 'poverty industry'.

SANDBOX SAILORS · US Naval (and, by extension, Air Force) personnel supplementing Army numbers in Iraq.

FoHo · Folk Bohemian fashion.

BULLYCIDE · the suicide of a child who has been bullied or harassed to death. *Also* E-THUGS · cyber-bullies [see p.199].

DARK TOURISM · travel to places associated with death, destruction, poverty, or tragedy. *Also* SLUM TOURISM.

PROSTITOTS · children who are dressed in sexually inappropriate clothing.

AGEOREXIA · ageorexia is to age, as anorexia is to weight.

GRAYFEVER · urban hayfever.

OBAMANATIONS · Barack Obama's gaffes and 'slips of the tongue' (e.g. announcing the deaths of 10,000 people in Kansas tornado, when the toll was just 12).

STUNT EATING · eating for media attention: [1] by celebrities, to disprove allegations of anorexia; [2] by officials, to reassure consumers about the safety of a food (e.g. poultry, post-avian flu); [3] by authors, to promote special diets.

LOCAVORES · those who eat only locally grown food.

QUIET RIOT · Obama's description of growing African American discontent.

SECURITY THEATER · the pretense of (airport) security.

72ed · Jihadi slang for death; a reference to the number of virgins that martyrs believe will greet them in Paradise.

FAMILY JEWELS · declassified documents relating to the CIA's extrajudicial 'black-ops' from the 1950s–70s.

AGFLATION · inflation in agriculture prices and, therefore, food.

RICHISTAN · the bubble of wealth the über-rich inhabit. *Also* BIZARRISTAN · Turkmenistan under (now dead) President Niyazov. *Also* OUTSOURCISTAN · areas dependent on outsourced contracts.

SeDS · Sedentary Death Syndrome · ailments and diseases caused or exacerbated by chronic inactivity.

FACTINESS · selective use of 'facts' as a political weapon, coined by Stephen Colbert in response to the Democrats' midterm victory.

WATER NEUTRAL · ensuring water-use is sustainable and recyclable.

SANDWICH GENERATION · those caring for young children and elderly parents at the same time.

THE SPLASHER · unknown assailant(s) defacing street art in NYC with splatterings of paint – supposedly attacking 'the commodification of art'.

———OBJECT OF THE YEAR: THE LIGHT BULB———

After 127 years in the spotlight, incandescent light bulbs may soon fade into history, as a host of initiatives seek to turn lighting eco-friendly. In February 2007, Australia announced that stricter energy standards would ban incandescent bulbs by 2010, forcing consumers to buy alternatives, like compact fluorescent light bulbs (CFLs). Australia's Environment Minister said, 'if the whole world switched to these bulbs today, we would reduce our consumption of electricity by an amount equal to five times Australia's annual consumption of electricity'. For a country that refused to sign the Kyoto Protocol, Australia's nationwide ban was dramatic and bold, but it was not made in isolation. In November 2006, Wal-Mart announced a campaign to sell 100m CFLs by 2008. In January 2007, a Bill was proposed to ban the sale of incandescents in California by 2012. In February 2007, similar legislation was proposed in a number of other US states. In March 2007, Philips announced it would phase out incandescents by 2016. In the same month, the EU discussed a ban on such bulbs by 2010. In April 2007, Canada imposed a federal ban on incandescents from 2012. ❦ Although dozens of people played a part in the invention of the light bulb (including Joseph Swan and Humphrey Davy), history's laurels rest on the head of Thomas Edison, not least because of his US Patent #223898, filed 1/27/1880. In fundamental design, the modern incandescent – with its finely coiled filament set within an inert-gas-filled glass bulb – differs little from those pioneered in the C19th. And, despite a range of modifications, incandescents still emit only 5% of the energy they consume as light; the rest is wasted as heat. CFLs are filled with a gas that emits UV light when excited by electricity. In turn, this UV light causes the bulb's interior coating to emit light visible to the human eye. Compared to incandescents, CFLs are 4× more efficient, last up to 10× longer, consume 50–80% less energy, and produce 75% less heat. And, although CFLs are currently more expensive to buy, the US Dept of Energy claims that >$30 in electricity can be saved over the lifetime of *each* bulb. ❦ While the cost- and energy-saving arguments for CFLs are powerful, public acceptance has been hindered by a sense that the quality of light CFLs emit is insufficiently 'soothing' or 'natural' – the so-called 'wife test'. Furthermore, because CFLs contain mercury, the safe disposal of spent or broken bulbs can be more complex and expensive. As the obligation to use CFLs becomes more widespread, it is clear that their price, quality, and ease of safe disposal will all have to improve. Indeed, they are likely to face competition from other forms of eco-lighting, such as light emitting diodes (LEDs). ❦ The demise of incandescents is part of a series of low-level 'eco-hardships' which are (more or less) consumer-approved or even consumer-driven. Other eco-hardships include removing 'standby' modes from appliances; charging for plastic bags (or banning them altogether, as in San Francisco); charging for the collection of (unrecyclable) waste; pricing drivers off congested roads; encouraging people to turn down domestic thermostats; &c. It remains to be seen, however, whether these individual acts can have an aggregate effect sufficient to counter environmental damage at an industrial and governmental level.

——————————2006 MIDTERM ELECTIONS——————————

In a dramatic rejection of the scandal-mired Republicans, the Democrats took control of the House of Representatives and the Senate at the November 2006 midterms. The result was a serious blow to the power and reputation of President George W. Bush – who was forced to accept the resignation of his controversial and bombastic Secretary of Defense, Donald Rumsfeld. Bush attempted to paint the individual races as narrowly lost, but admitted 'the cumulative effect, however, was not too close. It was a thumping'. Despite the conventional wisdom of 'its the economy, stupid', a Pew Research exit poll indicated that the electorate was at least as interested in the war in Iraq, corruption and scandals, terror, and immigration:

Top issues	*% all voters*		*% Democrats*		*% Republicans*	
War in Iraq	30		16		40	
Economy	20		17		25	
Values issues	16		30		8	
Corruption & scandals	10		4		14	
Terrorism	8		16		2	
Illegal immigration	7		11		2	
Other/don't know	9		6		9	

A breakdown of the Senate, House, and Gubernatorial results is tabulated below:

	SENATE			HOUSE		GOVERNOR		
	not up	*total*	±	*total*	±	*not up*	*total*	±
Republican	40	49	–6	202	–30	6	22	–6
Democrat	27	49	+5	233	+31	8	28	+6
Independent	0	2†	+1	0	–1	0	0	0

† The reported 51–49 Democratic majority in the Senate is premised on Joe Lieberman [CT-I] and Bernie Sanders [VT-I] both caucusing with the Democrats. [See also pp.298–99]

In the aftermath of the Democrats' win, both sides pledged a bipartisan approach. The White House promised Bush would 'extend a hand for cooperation to work on the issues facing our country'. And the new (first-ever female) Speaker of the House, Nancy Pelosi, promised 'integrity, civility, bipartisanship, and fiscal responsibility'. A common approach seemed just possible over issues like immigration, pork-barrel spending, and corruption. Yet, many of the policy debates seemed destined to test cross-party accord, including minimum wage, stem-cell research, climate change, and Bush's handling of the Iraq war. Nancy Pelosi pledged that the Democrats would tackle 6 priorities in the first 100 hours of the 110th Congress:

Increase the minimum wage to $7·25 per hour
Enact the recommendations of the 9/11 Commission
Allow the government to negotiate Medicare prescription drug prices
Eliminate numerous corporate subsidies for the oil industry
Cut in half the interest rate on federally subsidized college loans
Impose new restrictions on dealing with lobbyists

──────PRESIDENTIAL BID TIMELINE──────

Below are the dates when various presidential hopefuls formed their exploratory committee (where relevant), announced their bid, and withdrew (where relevant):

Candidate name	*Party allegiance*	*Exploratory committee*	*Announced bid*	*Withdrew from race*
Evan Bayh	Dem	12·05·06	–	12·15·06
Joe Biden	Dem	–	01·31·07	–
Sam Brownback	Rep	12·04·06	01·20·07	–
Hillary Clinton	Dem	01·22·07	01·20·07	–
John H. Cox	Rep	02·13·06	03·09·06	
Tom Daschle	Dem	–	–	12·02·06
Chris Dodd	Dem	–	01·11·07	–
John Edwards	Dem	–	12·28·06	–
Russ Feingold	Dem	–	–	11·11·06
Bill Frist	Rep	–	–	11·29·06
Jim Gilmore	Rep	01·09·07	04·26·07	07·14·07
Rudy Giuliani	Rep	11·20·06	–	–
Mike Gravel	Dem	–	04·17·06	–
Mike Huckabee	Rep	01·29·07	–	–
Duncan Hunter	Rep	01·12·07	01·25·07	–
John Kerry	Dem	–	–	01·24·07
Dennis Kucinich	Dem	–	12·12·06	
John McCain	Rep	11·16·06	04·25·07	
Barack Obama	Dem	01·16·07	02·10·07	–
Ron Paul	Rep	01·11·07	03·12·07	–
Bill Richardson	Dem	01·22·07	05·21·07	–
Mitt Romney	Rep	01·03·07	02·13·07	–
Tom Tancredo	Rep	01·22·07	04·02·07	–
Tommy Thompson	Rep	12·13·06	04·01·07	08·12·07
Tom Vilsack	Dem	–	11·09·06	02·23·07

As of 8/30/2007. ❦ The launching of a presidential bid is somewhat mysterious. Although federal law regulates campaign finance, the bid process, as understood by the press and public, is largely a creation of campaign strategists, and formal dates can be difficult to establish. For instance, by the end of August 2007 the Republican Fred Thompson was widely perceived as a candidate, but had not made a formal announcement nor filed with the FEC. ❦ 'Announced bid' dates are based on *Congressional Quarterly* and candidate reports of formal announcements – although these dates may be disputed. 'Exploratory committee' dates are based on FEC or state agency filing dates. ❦ Many 2008 presidential candidates attempted to exploit the popularity of social networking sites to further their campaigns. On Facebook, Barack Obama listed his interests as 'basketball, writing, loafing w/kids'. John Edwards was rather more serious: 'Fighting poverty. Raising the minimum wage. Stopping the genocide in Darfur'. Mitt Romney was one of the few pictured without a necktie, and his entry includes a link to the Elvis song 'A Little Less Conversation'. Under 'favorite foods' Hillary Clinton writes, 'I'm a lousy cook, but I make pretty good soft scrambled eggs'.

————— BAROMETER OF IRAQI OPINION 2004–07 —————

Below is a picture of the decline of Iraq – from three polls of >2,000 Iraqis across all 18 provinces, by D3 Systems for the BBC, ABC News, ARD TV, and *USA Today*:

Overall, how would you say things in your life are going these days?

(%)	'07	'05	'04
Very good	8	22	13
Quite good	31	49	57
Quite bad	32	18	14
Very bad	28	11	15
Refused/DK	–	1	1

Compared to the time before the war, how are things overall in your life?

(%)	'07	'05	'04
Much better	14	21	22
Somewhat better	29	31	35
About the same	22	19	23
Somewhat worse	28	19	13
Much worse	8	10	6
Refused/DK	–	1	2

What is the single biggest problematic issue you face these days?

(%)	'07	'05	'04
Security	48	18	25
Political/military	13	–	2
Economic	17	15	21
Social	22	16	18
Personal issues	1	7	4
Other	–	4	2
No problems	–	31	18
No opinion	–	9	8

From today's perspective, and all things considered, what do you think about the US-led coalition forces invasion of Iraq in spring 2003?

(%)	'07	'05	'04
Absolutely right	22	19	20
Somewhat right	25	28	29
Somewhat wrong	19	17	13
Absolutely wrong	34	33	26
Refused/DK	–	4	13

Do you support the presence of coalition forces in Iraq?

(%)	'07	'05	'04
Strongly support	6	13	13
Somewhat support	16	19	26
Somewhat oppose	32	21	20
Strongly oppose	46	44	31
Refused/DK	–	3	10

The % of those who in the last year (March '06–March '07) have …

Avoided leaving their home	78
Not sent their children to school	68
Avoided police stations, &c.	80
Avoided crowded areas, markets	83
Avoided coalition forces	91
Avoided travel	83
Avoided going to/seeking work	72
Watched what they told others	85

Conditions where you live (%2004 → %2007)	*very good*	*quite good*	*quite bad*	*very bad*	net decline 2004–07
Electricity supply	8→2	27→11	28→37	37→51	45% *worse*
Clean water	20→9	31→22	22→35	26→34	41% *worse*
Medical care	17→8	34→23	24→35	22→34	43% *worse*
Availability of jobs	7→3	19→17	23→44	46→35	16% *worse*
Security situation	20→17	29→30	21→21	29→32	5% *worse*
Local schools	37→12	35→31	15→35	11→21	59% *worse*

──── IRAQ CONFLICT · FATALITIES TO DATE ────

MONTH	IEDs	Car bombs	Mortars	RPGs	Helicopter	Hostile fire	Nonhostile	All	UK	Other	Min	Max
									COALITION FATALITIES		IRAQI CIVILIAN FATALITIES	
MAR '03	0	0	0	0	8	50	7	65	27	0	2,077	3,972
APR	0	0	3	4	8	41	18	74	6	0	2,647	3,433
MAY	0	0	0	0	7	6	24	37	4	1	499	540
JUN	0	0	0	4	0	14	12	30	6	0	541	572
JUL	4	0	0	9	0	15	20	48	1	0	593	632
AUG	7	0	0	2	0	7	19	35	6	2	735	780
SEP	5	0	2	2	1	9	12	31	1	1	525	542
OCT	13	0	4	2	0	14	11	44	1	2	461	484
NOV	20	0	1	1	39	8	13	82	1	27	433	459
DEC	18	1	2	0	0	4	15	40	0	8	504	523
JAN '04	20	3	4	1	14	4	1	47	5	0	541	561
FEB	9	0	2	0	2	3	4	20	1	2	560	578
MAR	19	0	4	0	0	12	17	52	0	0	917	951
APR	16	10	7	13	2	78	9	135	0	5	1,166	1,225
MAY	21	2	12	2	0	25	18	80	0	4	541	610
JUN	12	2	7	1	0	15	5	42	1	7	746	827
JUL	17	2	7	2	0	16	10	54	1	3	682	745
AUG	16	0	2	4	2	33	9	66	4	5	742	810
SEP	15	11	4	2	0	37	11	80	3	4	809	895
OCT	12	19	2	4	2	19	5	63	2	2	830	895
NOV	18	6	4	4	0	93	12	137	4	0	1,353	1,522
DEC	14	2	1	0	2	41	12	72	1	3	806	884
JAN '05	29	3	3	8	33	11	20	107	10	10	949	996
FEB	25	1	1	0	0	15	16	58	0	2	1,116	1,152
MAR	13	7	1	0	0	10	4	35	1	3	646	735
APR	20	7	5	2	0	12	6	52	0	0	852	974
MAY	33	10	6	2	2	14	13	80	2	6	1,030	1,187
JUN	36	8	2	3	2	18	9	78	1	4	1,077	1,203
JUL	36	2	3	0	0	4	9	54	3	1	1,355	1,411
AUG	40	7	1	0	0	27	10	85	0	0	1,982	2,118
SEP	37	0	2	0	0	3	7	49	3	0	1,163	1,264
OCT	57	2	7	0	0	11	19	96	2	1	982	1,115
NOV	40	6	0	0	2	24	12	84	1	1	1,008	1,171
DEC	42	3	2	1	2	9	9	68	0	0	854	942
JAN '06	24	3	0	1	13	10	11	62	2	0	1,320	1,407
FEB	36	2	1	0	0	7	9	55	3	0	1,386	1,442
MAR	12	1	3	1	0	9	5	31	0	2	1,594	1,713
APR	45	1	1	1	2	15	11	76	1	5	1,486	1,590
MAY	36	2	0	0	4	17	10	69	9	1	1,925	2,083
JUN	33	0	1	0	0	23	4	61	0	2	2,280	2,422
JUL	21	3	0	1	0	13	5	43	1	2	2,853	3,061
AUG	29	0	0	0	2	29	5	65	1	0	2,500	2,685
SEP	29	4	1	1	0	26	10	71	3	2	2,121	2,345
OCT	52	0	0	1	0	46	6	105	2	2	2,646	2,887
NOV	38	0	0	0	2	22	8	70	6	2	2,755	2,916
DEC	72	0	1	1	5	26	10	115	1	2	2,549	2,654
JAN '07	34	0	1	0	14	30	5	84	3	0	2,376	2,475
FEB	25	2	0	0	9	33	10	79	3	1	2,235	2,367
MAR	51	0	2	0	0	19	10	82	1	0	2,285	2,415
APR	60	0	1	1	0	34	8	104	12	1	2,480	2,590
MAY	82	0	0	0	2	37	6	127	3	2	2,643	2,770
JUN	57	0	0	4	0	31	8	100	7	0	1,997	2,092
JUL	46	0	2	1	1	19	11	80	8	1	2,500	2,600
AUG	28	0	0	3	19	17	7	74	4	0	1,800	2,011
%	39.5	3.5	3.1	2.4	5.4	31.2	14.9	...	...	...	...	...
TOTAL	1,474	132	115	89	201	1,165	556	3,733	168	129	75,453	83,233

(US TROOP FATALITIES BY CAUSE OF DEATH — columns: IEDs, Car bombs, Mortars, RPGs, Helicopter, Hostile fire, Nonhostile, All; COALITION FATALITIES — UK, Other; IRAQI CIVILIAN FATALITIES — Min, Max. APR–AUG '07 marked "troop surge".)

[US troop source: Brookings Institution; through 8/26/07. Helicopter losses include hostile and nonhostile deaths. Key: Improvised Explosive Devices; Rocket Propelled Grenades. UK & other coalition deaths source: icasualties.org, at 8/26/07. Iraqi civilian deaths source: Iraq Body Count, at 8/28/07: figures for April–August 2007 are provisional.]

DON IMUS AND 'SHOCK & JAW'

On April 12, 2007, CBS canceled the radio show *Imus in the Morning* after inflammatory remarks by its 'shock jock' host, 67-year-old Don Imus. ❧ On the morning of April 4, 2007, the banter on *Imus in the Morning* turned to the previous night's NCAA women's basketball final [where Tennessee beat Rutgers 59–46]. 'That's some rough girls from Rutgers', said Imus, 'Man, they got tattoos and ...'. 'Some hard-core hos', interjected producer Bernard McGuirk. Imus agreed: 'That's some nappy-headed hos there'. Later that day, the watchdog Media Matters for America posted online a transcript of this exchange, noting the Rutgers team comprised 8 African American and 2 white players. While the episode drew little attention at first, what the *Wall Street Journal* later called a 'digital brush fire' began to ignite, fueled by a slow Easter newscycle. Despite an apology from Imus ('our characterization was thoughtless and stupid, and we're sorry'), civil rights leaders Al Sharpton and Jesse Jackson held weekend protests, and on April 9, CBS and MSNBC (which aired a TV simulcast of the show) suspended Imus for a fortnight. On April 10, the Rutgers players held a news conference to 'express our team's great hurt, anger and disgust', describing how Imus had 'stolen a moment of pure grace from us'. The contrast between the injured dignity of the Rutgers team and the unthinking offensiveness of Imus turned the tide of public opinion even further. Major advertisers fled the now-toxic *Imus in the Morning*, and on April 11, MSNBC canceled its simulcast. On April 12, CBS cited 'the effect language like this has on our young people', and pulled the plug for good. ❧

Imus sought forgiveness by focusing on his charity work, but soon tired of defense ('I've apologized enough'). His critics argued that a history of dubious racist, sexist, and homophobic gibes made it impossible for Imus to excuse his comments as an aberration. For some, the fact that so many influential guests were willing to share a microphone with Imus lent his careless vitriol the disturbing aura of respectability. ❧ The 'shock and jaw' of 'i-Mess' played out against a backdrop of already impassioned debate as to the limits of free speech. A host of high-profile individuals had fallen foul of public sensibilities – from Michael Richards' racist outburst to Joe Biden's description of Barack Obama as 'articulate and bright and clean'. At the same time, audiences were squirming with laughter at the double-edged racism of Sacha Baron Cohen's bizarre Kazakh, Borat. As the April 12 cover of *Time* asked, 'Who can say what?' Recognizing that the problem may not be one-sided, a number of black leaders called for a ban on racist and sexist language, whatever its context. On April 23, hip-hop legend Russell Simmons called on the recording and broadcast industries voluntarily to ban 'nigger', 'bitch', and 'ho'. In July, the NAACP held a symbolic funeral for the word 'nigger', and NAACP Chairman Julian Bond conceded, 'while we are happy to have sent a certain radio cowboy back to his ranch, we ought to hold ourselves to the same standard'. ❧ At the time of writing, rumors of an Imus comeback were rife. If he does resurface, Imus will likely be forced to rethink an anachronistic shtick that for many has become simply unacceptable.

——————BAROMETER OF US MORALITY——————

The charts below give a snapshot of the (often contradictory) state of US morality:

66% think the death penalty morally acceptable †

65% think divorce morally acceptable †

64% think medical research using human embryo stem cells morally acceptable †

63% think gambling morally acceptable †

16% think suicide morally acceptable †

11% think cloning humans morally acceptable †

8% think polygamy morally acceptable †

6% think extramarital affairs morally acceptable †

59% think medical testing on animals morally acceptable †

59% think premarital sex morally acceptable †

58% think buying or wearing animal fur morally acceptable †

36% think cloning animals morally acceptable †

54% think having a baby outside marriage morally acceptable †

49% think doctor-assisted suicide morally acceptable †

47% think homosexual relations morally acceptable †

25% would not correct a restaurant bill that was too low §

36% think people should always live by God's teachings and principles §

74% think moral values in America are weaker now than 20 years ago §

68% think the media have a detrimental effect on moral values in America §

64% think the media are an important factor in shaping American morality §

4% reject the necessity of charity §

26% think it is acceptable to break outdated or harmless laws §

46% think lying acceptable, if the truth is 'too difficult or inconvenient' §

20% name religion as the most important factor in forming their values §

59% believe in making sacrifices to save for the future §

45% believe that, in general, most people can be trusted ‡

79% think women can lead complete and happy lives if single *

67% think men can lead complete and happy lives if single *

62% would not vote for an atheist political candidate ∞

26% said an atheist could not be a moral person ∞

[Key to sources: † = Gallup Poll, June 2007 · § = National Cultural Values Survey 2006–07
‡ Pew Research Center, February 2007 · * = Pew Research Center, July 2007 · ∞ = *Newsweek*, March 2007]

————————CLIMATE CHANGE · EXPERT OPINION————————

The near-unanimity of expert opinion on the reality of global warming (and mankind's role in it) was confirmed in 2006–07 by a series of reports. In late 2006, a UK government review by Nicholas Stern stated that 'the scientific evidence is now overwhelming: climate change presents very serious global risks, and it demands an urgent global response'. Stern predicted that, without action, there was a >75% chance of global temperatures rising 2–3°C by 2057, and a 50% chance of a 5°C rise. The impact of this would be more flooding and extreme weather, a decline in food supply, the extinction of ≤40% of species, and the displacement of millions. In the worst scenario, the global economy could shrink by 20%. 'All countries will be affected', Stern predicted, yet 'the most vulnerable – the poorest countries and populations – will suffer earliest and most, even though they have contributed least to … climate change'. Stern calculated it would cost 1% of global GDP to stabilize emissions (with a low-carbon route that could strengthen the world economy), and concluded, 'there is still time to avoid the worst impacts of climate change'. ❦ In a series of reports in 2007, the Intergovernmental Panel on Climate Change (IPCC) stated it was >90% certain that human activity, not least the burning of fossil fuels, caused global warming. And, the panel made some disheartening predictions for the C21st:

Warmer & fewer cold days & nights over most land areas........... probability >99%
Warmer & more frequent hot days & nights over most land areas................>99%
Frequency of warm spells/heat waves increases over most land areas..............>90%
Frequency of heavy precipitation events increases over most areas ....>90%
Area affected by droughts increases ....>66%
Intense tropical cyclone activity increases...>66%
Increased incidence of extreme high sea level (not tsunamis) ....>66%

Composed of hundreds of world experts, the IPCC is respected and influential. However, because IPCC reports are approved line-by-line by 113 governments, it was alleged that some of the panel's bolder findings were diluted, or even excised, at the insistence of China, America, India, &c. That said, the director of the UN Environment Program claimed the IPCC'S 2007 reports 'may go down in history as the day when the question mark was removed from … whether climate change has anything to do with human activities'. Curiously, as the scientific consensus becomes unequivocal, 39% of Americans still believe that 'there is a lot of disagreement among climate scientists' over global warming [8/07, *Newsweek*]. It seems that certain groups have a vested interest in nurturing the seeds of doubt – an echo, perhaps, of the 'debate' linking smoking and cancer. ❦ Governments that have hitherto resisted 'eco-vangelism' may increasingly be influenced by national security. Already, the world has been given a taste of the unrest caused by extreme weather (Katrina), desertification (Nigeria), displacement (Darfur, Tuvalu), water wars (Bolivia), heavy precipitation (2007 floods), and pandemics (SARS, avian flu). As the US Center for Naval Analyses stated in April 2007, climate change 'poses a serious threat to America's national security', 'acts as a threat multiplier for instability in some of the most volatile regions of the world', and 'will add to tensions even in stable regions of the world'. Also in April, at Britain's behest, the UN Security Council held its first-ever debate on the security threat of global warming. It is unlikely to be the last.

—————— CLIMATE CHANGE · US PUBLIC OPINION ——————

Which of the following statements reflects your view of when the effects of global warming will begin to happen? (1) They have already begun to happen. (2) They will start happening within a few years. (3) They will start happening within your lifetime. (4) They will not happen within your lifetime, but they will affect future generations. Or, (5) They will never happen. [†]

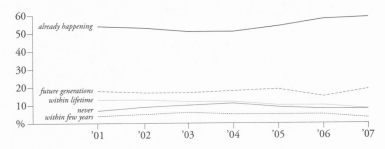

| | What in your opinion is the single biggest environmental problem the world faces at this time? [‡] | | | Do you think the world's temperature has been rising slowly over 100 years? [‡] | | |

What in your opinion is the single biggest environmental problem the world faces at this time? [‡]

Issue	2007	2006
Global warming/ Climate change	33	16
Air pollution	13	13
Pollution (misc.)	8	7
Energy problems	6	8
Toxins in environment	6	7
Water pollution	5	6
Loss of habitat/ over-development	4	7
Other	15	27
None	1	2
Unsure	8	7

Do you think the world's temperature has been rising slowly over 100 years? [‡]

Opinion	2007	2006
Has been	84	85
Has not been	13	13
Unsure	3	2

How would you rate the natural environment in the world today? [‡]

Condition	2007	2006
Excellent	3	3
Good	20	21
Fair	41	43
Poor	26	25
Very poor	9	8

%		*of American adults*
70	think the federal government should be doing more to deal with global warming [‡]
64	have installed energy-saving light bulbs [see p.15] [◊]
57	think global warming is a proven fact [37% think it an unproven theory] [§]
33	think news coverage of global warming is exaggerated [†]
30	favor increased taxes on gasoline to cut use or encourage fuel-efficient cars [‡]
20	favor increased taxes on electricity to cut use [‡]
23	think they understand the 'greenhouse effect' not very well, or not at all [†]

[Source: † Gallup, March 2007. ‡ ABC News/*Washington Post*/Stanford University, April 2007. § CNN/Opinion Research Corp., Jan 2007. ◊ Jon Dee/GMI, May 2007]

———————VIRGINIA TECH MASSACRE———————

On April 16, 2007, 23-year-old Seung-Hui Cho went on the deadliest 'shooting spree' in US history. He shot to death 32 and wounded 17 students and staff at the Virginia Polytechnic Institute and State University, where he was a senior, before committing suicide. This massacre, the latest in a long line of campus killings, catalyzed international shock and revulsion, and prompted introspection and debate over campus security, mental health care, the privacy of data, and gun laws.

Born in 1984 in Seoul, South Korea, Cho emigrated to the United States with his family aged 8. According to reports, Cho grew up a frail, shy, uncommunicative 'loner', with emotional and mental health problems. After being bullied at school, Cho enrolled at Virginia Tech in 2003 as a business information technology major, later switching to English. According to a state mental health report, while Cho did nothing to attract disciplinary attention in his first two years, his behavior from fall 2005 involved 'a significant number of incidents … in which other students and faculty members perceived or experienced his actions … as extremely odd, frightening and/or threatening'. At the insistence of a teacher, Cho was removed from some classes for one-on-one tuition. And, on a number of occasions Cho was warned by authorities for harassing and stalking female students. After one such warning, on 12/13/2005, Cho expressed suicidal thoughts to a roommate and was subsequently detained for a night at a psychiatric hospital. The next day, a judge concurred with an independent evaluation that Cho did not pose an imminent danger to himself or others, and ordered follow-up outpatient treatment. From then, apart from some relatively minor infractions, Cho attracted no further official attention until his attack 16 months later. ❦

At *c.*07:15 on April 16, 2007, Cho murdered 2 students in a nearby dorm before returning to his room to change clothes. At 09:01 he mailed a package to *NBC News* containing a 'multimedia manifesto' of text, photos, and video 'explaining' his attack. At 09:26, university officials sent the first in a series of emails warning students of the incident. At 09:40, Cho entered the classroom building Norris Hall and chained shut the doors. In *c.*11 minutes, Cho had fired 174 rounds with two semi-automatic pistols (purchased just months prior), killing 30 and wounding 17, before shooting himself at 09:51. ❦ Two days later, NBC controversially aired parts of Cho's disturbing and incoherent 'manifesto'. Railing against the 'rich' and 'debauched', Cho compared himself to Christ and said, 'you forced me into a corner and gave me only one option'. ❦ On April 23, Virginia Tech held a remembrance service for Cho's victims [see p.334]. Federal, state, and school inquiries were launched, and officials vowed to explore the causes of the tragedy. In June, after it was revealed that Cho's mental health treatment should have prevented him buying guns, the House legislated to improve nationwide background checks. ❦ VA Tech's President, Charles W. Steger, vowed, 'to the extent that rational conclusions can be drawn from irrational violence … we will learn and the world will learn from this'.

—————————— US SCHOOL SHOOTINGS ——————————

Below are some of the shooting incidents in educational establishments since 1966:

Date	location	perpetrator(s)	injured	killed
08·01·66	Austin, TX	Charles Whitman	31	16
12·30·74	Olean, NY	Anthony Barbaro	9	3
01·29·79	San Diego, CA	Brenda Spencer	7	2
01·21·85	Goddard, KA	James Alan Kearbey	2	1
05·20·88	Winnetka, IL	Laurie Dann†	6	1
09·26·88	Greenwood, SC	James Wilson	9	2
01·17·89	Stockton, CA	Patrick Purdy†	30	5
05·01·92	Olivehurst, CA	Eric Houston	10	4
01·18·93	Grayson, KY	Scott Pennington	0	2
02·02·96	Moses Lake, WA	Barry Loukaitis	1	3
02·19·97	Bethel, AK	Evan Ramsey	2	2
10·01·97	Pearl, MS	Luke Woodham	7	3
12·01·97	West Paducah, KY	Michael Carneal	5	3
12·15·97	Stamps, AR	Joseph 'Colt' Todd	2	0
03·24·98	Jonesboro, AR	A. Golden & M. Johnson	10	5
04·24·98	Edinboro, PA	Andrew Wurst	0	1
05·21·98	Springfield, OR	Kip Kinkel	>20	4
04·20·99	Littleton, CO	D. Klebold† & E. Harris†	23	13
05·20·99	Conyers, GA	T.J. Solomon	6	0
11·19·99	Deming, NM	Victor Cordova Jr	0	1
12·06·99	Fort Gibson, OK	Seth Trickey	4	0
03·10·00	Savannah, GA	Darrell Ingram	0	2
05·26·00	Lake Worth, FL	Nathaniel Brazill	0	1
03·05·01	Santee, CA	Charles Andrew Williams	13	2
03·07·01	Williamsport, PA	Elizabeth Catherine Bush	1	0
03·22·01	El Cajon, CA	Jason Hoffman	6	0
03·30·01	Gary, IN	Donald R. Burt Jr	0	1
04·24·03	Red Lion, PA	James Sheets†	0	1
09·24·03	Cold Spring, MN	John Jason McLaughlin	1	1
02·02·04	Ballou, DC	Thomas J. Boykin	0	1
03·21·05	Red Lake, MN	Jeff Weise†	7	9
11·08·05	Jacksboro, TN	Kenny Bartley	2	1
08·24·06	Essex, VT	Christopher Williams	1	2
09·27·06	Bailey, CO	Duane Morrison†	0	1
09·29·06	Cazenovia, WI	Eric Hainstock	0	1
10·02·06	Nickel Mines, PA	Charles Carl Roberts†	5	5
01·03·07	Tacoma, WA	Douglas S. Chanthabouly	0	1
04·02·07	Seattle, WA	Jonathan Rowan†	0	1
04·16·07	Blacksburg, VA	Seung-Hui Cho†	17	32

† Indicates the shooter committed suicide; these deaths are not accounted for under 'killed'.

For a number of entries, reports vary on the numbers killed or injured.

[Sources: BBC; *NYT*; *US News & World Report*; School Violence Watch Network; *Indianapolis Star*]

──────────OTHER MAJOR STORIES IN BRIEF──────────

Alexander Litvinenko

On 11/23/06, ex-KGB agent Alexander Litvinenko died in a London hospital. It soon emerged that his body contained a 'major dose' of the lethally radioactive element Polonium-210 – traces of which were later found at dozens of locations and in hundreds of people [see p.183]. The subsequent imbroglio, as macabre as it was complex, shed light on tensions between Russia and the West [see p.32]. In a letter he purportedly wrote while dying, Litvinenko accused President Putin of playing a part in his death. And a number of sources alleged that Litvinenko had been targeted for betraying Russia. On 12/6/06, after far-reaching inquiries, the British police announced that they were treating Litvinenko's death as a murder. On 5/22/07, the British announced there was sufficient evidence to charge the former KGB officer Andrei Lugovoi with deliberate poisoning, and to request his extradition from Russia. Lugovoi vigorously denied the charges, and accused the British of themselves killing Litvinenko who, he claimed, was a British spy. On 5/7, Russia refused Britain's extradition request, citing Article 61·1 of its Constitution. Britain responded on 7/16 by expelling 4 Russian diplomats. Russia countered three days later by expelling an equal number of British personnel, and threatening to end cooperation on visa applications and counterterrorism. ❦ At the time of writing, tensions between Britain and Russia were still high, though both countries saw the need to get over what Putin called a 'mini crisis'. However, Britain remained determined to prosecute whoever was responsible for what was, in effect, the deployment of a Weapon of Mass Destruction on British soil – albeit in nano-quantities.

China & Product Safety

In 2007, a slew of safety scares seriously undermined public confidence in imports – notably those from China. In March, several major suppliers initiated one of the largest-ever pet food recalls when >14 (and possibly hundreds) of cats and dogs died after eating contaminated food containing Chinese ingredients. Although FDA investigations failed to link any one chemical to the deaths, in May, China announced 2 companies were guilty of knowingly exporting pet food ingredients containing melamine – an industrial chemical banned from food, and allegedly used to raise protein content. After a host of further scandals (including $c.51$ deaths in Panama involving Chinese-made medicines, and a recall of millions of Chinese-made Mattel toys possibly coated in lead paint), China vowed to reform its regulatory systems. Yet byzantine supply chains and endemic corruption pose significant challenges to reform – despite the 7/10 execution of Zheng Xiaoyu, former head of the Chinese FDA, for accepting bribes. In America, scrutiny focused on the FDA and other regulatory agencies, already under fire following a spate of *E. coli* outbreaks [see p.110]. In July, the Consumer Product Safety Cmsn announced the drafting of new product inspection regulations, and Bush established a committee to recommend improvements to import safety. Yet despite such measures, America's reliance on cheap imports looks likely to leave consumers at the mercy of often less-than-rigorous foreign quality controls.

Zimbabwe's Stagflation

The catastrophic state of Zimbabwe's economy under the brutal kleptocracy of President Robert Mugabe spiraled

———————OTHER MAJOR STORIES IN BRIEF cont.———————

out of control in 2007. Sustained stag-flation resulted in unemployment of >80%, food and fuel shortages, and hyperinflation that rose faster than it could be tracked. In June, the US ambassador to Zimbabwe, Christopher Dell, told the *Guardian,* 'I believe inflation will hit 1·5m% [*sic*] by the end of 2007, if not before'. Dell said that Zimbabwe's government was 'committing regime change on itself'. Mugabe, who is standing for reelection in 2008, blamed British 'tricks, dishonesty, and hypocrisy' for his country's plight. In August it became clear that Mugabe's bizarre edict to shopkeepers to simply slash prices (on pain of arrest) had only exacerbated shortages and panic. 3m Zimbabweans are thought to have fled the country (*c.*23% of the population), and the UN estimated that >4m would require food aid during 2008.

Iran Hostage Crisis
On 3/23/07, 15 British sailors and Marines were seized at gunpoint by Iranian forces, after boarding a merchant ship in the northern Arabian Gulf. The exact location of the vessels in relation to the Shatt al-Arab median line that divides Iraqi and Iranian waters was the subject of heated disagreement: both countries claimed the other had crossed into its waters. Over the following days and weeks, intense diplomatic negotiations attempted to secure the release of the naval personnel. In retaliation for what they called an 'illegal act', the British government suspended bilateral contracts with Iran, and the EU called for the sailors' 'immediate release'. (The UN Security Council refused to 'deplore' Iran's action, expressing only 'grave concern'.) British outrage intensified when Iranian media broadcast interviews with the hostages, in which they 'admitted' to

being in Iranian waters. However, on 4/4, a day after the Foreign Sec. warned against hopes of a 'swift solution', President Ahmadinejad announced that he would release the hostages as a 'gift' to the people of Britain. The naval personnel returned home the next day, only to become embroiled in a controversy about selling their stories to the media.

US Attorney Firings
On 12/7/06, the Justice Dept asked 7 US Attorneys to submit their resignations. In January 2007, Congressional Democrats began hearings into the dismissals. While the Justice Dept maintained that these attorneys, and several others whose cases were later discussed, had been dismissed due to poor performance, critics charged the dismissals were politically motivated. Indeed, several attorneys alleged political interference, including pressure to pursue cases of voter fraud that may have harmed Democrats before the elections. A series of mini-scandals, including a row over 'millions' of lost emails possibly containing key evidence, ensued, amid a raft of Justice Dept resignations and waning support for Attorney General Alberto Gonzales. Gonzales continued to defend the dismissals, although in March 2007 he conceded certain 'mistakes were made'. Yet Gonzales was accused of providing misleading Congressional testimony regarding Bush administration involvement – uttering some form of 'I can't recall' 71 times during a single Senate Judiciary Cmte appearance in April. As the hearings continued, a controversy erupted over the administration's refusal to provide documents and sworn testimony. This led to debate on the limits of executive privilege, and exacerbated tensions between the White House and Congress.

──────── OTHER MAJOR STORIES IN BRIEF cont. ────────

Eventually, controversy over Gonzales's testimony overshadowed original concerns regarding the attorney dismissals, and his tenure at the Justice Dept became a lightning rod for wider criticism of the Bush government. After a series of high-profile departures from the administration (notably Karl Rove, announced 8/13), Gonzales announced his own resignation on 8/27.

Northern Ireland Power Sharing
On 5/8/07, Ian Paisley (DUP) was sworn in as First Minister of the Northern Ireland Assembly, and Martin McGuinness (Sinn Féin) as his Deputy in the new power-sharing executive. Upon taking office, Paisley said, 'I believe we're starting on a road which will bring us back to peace and prosperity'. McGuinness responded, 'We must overcome the difficulties which we face in order to achieve our goals and seize the opportunities that exist'. Greeting the return to devolved government (the Assembly was suspended in 2002), Tony Blair said, 'Look back and we see centuries marked by conflict, hardship, even hatred among the people of these islands; look forward and we see the chance to shake off those heavy chains of history'. Irish PM Bertie Ahern played tribute to Blair's role in bringing together old foes: 'I thank him for the true determination that he had, for just sticking with it for ten tough years'.

Hamas vs *Fatah*
The simmering violence between the secular Fatah and the Islamist Hamas – which began after Yasser Arafat's death in 2005, and worsened after the 2006 Palestinian elections – descended into all-out conflict in mid-2007. From 6/10, Hamas launched a series of successful attacks on Fatah positions in Gaza, and four days later, Hamas had control of the Gaza Strip. In response, Palestinian President (and Fatah leader) Mahmoud Abbas dissolved the elected unity government, declared a state of emergency, and announced that Gaza and the West Bank would be ruled by decree through an appointed government led by PM Salam Fayyad. The reality, however, was a Hamas-led Gaza and a Fatah-led West Bank. Israel, which had stood back during the fighting, sought to isolate Hamas by closing the checkpoints into Gaza, and signaled its support for Abbas by releasing hundreds of Palestinian prisoners and millions of dollars of frozen tax receipts. While expressing concern for the residents of Gaza, many in the international community, including the US and EU, sought to bolster Abbas by pledging millions in aid. At the time of writing, tensions in the region remained high. Although Hamas (which seeks Israel's destruction) had hoped to improve its reputation by securing the release of kidnapped BBC reporter Alan Johnston, it seemed that the international focus was on securing Fatah in the West Bank, while further isolating the Islamists in Gaza.

Immigration
To the chagrin of President Bush, for whom immigration reform has been a domestic priority, Congress failed to pass a major overhaul of the immigration system in 2007. The bipartisan Comprehensive Immigration Reform Act, introduced in the Senate on May 9, was designed to increase border security, establish a temporary guest-worker program, and provide a 'path to citizenship' for some of the US's *c.*12m illegal immigrants. Despite a major push from the President, and a series of

———————OTHER MAJOR STORIES IN BRIEF cont. ———————

amendments, the Bill finally collapsed in the Senate on June 28. Though conservatives were perhaps the loudest critics, the Bill was attacked by the left (who felt some penalties were too harsh) and the right (who claimed it provided 'amnesty' [or 'shamnesty'] for illegal immigrants). At time of writing, a series of Bills sought to resuscitate some of the Act's provisions, though it seemed likely the President would not see a resolution of many of the issues before the end of his term.

UK Terror Attacks

Within days of Gordon Brown replacing Blair as PM, Britain experienced a series of attempted terror attacks. In London, on 6/29/07, two car bombs (one parked outside a busy nightclub) containing gas cylinders, nails, and fuel failed to detonate and were defused by police. The next day, two men drove a burning SUV containing gas cylinders into the main doors of Glasgow's international airport. The SUV failed to explode, no-one was injured, and two men were arrested. The police stated that they believed the three attacks were linked, and the UK terror alert was raised to 'critical'. ❦ At the time of writing 3 men (all foreign-born doctors working in the National Health Service) had been charged and were awaiting trial. One of those allegedly involved in the Glasgow attack died in the hospital from his burns.

I. Lewis Libby's Trial & Commutation

On 3/6/07, Vice President Cheney's former chief of staff, I. Lewis 'Scooter' Libby, was convicted on two counts of perjury, one count of making a false statement to the FBI, and one count of obstruction of justice. Pending appeal, Libby's verdict closed another chapter of the investigation into the 2003 leak of Valerie Plame's undercover CIA identity. Although not charged with leaking Plame's identity, Libby was found guilty of lying about his role in the leak, which many allege was a deliberate attempt by the administration to discredit Plame's husband, Ambassador Joseph C. Wilson, who was a critic of the Iraq invasion. The trial forced top officials and prominent journalists to testify, and raised disturbing questions about the use of pre–Iraq War intelligence. On 6/5, Libby was sentenced to 30 months in prison and ordered to pay a fine of $250,000. On 7/2, after being denied bail by a federal appeals court, Libby was spared jail when President Bush commuted his prison sentence, deeming it 'excessive'. Although the President left the other elements of Libby's sentence intact, his commutation drew criticism from both Democrats (who saw it as a partisan move) and Republicans (who felt Libby should have been pardoned). Polls showed little public support for the President's clemency.

Darfur

On 7/31/07, the UN passed Resolution 1769, authorizing 26,000 UN and African Union (AU) peacekeepers to join the 7,000 AU troops already in the Sudanese province of Darfur. It was envisaged that the first wave of troops would deploy in 10/07, with the full force in place by early 2008. ❦ Darfur has been in crisis since at least 2003, when black African rebels attacked government targets in protest of their poor treatment. In response, Sudanese forces, in cahoots (it is alleged) with the Arab Janjaweed militia, launched a genocidal campaign of repression, ethnic cleansing, and human rights abuse,

──────────OTHER MAJOR STORIES IN BRIEF cont.──────────

resulting in >200,000 deaths and the displacement of *c*.2·5m. ❦ At Sudan's insistence, Resolution 1769 stopped short of authorizing sanctions, ensured the new force was mainly (entirely?) African, and prohibited the pursuit of suspected war criminals. ❦ At the time of writing, optimism about the UN's initiative was balanced by a host of doubts: Would even the world's largest peacekeeping force be sufficient for an area the size of France, with few roads and little infrastructure? Would the troops be properly trained, funded, and equipped, and would they be adequately mandated to protect civilians and aid workers? Would those countries with economic and military ties to Sudan (China and Russia) support the peace? Would the Darfurian rebel groups cease their internecine fighting? Would Sudan cooperate fully with the UN force? And, axiomatically, would there be a peace in Darfur to keep?

Subprime

Subprime loans are made to those with poor (or no) credit history, in return for higher interest rates, fees, and penalties. A range of subprime lending exists (from cash loans to credit cards), but the most dominant form has been mortgages – and it was this segment which went into 'meltdown' in 2006–07. Buoyed by rising house prices, lenders over-estimated the sums that could safely be lent. Keen to get on the housing ladder, borrowers 'overstated' how much they earned. So, as loans came off their initial low rates, and house prices weakened, many could not afford their repayments or to refinance their debt, and the incidence of delinquency, default, and foreclosure rocketed. In early 2007, a number of major lenders collapsed. This had a domino effect both on market confidence and on those hedge funds and investment banks with exposure to subprime loans – often in the form of complex 'bundles' of debt. In August, stockmarkets around the world reacted with such volatility that a number of Central Banks were forced to inject millions of dollars into the market to avoid a 'credit crunch'. At the time of writing, the Chairman of the Fed warned the crisis could cost $50–$100bn, and had been forced to cut the Fed's interbank 'discount' rate. CNN Money estimated that *c*.2·4m Americans might lose their homes. And this 'violent correction' in the US subprime market had begun spill over into the world's 'real economies'.

─────────────────────────────

US *retail gasoline prices* hit an all-time high on 5/18/2007, when the average gallon of regular reached $3·1827. Prices have since fallen – though they remain erratic.

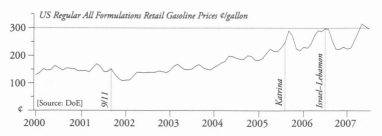

US Regular All Formulations Retail Gasoline Prices ¢/gallon
[Source: DoE]

———BAROMETER OF WORLD OPINION ON THE US———

OPINION OF AMERICA

*Ranked below are the
global views on the US*

	% favorable	% unfavorable
Ivory Coast	89	11
Kenya	87	11
Ghana	80	14
US	80	18
Israel	78	20
Nigeria	70	27
S. Africa	61	30
Poland	61	31
Peru	61	31
Japan	61	36
India	59	28
S. Korea	58	38
Venezuela	56	40
Mexico	56	41
Chile	55	35
Canada	55	42
Italy	53	38
UK	51	42
Lebanon	47	52
Kuwait	46	46
Czech Rep.	45	50
Brazil	44	51
Bolivia	42	52
Russia	41	48
France	39	60
China	34	57
Spain	34	60
Germany	30	66
Indonesia	29	66
Egypt	21	78
Jordan	20	78
Argentina	16	72
Morocco	15	56
Pakistan	15	68
Palestine	13	86
Turkey	9	83

[Pew Global Attitudes, June 2007]

AMERICA'S PLACE IN THE WORLD

*Do you think the US
is respected around the
world today?* (%)

Respected	24
Not respected	71
Respected by some	3
Unsure	2

*Do you think George W. Bush's
foreign policies have made
world leaders more or less
likely to cooperate with the US?*

More likely	10
Less likely	54
No difference	30
Unsure	6

[CBS News, June 2007]

GLOBAL RESPECT FOR GEORGE W. BUSH

*% of Americans who think
that leaders of other countries
around the world have respect
for George W. Bush*

Year	%		
2007	21	2004	39
2006	33	2003	40
2005	35	2002	75
		2001	49

[Gallup, all polls from February]

The Pew Global Attitudes Survey in 2007 found 45% of Americans had confidence in W. Bush's global leadership compared with: 30% of Italians; 29% of Canadians; 24% of British; 18% of Russians; and 14% of the French.

WORLD OPINION ON AMERICA'S INFLUENCE

*Ranked below are the global
views on whether the US has a
positive or negative influence*

	% mainly positive	% mainly negative
Philippines	72	11
Nigeria	72	20
Kenya	70	20
US	57	28
Poland	38	24
Italy	35	42
S. Korea	35	54
Canada	34	56
Lebanon	34	58
UK	33	57
Chile	32	51
India	30	28
Hungary	29	31
Portugal	29	55
Brazil	29	57
Australia	29	60
China	28	52
UAE	25	57
France	24	69
Indonesia	21	71
Russia	19	59
Germany	16	74
Argentina	13	64
Mexico	12	53
Greece	12	78
Egypt	11	59
Turkey	7	69
Average	30	51

The countries with the most negative international reputations were Israel, Iran, N Korea, US, Russia, Venezuela, India, and China.

[BBC World Service, March 2007]

————PERSON OF THE YEAR: VLADIMIR PUTIN————

Much of the recent posturing between Putin and the West has been decidedly reminiscent of the Cold War, not least: Moscow's objections to the US defense shield, and its threat to target missiles at Europe; the 'gas supply wars' with Ukraine and Belarus; withdrawal from the Conventional Forces in Europe Treaty; oil-related territorial shenanigans under the North Pole; Russia's resumption of long-range bomber patrols; disruption to Russian language BBC World Service broadcasts; and the Litvinenko affair [see p.26]. In July 2007, the *Economist* noted that 'Russia is no longer exporting a rival ideology ... nor fighting proxy wars with America around the globe'. However, Russia remains armed with the world's largest known gas reserves, strong political and economic influence over an archipelago of marginalized states, an Armageddonic nuclear arsenal, and a permanent seat (and veto) on the UN Security Council. Thus, whether the issue is terrorism, climate change, energy security, nuclear proliferation, Palestine, Iraq, Iran, Kosovo, or Darfur – Putin's Russia cannot be ignored. ❦ Vladimir Vladimirovich Putin was born in 1952 to working-class parents. He studied law at Leningrad University, where he was recruited by the KGB in 1975. After two years as a low-level spook, Putin was sent to Moscow for elite training. In 1985, he was assigned to the KGB office in Dresden, where he reportedly worked with the Stasi to gather Western technology secrets. In 1990, after the fall of the Berlin Wall, Putin was recalled to become Rector of Leningrad University – a thinly veiled KGB cover. Over the next few years, Putin climbed the political ladder in (the renamed) St Petersburg, before he was summoned to Moscow in 1996. In a vertiginous rise, Putin became Boris Yeltsin's deputy Chief of Staff in 1997, and head of the Federal Security Service in 1998. In 1999, Putin was appointed Secretary of the Security Council (March), PM (August), and Acting President (December). In March 2000, Putin was elected President – despite being as unknown to most Russians as he was to the rest of the world. ❦ The West welcomed Putin's early advocacy of democratic and economic reforms as much as his stylistic differences from the haphazard Yeltsin. Yet, by 2003, this optimism was overshadowed by Putin's quasi-Soviet clampdown on media freedoms and opposition protests, and his pursuit of foreign investors and Russia's newly minted oligarchs. Although he opposed the Iraq invasion, Putin used Bush's 'war on terror' to justify his Chechnya policy, and cited Guantánamo Bay to rebuff criticisms of his record on human rights. ❦ Putin has exploited Russia's petro-dollars (and US unpopularity) to renegotiate what he sees as the parlous deals Russia made as the Soviet Union collapsed. As he told Al-Jazeera, 'Russia knows its worth. We will work towards creating a multipolar world ... but Russia does have enough potential to influence the formation of the new world order'. ❦ Since Russia's constitution forbids 3 consecutive presidential terms, Putin must step down in 2008. Despite hinting he would like to stay on (and an approval rating of *c.*80%), few believe Putin will actually rewrite the law to do so. That said, aged just 55, it is implausible that he will simply fade into the background.

SCHEMATIC · WORLD EVENTS OF NOTE · 2006–07

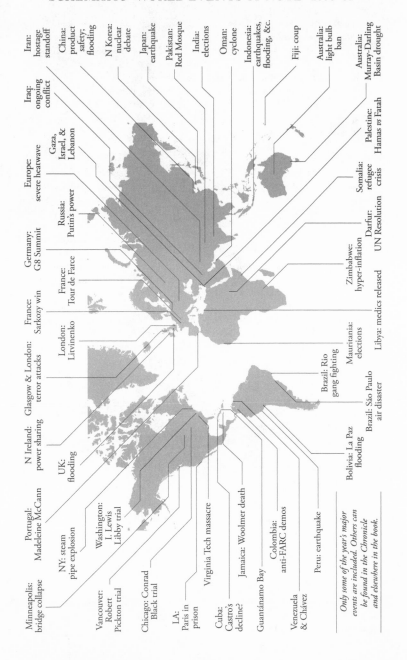

Iran: hostage standoff

China: product safety; flooding

N Korea: nuclear debate

Japan: earthquake

Pakistan: Red Mosque

India: elections

Oman: cyclone

Indonesia: earthquakes, flooding, &c.

Fiji: coup

Australia: light bulb ban

Australia: Murray–Darling Basin drought

Iraq: ongoing conflict

Gaza, Israel, & Lebanon

Europe: severe heatwave

Palestine: Hamas *vs* Fatah

Russia: Putin's power

Somalia: refugee crisis

Germany: G8 Summit

Darfur: UN Resolution

France: Tour de Farce

Zimbabwe: hyper-inflation

France: Sarkozy win

Libya: medics released

London: Litvinenko

Mauritania: elections

Glasgow & London: terror attacks

Brazil: Rio gang fighting

N Ireland: power sharing

Brazil: São Paulo air disaster

UK: flooding

Bolivia: La Paz flooding

Portugal: Madeleine McCann

Peru: earthquake

NY: steam pipe explosion

Colombia: anti-FARC demos

Washington: I. Lewis Libby trial

Venezuela & Chávez

Vancouver: Robert Pickton trial

Guantánamo Bay

Chicago: Conrad Black trial

Jamaica: Woolmer death

LA: Paris in prison

Cuba: Castro's decline?

Virginia Tech massacre

Minneapolis: bridge collapse

Only some of the year's major events are included. Others can be found in the Chronicle and elsewhere in the book.

—————— IN BRIEF · AUGUST – SEPTEMBER 2006 ——————

The daily chronicle below picks up from the 2007 edition of Schott's Almanac.

{AUGUST 23} Paramount cut ties with Tom Cruise, reportedly citing recent 'unacceptable' conduct. {24} The FDA approved over-the-counter sales of 'emergency contraceptive' Plan B for women >18. ❦ Apple recalled 1·8m laptop batteries over fire concerns. ❦ Pluto was stripped of its status as a planet. ❦ Austrian Natascha Kampusch was reunited with her parents after being kidnapped 8 years earlier. {25} 7 US flights were disrupted amid scares after the alleged transatlantic terror plot. {26} Iran inaugurated a heavy-water reactor. {27} 49 died in a KY plane crash, after pilots chose the wrong runway. ❦ 2 Fox journalists, kidnapped 8/14 in Gaza, were freed. {28} Prosecutors said DNA evidence failed to link John Mark Karr to JonBenet Ramsey's death, and dropped the case against him. {29} Britain charged 3 over the alleged transatlantic terror plot. ❦ >67 died when a Diwaniya, Iraq, gas pipeline exploded; looting was suspected. ❦ Sect leader Warren Jeffs was arrested near Las Vegas. {30} RIP @ 90, actor Glenn Ford. {31} The UN Security Council (UNSC) authorized a Darfur peacekeeping force; Sudan rejected it. ❦ Iran ignored a UN deadline to halt uranium enrichment. ❦ Munch's *The Scream* and *Madonna*, stolen in 2004, were recovered in Norway.

Tom Cruise

I have a slight tear in my eye today.
– astronomer IWAN WILLIAMS,
speaking about Pluto

killed a Canadian soldier in Afghanistan. {5} Mexico's top electoral court declared Felipe Calderón President-elect, following a contentious July election. ❦ The discovery of a major Gulf of Mexico oil source was announced. ❦ The FDA approved the first implantable artificial heart. {6} Princess Kiko of Japan gave birth to a boy. ❦ Former IL Gov. George Ryan was sentenced to 6·5 years' prison on corruption charges; he appealed. ❦ Bush acknowledged CIA use of secret prisons for the first time, and said 14 key terrorist suspects had been transferred to Guantánamo Bay. ❦ Bush proposed a draft Military Commissions Act defining rules for interrogating and trying terror suspects. {7} Israel lifted its air blockade of Lebanon. ❦ Former Deputy SoS Richard Armitage said he was the source for the leak of Valerie Plame's CIA identity. {8} The Senate Intelligence Cmte released a CIA report denying any evidence of formal links between Saddam Hussein and Al Qaeda before the 2003 war. ❦ Bombs near a Malegaon, India, mosque killed 31. ❦ Israel lifted its sea blockade of Lebanon. ❦ CA Gov. Schwarzenegger apologized for saying that Cubans and Puerto Ricans were 'all very hot'. {10} Montenegro held its first general elections as an independent state. {11} Ceremonies marked the 5th anniversary of 9/11; Bush said America was engaged in 'a struggle for civilization'. {12} 4 gunmen stormed the US embassy in Damascus, killing 1. ❦ *c.*50 were killed in a stampede during a Yemen election rally. ❦ During a speech in Germany, Pope Benedict XVI made controversial remarks on Islam. ❦ Amid a spying-allegation scandal, Hewlett-Packard said chairwoman

S EPTEMBER · {1} A Mashhad, Iran, plane accident killed >80. {3} RIP @ 44, 'Crocodile Hunter' Steve Irwin [see p.57]. {4} US warplanes

—— IN BRIEF · SEPTEMBER 2006 ——

Patricia C. Dunn would resign in January. {13} A gunman killed 1 and wounded *c.*20 at Dawson College, Montreal, before committing suicide. ❦ RIP @ 73, former TX Gov. Ann Richards. ❦ The Intl Astronomical Union named dwarf planet 2003 UB313 'Eris', and its moon 'Dysnomia'. {14} Andrei Kozlov, first deputy chairman of Russia's Central Bank, was murdered. {15} *Science* reported that a stone with the earliest known writing in the W Hemisphere had been found in Mexico. {17} The Pope apologized for his remarks on Islam. ❦ RIP @ 82, JFK's sister Patricia Kennedy Lawford. ❦ 5 basketball players were shot and wounded at Duquesne University, Pittsburgh. ❦ A tape was leaked to the media in which Hungarian PM Ferenc Gyurcsány admitted lying about the state of the economy; days of rioting followed. ❦ A 'Darfur Day of Action' was held in 30 cities worldwide. {18} A suicide bomb targeting the President of Somalia killed *c.*10 in Baidoa, Somalia. {19} RIP @ 83, photographer Martha Holmes. ❦ The Thai military overthrew PM Thaksin Shinawatra in a bloodless coup. {20} Venezuelan President Hugo Chávez called Bush 'the devil' in a UN General Assembly speech. ❦ The first-ever female space tourist, Anousheh Ansari, docked at the Intl Space Station. {21} The African Union extended the mandate of its peacekeeping force in Darfur until the end of 2006. ❦ The CDC recommended all teenagers and adults ≥13 be routinely tested for HIV. {22} Indonesia executed 3 Christians linked to the violence in central Sulawesi in 2000, despite an EU appeal. ❦ An elevated train crashed in NW Germany, killing 23. ❦

Benedict XVI

Yesterday the devil came here.
And it smells of sulfur still today.
– HUGO CHÁVEZ

Thailand's king gave the country's military coup formal approval. ❦ HP chairwoman Dunn resigned. {24} Bill Clinton accused Fox News host Chris Wallace of 'a conservative hit job' during a TV interview. {25} A federal judge granted class-action status to a lawsuit accusing tobacco companies of deceiving customers into thinking 'light' cigarettes were less harmful. ❦ Performances of a Berlin opera featuring the severed heads of Jesus and Muhammad were canceled amid security concerns. ❦ 47 were killed in a Quito, Ecuador, bus crash. ❦ Passengers were again allowed to carry liquids and gels onto airplanes, with restrictions. {26} Bush declassified parts of a National Intelligence Estimate after excerpts were leaked to newspapers; the report said 'jihadist activity' was increasing in 'both number and geographic dispersion'. ❦ Former Enron exec. Andrew Fastow was sentenced to 6 years' prison. ❦ Shinzo Abe was elected Japanese PM. ❦ RIP @ 90, 'Tokyo Rose' Iva Toguri D'Aquino. {27} The Hague war crimes tribunal sentenced Bosnian Serb leader Momčilo Krajišnik to 27 years' prison for crimes against humanity, but acquitted him of genocide. ❦ A gunman took 6 girls hostage at a Bailey, CO, high school, before killing 1, and then himself. ❦ John A. Gotti's alleged racketeering hearing was declared a mistrial. ❦ The House approved the Military Commissions Act; the compromise Act gave less leeway on the Geneva Conventions than originally proposed by Bush on 9/6. {28} The Senate approved the Military Commissions Act. ❦ The House approved a Bill granting legal status to the NSA warrantless wiretapping program,

—————— IN BRIEF · SEPTEMBER – OCTOBER 2006 ——————

with certain restrictions. {29} Rep. Mark Foley [FL-R] resigned from Congress amid a scandal over sexual electronic messages sent to teenage Congressional pages. ❦ The Senate passed a Bill to build 700 miles of US–Mexico border fencing. ❦ The House and Senate passed a $35bn Homeland Security spending Bill, including $1·2bn for border fencing. ❦ A crash involving 2 planes killed 155 over the Amazon jungle.

Patricia Dunn

OCTOBER · {1} Israel completed its withdrawal from Lebanon. ❦ Hamas–Fatah clashes in Gaza killed 10, over 2 days. {2} A gunman stormed an Amish schoolhouse in PA, killing 3 girls before committing suicide; 2 others later died of their injuries. ❦ 8 US soldiers were killed in Baghdad. {3} N Korea announced plans for a nuclear test. ❦ A Turkish man hijacked a plane and forced it to land in Italy; no passengers were hurt. ❦ Foley's lawyer said Foley had been abused as a teenager by a clergyman. ❦ The *Miami Herald*'s publisher resigned after firing 3 journalists for providing anti-Castro propaganda. {4} Bush signed the Homeland Security funding Bill. ❦ The US government said it was 'not going to live with' a nuclear-armed N Korea. ❦ CA prosecutors charged Dunn and 4 others with fraud and conspiracy in the alleged HP 'spying scandal'. ❦ Independent monitors said the IRA was committed to nonviolent politics and was no longer sponsoring criminal activities. ❦ The FBI began investigating 2 produce companies after an *E. coli* outbreak killed 1 and sickened *c.*192. {5} The House Ethics Cmte began investigating the Foley affair. ❦ A blast

at an NC chemical plant injured >18; 17,000 were evacuated. {6} Special assistant to Bush, and former Abramoff assistant, Susan Ralston resigned. ❦ US Navy medic Melson J. Bacos was sentenced to prison for his role killing an Iraqi civilian in April 2006. {7} Russian journalist Anna Politkovskaya was murdered in Moscow, amidst fears of a state crackdown on the media. {8} Iran refused to suspend uranium enrichment after 6 countries agreed to discuss sanctions. {9} S Korean foreign minister Ban Ki-moon was formally nominated as UN Sec. Gen. ❦ N Korea claimed to tested a nuclear device underground: the UNSC condemned the claim; the US proposed sanctions. ❦ Google bought YouTube for $1·65bn. {10} SoS Rice said the US would not attack N Korea, but the nation faced sanctions 'unlike anything that they have faced before'. {11} N Korea warned that sanctions would be considered a 'declaration of war', and threatened more nuclear tests; Japan imposed sanctions. ❦ Yankees pitcher Cory Lidle died after crashing his plane into a NYC building. ❦ The Justice Dept charged a CA man with treason for appearing in Al Qaeda videos; the first such charge since WWII. ❦ >129 Sri Lankan soldiers died fighting rebels in Jaffna, Sri Lanka. {12} Orhan Pamuk won the Nobel Prize in Literature [see p.161]. ❦ Madonna was granted interim adoption rights for a 1-year-old Malawi boy [see p.120]. {13} Muhammad Yunus won the Nobel Peace Prize [see p.66]. ❦ A Malawi human rights group attempted to delay Madonna's adoption bid. {14} The UNSC approved N Korean sanctions. {15} Israeli police said President Moshe Katsav

I know he will be very happy in America. – YOHANE BANDA
(father of Madonna's adopted son)

———— IN BRIEF · OCTOBER – NOVEMBER 2006 ————

should face rape charges. ✤ 2 days of violence in Iraq killed c.86. ✤ Hawaii declared a state of disaster after a 6·6 earthquake. ✤ Rep. Bob Ney [OH–R] pleaded guilty to bribery charges in the Abramoff investigation. {16} Lawyer Lynne F. Stewart was sentenced to 28 months' prison after distributing messages for a terrorist client. ✤ c.92 died in a Tamil Tiger attack in Dambulla, Sri Lanka. ✤ The US confirmed a N Korea nuclear explosion. ✤ Former FDA chief Lester M. Crawford was charged with conflict of interest and lying about stock he owned in FDA-regulated companies; he was later sentenced to 3 years' probation and fined. {17} Bush signed the Military Commissions Act. ✤ N Korea called the UN sanctions 'a declaration of war'. ✤ The US population officially hit 300m [see p.91]. ✤ Madonna's adopted child arrived in London. {18} The US military said 4 soldiers would be court-martialed over the March 2006 rape and murder of civilians in Mahmoudiya, Iraq. {19} A Catholic priest living in Malta acknowledged intimate contact with Foley. ✤ The Dow closed above 12,000 for the first time. {20} RIP @ 96, *Father Knows Best* actress Jane Wyatt. {22} Sudan expelled UN envoy Jan Pronk after he blogged about military defeat in the region. ✤ Senior State Dept official Alberto Fernandez apologized after telling Al-Jazeera the US acted with 'arrogance' and 'stupidity' in Iraq, in a 10/21 broadcast. ✤ Fighting between tribal factions in W Afghanistan killed 32. ✤ Panamanians voted in favor of a $5·25bn overhaul of the Panama Canal. {23} White House Press Sec. Tony Snow said Bush was no longer using the phrase 'stay the course' to refer to the

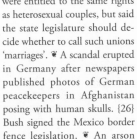
Ban Ki-moon

war in Iraq because it 'left the wrong impression'. ✤ Former Enron CEO Jeffrey Skilling was sentenced to 24 years' prison. {25} FL executed Danny Harold Rolling for killing 5 college students in 1990. ✤ NJ's highest court ruled same-sex couples were entitled to the same rights as heterosexual couples, but said the state legislature should decide whether to call such unions 'marriages'. ✤ A scandal erupted in Germany after newspapers published photos of German peacekeepers in Afghanistan posing with human skulls. {26} Bush signed the Mexico border fence legislation. ✤ An arson wildfire began in Cabazon, CA; in total, 4 firefighters died and c.40,200 acres razed. ✤ c.42 Iraqis died in insurgent ambushes near Baquba, Iraq. {27} The St Louis Cardinals won the World Series [see p.234]. ✤ Iran announced the installation of 164 new centrifuges. ✤ Amidst tensions with Bush, Iraqi PM Maliki said, 'I am a friend of the US, but I am not America's man in Iraq'. {29} Luiz Inácio Lula da Silva was reelected President of Brazil. {30} A military strike in the Bajaur region of Pakistan killed c.80. ✤ Sen. John Kerry warned a group of CA students to study or 'get stuck in Iraq'. He later claimed this was a botched joke. ✤ 46 Iraqis were killed in Baghdad bombings. {31} N Korea agreed to rejoin 6-nation disarmament talks. ✤ RIP @ 90, former S African leader P.W. Botha [see p.57]. ✤ >50 Iraqi civilians were kidnapped near Baghdad.

The members of the United States military are plenty smart.
– GEORGE W. BUSH

NOVEMBER · {1} Kerry apologized for his 'stuck in Iraq' gaffe. ✤ RIP @ 81, *Sophie's Choice* author William Styron. ✤

——————————IN BRIEF · NOVEMBER 2006——————————

Alexander Litvinenko was admitted to a London hospital with symptoms of poisoning [see p.26]. {2} United Artists announced Tom Cruise would join its management. ❦ Evangelical leader Rev. Ted Haggard resigned after a former male prostitute claimed a sexual relationship. {3} Rep. Ney resigned. ❦ Israeli attacks killed >20 Palestinians over several days in Beit Hanoun, Gaza. {4} Rev. Haggard was fired by his church. {5} Iraq's High Tribunal sentenced Hussein and 2 codefendants to death for the 1982 killings of 148 Shiites from Dujail; the verdict went to automatic appeal. {7} Panama was elected to the UNSC.

Michael Richards

❦ Democrats swept the US midterm elections, winning 233 House seats and 51 Senate seats for their first bicameral majority in 6 years [see p.16]. ❦ Britney Spears filed for divorce from Kevin Federline [see p.122]. ❦ Vietnam joined the World Trade Organization. {8} Defense Sec. Donald Rumsfeld resigned; Bush nominated former CIA Director Robert Gates as his replacement. ❦ Lee Boyd Malvo was sentenced to life for his role in the 2002 DC-area sniper killings. ❦ Israeli shells killed 18 Palestinian civilians in Gaza; Ehud Olmert called the shelling a mistake. ❦ A suicide bomber killed 42 at a military training site in Pakistan. {9} RIP @ 65, TV journalist Ed Bradley [see p.57]. ❦ RIP @ 83, former East German spymaster Markus Wolf. {12} >150 were killed or found dead across Iraq. {13} Chad declared a state of emergency after 10 days of attacks by Arab gunmen around the country killed >220. ❦ Bush met with members of the Iraq Study Group, but said any recommendations would be limited

It's been quite a time.
– DONALD RUMSFELD

by 'conditions on the ground'. {14} The S African parliament voted to legalize same-sex marriages. ❦ The IAEA said it had found enriched uranium and plutonium in Iran. ❦ *c.*80 gunmen stormed a Baghdad ministry and kidnapped (?) *c.*150. {15} Trent Lott was elected Senate minority whip and Mitch McConnell Senate minority leader. ❦ Rockets from Gaza killed 1 in Sderot, Israel. ❦ Spc. James P. Barker pleaded guilty to raping and helping to murder a 14-year-old girl in Mahmoudiya in March 2006. ❦ (?)*c.*70 Iraqis kidnapped in Baghdad the previous day were released. {16} The Senate approved a plan to share nuclear fuel and technology with India. ❦ RIP @ 94, Nobel Prize-winning economist Milton Friedman. {17} Former *Seinfeld* star Michael Richards unleashed a 'racist' outburst at an LA comedy club. {18} Tom Cruise and Katie Holmes wed in Italy. ❦ *c.*53 Iraqis were killed across the country. {19} Henry Kissinger said military victory was no longer possible in Iraq. ❦ *c.*112 were killed across Iraq. ❦ Russia and the US signed an agreement allowing Russia to join the WTO. {20} RIP @ 81, director Robert Altman [see p.57]. ❦ Richards apologized for his rant. ❦ After a public outcry, News Corp. canceled publication of a book by O.J. Simpson entitled *If I Did It.* {21} Anti-Syrian Lebanese cabinet minister and Christian leader Pierre Gemayel was assassinated near Beirut. ❦ >30 countries agreed to build the experimental nuclear fusion reactor ITER in France. {23} Litvinenko died at a London hospital [see p.26]. ❦ *c.*200 were killed and >250 wounded in coordinated bombings in Baghdad. {24} Polonium-

———IN BRIEF · NOVEMBER – DECEMBER 2006———

210 was found in Litvinenko's body; his alleged deathbed statement attacking Putin was released [see p.32]. {25} Israeli and Palestinian leaders agreed to a cease-fire in Gaza. {26} *c*.43 were injured in clashes during protests in Oaxaca, Mexico. {27} NBC began calling the violence in Iraq a 'civil war'. ❦ 91 Iraqis died in Iraq. ❦ The Justice Dept opened a review into its role in the NSA eavesdropping program. ❦ The Canadian parliament recognized Quebec as a nation 'within a united Canada'. {28} A memo was leaked in which national security adviser Stephen Hadley reportedly expressed doubts about Maliki. {29} Retiring Senate majority leader Bill Frist said he would not run for President in 2008. ❦ Ahmadinejad issued a letter appealing to 'noble Americans', and urging unity with Iran. ❦ The Supreme Court began a hearing over whether vehicle emissions must be regulated by the Clean Air Act. {30} Bush and Maliki met in Jordan; Bush said there would be no 'graceful exit' from Iraq. ❦ Benedict XVI prayed at Turkey's Blue Mosque, becoming the second Pope ever to enter a Muslim place of worship. ❦ Typhoon Durian struck the Philippines, killing *c*.500.

A. Litvinenko

ambassador to the UN John Bolton resigned. {5} In testimony before the Senate Armed Services Cmte, Gates said the US was 'not winning' the war in Iraq. ❦ US officials said N Korea had been offered an incentives package to renounce nuclear technology. ❦ Military commander Frank Bainimarama staged a coup in Fiji. {6} The Iraq Study Group released its report, calling for withdrawal of most US combat brigades by March 2008, among other recommendations. ❦ The Senate confirmed Gates as Defense Sec. ❦ NASA said Mars Global Surveyor pictures suggested the presence of water. {7} In a press conference with Blair, Bush said he was 'disappointed by the pace of success' in Iraq, but vowed to keep fighting. ❦ Russia announced a criminal investigation into Litvinenko's death. ❦ RIP @ 80, former UN Ambassador Jeane Kirkpatrick [see p.57]. {8} A House Ethics Cmte report said Republicans had been negligent in protecting pages from Foley's advances, but that no rules had been broken. ❦ In farewell remarks, Rumsfeld said his worst day in office had been learning of the Abu Ghraib abuse. {9} Congress approved a Bill to allow offshore drilling in the Gulf of Mexico. {10} Died @ 91, former Chilean dictator Gen. Augusto Pinochet [see p.57]. ❦ 3 climbers went missing during a heavy storm on Oregon's Mt Hood. {11} Iran convened a conference in Tehran to 'debate' the Holocaust. ❦ In his last address as UN chief, Annan warned the US not to 'abandon its own ideals and objectives' in the 'war on terror'. {12} *c*.63 Shiites were killed by a suicide bomber in Baghdad. ❦ Feds raided meat factories in 6 states and arrested >1,300

DECEMBER {1} >10,000 protesters in Beirut began a *c*.2-week sit-in. {2} Castro missed his 80th birthday celebrations in Havana, intensifying speculation as to his health. {3} Chávez won reelection for a further 6-year term in Venezuela. ❦ UN Sec. Gen. Annan said Iraq was in 'civil war'. {4} Rafael Correa officially won Ecuador's Presidential election. ❦ NASA announced plans for a permanent Moon base. ❦ US

The situation in Iraq is grave and deteriorating. – LEE H. HAMILTON, in the Iraq Study Group report

—————————— IN BRIEF · DECEMBER 2006 ——————————

illegal immigrants. ❦ RIP @ 71, actor Peter Boyle. {13} The NIH ended clinical trials in Africa after finding that circumcision halved a man's risk of HIV from heterosexual sex; the NIH said it would be unethical not to offer circumcision to all men in the study. ❦ A district judge ruled that Guantánamo detainees could not file habeas corpus challenges, thereby upholding the Military Commissions Act. ❦ RIP @ 74, founder of the AFL, Lamar Hunt. {14} The NJ legislature voted to recognize same-sex civil unions. ❦ Ban Ki-moon was sworn in as UN Sec. Gen. ❦ A British inquiry ruled that Princess Diana's death was a 'tragic accident', and found no evidence of murder. ❦ RIP @ 83, Atlantic records founder Ahmet Ertegun [see p.57]. ❦ Major storms hit the Pacific NW; 14 died over several days. ❦ Sen. Tim Johnson [SD-D] underwent emergency brain surgery, raising speculation about a rebalanced Senate. {15} FL suspended all executions, and CA's execution moratorium was extended after a judge ruled lethal injection unconstitutional [see p.118]. {16} Mahmoud Abbas ordered early elections, which Hamas rejected. ❦ A brawl erupted between Knicks and Nuggets players at Madison Square Garden. {17} Gunmen kidnapped 30 Red Crescent employees in Baghdad. ❦ Rescuers found the body of Kelly James, one of the Mt Hood climbers. {18} Gates was sworn in as Defense Sec. ❦ Rescuers called off the search for the remaining Mt Hood climbers. ❦ Bush signed the nuclear cooperation deal with India. ❦ RIP @ 95, Hanna-Barbera animator Joseph Barbera [see p.57]. {19} MD suspended executions. ❦ Bush backed increasing the size

Hugo Chávez

He was dramatic to the end, dying on Christmas Day.
— JESSE JACKSON on James Brown

of the armed forces to fight the 'war on terror'. ❦ Libya sentenced 5 nurses and a doctor to death for 'deliberately' infecting children with HIV in 1998. {20} Bush said victory in Iraq was 'achievable', but would require 'additional sacrifices'; *c.*100 died in Baghdad. ❦ A fragile Hamas–Fatah truce took hold in Gaza. {21} British authorities charged a man with the 'Suffolk strangler' murder of 5 women in Ipswich, England. ❦ 4 Marines were charged with murder in the 2005 Haditha killings; 4 officers were given lesser charges. ❦ RIP @ 66, president of Turkmenistan 'Turkmenbashi' Saparmurat Niyazov. ❦ *Harry Potter and the Deathly Hallows* was revealed as the title of HP7 [see p.166]. {22} 6-party talks with N Korea ended inconclusively. ❦ The Durham DA dropped rape charges against the former Duke lacrosse players, though other charges remained. {23} The UNSC imposed sanctions against Iran. {24} Ahmadinejad railed against the UN sanctions. ❦ Ethiopian forces bombed several locations in Somalia, escalating fears of a regional war. ❦ *c.*1,400 British and Iraqi troops freed 127 prisoners from a Basra jail allegedly run by criminals. {25} RIP @ 73, James Brown [see p.58]. {26} Israel approved a new West Bank settlement, provoking Palestinian condemnation. ❦ RIP @ 93, former President Gerald Ford [see p.58]. ❦ An Iraqi court upheld Hussein's death sentence, ordering his execution within 30 days. ❦ *c.*100 Iraqis and 7 US soldiers were killed in Iraq. ❦ A Spanish surgeon stated Castro did not have cancer. ❦ A gas pipeline exploded in Lagos, Nigeria, killing *c.*260. {27} The Pentagon said it would send *c.*3,500 troops to Kuwait as

———— IN BRIEF · DECEMBER 2006 – JANUARY 2007 ————

a standby force. ❦ Hussein posted a farewell letter on a Baath Party website, saying he was ready to die as a 'sacrifice'. {28} Islamist forces fled Mogadishu, and the transitional government took control of the city. ❦ John Edwards declared he was running for President in 2008. ❦ The FDA pronounced milk and meat from cloned animals safe to eat. {29} A ferry sunk near Java; 400 were feared dead. {30} Saddam Hussein was hanged. Cellphone footage of his death was leaked, and an outcry erupted over taunts directed at him during his execution. ❦ A Madrid airport car-park was bombed, killing *c*.2; Basque separatists ETA claimed responsibility. {31} Bombs at New Year's celebrations in Thailand killed 3. ❦ The military announced that the 3,000th US soldier had been killed in Iraq.

Nancy Pelosi

JANUARY · {1} Romania and Bulgaria joined the EU. ❦ An Indonesian plane disappeared; initial reports said its wreckage had been found and 90 killed. {2} Ford's funeral was held at Washington National Cathedral. ❦ Maliki ordered an investigation into Hussein's execution. ❦ Wesley Autrey heroically risked his life to rescue a man who had fallen onto the NYC subway tracks. {3} Iraqi officials arrested a guard believed to have filmed Hussein's execution. ❦ A student shot and killed another student in Tacoma, WA; he was later arrested. {4} The 110th Congress convened; Nancy Pelosi was elected the first female Speaker of the House. ❦ Harriet Miers resigned as White House Counsel. {5} Pelosi and Senate majority leader Harry Reid sent

He was very, very, very, broken.
– Iraqi official MOUWAFAK
AL-RUBAIE, on Saddam Hussein

Bush a letter requesting troop withdrawal from Iraq in 4–6 months. ❦ Bush named Lt. Gen. David Petraeus Commander of the Multi-National Force in Iraq. ❦ RIP @ 96, inventor of ramen noodles Momofuku Ando [see p.58]. {6} Abbas declared Hamas's paramilitary wing illegal; Hamas vowed to double the unit to 12,000 troops. {7} The Archbishop of Warsaw resigned after admitting Soviet-era collaboration with the Communist secret police. ❦ Part of Miami's port was closed and 3 men briefly detained in a terror scare. ❦ A US air strike targeting Al Qaeda militants in S Somalia killed *c*.12. {8} Bush said he would nominate Iraq ambassador Zalmay Khalilzad as US envoy to the UN, and Ryan Crocker as the new Iraq ambassador. ❦ A German court sentenced Mounir el-Motassadeq to 15 years' prison as an accessory to 9/11. ❦ A NY court sentenced Shahawar Matin Siraj to 30 years' prison for a 2004 NY subway bomb plot. ❦ Schwarzenegger proposed universal health coverage for CA residents. ❦ RIP @ 84, actress Yvonne 'Lily Munster' De Carlo. {9} Apple unveiled the iPhone, and changed its name from Apple Computer Inc. to Apple Inc. ❦ Chávez announced plans to nationalize telecommunications and power companies. ❦ The House passed a series of 9/11 Cmsn recommendations, including a Bill to screen all air cargo entering the US. ❦ RIP @ 94, producer and husband of Sophia Loren, Carlo Ponti. {10} Bush said he would send a 'surge' of >20,000 additional troops to Baghdad and Anbar; Democrats criticized the plan. ❦ The House voted to raise the federal minimum wage [see p.318]. {11} Sen. Chris Dodd [CT-D] announced he was running for President in 2008. ❦ The House voted to expand federal financing for stem cell research, but without the votes required to overturn a Presidential veto. ❦ Bangladesh declared a state of emergency and postponed elections after months of violent protests. ❦ The Los Angeles Galaxy announced David Beckham would join the team in June [see p.251]. {12} A rocket attack hit the US embassy in Athens; there were no casualties. ❦ 2 kidnapped MO boys were found alive; a local man was charged with their kidnapping. ❦ Durham County DA Mike Nifong asked to be removed from the Duke lacrosse 'rape' case. {14} The *New York Times* reported that the Pentagon and CIA were using 'national security letters' to obtain financial records of Americans suspected of terrorism or espionage; Cheney defended the practice. {15} Iraq hanged former intelligence chief Barzan Ibrahim al-Tikriti, and former head of the Revolutionary Court Awad Hamad al-Bandar; Ibrahim was accidentally decapitated. ❦ An ice storm in the Midwest and Plains states killed >41 over several days. ❦ The trial of 6 men charged with plotting unsuccessful 2005 suicide bombings in London began in Britain. {16} 3 bombs killed *c.*70 at a Baghdad university. ❦ Bush said the execution of Hussein and his 2 deputies had been 'fumbled'. ❦ Israeli military chief of staff Lt. Gen. Dan Halutz resigned amid criticism of the war with Hezbollah. ❦ Barack Obama formed a Presidential exploratory committee. ❦ I. Lewis Libby's trial began [see p.29]. {17} The Justice Dept agreed to give the Foreign Intelligence Surveillance Court jurisdiction over NSA domestic wiretapping.

Condoleezza Rice

One thing I'm convinced of … is that people want something new.
– BARACK OBAMA

❦ Senators Biden, Hagel, and Levin introduced a symbolic resolution opposing the troop 'surge'. ❦ Maliki said *c.*400 Shiite militants had been arrested in raids by US and Iraqi troops. {18} Bush signed a controversial executive order giving the White House more power to review federal agencies. ❦ The Senate passed an ethics and lobbying overhaul. ❦ RIP @ 81, humorist Art Buchwald. ❦ The House passed a Bill ending oil industry tax breaks and subsidies. ❦ Press reports said China destroyed one of its own satellites with a missile on 1/11/07; China refused to admit to the test. {19} Ney was sentenced to 30 months' prison for corruption. ❦ Rice returned from a Mideast trip, during which she secured agreements for renewed Israeli–Palestinian talks. ❦ Turkish newspaper editor Hrant Dink was murdered outside his office; a teenage suspect was later arrested. {20} 25 US soldiers died in Iraq. ❦ Bush announced a tax cut proposal to encourage health care. ❦ Hillary Clinton announced her Presidential bid. {21} Gov. Bill Richardson [NM-D] announced the creation of a Presidential exploratory committee. ❦ The Colts beat the Patriots to win the AFC title and entrance to the Super Bowl [see p.236]. {22} Bombs at a Baghdad market killed *c.*88. ❦ Sen. John Warner [VA-R] presented another symbolic resolution rejecting the troop 'surge'. ❦ Iran barred 38 nuclear inspectors in retaliation for UN sanctions. {23} Bush delivered his State of the Union address [see p.294]. ❦ Hezbollah led a violent general strike in Lebanon. ❦ Israel's attorney general said Katsav would be charged with rape, obstruction of justice, and fraud. ❦ China

———— IN BRIEF · JANUARY – FEBRUARY 2007 ————

confirmed its use of an anti-satellite missile, but denied the test was intended to intimidate. ❦ A US helicopter crashed in Baghdad, killing 5 security employees. ❦ RIP @ 88, Watergate plotter E. Howard Hunt. {24} Kerry said he would not run for President in 2008. ❦ The Senate Foreign Relations Cmte passed a nonbinding resolution opposing the troop 'surge'. {25} The Israeli parliament approved a 3-month leave of absence for Katsav, who continued to deny all charges. ❦ 30 countries pledged $7·6bn to strengthen the Lebanese government. ❦ A riot killed 4 and wounded *c.*150 in Beirut. {26} Army Lt. Gen. David Petraeus was confirmed by the Senate. ❦ Regarding the 'surge', Bush said 'I'm the decision-maker'. ❦ *c.*14 Palestinians died in fighting between Hamas and Fatah. {27} Tens of thousands protested the Iraq war in Washington, DC. {28} Iraqi and US forces killed *c.*250 militants in a major battle near Najaf, Iraq. {29} A suicide bombing at a bakery in Eilat, Israel, killed 3. ❦ Hamas and Fatah agreed to a cease-fire. ❦ Barbaro was euthanized [see p.58]. ❦ In a press interview, Chirac said that it would not be dangerous for Iran to have a nuclear bomb; he later retracted his remarks. ❦ The Hague's International Criminal Court ruled there was enough evidence against Congolese militiaman Thomas Lubanga to proceed with a trial, the ICC's first. {30} *c.*58 were killed in attacks across Iraq during a Shiite holy day. ❦ Ronell Wilson was sentenced to death for the 2003 murder of 2 detectives, the first death sentence in NY in >50 years. ❦ Archaeologists announced the discovery of the village where the workers who built

Barack Obama

Stonehenge likely lived. ❦ An explosion at a WV gas station killed 4. ❦ Microsoft launched its *Vista* operating system. {31} A German court issued arrest warrants for 13 involved in the 2003 CIA 'extraordinary rendition' of German citizen Khaled el-Masri. ❦ Roads were closed and parts of Boston gridlocked by a terror scare that turned out to be a guerrilla marketing campaign for a cartoon show; 2 men were arrested. ❦ Sen. Joseph Biden [DE-D] announced his Presidential bid, and was forced to defend remarks in which he called Barack Obama 'the first mainstream African American who is articulate and bright and clean and a nice-looking guy'. ❦ The Venezuelan legislature granted Chávez the power to rule by decree for 18 months.

FEBRUARY · {1} 2 suicide bombings at a market in Hilla, Iraq, killed >60. ❦ 6 were killed in Gaza as the Hamas–Fatah cease-fire collapsed. ❦ RIP @ 95, opera composer Gian Carlo Menotti. ❦ Senators Biden, Hagel, & Levin agreed to merge their resolution against the troop 'surge' with that proposed by Warner. ❦ SF Mayor Gavin Newsom apologized for an affair with the wife of his former campaign manager. ❦ Undersecretary of State Nicholas Burns warned Iran to stop aiding Iraqi militants, but said the US did not intend to attack the country. {2} A declassified National Intelligence Estimate expressed doubts about Iraq's ability to halt sectarian violence, saying coalition troops remained an essential stabilizing force. ❦ A major UN report claimed overwhelming evidence that global warming was worsening and

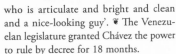

We apologize to the citizens of Boston that part of a marketing campaign was mistaken for a public danger.
— Turner CEO PHIL KENT

—————————— IN BRIEF · FEBRUARY 2007 ——————————

said humans were likely responsible [see p.22]. ❦ Hamas–Fatah fighting killed 17 in Gaza. ❦ IAEA investigators confirmed that Iran had begun installing equipment for large-scale uranium enrichment at Natanz. ❦ Storms killed *c.*20 in FL. {3} A truck bomb at a Shiite market in Baghdad killed *c.*137. {4} Floods in Jakarta left *c.*340,000 homeless. ❦ The Colts beat the Bears in the Super Bowl, 29–17 [see p.236]. {5} Bush submitted his FY2008 budget: the $2·9tr plan called for $145bn for the wars in Iraq and Afghanistan; projected an end to the deficit in 5 years without raising taxes; and extended controversial tax cuts. ❦ Turner Broadcasting and a marketing company agreed to pay $2m for funding the Boston cartoon ad scare. ❦ The resolution against the troop 'surge' failed to advance to debate in the Senate after it was blocked by Reps. ❦ Apple Inc. and the Beatles settled a dispute over use of the Apple name and logo. ❦ Michael Devlin was charged with 69 counts of sexual assault in the MO kidnapping cases. ❦ Astronaut Lisa Marie Nowak was arrested after allegedly confronting a rival at Orlando airport; she was later charged with attempted murder. {6} Apple's Steve Jobs issued an open letter calling for an end to Digital Rights Management (DRM) [see p.140]. ❦ Hamas and Fatah leaders began peace talks in Mecca, brokered by Saudi King Abdullah. ❦ The FDA approved a genetic test to predict whether breast cancer will return after treatment. ❦ British newspaper the *Sun* published a cockpit recording of US soldiers during a 2003 'friendly fire' incident that killed British soldier Matty Hull; the US then allowed the tape to be used in an

M. Ahmadinejad

inquest into Hull's death. ❦ Deputy Attorney Gen. Paul J. McNulty told a Senate Cmte that all but one of the fired prosecutors were dismissed for performance-related reasons. {7} A Marine helicopter crashed near Baghdad, killing 7; it was the 6th US helicopter to crash in Iraq in 3 weeks. ❦ 6-party talks on N Korea's nuclear program resumed. {8} Hamas and Fatah signed a power-sharing agreement in Mecca, and agreed to 'respect' peace deals with Israel. ❦ The Senate confirmed Gen. Casey as Army chief of staff. ❦ RIP @ 39, Anna Nicole Smith [see p.58]. ❦ Floyd Landis said he would not compete in the 2007 Tour de France. ❦ A Pentagon investigation into pre-Iraq war intelligence said former Pentagon official Douglas Feith acted inappropriately, but not illegally, in trying to establish a link between Iraq and Al Qaeda. {9} Clashes over Israeli construction near Jerusalem's Temple Mount wounded *c.*17 Palestinians. ❦ Defense Sec. Gates said serial numbers on explosives found in Iraq linked them to Iran. {10} In a speech at a Munich security conference, Putin accused the US of undermining global security. ❦ Obama formally announced his Presidential candidacy. ❦ Harvard named Drew Gilpin Faust its first female president. {11} Gates responded to Putin's charges, saying 'one Cold War was quite enough'. ❦ US military officials accused Iran of arming Iraqi Shiite militants, presenting a trove of weapons as evidence. ❦ Jerusalem's mayor postponed construction work near the Temple Mount after further Palestinian protests. {12} 3 car bombs in Iraq killed *c.*78. ❦ Ahmadinejad denied arming Iraqi militants. ❦ During

We have the right to ask, against whom is this expansion directed.
— VLADIMIR PUTIN

Libby trial testimony, several prominent reporters denied Libby had leaked Valerie Plame's identity. ❦ The Iraqi High Tribunal sentenced to death Hussein's VP, Taha Yasin Ramadan. {13} In a major breakthrough, N Korea agreed to close its main nuclear reactor in exchange for $400m in aid; the US agreed to discuss normalizing relations. ❦ Former MA governor Mitt Romney declared his Presidential candidacy. ❦ The House began debating a nonbinding resolution opposing the 'surge'. ❦ Bombs on minibuses killed 3 in Lebanon; the first attacks aimed at civilians since 1990. ❦ A shooting at a mall in Salt Lake City killed 6. {14} Bush said he was a certain Iran's Quds force was arming Iraqi Shiite militants, but said he did not know whether top officials were involved. ❦ The US said it would admit c.7,000 Iraqi refugees. ❦ Maliki launched a major security crackdown in Baghdad. {15} Pelosi said Bush would need Congressional authorization to attack Iran; Gates and other officials said the US had no intention of so doing. ❦ Bush warned of a renewed Taliban offensive in the Spring; the US diverted 3,200 troops from Iraq to Afghanistan. ❦ Palestinian PM Haniya and his Hamas-led government re-signed; Abbas reappointed Haniya as premier of a power-sharing government. ❦

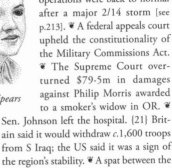

Britney Spears

The US introduced a Presidential dollar coin [see p.320]. {16} An Italian judge indicted 26 Americans in the 2003 'extraordinary rendition' of an Egyptian cleric. ❦ The House approved a nonbinding resolution criticizing the 'surge'. ❦ Britney Spears shaved her head [see p.122]. {17} A revised nonbinding resolution against the 'surge' again failed to advance to debate

The security plan has been a dazzling success during its first days.
– Iraqi PM NURI AL-MALIKI

in the Senate. ❦ A suicide bomber killed 16 in a Quetta, Pakistan, courtroom. {18} Car bombs in Baghdad killed c.60. ❦ 28 coordinated bombings in S Thailand killed c.60. {19} A train caught fire in N India, killing >66. ❦ Satellite radio providers Sirius and XM announced plans to merge. {20} JetBlue said operations were back to normal after a major 2/14 storm [see p.213]. ❦ A federal appeals court upheld the constitutionality of the Military Commissions Act. ❦ The Supreme Court overturned $79.5m in damages against Philip Morris awarded to a smoker's widow in OR. ❦ Sen. Johnson left the hospital. {21} Britain said it would withdraw c.1,600 troops from S Iraq; the US said it was a sign of the region's stability. ❦ A spat between the Obama and Clinton campaigns erupted after Hollywood executive David Geffen reportedly said that the Clintons lie 'with such ease, it's troubling'. ❦ Italian PM Romano Prodi resigned after his coalition lost a foreign policy vote in the Senate. {22} The IAEA said Iran had ignored a deadline to halt uranium enrichment, and had instead expanded its program; the US pressed for further sanctions. ❦ US soldier Sgt Paul E. Cortez was sentenced to 100 years' prison for March 2006 rape and murders in Mahmoudiya. ❦ Britain said Prince Harry would fight in Iraq. ❦ A FL judge settled a dispute over Anna Nicole Smith's burial place. ❦ A Presidential working group report rejected calls for further hedge fund regulation, but said companies should adhere to a set of nonbinding principles. {23} N Korea invited IAEA director El-Baradei to visit Pyongyang. {24} 52 died in a suicide bombing in Iraq's Anbar

─── IN BRIEF · FEBRUARY – MARCH 2007 ───

Province. ❧ Italian President Giorgio Napolitano asked Prodi to stay in office but submit to a vote of confidence. {25} Scorsese finally won the best director Oscar [see p.154]. {26} Britain confirmed it would send 1,400 additional troops to Afghanistan. ❧ The Hague's Intl Court of Justice ruled the 1995 Srebrenica massacre an act of genocide; Serbia was cleared of direct responsibility, but told it 'could and should' have prevented the massacre. ❧ Gunmen killed 4 French citizens near Medina, Saudi Arabia. ❧ *Titanic* director James Cameron held a press conference unveiling what he claimed was Jesus' family tomb. ❧ The Iraqi Cabinet passed draft legislation on oil revenue distribution. {27} A suicide bomber attacked the main US military base in Afghanistan during a Cheney visit: *c.*23 were killed; the Taliban claimed Cheney was the target. ❧ The Dow fell 416 points, the largest point drop in >5 years, catalyzed by a 9% fall in Shanghai stock prices. {28} Thieves broke into the apartment of Picasso's granddaughter, and stole 2 of his paintings worth *c.*$66m total. ❧ Prodi survived a vote of confidence in the Italian Senate. ❧ RIP @ 89, Pulitzer Prize-winning historian Arthur Schlesinger Jr.

I. Lewis Libby

A bus carrying an OH college baseball team crashed in Atlanta, killing 6. {4} US troops killed 16 civilians in E Afghanistan after their convoy was ambushed; a US air strike in central Afghanistan reportedly killed 9 civilians. {5} Veterans testified about conditions at Walter Reed before a House subcommittee; the acting Army Sec and Army Surgeon General accepted responsibility and vowed to improve conditions. ❧ Guantánamo detainees lodged a Supreme Court challenge to the December ruling upholding the Military Commissions Act. {6} Libby was convicted of 4 felony counts in the CIA leak trial, including perjury and obstruction of justice [see p.29]. ❧ 2 earthquakes in Sumatra killed >70. ❧ 2 CA women were treated in Moscow for apparent thallium poisoning. ❧ Bush appointed Bob Dole and Donna E. Shalala to lead a review of the army medical system. ❧ Suicide bombers and gunmen killed *c.*113 Shiite pilgrims across Iraq. ❧ RIP @ 97, CA winemaker Ernest Gallo. ❧ 6 federal prosecutors fired in late 2006 alleged political pressure prior to their dismissal [see p.27]. ❧ RIP @ 77, philosopher Jean Baudrillard [see p.58]. {7} A suicide bomber killed 30 at a café in Baquba, Iraq. ❧ NASA fired Lisa Marie Nowak. {8} House Dems unveiled a war-funding Bill calling for a troop withdrawal by the end of 2008. {9} A Justice Dept report claimed the FBI had misused national security letters; FBI Director Mueller admitted mistakes. ❧ The US began hearings into whether 14 Guantánamo detainees could be defined as enemy combatants. ❧ Pakistani President Musharraf suspended the country's chief justice on alleged misconduct

M ARCH · {1} 20 died in 3 S States during tornadoes. ❧ The army fired the head of the Walter Reed veteran's hospital, following an exposé of conditions there. ❧ Japanese PM Shinzo Abe denied the country's military had coerced women into sexual slavery during WWII, provoking international condemnation. {2} Army Sec. Francis Harvey resigned over Walter Reed conditions. ❧

Could you double-check the envelope, please?
– MARTIN SCORSESE

charges, leading to a major political backlash. {10} The US and Iran held direct talks at a Baghdad security conference. {11} Chirac announced his retirement but did not endorse a successor. ❧ Riot police in Zimbabwe arrested *c.*100 protesters, and severely beat opposition leader Morgan Tsvangirai. ❧ A suicide bomber killed 4 at an internet café in Casablanca. {12} Army Surgeon General Lt. Gen. Kevin C. Kiley resigned over Walter Reed conditions. ❧ Joint Chiefs of Staff chairman Gen. Pace said homosexuality was immoral and that openly gay people should not serve in the military. ❧ Attorney Gen. aide Kyle Sampson resigned amid continued fallout over the prosecutor firings. ❧ BBC reporter Alan Johnston was kidnapped in Gaza. {13} Attorney Gen. Alberto Gonzales admitted 'mistakes were made' in the prosecutor firings. ❧ Gen. Pace said he should have kept his personal views private. {14} The Pentagon released transcripts of a Khalid Sheikh Mohammed hearing in which he reportedly confessed to masterminding 9/11. ❧ A CA judge dismissed all charges against former HP chairwoman Dunn. {15} Hamas and Fatah formed a unity government. ❧ Maoist rebels killed 49 at a police post in Bijapur, India. ❧ The Senate rejected a Dem. resolution to withdraw most US combat troops from Iraq by March 2008. ❧ Schwarzenegger signed a Bill moving CA's Presidential primary from June to Feb 5. {16} A British coroner ruled that the US 2003 'friendly fire' attack that killed Matty Hull was unlawful and criminal. ❧ Menu Foods recalled 60m containers of pet food after the death of >14 animals [see p.26]. {18}

Alberto Gonzales

We pledge that we will never leave a fallen comrade.

– PETE GEREN, Secretary of the Army

Israel's cabinet voted to boycott the Palestinian unity government; the US agreed to maintain a ban on aid, but allowed for contact with non-Hamas ministers. ❧ Bob Woolmer, the coach of Pakistan's cricket team, was found dead during the Cricket World Cup; there was speculation of murder. {19} Thousands held protests across the US on the 4th anniversary of the Iraq invasion; Bush called for patience. ❧ US officials said $25m of N Korean funds in a Macao bank would be unfrozen. ❧ A mine explosion in the Kemerovo region of Siberia killed *c.*100. ❧ The Taliban released an Italian journalist captured 3/4/06. {20} Former Iraq VP Taha Yassin Ramadan was hanged. ❧ *c.*62 died at a home for the elderly and disabled in S Russia. ❧ The White House said Rove and other officials could provide private, unsworn testimony in the prosecutor firings inquiry; Congressional Dems rejected the offer. {21} Chirac endorsed formal rival Nicolas Sarkozy. ❧ A Veteran's Affairs investigation found widespread maintenance problems in clinics and hospitals. ❧ The House Judiciary Cmte approved subpoenas for top officials in the prosecutor firing inquiry. {22} A federal judge overturned the 1998 Child Online Protection Act. ❧ John Edwards said his wife's cancer had returned, but vowed his Presidential campaign would continue. ❧ The Senate Appropriations Cmte approved a $122bn war-funding measure, including a March 2008 Iraq withdrawal deadline. ❧ British police arrested 3 men in connection with the 7/7/05 London bombings. ❧ The N Korea 6-party talks were suspended after delays releasing the frozen $25m. {23} The House approved a

─────────── IN BRIEF · MARCH – APRIL 2007 ───────────

war spending Bill, including a September 2008 deadline for troop withdrawal from Iraq; Bush promised a veto. ❦ Iran seized 15 members of a British naval crew in the Persian Gulf [see p.27]. ❦ Former Interior Dept #2, J. Steven Griles, pleaded guilty to lying about his Abramoff ties. {24} The UNSC passed another round of sanctions against Iran, banning arms exports. {25} Iran declared the UN sanctions illegal, saying it would limit IAEA cooperation in response. ❦ Iran said the captured British crew had violated its waters and accused Britain of 'blatant aggression'. {26} N Ireland's rival

Hillary Clinton

factions held their first direct talks and agreed to form a joint administration. ❦ Guantánamo detainee David Hicks pleaded guilty to providing material support to Al Qaeda, in the first trial under revised military tribunal rules. ❦ Anna Nicole Smith's death was ruled an accidental drug overdose. ❦ The military said 9 officers had made critical reporting errors in the 2004 'friendly fire' death of Pat Tillman, but found no criminal wrongdoing. ❦ Gonzales' White House liaison refused to testify before the Senate panel on the prosecutor firings. {27} 2 suicide bombs in Tal Afar, Iraq, killed *c.*83. ❦ White House Press Sec. Snow revealed that his colon cancer had returned and spread to his liver. {28} *c.*70 Sunnis were killed in N Iraq in retaliation for the Tal Afar bombings. ❦ Zimbabwean police arrested Tsvangirai. {29} Suicide bombs killed *c.*122 at Shiite markets around Baghdad. ❦ The Senate approved a war-spending measure calling for Iraq troop withdrawals to begin in 120 days. ❦ Zimbabwe released Tsvangirai. ❦ In Senate Judiciary Cmte testimony,

From our perspective, there was no reason to stop.
– JOHN EDWARDS

Sampson contradicted Gonzales' account of his involvement in the prosecutor firings. {30} Australian Hicks was convicted of providing material support for terrorism and sentenced to 7 years as part of a plea agreement. ❦ The FDA reported it had found melamine in the recalled pet food, but the source of contamination remained unclear; more companies began recalling pet food. {31} The Pentagon released a hearing transcript in which a Guantánamo detainee claimed he had been tortured into admitting attacks.

APRIL · {1} Clinton's campaign said it raised $26m in Q1 of 2006. ❦ Former WI Gov. Tommy Thompson joined the Presidential race. {2} Florida beat Ohio State 84–75 in the NCAA basketball championship [see p.239]. ❦ The Supreme Court ruled that CO_2 and other greenhouse gases were air pollutants under the Clean Air Act, and subject to EPA regulation. ❦ The Supreme Court said it would not review whether Guantánamo detainees had the right to challenge their detention in federal courts. ❦ EMI said it would allow iTunes to sell its catalog without copying restrictions [see p.140]. {3} Colorado State U. forecasters predicted a 'very active' 2007 hurricane season. {4} Pelosi held a meeting with Syrian officials in Damascus; the White House criticized her visit. ❦ Obama's campaign said it had raised $25m in Q1 2006. Final reports showed that Democrats had raised a total of *c.*$78, and Republicans *c.*$51m. ❦ Iran released the 15 British captives as a 'gift' to Britain. {5} 22 brands of dog biscuits were added to the pet food recall. ❦ British police charged

—————————— IN BRIEF · APRIL 2007 ——————————

3 with conspiring with the 7/7/05 London subway bombers, the first charges in the attacks. {6} Gonzales's White House aide Monica Goodling resigned. {7} RIP @ 76, cartoonist Johnny 'B.C.' Hart. {8} Zach Johnson won the Masters [see p.242]. ❦ RIP @ 78, artist Sol LeWitt. ❦ Shiite cleric Moktada al-Sadr called for Iraqi forces to unite against the US; 10 US soldiers were killed over 2 days. {9} NBC News and CBS officials announced that radio host Don Imus's show would be suspended for 2 weeks after Imus called the Rutgers women's basketball team 'nappy-headed hos' [see p.20]. ❦ Tens of thousands of Shiites demonstrated against the US in Najaf, Iraq. {10} DNA results showed Larry Birkhead was the father of Anna Nicole Smith's daughter. ❦ 5 died in a Casablanca suicide bombing. {11} The US military extended Iraq and Afghanistan tours of duty for most active troops from 12 to 15 months. ❦ 2 suicide bombings in Algeria killed 33 and wounded 222. ❦ NC's attorney general dropped all charges against the Duke players. ❦ RIP @ 84, author Kurt Vonnegut [see p.58]. ❦ NBC canceled *Imus in the Morning*. ❦ The Senate approved the expanded federal financing for stem cell research. {12} CBS canceled *Imus in the Morning*. ❦ NJ Gov. Jon S. Corzine was critically injured in a car crash. ❦ World Bank President Paul Wolfowitz issued a statement apologizing for 'mistakes' made when his girlfriend was given a 2005 promotion. ❦ Student loan providers agreed to a code of conduct in a $2m settlement with the NY Attorney General, amid growing scrutiny into unethical college lending practices. ❦ White House spokeswoman Dana Perino

Paul Wolfowitz

You can't make fun of everybody, because some people don't deserve it.
— DON IMUS, apologizing

said the White House 'screwed up' by not saving millions of e-mails sent from Republican Party accounts. {14} N Korea missed a deadline to close its main nuclear reactor, part of the 2/13 deal with the US. ❦ RIP @ 76, singer Don 'Tiny Bubbles' Ho. {15} The World Bank's oversight committee expressed 'great concern' over the Wolfowitz controversy; Wolfowitz said he intended to stay in his post. ❦ In testimony prepared for the Senate inquiry into the prosecutor firings, Gonzales said he had 'nothing to hide'. ❦ Russian police arrested *c*.370 after 2 days of anti-Putin demonstrations. {16} In the worst shooting in US history, 32 were killed and 17 injured by a gunman at Virginia Tech [see p.24]. ❦ Sudan said it would accept 3,000 UN military police and other support in Darfur. {17} Police identified the Virginia Tech gunman as Seung-Hui Cho. Memorials and vigils were held across the country, and buildings evacuated in *c*.7 states amid fears of copycat attacks. ❦ The mayor of Nagasaki, Japan, was shot and killed by an organized crime boss over damage to his car. ❦ The FDA approved the first avian flu vaccine. {18} The Supreme Court upheld a federal ban on 'partial birth' abortions in a 5–4 decision. ❦ NBC aired a 'multimedia manifesto' by the Virginia Tech gunman [see p.24]. ❦ Bombs in Baghdad killed *c*.171. ❦ The IAEA confirmed Iran had begun enriching uranium in >1,300 centrifuges. {19} Amidst calls to resign, Gonzales testified before the Senate Judiciary Cmte over the prosecutor firings. ❦ Mary Winkler was convicted of voluntary manslaughter in the 3/2006 death of her preacher husband. ❦ Luis Posada Carriles, an anti-

Castro Cuban and ex-CIA officer linked to a 1976 airline bombing, was freed on bail, angering Cuba and Venezuela. ❧ A preliminary military investigation found marines had killed *c.*10 civilians near Jalalabad, Afghanistan, on 3/4. {20} A NASA worker killed 1 and then himself at the Johnson Space Center in Houston. ❧ The family of the VA Tech shooter issued an apology for his actions. {22} Nicolas Sarkozy and Ségolène Royal won the first round of France's presidential election. ❧ Maliki said construction of a controversial wall separating a Sunni area of Baghdad would stop. {23} RIP @ 76, former Russian President Boris Yeltsin [see p.59]. ❧ RIP @ 73, journalist David Halberstam. {24} Astronomers announced the discovery of a potentially 'Earthlike' planet 20 light-years away. ❧ The military wing of Hamas fired rockets and shells into Israel, and declared an end to the November cease-fire. ❧ Separatist rebels killed >70 at a Chinese-owned oil field in Ethiopia. ❧ Kevin Tillman told a Congressional committee the military had exploited his brother Pat's death for propaganda purposes; Jessica Lynch said the military had acted similarly during her 2003 capture. {25} McCain officially entered the Presidential race. ❧ The House approved a war spending Bill requiring troop withdrawal from Iraq by October 2008. ❧ After numerous feuds, Rosie O'Donnell said she would leave *The View*. {26} The Senate passed the war-spending Bill requiring troop withdrawal. ❧ Putin said Russia would no longer comply with the NATO Treaty on Conventional Armed Forces in Europe, in retaliation for a proposed US missile defense system in the region. {27} RIP

Rosie O'Donnell

The university was struck today with a tragedy of monumental proportions.
– VA Tech Pres. CHARLES STEGER

@ 80, cellist Mstislav Rostropovich [see p.59]. ❧ MIT's Dean of Admissions resigned after admitting to lying about her qualifications for 28 years. {28} A suicide car bomb attack in Karbala, Iraq, killed 68. ❧ A suicide attack in Charsadda, Pakistan, killed 28. {29} A shooting at a Kansas City shopping mall killed 3. {30} An Israeli government commission accused Olmert of 'severe failures' in the 2006 war with Hezbollah; Olmert said he would not resign. ❧ A British jury found 5 men guilty of plotting London bombings and linked them to the 7/7 subway bombers; the men were sentenced to life in prison. ❧ The VA Governor closed a state loophole that allowed VA Tech killer Cho to purchase guns despite having been treated for mental illness [see p.24].

MAY · {1} Bush vetoed the war-spending Bill, claiming it 'set a date for failure'. ❧ The FDA created a 'food safety czar' post. ❧ Rupert Murdoch made a surprise $6bn bid for Dow Jones & Co. ❧ Major immigration rallies were held around the US. {2} The House failed to override Bush's veto on the war-spending Bill. ❧ The Afghan government said a recent US bombing had killed >42 civilians; the US denied the charge. {3} The US military said it had killed Muharib Abdul Latif al-Jubouri, described as Al Qaeda's 'information minister'. ❧ Rice met with the Syrian Foreign Minister, the first high-level talks between the 2 countries in >2 years. ❧ Hillary Clinton and Sen. Byrd [WV-D] proposed a Bill to end Congressional authority for the war in Iraq on 10/11/07, 5 years after the original authorization. ❦ RIP @ 84, 'Mercury 7' astronaut Walter M. Schirra Jr. {4} A Greensburg, KS, tornado killed 12 and destroyed *c.*95% of the town's buildings. {5} A Cameroonian plane crash killed 114. {6} Nicolas Sarkozy was elected President of France. {7} Queen Elizabeth II visited the White House [see p.332]. ❦ The Senate approved a measure restricting the import of foreign drugs. ❦ NASA said a gigantic star had died in a 'monstrous explosion', the most powerful ever recorded. ❦ LA demoted a top police official amid controversy over forceful tactics used during a May 1 immigration rally. ❦ RIP @ 48, fashion icon Isabella Blow [see p.59]. {8} 6 alleged Islamic extremists living in the NE were charged with plotting to attack Fort Dix, NJ. ❦ The US military apologized to, and paid, families of the civilians killed in Jalalabad, Afghanistan, on 3/4/07. ❦ The heads of N Ireland's Sinn Féin and Democratic Unionists were sworn in as leaders of a historic power-sharing government. {9} The House voted to ban gifts and payments from student loan companies to universities. ❦ Afghan police said US air strikes killed 21 civilians in Helmand Province a day earlier. ❦ The Senate passed a Bill to increase FDA drug oversight. ❦ Putin made comments that seemed to compare the US to the Third Reich. {10} British PM Blair said he would leave office on June 27. ❦ The House passed a Bill to fund the Iraq war through July 13; a Bill to begin withdrawal in 90 days was defeated. ❦ Gonzales testified before the House Judiciary Cmte on the prosecutor firings. {11} A wildfire on Santa Catalina Island, CA, burned 4,200 acres and

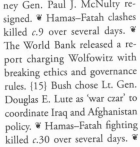

Nicolas Sarkozy

forced 3,200 to evacuate. {12} 3 US soldiers were abducted after an ambush S of Baghdad. ❦ A truck bomb at the Kurdistan Democratic Party offices in N Iraq killed *c.*50. ❦ Political clashes in Karachi, Pakistan, killed 39. {14} Deputy Attorney Gen. Paul J. McNulty resigned. ❦ Hamas–Fatah clashes killed *c.*9 over several days. ❦ The World Bank released a report charging Wolfowitz with breaking ethics and governance rules. {15} Bush chose Lt. Gen. Douglas E. Lute as 'war czar' to coordinate Iraq and Afghanistan policy. ❦ Hamas–Fatah fighting killed *c.*30 over several days. ❦ A suicide bomber in Peshawar, Pakistan, killed 22. ❦ Russia agreed to dampen anti-US rhetoric after a Rice–Putin meeting in Moscow. ❦ Former Justice Dept #2, James B. Comey, told the Senate Judiciary Cmte about a 2004 late-night visit in which Gonzales allegedly tried to persuade an ill John Ashcroft to recertify a classified intelligence program [see p.27]. ❦ RIP @ 73, evangelist Rev. Jerry Falwell [see p.59]. {16} Britain said Prince Harry would *not* serve in Iraq because conditions were too dangerous. ❦ RIP @ 51, actress and MLK's eldest child, Yolanda King. {17} Wolfowitz announced his resignation as World Bank President, effective June 30. ❦ Israeli air raids killed *c.*10 in Gaza. ❦ Senate Dems authorized a nonbinding, no-confidence vote on Gonzales. {18} Underwater explorers said they had found possibly the most valuable shipwreck ever, including *c.*$500m worth of Colonial-era coins. {19} ❦ Jimmy Carter was quoted in a press interview calling the W. Bush administration 'the worst in history'. {20} A battle between the Lebanese army and

Today, we will witness not hype, but history.
— MARTIN McGUINNESS, *Sinn Féin*

——————— IN BRIEF · MAY – JUNE 2007 ———————

militants near refugee camp Nahr al-Bared killed *c.*39. ❦ A gunman killed 3 in Moscow, ID. {21} Gov. Bill Richardson officially entered the Presidential race. ❦ Carter said his 'worst in history' remark had been 'careless or misinterpreted'. ❦ Israeli rocket attacks killed 5; a rocket from Gaza killed 1 Israeli. {22} British police said they had sufficient evidence to charge Russian Andrei Lugovoi with Litvinenko's murder and seek extradition. ❦ Congressional Dem leaders dropped their demand for a withdrawal time line in the war-funding Bill. {23} A body found in the Euphrates was identified as one of the missing US soldiers ambushed 5/12. ❦ In House testimony, former Justice Dept aide Monica Goodling admitted to using political criteria when hiring prosecutors; she also contradicted earlier Gonzales testimony. {24} Congress approved a $100bn war-funding Bill, including progress benchmarks but no withdrawal deadline; the Bill also raised the federal minimum wage [see p.318]. {25} N Korea test-fired a short-range missile. ❦ Moktada al-Sadr gave his first public sermon after months of hiding. ❦ Police discovered the bodies of pro wrestler Chris Benoit, his wife, and child, later ruling the incident a murder-suicide. {27} A Qassam rocket fired from Gaza killed 1 Israeli. {28} The US and Iran held direct talks on Iraq. ❦ Japan's agricultural minister hanged himself amid a campaign finance scandal. {29} Bush chose Goldman Sachs VP Robert Zoellick to head the World Bank. ❦ Bush ordered new economic sanctions against Sudan, aimed at stemming the violence in Darfur. ❦ Iran charged 3 Iranian Americans with spying. ❦ The Supreme

Moktada al-Sadr

I really believed that I wasn't putting people at risk.
— TB sufferer, ANDREW SPEAKER

Court ruled that employees must file discrimination charges within 180 days of a specific event, or lose their right to sue. {30} Officials began searching for air passengers who may have been exposed to drug-resistant TB, after an infected man took several flights [see p.111]. ❦ Bush asked Congress for $30bn to fight AIDS worldwide. {31} Bush proposed a 'long-term global goal' for cutting greenhouse emissions. ❦ Authorities arrested one of the world's 'top 10 spammers' in Seattle.

JUNE · {1} Jack Kevorkian was released from prison. {2} *c.*25,000 demonstrated in Germany against the G8 summit. ❦ Authorities charged 4 in an alleged plot to bomb fuel lines serving JFK airport. {3} Paris Hilton began a jail sentence for violating probation on a drunk-driving conviction. {4} Military judges dismissed charges against 2 Guantánamo detainees, arguing they were never declared 'unlawful' enemy combatants, as required by the Military Commissions Act. ❦ Rep. William J. Jefferson [LS-D] was indicted on 16 felony counts for bribery and other offenses. ❦ Pakistan arrested 2 in connection with Daniel Pearl's murder. ❦ An organ transplant team's plane crashed into Lake Michigan, killing 6. ❦ RIP @ 74, Sen. Craig Thomas [WY-R]. ❦ A federal appeals court overturned an FCC rule imposing fines for 'fleeting expletives' on live broadcasts. {5} Libby was sentenced to 30 months in prison for lying in the CIA leak case [see p.29]. ❦ Basque separatists ETA called-off a 15-month cease-fire. {6} Cyclone Gonu hit Oman, killing *c.*50. {7} The immigration Bill stalled in

──IN BRIEF · JUNE 2007──

the Senate. ❦ At the G8 meeting, the US agreed to 'consider seriously' a European plan to cut global greenhouse gas emissions in half by 2050. ❦ The House gave final approval to a Bill expanding stem cell research, but without sufficient votes to override a Bush veto. ❦ Hilton was released from jail due to an unspecified 'medical condition'. {8} Hilton was ordered back to jail. ❦ The G8 meeting ended with a $60bn pledge to fight disease in Africa. ❦ The *in absentia* trial of 26 Americans charged with the 2003 'extraordinary rendition' of a Muslim cleric began in Milan.

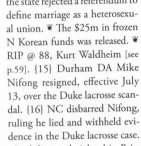

Ismail Haniya

❦ The administration said it would not renominate Gen. Pace for a second term. ❦ RIP @ 75, philosopher Richard Rorty. {10} Former SoS Colin Powell said Guantánamo should be closed. ❦ The final episode of *The Sopranos* aired. {11} A federal appeals court ruled that US residents could not be held indefinitely in military custody as 'enemy combatants'. ❦ A no-confidence vote on Gonzales failed in the Senate after being blocked by Reps. {12} Hamas seized Fatah's base in N Gaza; ongoing clashes killed >25; both sides accused the other of a coup. ❦ RIP @ 89, Don 'Mr Wizard' Herbert. ❦ Jamaican police concluded that cricket coach Woolmer died of natural causes. ❦ Sudan agreed to a joint UN–African Union peacekeeping force in Darfur, with certain conditions. {13} Sunni extremists bombed Iraq's al-Askari mosque for the second time since 2006. ❦ Shimon Peres was elected Israeli President. ❦ Congress issued subpoenas for Harriet Miers and top aide Sara Taylor to testify and provide documents in the prosecutor firings probe. ❦ In response to the VA Tech

shootings, the House voted to improve background-check information-sharing [see p.90]. {14} Hamas seized control of Gaza; Abbas fired PM Haniya, and declared a state of emergency [see p.28]. ❦ Gay marriage remained legal in MA, after the state rejected a referendum to define marriage as a heterosexual union. ❦ The $25m in frozen N Korean funds was released. ❦ RIP @ 88, Kurt Waldheim [see p.59]. {15} Durham DA Mike Nifong resigned, effective July 13, over the Duke lacrosse scandal. {16} NC disbarred Nifong, ruling he lied and withheld evidence in the Duke lacrosse case.

❦ Salman Rushdie was knighted in Britain, provoking protest from some Muslim groups. ❦ 6 were killed in TN after a race car spun out of control. ❦ *c.*500 were freed from forced labor at a Shanxi Province, China, brick kiln; the manager was arrested. {17} Abbas swore in an emergency Palestinian government and outlawed Hamas militias. ❦ RIP @ 62, fashion designer Gianfranco Ferré. ❦ A Kabul suicide bomber killed 35. {18} The US announced an end to its embargo of the Palestinian Authority. ❦ The Milan 'extraordinary rendition' trial was suspended. {19} A bomb at a Shiite mosque in Baghdad killed *c.*78. ❦ NYC Mayor Bloomberg quit the GOP, yet denied rumors of a Presidential bid. ❦ 9 firefighters died in a Charleston, SC, blaze. ❦ Nifong was suspended. {20} Bush vetoed the stem cell legislation. ❦ The US sent Asst SoS Christopher Hill to N Korea; the first top official sent for direct talks in 5 years. {21} The Senate passed a major energy Bill that included auto-efficiency standards. ❦ The Lebanese army said it had defeated militants at the

> *I'm going to do the time and I am going to do it the right way.*
> — PARIS HILTON

———————— IN BRIEF · JUNE – JULY 2007 ————————

Nahr al-Bared camp, and only 'clean-up' remained; the clashes killed *c.*170. {22} Hill returned from N Korea saying the country was ready to shut down its main nuclear reactor. {23} The EU dropped efforts to ratify a new constitution, and agreed to begin negotiating a new intergovernmental treaty. {24} An Iraqi court sentenced to death Ali Hassan al-Majid (aka 'Chemical Ali'). ❦ Israel agreed to release frozen Palestinian tax revenues. ❦ Johnston's kidnappers released a video of him wearing an explosives vest. {25} The Supreme Court ruled that a ban on pre-election 'issue ads' was a violation of free speech. ❦ Zoellick was approved World Bank president. {26} The CIA declassified 750 pages of documents [see p.14]. ❦ A Bill to allow employees to unionize without secret-ballot elections failed in the Senate. ❦ J. Steven Griles was sentenced to 10 months in prison for lying about his Abramoff connections. ❦ Hilton was released from jail. {27} Blair resigned as British PM, and was named special envoy for the Middle East 'Quartet'; he was replaced by Gordon Brown. ❦ The bald eagle was taken off the endangered species list [see p.256]. ❦ The Senate subpoenaed documents on the wiretapping program from the White House, Justice Dept, and Cheney's office. ❦ N Korea allowed UN inspectors to visit its Yongbyon reactor. ❦ RIP @ 78, fashion designer Liz Claiborne. {28} In a controversial decision, the Supreme Court ruled race could not be used as a factor in school assignment. ❦ The immigration Bill failed in the Senate [see p.28]. ❦ The White House rejected the Miers and Taylor subpoenas, invoking executive privilege. ❦ Lindsay Lohan

Gordon Brown

I'm going to do everything I can to stay out of trouble.
– ALAN JOHNSTON on his release

entered rehab after an alleged DUI arrest. ❦ Katsav resigned. {29} Apple's iPhone went on sale. ❦ Police discovered 2 car bombs in central London, but defused them before they could explode [see p.29]. ❦ The Supreme Court agreed to review the federal appeals court ruling that upheld the Military Commissions Act. {30} 2 men crashed a flaming SUV into the front doors of Glasgow Airport [see p.29]. British police arrested 5, and raised the threat alert level to 'critical'.

JULY · {1} Israel agreed to resume financial ties with the Palestinian Authority, and transferred *c.*120m in tax revenue. {2} Bush commuted Libby's sentence, calling it 'excessive' [see p.29]. ❦ Firefighters said they had contained a massive fire near Lake Tahoe, which razed >3,000 acres. ❦ RIP @ 78, opera singer Beverly Sills. {3} British police said the suspects in the failed car bombings were all doctors. ❦ America and Russia pledged to reduce nuclear stockpiles to the 'lowest possible level'. {4} 1,100 students surrendered amid an uprising at Pakistan's Red Mosque; a mosque leader was arrested trying to flee in a burka. ❦ Johnston was released to Hamas officials in Gaza. ❦ Britain lowered its threat level to severe, and said it would review screening procedures for foreign-born doctors. {5} Russia refused to extradite Lugovoi to Britain. {6} Musharraf survived an apparent assassination attempt when shots were fired at his plane outside Islamabad. ❦ A suspect was charged over the Glasgow attack. ❦ A federal appeals court overturned a challenge to the NSA wiretapping program. {7} Johnston returned to the UK. ❦

————— IN BRIEF · JULY 2007 —————

A suicide bomber killed *c.*105 N of Baghdad. {8} The Israeli government approved the release of 250 Fatah prisoners. {9} Claiming executive privilege once again, the White House rejected further subpoenas for prosecutor firing documents and said Taylor and Miers had been told not to testify. {10} Sen. John McCain's campaign said 2 top aides were leaving amid a funding crisis. ❦ Pakistani security forces stormed the Red Mosque. ❦ Former Surgeon General Richard H. Carmona told Congress he had been subject to political pressure and censorship during his term. {11} The battle at the Red Mosque ended; *c.*87 total were killed during the 8-day siege. Al Qaeda #2, al-Zawahiri, called for revenge. ❦ The Libyan Supreme Court upheld death sentences for the 6 medical workers accused of intentionally infecting children with HIV. ❦ RIP @ 94, LBJ's widow Lady Bird Johnson. ❦ A British court convicted 4 over the failed 7/21/05 London bombings. ❦ Taylor testified before the Senate Judiciary Cmte, but invoked executive privilege for some questions. {12} Bush released an interim Iraq report to Congress, showing 'satisfactory' progress on 8 of 15 benchmarks. The House voted to withdraw combat troops from Iraq by April 1. ❦ Miers refused to testify before the Con-

Lindsay Lohan

This earthquake was stronger than the reactor was designed for.
– MOHAMED ELBARADEI, IAEA

gressional panel on the prosecutor firings. {13} Former Hollinger Chairman Conrad Black was convicted of fraud and obstruction of justice; he vowed to appeal. ❦ Lohan left rehab. {14} The LA Archdiocese agreed to a $660m settlement for 508 victims of sexual abuse. {15} *c.*70 were killed over 2 days of bombing in NW Pakistan. {16} The IAEA confirmed

N Korea had shut its main nuclear reactor and allowed in a permanent inspection team. ❦ Bush announced renewed efforts to build a Palestinian state, including a Rice-led peace conference. ❦ An earthquake in Japan killed 10, injured >900, and leaked radioactive material from a nuclear plant. ❦ Suicide bombers killed *c.*100 in Kirkuk and Diyala Province, Iraq. {17} A major US intelligence report said Al Qaeda was resurgent, and the US was in a 'heightened threat environment'. ❦ *c.*200 were killed in a São Paulo plane crash. ❦ Libya commuted the death sentences of the 6 medical workers. ❦ The Dow Jones & Co. Board endorsed News Corp.'s takeover bid. ❦ A federal grand jury indicted Atlanta Falcons' quarterback Michael Vick for dog-fighting. {18} An Iraq troop withdrawal amendment failed in the Senate after an all-night debate session. ❦ A Manhattan steam-pipe explosion killed 1, wounded *c.*20, and rattled nerves. {19} Suicide bombers in Pakistan killed *c.*51. ❦ A federal district judge dismissed Valerie Plame's suite against Cheney and 3 others for the disclosure of her CIA identity, saying there was no legal basis for damages. ❦ The Taliban kidnapped 18 S Koreans in Afghanistan. {20} Bush signed an executive order banning cruel treatment of terrorism suspects in CIA detention and interrogation, while authorizing some harsh techniques. ❦ Pakistan's high court reinstated the Chief Justice. ❦ Israel freed 250 Palestinian prisoners. ❦ Russia blocked a UN vote on Serbian independence. {21} *Harry Potter and the Deathly Hallows* went on sale at 12:01am [see p.166]. {22} Turkey's 'Islamic-rooted' AK Party won parliamentary elections.

IN BRIEF · JULY – AUGUST 2007

{24} In Senate Judiciary Cmte testimony, Gonzales defended his 2004 visit to an ill Ashcroft. ❦ Libya freed the 6 medical workers. ❦ An LA grand jury refused to indict a doctor accused of Katrina 'mercy killings'. ❦ The Senate passed an ethics overhaul targeting student loan companies, following investigations that uncovered considerable corruption in the industry. ❦ Lohan was again arrested on drunk driving charges. {25} A House Cmte voted to hold Miers and another aide in contempt. ❦ The Taliban killed one of its Korean hostages. ❦ Bombs killed *c.*50 in Baghdad as crowds cheered the Iraqi soccer team's victory in the Asian Cup semifinals. ❦ Tour de France leader Michael Rasmussen was banished from the race [see p.242]. ❦ The Presidential commission on the Army medical system recommended an overhaul. {26} FBI chief Mueller gave testimony contradicting Gonzales's account of the 2004 meeting with Ashcroft. ❦ 13 were killed in a suicide bombing as Pakistan's Red Mosque reopened. {27} Wall Street numbers fell sharply, ending a volatile week amid concerns over credit, growth, and housing. ❦ Nicole Richie was sentenced to 4 days in jail for a February DUI charge. ❦ The US and India agreed on a nuclear cooperation deal. {29} Alberto Contador won the Tour de France [see p.242]. {30} Chief Justice John Roberts was hospitalized after a seizure. ❦ A second Korean hostage was reportedly executed. ❦ RIP @ 89, filmmaker Ingmar Bergman [see p.59]. {31} Rupert Murdoch secured a deal to buy the *Wall Street Journal* after gaining approval from longtime shareholders, the Bancroft family. ❦ The Army censured a

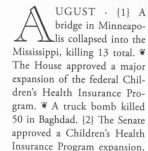

Rupert Murdoch

retired general over the 2004 handling of Cpl. Pat Tillman's 'friendly fire' death. ❦ The House passed a major ethics and lobbying overhaul. ❦ RIP @ 94, filmmaker Michelangelo Antonioni.

AUGUST · {1} A bridge in Minneapolis collapsed into the Mississippi, killing 13 total. ❦ The House approved a major expansion of the federal Children's Health Insurance Program. ❦ A truck bomb killed 50 in Baghdad. {2} The Senate approved a Children's Health Insurance Program expansion, with enough votes to override a threatened Bush veto. ❦ Russia planted a flag on the seabed under the North Pole, to Canadian and other objections. ❦ The Senate gave final Congressional approval to a major ethics and lobbying overhaul. {3} Britain announced a foot-and-mouth disease outbreak. {4} Major energy legislation passed the House. {5} Bush signed an amendment to the Foreign Intelligence Surveillance Act. {6} 6 were trapped in a UT coal mine. {7} Bonds hit his 756th home run [see p.250]. {8} *Endeavour* launched. {9} Mitt Romney won the Iowa Straw Poll. {12} RIP @ 82, entertainer Merv Griffin. {13} Rove announced his resignation. {14} RIP @ 89, beloved Yankee Phil Rizzuto. ❦ Truck bombs killed *c.*500 in N Iraq. ❦ Imus settled with CBS. {15} Former NBA ref Tim Donaghy pleaded guilty to gambling. ❦ Chávez announced plans to remake the Venezuelan constitution. ❦ An earthquake in Peru killed *c.*450.

All the secrets I have been carrying around for so long will be yours, too.
— J.K. ROWLING

The Daily Chronicle will be continued in the 2009 edition of *Schott's Miscellany*.

──────────SOME GREAT LIVES IN BRIEF──────────

STEVE IRWIN
2·22·1962–9·4·2006 (44)

Known around the world as 'the crocodile hunter', Irwin was a fearless showman of animal stunts and a tireless champion of conservation. In his trademark khaki clothes, with his trademark cry of 'crikey!', Irwin captured TV's fascination with venomous and dangerous animals. He died after being stabbed in the heart by a stingray's barb.

PIETER WILLEM BOTHA
1·12·1916–10·31·2006 (90)

As PM and President of South Africa from 1978–89, P.W. Botha maintained apartheid, ordered murderous attacks on political opponents, and attempted to destabilize neighboring countries. The so-called Great Crocodile refused even to appear before the Truth & Reconciliation Commission. His death was little mourned.

ED BRADLEY
6·22·1941–11·9·2006 (65)

Bradley's broadcasting talent was such that what might have caused comment (not least his beard and earring) were footnotes to a remarkable career in which he won 19 Emmys. A war correspondent in Vietnam, and a member of the White House press corps, Bradley joined *60 Minutes* in 1981 and stayed for 26 years.

ROBERT ALTMAN
2·20·1925–11·20·2006 (81)

Altman's unique style of film directing tended to be somewhat hit (*M*A*S*H*, *Nashville*, *The Player*, *Gosford Park*) and miss (*Quintet*, *Popeye*, *Prêt-à-Porter*). Yet by creating ambitious narrative tapestries and allowing his actors to improvise, Altman's 'pursuit of the imperfect moment' ensured his films were never ignored.

JEANE KIRKPATRICK
11·19·1926–12·7·2006 (80)

Reagan's first ambassador to the UN (and the first woman in that role), Kirkpatrick became known for her undiplomatic approach to diplomacy. Originally a Democrat, Kirkpatrick established a powerful and lasting influence over Republicans and neocons – famously asserting that 'traditional authoritarian governments are less repressive than revolutionary autocracies'.

AUGUSTO PINOCHET
11·25·1915–12·10·2006 (91)

After overthrowing Allende in 1973, General Pinochet presided over a brutal regime during which >3,000 Chileans were executed and many thousands were tortured or 'disappeared'. Claiming to be saving Chile from communism, Pinochet implemented harsh economic reforms that, despite a recession in the 1980s, were ultimately successful in making Chile one of the wealthiest Latin American states. The (disputed) ill-health of his old age saved Pinochet from standing trial for the human rights abuses many alleged he had instigated.

AHMET ERTEGUN
7·31·1923–12·14·2006 (83)

Cofounder of Atlantic Records (alongside his brother Nesuhi), Ertegun was one of the defining forces in American blues, jazz, rock, and soul. His roster of artists (Wilson Pickett, Ray Charles, Bobby Darin, Led Zeppelin, Stevie Wonder, Aretha Franklin, John Coltrane, &c.) reads like the Rock & Roll Hall of Fame he also helped to found.

JOSEPH BARBERA
3·24·1911–12·18·2006 (95)

As one half of the duo Hanna-Barbera, Barbera was responsible for some of the

─────────────SOME GREAT LIVES IN BRIEF cont.─────────────

best-loved cartoon characters, including: Yogi Bear, Scooby-Doo, Dastardly & Mutley, the Flintstones, and Tom & Jerry – which won more Oscars (7) than any other animation series in history.

JAMES BROWN
5·3·1933–12·25·2006 (73)

Brown's role in creating funk, fathering disco, and supplying the beat for rap and R&B truly earned him his many (self-appointed) titles – not least 'The Godfather of Soul'. A checkered personal life and time in prison dampened neither the spirit nor the appeal of this Black American icon – 'The Hardest Working Man in Show Business'.

GERALD FORD
7·14·1913–12·26·2006 (93)

Sworn in as the 38th President after Nixon's dramatic resignation, Ford became the only man to serve as President and Vice President without winning a single vote. Although controversial at the time, Ford's grant to Nixon of a full pardon was later seen as a vital step in rehabilitating America's body politic. While sometimes criticized for naïveté, Ford's plainspoken familiarity helped calm a nation struggling through recession and rattled by the horrors of Vietnam. Ford's standing rose after his presidency ended.

MOMOFUKU ANDO
3·5·1910–1·5·2007 (96)

Spurred by the sight of long queues for black market noodle soup in postwar Japan, Ando developed a range of instant ('just add boiling water') noodles that became an astounding international success. More than 85bn servings of Cup Noodles are slurped each year, justifying Ando's description of his culinary invention as 'magic noodles'.

BARBARO
4·29·2003–1·29·2007 (3)

Barbaro's injury at the 2006 Preakness catalyzed an unprecedented outpouring of affection for the 3-year-old colt who had won the Kentucky Derby (by 6½ lengths) just weeks earlier. Although the breaks in his right hind leg successfully healed, the resulting changes in weight distribution led to complications so debilitating that he was euthanized.

ANNA NICOLE SMITH
11·28·1967–2·8·2007 (39)

A model, actress, stripper, and reality TV star, Smith was 'famous for being infamous'. Her life vacillated between oddity (her marriage to an oil billionaire 60 years her senior) and tragedy (the death of her 20-year-old son). A paternity 'tug of love' over her 5-month-old daughter ensured that Smith remained in the headlines long after her death from a drug overdose.

JEAN BAUDRILLARD
7·29·1929–3·6·2007 (77)

A French social theorist and philosopher of postmodernism, Baudrillard was primarily concerned with consumerism and mass communication. These, he claimed, created a state of simulation and 'hyper-reality', more real than real life. Expanding on this thesis, he provocatively suggested that the 1991 Gulf War and the 9/11 attacks might be more explicable as symbolic events.

KURT VONNEGUT
11·11·1922–4·11·2007 (84)

Vonnegut is famed for his antiwar classic *Slaughterhouse-Five* (1969) – based on his experience of surviving the 1945 Dresden 'firestorm' by hiding in a subterranean meat locker. Combining science fiction with a pithy, cynical style,

———————— SOME GREAT LIVES IN BRIEF cont. ————————

Vonnegut's prolific output survived some critical derision and joined the pantheon of American literature.

BORIS YELTSIN
2·1·1931–4·23·2007 (76)

Russia's first elected President, Yeltsin rose to power as a populist reformer, but left a troubled legacy. After helping to orchestrate the dissolution of the Soviet Union, his economic 'shock therapy' led to rapidly declining living conditions, widespread resentment by many Russians, and a 1993 political crisis. After the disastrous invasion of Chechnya in 1994 and a second term marked by failing health, he resigned unexpectedly on New Year's Eve 1999, transferring power to Putin [see p.32].

MSTISLAV ROSTROPOVICH
3·27·1927–4·27·2007 (80)

Widely acclaimed as the greatest cellist since Pablo Casals, Rostropovich combined musical excellence with a deep commitment to humanitarian causes. Exiled from the Soviet Union in 1974, Rostropovich went to America until the Cold War thaw allowed him to re-establish relations with his homeland.

ISABELLA BLOW
11·19·1958–5·7·2007 (48)

One of fashion's genuine iconoclasts, Blow worked for a host of magazines, and with many of the industry's most respected names. Revolving around style and the stylish, her life was eccentric, aristocratic, creative, generous, impoverished, and, finally, suicidally tragic. Blow is credited with 'discovering' a constellation of stars, including Philip Treacy, Stella Tennant, Sophie Dahl, and Alexander McQueen – who once described her as 'a cross between a Billingsgate fishwife and Lucretia Borgia'.

JERRY FALWELL
8·11·1933–5·15·2007 (73)

By combining (tel)evangelism with attacks on liberalism, Falwell is credited with shaping Christian conservatism into a political force, and aiding the fortunes of Reagan. Equally loved and loathed, Falwell courted controversy, calling AIDS God's punishment for homosexuals, denouncing Muhammad as a terrorist, and claiming that feminists, abortionists, gays, liberals, the ACLU, &c., 'helped 9/11 to happen'.

KURT WALDHEIM
12·21·1918–6·14·2007 (88)

Waldheim's distinguished career as an Austrian diplomat and then Secretary General of the UN (1972–82) ended in ignominy, when his previously denied wartime service in the German Army was exposed. Despite a number of allegations against him, Waldheim was elected Austrian President in 1985. Yet, ostracism by the international community made his position untenable, and he did not seek reelection in 1992. Three years later, on the basis of his war record, he was denied entry into the US to celebrate the UN's 50th anniversary.

INGMAR BERGMAN
7·14·1918–7·30·2007 (89)

With films like *The Seventh Seal* and *Through a Glass Darkly*, Bergman established an indelible reputation for spare, powerful meditations on existential themes. He wrote and directed >50 films in *c*.40 years, winning 3 Oscars for best foreign film. After being charged in Sweden with tax evasion in 1976, he lived in self-imposed exile in Germany until the mid-'80s, and declared an 'official' retirement in 1982 after writing and directing one of his finest films, *Fanny & Alexander*.

The World

*Physicists and astronomers see their own implications in the world being round,
but to me it means that only one-third of the world is asleep at any given time
and the other two-thirds is up to something.*
— DEAN RUSK, Secretary of State, 1964

ASYLUM LEVELS & TRENDS · 2006

In 2006, the United States became the most popular destination for asylum seekers – receiving an estimated 51,500 applications. Figures from the United Nations High Commissioner for Refugees (UNHCR), released in March 2007, revealed the industrialized countries that received the largest share of asylum applications:

Country (%)	2005	2006			
United States	14·4	17·0	Sweden	5·2	8·0
France	14·7	10·1	Canada	5·8	7·6
UK	9·1	9·2	Germany	8·5	7·0
			Netherlands	3·7	4·8

In 2006, the top ten nationalities applying for asylum in the United States were:

Country	applicants				
China	9,706	Mexico	1,827	Indonesia	1,106
Haiti	4,475	Colombia	1,791	Honduras	1,076
El Salvador	2,734	Guatemala	1,731	Venezuela	902
		Ethiopia	1,173	[Source: UNHCR]	

INTERNATIONAL DEVELOPMENT & AID

Organization for Economic Cooperation and Development (OECD) figures show that development aid has fallen by 5·1% since 2005, to $103·9bn in 2006. This fall in aid was due to the exceptionally high levels donated in 2005, mainly in the form of debt relief for countries such as Iraq and Nigeria. The US was the largest donor in 2006. As before, only 5 of the 22 major donors managed to hit the UN target of giving 0·7% of their Gross National Income to Overseas Development Aid:

Country	ODA $m	% GNI			
Australia	2,128	0·30	Luxembourg	291	0·89
Canada	3,713	0·30	Netherlands	5,452	0·81
Denmark	2,234	0·80	Norway	2,946	0·89
France	10,448	0·47	Spain	3,801	0·32
Germany	10,351	0·36	Sweden	3,967	1·03
Ireland	997	0·53	UK	12,607	0·52
Japan	11,608	0·25	US	22,739	0·17
			[Provisional figures, 2006]		

THE DOOMSDAY CLOCK

In 1947, the *Bulletin of the Atomic Scientists* established its 'Doomsday Clock' – the hands of which move to and from midnight (the figurative end of civilization), as the threat of nuclear devastation ebbs and flows. In 2007, the clock hit '5 minutes to midnight', reflecting the growing threat of nuclear proliferation and, significantly, the threats posed by climate change. Below are the time changes since the clock was established at '7 minutes to midnight'.

-7 **(1947)** The Doomsday Clock appears on the cover of the *Bulletin of the Atomic Scientists* for the first time, in the wake of the Hiroshima and Nagasaki bombs.

-3 **(1949)** President Truman tells the American public that, despite official denials, the Soviets have tested their first nuclear device, thereby starting the arms race.

-2 **(1953)** International security is thrown into disarray, as the US and the Soviets test thermonuclear hydrogen bombs within months of each other during 1952–53.

-7 **(1960)** A number of political and scientific interactions signal that the US and the Soviets are keen to avoid confrontation and quell diplomatic hostilities.

-12 **(1963)** The US and the Soviets sign the Partial Test Ban Treaty ending all atmospheric testing, and signaling an awareness of the risks of nuclear conflict.

-7 **(1968)** France and China both develop nuclear weapons; regional wars include the US and Vietnam, India and Pakistan, and Israel with its Arab neighbors.

-10 **(1969)** Tensions are reduced when most of the world's nations sign the Nuclear Non-Proliferation Treaty – significantly not India, Pakistan, nor Israel.

-12 **(1972)** The US and the Soviets sign the Strategic Arms Limitation Treaty and the Anti-Ballistic Missile Treaty, signaling a slowing of the arms race.

-9 **(1974)** India tests its first nuclear device, bringing the bomb to South Asia. Both the US and the Soviets appear to be modernizing their nuclear arsenals.

-7 **(1980)** Some promising moves towards disarmament fail to end the superpowers' reliance on nuclear weapons as an integral part of their national security.

-4 **(1981)** The Soviet invasion of Afghanistan hardens the US nuclear position; Carter pulls the US from the Moscow Olympics; Reagan vows to win the Cold War.

-3 **(1984)** US–Soviet relations sink to a low as negotiations all but cease. The US pursues a space-based anti-ballistic capability, raising fears of a new arms race.

-6 **(1988)** The US and the Soviets sign the historic Intermediate-Range Nuclear Forces Treaty, banning for the first time a whole category of nuclear weapons.

-10 **(1990)** The risk of nuclear war diminishes with the collapse of the Soviet Union, the fall of the Berlin Wall in 1989, and the end of the Cold War.

-17 **(1991)** The Cold War's end; Strategic Arms Reduction Treaty, and unilateral measures lower tensions and cast doubt on the reliance on nuclear weapons.

-14 **(1995)** Hopes fade for a Cold War peace dividend as US hawks view Russia with suspicion; concern grows over unsecured nukes in the former Soviet Union.

-9 **(1998)** India and Pakistan stage nuclear tests within weeks of each other; Russia and the US still maintain 7,000 warheads ready to fire within 15 minutes.

-7 **(2002)** Concern grows about terrorist groups acquiring unsecured nuclear material; the US expresses a more dogmatic attitude to nuclear proliferation.

-5 **(2007)** US & Russia stand ready to attack; N. Korea conducts tests; Iran threatens to acquire a nuclear bomb; damage to ecosystems is causing environmental crises.

[Source: *Bulletin of the Atomic Scientists*]

———————INTERNATIONAL OPINIONS ON TORTURE———————

A BBC World Service survey published in October 2006 suggested that nearly one third of people around the world supported some use of torture. 27,000 people in 25 countries were asked which of two statements was closest to their opinion:

'Terrorists pose such an extreme threat that governments should now be allowed to use some degree of torture if it may gain information that saves innocent lives'	*'Clear rules against torture should be maintained because any use of torture is immoral and will weaken international human rights'*

Internationally, 59% of respondents opposed torture under any circumstances, and 29% considered some degree of torture acceptable. Below is a country breakdown:

Country	against all torture	allow some torture	don't know
Australia	75%	22	3
Canada	74	22	4
China	49	37	13
Egypt	65	25	9
France	75	19	6
Germany	71	21	7
Great Britain	72	24	4
India	23	32	45
Indonesia	51	40	8
Iraq	55	42	1
Israel	48	43	9
Italy	81	14	6
Russia	43	37	19
Turkey	62	24	14
USA	58	36	7

[Source: BBC/Globescan/PIPA · Some figures do not add up to 100% due to rounding]

———————————— THE DEATH PENALTY ————————————

Amnesty International's annual Death Penalty Statistics, released in April 2007, indicated a 25% fall in executions and death sentences around the world in 2006. During 2006, the Philippines abolished the death penalty for ordinary crimes, and both Georgia and Moldova removed death penalty provisions from their constitutions. However, more than 1,591 people were executed in 25 countries that year; 3,861 death sentences were passed in 55 countries; and more than 20,000 prisoners were held on 'death row'. Since 1990, >45 countries have abolished the death penalty, though it is still in force in 69 countries. Below is Amnesty's estimate of the countries that executed the greatest number of people during 2006:

China.......1,010	Pakistan 82	Sudan...........65	Saudi Arabia....39
Iran...........177	Iraq.............65	USA.............53	Yemen..........30

---------------WOMEN IN POLITICS WORLDWIDE---------------

Women continue to struggle against inequality, according to a UN report released in December 2006 – *The State of the World's Children 2007: Women & Children, the Double Dividend of Gender Equality*. The study indicated that women's lack of access to education and employment contributed to poverty and disenfranchisement. Symptomatic of the gender divide is women's lack of representation at government level. The public's attitude to female politicians may go some way towards explaining this inequality. The chart below shows the percentage of the public (by region) who agreed, or strongly agreed, that men make better political leaders than women:

Region	*% agreeing that men make better politicians*
Middle East & North Africa	77
Sub-Saharan Africa	59
South Asia	58
East Asia & Pacific	55
Latin America & Caribbean	35

Women are underrepresented in every national parliament in the world – 10 countries have no female MPs, and in 40 others women account for less than 10% of parliamentarians. The worldwide average percentage of women in government:

In parliament.......17% | Female ministers ...14% | Heads of govt 6%

The following table from the Inter-Parliamentary Union shows the countries with the highest percentage of women in the lower or single chamber, as of 10·31·2006:

Country	*elections*	*% women*				
1 Rwanda	09/2003	48·8	5	Norway	09/2005	37·9
2 Sweden	09/2006	47·3	(15	Germany	09/2005	31·8)
3 Costa Rica	02/2006	38·6	(50	UK	05/2005	19·7)
4 Finland	03/2003	38·0	(67	USA	11/2004	15·2)

[Sources: UN *State of the World's Children 2007*; World Values Survey; Inter-Parliamentary Union]

---------------GLOBAL GENDER GAP---------------

In 2006, the World Economic Forum released a Gender Gap Index that ranked 115 countries according to their levels of gender equality. Scores between 0 (inequality) and 1 (equality) were assigned in four areas: economic participation and opportunity; educational attainment; political empowerment; and health and survival. Nordic countries came at the top of the list, while the US ranked 22nd:

Rank country	*score*	4	Iceland	0·7813	8	Denmark	0·7462
1 Sweden	0·8133	5	Germany	0·7524	9	UK	0·7365
2 Norway	0·7994	6	Philippines	0·7516	10	Ireland	0·7335
3 Finland	0·7958	7	N. Zealand	0·7509	(22	US	0·704)

———————SIGNIFICANT ONGOING CONFLICTS———————

The Quaker lobby group Friends Committee on National Legislation (FCNL) classifies significant ongoing conflicts as those in which ≥1,000 have been killed. As of January 2007, the FCNL and the Center for Defense Information reported there were fifteen significant ongoing armed conflicts in the world – they are:

Middle East   *began*
US global 'war on terror' & 'terrorists with global reach' 2001
Iraq government and allies & Iraqi and foreign resistance 2003
Israel & Hamas, Hezbollah, Islamic Jihad, &c. 1975
Asia
Afghanistan: Kabul government & Al Qaeda and Taliban. 1978
India & Assam (ULFA) insurgents, &c. 1986
Sri Lanka & Tamil Eelam 1978; 2002
Philippines & New People's Army 1969
Latin America
Colombia & National Liberation Army (ELN) 1978
Colombia & Revolutionary Armed Forces of Colombia (FARC) 1978
Europe
Russia & Chechnya 1994; 1996
Africa
Democratic Republic of Congo & indigenous insurgents 1997
Nigeria: ethnic and religious communal violence 1970
Somalia: Somaliland, Puntland, and other factions 1978; 2005
Sudan & Sudan Liberation and Justice and Equality Movements 2003
Uganda & Lord's Army 1986

[Source: Center for Defense Information, as at January 1, 2007]

———————THE UN SECURITY COUNCIL———————

The United Nations Security Council (UNSC) has a mandate under the 1945 United Nations Charter to maintain international peace and security. The Council held its first meeting in London in January 1946, and has been in continuous session ever since (a representative of each of the member nations is present at the UN's headquarters at all times). The Council has five permanent members: China, France, the Russian Federation, the UK, and the US. Alongside these serve ten nonpermanent members, who are elected for 2-year terms by the UN General Assembly. In 2007–08 the nonpermanent members were: Belgium, Congo, Ghana, Indonesia, Italy, Panama, Peru, Qatar, Slovakia, and South Africa. The 1-month Presidency of the Security Council rotates among members of the Council, according to the English alphabetical order of country names. Each Council member may cast one vote. For a resolution [see p.65] to be passed, at least nine of the fifteen must vote 'yes'. All permanent members of the Council must vote in the affirmative for substantive matters to pass, giving all five a veto. The United Nations Charter states that all members are obliged to accept and enforce decisions made by the Security Council – it is the only UN body which has such powers.

UN SECURITY COUNCIL RESOLUTIONS OF NOTE

Year	resolution number	called for
1947	27	an immediate cessation of hostilities between troops from the Netherlands and the Republic of Indonesia
1948	50	a cessation of hostilities in Palestine, without prejudice to the rights, claims, and position of either Arabs or Jews
1950	82	North Korea to cease hostilities against the Republic of Korea and withdraw to the 38th parallel
1956	118	the operation of the Suez Canal to be insulated from the politics of any country
1963	181	the government of South Africa to abandon the policies of apartheid and release all political prisoners
1967	242	withdrawal of Israel from the occupied territories, in exchange for a peace settlement
1973	338	a cease-fire between Israeli and Arab forces to end the Yom Kippur War
1974	353	Turkey to respect the independence of Cyprus and the withdrawal of all troops of every nationality
1982	502	an immediate cessation of hostilities and the withdrawal of all Argentine troops from the Falklands
1982	514	Iran and Iraq to suspend hostilities and withdraw to internationally recognized borders
1990	660	the immediate withdrawal of all occupying Iraqi forces from Kuwait
1994	955	the establishment of an international tribunal to bring to justice those who committed atrocities in Rwanda
1998	1172	India and Pakistan to cease the development of nuclear weapons
1999	1244	Kosovo to be placed under transitional UN administration, and a NATO-led peacekeeping force to be deployed
1999	1264	the establishment of a multinational force to restore peace and security in East Timor
1999	1267	the Taliban in Afghanistan to stop supporting terrorism, and surrender Osama bin Laden
2001	1373	condemnation of the 9/11 attacks and for states to work together to prevent terrorist acts
2002	1441	Iraq to comply with all previous calls for disarmament, and disclose and surrender all WMD
2003	1515	the Roadmap to a permanent two-state solution to the Israeli–Palestinian conflict to be adhered to
2004	1556	the Sudanese government to disband the Janjaweed, and bring to justice those who committed atrocities in Darfur
2006	1701	full cessation of hostilities between Israel and Hezbollah in Lebanon
2006	1718	sanctions to be imposed against North Korea, in response to their nuclear test
2006	1737	Iran to suspend nuclear activities, sanctions imposed to prevent the supply of nuclear-related technology to Iran
2007	1769	a peace-keeping force of 20,000 military personnel be deployed to the Darfur region of Sudan [see pp.29–30]

──────────── NOBEL PEACE PRIZE ────────────

The 2006 Nobel Peace Prize was awarded in equal parts to the GRAMEEN BANK and its founder and managing director, MUHAMMAD YUNUS (1940–)

for their efforts to create economic and social development from below

Muhammad Yunus was born in Chittagong, Bangladesh, in 1940. He was a Fulbright Scholar at Vanderbilt University, where he earned his PhD in economics in 1969, and later joined the Chittagong University Economics Dept. Before founding the Grameen Bank, Yunus developed a form of village government and a system of cooperative farming, both of which were later adopted by the Bangladeshi government. ❦ Grameen Bank was founded as an independent bank by government legislation in 1983. Grameen (meaning 'village' or 'rural' in Bengali) offers small, collateral-free loans to the 'poorest of the poor' in rural Bangladesh. The bank's philosophy deems credit a basic human right, and challenges the traditional wisdom that the poor are not 'creditworthy'. Loans are offered alongside institutional support, such as weekly meetings for groups of borrowers. The bank has so far disbursed over $5·3bn to *c*.6·67m borrowers and, unlike most Third World banks, it lends almost exclusively to women. The bank claims repayment rates of *c*.98%. ❦ Yunus became frustrated with teaching economic theories during the 1974 Bangladesh famine, in which hundreds of thousands died. He began an 'action research' project in the nearby village of Jobra, where he interviewed villagers about the 'real-life economics' of their existence. Yunus and his students discovered that many in Jobra were so poor they had to depend on usurious middlemen for the materials of their

Muhammad Yunus

trade, leaving them with only the basics of survival. Sickened, Yunus loaned the villagers enough money ($27) to buy their own materials and cut out the middlemen. All the loans were repaid, and Yunus' generosity grew into a full-fledged business plan, which expanded to other villages with the help of Bangladesh's Central Bank. As of May 2006, Grameen had 2,247 branches, covering >86% of the villages in Bangladesh. Grameen is nonprofit: 90% of the bank's shares are owned by its borrowers; the balance is held by the government. Yunus claims that within 5 years, 50% of Grameen's borrowers have escaped poverty, in that they now possess, among other essentials, clean drinking water, warm clothes in winter, mosquito netting in summer, a sanitary latrine, a house with a tin roof, schooling for children, and ≥$75 in savings. ❦ Grameen has catalyzed what some call a 'microfinance revolution'. Over 250 institutions in *c*.100 countries have reportedly established microcredit programs based on the Grameen model. In the last decade, organizations have expanded the idea of microcredit to include profit-making commercial ventures. Recently, foundations established by tech billionaires (like the Michael and Susan Dell Foundation, the Bill and Melinda Gates Foundation, and Google. org) have contributed major microfinance funding. Yet only time will tell whether microcredit can eradicate poverty, as Yunus earnestly believes.

———————— CHILD WELL-BEING ————————

The well-being of children in 21 industrialized nations was ranked by a UNICEF report published in February 2007. The study used more than 40 indicators to assess children including: their relationship with their parents; rates of teenage pregnancy; drug use; and levels of literacy. The Netherlands ranked top overall, and the US languished in most areas, coming in the bottom third of results for five out of the six main categories [see also p.95]. The overall and category rankings are below:

overall rank		material well-being	health & safety	educational well-being	behaviors & risks	subjective well-being	family & friends
1st	Netherlands	10th	2nd	6th	3rd	1st	3rd
2nd	Sweden	1st	1st	5th	1st	7th	15th
3rd	Denmark	4th	4th	8th	6th	12th	9th
4th	Finland	3rd	3rd	4th	7th	11th	17th
5th	Spain	12th	6th	15th	5th	2nd	8th
6th	Switzerland	5th	9th	14th	12th	6th	4th
7th	Norway	2nd	8th	11th	13th	8th	10th
8th	Italy	14th	5th	20th	10th	10th	1st
9th	Ireland	19th	19th	7th	4th	5th	7th
10th	Belgium	7th	16th	1st	19th	16th	5th
11th	Germany	13th	11th	10th	11th	9th	13th
12th	Canada	6th	13th	2nd	17th	15th	18th
13th	Greece	15th	18th	16th	8th	3rd	11th
14th	Poland	21st	15th	3rd	2nd	19th	14th
15th	Czech Rep.	11th	10th	9th	9th	17th	19th
16th	France	9th	7th	18th	14th	18th	12th
17th	Portugal	16th	14th	21st	15th	14th	2nd
18th	Austria	8th	20th	19th	16th	4th	16th
19th	Hungary	20th	17th	13th	18th	13th	6th
20th	USA	17th	21st	12th	20th	—	20th
21st	UK	18th	12th	17th	21st	20th	21st

[Source: UNICEF, *Report Card 7: An Overview of Child Well-being in Rich Countries*, 2007]

———————— SAKHAROV PRIZE ————————

Presented by the European Union since 1988, the Sakharov Prize for Freedom of Thought aims to reward individuals who challenge oppression and campaign for human rights. It is named in honor of Soviet physicist Andrei Sakharov (1921–89), who helped to develop the hydrogen bomb but later won the Nobel Peace Prize for his work campaigning against nuclear weapons. In 2006, the €50,000 prize was awarded to leader of the Belarusian opposition ALIAKSANDR MILINKEVICH, for his fight to bring democracy to his country despite an oppressive political climate.

———————————— THE FBI'S MOST WANTED ————————————

Fugitive [as at 8·13·07]	*allegation*	*reward*
Osama bin Laden	terrorism	$25,000,000
Diego Leon Montoya Sanchez	drug running	$5,000,000
James J. Bulger	murder; racketeering	$1,000,000
Victor Manuel Gerena	armed robbery	$1,000,000
Robert William Fisher	murder; arson	$100,000
Alexis Flores	kidnapping; murder	$100,000
Glen Stewart Godwin	murder; prison escape	$100,000
Jorge Alberto Lopez-Orozco	murder	$100,000
Emigdio Preciado Jr	attempted murder; assault	$100,000
Richard S. Goldberg (captured 5·12·07)	child abuse	$100,000

———————————— WORLD DEATH WATCH ————————————

In 2006, the World Health Organization forecast the leading causes of death in 2030 based on 2002 statistics. Overall trends show a shift from communicable, maternal, and nutritional diseases towards noncommunicable illnesses – although AIDS is predicted to become the 3rd worst killer, after heart disease and stroke.

2002 actual causes of death		*2030 predicted causes of death*
Ischemic heart disease	1	ischemic heart disease
Cerebrovascular disease (stroke)	2	cerebrovascular disease (stroke)
Lower respiratory infections	3	HIV/AIDS
HIV/AIDS	4	COPD[†]
COPD[†]	5	lower respiratory infections
Perinatal conditions	6	trachea, bronchus, lung cancer
Diarrheal diseases	7	diabetes
Tuberculosis	8	road traffic accidents
Trachea, bronchus, lung cancer	9	perinatal conditions
Road traffic accidents	10	stomach cancer

The WHO also predicts that in 2030 1·1m people worldwide will die from self-inflicted injuries, 0·8m from violence, and 0·3m from war. † Chronic Obstructive Pulmonary Disease; a group of lung diseases primarily caused by smoking. [Source: WHO, 2006. Projections according to a baseline scenario.]

———————————— SUICIDE RATES WORLDWIDE ————————————

suicides per million pop.	Poland	13·6	Canada	10·6
Japan	20·3	New Zealand	12·0	Germany	10·3
Korea	18·7	Australia	11·1	USA	10·2
France	15·1	Ireland	11·1	UK	6·3

[Source: OECD. Figures are the most recent available: data from Germany are 2004; Poland and Japan, 2003; UK, USA, Ireland, France, Korea, Australia, and Canada, 2002; and New Zealand, 2000.]

—————————— WORLD'S TEN WORST DICTATORS ——————————

American magazine *Parade* annually publishes a list of the world's worst dictators, based on their record of human rights abuse. The 2007 top ten ('06 rank in brackets):

No.	dictator	age	country	years' reign	facial hair?
1 (1)	Omar al-Bashir	63	Sudan	18	goatee†
2 (2)	Kim Jong-il	64	North Korea	13	none
3 (9)	Sayyid Ali Khamenei	67	Iran	18	bushy beard
4 (6)	Hu Jintao	64	China	5	none
5 (7)	King Abdullah	83	Saudi Arabia	12	cavalier beard
6 (3)	Than Shwe	74	Burma	15	none
7 (4)	Robert Mugabe	82	Zimbabwe	27	Hitler-esque
8 (5)	Islam Karimov	69	Uzbekistan	18	none
9 (11)	Muammar al-Qaddafi	64	Libya	38	none
10 (16)	Bashar al-Assad	41	Syria	7	mustache

† 'A beard trimmed in the form of a tuft hanging from the chin, resembling that of a he-goat' [*OED*].

—————————————— PRIVACY RANKINGS ——————————————

In November 2006, the human rights organization Privacy International ranked 36 countries on their record of protecting privacy. Scores were awarded in 13 categories including: constitutional protections; extent of visual surveillance; law enforcement's access to data; communications interception; workplace monitoring; and data-sharing provisions. Category scores were averaged to create an overall country score, which Privacy International characterized using the following scale:

4·1–5·0 .... consistently upholds human rights standards
3·6–4·0 .... significant protections and safeguards
3·1–3·5 .... adequate safeguards against abuse
2·6–3·0 .... some safeguards but weakened protections
2·1–2·5 .... systemic failure to uphold safeguards
1·6–2·0 .... extensive surveillance societies
1·1–1·5 .... endemic surveillance societies

Germany ranked at the top of the scale (3·9), while Malaysia and China were tied at the bottom (1·3). Below are the overall scores for some other countries of note:

Canada .... 3·6	New Zealand........ 2·5	USA .... 2·0†
France .... 2·9	Australia............. 2·4	UK................... 1·5
Ireland.............. 2·5	Israel................. 2·2	Russia............... 1·4

† The US scored the lowest of any democratic country for statutory protection and privacy enforcement. However, America received top marks in the democratic safeguards category, which looked at public consultation processes and levels of accountability, as well as in the communications data retention category, which looked both at legal conditions and the extent of data retention.

2006 GLOBAL HUNGER INDEX

In October 2006, the International Food Policy Research Institute released its 2006 Global Hunger Index (GHI) which ranked levels of hunger in 94 'developing' and 22 'transitional' countries. Three indicators were used to rank the countries on a 0–100 scale: the proportion of people who are food-energy deficient; infant mortality rates; and the prevalence of underweight children under five years old. Twelve countries with values exceeding 30 displayed 'extremely alarming' rates of hunger:

Country	hunger level				
Burundi	42·70	Sierra Leone	35·20	Comoros	30·81
Eritrea	40·37	Niger	33·43	Cambodia	30·73
Congo DR	37·60	Angola	32·17	Tajikistan	30·25
Ethiopia	36·70	Liberia	32·00		
		Zambia	31·77	Data from 2003. [See p.101]	

The GHI was calculated in 1981, 1992, 1997, and (most recently) 2003. As conditions have improved, so too have the rankings of a number of countries, including Mozambique, Ghana, and Guatemala.

THE WORLD'S FATTEST COUNTRIES

According to the World Health Organization, there are 1·6bn overweight adults worldwide – a figure that is predicted to swell by 40% in the next decade. *Forbes* compiled a list of the countries with the highest percentage of overweight adults[†]:

Country	%				
1 ... Nauru[‡]	94·5	4 ... Tonga	90·8	8 ..... Kuwait	74·2
2 ... Micronesia	91·1	5 ... Niue	81·7	9 ..... USA	74·1
3 ... Cook Islands	90·9	6 ... Samoa	80·4	10 .... Kiribati	73·6
		7 ... Palau	78·4	(28 ... UK	63·8)

† Adults with a Body Mass Index >25. ‡ Island republic on a coral atoll halfway between Australia and Hawaii. [Figures based on latest WHO estimates. Source: Forbes.com, February 2007]

CLIMATE CHANGE & GLOBAL MIGRATION

Christian Aid warned that an estimated 1bn people will be displaced by 2050 because of the effects of climate change and a developing migration crisis. Their report, *Human Tide: The Real Migration Crisis*, released to mark Christian Aid Week in May 2007, revealed that 155m people are currently displaced by conflicts, natural disasters, and the effects of large-scale development projects (like dams and plantations). This figure is likely to grow as the effects of climate change are felt, and the causes of internal displacement are magnified. The countries worst affected by mass displacement are often those least able to cope, and security experts warn that future conflicts are likely to develop over competition for scarce resources [see p.22]. Christian Aid identified six states that are currently experiencing serious levels of internal displacement which, as a result, are at greatest risk from a future migration crisis. They are: SUDAN, COLOMBIA, UGANDA, SRI LANKA, BURMA, and MALI.

———————— BIG GAME HUNTING & CONSERVATION ————————

A study by the conservation biologist Dr Peter Lindsey, published in *Biological Conservation* in January 2007, suggested that big game hunting may be good for conservation. When managed properly, hunting provides economic motivation for the local population to protect the environment and combat poaching. Trophy hunting is a growing market in southern Africa, annually contributing $28·5m to Namibia, $27·6m to Tanzania, and $100m to South Africa. The table below reveals some of the animals available to hunt in Namibia, and their trophy cost in 2007:

Animal	trophy cost (US$)	Animal	trophy cost (US$)
		Blue Wildebeest	800
Jackal	100	Hartmann Zebra	1,000
Baboon	110	Black Wildebeest	1,100
Ostrich	310	Giraffe	2,500
Springbok	350	Leopard	3,400
Impala	520	Cheetah	3,400

[Source: Kowas Adventure Safaris, Namibia] · In 2003, Marco Festa-Bianchet, a wildlife biologist at Univ. of Sherbrooke, Quebec, reported in *Nature* that hunting of bighorn sheep in Canada may have harmed the gene pool. This research suggested that since hunters generally targeted animals with the largest horns or antlers, the sheep with the best genes were threatened. Due to pressure from hunting, bighorn sheep in Alberta, Canada, were increasingly found to have smaller horns and poorer genes.

———————————— LAZARUS SPECIES ————————————

In July 2007, David Attenborough's long-beaked echidna (*Zaglossus attenboroughi*), long-thought extinct, was 're-discovered' by scientists in Papua. A team of researchers noted burrows and tracks made by the echidna – its continued existence was then confirmed by local tribespeople, who admitted they recently ate one of the beasts. The rare echidna was last seen in the Cyclops mountains of Papua in 1961, when a Dutch botanist captured the only known specimen. Cases such as this, when a previously extinct animal is found alive and well, are sometimes called 'Lazarus species' after the biblical Lazarus brought back from the dead by Jesus. Some other Lazarus species, recently re-listed on the IUCN Red List, are below:

Species	Latin name	classed extinct	re-listed
Painted frog	*Atelopus ebenoides marinkellei*	1995	2006
Caatinga Woodpecker	*Celeus obrieni*	1926	2006
N Zealand storm-petrel	*Oceanites maorianus*	2000	2004
Lord Howe Isld stick-insect	*Dryococelus australis*	1986	2001
Ivory-billed woodpecker	*Campephilus principalis*	1994	2000
Negros naked-backed bat	*Dobsonia chapmani*	1988	2000
Madeiran land snail	*Discus guerinianus*	1994	1999
Wollemi pine†	*Wollemia nobilis*	200m years ago	1994

[Source: IUCN Red List · BBC & various] † After the Wollemi pine was rediscovered, scientists began to cultivate the ancient tree commercially; from 2005, saplings have been available as potted plants.

OCEANIC DEAD ZONES

Oceanic 'dead zones' are regions of low oxygen in which most fish and plants cannot survive. While some dead zones occur naturally, pollution has caused their number to double in every decade since the 1960s. New dead zones are formed when pollution encourages blooms of algae that die and fall to the seabed; there they are consumed by bacteria which choke the water's supply of oxygen. While some fast-swimming fish can escape dead zones, bottom-dwellers like shellfish frequently die. A number of species face extinction if dead zones continue to spread. In October 2006, the UN Environmental Program estimated there may be 200 dead zones worldwide, up from 149 in 2004. Newly detected zones announced in October 2006 include:

Archipelago Sea .... Finland	*Mondego River* .... Portugal
Elefsis Bay .... Greece	*Montevideo Bay* .... Uruguay
Fosu Lagoon .... Ghana	*Paracas Bay* .... Peru
Mersey Estuary .... United Kingdom	[Source: UNEP, 2006]

As of autumn 2006, the Census of Marine Life had counted *c.*75,000 species of marine mammals living in the world's oceans – including *c.*16,000 species of fish. 2006 discoveries of note included the 'Jurassic shrimp', thought to have died out 50 million years ago; a species of 'hairy crab' named *kiwa hirsuta*; and 8 million herring swimming in a school the size of Manhattan, discovered off New Jersey.

GREEN GUILT

14% of Americans admit they recycle nothing, and 20% suffer 'green guilt' about the state of the environment, according an April 2007 survey by the Rechargeable Battery Recycling Corporation. The research also showed that 52% of Americans claimed to recycle glass and cardboard, and 60% recycled newspapers. Those who recycled claimed that their main motivation was to improve the environment; those who did not recycle blamed unclear local recycling regulations and uncertainty about the location of recycling facilities. 34% of those questioned said that they did not recycle because it took long to separate the trash, and 43% doubted that recycling would have any impact on the world's future environment. The 'green' actions that most people felt they could easily adopt were: unplugging appliances when not in use (19%); recycling used batteries and old cell phones (15%); and bringing a coffee mug to the local coffeehouse instead of using disposable cups (12%).

TOP TEN RECIPIENTS OF US AID

The 10 top beneficiaries of US aid, according to latest figures from the OECD:

Iraq $6,926m	Jordan $368m	[Source: OECD, 2005 · In
Afghanistan ... $1,060m	Colombia $366m	2005, the US's net Official
Egypt $750m	Palestinian Adm. $227m	Development Assistance
Sudan $575m	Uganda $225m	budget increased 40·2% since
Ethiopia $552m	Pakistan $224m	2004 to $27,622m]

———————————CO$_2$ & CLIMATE CHANGE———————————

The 2007 Climate Change Performance Index (CCPI), produced by GermanWatch (an independent, nonprofit, nongovernmental organization), indicated that c.65% of all global carbon dioxide (CO$_2$) emissions come from just ten countries – they are:

Country	% global CO$_2$ emissions				
USA	21·82	Russia	5·75	Canada	2·07
China	17·94	Japan	4·57	UK	2·02
		India	4·15	South Korea	1·74
		Germany	3·19	Italy	1·74

The CCPI ranked 56 industrialized countries by comparing their environmental policies and emissions. According to the 2007 index, the best and worst nations are:

The best climate change records		The worst climate change records	
1 ....Sweden	6 ..... Argentina	56.. Saudi Arabia	51........Canada
2 ....UK	7 .... Hungary	55...... Malaysia	50..... Thailand
3 ...... Denmark	8 ....Brazil	54......... China	49........... Iran
4 ....Malta	9 .... India	53...........USA	48.. South Korea
5 ......Germany	10... Switzerland	52... Kazakhstan	47...... Australia

In April 2007, the Center for Naval Analyses warned the US government that global warming should be considered a threat to national security. The study showed that climate change can cause large-scale migrations, increase the spread of disease, and cause conflict over scarce resources [see also p.22].

——————US OIL IMPORTS BY COUNTRY OF ORIGIN——————

OPEC *countries* 2005	barrels	Non-OPEC *countries* 2005	barrels
Saudi Arabia	561m	Canada	796m
Venezuela	558m	Mexico	607m
Nigeria	425m	Angola	173m
Iraq	194m	Russia	150m
Algeria	175m	UK	145m

[Source: Energy Information Administration; most current figures available]

——————WORLD ECOLOGICAL DEBT 'OVERSHOOT' DAY——————

The US think tank Global Footprint Network regularly assesses the date on which human consumption outstrips the Earth's ability to supply resources sustainably. By living beyond its environmental means, mankind is placing such pressure on the Earth's resources that this so-called 'ecological debt day' is falling ever earlier:

Year	debt day				
1987	December 19	1995	November 21	2006	October 9
1990	December 7	2000	November 1	[Source: Global Footprint	
		2005	October 11	Network/NEF]	

——— KÖPPEN'S CLIMATIC CLASSIFICATION SYSTEM ———

In *c.*1900, Russian-born climatologist Wladimir Köppen (1846–1940) developed a system to classify world climates. Köppen's classification system has been updated over the years, but it is usually broken down into the following five categories:

Category		specifications
A	Tropical humid	*rainy climate, no winter, coolest month >18ºC*
B	Dry	*arid climate*
C	Warmer temperate	*rainy, coolest month >0ºC but <18ºC, warmest >10ºC*
D	Colder temperate	*rainy, severe winter, coldest month <0ºC, warmest >10ºC*
E	Polar	*polar climate, no warm season, warmest month <10ºC*

Some examples: [A]: Brazil, Indonesia, Thailand · [B]: Yemen, Libya, most of Australia · [C]: UK, Spain, Hong Kong · [D]: Norway, most of Canada, Latvia · [E]: Greenland, parts of Chile, parts of Russia. ❦ By 2100, many of the world's climates will have disappeared due to the effects of global warming, according to a study published in the *Proceedings of the National Academy of Sciences* in March 2007. Researchers indicated that, as the world heats up, many climates will be lost, replaced by new ones with higher temperatures and greater rainfall. Shifting climate zones are likely to have the greatest impact on endangered animals that depend on the Arctic ice, such as the polar bear and ring seals.

——————— MAMMALS AT RISK ———————

In January 2007, the Zoological Society of London created the EDGE project to conserve the most genetically unique mammals which usually receive little or no conservation attention. Each year, the project implements research for ten different species considered to be at risk. The species earmarked for research in 2007 were:

1 . . . . Yangtze River dolphin	6 . . . . Slender loris
2 . . . . Long-beaked echidna [see p.71]	7 . . . . Hirola
3 . . . . Hispaniolan solenodon	8 . . . . . . Golden-rumped elephant shrew
4 . . . . Bactrian camel	9 . . . . Kitti's hog-nosed bat
5 . . . . Pygmy hippopotamus	10 . . . . Long-eared jerboa

——————— GLOBAL ENVIRONMENTAL CITIZEN PRIZE ———————

Prince Charles accepted the 2006 Global Environmental Citizen Prize from Harvard Medical School's Center for Health and the Global Environment in January 2007. Awarded since 2001, the prize rewards outstanding achievement in raising awareness of global environmental change. Previous winners include:

2005 . . . . Al Gore	2003 . . . . . . Jane Goodall	2001 . . . .
2004 . . . . Bill Moyers	2002 . . . . . Harrison Ford	Edward O. Wilson

The Prince was branded a hypocrite by some environmental campaigners for flying with a 20-strong entourage to New York to collect the prize, when he could have accepted it via a video-link.

──────── ASTEROID IMPACT HAZARD SCALE ────────

The Torino Scale categorizes the 'impact hazard' of asteroids and comets on a scale of 1–10. Values are assigned on the probability of an object's collision and its kinetic energy (*mass × encounter velocity²*). The scale is intended as a tool for public communication and government planning should a potentially calamitous asteroid be discovered. At the time of writing, no asteroid or comet was rated above zero:

0	*collision likelihood is zero or effectively zero, or object will burn up in the earth's atmosphere*	no hazard	WHITE
1	*chance of collision is extremely unlikely*	normal	GREEN
2	*somewhat close but not highly unusual pass*	merits astronomer's attention	YELLOW
3	*close encounter, ≥1% chance of localized destruction*		
4	*close encounter, ≥1% chance of regional devastation*		
5	*close encounter, serious but uncertain threat of regional devastation*		
6	*close encounter by large object; serious but uncertain threat of global catastrophe*	threatening	ORANGE
7	*very close encounter by large object; unprecedented but uncertain threat of global catastrophe*		
8	*certain collision; localized destruction on land, possible tsunami*		
9	*certain collision; unprecedented regional destruction or possible major tsunami*	certain collisions	RED
10	*certain collision; global climatic catastrophe that may threaten the future of civilization*		

The highest-ever Torino rating was given to the asteroid Apophis, which was assigned a value of 4 in December 2004. At the time, the odds of Apophis striking Earth were thought to be 60-to-1. After further study, Apophis was deemed not to be a threat, and its rating was downgraded to 0 in 2006.

──────── SAFFIR-SIMPSON HURRICANE INTENSITY SCALE ────────

Category	wind (mph)	storm surge (ft)	description	example
1	74–95	3–5	Minimal	Gaston (2004)
2	96–110	6–8	Moderate	Frances (2004)
3	111–130	9–12	Extensive	Ivan (2004)
4	131–155	13–18	Extreme	Charley (2004)
5	>156	>18	Catastrophic	Katrina (2005)

According to NOAA, 'hurricane' is a regional name for a strong 'tropical cyclone', defined as a '*non-frontal synoptic scale low-pressure system over tropical or sub-tropical waters with organized convection (i.e. thunderstorms) and definite cyclonic surface wind circulation*'. Tropical cyclones with windspeeds >39mph are technically 'tropical depressions'; those with windspeeds 34–73mph are 'tropical storms'. Those with windspeeds ≥74 are named depending on the ocean they hit: 'hurricane' in the N Atlantic, NE Pacific, or S Pacific; 'typhoon' in the NW Pacific; 'severe tropical cyclone' in the SW Pacific or SE Indian; 'severe cyclonic storm' in the N Indian; and 'tropical cyclone' in the SW Indian.

——————GROWING & SHRINKING FORESTS——————

Many forests have expanded in size between 1990–2005, according to a November 2006 report in the *Proceedings of the National Academy of Sciences*. 22 of the 50 countries investigated by Pekka Kauppi at the University of Helsinki had a growing tree population. The greatest improvements were seen in China and the western industrialized states, whereas Brazil and Indonesia persisted in their ruthless clearing of forests. Kauppi's study proposed a relationship between 'wealth and woods', suggesting that countries with an annual per capita GNP ≥$4,600 usually had a tree population that was stable or increasing. In contrast, countries with lower annual per capita GNPs tended to continue clearing forests – an act likely to accelerate the greenhouse effect. Below are the areas with growing and shrinking forests:

Growing forests	*Shrinking forests*
USA · Western Europe	Indonesia · Brazil
China · India	Nigeria · Philippines

——————————— iPODS, KIM, & COGNAC ———————————

In the wake of North Korea's first nuclear test in October 2006, a number of countries, including America and Japan, applied sanctions halting the export of a range of luxury goods to Kim Jong-il's poverty-stricken state. Below are some of the items from which the dictator and his friends will (theoretically) have to abstain:

Swiss watches · works of art · Cognac · cigarettes · sporting goods[†] · diamonds
musical instruments[‡] · Sony PlayStations · MP3 players (iPods &c.)[§]
gemstones · luxury cars · caviar · tuna steaks · fountain pens

[†] Kim is a sports fan and owns a basketball inscribed with Michael Jordan's signature (a gift from former US Secretary of State Madeleine Albright). [‡] Kim's new wife, Kim Ok, is said to be a devoted pianist. [§] Despite the sanctions, the illegal trade of consumer electronics and DVDs is highly likely; Kim's video collection is said to include >20,000 titles. He is rumored to be a fan of James Bond and Godzilla, and to have a soft spot for Whitney Houston's emetic film *The Bodyguard* (1992).

——————————— WORLD'S TOP TEN RIVERS AT RISK ———————————

Pollution, climate change, and shipping are pushing many rivers towards crisis, according to a 2007 WWF report, which listed the river systems at greatest risk:

River system	*key risk from*		
Danube	shipping	Nile	climate change
Ganges	water extraction	Rio Grande	water extraction
Indus	climate change	Salween	16 proposed dams
La Plata	27 proposed dams	Yangtze	pollution
Mekong	overfishing	[Source: WWF *Rivers at Risk*, Mar 2007] In	
Murray-Darling	invasive species	June 2007, researchers in Brazil asserted that	
		the Amazon was 105km longer than the Nile.	

THE CLASSICAL PLANETS

symbol	name	diameter	no. of moons	surface gravity	rings?	distance from Sun	mean temp.	day length
		km		m/s²		x10⁶ km	°C	hours
☿	Mercury	4,879	0	3·7	N	57·9	167	4,222·6
♀	Venus	12,104	0	8·9	N	108·2	457	2,802·0
⊕	Earth	12,756	1	9·8	N	149·6	15	24·0
♂	Mars	6,794	2	3·7	N	227·9	–63	24·6
♃	Jupiter	142,984	63	23·1	Y	778·4	–110	9·9
♄	Saturn	120,536	60	9·0	Y	1,426·7	–140	10·7
♅	Uranus	51,118	27	8·7	Y	2,871·0	–195	17·2
♆	Neptune	49,532	13	11·0	Y	4,498·3	–200	16·1

In June 2007, non-planet Pluto suffered a further blow when astronomers revealed Eris had a greater diameter. Consequently, Pluto could no longer claim even to be the largest of the dwarf planets.

CLASSICAL PLANETARY MNEMONIC

Many **V**ery **E**ducated **M**en **J**ustify **S**tealing **U**nique **N**inth
Mercury *Venus* *Earth* *Mars* *Jupiter* *Saturn* *Uranus* *Neptune*

THE CONTINENTS

Continent	area square miles	est. population	population density
Asia	17,212,000	3,959m	88·8
Africa	11,608,000	910m	30·3
North America	9,449,000	331m	13·6
South America	6,879,000	561m	31·5
Antarctica	5,100,000	(a scientist or two)	—
Europe	3,837,000	729m	73·4
Australia	3,132,000	33m	4·3

THE OCEANS

Oceans make up *c.*70% of the globe's surface. The five oceans are detailed below:

Ocean	area square miles	greatest known depth at	depth (ft)
Pacific	60,045,000	Mariana Trench	36,220
Atlantic	29,630,000	Puerto Rico Trench	28,232
Indian	26,463,000	Java Trench	23,812
Southern	7,846,000	South Sandwich Trench	23,737
Arctic	5,426,000	Fram Basin	15,305

———————————— A WORLD OF SUPERLATIVES ————————————

Highest city .... La Paz, Bolivia 11,926ft
Highest mountain .... Everest, Nepal/Tibet 29,028ft
Highest volcano .... Ojos del Salado, Chile 22,595ft
Highest dam .... Rogun, Tajikistan 1,099ft
Highest waterfall .... Angel Falls, Venezuela 3,212ft
Biggest waterfall (volume) ..... Inga, Dem. Rep. of Congo 1,500,000ft³/s
Lowest point .... Dead Sea, Israel/Jordan .... −1,300ft
Deepest point .... Challenger Deep, Mariana Trench .... −36,220ft
Deepest ocean .... Pacific .... average depth −14,040ft
Deepest freshwater lake .... Baikal, Russia 5,371ft
Largest lake .... Caspian Sea 143,200mi²
Largest desert .... Sahara 3,500,000mi²
Largest island .... Greenland 836,109mi²
Largest country .... Russia 6,592,800mi²
Largest population .... China .... 1·3bn
Largest monolith .... Uluru, Australia .... 1,114ft high; 5·8mi base
Largest landmass .... Eurasia 21,137,357mi²
Largest river (volume) .... Amazon .... 28bn gal/min
Largest peninsula .... Arabian 900,000mi²
Largest rain forest .... Amazon, South America .... 1·2bn acres
Largest forest .... Northern Russia .... 2·7bn acres
Largest atoll .... Kwajalein, Marshall Islands .... 6·5mi²
Largest glacier .... Vatnajökull, Iceland 3,127mi²
Largest concrete artichoke ...... Castroville, USA .... 20ft×12ft
Largest archipelago .... Indonesia .... 17,508 islands
Largest lake in a lake .... Manitou, on an island in Lake Huron 60mi²
Largest city by area .... Mount Isa, Australia 15,821mi²
Smallest country .... Vatican City .... 0·17mi²
Smallest population .... Vatican City .... 821 people
Smallest republic .... Republic of Nauru [see p.70] 8mi²
Longest coastline .... Canada 125,567mi
Longest mountain range .... Andes 5,500mi
Longest suspension bridge ..... Akashi-Kaikyo, Japan 6,529ft
Longest rail tunnel .... Seikan, Japan 33mi
Longest road tunnel .... Lærdal, Norway .... 15·2mi
Longest river .... Nile [see p.76] 4,185mi
Tallest inhabited building ...... Dubai Tower, UAE 1,680ft
Tallest structure .... KVLY-TV Mast, USA 2,063ft
Most land borders .... China & Russia .... 14 countries
Most populated urban area ..... Tokyo, Japan .... 35·2m
Most remote settlement .... Tristan da Cunha .... 1,450mi from neighbors
Least populous capital city ..... San Marino, San Marino .... pop. 4,482
Warmest sea .... Red Sea .... Average temp. *c*.77°F
Longest bay .... Bay of Bengal 1,150mi
Largest banknote .... Brobdingnagian bills, Philippines .... 14"×8½"

Unsurprisingly, a degree of uncertainty and debate surrounds some of these entries and their specifications.

POPULATION BY CONTINENT

Year	World	Africa	N. America	S. America	Asia	Europe	Oceania
Millions							
1980	4,447	472	371	242	2,645	694	23
1990	5,274	626	424	296	3,181	721	27
2000	6,073	801	486	348	3,678	730	31
2010	6,838	998	540	393	4,148	726	35
2020	7,608	1,220	594	431	4,610	715	38
2030	8,296	1,461	645	461	4,991	696	41
2040	8,897	1,719	692	481	5,291	671	43
2050	9,404	1,990	734	490	5,505	640	45
Percentage distribution							
1980	100%	10·6	8·4	5·4	59·5	15·6	0·5
2000	100%	13·2	8·0	5·7	60·6	12·0	0·5
2050	100%	21·2	7·8	5·2	58·5	6·8	0·5

WORLD BIRTH & DEATH RATES

Births	time unit	deaths	change
133,201,704	*per* YEAR	55,490,538	+77,711,166
11,100,142	*per* MONTH	4,624,212	+6,475,931
364,936	*per* DAY	152,029	+212,907
15,206	*per* HOUR	6,335	+8,871
253	*per* MINUTE	106	+148
4·2	*per* SECOND	1·8	+2·5

[Source: US Census Bureau, 2007 · Figures may not add up to totals because of rounding]

URBAN POPULATION

Tabulated below are the percentages of the urban population, across various regions:

Region % of population in urban areas · 1975	2005	2030 (est.)
Africa 25·3	38·3	50·7
Asia 24·0	39·8	54·1
Europe 66·0	72·2	78·3
Latin America & Caribbean 61·2	77·4	84·3
North America 73·8	80·7	86·7
Oceania 71·7	70·8	73·8
World 37·3	48·7	59·9

[Source: United Nations Department of Economic and Social Affairs, 2005]

MEGACITIES

The term 'megacity' is used by the UN for cities or metropolitan areas with >10m people. Below are the largest megacities (2003), with their estimated 2015 populations:

Megacity	country	pop. 2003 (m)	est. pop. 2015
Tokyo	Japan	35.0	36.2
New York	USA	21.2	22.8
Seoul-Inchon	South Korea	20.3	24.7
Mexico City	Mexico	18.7	20.6
São Paulo	Brazil	17.9	20.0
Mumbai	India	17.4	22.6
Los Angeles	USA	16.4	17.6
Delhi	India	14.1	20.9
Manila, Quezon City	Philippines	13.9	16.8
Calcutta	India	13.8	16.8

[Source: Münchener Rück, 2005]

MISS EARTH

22-year-old Hil Yesenia Hernandez Escobar from Chile was crowned Miss Earth in a ceremony in Manila in November 2006. The beauty pageant has ecological ambitions, with the winning beauty traveling the world for a year to 'actively promote and get involved in the preservation of the environment and the protection of Mother Earth'. In addition to posing in skimpy swimsuits, contestants had also to plant young trees. The official theme song '*Woman of the Earth*' represents one of the highlights of the award ceremony; it includes the following moving lyrics:

> *I am a woman of the earth, Spreading love and joy, fun and laughter*
> *Woman of the earth, Making miracles forever after*

THE NEW SEVEN WORLD WONDERS

The New 7 Wonders Foundation is a privately funded group that organized the selection of a new list of world wonders. Since 2001, more than 100 million people worldwide have voted online and by telephone for their favorite global landmarks. The new list was announced on 07·07·07 to a worldwide television audience of 1·6bn people in 170 countries. The seven new wonders the public selected were:

Chichén Itzá, Mexico	Great Wall, China	Taj Mahal, India
Christ Redeemer, Brazil	Machu Picchu, Peru	The Giza pyramids were given
Colosseum, Italy	Petra, Jordan	'honorary wonder' status

The 7 ancient wonders: pyramids of Egypt, colossus of Rhodes, hanging gardens of Babylon, mausoleum of Halicarnassus, statue of Zeus at Olympia, temple of Artemis at Ephesus, pharos of Alexandria.

—DEVELOPMENT INDEX—

The UN Human Development Index annually ranks 177 countries by health, life expectancy, income, education, and environment. The 2006 ranking was:

Most developed	Least developed
1 . . . . Norway	177 . . . . Niger
2 . . . . Iceland	176 . . . . Sierra Leone
3 . . . . Australia	175 . . . . Mali
4 . . . . Ireland	174 . . . Burkina Faso
5 . . . . Sweden	173 . . Guinea-Bissau
6 . . . . Canada	172 . . C African Rep
7 . . . . Japan	171 . . . . Chad
8 . . . . USA	170 . . . . Ethiopia
9 . . . . . . Switzerland	169 . . . . Burundi
10 . . . . . Netherlands	168 . . . Mozambique

———FAILED STATES———

Research organization Fund for Peace, in association with *Foreign Policy*, annually compiles an index of failed states. Twelve social, economic, military, and political factors are used to rank the states most vulnerable to 'violent internal conflict and societal deterioration'. The most failing states in 2007 were:

1 . . . . Sudan	8 . . . . Afghanistan
2 . . . . Iraq	9 . . . . Guinea
3 . . . . Somalia	10 . C African Rep
4 . . . . . Zimbabwe	11 . . . . Haiti
5 . . . . Chad	12 . . . . . . Pakistan
6 . . . . Ivory Coast	13 . . . . . . N Korea
7 . . . . DR Congo	14 . . . . Burma

——————— NOTES TO THE GAZETTEER ———————

As I walked through the wilderness of this world. — JOHN BUNYAN (1628–88)

The gazetteer on the following pages is designed to allow comparisons to be made between countries around the world. As might be expected, some of the data are tentative and open to debate. A range of sources has been consulted, including the CIA's *World Factbook*, Amnesty International, the US Treasury Dept, &c.

Size km²	*sum of all land and water areas delimited by international boundaries and coastlines*
Population	*July 2007 estimate*
GMT	*based on capital city; varies across some countries; varies with daylight saving*
Life expectancy at birth	*in years; 2007 estimate*
Infant mortality	*deaths of infants <1, per 1,000 live births, per year; 2007 estimate*
Median age	*in years; 2007 estimate*
Birth & death rates	*average per 1,000 persons in the population at midyear; 2007 estimate*
Fertility rate	*average theoretical number of children per woman; 2007 estimate*
HIV rate	*percentage of adults (15–49) living with HIV/AIDS; mainly 2003 estimate*
Literacy rate	*%; definition (especially of target age) varies; mainly 2003 estimate*
Exchange rate	*spot rate at 6·30·07*
GDP per capita	*($) GDP on purchasing power parity basis/population; from 2006*
Inflation	*annual % change in consumer prices; years vary, from 2006*
Unemployment	*% of labor force without jobs; years vary, generally from 2006*
Voting age	*voting age; (U)niversal; (C)ompulsory for at least one election; *=entitlement varies*
Military service	*age, length of service, sex and/or religion required to serve vary*
Death penalty	*(N) no death penalty; (N*) death penalty not used in practice;*
	(Y) death penalty for common crimes; (Y) death penalty for exceptional crimes only*
National Day	*some countries have more than one; not all are universally recognized*

—— GAZETTEER · ALGERIA – SOUTH KOREA · [1/4] ——

Country	Size (km²)	Population (m)	Capital city	± GMT	Inhabitants
United States	9,826,630	301·1	Washington, DC	–5	Americans
Algeria	2,381,740	33·3	Algiers	+1	Algerians
Argentina	2,766,890	40·3	Buenos Aires	–3	Argentines
Australia	7,686,850	20·4	Canberra	+10	Australians
Austria	83,870	8·2	Vienna	+1	Austrians
Belarus	207,600	9·7	Minsk	+2	Belarusians
Belgium	30,528	10·4	Brussels	+1	Belgians
Bolivia	1,098,580	9·1	La Paz	–4	Bolivians
Brazil	8,511,965	190·0	Brasilia	–3	Brazilians
Bulgaria	110,910	7·3	Sofia	+2	Bulgarians
Burma/Myanmar	678,500	47·4	Rangoon	+6½	Burmese
Cambodia	181,040	14·0	Phnom Penh	+7	Cambodians
Canada	9,984,670	33·4	Ottawa	–5	Canadians
Chile	756,950	16·3	Santiago	–4	Chileans
China	9,596,960	1·3bn	Beijing	+8	Chinese
Colombia	1,138,910	44·4	Bogotá	–5	Colombians
Cuba	110,860	11·4	Havana	–5	Cubans
Czech Republic	78,866	10·2	Prague	+1	Czechs
Denmark	43,094	5·5	Copenhagen	+1	Danes
Egypt	1,001,450	80·3	Cairo	+2	Egyptians
Estonia	45,226	1·3	Tallinn	+2	Estonians
Finland	338,145	5·2	Helsinki	+2	Finns
France	547,030	60·9	Paris	+1	French
Germany	357,021	82·4	Berlin	+1	Germans
Greece	131,940	10·7	Athens	+2	Greeks
Haiti	27,750	8·7	Port–au–Prince	–5	Haitians
Hong Kong	1,092	7·0	—	+8	Hong Kongers
Hungary	93,030	10·0	Budapest	+1	Hungarians
India	3,287,590	1·1bn	New Delhi	+5½	Indians
Indonesia	1,919,440	234·7	Jakarta	+7	Indonesians
Iran	1,648,000	65·4	Tehran	+3½	Iranians
Iraq	437,072	27·5	Baghdad	+3	Iraqis
Ireland	70,280	4·1	Dublin	0	Irish
Israel	20,770	6·4	Jerusalem/Tel Aviv	+2	Israelis
Italy	301,230	58·1	Rome	+1	Italians
Japan	377,835	127·4	Tokyo	+9	Japanese
Jordan	92,300	6·1	Amman	+2	Jordanians
Kazakhstan	2,717,300	15·3	Astana	+6	Kazakhstanis
Kenya	582,650	36·9	Nairobi	+3	Kenyans
Korea, North	120,540	23·3	Pyongyang	+9	Koreans
Korea, South	98,480	49·0	Seoul	+9	Koreans

——— GAZETTEER · KUWAIT – ZIMBABWE · [1/4] ———

Country	Size (km²)	Population (m)	Capital city	+ GMT	Inhabitants
United States	9,826,630	301·1	Washington, DC	−5	Americans
Kuwait	17,820	2·5	Kuwait City	+3	Kuwaitis
Latvia	64,589	2·3	Riga	+2	Latvians
Lebanon	10,400	3·9	Beirut	+2	Lebanese
Liberia	111,370	3·2	Monrovia	0	Liberians
Lithuania	65,200	3·6	Vilnius	+2	Lithuanians
Malaysia	329,750	24·8	Kuala Lumpur	+8	Malaysians
Mexico	1,972,550	108·7	Mexico City	−6	Mexicans
Monaco	1·95	32·7k	Monaco	+1	Monegasques
Morocco	446,550	33·8	Rabat	0	Moroccans
Netherlands	41,526	16·6	Amsterdam	+1	Dutch
New Zealand	268,680	4·1	Wellington	+12	New Zealanders
Nigeria	923,768	135·0	Abuja	+1	Nigerians
Norway	323,802	4·6	Oslo	+1	Norwegians
Pakistan	803,940	164·7	Islamabad	+5	Pakistanis
Peru	1,285,220	28·7	Lima	−5	Peruvians
Philippines	300,000	91·1	Manila	+8	Filipinos
Poland	312,685	38·5	Warsaw	+1	Poles
Portugal	92,391	10·6	Lisbon	0	Portuguese
Romania	237,500	22·3	Bucharest	+2	Romanians
Russia	17,075,200	141·4	Moscow	+3	Russians
Rwanda	26,338	9·9	Kigali	+2	Rwandans
Saudi Arabia	2,149,690	27·6	Riyadh	+3	Saudis
Singapore	692·7	4·6	Singapore	+8	Singaporeans
Slovakia	48,845	5·4	Bratislava	+1	Slovaks
Slovenia	20,273	2·0	Ljubljana	+1	Slovenes
Somalia	637,657	9·1	Mogadishu	+3	Somalis
South Africa	1,219,912	44·0	Pretoria/Tshwane	+2	South Africans
Spain	504,782	40·4	Madrid	+1	Spaniards
Sudan	2,505,810	39·4	Khartoum	+3	Sudanese
Sweden	449,964	9·0	Stockholm	+1	Swedes
Switzerland	41,290	7·6	Bern	+1	Swiss
Syria	185,180	19·3	Damascus	+2	Syrians
Taiwan	35,980	22·9	Taipei	+8	Taiwanese
Thailand	514,000	65·1	Bangkok	+7	Thai
Turkey	780,580	71·2	Ankara	+2	Turks
Ukraine	603,700	46·3	Kiev/Kyiv	+2	Ukrainians
United Kingdom	244,820	60·8	London	n/a	British
Venezuela	912,050	26·0	Caracas	−4	Venezuelans
Vietnam	329,560	85·3	Hanoi	+7	Vietnamese
Zimbabwe	390,580	12·3	Harare	+2	Zimbabweans

—— GAZETTEER · ALGERIA – SOUTH KOREA · [2/4] ——

Country	Male life expectancy	Female life expectancy	difference	Infant mortality	Median age	Birth rate	Death rate	Fertility rate	Adult HIV rate	Literacy
United States	75·1	81·0	−5·9	6·4	36·6	14·2	8·3	2·1	0·6	99
Algeria	71·9	75·2	−3·3	28·8	25·5	17·1	4·6	1·9	0·1	70
Argentina	72·6	80·2	−7·6	14·3	29·9	16·5	7·6	2·1	0·7	97
Australia	77·7	83·6	−5·9	4·6	37·1	12·0	7·6	1·8	0·1	99
Austria	76·3	82·3	−6·0	4·5	41·3	8·7	9·8	1·4	0·3	98
Belarus	64·3	76·1	−11·8	6·6	38·2	9·5	14·0	1·2	0·3	100
Belgium	75·7	82·2	−6·5	4·6	41·1	10·3	10·3	1·6	0·2	99
Bolivia	63·5	69·0	−5·5	50·4	22·2	22·8	7·4	2·8	0·1	87
Brazil	68·3	76·4	−8·1	27·6	28·6	16·3	6·2	1·9	0·7	89
Bulgaria	68·9	76·4	−7·5	19·2	40·9	9·6	14·3	1·4	0·1	98
Burma/Myanmar	60·3	64·8	−4·5	50·7	27·4	17·5	9·3	2·0	1·2	90
Cambodia	59·3	63·4	−4·1	58·5	21·3	25·5	8·2	3·1	2·6	74
Canada	77·0	83·9	−6·9	4·6	39·1	10·8	7·9	1·6	0·3	99
Chile	73·7	80·4	−6·7	8·4	30·7	15·0	5·9	2·0	0·3	96
China	71·1	74·8	−3·7	22·1	33·2	13·5	7·0	1·8	0·1	91
Colombia	68·4	76·2	−7·8	20·1	26·6	20·2	5·5	2·5	0·7	93
Cuba	74·8	79·4	−4·6	6·0	36·3	11·4	7·1	1·6	0·1	100
Czech Republic	73·1	79·9	−6·8	3·9	39·5	9·0	10·6	1·2	0·1	99
Denmark	75·6	80·4	−4·8	4·5	40·1	10·9	10·3	1·7	0·2	99
Egypt	69·0	74·2	−5·2	29·5	24·2	22·5	5·1	2·8	0·1	71
Estonia	66·9	78·1	−11·2	7·6	39·4	10·2	13·3	1·4	1·1	100
Finland	75·1	82·3	−7·2	3·5	41·6	10·4	9·9	1·7	0·1	100
France	77·3	84·0	−6·7	3·4	39·0	12·9	8·6	2·0	0·4	99
Germany	76·0	82·1	−6·1	4·1	43·0	8·2	10·7	1·4	0·1	99
Greece	76·8	82·1	−5·3	5·3	41·2	9·6	10·3	1·4	0·2	96
Haiti	55·3	58·7	−3·4	63·8	18·4	35·9	10·4	4·9	5·6	53
Hong Kong	79·0	84·6	−5·6	2·9	41·2	7·3	6·5	1·0	0·1	94
Hungary	68·7	77·4	−8·7	8·2	38·9	9·7	13·1	1·3	0·1	99
India	66·3	71·2	−4·9	34·6	24·8	22·7	6·6	2·8	0·9	61
Indonesia	67·7	72·8	−5·1	32·1	26·9	19·7	6·3	2·4	0·1	90
Iran	69·1	72·1	−3·0	38·1	25·8	16·6	5·7	1·7	0·1	77
Iraq	68·0	70·6	−2·6	47·0	20·0	31·4	5·3	4·1	0·1	74
Ireland	75·3	80·7	−5·4	5·2	34·3	14·4	7·8	1·9	0·1	99
Israel	77·4	81·8	−4·4	6·8	29·9	17·7	6·2	2·4	0·1	97
Italy	77·0	83·1	−6·1	5·7	42·5	8·5	10·5	1·3	0·5	98
Japan	78·7	85·6	−6·9	2·8	43·5	8·1	9·0	1·2	0·1	99
Jordan	76·0	81·2	−5·2	16·2	23·5	20·7	2·7	2·6	0·1	90
Kazakhstan	61·9	72·8	−10·9	27·4	29·1	16·2	9·4	1·9	0·2	100
Kenya	55·2	55·4	−0·2	57·4	18·6	38·9	11·0	4·8	6·7	85
Korea, North	69·2	74·8	−5·6	22·6	32·4	15·1	7·2	2·1	—	99
Korea, South	73·8	80·9	−7·1	6·1	35·8	9·9	6·0	1·3	0·1	98

————— GAZETTEER · KUWAIT – ZIMBABWE · [2/4] —————

Country	Male life expectancy	Female life expectancy	difference	Infant mortality	Median age	Birth rate	Death rate	Fertility rate	Adult HIV rate	Literacy
United States	75·1	81·0	−5·9	6·4	36·6	14·2	8·3	2·1	0·6	99
Kuwait	76·2	78·5	−2·3	9·5	26·0	22·0	2·4	2·9	0·1	93
Latvia	66·4	77·1	−10·7	9·2	39·6	9·4	13·6	1·3	0·6	100
Lebanon	70·7	75·8	−5·1	23·4	28·3	18·1	6·1	1·9	0·1	87
Liberia	38·9	41·9	−3·0	149·7	18·1	43·8	22·2	5·9	5·9	58
Lithuania	69·5	79·7	−10·2	6·7	38·6	8·9	11·1	1·2	0·1	100
Malaysia	70·0	75·6	−5·6	16·6	24·4	22·7	5·1	3·0	0·4	89
Mexico	72·8	78·6	−5·8	19·6	25·6	20·4	4·8	2·4	0·3	91
Monaco	76·0	83·8	−7·8	5·3	45·5	9·1	12·9	1·8	—	99
Morocco	68·9	73·7	−4·8	38·9	24·3	21·6	5·5	2·6	0·1	52
Netherlands	76·5	81·8	−5·3	4·9	39·7	10·7	8·7	1·7	0·2	99
New Zealand	76·0	82·1	−6·1	5·7	34·2	13·6	7·5	1·8	0·1	99
Nigeria	46·8	48·1	−1·3	95·5	18·7	40·2	16·7	5·5	5·4	68
Norway	77·0	82·5	−5·5	3·6	38·7	11·3	9·4	1·8	0·1	100
Pakistan	62·7	64·8	−2·1	68·8	20·9	27·5	8·0	3·7	0·1	50
Peru	68·3	72·0	−3·7	30·0	25·5	20·1	6·2	2·5	0·5	88
Philippines	67·6	73·5	−5·9	22·1	22·7	24·5	5·4	3·1	0·1	93
Poland	71·2	79·4	−8·2	7·1	37·3	9·9	9·9	1·3	0·1	100
Portugal	74·6	81·4	−6·8	4·9	38·8	10·6	10·6	1·5	0·4	93
Romania	68·4	75·6	−7·2	24·6	36·9	10·7	11·8	1·4	0·1	97
Russia	59·1	73·0	−13·9	11·1	38·2	10·9	16·0	1·4	1·1	99
Rwanda	47·9	50·2	−2·3	85·3	18·6	40·2	14·9	5·4	5·1	70
Saudi Arabia	73·8	78·0	−4·2	12·4	21·4	29·1	2·6	3·9	0·01	79
Singapore	79·2	84·6	−5·4	2·3	37·8	9·2	4·4	1·1	0·2	93
Slovakia	71·0	79·1	−8·1	7·1	36·1	10·7	9·5	1·3	0·1	100
Slovenia	72·8	80·5	−7·7	4·4	41·0	9·0	10·4	1·3	0·1	100
Somalia	47·1	50·7	−3·6	113·1	17·6	44·6	16·3	6·7	1·0	38
South Africa	43·2	41·7	1·5	59·4	24·3	17·9	22·5	2·2	21·5	86
Spain	76·5	83·3	−6·8	4·3	40·3	10·0	9·8	1·3	0·7	98
Sudan	48·2	50·0	−1·8	91·8	18·7	34·9	14·4	4·7	2·3	61
Sweden	78·4	83·0	−4·6	2·8	41·1	10·2	10·3	1·7	0·1	99
Switzerland	77·8	83·6	−5·8	4·3	40·4	9·7	8·5	1·4	0·4	99
Syria	69·3	72·0	−2·7	27·7	21·1	27·2	4·7	3·3	0·1	80
Taiwan	74·6	80·7	−6·1	5·5	35·5	9·0	6·5	1·1	—	96
Thailand	70·2	75·0	−4·8	18·9	32·4	13·7	7·1	1·6	1·5	93
Turkey	70·4	75·5	−5·1	38·3	28·6	16·4	6·0	1·9	0·1	87
Ukraine	62·2	74·0	−11·8	9·5	39·2	9·5	16·1	1·2	1·4	99
United Kingdom	76·2	81·3	−5·1	5·0	39·6	10·7	10·1	1·7	0·2	99
Venezuela	70·2	76·5	−6·3	22·5	24·9	21·2	5·1	2·6	0·7	93
Vietnam	68·3	74·1	−5·8	24·4	26·4	16·6	6·2	1·9	0·4	90
Zimbabwe	40·6	38·3	2·3	51·1	20·1	27·7	21·8	3·1	24·6	91

—— GAZETTEER · ALGERIA – SOUTH KOREA · [3/4] ——

Country	Currency	Currency code	$1 =	GDP per capita $	Inflation %	Unemployment %	Fiscal year end
United States	Dollar=100 Cents	USD	—	44,000	2·5	4·8	Sep 30
Algeria	Dinar=100 Centimes	DZD	69·8	7,600	3·0	15·7	Dec 31
Argentina	Peso=10,000 Australes	ARS	3·1	15,200	9·8	8·7	Dec 31
Australia	Dollar=100 Cents	AUD	1·2	33,300	3·8	4·9	Jun 30
Austria	euro=100 cent	EUR	0·8	34,600	1·6	4·9	Dec 31
Belarus	Ruble=100 Kopecks	BYR	2,143·0	8,100	9·5	1·6	Dec 31
Belgium	euro=100 cent	EUR	0·8	33,000	2·1	8·1	Dec 31
Bolivia	Boliviano=100 Centavos	BOB	7·9	3,100	4·3	7·8	Dec 31
Brazil	Real=100 Centavos	BRL	2·1	8,800	3·0	9·6	Dec 31
Bulgaria	Lev=100 Stotinki	BGN	1·5	10,700	6·5	9·6	Dec 31
Burma/Myanmar	Kyat=100 Pyas	MMK	450·0	1,800	21·4	10·2	Dec 31
Cambodia	Riel=100 Sen	KHR	4,067·0	2,700	5·0	2·5	Dec 31
Canada	Dollar=100 Cents	CAD	1·2	35,600	2·0	6·4	Mar 31
Chile	Peso=100 Centavos	CLP	531·0	12,700	2·6	7·8	Dec 31
China	Renminbi Yuan=100 Fen	CNY	7·7	7,700	1·5	4·2	Dec 31
Colombia	Peso=100 Centavos	COP	2,149·7	8,600	4·3	11·1	Dec 31
Cuba	Peso=100 Centavos	CUP/C	0·9	4,000	5·0	1·9	Dec 31
Czech Republic	Koruna=100 Haléru	CZK	20·7	21,900	2·7	8·4	Dec 31
Denmark	Krone=100 Øre	DKK	5·6	37,000	1·8	3·8	Dec 31
Egypt	Pound=100 Piastres	EGP	5·7	4,200	6·5	10·3	Jun 30
Estonia	Kroon=100 Sents	EEK	11·7	20,300	4·4	4·5	Dec 31
Finland	euro=100 cent	EUR	0·8	33,700	1·7	7·0	Dec 31
France	euro=100 cent	EUR	0·8	31,100	1·5	8·7	Dec 31
Germany	euro=100 cent	EUR	0·8	31,900	1·7	7·1	Dec 31
Greece	euro=100 cent	EUR	0·8	24,000	3·3	9·2	Dec 31
Haiti	Gourde=100 Centimes	HTG	36·7	1,800	14·4	c.65	Sep 30
Hong Kong	HK Dollar=100 Cents	HKD	7·8	37,300	2·2	4·9	Mar 31
Hungary	Forint=100 Fillér	HUF	186·5	17,600	3·7	7·4	Dec 31
India	Rupee=100 Paisa	INR	42·9	3,800	5·3	7·8	Mar 31
Indonesia	Rupiah=100 Sen	IDR	9,120·0	3,900	13·2	12·5	Dec 31
Iran	Rial	IRR	8,229·0	8,700	15·8	15·0	Mar 20
Iraq	New Iraqi Dinar	NID	1,272·3	2,900	64·8	c.27·5	Dec 31
Ireland	euro=100 cent	EUR	0·8	44,500	3·9	4·3	Dec 31
Israel	Shekel=100 Agora	ILS	4·2	26,800	−0·1	8·3	Dec 31
Italy	euro=100 cent	EUR	0·8	30,200	2·3	7·0	Dec 31
Japan	Yen=100 Sen	JPY	117·9	33,100	0·3	4·1	Mar 31
Jordan	Dinar=1,000 Fils	JOD	0·7	5,100	6·3	15·4	Dec 31
Kazakhstan	Tenge=100 Tiyn	KZT	124·0	9,400	8·6	7·4	Dec 31
Kenya	Shilling=100 Cents	KES	68·7	1,200	10·5	40·0	Jun 30
Korea, North	NK Won=100 Chon	KPW	—	1,800	—	—	Dec 31
Korea, South	SK Won=100 Chon	KRW	940·3	24,500	2·2	3·3	Dec 31

—————— GAZETTEER · KUWAIT – ZIMBABWE · [3/4] ——————

Country	Currency	Currency code	$1 =	GDP per capita $	Inflation %	Unemployment %	Fiscal year end
United States	Dollar=100 Cents	USD	—	44,000	2·5	4·8	Sep 30
Kuwait	Dinar=1,000 Fils	KWD	0·3	23,100	3·0	2·2	Mar 31
Latvia	Lats=100 Santims	LVL	0·5	16,000	6·8	6·5	Dec 31
Lebanon	Pound=100 Piastres	LBP	1,510·0	5,700	4·8	20·0	Dec 31
Liberia	Dollar=100 Cents	LRD	49·0	900	15·0	85·0	Dec 31
Lithuania	Litas=100 Centas	LTL	2·6	15,300	3·8	5·7	Dec 31
Malaysia	Ringgit=100 Sen	MYR	3·5	12,900	3·8	3·5	Dec 31
Mexico	Peso=100 Centavos	MXN	11·1	10,700	3·4	3·2	Dec 31
Monaco	euro=100 cent	EUR	0·8	30,000	1·9	—	Dec 31
Morocco	Dirham=100 centimes	MAD	8·4	4,600	2·8	7·7	Dec 31
Netherlands	euro=100 cent	EUR	0·8	32,100	1·4	5·5	Dec 31
New Zealand	Dollar=100 Cents	NZD	1·4	26,200	3·8	3·8	Mar 31
Nigeria	Naira=100 Kobo	NGN	128·0	1,500	10·5	5·8	Dec 31
Norway	Krone=100 Øre	NOK	6·1	46,300	2·3	3·5	Dec 31
Pakistan	Rupee=100 Paisa	PKR	60·7	2,600	7·9	6·5	Jun 30
Peru	New Sol=100 Cents	PEN	3·2	6,600	2·1	7·2	Dec 31
Philippines	Peso=100 Centavos	PHP	48·1	5,000	6·2	7·9	Dec 31
Poland	Zloty=100 Groszy	PLN	2·9	14,300	1·3	14·9	Dec 31
Portugal	euro=100 cent	EUR	0·8	19,800	2·5	7·6	Dec 31
Romania	New Leu=100 New Bani	RON	2·5	9,100	6·8	6·1	Dec 31
Russia	Ruble=100 Kopecks	RUR	26·0	12,200	9·8	6·6	Dec 31
Rwanda	Franc=100 Centimes	RWF	546·2	1,600	6·7	—	Dec 31
Saudi Arabia	Riyal=100 Halala	SAR	3·8	13,600	1·9	c.25	Dec 31
Singapore	Dollar=100 Cents	SGD	1·5	31,400	1·0	3·1	Mar 31
Slovakia	Koruna=100 Halierov	SKK	25·0	18,200	4·4	10·2	Dec 31
Slovenia	euro=100 cent	EUR	0·8	23,400	2·4	9·6	Dec 31
Somalia	Shilling=100 Cents	SOS	—	600	—	—	—
South Africa	Rand=100 Cents	ZAR	7·3	13,300	5·0	25·5	Mar 31
Spain	euro=100 cent	EUR	0·8	27,400	3·5	8·1	Dec 31
Sudan	Dinar=100 Piastres	SDD	200·0	2,400	9·0	18·7	Dec 31
Sweden	Krona=100 Øre	SEK	7·0	32,200	1·4	5·6	Dec 31
Switzerland	Franc=100 Centimes	CHF	1·2	34,000	1·2	3·3	Dec 31
Syria	Pound=100 Piastres	SYP	50·7	4,100	8·0	12·5	Dec 31
Taiwan	Dollar=100 Cents	TWD	33·1	29,500	1·0	3·9	Jun 30
Thailand	Baht=100 Satang	THB	35·0	9,200	5·1	2·1	Sep 30
Turkey	New Lira=100 New Kurus	TRY	1·4	9,000	9·8	10·2	Dec 31
Ukraine	Hryvena=100 Kopiykas	UAH	5·0	7,800	11·6	c.10	Dec 31
United Kingdom	Pound=100 Pence	GBP	0·5	31,800	3·0	2·9	Apr 5
Venezuela	Bolivar=100 Centimos	VEB	2,150·0	7,200	15·8	8·9	Dec 31
Vietnam	Dong=100 Xu	VND	16,010·0	3,100	7·5	2·0	Dec 31
Zimbabwe	Dollar=100 Cents	ZWD	—	2,100	p.26	80·0	Dec 31

—— GAZETTEER · ALGERIA – SOUTH KOREA · [4/4] ——

Country	Voting age	Driving side	UN vehicle code	Internet country code	Military service	Death penalty	National Day
United States	18 U	R	USA	.us	N	Y	Jul 4
Algeria	18 U	R	DZ	.dz	Y	N*	Nov 1
Argentina	18 UC	R	RA	.ar	N	Y*	May 25
Australia	18 UC	L	AUS	.au	N	N	Jan 26
Austria	18 U	R	A	.at	Y	N	Oct 26
Belarus	18 U	R	BY	.by	Y	Y	Jul 3
Belgium	18 UC	R	B	.be	N	N	Jul 21
Bolivia	18 UC*	R	BOL	.bo	N/Y	Y*	Aug 6
Brazil	16 U*	R	BR	.br	Y	Y*	Sep 7
Bulgaria	18 U	R	BG	.bg	Y	N	Mar 3
Burma/Myanmar	18 U	R	BUR	.mm	N	N*	Jan 4
Cambodia	18 U	R	K	.kh	Y	N	Nov 9
Canada	18 U	R	CDN	.ca	N	N	Jul 1
Chile	18 UC	R	RCH	.cl	Y	Y*	Sep 18
China	18 U	R	RC	.cn	Y	Y	Oct 1
Colombia	18 U	R	CO	.co	Y	N	Jul 20
Cuba	16 U	R	CU	.cu	N	Y	Jan 1
Czech Republic	18 U	R	CZ	.cz	N	N	Oct 28
Denmark	18 U	R	DK	.dk	Y	N	Jun 5
Egypt	18 UC	R	ET	.eg	Y	Y	Jul 23
Estonia	18 U	R	EST	.ee	Y	N	Feb 24
Finland	18 U	R	FIN	.fi	Y	N	Dec 6
France	18 U	R	F	.fr	N	N	Jul 14
Germany	18 U	R	D	.de	Y	N	Oct 3
Greece	18 UC	R	GR	.gr	Y	N	Mar 25
Haiti	18 U	R	RH	.ht	N	N	Jan 1
Hong Kong	18 U*	L	—	.hk	N	N	Oct 1
Hungary	18 U	R	H	.hu	N	N	Aug 20
India	18 U	L	IND	.in	N	Y	Jan 26
Indonesia	17 U*	L	RI	.id	Y	Y	Aug 17
Iran	18 U	R	IR	.ir	Y	Y	Apr 1
Iraq	18 U	R	IRQ	.iq	N	Y	Jul 17
Ireland	18 U	L	IRL	.ie	N	N	Mar 17
Israel	18 U	R	IL	.il	Y	Y*	May 14
Italy	18 U*	R	I	.it	N	N	Jun 2
Japan	20 U	L	J	.jp	N	Y	Dec 23
Jordan	18 U	R	HKJ	.jo	N	Y	May 25
Kazakhstan	18 U	R	KZ	.kz	Y	Y	Dec 16
Kenya	18 U	L	EAK	.ke	N	N*	Dec 12
Korea, North	17 U	R	—	.kp	N	Y	Sep 9
Korea, South	19 U	R	ROK	.kr	Y	Y	Aug 15

—————— GAZETTEER · KUWAIT – ZIMBABWE · [4/4] ——————

Country	Voting age	Driving side	UN vehicle code	Internet country code	Military service	Death penalty	National Day
United States	18 U	R	USA	.us	N	Y	Jul 4
Kuwait	16 U*	R	KWT	.kw	Y	Y	Feb 25
Latvia	18 U	R	LV	.lv	Y	Y*	Nov 18
Lebanon	21 C*	R	RL	.lb	Y	Y	Nov 22
Liberia	18 U	R	LB	.lr	N	N	Jul 26
Lithuania	18 U	R	LT	.lt	Y	N	Feb 16
Malaysia	21 U	L	MAL	.my	N	Y	Aug 31
Mexico	18 UC	R	MEX	.mx	Y	N	Sep 16
Monaco	18 U	R	MC	.mc	—	N	Nov 19
Morocco	18 U	R	MA	.ma	Y	N*	Jul 30
Netherlands	18 U	R	NL	.nl	N	N	Apr 30
New Zealand	18 U	L	NZ	.nz	N	N	Feb 6
Nigeria	18 U	R	WAN	.ng	N	Y	Oct 1
Norway	18 U	R	N	.no	Y	N	May 17
Pakistan	18 U	L	PK	.pk	N	Y	Mar 23
Peru	18 UC*	R	PE	.pe	Y	Y*	Jul 28
Philippines	18 U	R	RP	.ph	Y	N	Jun 12
Poland	18 U	R	PL	.pl	Y	N	May 3
Portugal	18 U	R	P	.pt	N	N	Jun 10
Romania	18 U	R	RO	.ro	N	N	Dec 1
Russia	18 U	R	RUS	.ru	Y	N*	Jun 12
Rwanda	18 U	R	RWA	.rw	N	Y	Jul 1
Saudi Arabia	21 C	R	SA	.sa	N	Y	Sep 23
Singapore	21 UC	L	SGP	.sg	Y	Y	Aug 9
Slovakia	18 U	R	SK	.sk	N	N	Sep 1
Slovenia	18 U*	R	SLO	.si	N	N	Jun 25
Somalia	18 U	R	SO	.so	N	Y	Jul 1
South Africa	18 U	L	ZA	.za	N	N	Apr 27
Spain	18 U	R	E	.es	N	N	Oct 12
Sudan	17 U	R	SUD	.sd	Y	Y	Jan 1
Sweden	18 U	R	S	.se	Y	N	Jun 6
Switzerland	18 U	R	CH	.ch	Y	N	Aug 1
Syria	18 U	R	SYR	.sy	Y	Y	Apr 17
Taiwan	20 U	R	—	.tw	Y	Y	Oct 10
Thailand	18 UC	L	T	.th	Y	Y	Dec 5
Turkey	18 U	R	TR	.tr	N	N	Oct 29
Ukraine	18 U	R	UA	.ua	Y	N	Aug 24
United Kingdom	18 U	L	GB	.uk	N	N	—
Venezuela	18 U	R	YV	.ve	Y	N	Jul 5
Vietnam	18 U	R	VN	.vn	Y	Y	Sep 2
Zimbabwe	18 U	L	ZW	.zw	N	Y	Apr 18

Society & Health

What is not good for the beehive, cannot be good for the bees.
— MARCUS AURELIUS (AD 121–180)

―――――――――――――――――GUN CONTROL―――――――――――――――――

Inevitably, in the aftermath of the April 2007 VA Tech massacre [see p.24], the issue of gun control hit the headlines once again. Yet for all the expressions of sadness and shock, even the worst shooting incident in US history did little to shift significantly the now ossified positions on the 2nd Amendment and its ramifications. As the *LA Times* noted, 'gun control advocates said the shootings pointed to the need for tougher laws, while supporters of gun rights generally kept their heads down. And leaders of both major political parties expressed sympathy for victims and their families, while avoiding comment on gun control'. That said, a number of pro-gun lobbyists argued that if students or faculty had been carrying weapons, Seung-Hui Cho's attack would not have been so catastrophic. ❦ In June 2007, the House passed a compromise Bill that (if approved by the Senate) would tighten and automate the process by which states share data with the FBI's National Instant Criminal Background Check System, which prevents criminals and the mentally ill from purchasing guns. However, in supporting the Bill, the NRA reassured its members that the measures were not 'gun control', and would not disqualify anyone currently legally able to buy a weapon. ❦ Below are some recent data on guns in the US:

According to the GSS, the percentage of US adults with a firearm in their house is:

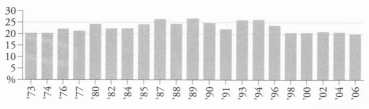

%	*of adult Americans*	*source & month 2007*
71	think people like Seung-Hui Cho 'will always find guns'	[Fox/Opinion Dynamics; April]
67	support a ban on the sale of assault weapons	[ABC; April]
62	think gun violence is a 'very serious' problem today	[AP/Ipsos; April]
55	support a ban on the sale of semi-automatic handguns	[ABC; April]
50	would like to see US gun laws made more strict	[CNN/Opinion Research Corp.; May]
50	think stricter gun laws would not reduce violent crime in the US	[ABC; April]
42	support a ban on the carrying of concealed weapons	[ABC; April]
35	worry about being the victim of gun crime	[AP/Ipsos; April]
22	personally know a victim [in the last 3 years] of gun crime	[AP/Ipsos; April]

———————THE 300 MILLIONTH AMERICAN———————

The American population reached 300 million people at approximately 07:46 EDT on October 17, 2006, according to Census Bureau estimates. Although many demographers agreed that the milestone was most likely to have been hit by a Hispanic boy born in the Southwest, no official government designations were made nor ceremonies held†. However, hospitals and news organizations around the country named babies born at or near the designated time the '300 millionth', including:

Anthony Anton (*Magee-Womens Hospital, Pittsburgh*) · Caitlin Warner (*Rex Hospital, Raleigh*) · Emanuel Plata (*Elmhurst Hospital Center, Queens*) · Emily A. Dierna (*Glens Falls Hospital, Glens Falls, NY*) · Hannah Romero (*Tucson Medical Center, Tuscon*) Joana Palaguachi (*Flushing Hospital, Queens*) · Katie Sikkema (*Saint Mary's, Grand Rapids*) · Kiyah L. Boyd (*Northside Hospital, Atlanta*) · Maria Byron (*St Luke's, Boise*) · Mystique Alyzha Agueda (*Lutheran Med. Center, Brooklyn*) · Zoë E. Hudson (*New York–Presbyterian/ Weill Cornell Hospital, Manhattan*)

† When the 200 millionth American was born on November 20, 1967, the 'population clock' was artificially slowed so that President Lyndon B. Johnson could attend a special ceremony. Some speculated that the lack of official celebration in 2006 might be linked to illegal immigration, a significant contributor to US population growth. However, Census Bureau employees revealed that they planned to celebrate the landmark 2006 birth with a private party featuring cake and punch.

Each year, the US population grows by *c*.2·8m – an annual growth rate of *c*.1%. Each day, an average of 11,000 babies are born, and 3,000 immigrants arrive. Other growth rates according to the US Census population clock (as of January 2007):

1 birth every .... 8 secs		*1 net foreign migrant every* ...... 27 secs
1 death every .... 11 secs		*Net gain of 1 person every* .... 15 secs

The chart below shows the growth in the US resident population in 1900–2050, based on Census Bureau population estimates (2000–2050 counts are projected):

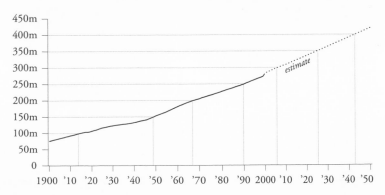

[1900–49 data exclude Alaska and Hawaii, and 1940–1979 data include overseas Armed Forces.]

ANCESTRY OF US CITIZENS

Ancestry	millions	%
German	42·9	15·2
Irish	30·6	10·9
English	24·5	8·7
US or American	20·6	7·3
Italian	15·7	5·6
Polish	9·0	3·2
French	8·3	3·0
Scottish	4·9	1·7
Dutch	4·5	1·6
Norwegian	4·5	1·6
Scotch-Irish	4·3	1·5
Swedish	4·0	1·4
Russian	2·7	0·9
French Canadian	2·4	0·9
West Indian	1·9	0·7
Sub-Saharan African	1·8	0·6
Welsh	1·8	0·6
Czech	1·7	0·6
Danish	1·4	0·5
Hungarian	1·4	0·5

Ancestry	millions	%
Arab	1·2	0·4
Portuguese	1·2	0·4
Greek	1·2	0·4
Swiss	0·9	0·3
Ukrainian	0·9	0·3
Slovak	0·8	0·3
Lithuanian	0·7	0·2
Other ancestries	91·6	32·6
Total population	281·4	100·0
Total reported	287·3	102·1

Includes both single and multiple ancestries. French includes Alsatian but excludes Basques. French Canadian includes Acadian/Cajun. West Indian excludes Hispanic groups. Irish includes Celtic. Czech includes Czechoslovakian.

[Source: US Census, 2000]

TOP LANGUAGES SPOKEN AT HOME

Speak only English	80·6%
Speak another language	19·4
of which	
Spanish or Spanish Creole	62·0
Chinese	4·4
French (incl. Patois, Cajun)	2·7
Tagalog	2·6
German	2·2
Vietnamese	2·2
Korean	2·0
Italian	1·9
Russian	1·6
Polish	1·2
Arabic	1·3
Portuguese or Portuguese Creole	1·3
French Creole	1·1

[Source: American Community Survey, 2005, based on a sample of households. For population age >5]

NATIVE vs FOREIGN-BORN POPULATION

Native population
252,688,295 (87·6%)

Foreign-born pop.
35,689,842 (12·4%)

Below are the states with the highest and lowest % foreign-born population:

California	27·2%
New York	21·4
New Jersey	19·5
Florida	18·5
Nevada	17·4
North Dakota	2·0
Montana	1·8
Mississippi	1·5
West Virginia	1·1

[Source: American Community Survey, 2005]

──────US POPULATION BY RACE & ETHNICITY──────

The racial and ethnic breakdown of the US, according to the latest (2000) Census:

	%	
TOTAL POPULATION		281,421,906
ONE RACE	97·6	274,595,678
· White	75·1	211,460,626
· Black or African American	12.3	34,658,190
· American Indian and Alaska Native	0·9	2,475,956
· Asian	3·6	10,242,998
Asian Indian	0·6	1,678,765
Chinese	0·9	2,432,585
Filipino	0·7	1,850,314
Japanese	0·3	796,700
Korean	0·4	1,076,872
Vietnamese	0·4	1,122,528
Other Asian	0·5	1,285,234
· Native Hawaiian & other	0·1	398,835
Native Hawaiian	<0·1	140,652
Guamanian/Chamorro	<0·1	58,240
Samoan	<0·1	91,029
Other Pacific Islander	<0·1	108,914
· Some other race	5·5	15,359,073
TWO OR MORE RACES	2·4	6,826,228

Race alone or with >1 other race

	%	
Total population		281,421,906
White	77·1	216,930,975
Black or African American	12·9	36,419,434
American Indian and Alaska Native	1·5	4,119,301
Asian	4·2	11,898,828
Native Hawaiian & other	0·3	874,414
Some other race	6·6	18,521,486

Hispanic or Latino & Race

	%	
Total population		281,421,906
Hispanic or Latino (of any race)	12·5	35,305,818
Mexican	7·3	20,640,711
Puerto Rican	1·2	3,406,178
Cuban	0·4	1,241,685
Other Hispanic or Latino	3·6	10,017,244
Not Hispanic or Latino	87·5	246,116,088
White alone	69·1	194,552,774

According to the 2006 US Census Special Report into American Indians and Alaska Natives, 4,315,865 people (1·53% of the entire US population) reported that they were American Indian or Alaska Native, of whom 2,447,989 (0·87% of the population) reported only American Indian or Alaska Native as their race.

───────────── IMMUNIZATION SCHEDULE ─────────────

The following is a basic immunization schedule for children from birth to age 6:

Vaccine	*standard dose(s)*	*age of child*
Hepatitis B	3	birth · 1–2 months · 6–18 months
Rotavirus	3	2 months · 4 months · 6 months
DTaP	5	2 months · 4 months · 6 months · 15–18 months · 4–6 years
Hib	4	2 months · 4 months · (6 months) · >12–15 months
Pneumococcal	4	2 months · 4 months · 6 months · 12–15 months
Polio	4	2 months · 4 months · 6–18 months · 4–6 years
Influenza	6	yearly from 6–59 months
MMR	2	12–15 months · 4–6 years
Varicella	2	12–15 months · 4–6 years
Hepatitis A	2	2 doses >6 months apart, both between 12–23 months

This chart is based upon the Dept of Health & Human Services schedule, 2007. Parents should *always* check with the CDC or their pediatrician, especially for children >6 and for advice on high-risk groups. ❦ In 2007, the CDC added the controversial human papillomavirus (HPV) vaccine to its immunization schedule for girls aged 11–12. (HPV is a sexually transmitted disease that can cause cervical cancer.) Although many states are considering making this vaccine mandatory, Conservatives have questioned whether it may encourage sexual activity, while others have questioned its efficacy.

───────────── NEW FIRST NAMES OF THE YEAR ─────────────

The Social Security Administration annually lists the most popular names given to babies, based on applications for Social Security cards. The top 2006 names were:

Jacob	*from Hebrew Yaakov*	1	*from the Latin Aemilia*	Emily
Michael	*who is like God*	2	*from Germanic ermen, 'universal'*	Emma
Joshua	*Jehovah saves*	3	*son of Maud*	Madison
Ethan	*Hebrew for solid, enduring*	4	*Spanish form of Elizabeth*	Isabella
Matthew	*God's gift*	5	*possible variant of Eve*	Ava
Daniel	*God is my judge*	6	*my father is joy*	Abigail
Christopher	*bearer of Christ*	7	*feminine form of Oliver*	Olivia
Andrew	*from Greek for 'warrior' or 'man'*	8	*from Hebrew for 'grace'*	Hannah
Anthony	*from the Latin Antonius*	9	*wisdom*	Sophia
William	*protector*	10	*combination of Sam and Anthea*	Samantha

In the 1980s, Katrina was one of the most popular names for girls. Yet, because of associations with the hurricane, Katrina fell from 247th to 382nd on the SSA's list in 2006, with only 850 baby girls so named, according to the *New York Times*. Below are the most popular names from past decades:

1890s	*1940s*	*1990s*
John & Mary	James & Mary	Michael & Jessica
William & Anna	Robert & Linda	Christopher & Ashley
James & Margaret	John & Barbara	Matthew & Emily

──────── AMERICAN YOUTH ────────

The Census Bureau report *A Child's Day* examines the well-being and daily activity of American children. Below are some selected indicators from the 2007 report:

Children aged 6–11 who ...	%
Ate breakfast with a parent 7 days a week	36·5
Ate dinner with a parent 7 days a week	72·8
Were *never* praised by a parent, or were praised *once a week*	2·2
– *a few times a week*	17·2
– *once or twice a day*	30·2
– ≥3 *times a day*	50·5
Were *never* talked to/played with for ≥5 min. *just for fun*, or *once a week*	2·9
– *a few times a week*	16·8
– *once or twice a day*	31·0
– ≥3 *times a day*	49·3
Have household rules about the hours of television allowed	72·0
Have rules about the type of television programs they can watch	85·8
Were enrolled in gifted classes	13·4
Had to repeat a grade	5·7

[9,925 parents were asked about a 'typical week' with their child; sample represents 72·7m children.]

The annual Youth Risk Behavior Surveillance System (YRBSS) monitors a range of risk behaviors that contribute to unintentional injury and violence amongst those in grades 9–12. Below are some results from the most recent (2005) YRBSS study:

Children in grades 9–12 who ...	%
Had rarely or never worn a seat belt as a car passenger†	10·2
Of the 67·9% who rode bicycles, rarely or never wore a helmet†	83·4
Of the 27·9% who rode motorbikes, rarely or never wore a helmet†	36·5
Had ridden in a car driven by someone who had been drinking alcohol‡	28·5
Had driven a car after drinking alcohol‡	9·9
Had carried a weapon (gun, knife, club, &c.) at least once‡	18·5
Had carried a gun at least once‡	5·4
Had been in at least one physical fight†	35·9
Had been in at least one physical fight on school property†	13·6
Had been threatened or injured with a weapon on school property†	7·9
Had received injuries in a physical fight requiring a doctor or nurse†	3·6
Had been physically hurt by a dating partner†	9·3♀, 9·0♂
Had been forced to have sexual intercourse against their will§	10·8♀, 4·2♂
Had not gone to school because of fears for their safety‡	6·0
Had smoked cigarettes on school property‡	6·8
Had drunk alcohol on school property‡	4·3
Had been offered, sold, or given drugs on school property†	25·4
Regularly used sunscreen (≥SPF15) when in sunny conditions†	9·0

† During the 12 months preceding the survey; ‡ During the 30 days preceding the survey; § Ever.

—————ELEMENTARY & SECONDARY SCHOOLS—————

97,382 public elementary and secondary schools were in operation during the 2005–06 school year, according to the National Center for Education Statistics (NCES). Further recent statistics regarding public K–12 education are shown below:

School type (2005–06)	no. of schools
Regular	87,585
Alternative	6,448
Charter	3,780
Magnet	2,736
Special education	2,128
Vocational	1,221
Opened in 2005–06	2,291
Closed in 2005–06	1,553
Planned to open within 2 years	951

School location (2005–06)	% of students
Suburban	40·6
Urban	29·7
Rural	21·7
Town	8·1

Average minutes per day of recess (2005)

Grade 1	27·8
Grade 3	26·7
Grade 6	23·8

Average student:teacher ratio (2005–06)	
All regular public schools	16·2:1
– primary school	15·9:1
– middle school	16·1:1
– high school	17·1:1

Students bullied (2005)	% of students
Inside school	79
Outside on school grounds	28
On school bus	8

[Ages 12–18; self-reported; in previous 6 mths]

—————————CHEATING IN SCHOOLS—————————

60% of high school students, and 38% of middle school students, admitted to cheating on a test at least once in the past year, according to a 2006 survey by the Josephson Institute of Ethics. Below are rates of cheating by gender and grade:

No. of times cheated	never	once	≥twice	'at least once'
Middle school total	62·3	23·5	14·2	37·7
Middle school ♀	62·9	23·7	13·5	37·1
Middle school ♂	61·4	23·5	15·1	38·6
High school total	39·8	25·0	35·2	60·2
High school ♀	41·5	27·6	30·8	58·5
High school ♂	38·2	22·2	39·6	61·8

33% of high school students surveyed admitted to copying an internet document for a class assignment at least once in the past year; 24% of middle school students admitted the same. 7% of high school students said that their parents would rather they cheat than get bad grades, compared with 4·7% of middle school students. Disconcertingly, 27% of all students surveyed admitted to having lied at least once when completing the survey itself.

A 2006 *Academy of Management Learning and Education* study found that MBA candidates were more likely to cheat than other graduate students. 56% said they had done so in the past year, compared with: 54% of engineering students; 50% in physical sciences; 49% of medicine; 45% in law; 43% in the arts; and 39% in the social sciences and humanities. (Cheating was defined as plagiarism, copying work, or bringing prohibited materials into exams.)

―――――――――――――COLLEGE TUITION―――――――――――――

NCES statistics reveal the rise in tuition and fees at public and private US colleges. In 1970, the annual cost for a full-time in-state student was $323 at public institutions, and $1,533 at private schools; in 2005, the cost was $3,638 at public schools, and $18,374 at private schools. (Averages include both two-year and four-year schools.)

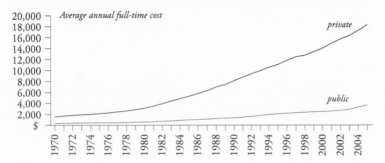

―――――TOP US COLLEGES――――― │ ―――TOP WORLD COLLEGES――

US News & World Report · 2007 │ *Times Educational Supplement* · 2006

1 . . . . .Princeton University · NJ │ 1 . . . . .Harvard University · US
2 . . . . Harvard University · MA │ 2 . . . . Cambridge University · UK
3 . . . . Yale University · CT │ 3 . . . . Oxford University · UK
4 . . . California Institute of Technology │ 4 . . . . Massachusetts Inst. of Tech. · US
4 . . . . Stanford University · CA │ 4 . . . . .Yale University · US
4 . . . Massachusetts Inst. of Technology │ 6 . . . . .Stanford University · US
7 . . . . .University of Pennsylvania │ 7 . . . . .California Inst. of Tech. · US
8 . . . . Duke University · NC │ 8 . . . . . . .U. of California, Berkeley · US
9 . . . . Dartmouth College · NH │ 9 . . . . . . .Imperial College London · UK
9 . . . . .Columbia University · NY │ 10 . . . . Princeton University · US

―――――――――――――――― HONORARY DEGREES―――――――――――――

Some of the honorary degrees conferred upon notable public figures during 2007:

Bob Barker (*Drury University*) · Dick Cheney (*Brigham Young University*)
Bill Cosby (*Carnegie Mellon University*) · Aretha Franklin (*Univ. of Pennsylvania*)
Bill Gates (*Harvard*) · Ruth Bader Ginsburg (*University of Pennsylvania*)
Loretta Lynn (*Berklee College of Music*) · Barack Obama (*Sthrn New Hampshire U.*)
Harold Pinter (*Leeds University*) · Elie Wiesel (*University of Vermont*)

In 2007, Edinburgh University stripped Zimbabwean President Robert Mugabe of a 1984 honorary degree after reviewing evidence of his alleged human rights abuses (two US schools are considering similar actions). Zimbabwean officials said Mugabe had 7 degrees, and could 'do without' the honors.

MARRIAGE & DIVORCE

Below are the US Census rates (per 1,000) of US marriage and divorce (1970–2003):

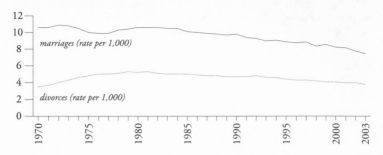

MARITAL STATUS OF THE US POPULATION

Marital status 2006	% all	% ♂	% ♀
Married, spouse present	51·1	52·6	49·6
Married, spouse absent	1·6	1·9	1·4
Widowed	6·0	2·3	9·4
Divorced	9·8	8·6	10·9
Separated	2·1	1·8	2·4
Never Married	29·4	32·8	26·2

[Source: US Census. Marital status of people ≥15]

HAPPINESS OF MARRIAGE

General Social Survey data for those who describe their marriage as 'very happy':

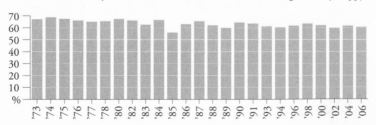

SUPERSTITION AFTER THE WEDDING DAY

The day after the wedding is the *bride's day* – its weather foretells the wife's married life. The day after that is the *groom's day* – its weather foretells the husband's married life. The weather on the third day after the wedding foretells the marriage's length.

———————— DOMESTIC VIOLENCE ————————

In 2006, the Bureau of Justice Statistics released a study showing that rates of domestic violence fell by over 50% between 1993–2004. In 1993, there were 5·8 victims of (nonfatal) domestic violence per 1,000 US adults; by 2004, the rate had fallen to 2·6 victims per 1,000 adults. Homicide rates show a similar fall: 2,269 people were murdered by an intimate partner in 1993, compared to 1,544 in 2004. Some attribute these declines to the 1994 Violence Against Women Act, which improved training for police and increased funding for prosecution. Below are the 1993 and 2004 rates of nonfatal domestic violence in various demographic groups:

Rates of nonfatal domestic violence per 1,000 people >12 years old

Victims	'93 rate	'04 rate
White ♀	9·8	3·4
White ♂†	1·6	1·1
Black ♀	11·9	6·6
Hispanic ♀	11·8	4·6
Non-Hispanic ♀	9·6	3·7

Female victims	'93 rate	'04 rate
Married	3·1	1·0
Divorced	26·2	9·3
Separated	92·3	41·8
Never married	11·5	5·0

Rates of nonfatal domestic violence per 1,000 women in age group:

Female victims	'93 rate	'04 rate
12–15 years	3·8	1·6
16–19 years	16·4	4·2
20–24 years	24·1	11·5
25–34 years	14·7	7·5
35–49 years	12·2	3·9
50–64 years	1·7	1·3
≥65 years	0·6	0·1

† The Justice Department did not provide data for black and Hispanic males, due to the statistically insignificant number of cases.

'Intimate partner violence' is defined as homicides, rapes, robberies, and assaults committed by current or former spouses, boyfriends, or girlfriends, including those in same-sex relationships.

———————— ADOPTION & FOSTER CARE ————————

ADOPTED in 2005	51,000
– Mean age	6·7 years old
– Sex	51% ♂ · 49% ♀
Adopted by · Married couple	68%
Unmarried couple	2%
Single ♀	27%
Single ♂	3%
Relationship to adoptive parents	
Foster parent	60%
Other relative	25%
Non-relative	15%
Receiving adoption subsidy	89%
WAITING to be adopted	114,000
– Sex	53% ♂ · 47% ♀
– Mean months in foster care	41·6

In FOSTER CARE in 2005	513,000
– Mean age	10 years old
– Sex	52% ♂ · 48% ♀
– Mean length of stay	28·6 months
Entered foster care in 2005	311,000
Exited foster care in 2005	287,000
– Reunited with parent/caretaker	54%
– Adopted	18%
– Living with other relative	11%
– Emancipation (i.e. adulthood)	9%
– Guardianship	4%

[Source: Dept of Health & Human Services, prelim. 2005 data. Adoption data only include cases in which public agencies were involved.]

———————— AVERAGE US HOUSEHOLD & FAMILY SIZE ————————

Size	1980	1990	1995	2000	2002	2003	2005
Household	2·76	2·63	2·65	2·62	2·58	2·57	2·57
Family	3·29	3·17	3·19	3·17	3·15	3·13	3·13

———— HOUSEHOLD TYPE ————

Family households ..... 77,010,000 *total*
· Married couple .... 75·5%
· Male householder† .... 6·4%
· Female householder† .... 18·2%
· With own children >18 .... 47·4%
· Without own children >18 .... 52·6%

Nonfamily h/holds .... 36,136,000 *total*
· Male householder† .... 45·2%
· Female householder† .... 54·8%

† The 'householder' is the person/s in
whose name the house is owned or rented.

———— SIZE OF HOUSEHOLD ————

Persons	%		
1	29·9	4	16·5
2	37·2	5	7·2
3	18·3	6	2·5
		≥7	1·4

— AGE OF HOUSEHOLDER —

Age	%		
15–24	6	55–64	15
25–29	8	65–74	10
30–34	9	≥75	10
35–44	21	[US Stat. Abs., 2007
45–54	21	· All figures 2005]

———————————— OVERSEAS ADOPTION ————————————

According to State Department statistics, the number of foreign children adopted by Americans declined by 9% in 2006 – the first significant drop since 1992. Increasingly strict eligibility rules set by foreign countries were one factor in the decline. Below are the top countries for overseas adoptions in 2005 and 2006, based on the number of immigrant visas issued to orphans by the State Department:

2005 countries	*visas issued*	*2006 countries*	*visas issued*
China (mainland)	7,906	China (mainland)	6,493
Russia	4,639	Guatemala	4,135
Guatemala	3,783	Russia	3,706
South Korea	1,630	South Korea	1,376
Ukraine	821	Ethiopia	732
Kazakhstan	755	Kazakhstan	587
Ethiopia	441	Ukraine	460

It seems likely that adoption statistics for 2007 will show a similar trend. Since 2000, China has been the top source for US adoptions, but as of May 2007, Beijing forbade those who are unmarried, obese, have a criminal record, are over 50, or have a net worth of <$80,000 from adopting children.

─────────────── FOOD & HUNGER ───────────────

According to the Dept of Agriculture (USDA), the number of hungry[†] Americans fell in 2005, for the first time in 6 years, yet 35·1m suffered some food insecurity:

Food security definitions	Low Food Security	Very Low Food Security
Food Secure	*at times, uncertain of having, or unable to acquire, enough food for all household members because of insufficient money or other resources*	*eating patterns of one or more household members were disrupted and their food intake reduced because they couldn't afford enough food*
access by all people at all times to enough food for an active, healthy life		

In 2005, although 89% of households were food secure, 7·1% suffered from low food security, and 3·9% from very low food security. Usually, in food insecure households containing children, the adults bore the brunt of hunger. However, in about 270,000 households one or more children suffered from reduced food intake or disrupted eating patterns at some stage during the year.

As might be expected, certain types of household were more likely to experience hunger. The national average rate of food insecurity in 2005 was 11%, but black households experienced a rate of 22·4%, Hispanic households a rate of 17·9%, and households with children headed by a single woman a rate of 30·8%. Of the 4·4m very food insecure households (3·9% of all households) in the United States:

98% .... *worried food would run out before they got money to buy more*
96% .... *reported the food they bought did not last and they could not afford more*
96% .... *reported an adult had cut the size of meals or skipped meals due to poverty*
94% .... *reported they could not afford to eat balanced meals*
94% .... *reported they had eaten less than they should have because of poverty*
44% ... *reported they had lost weight because they did not have enough money for food*

According to the USDA, the typical US household spent $40 per person per week on food in 2005. On average, in food secure households this figure was $42·50, in households with low food security it was $30, and in households with very low food security it was $32·50 [*sic*]. ❦ In 2005, 6·9m adults and 4·1m children obtained food from 'food pantries' that supply unprepared food for consumption off-site. In that year, 1m adults and 0·4m children received food from 'emergency kitchens' (also known as 'soup kitchens'), that provide prepared meals to consume on-site.

[†] Controversially, the USDA's 2006 report omitted the word 'hunger'. Previously, 'very low food security' was termed 'food insecurity with hunger'. The USDA made this change in response to the recommendation of an expert panel of academics and statisticians, that stated, 'the word "hunger" should refer to a potential consequence of food insecurity that, because of prolonged, involuntary lack of food, results in discomfort, illness, weakness, or pain that goes beyond the usual uneasy sensation'. The USDA claimed that to measure hunger in this way would require detailed personal and psychological research beyond the scope of its current survey. In an editorial, the *New York Times* said, 'to the extent that more public empathy is needed to prod a stronger attack on low food security, we opt for "hunger" as a most stirring word'.

—————————— LOYALTY IN RELATIONSHIPS ——————————

The loyalty of those in relationships was tested by a 2007 MSNBC/iVillage poll:

77%♂	89%♀	*considered kissing another person romantically to be cheating*
6%♂	16%♀	*considered viewing pornography to be cheating*
19%♂	12%♀	*had had sex with another partner during a relationship*
67%♂	41%♀	*had sexually fantasized about someone they knew*
44%♂	26%♀	*had sexually fantasized about a celebrity*

Of those who would commit adultery with a celeb, 21% of women chose Matthew McConaughey; 17% of men chose Jessica Alba. Angelina Jolie was the partner of choice for 10% of men and women.

—————————— SEX BEFORE MARRIAGE ——————————

% of Americans who think sex before marriage is 'always wrong'
[Source: General Social Survey]

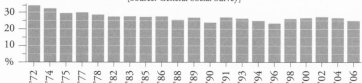

—————————— FREQUENCY OF SEX BY COUNTRY ——————————

% *having sex weekly*	China 78	France 70	Australia 60
Greece 87	Italy 76	India 68	Canada 59
Brazil 82	Spain 72	Germany 68	UK 55
Russia 80	Mexico 71	Netherlands .. 63	USA 53

Also reported: Americans have sex 114 times per year (the global average is 103), and spend 20 minutes per 'session' (the global average is 18). [Source: Durex Sexual Wellbeing Global Survey, 2007]

—————————— FAVORITE FETISH ——————————

Results from a global survey into sexual fetishes indicated that feet and shoes are the most commonly cited kink. Researchers from the University of Bologna, writing in the *International Journal of Impotence Research*, monitored activity in fetish-related internet discussion groups to gather information on the sexual preferences of the general population. When discussing favorite body parts, 47% opted for feet and toes, compared with just 3% who favored (the more mainstream) breasts. 64% of those asked to name their favorite object associated with the body claimed to be most turned on by shoes or boots; 12% by underwear; 7% by hair; and 5% by muscles. 150 of the *c.*5,000 questioned admitted to having a thing for hearing aids.

———————————— ABORTION ————————————

Since 1972, the General Social Survey has polled US public opinion on abortion, asking which, if any, circumstances justify terminating a pregnancy. Charted below are those who favor legal abortions for these reasons: because of risk to the mother's health; because of a strong chance of a serious birth defect; because the child was conceived as a result of rape; because the mother is unmarried; or, for any reason:

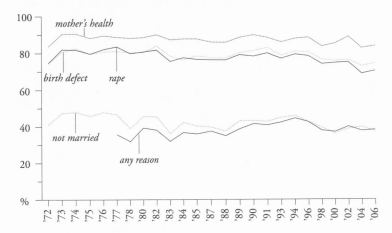

According to the US Census, 1,293,000 legal abortions were performed in the US in 2002: 20·8 per 1,000 women (15–44) and 319 per 1,000 live births. 2005 Guttmacher Institute data show that half of all pregnancies to US women are un-intended, of which 4 in 10 end in abortion. At current rates, *c.*33% of American women will have had an abortion by the age of 45. 88% of abortions occur in the first 12 weeks of pregnancy. And, of those women who have had abortions:

88% .... live in a metropolitan area	61% .... have one or more children
78% .... report a religious affiliation	57% .. are economically disadvantaged
67% .... have never married	56% .... are in their 20s

Below are the rates of abortion (per 1,000 women) by racial group (1975–2002):

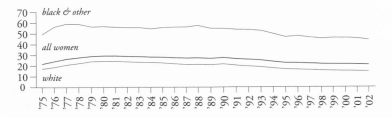

[Sources: US Census & the Guttmacher Institute]

———————————HOMELESSNESS———————————

An estimated 754,147 people (*c.*0·3% of the population) were homeless in the US on January 5, 2005, according to the first Annual Homelessness Assessment Report to Congress (AHAR) in 2007. However, data on homelessness are problematic to collect, and tend to be prone to seasonal variations – not least because some shelters operate only during the colder months. Roughly 45% of the homeless population were considered *unsheltered* – in that they lived on the streets, in cars, or in other places 'not meant for human habitation'. The rest were *sheltered* in emergency or transitional housing. Below are the characteristics of the sheltered homeless population, compared to the characteristics of the American population as a whole:

% sheltered homeless	group	% general US population
34·7	♀ adults	51·7
65·3	♂ adults	48·3
51·9	♀ children	48·7
48·1	♂ children	51·3
22·1	Hispanic/Latino	12·5
41·1	White†	69·1
45·0	Black/African Amer.	12·3
1·2	Asian	3·6
1·7	Amer. Indian/Alaska Nat.	0·9
0·2	Nat. Hawaiian/other‡	0·1
5·1	Multiple races	2·4
2·4	Under 1 year old	1·4
8·7	1–5 years old	6·9
7·5	6–12 years old	10·3
4·0	13–17 years old	7·1
21·3	18–30 years old	18·1
41·3	31–50 years old	30·3
10·3	51–61 years old	11·3
1·8	62 and older	14·6
66·2	1-person household	43·6
10·6	2-person household	2·0
10·3	3-person household	12·3
6·8	4-person household	19·3
6·1	≥5-person household	22·8
8·7	Veteran	12·6
25·0	Disabled (adults)	19·3

† Non-Hispanic and non-Latino whites.
‡ Native Hawaiian or other Pacific Islander.
[Homeless pop. averages based on data collected February–April 2005. Source: HUD, 2007]

A 2007 survey by the National Alliance to End Homelessness showed the number of homeless people in each state. The states with the highest % of the homeless are:

State	sheltered	unsheltered	total no. homeless	% of state pop.
Washington, DC	5,164	354	5,518	1·00
Nevada	6,700	9,702	16,402	0·68
Rhode Island	6,758	108	6,866	0·64
California	46,940	118,275	170,270	0·47
Colorado	7,436	14,294	21,730	0·47
Hawaii	2,448	3,495	5,943	0·47
Oregon	7,775	8,446	16,221	0·45
Alaska	1,431	1,318	2,749	0·41
Idaho	5,092	332	5,424	0·38

A US Conference of Mayors survey of officials in 23 cities found that 68% of the cities reported an increase in requests for emergency shelter in 2006. The average increase in requests was 9%, and 23% of the requests went unmet. Officials said the average time spent homeless was eight months; 32% said that this duration had increased in the past year. Mental illness, lack of services, lack of affordable housing, substance abuse, and low-paying jobs were cited as the leading factors driving homelessness.

——————————UNEMPLOYMENT RATE——————————

The unemployment rate of the civilian noninstitutional population ≥16 (1969–):

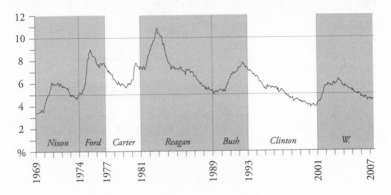

——————OCCUPATIONAL EMPLOYMENT & WAGES——————

Below are the percent of workforce and mean hourly wages, by occupational group:

% of workforce	major occupational group	mean wage/hour
4.6	Management	$42.52
0.8	Legal	$38.98
2.3	Computer and mathematical science	$32.26
1.8	Architecture and engineering	$30.73
5.0	Health care practitioner and technical	$28.45
0.9	Life, physical, and social science	$27.90
4.2	Business and financial operations	$27.85
1.3	Arts, design, entertainment, sports, and media	$21.30
6.2	Education, training, and library	$20.89
4.9	Construction and extraction	$18.39
4.1	Installation, maintenance, and repair	$18.30
1.3	Community and social services	$18.04
2.3	Protective service	$17.19
10.7	Sales and related	$15.77
7.9	Production	$14.37
17.5	Office and administrative support	$14.28
7.4	Transportation and material moving	$13.85
2.6	Health care support	$11.47
2.4	Personal care and service	$10.67
3.3	Building and grounds cleaning and maintenance	$10.55
0.3	Farming, fishing, and forestry	$10.10
8.3	Food preparation and serving related	$8.58

[Source for graph & table: Bureau of Labor Statistics · Table data as of May 2005]

DANGEROUS JOBS

Below are the occupations with the highest rates of fatal injuries, as well as fatal injury rates for each major occupational group, according to the latest (2005) data:

Occupation	fatality rate†
Fishers, related fishing workers	118·4
Logging workers	92·9
Aircraft pilots, flight engineers	66·9
Structural iron and steel workers	55·6
Refuse, recycling collectors	43·8
Farmers and ranchers	41·1
Power-line installers, repairers	32·7
Truck drivers	29·1
Misc. agricultural workers	23·2
Construction laborers	22·7

† Deaths per 100,000 workers

Occupational group	fatality rate†
Farming, fishing, forestry	31·4
Transportation, material moving	17·8
Construction, extraction	12·9
Installation, maintenance, repair	7·6
Military	4·0
Management, business, financial	2·9
Production	2·9
Service	2·8
Sales and related	1·9
Professional and related	0·8
Office and admin. support	0·5
Average worker fatality rate	4·0

Beet sugar manufacturing claimed the unfortunate distinction of having the highest workplace injury rate in 2005:16·6 injuries per 100 workers. Light truck and utility vehicle manufacturing reported the highest illness rate: 701·5 illnesses per 10,000 workers. [Source: Bureau Labor Stats & MSN Careers]

WEEKLY HOURS OF WORK

Industry	average weekly hours
Natural resources & mining	41·8
Manufacturing†	39·6
Goods-producing	38·8
Construction	37·0
Financial activities	36·4
Information	35·8
Professional & business services	34·7

Trade, transportation, utilities	33·9
Education & health services	33·3
Private service-providing	33·0
Other services	32·7
Leisure & hospitality	25·4

† Also worked an average 3 hours of overtime a week. [Source: BLS, Jan 2007 averages]

UNION MEMBERSHIP

According to the Bureau of Labor Statistics, 12% of employees belonged to a union in 2006, compared with 12·5% in 2005, 20·1% in 1983, and 35% in the 1950s.

2006 union membership	%
Men	13·0
Women	10·9
Blacks & African Americans	14·5
Whites	11·7
Asians	10·4
Hispanics & Latinos	9·8

Full-time workers	13·1
Part-time workers	6·3
Age 16–24	4·4
Age ≥25	13·3

In 2006, full-time union workers had median weekly earnings of $833 – compared to a nonunion median of $642.

CONFIDENCE IN INSTITUTIONS

Below are the percentages of US adults with 'a great deal of confidence' in the following institutions: medicine, organized religion, the military, the press, and Congress. [Source: General Social Survey]

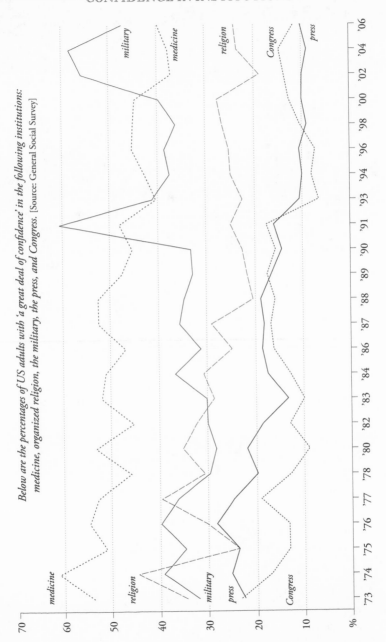

———————AMERICA'S BEST HOSPITALS · 2006———————

The top 10 from the 'honor roll'[†] of *US News & World Report*'s Best Hospitals list:

1 . .Johns Hopkins . . . . .Baltimore	7 . .UCSF Medical Center . . . .
2 . .Mayo Clinic . . . . Rochester, MN	San Francisco
3 . .UCLA Med. Center . . . . .Los Angeles	9 . .Barnes–Jewish Hospital . . . .St Louis
4 . .Cleveland Clinic . . . . .Cleveland	10.Brigham & Women's . . . . .Boston
4 . .MA General Hospital . . . . . . .Boston	
6 . .New York–Presbyterian . . . . . . .NYC	† The honor roll ranks the hospitals that
7 . .Duke Med. Center. . . Durham, NC	received top scores in ≥6 specialities.

———————PANDEMIC SEVERITY INDEX———————

In February 2007, the federal government released guidelines to help cities and states prepare for a flu pandemic. The guidelines included a Pandemic Severity Index (similar to the Saffir-Simpson Hurricane Intensity Scale, see p.75) designed to help officials predict the severity of an outbreak (based on early cases) and enact appropriate 'mitigation strategies'. All future pandemics in the United States will be assigned one of five categories by the Centers for Disease Control and Prevention:

Cat.	case fatality[†]	excess death rate[‡]	potential no. deaths	US C20th experience
1	<0·1	<30	<90,000	seasonal influenza
2	0·1–<0·5	30–<150	90,000–<450,000	1957 & 1968
3	0·5–<1·0	150–<300	450,000–<900,000	none
4	1·0–<2·0	300–<600	900,000–<1·8m	none
5	≥2·0	≥600	≥1·8m	1918

† The proportion of deaths among the critically ill. ‡ The rate of death per 10,000 people compared to the normal 'nonpandemic' rate. [Source: US Department of Health & Human Services, 2007]

———————EMERGENCY ROOM VISITS———————

Top 'principal reasons' for 2004 ER visits

Stomach pain &c. . . . . .6·8%
Chest pain & related . . . . .5·4
Fever . . . . .3·8
Back symptoms . . . . .2·6
Headache/pain in head . . . . .2·6
Cough . . . . .2·5
Shortness of breath . . . . .2·3
Vomiting . . . . .2·3
Pain (general) . . . . .2·1
Lacerations/cuts, upper extremity . . 1·9
Accidents (unspecified) . . . . .1·9

Pain levels reported at time of visit

None . . . . 16·8%
Mild . . . . 16·5
Moderate . . . . 23·7
Severe . . . . 15·1
Unknown/blank . . . . 28·0

ER visits related to work

Yes	No	Unknown
2·9%	91%	5·3%

[Source: CDC 2004 data, released 2006]

──────────HEALTH (CARE) OF THE NATION──────────

The US spent 16% of its GDP on health care in 2004 ($1·9tr) – 7·9% more than in 2003. Americans made 1,106,067,000 visits to doctors, outpatient departments, and emergency rooms the same year – 3·8 visits per person (4·3 for women, and 3·3 for men). Below are some other figures relating to the health care of the nation:

❦ In 2003, LIFE EXPECTANCY was 74·8 years for men, and 80·1 years for women (+3 years for men, and +1 year for women, compared to 1990). However, 11·9% (23% below the poverty level) reported a limitation in their activities due to chronic physical, mental, or emotional problems, and 26% of Americans >20 years old reported experiencing pain for >24 hours in the last month.

❦ 744,143 medical DOCTORS were practicing in the US in 2004 – a rate of 26·3 physicians per 10,000 population. 141,730,000 CIVILIANS worked in health service sites – 9·9% of all US workers. There were 5,759 hospitals in the US, offering 955,768 beds, with an average occupancy rate of 68·9%. 36,942,000 hospital visits were made; the average length of stay was 6·5 days.

❦ A breakdown of the major sources of national health care SPENDING:

Hospital care	30·4%
Physician and clinical services	21·3
Prescription drug sales	10·0
Nursing home & home care	8·4
Gov. administration & net cost of private health insurance	7·3
Dental services	4·3
Research	2·1

❦ According to a CDC survey, 43·6m Americans (14·8%) had no HEALTH INSURANCE in 2006, a 6% rise from 2005. 54·5m Americans (18·6%) were without health insurance for at least part of the year. Among the 20 largest states, Texas had the highest rate of uninsured (23·8%), and Michigan the lowest (7·7%). 9·3% of the nation's children were uninsured in 2006.

Below are some of the leading causes of death in the US (2003), broken down by sex:

Leading cause of death	♀ deaths	♂ deaths	Leading cause of death
Diseases of heart	348,994	336,095	*diseases of heart*
Malignant neoplasms (i.e. cancer)	268,912	287,990	*malignant neoplasms (i.e. cancer)*
Cerebrovascular diseases	96,263	70,532	*unintentional injuries*
Chronic lower respiratory diseases	65,668	61,426	*cerebrovascular diseases*
Alzheimer's disease	45,122	60,714	*chronic lower respiratory diseases*
Diabetes mellitus	38,781	35,438	*diabetes mellitus*
Unintentional injuries	38,745	28,778	*influenza and pneumonia*
Influenza and pneumonia	36,385	25,203	*suicide*
Nephritis, nephrosis, &c.	21,972	20,481	*nephritis, nephrosis, &c.*
Septicemia	19,082	18,335	*Alzheimer's disease*

Unintentional fatal drug overdoses overtook *falls* as the second leading cause of accidental death in 2004; there were 19,838 that year. Car crashes remained the leading cause (43,432 deaths in 2004).

[Sources for the page: *Health, US*, 2006; Centers for Disease Control & Prevention]

─────SOME HEALTH SCARES OF NOTE─────

{SEPT 2006} An *E. coli* outbreak traced to spinach grown in California sickened *c.*200 and killed 3 during September and early October; the FDA warned consumers against eating raw spinach. {OCT} Carrot juice containing botulism paralyzed *c.*2 women and hospitalized several others; the FDA issued a warning about the juice. ❦ 8,500 cartons of lettuce were recalled by a CA company as a precautionary measure against *E. coli* infection. ❦ Cincinnati Children's Hospital researchers suggested that up to a third of ADHD cases in the US might be caused by toxic lead or cigarette smoke. ❦ A controversial study by a Cornell economist found evidence that early childhood TV viewing could trigger autism. {NOV} Mayo Clinic researchers suggested that common picornaviruses, like those that cause colds and diarrhea, may cause lasting memory damage. ❦ Czech researchers discovered that women infected with the cat parasite toxoplasma were more likely to give birth to boys, and theorized that the parasite (found in feline feces and raw meat) harms female embryos. ❦ During November and early December, *c.*71 people were sickened by *E. coli* traced to Taco Bell restaurants in NE states. ❦ The FDA announced that patients taking Tamiflu should be closely monitored for abnormal behavior, after 103 reports of delirium and hallucination in children taking the drug. {DEC} The American College of Obstetricians and Gynecologists warned that pregnant women should avoid the antidepressant Paxil, because of possible risks of birth defects. ❦ A study commissioned by the UK's Miscarriage Association suggested that underweight women

E. coli

are 72% more likely to miscarry than overweight women. {JAN} Research published in the *American Journal of Clinical Nutrition* found that even small amounts of trans fats can increase a woman's risk of fertility problems by ≥70% [see p.219]. ❦ A Rhode Island school was closed after a rare outbreak of encephalitis killed a second grader. ❦ A German study found that adding milk to tea destroyed tea's ability to guard against heart disease. ❦ A report in the *New England Journal of Medicine* said that frequent use of lavender and tea tree oil had caused 3 young boys to grow breasts. ❦ Results from a study published in the *Lancet* suggested that growing up near major roads could affect the development of children's lungs. The study indicated that children who lived up to 500 meters from a motorway had significantly lower lung volume and peak flow than those who lived >1,500m away. {FEB} Research from the Saint Louis University School of Medicine found that those who spent a lot of time driving were more likely to develop skin cancer on the left side of their bodies. ❦ Several brands of peanut butter were recalled after a salmonella outbreak sickened 288 people in 39 states over several months. ❦ A study in the *British Journal of Sports Medicine* suggested those playing contact sports were at an increased risk of contracting hepatitis B through sweat. {MAR} The US Preventative Services Task Force warned that those with a family history of colon cancer should not take aspirin to prevent the disease, due to increased risks of internal bleeding, stroke, and kidney failure. ❦ A study published in the *Archives of Pediatric and Adolescent*

——————SOME HEALTH SCARES OF NOTE cont.——————

Medicine found that white teenagers with the highest exposure to R-rated movies were nearly 7 times more likely to start smoking than those with less exposure; however, the same effect was not found in black teenagers [see p.139].
❧ A *Journal of the American Medical Association* study suggested that lung cancer screening with CT scans might not save lives and may lead to injuries and deaths from needless surgery. ❧ Research published in the *Journal of the American Medical Association*, which reviewed 68 clinical trials of vitamin supplements,

Drugs

indicated that those taking vitamin supplements were 16% more likely to die within the trial period than those taking nothing. {APR} A University of Rochester Medical Center study found that men whose mothers consumed large amounts of beef during pregnancy averaged a 24.3% lower sperm count. ❧ The CDC warned that gonorrhea was increasingly becoming a drug-resistant 'superbug', and advised doctors to switch to a different class of antibiotics. ❧ A journal published by the American Thoracic Society warned that the high levels of nitrites in cured meats might be associated with an increased risk of developing lung disease. ❧ A study published in *Public Health* suggested that inhalation of air pollution in cities may be more detrimental to health than the fallout from an atomic bomb. ❧ Research published in the *Lancet* indicated that hormone replacement therapy significantly increased the risks of developing ovarian, breast, and womb cancer. {MAY} After reviewing 900 studies, researchers at the Silent Spring Institute created a list of chemicals in food and the environment that might

cause breast cancer. The research found that at least 29 of the chemicals were widely produced in the US, including 10 food additives registered with the US Food and Drug Administration.
❧ An Atlanta man caused an international health scare after flying from Europe to Canada while suffering from tuberculosis. After an international outcry, the patient apologized, but said he had never been forbidden from flying. While it was initially believed that the man suffered from an extremely drug-resistant form of TB, tests later found a less severe strain. ❧ The FDA warned consumers that some brands of imported monkfish actually contained potentially deadly puffer fish. ❧ An analysis issued by the CDC found while the the oral health of most Americans had improved, the number of cavities in the baby teeth of children 2–5 had risen by 4%, 1999–2004. {JUN} · An analysis by the French Inst. of Public Health, Epidemiology & Dev. suggested that agricultural workers exposed to high levels of pesticides had a greater risk of brain tumors. ❧ The FDA warned consumers to avoid toothpaste from China after a shipment was found to contain a poisonous chemical. ❧ United Arab Emirates University researchers found that women whose conservative dress limits their exposure to sunlight may suffer from Vitamin D deficiencies. ❧ The FDA banned the import of 5 types of seafood from China after finding harmful chemicals. {JUL} · Danish researchers reported that vacuum-packed foods encourage the growth of Listeria bacteria, which can become 100 times more invasive because the contents are not exposed to oxygen.

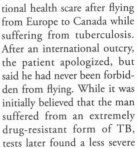

———————————SELECTED US HEALTH RISKS———————————

Since 1983, Harris Interactive has annually polled US adults about their weight, seat belt use, and smoking habits. Charted below are the trends from 1983 to 2007:

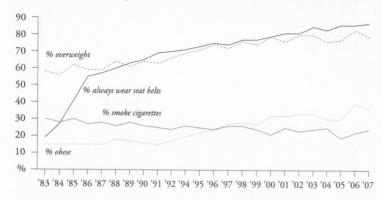

The Harris poll also found that the more educated Americans are, the less likely they are to smoke, be obese, or not wear seat belts. In 2007 the percentages were:

Level of education (%)	smoke	obese	wear seat belts
High school or less	34	41	83
Some college	23	39	88
College graduate	10	24	90
Post-grad	8	22	93
All adults	24	36	87

[Obese: adults ≥25 who weigh ≥20% more than their recommended weight based on height and body frame, using the Metropolitan Life tables. Overweight: adults ≥25 who weigh more than their recommended weight based on the same specifications. Seat belt wearing when in front seat of a car.]

———————————DRINKING———————————

Below are the latest (2004) DOH figures for the alcohol consumption of those ≥18:

Characteristic	All %	♂ %	♀ %
DRINKERS	60·8	67·3	54·9
regular	47·1	56·7	38·3
infrequent	13·3	10·0	16·4
light	69·7	60·8	79·7
moderate	23·1	31·5	13·6
heavy	7·2	7·7	6·7
NON-DRINKERS	39·1	32·7	45·0
lifetime abstainers	24·6	17·8	30·6
former drinkers	14·5	14·9	14·4

DRUG ABUSE

The most recent findings on drug abuse from the US Substance Abuse and Mental Health Services Administration (SAMHSA) show that, in 2005, 8·1% of Americans aged ≥12 had used illicit drugs (marijuana/hashish, cocaine, crack, hallucinogens, heroin, inhalants, psychotherapeutics, &c.) during the past *month*. This was similar to the rate in 2004 (7·9%), 2003 (8·2%), and 2002 (8·3%). The drugs used were:

2005	*No. of users in past month*	%			
Marijuana/hashish	14,626,000	6·0	Inhalants	611,000	0·3
Cocaine	2,397,000	1·0	Psychotherapeutics	6,405,000	2·6
Crack	682,000	0·3	Pain relievers	4,658,000	1·9
Heroin	136,000	0·1	OxyContin	334,000	0·1
Hallucinogens	1,088,000	0·4	Tranquilizers	1,817,000	0·7
LSD	104,000	–	Stimulants	1,067,000	0·4
PCP	48,000	–	Methamphetamine	512,000	0·2
Ecstasy	502,000	0·2	Sedatives	272,000	0·1
			Any illicit drug	19,720,000	8·1

Below are further findings from SAMHSA's 2005 Survey of Drug Use and Health:

22·2m (9·1%) of US ≥12s were classified with substance dependence or abuse in the past year. ❦ 6·4m (2·6% of ≥12s) regularly used prescription-type psychotherapeutic drugs nonmedically. Of these, 4·7m used pain relievers; 1·8m, tranquilizers; 1·1m, stimulants; and 272,000, sedatives. ❦ 51% of those aged 12–17 reported that it would be 'fairly' or 'very' easy for them to obtain marijuana if they wanted to; 24·9% reported it would be easy to get cocaine; 25·3%, crack; 15·7%, LSD; and 14%, heroin. 90·2% said that their parents would strongly disapprove of their trying marijuana or hashish once or twice.

❦ Males were more likely to report current illicit drug use than females (10·2% and 6·1% respectively). ❦ 3·9m people (1·6% of the US population ≥12) received some kind of treatment for a problem related to the use of alcohol or illicit drugs. ❦ Amongst those adults suffering from 'serious psychological distress', 21·3% were dependent on or abused illicit drugs or alcohol; the rate of abuse amongst healthy adults was 7·7%. ❦ Amongst those adults who suffered a 'major depressive episode', 19·9% were dependent on or abused alcohol or illicit drugs; the rate of abuse amongst healthy adults was 8·4%.

Below are the mean ages of first use for a range of drugs amongst those (aged 12–49) who started using drugs in 2005 (e.g. the average first use of heroin was 22·2).

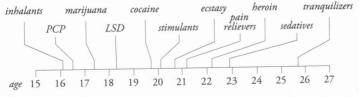

SAMHSA cautions against inferring a *sequence* of drug use (e.g. 'soft' to 'hard') from these data.

——————————————SUICIDE & DEPRESSION——————————————

Suicide was the third leading cause of death among youths aged 15–24, and the eleventh leading cause of death among adults in 2004, the latest year for which data are available. Below are further data from the American Association of Suicidology:

Group	2004 suicides	suicides per day	rate/100,000	% of all deaths
All	32,439	88·6	11·1	1·4
Male	25,566	69·9	17·7	2·2
Female	6,873	18·8	4·6	0·6
White	29,251	79·9	12·3	1·4
Non-white	3,188	8·7	5·8	0·9
– black	2,019	5·5	5·2	0·7
Elderly (≥65)	5,198	14·2	14·3	0·3
Young (15–24)	4,316	11·8	10·4	12·9

SUICIDE METHODS 2004		
Method	suicides	%†
Firearms	16,750	51·6
Suffocation/hanging	7,336	22·6
Poisoning	5,800	17·9
Cut/pierce	590	1·8
Drowning	365	1·1

STATE RANK BY SUICIDE RATE 2004		
State	suicides	rate‡
Alaska	155	23·6
Montana	175	18·9
Nevada	440	18·9
New Mexico	356	18·7
DC [lowest]	33	6·0

† Percent of 2004 suicides   ‡ Rate per 100,000 population

The National Survey on Drug Use and Health (NSDUH) provides data on suicidal thoughts and attempts. The NSDUH asks Americans about their experiences with major depressive episodes (MDEs), defined, using the criteria in the 4th *Diagnostic & Statistical Manual of Mental Disorders*, as a period of two weeks or more 'during which there is either depressed mood or loss of interest or pleasure' and other symptoms. Of the 7·6% of adults reporting an MDE in the past year, the following:

Felt they would be better dead	56·3%	Made a suicide plan	14·5%
Had suicidal thoughts	40·3%	Attempted suicide	10·4%

Women were almost twice as likely as men to report an MDE in the past year, but men were more likely than women to think about committing suicide (45·5% *vs* 37·6%), or to make a suicide plan (17·9% *vs* 12·7%). Respondents were asked to report on their worst MDE. [Source: SAMHSA, 2006]

In 2007, the CDC reported that suicides among American youth (<20) climbed 18% between 2003–04, from 1,737 deaths in 2003, to 1,985 in 2004. Some experts noted a concurrent decline in antidepressant prescriptions, which fell by 6·8% during the same period. According to the 2005 YRBSS [see p.95], 36·7% of female students in grades 9–12 reported feeling 'so sad or hopeless that it disrupted their normal life' in the past year; 20·4% of boys said the same. Furthermore, 16·2% of girls reported making a suicide plan in the last year (9·9% of boys), while 10·8% of girls said they had actually attempted suicide at least once (6% of boys).

─────────FIRE IN THE US─────────

In 2005, the US had *c.*30,300 fire departments, staffed by 1,136,650 uniformed (public municipal) firefighters – of whom 12·6% were 'career' firefighters, and 87·4% were volunteers of some sort. 76% of career firefighters protect communities with populations >25,000; 95% of volunteers protect populations <25,000; and more than half of volunteers protect populations <2,500. In 2005, they responded to:

Number	response	% change from 2004
1,602,000	fires	+3·3
14,373,500	medical aid	+1·9
2,134,000	false alarms	+1·3
1,091,000	mutual aid/assistance	+10·9
375,000	hazardous materials	+5·9
667,000	other hazardous (arcing wires, bomb removal, &c.)	–0·6
3,009,000	all other (smoke scares, lockouts, &c.)	+5·5
23,251,500	TOTAL	+2·8

Below is the National Fire Protection Association's (NFPA) 2005 'fire loss clock':

Fire event	every		
Fire dept responded to a fire	20 sec	Home structure fire reported	83 sec
Outdoor fire reported	39 sec	Vehicle fire reported	109 sec
Structure fire reported	62 sec	Civilian fire injury reported	29 min
		Civilian fire death	2 hr 23 min

The NFPA estimates that the 1·6m reported fires in 2005 were responsible for 3,675 civilian deaths, 17,925 civilian injuries, 115 firefighter deaths, 80,100 firefighter injuries, and *c.*$10·7bn of damage to property. In the same year, *c.*31,500 acts of structural arson were thought to be responsible for 315 civilian deaths. ❦ By 2004, 96% of US households were fitted with smoke alarms. However, a 2006 report by the US Fire Administration indicated that between 2001–04, smoke alarms were present in *c.*60% of fatal residential fires. And, where fatal fires broke out in homes with smoke alarms, those alarms operated properly just 39% of the time. ❦ Below are the ten deadliest fires and explosions in the US, according to the NFPA.

Date	event	fatalities†
09·11·2001	The World Trade Center, New York, NY	2,666
04·27·1865	*SS Sultana* boiler explosion and fire, Mississippi River	1,547
10·08·1871	Forest fire, Peshtigo, WI, and environs	1,152
06·15·1904	*General Slocum* excursion steamship fire, New York, NY	1,030
12·30·1903	Iroquois Theater, Chicago, IL	602
10·12·1918	Forest fire, Cloquet, MN, and environs	559
11·28·1942	Cocoanut Grove nightclub, Boston, MA	492
04·16·1947	*SS Grandcamp* and Monsanto plant, Texas City, TX	468
09·01·1894	Forest fire, Hinckley, MN, and environs	418
12·06·1907	Monongha Mine coal mine explosion, Monongha, WV	361

[Sources: US Fire Administration; FEMA; The National Fire Protection Association. † NFPA figures.]

——————— MURDER ———————

An estimated 16,692 people were murdered in the US in 2005 (5·6 per 100,000 inhabitants), an increase of 3·4% over 2004. Below are some of the statistics pertaining to murder perpetrators and their victims in 2005:

murder victims by race and sex

%	all	♂	♀	?
White	48·0	44·6	61·1	0
Black	47·9	51·7	34·3	4·5
Other	2·6	2·4	3·3	0
?	1·4	1·3	1·3	95·5
Total	—	78·6	21·2	0·2

murder offenders by race, sex, and age %

♂	65·3	White	32·0
♀	7·3	Black	37·6
? sex	27·4	Other race	2·0
<18-yr-old	5·54†	? race	28·8
>18-yr-old	60·8†	† *Where age is known*	

murder weapons by % killed

Firearms	68·0	Strangulation	0·8
Knives &c.	12·9	Narcotics	0·3
Blunt objects	4·0	Poison	0·1
Bodily†	6·0	*Where weapon known*	
Fire	0·8	† *Fists, feet, &c.*	

27% of murder circumstances involved arguments; 6·2%, robberies; 5·1%, juvenile gang killings; and 3·9%, drug felonies. ❦ In single victim–offender murders, 92·6% of blacks were killed by blacks; 84·8% of whites by whites. ❦ Only 25·4% of victims were killed by strangers. [Source: Crime in the US, 2005]

DEGREES OF MURDER

Although laws vary by state, *first degree* murder is generally a deliberate and premeditated killing, or one that occurs alongside certain felonies; while *second degree* murder is a nonpremeditated killing. Some states also have the lesser charge of *third degree* murder.

——————— LAW ENFORCERS ———————

2005 law enforcement personnel data:

Total law enforcement		969,070
– civilians	(30·5%)	295,924
– sworn officers	(69·5%)	673,146
Personnel/1,000 pop.		3·5

Sworn officers are defined as those '*who ordinarily carry a firearm and a badge, have full arrest powers, and are paid from governmental funds set aside specifically for sworn law enforcement representatives*'. ❦ 61·8% of full-time civilian law enforcement employees were female, along with 11·6% of full-time sworn officers. ❦ In 2005, 55 law enforcement officers were killed in 53 incidents; 67 officers died as a result of accidents in the line of duty. [Sources: Crime in the US, 2005; Law Enforcement Officers Killed & Assaulted, 2005]

——————— HATE CRIMES ———————

The 1990 Hate Crime Statistics Act requires the Attorney General to collect data '*about crimes that manifest evidence of prejudice based on race, religion, sexual orientation, or ethnicity*'. In 2005, police reported 7,163 hate crime incidents; 7,160 were said to be motivated by a single bias, while 3 were said to involve multiple biases. Below are the single-bias *incidents*, by type of bias involved:

54·7%	*were motivated by*	racial bias
17·1		religious bias
14·2		sexual-orientation bias
13·2		ethnicity/national origin bias
0·7		anti-disability bias

Intimidation accounted for 30·3% of hate crime *offenses*; destruction, damage, or vandalism, 30·2%; simple assault, 18·7%; and aggravated assault, 12·7%. [Source: Hate Crime Statistics, 2005]

PRISONS & PRISONERS

In December 2005, US federal, state, and local jails held the following prisoners:

1,446,269	73,097	107,500	737 inmates	1 in 136
in state &	*in local*	*in private*	*per 100,000*	*of population*
federal prison	*jails*	*prisons*	*population*	*in prison*

The total of all those incarcerated in the US (including military and juvenile facilities, territorial prisons, immigration facilities, &c.) was 2,320,359. Including probation and parole, the US 'correctional population' totals >7 million. At the end of 2005, state prisons were operating between 1% under and 14% over capacity, while the federal system was at 34% over capacity. [Source: Bureau of Justice Statistics, 2006]

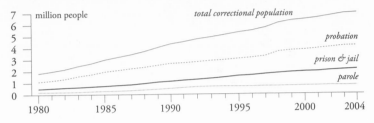

The Federal Bureau of Prisons operates institutions at 5 different levels of security 'in order to confine offenders in an appropriate manner'. These security levels are:

MINIMUM SECURITY · (also known as Federal Prison Camps) have dormitory housing, a low staff-to-inmate ratio, and limited or no perimeter fencing. They are work- and program-oriented, and many are located adjacent to institutions or military bases, whose labor needs inmates serve.

LOW SECURITY · have double-fenced perimeters, mostly dormitory or cubicle housing, and strong work and program components. The staff-to-inmate ratio is higher than in minimum security.

MEDIUM SECURITY · have strengthened perimeters (often double fences with electronic detection), mostly cell-type housing, a wide variety of work and treatment programs, a higher staff-to-inmate ratio, and even greater internal controls.

HIGH SECURITY · (also known as US Penitentiaries) have highly secured perimeters (featuring walls or reinforced fences), multiple- and single-occupant cells, the highest staff-to-inmate ratio, and close control of inmate movement.

ADMINISTRATIVE · institutions with special missions: e.g. detention of pre-trial offenders; treatment of inmates with serious medical problems; or the containment of extremely dangerous, violent, or escape-prone inmates. Such facilities are capable of holding inmates in all security categories.

The Bureau of Prisons' breakdown of inmates by security level (at June 2007):

Security level	%		
Minimum	18·3	Medium	27·8
Low	38·4	High	10·7
		Unclassified	4·6

CAPITAL PUNISHMENT

53 prisoners in 14 states were executed during 2006 (compared to 60 in 2005) – of whom, 32 were white and 21 black. All of those executed were male; 52 died from lethal injection, and 1 from electrocution. According to the State Dept, 'the number of executions in the United States in 2006 dropped to its lowest number in 10 years, in part due to legal challenges resulting in many states reviewing their capital punishment policies and procedures'. According to the Death Penalty Information Center (DPIC), as of July 2007, 12 states had suspended executions due to concerns over lethal injection, and New Jersey was considering abolishing the death penalty entirely. Currently, the death penalty is legal in 38 states, while 12 states and the District of Columbia have abolished it. An October 2006 Gallup poll showed that most Americans support the death penalty for those convicted of murder:

favor 67% · *oppose* 28% · *unsure* 5%

However, a 2007 DPIC poll also found that 58% of those surveyed supported a moratorium on executions so the entire process can be reviewed.

The table opposite gives a snapshot of the death penalty in the 50 states, DC, the federal system, and the US. It shows: the methods allowed by state statute; state minimum age; the number of prisoners on death row [as of 1·1·2007]; the number executed since 1977 [as of 6·20·2007]; the number executed in 2006; and the state's 2005 murder rate per 100,000 population.

Key to table – Lethal [I]njection · [G]assing [E]lectrocution · [H]anging · [F]iring squad
ns=not stated · *na*=not applicable
[Sources: DoJ; FBI; Death Penalty Information Center. For worldwide death penalty statistics, see p.62]

	legal methods	minimum age	on death row	executed post '77	executed in '06	murder rate '05
AL	I·E	16	195	36	1	8·2
AK	·	·	·	·	·	4·8
AZ	I·G	ns	124	23	0	7·5
AR	I·E	14	37	27	0	6·7
CA	I·G	18	660	13	1	6·9
CO	I	18	2	1	0	3·7
CT	I	18	8	1	0	2·9
DC	·	·	·	·	·	35·4
DE	I·H	16	18	14	0	4·4
FL	I·E	17	397	64	4	5·0
GA	I	17	107	40	0	6·2
HI	·	·	·	·	·	1·9
ID	I·F	ns	20	1	0	2·4
IL	I	18	11	12	0	6·0
IN	I	18	23	19	1	5·7
IA	·	·	·	·	·	1·3
KS	I	18	9	0	0	3·7
KY	I·E	16	41	2	0	4·6
LA	I	ns	88	27	0	9·9
ME	·	·	·	·	·	1·4
MD	I	18	8	5	0	9·9
MA	·	·	·	·	·	2·7
MI	·	·	·	·	·	6·1
MN	·	·	·	·	·	2·2
MS	I	16	66	8	1	7·3
MO	I·G	16	51	66	0	6·9
MT	I	ns	2	3	1	1·9
NE	E	18	9	3	0	2·5
NV	I	18	80	12	1	8·5
NH	I·H	17	0	0	0	1·4
NJ	I	18	11	0	0	4·8
NM	I	18	2	1	0	7·4
NY	I	18	1	0	0	4·5
NC	I	17	185	43	4	6·7
ND	·	·	·	·	·	1·1
OH	I	18	191	26	5	5·1
OK	I·E·F	13	88	85	4	5·3
OR	I	18	33	2	0	2·2
PA	I	ns	226	3	0	6·1
RI	·	·	·	·	·	3·2
SC	I·E	ns	67	37	1	7·4
SD	I	18	4	1	0	2·3
TN	I·E	18	107	3	1	7·2
TX	I	17	393	397	24	6·2
UT	I·F	14	9	6	0	2·3
VT	·	·	·	·	·	1·3
VA	I·E	14	20	98	4	6·1
WA	I·H	18	9	4	0	3·3
WV	·	·	·	·	·	4·4
WI	·	·	·	·	·	3·5
WY	I·G	18	2	1	0	2·7
Fed.	I	18	44	3	0	na
USA	na	na	3,348	1,087	53	5·6

Media & Celebrity

I would much rather have men ask why I have no statue than why I have one.
— CATO THE ELDER (234–149 BC)

———— 'PEOPLE' vs 'US WEEKLY' COVER STARS ————

Date	People	Us Weekly
1·01·07	*No issue published*	Jennifer Aniston
1·08·07	People who lost 'half their size'	Carrie Underwood
1·15·07	Oprah Winfrey	Kate Hudson & Owen Wilson
1·22·07	Michelle Young	Scarlett Johansson & Justin Timberlake
1·29·07	Pam & Shawn Hornbeck	Britney Spears & Isaac Cohen
2·05·07	Tyra Banks	Justin Timberlake & Cameron Diaz
2·12·07	Angelina Jolie	Jessica Biel
2·19·07	Lisa Nowak	Reese Witherspoon
2·26·07	Anna Nicole Smith	Britney Spears
3·05·07	Britney Spears	Britney Spears
3·12·07	Patrick Dempsey	Britney Spears & Kevin Federline
3·19·07	Brad Pitt & Angelina Jolie	Brad Pitt & Angelina Jolie
3·26·07	Sandra Bullock	Paris Hilton, Britney Spears, Lindsay Lohan
4·02·07	Angelina Jolie & Pax Thien	Katie Holmes & Suri Cruise
4·09·07	*American Idol* finalists	Angelina Jolie
4·16·07	Valerie Bertinelli	Tori Spelling & Liam Aaron
4·23·07	Marcia Cross & twins	Reese Witherspoon & Jake Gyllenhaal
4·30·07	Virginia Tech mourning	Prince William & Kate Middleton
5·07·07	Drew Barrymore	Tom Cruise & Katie Holmes
5·14·07	Rachael Ray	Vanessa Minnillo
5·21·07	Women who lost 100lbs	Ricki Lake
5·28·07	Madeleine McCann	Angelina Jolie & Jennifer Aniston
6·04·07	Princess Diana & Princes William and Harry	Janet Jackson
6·11·07	Lindsay Lohan	Shiloh Jolie-Pitt
6·18·07	Jennifer Aniston	Vanessa Minnillo & Nick Lachey
6·25·07	Matthew McConaughey	Britney & Lynne Spears
7·02·07	Billy Ray & Miley Cyrus	Jessica Simpson
7·09·07	Paris Hilton	Suri Cruise
7·16·07	Chris Benoit	Nicole Richie
7·23·07	Daniel Radcliffe	Hilary Duff
7·30·07	Katie Holmes & Suri	Jenn. Aniston, Cameron Diaz, Jessica Simpson
8·06·07	Lindsay Lohan	Jason Priestley & Naomi Lowde-Priestley
8·13·07	Hawke-Petit family	Jayden & Sean Preston Federline, Britney Spears
8·20·07	Valerie Bertinelli & Kirstie Alley	Britney Spears & Matt Encinas

Spears graced the cover of *Us Weekly* 8 times in the months surveyed. For a look at her year, see p.122.

—SOME HATCHED, MATCHED, & DISPATCHED · 2006–07—

HATCHED

Angel Iris	*born to* Melanie Brown & Eddie Murphy
Cayden Wyatt	Christine Baumgartner & Kevin Costner
Dannielynn Hope	Anna Nicole Smith & Larry Birkhead
Eden & Savannah	Marcia Cross & Tom Mahoney
Henry Daniel	Julia Roberts & Danny Moder
Jayden James	Britney Spears & Kevin Federline
Jessie James & D'Lila Star	Sean 'Diddy' Combs & Kim Porter
Johan Riley Fyodor Taiwo	Heidi Klum & Seal
Liam Aaron	Tori Spelling & Dean McDermott
Ramona	Maggie Gyllenhaal & Peter Sarsgaard
Sam Alexis	Elin Nordegren & Tiger Woods
Sullivan Patrick & Darby Galen	Patrick & Jillian Dempsey
Thijs	Matt & Annette Lauer

MATCHED

Elizabeth Hurley & Arun Nayar	Sudeley Castle, UK, & Jodhpur, India
Eva Longoria & Tony Parker	Paris, France
Neve Campbell & John Light	Malibu, California
Rebecca Romijn & Jerry O'Connell	Calabasas, California
Rod Stewart & Penny Lancaster	Portofino, Italy
Steve Martin & Anne Stringfield	Los Angeles, California
Tim Allen & Jane Hajduk	Grand Lake, Colorado
Tom Cruise & Katie Holmes	Bracciano, Italy
Usher & Tameka Foster	Atlanta, Georgia

DISPATCHED

Britney Spears & Kevin Federline (*married for* 2 years)	divorced
Carmen Electra & Dave Navarro (3 years)	divorced
Dita Von Teese & Marilyn Manson (1 year)	filed for divorce
Pamela Anderson & Kid Rock (4 months)	filed for divorce
Reese Witherspoon & Ryan Phillipe (7 years)	filed for divorce
Whitney Houston and Bobby Brown (14 years)	filed for divorce

—————— CELEBRITY ADOPTIONS ——————

Celebrity	adopted	year	from
Sheryl Crow	Wyatt Steven	2007	USA
Angelina Jolie	Pax Thien	2007	Vietnam
	Zahara, Maddox	2005, 2002	Ethiopia, Cambodia
Meg Ryan	Daisy	2006	China
Madonna	David	2006	Malawi
Ewan McGregor	Jamiyan	2006	Mongolia
Sharon Stone	Quinn, Laird, Roan	2006, 2005, 2002	USA
Calista Flockhart	Liam	2001	USA

VANITY FAIR'S HOLLYWOOD · 2007

The stars featured on the cover of the 2007 *Vanity Fair* 'Hollywood issue' were:

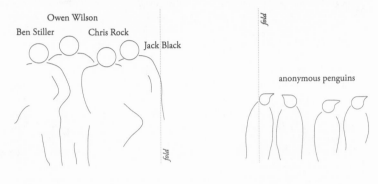

REHAB

In 2007, a rash of high-profile stars suffered particularly public meltdowns and took themselves off to rehab. Below is a summary of some celeb-attended rehab centers:

BETTY FORD CENTER
Rancho Mirage, CA · *founded*: 1982
Treatment: Old-fashioned approach to detox based on the 12-step recovery program. Clients perform chores, such as cleaning the lavatories.
Cost: $21,000 a month
Celeb clients: Elizabeth Taylor, Ozzy Osbourne, Drew Barrymore, Keith Urban, David Hasselhoff, Billy Joel

PROMISES
Malibu, CA · *founded*: 1997
Treatment: Luxury spa-style center with new-age treatments offered alongside addiction counseling.
Cost: $48,000 a month
Celeb clients: Mel Gibson, Charlie Sheen, Diana Ross, Britney Spears

THE MEADOWS
Wickenburg, AZ · *founded*: 1976
Treatment: Desert-based center that 'provides a path to personal completeness and integrity, for those seeking treatment for trauma and addictions'.
Cost: $4,000 a night
Celeb clients: Kate Moss, Elle McPherson, Whitney Houston

WONDERLAND CENTER
Los Angeles, CA · *founded*: 2006
Treatment: All patients must undergo a 3-day detox, but clients can then come and go because 'recovery does not need to isolate you from your friends, family or career'.
Cost: $80,000 a month
Celeb clients: Lindsay Lohan, Mike Tyson

[Sources: *Us Weekly*; *The Independent*; &c. · Costs are approximate and depend on treatment.]

CELEBRITY REHAB QUOTES: *Other than smoking cigarettes, I've got no real bad vices left.* [Marc Jacobs to *Fashion Week Daily*] · *I always said I would die before I went to rehab.* [Lindsay Lohan to *Allure*] · *I was sent to a very humbling place called rehab. I truly hit rock bottom.* [Britney Spears on BritneySpears.com] · *They tried to make me go to rehab, I said no! No! No!* [Amy Winehouse]

—BRITNEY—

A timeline of Britney Spears' curious year:

11/6/06: Britney appears on *Letterman* with new haircut · 11/7: files for divorce from Kevin Federline; goes ice-skating · 11/27: 'revealing' photos appear online · 12/31: hosts Las Vegas New Year's party; 'falls asleep' · 1/9/07: tops Blackwell's Worst Dressed List [see p.123] · 1/13: stays in $40,000-a-night Las Vegas hotel room with Isaac Cohen · 2/7: reportedly breaks up with Cohen · 2/15: press reports on 24-hour rehab stint · 2/16: shaves head · 2/20: enters *Promises* rehab · 2/21: checks out of *Promises* · 2/22: re-enters *Promises* · 3/20: finishes treatment at *Promises* · 3/29: reaches divorce settlement with Federline · 5/1: first live performance in *c*.3 years · 5/19: reportedly lip-synching when record skips in Orlando · 6/28: delivers 'warning letter' to mother, Lynne Spears · 7/4: apologizes to the paparazzi for Feb shenanigans with umbrella · 7/19: 'disastrous' *Ok!* magazine photo shoot, and 'stripper-pole' video shoot · 7/30: divorce from Federline finalized · 8/29 Comeback single 'Gimme More' debuted online [Sources: many & various]

—CELEBRITY RANKINGS—

· MAXIM's HOT 100 ·

1 .... Lindsay Lohan
2 .... Jessica Alba
3 ...... Scarlett Johansson
4 ...... Christina Aguilera
5 .... Jessica Biel
6 .... Ali Larter
7 .... Eva Mendez
8 .... Rihanna
9 .... Eva Longoria
10 .... Fergie

· PEOPLE's SEXIEST ♂ ·

1 .... George Clooney
2 .... Patrick Dempsey
3 .... Ashton Kutcher
4 .... Taye Diggs
5 .... Johnny Depp
6 .... Josh Duhamel
7 ...... Enrique Murciano
8 .... Leonardo DiCaprio
9 .... John Krasinski
10 .... Jake Gyllenhaal

· PEOPLE's 100 MOST BEAUTIFUL ·

People magazine named Drew Barrymore the 'World's Most Beautiful' person in 2007. The actress was one of eleven stars to appear without makeup in the issue, which also included a spotlight on celebrity humanitarians. Other celebs said to be among the 'Most Beautiful' were Halle Berry, Eric Bana, Jennifer Aniston, Scarlett Johansson, Patrick Dempsey, Kerry Washington, Matthew McConaughey, Reese Witherspoon, and Jennifer Garner.

· FORBES CELEBRITY POWER RANKING ·

The world's most powerful media figures in 2007:

1 .... Oprah Winfrey
2 .... Tiger Woods
3 .... Madonna
4 ..... The Rolling Stones
5 .... Brad Pitt
6 .... Johnny Depp
7 .... Elton John
8 .... Tom Cruise
9 .... Jay-Z
10 ...... Steven Spielberg

· FILM THREAT's FRIGID 50 ·

The 'coldest, least powerful people in Hollywood':

1 .... Mel Gibson
2 .... Jennifer Aniston
3 .... Borat
4 .... Lindsay Lohan
5 .... Wesley Snipes
6 .... Mark Cuban
7 .... Tara Reid
8 .... Lonelygirl15
9 .... Movie critics
10 .... TomKat

· POPSUGAR's TOP 10 ·

The tops for talent, looks, &c., based on 4m votes:

1 .... Brad Pitt
2 .... Angelina Jolie
3 .... Oprah Winfrey
4 .... Madonna
5 .... Tom Cruise
6 .... Britney Spears
7 .... Jennifer Aniston
8 .... Julia Roberts
9 .... George Clooney
10 .... Johnny Depp

——————HOLLYWOOD'S WORST-DRESSED WOMEN——————

Former designer Richard Blackwell has issued his annual 'Worst Dressed Women List' for 47 years. In 2006, Paris Hilton and Britney Spears (nicknamed 'The Screamgirls' by Mr Blackwell) tied for number one. The rest of the 2006 top 10:

1 ....Britney Spears/Paris Hilton		6 .... Paula Abdul
2 ....Camilla Parker-Bowles		7 ....Sharon Stone
3 .... Lindsay Lohan		8 ....Tori Spelling
4 .... Christina Aguilera		9 ....Sandra Oh
5 .... Mariah Carey		10........................ Meryl Streep

Mr Blackwell's 2006 list of *best*-dressed women included: Beyoncé, Marcia Cross, Katie Holmes, Angelina Jolie, Heidi Klum, Helen Mirren, Princess Charlotte of Monaco, Speaker of the House Nancy Pelosi, Barbra Streisand, and Kate Winslet.

——CELEBRITY SCENTS——

Below are some celebrity fragrances launched during 2006 and 2007:

Prince.............................*3121*
C. Aguilera.. *Simply Christina Aguilera*
Sean Combs...... *Unforgivable Woman*
Shania Twain.......... *Shania Starlight*
Mariah Carey ..... *M by Mariah Carey*
Celine Dion.............*Spring in Paris*
Kylie Minogue ....*Sweet Darling*
Paris Hilton ....*Can Can*
Derek Jeter ....*Driven*

——US WEEKLY AWARDS——

HOT HOLLYWOOD
Style Icon of the Year · Jennifer Lopez
Red Carpet Style · Lindsay Lohan

BEST MAKEOVERS
Reese Witherspoon,
Katherine McPhee, Kate Walsh,
Drew Barrymore, Katie Holmes

HOTTEST BODIES
Janet Jackson, Rihanna,
Jenny McCarthy, Christina Milian,
Diana DeGarmo

——WHAT IS SEXY?——

The Victoria's Secret 2007 'What Is Sexy?' list, as adjudicated by the company's executives, designers, and models:

Actor .... Eric Dane
Actress.......................Jessica Alba
♂ *musician* ....Justin Timberlake
♀ *musician* ....Carrie Underwood
♂ *athlete*.................... Derek Jeter
♀ *athlete*................ Danica Patrick
Mom......................Kate Hudson
Dad....................David Beckham
City.......................... Las Vegas
Legs .... Cameron Diaz
Lips .... Jennifer Hudson

——MILK MUSTACHES——

The following celebrities sported 'Got Milk?' mustaches during 2006–07:

Sasha Cohen · Alex Rodriguez
Carrie Underwood · David Beckham
Beyoncé, Solange, and Tina Knowles
Vince Carter · Kathy Smith · Mariska
Hargitay · Rex Grossman and Marvin
Harrison · 'Fantastic Four' · *High
School Musical* cast · Sara Ramirez

————— CELEBRITY BLOGS AND QUOTES OF NOTE —————

*Wisdom from celebrity
interviews and blogs:*

TYRESE GIBSON
(to *Elle*)
I'm very intelligent
beyond my years. The
beautiful thing about
my intelligence is that
it doesn't really come in
one specific department.

TONY PARKER
(to *AP*, on sleeping with his
NBA championship trophy)
I put Eva on the couch.

BRITNEY SPEARS
(BritneySpears.com)
Till this day I don't
think that it was alcohol
or depression. I was
like a bad kid running
around with ADD.

NICOLE RICHIE
('joke' Memorial Day party
invitation, widely reported)
There will be a scale at
the front door. No girls
over 100 pounds allowed
in. Start starving
yourself now.

ISAIAH WASHINGTON
(statement after being fired
from *Grey's Anatomy*)
I'm mad as hell,
and I'm not going to
take it anymore.

PRESIDENT BUSH
(to aide before G8 summit,
widely reported)
Where's Bono?
Bono for president!

JESSICA SIMPSON
(to *Us Weekly*)
I think I do have a little
bit more fun as a blonde
... People take me a
little too seriously when
I'm a brunette.

HEATHER MILLS
(to *Extra*, regarding
Dancing with the Stars)
Hopefully my leg will
stay on. It's very unlikely
my leg is going to fly off,
although it would
be quite funny.

GISELE BÜNDCHEN
(to Italian *Vanity Fair*)
The only difference
between me and other
people is that I travel
a lot more.

PARIS HILTON
(on adversity, to Larry King)
It's a process, a gift, and
a journey, and if we can
travel it alone, although
the road may be rough
at the beginning, you
find an ability to walk it.

MADONNA
(to Sirius Satellite Radio)
I want to be like Gandhi
and Martin Luther King
and John Lennon – but
I want to stay alive.

PAULA ABDUL
(to *Us Weekly*)
I've never been drunk.
I have never done recrea-
tional drugs. Just look at
my 20-year career.

ANGELINA JOLIE
(to UK *Elle*)
Shiloh seemed so privi-
leged from the moment
she was born. I have less
inclination to feel for
her ... A newborn really
is this ... Yes, a blob!

GEORGE CLOONEY
(to David Letterman, on being
named *People's* Sexiest Man)
I felt bad for Matt
Damon, because he
really wanted it. He
campaigned hard for it,
but he came up short.

VICTORIA BECKHAM
(to UK's *Sun*)
I've been practising for
years to keep that pout.
I learned how to do it
and stuck with it.

LIV TYLER
(to *Us Weekly*, on surgery)
I'm definitely going to
have some ... especially
when you see what
happens to your body
after you have a baby.

CHRISTINA AGUILERA
(to *Access Hollywood*)
There's a proper way
to make sure privates
are kept private.
That's just my personal
take on exiting a limo.

BRITNEY SPEARS
(BritneySpears.com)
Thank God for
Victoria's Secret's
new underwear line!

THE FACE OF …

The following are some selected celebrity endorsements from late 2006 and 2007:

Tom Brady .... *Stetson fragrances*	Carmen Electra .... *Max Factor*
Jay-Z...................... *Cherry Coke*	Jennifer Aniston........... *SmartWater*
Salma Hayek .... *Campari*	Rachel Hunter .... *SlimFast*
Lindsay Lohan .... *Jill Stuart*	Rachael Ray .... *Dunkin' Donuts*
Drew Barrymore .... *Gucci* [jewelry]	Ashlee Simpson .... *Skechers*
Sienna Miller..................... *Tod's*	Michael Jordan & Cuba Gooding Jr..
Kate Winslet .... *Lancôme Trésor*	*Hanes*

Cover Girl, L'Oréal Paris, and Revlon employ a veritable army of spokesmodels. At the time of writing, the faces of Revlon included Jessica Alba, Eva Mendes, Beau Garrett, Julianne Moore, Susan Sarandon, and Sheryl Crow. Cover Girl employed Rihanna, Keri Russell, Christie Brinkley, Molly Sims, Drew Barrymore, and Queen Latifah, while in 2007 L'Oréal was represented by Beyoncé, Eva Longoria, Scarlett Johansson, Andie McDowell, Heather Locklear, and Diane Keaton – among others.

MOST-DESIRED CELEB FEATURES

Each year plastic surgeons Toby G. Mayer and Richard W. Fleming poll their *c*.1,500 clients at the Beverly Hills Institute of Aesthetic & Reconstructive Surgery about the celebrity features they consider to be the most desirable. The 2007 list:

WOMEN	MEN
Nose.. *Jennifer Connelly, Jennifer Lopez*	Nose..... *Jude Law, Leonardo DiCaprio*
Eyes..... *Penélope Cruz, Cameron Diaz*	Eyes..... *J. Timberlake, Patrick Dempsey*
Lips.... *Kate Winslet, Scarlett Johansson*	Lips.......... *Ashton Kutcher, Brad Pitt*
Jaw/chin... *Sharon Stone, Katie Holmes*	Jaw/chin... *Matt Damon, Jeremy Piven*
Cheeks. *Keira Knightley, Cate Blanchett*	Cheeks....*George Clooney, Johnny Depp*
Body..... *Beyoncé Knowles, Halle Berry*	Body....... *Mark Wahlberg, Will Smith*
Skin.... *Reese Witherspoon, Paris Hilton*	Skin...... *Ryan Seacrest, Orlando Bloom*

HASTY PUDDING MAN & WOMAN OF THE YEAR

Harvard University's Hasty Pudding Theatricals presents Man and Woman of the Year awards annually to celebrities who have made a 'lasting and impressive contribution to the world of entertainment'. In February 2007, the Puddings were presented to Scarlett Johansson and Ben Stiller. Johansson led a parade through the streets of Cambridge, before being roasted by the troupe and presented with a golden pudding pot. Previous Hasty Pudding recipients include Halle Berry and Richard Gere [2006]; Catherine Zeta-Jones and Tim Robbins [2005]; Sandra Bullock and Robert Downey Jr [2004]; and Anjelica Huston and Martin Scorsese [2003].

The Harvard troupe takes its unusual name from the pledge made when the society was created in 1795 – 'the members in alphabetical order shall provide a pot of hasty pudding for every meeting'.

MAX CLIFFORD'S GUIDE TO FAME

In December 2006, the influential British 'PR guru' Max Clifford offered Fame TV his advice to those in search of fame. Clifford's top tips for making it big were:

1 . . . . appear on a reality TV show	6 . . . . flaunt your body
2 . . . . enter a talent contest	7 . . . . date a Royal family member
3 . . . . be abysmal on a talent show	8 . . . . make a home sex tape
4 . . . . gain fame by association	9 . . . . be a success on MySpace
5 . . . . date a celebrity	10. . . be in right place at the right time

MISS AMERICA · 2007

20-year-old blonde Lauren Nelson, an aspiring Broadway performer, was crowned Miss America on January 29, 2007, in Las Vegas. She was the second Miss Oklahoma in a row to win the award, following Jennifer Berry's win in 2006. Nelson sang *You'll Be in My Heart* (from *Tarzan*) during the talent portion of the competition, and during her interview she was questioned about how to close the salary gap between men and women. She replied: 'I think by being a good role model we can change that'. Nelson received $50,000 to continue her education, and embarked on a yearlong tour in support of the Children's Miracle Network and her platform issue: 'Be NetSmart – Protecting Kids Online'†. Miss Alabama, Melinda Toole, was named Miss Congeniality; and Miss Missouri, Sarah French, won Best Smile.

† In April 2007, Nelson went undercover posing as a 14-year-old girl during a New York police operation targeting online pedophiles. The sting (which was filmed by *America's Most Wanted*) led to the arrest of 11 men, who were lured to Nelson's house. ❦ The pageant world suffered several scandals in 2006–07. Miss USA Tara Conner's crown was threatened in December after reports of underage drinking and other activities surfaced in the press, but pageant owner Donald Trump allowed her to keep the title. However, Trump's organization fired Miss Nevada in December, after indecent photos were found online. In January 2007, Miss New Jersey quit after announcing her pregnancy.

10 MOST INFLUENTIAL PEOPLE WHO NEVER LIVED

Recognition, popularity, and persistence were the traits required for fictitious characters to enter Lazar, Karlan, and Salter's splendid book, *101 Most Influential People Who Never Lived*. Their top 10 imaginary, yet consequential, characters were:

1 . . . . Marlboro Man	6 . . . . Frankenstein's Monster
2 . . . . George Orwell's Big Brother	7 . . . . Siegfried
3 . . . . King Arthur	8 . . . . Sherlock Holmes
4 . . . . Santa Claus	9 . . . . Romeo & Juliet
5 . . . . Hamlet	10. . . . . Dr Jekyll & Mr Hyde

—————————————AMERICAN IDOL 6————————————

Jordin 'Just 17' Sparks was crowned the sixth American Idol on May 23, 2007, beating the 'beatboxer from Seattle', Blake Lewis, to become the youngest American Idol to date. While some complained the sixth season's crop lacked the raw talent of previous years, Sanjaya Malakar's ever-changing hairstyles (from ponyhawk to flatiron) and his No. 1 fan ('crying girl' Ashley Ferl†) sparked plenty of water-cooler conversation. Many were surprised to see Simon Cowell favorite Melinda Doolittle sent home May 16, although recent triumphs from past *Idol* also-rans (viz Oscar-winner Jennifer Hudson) indicate that winning is not the only path to success. The top 12 contestants on *American Idol* 6 were voted off in the following order:

March 14	Brandon Rogers	May 2	Phil Stacey
March 21	Stephanie Edwards	May 2	Chris Richardson
March 28	Chris Sligh	May 9	LaKisha Jones
April 4	Gina Glocksen	May 16	Melinda Doolittle
April 11	Haley Scarnato	May 23	Blake Lewis
April 18	Sanjaya Malakar	WINNER	Jordin Sparks

† 13-year-old Ashley Ferl from Riverside, California, was an *American Idol* audience member who became known as 'the crying girl' after sobbing inconsolably on the March 20 episode. She began crying during Sanjaya Malakar performance's of 'You Really Got Me', and was later invited onstage. Asked to explain her tears, she told a *Los Angeles Times* reporter, 'that was the coolest thing ever'.

QUOTES OF NOTE

CHRIS RICHARDSON · [to Simon Cowell] Nasally is a form of singing. ❦ SANJAYA MALAKAR · [singing] Let's give them something to talk about ... other than hair. ❦ SIMON COWELL · LaKisha, I actually could kiss you after that. ❦ SIMON COWELL · I think you have a very good tactic at the moment, Haley: wear [the] least amount of clothes possible. ❦ RYAN SEACREST · [to Cowell] Stay out of my closet! ❦ SIMON COWELL · [to Seacrest] Come out! ❦ SANJAYA MALAKAR · I definitely hoped that Jennifer Lopez picked up on my passion and um ... maybe I'll get her number later and we won't have to tell Marc Anthony. ❦ MELINDA DOOLITTLE · I like church! ❦ BLAKE LEWIS · [whispered at the finale] I love you, Jordin Sparks!

—————————OTHER REALITY SHOW WINNERS————————

Network	show	winner (prize)
ABC	*Dancing with the Stars 4*	Apolo Anton Ohno (disco ball trophy)
VH1	*Flavor of Love 2*	Deelishis (set of gold teeth; Flavor Flav's lurve)
UPN	*Next Top Model 8*	Jaslene Gonzalez (Elite & CoverGirl contracts; *Seventeen* shoot)
CBS	*Survivor: Fiji*	Earl Cole ($1m)
BRAVO	*Top Chef 2*	Ilan Hall (new kitchen; $100,000; &c.)
NBC	*The Apprentice: Los Angeles*	Stefani Schaeffer (job with Donald Trump)
BRAVO	*Project Runway 3*	Jeffrey Sebelia ($100,000 for a clothing line; *Elle* spread; &c.)
ABC	*The Bachelor: Officer and a Gentleman*	Tessa Horst (marriage to Andy Baldwin)
Fox	*So You Think You Can Dance 3*	Sabra Johnson ($250,000)

THE 'BIG 3' NEWS ANCHORS

BRIAN WILLIAMS *NBC Nightly News with Brian Williams*	CHARLES GIBSON *ABC World News with Charles Gibson*	KATIE COURIC *CBS Evening News with Katie Couric*
Since · 12/02/2004	Since · 5/29/2006	Since · 9/05/2006
Average viewers[†] · *c*.9·5m	Average viewers[†] · *c*.8·8m	Average viewers[†] · *c*.7·8m
Salary · reportedly $10m	Salary · reportedly $7m	Salary · reportedly $15m
Prior jobs · Anchor & Managing Editor *The News with Brian Williams*; Anchor & Managing Editor *NBC Nightly News* [Sat. edition]; NBC News Chief White House Correspondent; Pancake House busboy	Prior jobs: Co-anchor *Good Morning America*; Co-anchor *Primetime Thursday*; Correspondent *World News Tonight with Peter Jennings*; Substitute Anchor *Nightline* & *World News This Morning*	Prior jobs · Co-anchor NBC News *Today*; Contributing Anchor *Dateline NBC*; NBC Deputy Pentagon Reporter & Correspondent
Born · 05/05/1959	Born · 03/09/1943	Born · 01/07/1957
[in Elmira, New York]	[in Evanston, Illinois]	[in Arlington, Virginia]
Marital status · married, 2 children	Marital status · married, 2 children	Marital status · widowed[‡], 2 children
Hair color · brunette	Hair color · salt-and-pepper	Hair color · honey-blond
Predecessor · Tom Brokaw	Predecessor · Elizabeth Vargas & Bob Woodruff	Predecessor · Bob Schieffer
		[Sources: Proj. for Excellence in Journalism; various]

† Viewer figures are for November 2006. Year-on-year figures show that NBC's ratings have fallen since 2005, while ABC's remained roughly level. Couric drew 13·6m viewers to her first CBS broadcast, but her viewership has since declined. ‡ Couric's husband died of colon cancer in 1998. Her on-air colonoscopy in 2000 led to a *c*.20 percent rise in the procedures – nicknamed 'the Couric effect'.

NEWS ANCHOR SIGN-OFFS OF NOTE

The sign-offs of some venerable anchors, with their network and years as anchor:

Edward R. Murrow .... CBS .... 1937–61[†] .... *Good night and good luck*
John Cameron Swayze .... NBC .... 1949–56 .... *Glad we could get together*
Dave Garroway .... NBC .... 1949–61 .... *Peace*
C. Huntley/D. Brinkley .. NBC .... 1956–70[‡] .... *Good night, Chet. Good night, David. And good night for NBC News*
Walter Cronkite........... CBS .... 1962–81 .... *And that's the way it is*
Dan Rather................ CBS .... 1981–2005 .... *Courage*[§]

† Murrow became director of the CBS European Bureau in London in 1937, but began his famous London broadcasts in 1938. ‡ The *Huntley–Brinkley Report* aired on NBC from 1956 to 1970; but Brinkley's career continued into the 1990s. § Dan Rather began ending his *CBS Evening News* broadcasts with the word 'courage' in September 1986, but discontinued the practice after a week. He also ended his last-ever broadcast, on March 9, 2005, with the word. ❧ In September 2006, Katie Couric began soliciting suggestions for a new sign-off. She later said 50,000 people had sent suggestions, and told David Letterman in October 2006 her favorite was 'Here, kitty kitty kitty'.

——TV HOUSEHOLDS——

Of the 111,400,000 homes with TV:

Have a color TV	99%
– have ≥2 sets	82%
– have ≥3 sets	52%
Have a VCR	85%
Have a DVD player	84%
Have wired cable	64%
Have wired pay cable	32%

–NUMBER OF CHANNELS–

TV channels in the average US home:

Year	No. channels	No. viewed
2006	104·2	15·7
2005	96·4	15·4
2004	92·6	15·0
2000	61·4	13·6
1995	41·1	10·1

——VIEWING DURATION——

Daily TV viewing per US household:

2005–06 [through 1/1/06]	8h 21m
2004–05	8h 11m
2003–04	8h 01m
2002–03	7h 55m
2001–02	7h 42m
2000–01	7h 39m
1999–2000	7h 31m
1998–99	7h 24m
1997–98	7h 15m
1996–97	7h 12m
1995–96	7h 15m
1994–95	7h 15m
1993–94	7h 16m
1992–93	7h 12m
1991–92	7h 05m
1990–91	6h 56m
1989–90	6h 55m

——TOP SHOWS——

The top 15 prime-time programs of September 2006–May 2007:

Network	show	share %
Fox	*American Idol* [Wed]	26
Fox	*American Idol* [Tue]	26
ABC	*Dancing with the Stars*	20
ABC	*Dancing with the Stars* [Mon]	20
ABC	*Dancing with the Stars* [results]	20
CBS	*CSI*	19
ABC	*Grey's Anatomy* [Thur 9pm]	18
ABC	*Dancing with the Stars* [Tue res.]	18
Fox	*House*	17
ABC	*Desperate Housewives*	16
NBC	*Sunday Night Football*	17
CBS	*CSI: Miami*	18
CBS	*Without a Trace*	16
NBC	*Deal or No Deal* [Mon]	14
CBS	*Survivor: Cook Island*	14

——PROGRAM GENRES——

Prime-time, English-language shows in each genre during the 2006–07 season:

Drama	67 *shows*
Situation comedy	28
Other (sports, cartoons, quiz)	14
Variety	13
Adventure, sci-fi, western	5
Feature film	3
News	4

–PRODUCT PLACEMENTS–

Top brands by placement during 2006:

Coca-Cola	*placements* 3,346
Chef Revival apparel (aprons &c.)	1,592
Nike apparel	1,245
24 Hour Fitness Centers	858
Chicago Bears football	600

[Source for page: Nielsen Media Research ©]

PRIMETIME EMMYS · 2006

Award	winner
Drama series	*24* · Fox
Drama, actor	Kiefer Sutherland · *24*
Drama, actress	Mariska Hargitay · *Law & Order: Special Victims Unit*
Drama, directing	Jon Cassar · *24*, '7:00–8:00'
Drama, writing	Terence Winter · *The Sopranos*, 'Members Only'
Comedy series	*The Office* · NBC
Comedy, actor	Tony Shalhoub · *Monk*
Comedy, actress	Julia Louis-Dreyfus · *The New Adventures of Old Christine*
Comedy, directing	Marc Buckland · *My Name Is Earl*, 'Pilot'
Comedy, writing	Greg Garcia · *My Name Is Earl*, 'Pilot'
Miniseries	*Elizabeth I* · HBO
Made-for-TV movie	*The Girl in the Café* · HBO
Miniseries or movie, actor	Andre Braugher · *Thief*
Miniseries or movie, actress	Helen Mirren · *Elizabeth I*
Variety, music, or comedy series	*The Daily Show w. Jon Stewart* · Comedy Central
Reality-competition program	*The Amazing Race* · CBS

The 59th Primetime Emmys were scheduled to take place in LA on September 16, 2007. The following programs were honored with the most 2007 nominations:

Bury My Heart at Wounded Knee	17	*Ugly Betty*	11
Broken Trail	16	*Grey's Anatomy; The Starter Wife;*	
The Sopranos	15	*30 Rock*	10 [each]

DAYTIME EMMYS · 2007

Award	winner
Drama series	*Guiding Light* · CBS; and *The Young & the Restless* · CBS
Drama, lead actress	Maura West · *As the World Turns*
Drama, lead actor	Christian LeBlanc · *The Young & the Restless*
Drama, supporting actress	Genie Francis · *General Hospital*
Drama, supporting actor	Rick Hearst · *General Hospital*
Children's series	*Reading Rainbow* · PBS
Children's series, performer	Kevin Clash · Elmo, *Sesame Street*; and Caroll Spinney · Oscar the Grouch, *Sesame Street*
Preschool children's series	*Sesame Street* · PBS
Talk show	*The Ellen DeGeneres Show* · Syndicated
Talk show host	Ellen DeGeneres · *The Ellen DeGeneres Show*
Game show	*The Price Is Right* · CBS
Game show host	Bob Barker · *The Price Is Right*
Lifestyle show	*Paula's Home Cooking* · Food Network
Lifestyle host	Paula Deen · *Paula's Home Cooking*
Children's animated program	*Arthur* · PBS
Original song	*Love Is Ecstasy* · *Passions*

RADIO LISTENING

93% of Americans over age 12 listen to the radio at least once a week, and the average adult spends 19 hours per week tuning in – most of the time, away from home. Below are other key facts on US radio listening from a 2007 Arbitron Inc. report:

Radio listening location, 6am–midnight		Top listening hour, *weekday* ... 7–8 am
		– *weekend*......................12–1 pm
Home	39.0%	Group listening the most† .....25–34♀
Car	34.8%	Group listening the least† .... ≥65♀
Work	23.6%	
Other	2.6%	† Based on the % of listeners in demographic.

Below are the number of US radio stations in various genres, according to Arbitron:

Genre	*no. stations*	Contemp. Christ....677	Adult standards 314
Country	1,704	Sports................527	Classical 291
News, talk, info	1,503	Classic rock.........512	Classic country......287
Religious	948	Hot adult contemp. 447	Mexican regional....277
Adult contemp.	822	Pop contemp. 386	Classic hits 264
Oldies	780	Alternative...........321	Talk & 'personality' .204
Variety	748	Gospel...............320	Album rock 197

PODCASTING

11% of Americans over age 12 have listened to a podcast†, according to data from Arbitron and Edison Media Research. Despite this low overall figure, the growth in podcasting has been phenomenal. In November 2004, the directory Podcast Alley listed fewer than 1,000 podcasts; as of April 2007, 30,948 were available. Arbitron data show that young people are more likely to listen to podcasts than older people:

Group	*% of podcast listeners*	25–34 years old	20
♂	52	35–44 years old	21
♀	48	45–54 years old	17
12–17 years old	21	55–64 years old	17
18–24 years old	12	65+ years old	2

Podcast listeners are more likely to have experience online, and to have more years of formal education, as data from the Pew Internet & American Life Project show:

Group	*% listening to podcasts*	3 years or less of online experience ... 6
High school grad.	9	4–5 years of online experience........7
Some college	13	6+ years of online experience........13
College graduate	13	[August 2006 data · of internet users]

† 'Podcasts' are generally defined as subscription-based audio programs downloaded from the internet. The term was reportedly coined by journalist Ben Hammersley in a February 2004 *Guardian* article.

──────────────NEWSPAPER READERSHIP──────────────

76% of American adults read a newspaper at least once a week, according to a 2006 Newspaper Association of America survey†. On an average weekday, 50% of adults read the paper; 57% on an average Sunday. Below are the newspaper readership rates for an average weekday and average Sunday across various demographic groups:

% weekday	group	% Sunday			
48	♀	58	45	35–44	54
52	♂	56	55	45–54	63
36	18–24	43	61	55–64	67
35	25–34	44	68	65+	72

† In the top 50 'Designated Market Areas'

Below is a breakdown of the sections that readers of weekday papers actually read:

Section (% who read)	all	♂	♀		all	♂	♀
Main news/front page	87	85	90	Classifieds	39	37	41
Local news	85	82	88	Comics	39	40	38
Intnl/national news	56	59	53	Food/cooking	38	23	53
Sports	55	75	35	Movie listings/reviews	34	29	38
Editorial page	44	42	45	TV listings	30	27	33
Entertainment/lifestyle	44	35	53	Travel	29	27	30
Business/finance	42	49	36	Home/gardening	28	18	38
Circulars/inserts/flyers	39	29	49	Science & technology	25	30	19
				Fashion	19	9	30

In a 2005 Scarborough Research study, 74% of adult US newspaper readers said they had a favorite section of the newspaper. The most popular sections included:

Local news	19	Arts & entertain.	9	Classifieds	5
Sports	19	Comics	7	Ads/coupons	3
Front-page news	10	Editorial/opinion	6	Business	3

3% said the crossword puzzle/other puzzles was their favorite section; 2% chose the obituaries. The same study found that most respondents (45%) spent >30 mins reading the weekday paper, and >60 mins reading the Sunday paper; 56% said reading a newspaper made them a smarter person.

Since 1972, the General Social Survey has tracked the daily readership of papers:

% of US adults who read a newspaper every day

―――――――――FREE NEWSPAPERS WORLDWIDE―――――――――

The worldwide circulation of free daily newspapers increased 137% between 2001–05 – from 12m copies a day to 28m. Below are the world's top 5 free dailies:

Title	country	circulation	Que! [That!]	Spain	964,000
Leggo [I read]	Italy	1,050,000	*20 Minutos*	Spain	920,000
Metro	UK	977,000	*Metro*	Italy	850,000

The number of free daily titles in 2005 for selected countries is tabulated below:

Country	No. titles 2005	Adult population	No. titles/adult pop.
Canada	30	25,885,000	1·2
USA	34	213,453,000	0·2
Rep. Korea	9	36,344,000	0·2
France	8	48,911,000	0·2
Germany	3	70,576,000	<0·1
Ireland	3	3,262,000	0·9
Spain	23	37,084,000	0·6
UK	8	47,391,000	0·2

[Source: World Association of Newspapers, World Press Trends 2006]

――――PAID-FOR DAILY PAPERS · TITLES & CIRCULATION――――

Paid-for newspaper circulation is in decline worldwide, with only Africa and Asia reporting any growth in circulation during 2005. Despite this, most regions reported a rise in the number of newspapers, with 10,104 titles currently on sale worldwide:

Number of titles	2001	2002	2003	2004	2005	±%†
Africa	266	273	285	297	308	+15·8
America, North	2,000	1,946	1,945	1,947	1,939	–3·1
America, South	807	852	939	960	970	+20·2
Asia	3,765	3,622	4,347	4,237	4,522	+20·1
Australia & Oceania	88	86	85	84	85	–3·4
Europe	2,004	2,205	2,253	2,306	2,280	+13·8

Circulation, dailies (m)	2001	2002	2003	2004	2005	±%†
Africa	2·8	2·8	2·9	3·1	3·1	+11·6
America, North	61·5	60·9	60·8	60·3	58·7	–4·5
America, South	12·0	11·2	10·7	10·9	11·2	–7·3
Asia	246·8	248·4	267·6	278·2	283·4	+14·9
Australia & Oceania	3·8	3·8	3·8	3·8	3·7	–3·0
Europe	96·8	95·2	93·2	91·3	90·7	–6·34

† % change 2001–05. A worldwide June 2007 poll by Harris International indicated the key reason why people do not read newspapers is lack of time. [Source: WAN, World Press Trends 2006]

THE PULITZER PRIZE · JOURNALISM · 2007

PUBLIC SERVICE AWARD
The Wall Street Journal for its *'creative and comprehensive probe into backdated stock options for business executives that triggered investigations, the ouster of top officials and widespread change in corporate America'*

BREAKING NEWS REPORTING
The Oregonian staff for its *'skillful and tenacious coverage of a family missing in the Oregon mountains, telling the tragic story both in print and online'*

INVESTIGATIVE REPORTING
Brett Blackledge of the *Birmingham News* for his *'exposure of cronyism and corruption in the state's two-year college system, resulting in the dismissal of the chancellor and other corrective action'*

INTERNATIONAL REPORTING
The Wall Street Journal staff for its *'sharply edged reports on the adverse impact of China's booming capitalism on conditions ranging from inequality to pollution'*

BREAKING NEWS PHOTOGRAPHY
Oded Balilty of the Associated Press for his *'powerful photograph of a lone Jewish woman defying Israeli security forces as they remove illegal settlers in the West Bank'*

EXPLANATORY REPORTING
Kenneth R. Weiss, Usha Lee McFarling, & Rick Loomis of the *Los Angeles Times* for their *'richly portrayed reports on the world's distressed oceans, telling the story in print and online, and stirring reaction among readers and officials'*

66th PEABODY AWARDS

Some of the programming chosen by the Peabody Awards, which honor the previous year's best in electronic media. (The awards do not recognize specific categories.)

Mental Anguish and the Military · NPR
This American Life: Habeas Schmabeas
WBEZ, CHICAGO
StoryCorps · NPR
The Education of Ms. Groves · NBC
60 Minutes: The Duke Rape Case · CBS
ABC News Brian Ross Investigates: Conduct Unbecoming · ABC
Galapagos: Born of Fire · BBC TWO
American Masters: Andy Warhol · PBS
Baghdad ER · HBO
When the Levees Broke: A Requiem in Four Acts · HBO
Out of Control: AIDS in Black America · ABC
Why We Fight · CBC
Brotherhood · SHOWTIME
Billie Jean King: Portrait of a Pioneer · HBO

Elizabeth I · HBO
Boondocks: Return of the King
CARTOON NETWORK
Scrubs · NBC
Ugly Betty · ABC
Gideon's Daughter · BBC AMERICA
The Office · NBC
Friday Night Lights · NBC
Good Eats · FOOD NETWORK
The Music in Me · HBO
Being a Black Man
WASHINGTONPOST.COM
FourDocs
CHANNEL4.COM/FOURDOCS
For My Country? Latinos in the Military · MUN2
Prescription Privacy/Cause for Alarm
WTHR-TV

——————————ON ADVERTISING——————————

2006 TOP ADVERTISERS

Procter & Gamble Co...........$3,339m
General Motors Corp. 2,295
AT&T Inc......................... 2,204
Verizon Comm. Inc.............. 1,944
Time Warner..................... 1,825

2006 AD-SPENDING BY MEDIUM

Television...................... $65,373
Magazines.......................29,833
Newspapers 27,972
All other media.................15,416
Radio...........................11,055

All figures are for the US market.
[Source: TNS Media Intelligence, 2007]

BRAND WINNERS & LOSERS
Top and bottom brands as ranked by consumers, based on 2006 performance

WINNERS	LOSERS
Google	Nicole Richie
Las Vegas	Britney Spears
iPod	Havana
YouTube	Paris Hilton
eBay	Hand-to-Hand combat
Yahoo!	Mumbai
Target	Boxing
Oprah Winfrey	W Hotels

[Source: Landor Assocs] Respondents forecasted that Google, Las Vegas, and the NFL would do well in 2007, but the fates of Paris Hilton, Nicole Richie, and Britney Spears would suffer.

——————————DO NOT CALL REGISTRY——————————

The *National Do Not Call Registry* was created in 2003 by the FCC and the FTC. Over 10 million telephone numbers were registered within four days of the June 2003 launch; by June 2006 over 125 million numbers had been registered. A December 2005 survey found that 76% of all US adults were on the list, and that 92% of those reported receiving fewer telemarketing calls after registering. Not all telemarketers are restricted by the registry – political organizations, charities, and telephone surveyors are exempt, and several other restrictions apply. However, the vast majority of telemarketers are required to search the registry and update their calling lists accordingly. (In FTC parlance, lists free of Do Not Call numbers are said to be 'scrubbed'.) Telemarketers found in violation of this rule can be fined $11,000 per call.

A persistent chain email (circulated since at least 2004) warns that cell phone owners will soon face a barrage of telemarketing calls unless they immediately register their cells on the Do Not Call list. Yet, there has never been a deadline to register cell phones, and because FTC regulations prohibit the use of automated dialers (standard in the industry) to call cells, these numbers are less often targeted by telemarketers – a situation not likely to change soon. ❧ Although less well known, other FTC rules require that telemarketers: restrict calling times to 8am–9pm; promptly declare the identity of the seller or charitable organization; connect their calls within 2 seconds of the consumer's greeting; transmit their numbers to Caller ID services; and obtain express informed consent before making any charges.

[Home and cell numbers can be registered online at donotcall.gov or at 1-888-382-1222.]

JOURNALIST DEATHS

At least 1,000 journalists have been killed around the world in the past 10 years, according to a survey released in 2007 by the International News Safety Institute. Surprisingly, only a quarter died covering wars and armed conflicts; the majority were killed in peacetime, often covering news in their own countries. According to the report, their killers were frequently hostile authorities or criminals intent on silencing press coverage. 90% of the murders have not been prosecuted. The countries with the most deaths were Iraq (138), Russia (88), Colombia (72), the Philippines (55), and Iran (54). Below is a breakdown of journalist deaths since 1997:

Employer	
Press	435
TV	279
Radio	162
News agency	62
Unknown	56
Online	6

Context of death	
Peacetime	731
International armed conflict	167
National armed conflict	102

Peacetime deaths by topic of coverage†	
Corruption	97
Politics	46
Insurgency	39
Civil unrest	21
Investigating drugs	21
Terrorism	14
Investigating crime	14
Investigating paramilitary	4

† 325 deaths were unspecified. 150 also died in accidents. Remaining deaths were in wartime.

KNOWLEDGE & THE NEWS

The disappointing level of basic news literacy among many Americans was revealed in an April 2007 survey by the Pew Research Center for the People and the Press. The survey results also show a decline in news literacy levels since 1989, and some (perhaps unexpected) correlations between news knowledge and media diet:

2007 NEWS KNOWLEDGE

Americans aware of ...	%
Bush's troop 'surge'	88
Hillary Clinton pres. candidacy	73
Civilian deaths in Iraq outnumber troop deaths	69
Sunnis are major branch of Islam	32

1989/2007 NEWS KNOWLEDGE

Americans who ... (%)	'89	'07
Can name the Vice Pres.	74	69
Can name their state Gov.	74	66
Knew US has a trade deficit	81	68
Knew party controlling House	68	76
Could name Russian Pres.	47†	36

† Question asked in 1994.

KNOWLEDGE BY SOURCE

Regular viewers of ...	% *high score*‡
Daily Show/Colbert Report	54
Major newspaper websites	54
O'Reilly Factor	51
NPR	51
Rush Limbaugh radio show	50
News magazines	48
Local daily newspaper	43
Network evening news	38
News discussion blogs	37
Local TV News	35
Network morning shows	34

‡ Percent with ≥15 of 23 answers correct, among regular viewers/readers &c. of above.

———————————MEDIA & THE MIDTERMS———————————

Although US adults still overwhelmingly choose TV as their main source for election news, surveys by the Pew Internet & American Life Project show that the percentage who turn to the internet for such news has more than doubled since 2002.

Election news sources[†]	1992	1996	2000[‡]	2002	2004	2006
Television	82%	72%	70%	66%	78%	69%
Newspapers	57	60	39	33	39	34
Radio	12	19	15	13	17	17
Internet	–	3	11	7	18	15
Magazines	11	11	4	1	3	2

† Respondents were asked how they got 'most of their news', and allowed 2 responses. Totals do not add to 100% because of rounding & multiple answers. ‡ 2000 results based on registered voters only.

Interestingly, preferences for news sources tended to divide along partisan lines:

Rep. %	2006 elections news source	Dem. %
69	ALL FORMS OF TV	74
24	– Fox Cable –	10
22	– Local news –	25
11	– ABC Network –	13
10	– NBC Network –	14
8	– CNN Cable –	17
7	– CBS Network –	11
3	– MSNBC Cable –	6
38	NEWSPAPERS	44
21	RADIO	14
17	INTERNET	17
2	MAGAZINES	2

31% of Americans (*c.*60m) went online to get information or send emails about the midterm elections. Below is a breakdown of the type of websites they visited:

News portals[†]	60%	Blogs & online journals	20%
TV network websites	60%	Candidate websites	20%
Local news organization websites	48%	Intnl news organization websites	20%
National newspaper websites	31%	Humor websites	19%
State/local government websites	28%		
Issue-oriented websites	24%	† Google News, Yahoo! News, &c.	

23% of those who used the internet as a news source during the midterms also created or shared online political content, of which: 8% posted political commentary; 13% forwarded or posted someone else's commentary; 1% created either audio or video recordings; and 8% forwarded or posted someone else's audio or video recordings.

'Googlebombing' gained attention as a controversial form of online activism during the 2006 midterms. Googlebombing is the practice of forcing certain results to the top of a search query by repeatedly linking a search term to a specific site (an early 'Googlebomb' linked searches for 'miserable failure' to George W. Bush's White House biography). In 2006 a group of liberal bloggers attempted to Googlebomb *c.*50 Republican candidates for Congress by linking their names to unflattering news sources; results were mixed. In January 2007, Google announced it had altered its algorithms so that Googlebombs directed searchers to articles primarily about the Googlebombs themselves.

TOP BLOGS

Below are the top blogs tracked by Technorati, which monitors *c.*57m such sites. The rankings are based on the number of blogs linking to each site within 6 months:

Engadget .. 27,721 *links*	Gizmodo 19,109	Huffington Post. 16,006
Boing Boing..... 21,029	Techcrunch...... 18,479	[Ranks as of 5·17·2007]

In March 2007, Tim O'Reilly [see p.199] and other prominent bloggers called for a blogging code of conduct in response to a series of online death threats and alarming messages targeting popular blogger Kathy Sierra. Among among other stipulations, the code requires that users not say anything online they wouldn't say in person. The code was still being vigorously debated at the time of writing.

CYBER-DISSIDENTS & ENEMIES OF THE INTERNET

In November 2006, Reporters Without Borders released its annual list of 'internet enemies' – countries with repressive internet policies that restrict 'freedom of expression' and allow website filtering. Egypt appeared on the list for the first time; Nepal, Libya, and the Maldives were removed. The 13 'enemies' of the internet were:

Belarus · Burma · China · Cuba · Egypt · Iran · North Korea
Saudi Arabia · Syria · Tunisia · Turkmenistan · Uzbekistan · Vietnam

As the internet becomes increasingly open to user-generated content, so restrictive regimes have become concerned about the subversive potential of blogs, chatrooms, instant messaging, &c. A number of states have developed techniques to monitor their subjects – including Cuba, which has installed spyware in cybercafe computers to shut down web browsers if certain prohibited words are entered. Infamously, the Chinese government has pressured companies like Google and Yahoo! to facilitate censorship, and has an agreement with MSN Messenger to ban keywords relating to Taiwanese independence and the Dalai Lama. When censorship fails, repressive regimes take more drastic action. Reporters Without Borders estimated that, as of February 2007, at least 60 'cyber-dissidents' were incarcerated in jails worldwide:

Country cyber-dissidents		
China................50	Syria...................2	Iran....................1
Vietnam...............4	Tunisia................1	Libya 1
	Egypt.................1	*Total incarcerated*.....60

BLOGGING LANGUAGES

The most commonly used blogging languages, as charted by Technorati in 2006:

Language	*% of posts*		
English 39	Spanish...............3	French.................2
Japanese 33	Italian.................2	German...............1
Chinese..............10	Russian 2	Farsi 1
	Portuguese............2	Other..................5

Music & Movies

You must remember this, A kiss is just a kiss, a sigh is just a sigh
— HERMAN HUPFELD, *As Time Goes By*, 1942

SMOKING IN MOVIES

In May 2007, the Motion Picture Association of America (MPAA) warned that movies which 'glamorize smoking or ... feature pervasive smoking outside of an historic or other mitigating context may receive a higher rating'. In July, Disney became the first major studio to ban smoking from its films (and 'discourage' it in its adult divisions Touchstone and Miramax). Subsequently, a number of other studios intimated they would follow suit. ❦ Theorists have traditionally resisted 'magic bullet' links between media consumption and social behavior – cautioning against, for example, blaming violent films for violent crime. Yet the evidence linking tobacco in movies with youth smoking is increasingly compelling. In 2005, *Pediatrics* printed a magisterial review of 40 studies, which concluded 'strong empirical evidence indicates that smoking in movies increases adolescent smoking initiation'. In 2007, the Institute of Medicine of the National Academy of Sciences stated that 'studies show a clear dose effect, whereby greater exposure to smoking in the movies is associated with a greater chance of smoking'. According to a 2003 CDC backgrounder: current movie heroes are 3–4× more likely to smoke than people in real life; a teen whose favorite star smokes on-screen is significantly more likely to be a smoker; and, bizarrely, US adolescents may see more smoking onscreen than in real life. ❦ One of the most persuasive arguments for smokefree movies is the precedent set by TV's promotion of 'designated drivers'. In a February 2007 speech to the MPAA, Dr Jay Winsten of the Harvard School of Public Health described how, in the late 1980s, he asked TV execs and writers to consider 'incorporating a line or two of dialogue to reflect the evolution of a new social norm about drinking-and-driving ... and to depict the use of designated drivers'. The response was 'overwhelmingly positive', according to Winsten, who stated that from 1988–89, '160 prime time episodes incorporated the designated driver message'. Polls found 'sharp increases in the use of designated drivers', and Winsten asserted that his campaign contributed to the 25% fall in alcohol-related traffic deaths, 1990–93. Clearly, there are differences between designated drivers and smoking, and between the cultures of TV and Hollywood. Yet Winsten's success shows how media action can wreak good. ❦ Although some were disappointed that the MPAA decided not to R-rate all movies featuring smoking, its decision was widely welcomed. The Directors Guild of America said, 'they, like us, are working to find the delicate balance between addressing important health concerns and safeguarding free expression'.

─────── DIGITAL MUSIC WORLDWIDE ───────

Record company revenues from worldwide digital sales nearly doubled from $1·1bn to c.$2bn between 2005 and 2006, according to the International Federation of the Phonographic Industry (IFPI). Digital sales grew from 5·5% of total industry sales in 2005 to c.10% in 2006, and the IFPI forecasts that digital will account for 25% of all music sales by 2010. Other figures on the global digital music market:

	2005	2006	% change
Tracks available for download†	2m	4m	+100
Single tracks downloaded	420m	795m	+89
Subscription service users	2·8m	3·5m	+25
3G cell phone subscriptions‡	90m	137m	+52
Portable player sales (iPod &c.)	84m	120m	+43

† Songs on 500 leading online services in 40 countries. ‡ Third-generation cell phone technology, which allows for advanced services such as music and video downloads. [Source: IFPI, Jan 2007]

─────── DIGITAL MUSIC IN THE US ───────

The US market for music and music video downloads continued to rise in 2006 – as illustrated by the Recording Industry Association of America statistics below:

DOWNLOADS	2005	2006	% change
Singles (units)	366·9m	586·4m	+59·8
Albums (units)	13·6m	27·6m	+103·3
Music videos (units)	1·9m	9·9m	+434·3
Total value	$503·6m	$878·0m	+74·4

This rise in digital music sales was at the inevitable expense of physical music sales:

PHYSICAL SALES	2005	2006	% change
CDs (units)	705·4m	614·9m	−12·8
Music videos (units)	33·8m	23·1m	−31·8
Other, albums (units)	4·4m	1·7m	−61·6
Other, singles (units)	5·0m	2·9m	−41·4
Total value	$111·9bn	$96·5bn	−13·6

Figures are net after returns. ❦ Digital Rights Management (technology that prevents the unauthorized copying and sharing of digital goods) became one of the most talked-about music issues of 2007, as major music business players abandoned its use. Until May 2007, all music purchased via Apple's iTunes was enveloped, in the words of CEO Steve Jobs, by 'special and secret' DRM software that severely restricted copying and playing. But in February 2007, Jobs penned an open letter, declaring Apple would 'embrace' an end to DRM if music publishers made such a move possible. In response, EMI announced in April that it would sell its entire digital catalog DRM-free on iTunes and elsewhere. Yet, while Jobs expected that half the iTunes catalog would be sold DRM-free by the end of 2007, at the time of writing only Universal had followed EMI's lead, and then not via iTunes.

CD PIRACY

The 2006 Piracy Report of the International Federation of the Phonographic Industry estimated that 37% of all CDs purchased worldwide in 2005 were pirated – amounting to 1·2bn CDs, with a total market value of $4·5bn. In the same year, the IFPI estimated 20bn tracks were illegally downloaded or swapped on the web. The IFPI report suggested that the bulk of piracy currently takes place in three distinct ways, although three new methods were increasingly prevalent:

Current methods of piracy	*Newer methods of piracy*
CD-R PIRACY · using a CD burner attached to a PC; currently the most common method of piracy.	LAN FILE SHARING · sharing tracks through a Local Area Network, e.g. at a university campus or business.
PRESSED · employing professional CD-making equipment to create multiple copies.	DIGITAL STREAM RIPPING · converting streamed radio or webcasts into individual MP3 files.
INTERNET PIRACY · downloading and sharing of tracks over the internet.	MOBILE PIRACY · transferring music phone-to-phone via Bluetooth.

The IFPI report also identified ten 'priority countries' in which piracy had become a serious problem. These countries are ranked below by their 'physical piracy level' – the number of pirated hard-copy CDs sold as a percentage of the total market:

% physical piracy level			
Indonesia..... 88	Mexico 65	Spain 22	Bulgaria, Pakistan,
China......... 85	Greece 50	Canada ......N/A	Taiwan, and Ukraine
Russia......... 67	Brazil 40	S Korea ......N/A	all warranted 'special
	Italy........... 26		focus' status.

CELEBRITY BANDS

In 2006–07, Steven '*Under Siege*' Seagal and his band *Thunderbox* toured the globe to promote their album *Mojo Priest*, drawing attention to a range of celebrities who have played or still perform with a band. Other celebrity musicians include:

Celeb	band
Kevin Bacon........	*The Bacon Brothers*
Russell Crowe ...	*The Ordinary Fear of God*[†]
Jared Leto	*30 Seconds to Mars*
Jeff Goldblum....	*The Mildred Snitzer Orch.*
Bruce Willis...........	*The Accelerators*
Keanu Reeves	*Dogstar*
Gary Sinise[‡]	*Lt Dan Band*
Jamie Oliver...........	*Scarlet Division*
Tony Blair...............	*Ugly Rumours*

Dennis Quaid............... *The Sharks*
Billy Bob Thornton...... *Tres Hombres*
Juliette Lewis.................. *The Licks*

[†] Renamed from *Thirty Odd Foot of Grunts* (still TOFOG). [‡] Played character of Lt Dan in *Forrest Gump*. ❦ Additionally, the model Karen Elson, musician Rain Phoenix, and actress Zooey Deschanel (among others) have performed in the cabaret *The Citizens Band*.

MUSIC SALES AWARDS

The highest-certified albums of 2006 were the *High School Musical* soundtrack and the fourth release from Nashville stars Rascal Flatts. Both earned triple platinum designations from the Recording Industry Association of America (RIAA). Overall, in 2006, the RIAA awarded 74 albums and 14 ringtones *multiplatinum* designation; 108 albums, 65 ringtones, and 21 downloads *platinum* certification; and 224 albums, 160 ringtones, 142 downloads, and 1 single *gold* certification. Below are the number of units that must be sold in order to qualify for each of the various RIAA awards:

Album, singles, or ringtones sold	Recording Industry Association of America Award	Internet downloads (singles only)
500,000	Gold	100,000
1,000,000	Platinum	200,000
2,000,000	Multiplatinum	400,000
10,000,000	Diamond [albums & singles only]	—

ROCK & ROLL HALL OF FAME

The following were inducted into the American *Rock & Roll Hall of Fame* in 2007:

Grandmaster Flash and the Furious Five (Grandmaster Flash, Cowboy,
Kidd Creole, Melle Mel, Raheim, Mr Ness/Scorpio)
R.E.M. (Bill Berry, Peter Buck, Mike Mills, Michael Stipe)
The Ronettes (Veronica 'Ronnie' Spector, Estelle Bennett, Nedra Talley)
Patti Smith · Van Halen (Michael Anthony, Sammy Hagar,
David Lee Roth, Alex Van Halen, Eddie Van Halen)

BEST-SELLING ALBUMS · 2006

WORLD	RANK	UNITED STATES
Various · *High School Musical*†	1	Various · *High School Musical*†
Red Hot Chili Pep. · *Stadium Arcadium*	2	Rascal Flatts · *Me and My Gang*
Beatles · *Love*	3	Carrie Underwood · *Some Hearts*
James Blunt · *Back to Bedlam*	4	Nickelback · *All the Right Reasons*
J. Timberlake · *FutureSex/LoveSounds*	5	J. Timberlake · *FutureSex/LoveSounds*
Beyoncé · *B'Day*	6	James Blunt · *Back to Bedlam*
U2 · *U218 Singles*	7	Beyoncé · *B'Day*
Rascal Flatts · *Me and My Gang*	8	Various · *Hannah Montana*
Il Divo · *Siempre*	9	Dixie Chicks · *Taking the Long Way*
Andrea Bocelli · *Amore*	10	Hinder · *Extreme Behavior*

† *High School Musical* is a Disney boy-meets-girl TV-movie about resisting peer pressure and following your dreams. The soundtrack sold 7·2m copies around the world in 2006 (3·7m in the US), and was turned into a novel, video game, touring stage show, *actual* school musical, and 'on ice' extravaganza in 2006–07. There is also a sequel. [Source for ranking: IFPI · Global sales are for physical copies only.]

————————— MOST EXPENSIVE RECORD EVER? —————————

In 2002, Montreal record collector Warren Hill discovered a strange, sleeveless Velvet Underground album at a Manhattan flea market. Hill purchased the record for 75 cents and, after some investigation, discovered that it was an acetate master of the band's first studio recording in 1966. Early press reports speculated that the album could become the most expensive of all time, a conjecture that a winning December 2006 eBay bid of $155,401[†] looked set to realize. However, the next day the eBay buyer confessed that his offer had been an office joke, and he could not even afford gas for his car. Hill relisted the album, which sold for 'only' $25,200, and claimed to be satisfied – despite losing this shot at music history. Hill said he just wanted to be rid of the record, and that he actually preferred gospel.

[Sources: *Globe & Mail*; CBC; *Washington Post*]
[†] Several albums lay claim to the 'most expensive in the world' title. Many sources give the honor to the copy of John Lennon and Yoko Ono's *Double Fantasy* Lennon signed for his killer just before being shot, which sold for $525,000 in 2003. Others favor the Quarry Men (later the Beatles), whose demo was valued at *c.*$200,000 and declared most expensive record of all time by *Record Collector* magazine in 2004.

————————————————— PAZZ & JOP —————————————————

Pazz & Jop[†] is a critics' poll originally created by music writer Robert Christgau for the *Village Voice* newspaper in 1971. Each year, critics are asked to vote for their top 10 favorite albums and songs, and the results are compiled to create an overall list of the year's 'most critically acclaimed' music. Critics pick their favorite albums by dividing 100 points among 10 albums of their choice, while the year's top songs are derived using a 'one vote = one vote' formula. The top 2006 albums and singles were:

2006 ALBUMS OF THE YEAR

1 ......Bob Dylan...................... *Modern Times*...................1,123 *points*
2 ......TV on the Radio .... *Return to Cookie Mtn*............... 1,109
3 ......Ghostface Killah................ *Fishscale* 1,031
4 ......The Hold Steady .... *Boys and Girls in America*............983
5 ......Gnarls Barkley.................. *St Elsewhere* 791

2006 SINGLES OF THE YEAR

1 ......Gnarls Barkley.................. *Crazy*............................ 151 *votes*
2 ......T.I.............................. *What You Know*...........................55
3 ......Christina Aguilera.............. *Ain't No Other Man*......................54
4 ......Justin Timberlake feat. T.I...... *My Love* 53
5 ......The Raconteurs................. *Steady, As She Goes*......................43

[Source: *Village Voice*, 2006] [†] 'Pazz & Jop' is a splendid example of a spoonerism, a transposition of sounds within a single phrase frequently used to comic effect. The term is named for Anglican cleric Rev. William A. Spooner (1844–1930), Warden of New College, Oxford, known for his frequent slips of the tongue. Legend has collected many of his attributed slips into this unlikely line: 'You have tasted two whole worms, hissed all my mystery lectures, and have been caught fighting a liar in the quad'.

——————————GRAMMY AWARDS · 2007——————————

The Dixie Chicks found vindication at the 49th Grammy Awards in LA on February 11, 2007. Four years after controversial comments in London about George W. Bush led to death threats and a Nashville blacklisting, the Chicks swept the Grammys with 5 awards, including the trifecta of record, album, and song of the year. Mary J. Blige was honored with 8 nominations and 3 wins for her aptly titled comeback album, *The Breakthrough*. Blige wept as she described her win as a personal triumph. For many, the high point of the ceremony was an energetic (if idiosyncratic) performance of *Roxanne* by the Police, who had reunited just in time for the awards.

Record of the year............................Dixie Chicks · *Not Ready to Make Nice*
Album of the year.............................. Dixie Chicks · *Taking the Long Way*
Song of the year.............................Dixie Chicks · *Not Ready to Make Nice*
New artist.. Carrie Underwood
Female pop vocal performance............ Christina Aguilera · *Ain't No Other Man*
Male pop vocal performance .... John Mayer · *Waiting on the World to Change*
Pop vocal album .... John Mayer · *Continuum*
Dance recording ....Justin Timberlake & Timbaland · *SexyBack*
Electronic/dance album....................Madonna · *Confessions on a Dance Floor*
Solo rock vocal performance ....Bob Dylan · *Someday Baby*
Rock song................................Red Hot Chili Peppers · *Dani California*
Rock album ....Red Hot Chili Peppers · *Stadium Arcadium*
Alternative music album................................Gnarls Barkley · *St Elsewhere*
Female R&B vocal performance ....Mary J. Blige · *Be Without You*
Male R&B vocal performance......................John Legend · *Heaven*
R&B song.. Mary J. Blige · *Be Without You*
R&B album.....................................Mary J. Blige · *The Breakthrough*
Contemporary R&B album .... Beyoncé · *B'Day*
Rap song ....Ludacris · *Money Maker*
Rap album .... Ludacris · *Release Therapy*
Country song .... Carrie Underwood · *Jesus, Take the Wheel*
Country album .... Dixie Chicks · *Taking the Long Way*
Bluegrass album.............. Ricky Skaggs and Kentucky Thunder · *Instrumentals*
Traditional blues album............................ Ike Turner · *Risin' with the Blues*
Contemporary jazz album ....Bela Fleck and the Flecktones · *The Hidden Land*
Gospel performance .... Yolanda Adams · *Victory*
Latin pop album .... Arjona · *Adentro*; Julieta Venegas · *Limón y Sal* [TIE]
Reggae album .... Ziggy Marley · *Love Is My Religion*
Polka album....................Jimmy Sturr and His Orchestra · *Polka in Paradise*
Spoken word album Jimmy Carter · *Our Endangered Values: America's Moral Crisis*
          Ossie Davis & Ruby Dee · *With Ossie and Ruby: In This Life Together* [TIE]
Compilation soundtrack album..............Joaquin Phoenix *et al.* · *Walk the Line*
Score soundtrack album ....John Williams · *Memoirs of a Geisha*
Classical album............ *cond.* Michael Tilson Thomas · *Mahler: Symphony No. 7*
Opera recording....... *cond.* Robert Spano · *Golijov: Ainadamar: Fountain of Tears*
Producer of the year, non-classical .... Rick Rubin
Short-form music video ....OK Go · *Here It Goes Again*

———OTHER NOTABLE MUSIC AWARDS———

Awards	prize	winner
American Music ['06]	Pop album	Nickelback · *All the Right Reasons*
	Country album	Tim McGraw · *Greatest Hits, Volume 2*
	Soul/R&B album	Mary J. Blige · *The Breakthrough*
	Rap/hip-hop album	The Black Eyed Peas *Monkey Business*
	Artist, adult contemporary	Kelly Clarkson
	Artist, Latin	Shakira
	Artist, alternative	Red Hot Chili Peppers
	Century award	Tony Bennett
	Artist, duo/group	Nickelback
	Artist of the year, male	Chris Brown
	Artist of the year, female	Rihanna
	Artist, R&B/hip-hop	Mary J. Blige
Billboard Music ['06]	Artist of the year	Chris Brown
	New artist of the year	Chris Brown
	Artist of the year, male	Chris Brown
	Artist of the year, female	Rihanna
	Album of the year	Carrie Underwood · *Some Hearts*
	Artist, country	Kenny Chesney
	Artist, rap	T.I.
	Hot 100 airplay song	Mary J. Blige · *Be Without You*
Country Music ['06]	Entertainer of the year	Kenny Chesney
	Vocalist of the year, female	Carrie Underwood
	Vocalist of the year, male	Keith Urban
	Single	Brooks & Dunn · *Believe*
	Album	Brad Paisley · *Time Well Wasted*
	Vocal group	Rascal Flatts
People's Choice ['07]	Artist, female	Carrie Underwood
	Artist, male	Kenny Chesney
	Song, R&B	Justin Timberlake · *SexyBack*
	Song, pop	Shakira · *Hips Don't Lie*
	Song, country	Carrie Underwood · *Before He Cheats*
Soul Train ['07]	Single, female	Beyoncé · *Irreplaceable*
	Single, male	John Legend · *Save Room*
	Album, female	Mary J. Blige · *The Breakthrough*
	Album, male	Jamie Foxx · *Unpredictable*
	Song	India.Arie · *I Am Not My Hair*
NAACP Image ['07]	Album	Various artists · *Dreamgirls* (soundtrack)
	Artist, male	Prince
	Artist, female	Mary J. Blige
MTV VMAs ['06]	Video of the year	Panic! At the Disco *I Write Sins Not Tragedies*
	Video, male	James Blunt · *You're Beautiful*
	Video, female	Kelly Clarkson · *Because of You*
	Viewers' choice award	Fall Out Boy · *Dance, Dance*

─────────── NATIONAL RECORDING REGISTRY ───────────

The National Recording Registry, within the Library of Congress, was established by Congress in 2000 to maintain and preserve sound recordings deemed 'culturally, historically, or aesthetically significant'. Each year, 25 recordings enter the Registry, after being nominated by the public and vetted by the National Recording Preservation Board. Below is a selection of the recordings added in 2006:

John McCormack; *cond.* W. Rogers, *Il mio tesoro* [1916] · National Defense Test [1924][†]
Charley Patton, *Pony Blues* [1929] · Cole Porter, *You're the Top* [1934]
The Lone Ranger, The Osage Bank Robbery ep. [1937] · FDR, *Address to Congress* [1941]
Red Foley and the Sunshine Boys, *Peace in the Valley* [1951]
A. Rubinstein, *Chopin Polonaise, op. 40, no. 1* [1952] · C. Perkins, *Blue Suede Shoes* [1955]
A. Ginsberg, *Howl* [1959] · B. Newhart, *The Button-Down Mind of Bob Newhart* [1960]
The Ronettes, *Be My Baby* [1963] · Pete Seeger, *We Shall Overcome* [1963]
Rolling Stones, (*I Can't Get No) Satisfaction* [1965] · Sam Cooke, *A Change Is Gonna Come* [1964] · Velvet Underground, *Velvet Underground and Nico* [1967; see p.143]
The Wailers, *Burnin'* [1973] · Paul Simon, *Graceland* [1986]

† A real-time test of how the nation might respond in an emergency, featuring conversations between General John J. Pershing and military personnel in various cities. [Source: Library of Congress]

─────────── APPLAUSE AT CONCERTS ───────────

In recent years, commentators have discussed an evolution in the unwritten rules governing applause at classical music concerts. Since *c.*1900, it has been customary for audiences to hold their applause until the end of the final movement – lest they break the concentration of performers. Applause at other times has met glares (or worse) from fellow patrons and conductors. Yet, nowadays, 'premature clapping' is an increasingly frequent occurrence – and one that has been embraced by those who worry that an overly stuffy atmosphere discourages younger fans. In September 2006, the internationally renowned conductor Leonard Slatkin penned an essay entitled *To Clap or Not to Clap?*, in which he encouraged audiences to applaud whenever they felt so moved, whether or not the final movement had ended. An October 2006 poll on the music blog *Adaptistration* discovered that 74% felt audiences should 'feel free to applaud after a movement if they wish', so long as a conductor can make it clear when applause should be held. Inevitably, there remain some who detest premature clapping as a distraction, while others argue that an applause-free experience can easily be enjoyed for nothing in one's living room.

Audiences at Milan's La Scala opera house need no encouragement in expressing their feelings about a performance. In December 2006, the 'Loggionisti', fanatical opera buffs who sit in La Scala's upper gallery, heckled tenor Roberto Alagna so aggressively during the first act of *Aïda* that he stalked offstage. (His understudy, Antonello Palombi, was rushed onto the stage in his jeans.) The La Scala audience expressed warmer feelings towards tenor Juan Diego Flórez, whose 2007 performance of the aria 'Ah! mes amis' from Donizetti's *La fille du régiment* drew so much applause that the conductor was forced to ask him to sing it again – breaking a 70-year-old rule at La Scala forbidding encores.

——SOME CLASSICAL MUSIC USED IN ADVERTISING——

Got Milk? [2007] .... Górecki · *For You Ann Lill*
Ghirardelli [2006].................................Delibes · *Flower Duet* from *Lakme*
Nike [2006] .... Mozart · *Lacrimosa* from *Requiem*
Nasonex [2006] .... Rimsky-Korsakov · *The Flight of the Bumblebee*
Gap [2005]................. Grieg · *In the Hall of the Mountain King* from *Peer Gynt*
Capitol One [2004]...........................Orff · *O Fortuna* from *Carmina Burana*
K9 Advantix [2004]....................................Ponchielli · *Dance of the Hours*
American Express [2004] .... Tchaikovsky · *1812 Overture*
Pampers [2004] .... Rossini · *La gazza ladra*
AT&T [2003]................................Handel · *Ombra mai fù* from *Xerxes*
Samsung [2002]....................... Beethoven · *Ode to Joy* from *Symphony No. 9*
Levi's [2002]...Handel · *Sarabande in D minor*

[Sources: National Endowment for the Arts & various]

—————————— 'HATTOGATE' ——————————

When Joyce Hatto died of cancer in June 2006, critics hailed her as 'one of the greatest pianists Britain has ever produced', and lauded the astonishing range of her 119 albums. Yet doubts as to the authenticity of her virtuosic recordings had long simmered, not least because of her retirement from public life. In February 2007, *Gramophone* magazine was contacted by a reader who observed that Apple iTunes had identified a Hatto recording as belonging to the pianist László Simon. (iTunes automatically identifies music based on its 'mathematical footprint'.) A subsequent investigation by *Gramophone* confirmed that 10 tracks on one of Hatto's album were in fact recorded by Simon. After further inquiries found more examples of 'borrowing', Hatto's husband (and her sole engineer) admitted to using recordings by others to 'patch' his wife's work – initially to cover her groans of pain while she played. At the time of writing, the British Phonographic Industry had launched its own inquiry, telling *Time* that Hattogate could become 'one of the most extraordinary cases of piracy the record industry has ever seen'. Hatto's widower maintains his only motive was to assure his wife of the critical acclaim denied to her by cancer.

——SOME CLASSICAL MUSIC ANNIVERSARIES · 2008——

2008 marks two major classical music anniversaries: the 150th anniversary of the birth of Italian opera composer GIACOMO PUCCINI (12·22·1858), and the 170th anniversary of the untimely death, at the age of 31, of Austrian composer FRANZ SCHUBERT (11·19·1828). Other notable classical music anniversaries in 2008 are:

b. 1658	Giuseppe Torelli		*b.* 1908	Herbert von Karajan
b. 1678	Antonio Vivaldi		*b.* 1918	Leonard Bernstein
d. 1708	John Blow		*d.* 1918	Claude-Achille Debussy
b. 1838	Georges Bizet		*d.* 1958	Ralph Vaughan Williams
d. 1868	Gioacchino Rossini		*d.* 1958	Artur Rodziński

THE FACH SYSTEM

The Fach System is a German method of categorizing opera singers according to the range, color, and character of their voice, as well as their acting ability and physical appearance. The system was once used to facilitate casting in European repertory opera houses, although it is used less frequently today. Below is an adaptation of the system based on information compiled by the singer and teacher Bard Suverkrop:

	Fach	description	role example
Soprano	Soubrette	mellow, light, supple	Adèle, *Die Fledermaus*
	Lyric Coloratura	flexible, bright	Zerbinetta, *Ariadne auf Naxos*
	Dramatic Coloratura	dramatic, rich	Violetta, *La Traviata*
	Full Lyric Soprano	supple, feminine	Michaela, *Carmen*
	Spinto Soprano	powerful, intense	Desdemona, *Othello*
	Charaktorsopran	lyric with dramatic abilities	Tosca, *Tosca*
	Dramatic Soprano	intense, metallic, emotional depth	Aïda, *Aïda*
	Wagnerian Soprano	large, heavy	Brünnhilde, *Die Walküre*
Mezzo/	Lyric Mezzo	light, expressive	Cherubino, *Le nozze di Figaro*
Alto	Dramatic Mezzo I	flexible, metallic, dark	Carmen, *Carmen*
	Dramatic Mezzo II	flexible, metallic, dramatic	Herodias, *Salome*
	Alto	rich, extended bottom range	Erda, *Das Rheingold*
Tenor	Buffo Tenor	smaller voice, good acting skills	Jacquino, *Fidelio*
	Light Lyric Tenor	mellow, extended top range	Alfredo, *La Traviata*
	Full Lyric Tenor	heavier lyric tenor	Des Grieux, *Manon*
	Charaktertenor	large voice, good characterization	Herodes, *Salome*
	Spinto Tenor	noble, staying power	Max, *Der Freischütz*
	Dramatic Tenor	full, baritonal ability	Siegfried, *Götterdämmerung*
Baritone	Lyric Baritone	mellow, good actor	Malatesta, *Don Pasquale*
	Kavalierbariton	manly, good looks	Don Juan, *Don Giovanni*
	Verdi Baritone	powerful, nuanced	Scarpia, *Tosca*
	Heldenbaritone	heavy, projecting	Kurvenal, *Tristan*
Bass	Buffo Bass	smaller, flexible, expressive	Pasquale, *Don Pasquale*
	Heavy Buffo	large, imposing	Baron Ochs, *Der Rosenkavalier*
	Bass Baritone	refined, good characterization	Zuniga, *Carmen*
	Basso Cantabile	full, dark, low	Phillip, *Don Carlos*

The following are some popular opera singers known to perform in various Fachs:

Soubrette . . . . Dawn Upshaw	Dramatic Mezzo II . . . . .Christa Ludwig
Lyric Coloratura . . . . Beverly Sills	Alto. . . . . .Clara Butt
Dramatic Coloratura . . . . . .Maria Callas	Light Lyric Tenor . . . . . .Rockwell Blake
Full Lyric Soprano	Full Lyric Tenor . . . . . .Fritz Wunderlich
Elizabeth Schwarzkopf	Spinto Tenor . . . . . Luciano Pavarotti &
Spinto soprano. . . . . .Aprile Millo	Plácido Domingo
Dramatic soprano. . . . . . . Birgit Nilsson	Lyric Baritone. . . . . . . Lawrence Tibbett
Lyric Mezzo . . . . .Cecilia Bartoli	Basso Cantabile . . . . . .Nicolai Ghiaurov

[Sources: Bard Suverkrop & IPASource.com; *The New Grove Dictionary of Opera*; Vocalist.org]

GRAMOPHONE AWARDS · 2006

The Gramophone Awards, presented annually by *Gramophone* magazine, are chosen by a panel of critics, members of the industry, broadcasters, and 'celebrity' jurors.

Record of the year & Best of category (orchestral)............*cond.* Claudio Abbado, Berlin Philharmonic Orchestra · Mahler *Symphony No. 6*
Artist of the year ....Angela Hewitt
Label of the year ....Virgin Classics
Best of category, chamber............ Vadim Repin *et al.* · Taneyev *Chamber Music*
Best of category, instrumental..... Piotr Anderszewski · Szymanowski *Piano Works*
Best of category, solo vocal ....Christian Gerhaher & Gerold Huber · Schubert *Abendbilder*
Best of category, contemporary.................. Kari Kriikku, *cond.* Sakari Oramo, Finnish RSO · Magnus Lindberg *Clarinet Concerto*
Best of category, historic archive ... *cond.* J. Keilberth, Bayreuth · Wagner *Siegfried*

OPERA'S 'GRAND SLAM'

For opera singers to score a 'Grand Slam', they must perform at these four venues:

LA SCALA · Milan
opened 1778 · capacity: 2,400
Musical director: Stéphane Lissner
Notable premieres:
Verdi – *Otello* (1887)
Puccini – *Madama Butterfly* (1904)

STATE OPERA HOUSE · Vienna
opened 1869 · capacity: 2,282
Musical director: Seiji Ozawa
Notable premieres: R Strauss –
Die Frau ohne Schatten (1919)
Meyerbeer – *Le Prophète* (1998)

ROYAL OPERA HOUSE · London
opened 1732 · capacity: 2,267
Music director: Antonio Pappano
Notable premieres:
Birtwistle – *Gawain* (1991)
Maw – *Sophie's Choice* (2002)

METROPOLITAN OPERA · New York
opened 1883 · capacity: 3,995
Musical director: James Levine
Notable premieres: R Strauss –
Salome (1907) · Puccini – *The Girl of the Golden West* (1910)

MOST-PERFORMED OPERAS

The operas most frequently staged by members of OPERA America and Opera.ca during the 2005–06 season, with the number of productions during the season:

Bizet · *Carmen* .... 12 productions
Puccini · *La Bohème*...................11
Puccini · *Tosca*........................11
Rossini · *The Barber of Seville*........10
Puccini · *Turandot*....................10
Puccini · *Madame Butterfly* 9

Verdi · *Rigoletto* 9
Verdi · *La Traviata* 9
Donizetti · *Lucia di Lammermoor* 9
Verdi · *Aïda*............................9

[Source: OPERA America]

─────────────── BEST NUDE SCENES ───────────────

Each year, the infamous 'Mr Skin', and his team of self-styled screen nudity experts, award the best in cinematic nudity. Below are Mr Skin's top nude scenes of 2006:

Salma Hayek & Colin Farrell .... *Ask the Dust*
Gretchen Mol .... *The Notorious Betty Page*
Brittany Daniel .... *Rampage: The Hillside Strangler Murders*
Bai Ling .... *Edmond*
Jennifer Aniston .... *The Break-Up*
Barbara Nedeljakova .... *Hostel* (unrated version)
Kelly Brook .... *Survival Island*
Kyra Sedgwick .... *Loverboy*
Amanda Righetti .... *Angel Blade*†
Lauren Lee Smith .... *Lie with Me*

[Mr Skin's team views only nonadult titles.] † DVD release in 2006; original release in 2002.

─────────────── BEST BATHING SUITS ───────────────

2006 was a good year for the cinematic display of bathing trunks. Consequently, the German newspaper *Frankfurter Allgemeine Sonntagszeitung* compiled a list of the 'best male swimsuits', and the actors sporting them, in films during that year:

1 ... Sacha Baron Cohen .... *Borat*	4 ... Woody Allen .... *Scoop*
2 ... Daniel Craig .... *Casino Royal*	5 ... Rudy Youngblood ...... *Apocalypto*
3 ... Hugh Jackman .... *Scoop*	6 ... Pierce Brosnan .... *The Matador*

─────────────── JAMES BOND AND DRINKING ───────────────

James Bond is forever associated with his order of 'a vodka martini – shaken, not stirred' and, as a result, he has become something of a poster-boy for the cocktail. However, heroic research by *atomicmartini.com* proved that over the course of the 22 Bond films, 007 is more commonly seen quaffing champagne (35 times) than vodka martinis (22 times). The drink-per-film average for each 007 is shown below:

James Bond	films	drinks	drink/film		films	drinks	drink/film
Daniel Craig	1	12	12·0	Timothy Dalton	2	10	5·0
George Lazenby	1	7	7·0	Pierce Brosnan	4	20	5·0
Sean Connery	7	36	5·1	Roger Moore	7	29	4·1
				Total	22	114	5·2

Over the course of 22 films, Bond averages one drink every 24·3 minutes. 007 also carelessly placed 7 orders that he either did not receive or did not drink, including: 2 martinis, 2 bottles of champagne (Dom Perignon, naturally), a bourbon with water, a Sazerac, and a bottle of Budweiser. (Sazerac is the name of a venerable cognac; an 18-year-old rye; and a foul-tasting cocktail comprising rye, brandy, and absinthe.) For further analysis of the vodka martini, see *Schott's Food & Drink Miscellany*.

US TOP-GROSSING MOVIES · 2006

Film	US box-office gross ($m)	director
Pirates of the C.: Dead Man's Chest†	423·3	Gore Verbinski
Cars	244·1	John Lasseter & Joe Ranft
X-Men: The Last Stand†	234·4	Brett Ratner
Night at the Museum	218·6	Shawn Levy
The Da Vinci Code	217·5	Ron Howard
Superman Returns	200·1	Bryan Singer
Ice Age: The Meltdown†	195·3	Carlos Saldanha
Happy Feet	192·1	George Miller
Casino Royale	165·5	Martin Campbell
Over the Hedge	155·0	T. Johnson & Karey Kirkpatrick

MPAA analysis of the 20 top-grossing films shows the following ratings breakdown:

Rating	G	PG	PG-13	R
2006	5%	20%	65%	10%
2005	5%	25%	60%	10%
2004	5%	25%	55%	15%
2003	5%	15%	60%	20%
2002	5%	30%	65%	

[Source: Motion Picture Association of America] · † Indicates a prequel or sequel.

STUDIO MARKET SHARE · 2006

	Distributor	total gross ($bn)	market share	No. 2006 movies
1	Sony/Columbia	1·7	18·6%	27
2	Buena Vista	1·5	16·2%	19
3	20th Century Fox	1·4	15·2%	24
4	Warner Bros.	1·1	11·6%	21
5	Paramount	0·9	10·3%	16

[Source: Box Office Mojo. Total gross for all distributors was $9·2 billion.]

DOMESTIC BOX OFFICE SHARE

The market share of domestic films as a % of the total box-office in various nations:

% market share of domestic films			
Australia	3	Japan	41
Canada	5	South Korea	57
France	38	UK	34
Germany	17	USA	93
Italy	25		

[Source: Australian Film Comm., 2007. 2005 data, from *Screen Digest* & various]

—————————— THE 64th GOLDEN GLOBES · 2007 ——————————

No single film swept the 64th Golden Globes, although the musical *Dreamgirls* won three trophies, and Helen Mirren managed to win two best actress awards playing queens named Elizabeth. *Babel* took best dramatic picture despite modest US box-office success, and *Cars* won in a new Golden Globes category – best animated feature film. The relatively staid ceremony saw teary acceptance speeches from Forest Whitaker and former *American Idol* finalist Jennifer Hudson, while British comedian Sacha Baron Cohen's speech was predictably (and hilariously) off-color.

[This] makes me feel like I'm part of a community, it makes me feel like an actress, and you don't understand how much that feels good today. — JENNIFER HUDSON

Award	winner
Dramatic picture	*Babel*
Dramatic actress	Helen Mirren · *The Queen*
Dramatic actor	Forest Whitaker · *The Last King of Scotland*
Picture, musical or comedy	*Dreamgirls*
Actress, musical or comedy	Meryl Streep · *The Devil Wears Prada*
Actor, musical or comedy	Sacha Baron Cohen · *Borat*
Supporting actress	Jennifer Hudson · *Dreamgirls*
Supporting actor	Eddie Murphy · *Dreamgirls*
Director	Martin Scorsese · *The Departed*
Screenplay	Peter Morgan · *The Queen*
Original score	Alexandre Desplat · *The Painted Veil*
Original song	*The Song of the Heart* · *Happy Feet*
Animated feature film	*Cars*
Foreign language film	*Letters from Iwo Jima*
Dramatic TV series	*Grey's Anatomy*
Actress, dramatic TV series	Kyra Sedgwick · *The Closer*
Actor, dramatic TV series	Hugh Laurie · *House*
TV series, musical or comedy	*Ugly Betty*
TV actress, musical or comedy	America Ferrera · *Ugly Betty*
TV actor, musical or comedy	Alec Baldwin · *30 Rock*
TV miniseries or movie	*Elizabeth I*
TV actress, miniseries or movie	Helen Mirren · *Elizabeth I*
TV actor, miniseries or movie	Bill Nighy · *Gideon's Daughter*
TV supporting actress, miniseries or movie	Emily Blunt · *Gideon's Daughter*
TV supporting actor, miniseries or movie	Jeremy Irons · *Elizabeth I*
Cecil B. De Mille award	Warren Beatty

NOTABLE QUOTES ❦ MERYL STREEP · I think I've worked with everybody in the room. ❦ HUGH LAURIE · My goodness, this is stunning, absolutely stunning. I am speechless. I am literally without a speech. ❦ ALEJANDRO GONZALEZ IÑÁRRITU (*to* Schwarzenegger) · I swear I have my papers in order, Governor. ❦ HELEN MIRREN · [Elizabeth] walked into literally the role of a lifetime, and I honestly think this award belongs to her, because I think you fell in love with her, not with me. ❦ SACHA BARON COHEN · Thank you to every American who has not sued me so far.

BLOCKBUSTERS

The term *blockbuster* was first used to describe a class of bombs dropped by the British Royal Air Force during WWII. These extremely heavy, vastly powerful incendiaries were capable of destroying an entire block of buildings at a time. (The 4,000lb blockbuster was first dropped on Emden, Germany, in 1941; the 12,000lb blockbuster on Germany's Dortmund–Ems Canal in 1943.) The term has evolved to describe anything of great size or power, but is most frequently applied to entertainment productions such as books, plays, museum exhibits, and especially movies. (Extremely successful prescription medications are also sometimes called *blockbuster* drugs; in music, the term *chartbuster* was coined to describe a best-selling song or group. Blockbuster's meaning in real estate circles is less pleasant; see below.) ❦ The first blockbuster film is generally said to be Steven Spielberg's *Jaws* (1975), which grossed $260m and (by some accounts) inaugurated the tradition of summer blockbuster thrillers. According to the Internet Movie Database, a movie is generally said to be a blockbuster once it grosses $100m in North America. IMDb maintains a list of films with the highest domestic box-office grosses of all time:

Movie	domestic gross $	year released
Titanic	600,779,824	1997
Star Wars	460,935,665	1977
Shrek 2	436,471,036	2004
E.T. the Extra-Terrestrial	434,949,459	1982
Star Wars: Episode I – The Phantom Menace	431,065,444	1999
Pirates of the Caribbean: Dead Man's Chest	423,032,628	2006
Spider-Man	403,706,375	2002
Star Wars: Episode III – Revenge of the Sith	380,262,555	2005
The Lord of the Rings: The Return of the King	377,019,252	2003
Spider-Man 2	373,377,893	2004

In real estate, *Blockbusting* was the practice in which agents or speculators trigger neighborhood turnover through the exploitation of racial prejudice. The term is associated with the 1940s and 1950s, when unscrupulous realtors used questionable tactics to convince white homeowners of growing black 'encroachment' (for instance, hiring blacks to drive through the neighborhood). After property owners sold their houses at devalued prices, agents would profit by charging high prices to resell the homes to blacks, who often had few other housing choices. ❦ A *bonkbuster* is a genre of novel noted for its sexual escapades. A *bronco buster* is one who breaks horses; a *baby buster* is one born during a time of low birth rate (the opposite of a *baby boomer*). *Filibuster* has an entirely different etymology; see p.296.

'THREE-QUELS'

The summer of 2007 was all about the 'three-quel' – a neologism coined to describe the third episode in a movie franchise. Key three-quels released in 2007 included:

Spider-Man 3 · *Shrek the Third* · *Pirates of the Caribbean: At World's End*
Ocean's Thirteen · *Rush Hour 3* · *Resident Evil: Extinction*
The Bourne Ultimatum

————79TH ACADEMY AWARD WINNERS · 2007————

Comedian Ellen DeGeneres gave a low-key, safe, and unpretentious performance when she became only the second woman to single-handedly host the Academy Awards. Predictions that the 79th Oscars would be lucky for Helen Mirren[†] and eight-time nominee Martin Scorsese were proved right. And the winners were ...

Leading actor	Forest Whitaker · *The Last King of Scotland*
Leading actress	Helen Mirren · *The Queen*
Supporting actor	Alan Arkin · *Little Miss Sunshine*
Supporting actress	Jennifer Hudson · *Dreamgirls*
Best picture	*The Departed*
Directing	Martin Scorsese · *The Departed*
Animated feature	George Miller · *Happy Feet*
Art direction	Eugenio Caballero & Pilar Revuelta · *Pan's Labyrinth*
Cinematography	Guillermo Navarro · *Pan's Labyrinth*
Costume design	Milena Canonero · *Marie Antoinette*
Doc. feature	Davis Guggenheim · *An Inconvenient Truth*
Doc. short subject	Yang & Lennon · *The Blood of Yingzhou District*
Film editing	Thelma Schoonmaker · *The Departed*
Foreign language film	Florian Henckel von Donnersmarck · *The Lives of Others*
Makeup	David Martí & Montse Ribé · *Pan's Labyrinth*
Music (score)	Gustavo Santaolalla · *Babel*
Music (song)	Melissa Etheridge *I Need to Wake Up* · *An Inconvenient Truth*
Short film (animated)	Torill Kove · *The Danish Poet*
Short film (live)	Ari Sandel · *West Bank Story*
Sound mixing	Michael Minkler, Bob Beemer, & Willie Burton · *Dreamgirls*
Sound editing	Alan Robert Murray & Bub Asman · *Letters from Iwo Jima*
Visual effects	Knoll, Hickel, Gibson & Hall *Pirates of the Caribbean: Dead Man's Chest*
Screenplay (adapted)	William Monahan · *The Departed*
Screenplay (original)	Michael Arndt · *Little Miss Sunshine*
Honorary award	Ennio Morricone

[†] As the odds reached 1/66 for Helen Mirren to win the Best Actress Oscar, UK bookie William Hill paid out £50,000 ahead of the ceremony. Ladbrokes also stopped taking bets on the actress's victory.

NOTABLE QUOTES ❦ FOREST WHITAKER · I want to thank the people of Uganda who helped this film have a spirit. ❦ HELEN MIRREN · For 50 years and more, Elizabeth Windsor has maintained her dignity, her sense of duty, and her hairstyle. She's had her feet planted firmly on the ground, her hat on her head, her handbag on her arm, and she has weathered many, many storms, and I salute her courage and her consistency. ❦ MARTIN SCORSESE · Could you double-check the envelope? ❦ ELLEN DEGENERES · No one knows who's going to win, unless you're British, and then you know you have a good shot. ❦ AL GORE · People all over the world, we need to solve the climate crisis. It's not a political issue. It's a moral issue ❦ GEORGE MILLER (director of animated film *Happy Feet*) · I asked my kids, 'What should I say?' They said, 'Thank all the men for wearing penguin suits' ❦

OSCAR NIGHT FASHION · 2007

Star	dress	designer
Nicole Kidman	*bright red, halter-necked, oversize shoulder bow*	Balenciaga
Reese Witherspoon	*indigo, strapless, scalloped layers*	Nina Ricci
Cate Blanchett	*charcoal, crystal mesh with single strap*	Armani Privé
Gwyneth Paltrow	*peach, multi-pleated, fish-tailed dress*	Zac Posen
Kate Winslet	*pistachio silk dress, with draped single strap*	Valentino
Naomi Watts	*pale lemon strapless, empire-line, dropped sleeves*	Escada
Helen Mirren	*pale gold lace V-neck, full patterned skirt*	Christian Lacroix
Penélope Cruz	*nude fitted bodice with full ruched organza skirt*	Versace
Jennifer Lopez	*Grecian-style empire line, with jeweled boat neck*	Marchesa
Jennifer Hudson	*dark brown silk dress with gold bolero*	Oscar de la Renta

THE ACADEMY & OSCAR VOTING

The Academy of Motion Picture Arts and Sciences was formed in 1927 as a nonprofit organization to promote the film industry. Academy membership is divided into 15 branches: actors; animators and short-film makers; art directors and costume designers; cinematographers; composers; documentary filmmakers; directors; executives; editors; makeup artists; producers; PR specialists; sound technicians; visual effect artists; and writers. Membership is by invitation, and candidates must be sponsored by at least two members from the branch to which they are applying; anyone nominated for an Oscar is automatically considered for membership. The Academy currently has *c*.6,500 members – *c*.25% of whom are actors. ❦ One of the greatest privileges of membership is the right to vote on the annual Academy Awards. In January each year, members are asked to nominate, in rank, up to five candidates for each award in their branch (e.g. only actors are allowed to nominate for the Best Actor categories); additionally, every member is entitled to nominate up to five movies for Best Picture. The five most popular candidates in each category are selected using a system of proportional representation whereby any candidate with 20% of nominations will go through. In the second round of voting, all Academy members are sent a ballot with the five nominations in each category. Members can only vote once for each award, and the nominee with the most votes win the Oscar[†]. This complex and highly secretive voting process is run by the accountants PricewaterhouseCoopers. In 2007, PwC partners Brad Oltmanns and Rick Rosas were the only two people to know the winners before the envelopes were opened live onstage[‡].

[†] Votes have been tied on two occasions: in 1932, the Best Actor Oscar was shared by Wallace Beery and Frederic March; and in 1968, Barbra Streisand and Katharine Hepburn were presented with Best Actress Oscars. [‡] As a precautionary measure, one of these partners carries a duplicate set of winning envelopes and travels to the ceremony in a separate car, on a secret route. As an additional safeguard, the partner memorizes the names of all of the winners – no mean feat, given the number – just in case.

———————OTHER MOVIE AWARDS OF NOTE———————

ANNIE AWARDS 2007 · *annieawards.com*

Best animated feature..*Cars*
Best animated television production............*Foster's Home for Imaginary Friends*

DIRECTORS GUILD AWARDS 2007 · *dga.org*

Feature ....Martin Scorsese · *The Departed*
Documentary ....Arunas Matelis · *Before Flying Back to the Earth*
Comedy series.................................Richard Shepard · *Ugly Betty* (pilot)
Reality............................... Tony Sacco · *Treasure Hunters* (episode 101)
Commercials...............................Dante Ariola · *'First Taste'* (Coca-Cola);
'Human' (Johnnie Walker); *'Snowball'* (Travelers Insurance)

GOLDEN RASPBERRIES 2007 · *razzies.com*

Worst picture ....*Basic Instinct 2*
Worst director........................... M. Night Shyamalan · *Lady in the Water*
Worst actor........................ Marlon Wayans & Shawn Wayans · *Little Man*
Worst actress...Sharon Stone · *Basic Instinct 2*
Worst Excuse for Family Entertainment[†]....................................... *RV*

INDEPENDENT SPIRIT AWARDS 2007 · *filmindependent.org*

Best feature..*Little Miss Sunshine*
Best director...............Jonathan Dayton & Valerie Faris · *Little Miss Sunshine*
Best male lead...Ryan Gosling · *Half Nelson*
Best female lead..................................... Shareeka Epps · *Half Nelson*

MTV MOVIE AWARDS 2007 · *mtv.com*

Best movie..............................*Pirates of the Caribbean: Dead Man's Chest*
Best performance ....Johnny Depp · *Pirates of the Caribbean: Dead Man's Chest*
Best villain ....Jack Nicholson · *The Departed*
Best fight...............................Gerard Butler *vs* 'The Über Immortal' · *300*
Best comedic performance ....Sacha Baron Cohen · *Borat*
Best kiss ....Will Ferrell & Sacha Baron Cohen · *Talladega Nights*

NATIONAL BOARD OF REVIEW 2006 · *nbrmp.org/awards*

Best film...*Letters from Iwo Jima*
Best actor................................Forest Whitaker · *The Last King of Scotland*
Best actress..Helen Mirren · *The Queen*
Career achievement award... Eli Wallach

SCREEN ACTORS GUILD AWARDS 2007 · *sagawards.org*

Cast performance..*Little Miss Sunshine*
Best actor................................Forest Whitaker · *The Last King of Scotland*
Best actress..Helen Mirren · *The Queen*
Life achievement award...Julie Andrews

[†] New for 2007, this Razzie saluted the 'dearth of quality G- and PG-rated movie fare in 2006'.

HOLLYWOOD WALK OF FAME

Some of the celebrities awarded a star on the Hollywood Walk of Fame in 2007:

Robert Altman · Michael Caine · Mariah Carey · Sean 'Diddy' Combs
Matt Damon · The Doors · Erik Estrada · Jamie Foxx · John Goodman
Michele Pfeiffer · Leann Rimes · Kiefer Sutherland
Lily Tomlin · Shania Twain · Barbara Walters

SOME 2007 MOVIE TAGLINES OF NOTE

At the end of the world, the adventure begins .. Pirates of the Caribbean: At World's End
Tradition prepared her. Change will define her .... The Queen
The greatest battle lies within .... Spider-Man 3
A family on the verge of a breakdown .... Little Miss Sunshine
Cops or Criminals. When you're facing a loaded gun, what's the difference? . The Departed
What are the odds of getting even? 13 to one .... Ocean's Thirteen
Innocence has a power evil cannot imagine .... Pan's Labyrinth
If you want to be understood ... listen .... Babel
WARNING: May cause toe-tapping. .... Happy Feet
A global warning .... An Inconvenient Truth
The rebellion begins .... Harry Potter and the Order of the Phoenix
Their war. Our world. .... Transformers
There are worlds beyond our own – the compass will show the way . The Golden Compass
See our family. And feel better about yours .... The Simpsons Movie
Come watch my movie film · High Five! .... Borat

FILM GUILDS AND SOCIETIES

Film guilds exist to promote high standards throughout the movie industry and
to encourage technological and artistic development. Most have no trade union
alliance; instead, membership is achieved through nomination and approval by
a committee. Listed below are some of the most notable current US film guilds:

Guild/Film Society	*abbreviation*	*membership*
American Cinema Editors	ACE	.500
Art Directors Guild	ADG	.850
Casting Society of America.	CSA	.385
Directors Guild of America	DGA	13,460
Motion Picture Sound Editors	MPSE	.400
Producers Guild of America	PGA	3,500
Set Decorators Society of America.	SDSA	.300
Society of Camera Operators	SOC	.500
Stuntmen Association of Motion Pictures	SAMP	.120

Guild members are able to use the appropriate society abbreviation after their name in film credits.

THE ORACLE OF BACON

The University of Virginia's computer science department has developed an algorithm based on the enduring game 'six degrees of Kevin Bacon'. The game tests which actors can be linked to Kevin Bacon within six career moves. (For example, Keira Knightley is two moves away from Kevin Bacon, since she was in *Love Actually* (2003) with Colin Firth, who was in *Where the Truth Lies* (2005) with Kevin Bacon). The algorithm (or 'Oracle of Bacon') employs the >800,000 Internet Movie Database (IMDb) records to create a map that tracks the shortest path from one actor to another, and calculates a 'Bacon Number' indicating how many actors are linked to Kevin in 0–8 moves. Naturally, these Bacon Numbers are constantly changing; as of January 2007, the breakdown of actors by Bacon Number was:

Bacon No.	No. people				
0	1†	4	129,381	† Naturally, only 1 person
1	1,920	5	9,147	can be zero moves from
2	173,757	6	931	Kevin Bacon: Kevin himself.
3	517,654	7	96	The average *Bacon Number*
		8	17	is currently 2·968.

The database can also be used to calculate the 'center of the Hollywood Universe', which is the actor who can be linked to the most other performers in the least moves. In January 2007, the top 5 were: Rod Steiger (average 2·67), Christopher Lee (2·68), Dennis Hopper (2·69), Donald Sutherland (2·70), and Harvey Keitel (2·70).

The concept of 'six degrees of separation' was popularized by psychologist Stanley Milgram (1933–84), who used the American postal service to test the 'small world theory' that the world is more interconnected than it seems. ❦ A similar principle has been applied to the late Hungarian mathematician Paul Erdös (1913–96), who was a prolific contributor to academic journals. The Erdös Number is used to describe the 'collaborative distance' between academics. Inevitably, someone with much time on their hands has merged the Bacon Number with the Erdös Number to create the hybrid (and deliciously obscure) Erdös–Bacon. This allows academics who have appeared in a film *and* published a paper that links to Erdös to claim an Erdös–Bacon Number (Stephen Hawking apparently has an Erdös–Bacon number of 3.)

IMDb PLOT KEYWORDS

The Internet Movie Database (IMDb) classifies every film with a list of plot 'keywords'. Below is a selection of recent movies with some of their keywords:

Movie *some plot keywords*
Borat............racist, on the road, male frontal nudity, retardation, homophobia
X-Men 3......... presumed dead, prison escape, surprise after end credits, blue fur
Casino Royale...........shot in the head, super villain, lost love, gadget, henchmen
The Da Vinci Code ....monk, secret passage, albino, religion, twist at the end
The Queen ....royalty, London, England, critically acclaimed, based on fact
Little Miss Sunshine ....pageant, car trouble, quirky, dysfunctional, loser
An Inconvenient Truth.. glacier, presidential election, armageddon, humanity, hope

SUNDANCE · 2007

The Sundance Film Festival is a showcase of American and international independent film held each year in snowy Park City, Utah. The 2007 festival took place January 18–27, and included 125 feature films, shown to a total audience of *c*.52,000. Although Sundance was founded by Robert Redford with the goal of exhibiting independent filmmakers, many have noted the increasing presence of Hollywood studios and celebrities – and the attendant media glare. Interest in the festival was heightened in 2007 by the breakout success of *Little Miss Sunshine*, which achieved commercial success after playing Sundance in 2006, and was sold to Fox Searchlight for $10·5m. 2007 Sundance deals of note included a reported $7·75m for quirky coming-of-age comedy *Son of Rambow*; *c*.$5m for Mexican tearjerker *La Misma Luna*; *c*.$4m for poignant drama *Grace Is Gone*; and *c*.$5m for romantic comedy *Waitress*. A number of commentators noticed particularly dark themes in the 2007 films, which grappled with rape and child abuse as well as the horrors of Darfur, Iraq, Hiroshima, and elsewhere. Major 2007 awards included:

Grand jury prize, documentary .... *Manda Bala (Send a Bullet)* · Jason Kohn
Grand jury prize, dramatic .... *Padre Nuestro* · Christopher Zalla
World cinema jury prize, documentary .... *Enemies of Happiness*
Eva Mulvad & Anja Al Erhayem (Denmark)
World cinema jury prize, dramatic .... *Sweet Mud* · Dror Shaul (Israel)
Audience award, documentary .... *Hear and Now* · Irene Taylor Brodsky
Audience award, dramatic .... *Grace Is Gone* · James C. Strouse
World cin. aud. award, doc. ...... *In the Shadow of the Moon* · David Sington (UK)
World cinema audience award, dramatic .... *Once* · John Carney (Ireland)

FILM FESTIVAL PRIZES · 2007

Berlin · Golden Bear [FEB] .... *Tu ya de hun shi (Tuya's Marriage)* · Wang Quan'an
Tribeca · Best Narrative Feature [MAY] .... *My Father My Lord* · David Volach
Cannes · Palme d'Or [MAY] ..... *4 Months, 3 Weeks and 2 Days* · Cristian Mungiu
Moscow · Golden St George [JUN] .... *Travelling with Pets* · Vera Storozheva
Venice · Golden Lion [SEP '06] .... *Still Life* · Jia Zhang-ke
Toronto · People's Choice Award [SEP '06] ... *Bella* · Alejandro Gomez Monteverde
London · Sutherland Trophy [OCT '06] .... *Red Road* · Andrea Arnold

POPCORN & SADNESS

A January 2007 *Journal of Marketing* study found that people watching sad movies tended to consume more popcorn than those watching happy movies. 38 subjects were asked to view either the 2002 upbeat comedy *Sweet Home Alabama* or the 1970 tearjerker *Love Story*. By the end of the movies, subjects watching *Love Story* had consumed 36% more 'buttered' popcorn than those watching *Sweet Home Alabama*. Researchers theorized that, when sad, people may be more likely to seek momentary satisfaction in food – regardless of its (lack of) nutritional content.

TOP 100 AMERICAN FILMS

In June 2007, the American Film Institute (AFI) released its top 100 films of the first century of American cinema (1896–1996). The list was a '10th anniversary' update of a previous ranking released in 1998. For both lists, a jury of 1,500 filmmakers, screenwriters, executives, critics, and historians selected their top 100 films from 400 AFI nominations. Below are 2007's top 10 films – with some memorable lines:

1 ...*Citizen Kane* (1941) ....Rosebud ...
2 ...*The Godfather* (1972) ....I'm gonna make him an offer he can't refuse
3 ...*Casablanca* (1942) ....Play it, Sam†
4 ...*Raging Bull* (1980)..................... You win, you win. You lose, you still win
5 ...*Singin' in the Rain* (1952) ....'People'? I ain't 'people'
6 ...*Gone with the Wind* (1939)................ Frankly, my dear, I don't give a damn
7 ...*Lawrence of Arabia* (1962).....................The truth is: I'm an ordinary man
8 ...*Schindler's List* (1993) .... The list is life. All around its margins lies the gulf
9 ...*Vertigo* (1958)............................You and I know who killed Madeleine
10 ..*The Wizard of Oz* (1939) .. Toto, I've got a feeling we're not in Kansas anymore

† Often misquoted as 'Play it again, Sam'. ❦ The AFI has produced a series of other 'Top 100' lists and accompanying television specials. A selection of the top picks from some recent lists appears below:

Most memorable movie quote ['05] .... Frankly, my dear, I don't give a damn
Top movie song ['04] ....*Over the Rainbow*
Top hero & villain ['03].... Atticus Finch (*To Kill a Mockingbird*); Hannibal Lecter (*Silence of the Lambs*)
Greatest movie love story of all time ['02] ....*Casablanca*
Funniest movie of all time ['00]...*Some Like It Hot*

WHITE HOUSE CINEMA

The White House 'family theater' is a luxury 40-seat cinema constructed in 1942. Jimmy Carter held the most screenings (480 in 4 years), and the classic western *High Noon* is the most-seen film. Other films watched in the White House include:

John F. Kennedy .... *Expresso Bongo · Roman Holiday*
Lyndon B. Johnson .... *The President*†
Richard Nixon ....*Patton · Yankee Doodle Dandy*
Jimmy Carter ....*All the President's Men · Midnight Cowboy*
Ronald Reagan....................... *Gandhi · Stagecoach · Ragtime · Top Hat · Reds*
Bill Clinton .... *Schindler's List · American Beauty ·* the *Naked Gun* series
George W. Bush............ *Black Hawk Down ·* the *Austin Powers* series *· Flight 93*

The first film screened in the White House, though not in the family theater, was *Birth of a Nation*, watched by Woodrow Wilson in 1915. Incidentally, Stalin took a great interest in film and commissioned many himself. He is said to have enjoyed films by John Ford, as well as Tarzan movies. For Kim Jong-il's cinematic preferences, see p.76. † A 10-minute homage to LBJ himself, narrated by Gregory Peck. [Sources: Ronald Reagan Presidential Library; White House Museum; *Guardian*]

Books & Arts

A man will turn over half a library to make one book.
— SAMUEL JOHNSON

NOBEL PRIZE IN LITERATURE

The 2006 Nobel Prize in Literature was awarded to ORHAN PAMUK (1952–),

*who in the quest for the melancholic soul of his native city has
discovered new symbols for the clash and interfacing of cultures*

Turkish writer Orhan Pamuk is celebrated for novels that explore themes of identity through an examination of the transformation of modern Turkey. Writing in the *Guardian*, Margaret Atwood said of Pamuk's award, 'it would be difficult to conceive of a more perfect winner for our catastrophic times'. ❦ In February 2005, Pamuk attracted worldwide media attention when the Turkish government tried to prosecute him for comments that they alleged were an 'insult to Turkishness'. During an interview with a Swiss newspaper, Pamuk stated that 'thirty thousand Kurds and a million Armenians were killed in these lands, and nobody but me dares to talk about it'. The case against him was only dropped after international outcry over freedom of speech. Pamuk's criticisms of his country's past meant that Turkish reaction to his win was ambivalent – many rejoiced in the recognition of Turkish literature while others questioned his 'Turkishness', suggesting his flirtation with controversy signified a dissident nature. ❦ Pamuk used his experiences of growing up in Turkey – a simultaneously secular and Muslim society that straddles Europe and Asia – to inform his work. He drew on personal experiences for his first novel, *Cevdet Bey Ve Oğullari* (1982; Cevdet Bey and His Sons), a work that chronicled the increasing Western influences on traditional Ottoman family life. But Pamuk came to international attention with his third novel, *Beyaz Kale* (1985; The White Castle, 1992), which established his reputation as a novelist who liked to play with identities, a theme that he revisited in his subsequent novel *Kara Kitap* (1990; The Black Book, 1995). More recently, Pamuk's work has examined the religious conflicts and contradictions that dog Turkish society, notably in his latest novel, *Kar* (2002; Snow, 2005). ❦ After Pamuk's Laureate was announced, the Swedish Academy faced accusations that it was abandoning literature for politics – a reference both to Pamuk's recently politicized position, and Harold Pinter's award in 2005 (which he used as a platform to attack American foreign policy). Despite a reputation in some quarters as a political agitator, Pamuk claims he has no partisan agenda, describing himself as principally a writer of fiction.

——————— TOP 10 BEST-SELLING US BOOKS · 2007 ———————

Title	author	sales
Harry Potter and the Deathly Hallows	J.K. Rowling	7,284,237
The Secret	Rhonda Byrne	2,481,470
A Thousand Splendid Suns	Khaled Hosseini	856,371
The Memory Keeper's Daughter	Kim Edwards	664,249
The Road	Cormac McCarthy	592,954
You: On a Diet: The Owner's Manual	Michael F. Roizen	590,341
The Measure of a Man: A Spiritual Autobiography	Sidney Poitier	529,763
The Kite Runner	Khaled Hosseini	512,367
Eat, Pray, Love: One Woman's Search for Everything	Elizabeth Gilbert	510,059
The Best Life Diet	Bob Greene	487,747

[Source: Nielsen BookScan © · January–August 2007] Americans bought $10·023bn worth of books in 2006, a negligible decline of 0·2% from the $10·044bn sold in 2005, according to the Association of American Publishers. Sales of adult hardcover books increased by 4%, and adult paperback sales increased by 8·5%. E-books posted the highest growth rate, with sales increasing by 24% for the year. However, bookstore sales declined by almost 3% according to the Census Bureau, from $16·977bn in 2005 to $16·589bn in 2006, perhaps reflecting a rise in e-commerce.

——————— 'ONE BOOK' PROGRAMS ———————

Many American cities and states have created 'One Book' programs which encourage residents to read the same book at the same time – as a form of 'mass book club'. The programs are usually sponsored by local libraries, which host author readings, discussions, and other activities to foster 'civic unity through reading'. Below are some of the books read in 'One Book' programs throughout America in 2007:

Region	title
Arizona	*Going Back to Bisbee* · Richard Shelton
Bowling Green, KY	*The Memory Keeper's Daughter* · Kim Edwards
Huntsville, AL	*To Kill a Mockingbird* · Harper Lee
Iowa	*Splendid Solution: Jonas Salk and the Conquest of Polio* · Jeffrey Kluger
Kalamazoo, MI	*The Curious Incident of the Dog in the Night-Time* · Mark Haddon
Miami	*The Color Purple* · Alice Walker
Orlando, FL	*Mr Popper's Penguins* · Richard & Florence Atwater
Pasadena, CA	*The Distant Land of My Father* · Bo Caldwell
Rockford, IL	*Kitchen Confidential* · Anthony Bourdain
San Diego	*Enrique's Journey* · Sonia Nazario
Savannah, GA	*Their Eyes Were Watching God* · Zora Neale Hurston
Seattle	*The Namesake* · Jhumpa Lahiri
Sierra Madre, CA	*The Wonderful Wizard of Oz* · L. Frank Baum
Silicon Valley	*The Tortilla Curtain* · T.C. Boyle
Topeka, KS	*Fahrenheit 451* · Ray Bradbury

[Sources: The Center for the Book at the Library of Congress; various]

―――――――PULITZER PRIZES · LETTERS & DRAMA―――――――

The 2007 Pulitzers awarded Special Citations to *Ray Bradbury* for his 'distinguished, prolific and deeply influential career as an unmatched author of science fiction and fantasy', and *John Coltrane* for his 'masterful improvisation, supreme musicianship and iconic centrality to the history of jazz' (Coltane's award was posthumous; he died in 1967). The other 2007 Pulitzer Prizes in Letters, Drama, and Music were:

Fiction...Cormac McCarthy · *The Road*
Drama...David Lindsay-Abaire · *Rabbit Hole*
History..............................Gene Roberts & Hank Klibanoff · *The Race Beat*
Biography....................Debby Applegate · *The Most Famous Man in America*
Poetry...Natasha Trethewey · *Native Guard*
General nonfiction.........................Lawrence Wright · *The Looming Tower*
Music.......................................Ornette Coleman · *Sound Grammar*

―――――――――――BEST YOUNG NOVELISTS―――――――――――

The best US novelists under 35, as named by the magazine *Granta* in March 2007:

Daniel Alarcón	Olga Grushin	Maile Meloy
Kevin Brockmeier	Dara Horn	ZZ Packer
Judy Budnitz	Gabe Hudson	Jess Row
Christopher Coake	Uzodinma Iweala	Karen Russell
Anthony Doerr	Nicole Krauss	Akhil Sharma
Jonathan Safran Foer	Rattawut Lapcharoensap	Gary Shteyngart
Nell Freudenberger	Yiyun Li	John Wray

―――――――――――LITERATURE & MEMORY―――――――――――

In 2006, a group of psychiatrists and literary scholars led by Dr Harrison Pope of Harvard offered $1,000 to the first person who found an account of 'repressed memory' written prior to 1800. The group theorized that if repressed memory was a natural function of the human brain, it should appear in literature before becoming a fashionable plot device *c.*1800. To qualify, the account had to describe a healthy, lucid adult with amnesia for a specific traumatic event. In a paper published in December 2006, the researchers said that none of the responses offered met their criteria, giving these explanations for frequently cited memory lapses in literature:

Euripides' Heracles...simple delirium
Shakespeare's Hotspur in *Henry IV, Part I*...................'ordinary forgetfulness'
Sophocles' Oedipus...infantile amnesia
The Arthurian knight Ivain...simple delirium
Shakespeare's King Lear..simple delirium

[Rebuttals were ongoing at the time of writing.]

————————BULWER-LYTTON FICTION CONTEST————————

In 1982, the Department of English and Comparative Literature at San José State University created a literary contest in honor of E.G.E. Bulwer-Lytton (1803–73), who infamously opened his book *Paul Clifford* with 'It was a dark and stormy night'. The contest rewards the best 'bad' opening line to an imaginary novel. The 2007 winner was Jim Gleeson, a 47-year-old media technician, whose entry was:

> *Gerald began – but was interrupted by a piercing whistle which cost him ten percent of his hearing permanently, as it did everyone else in a ten-mile radius of the eruption, not that it mattered much because for them 'permanently' meant the next ten minutes or so until buried by searing lava or suffocated by choking ash – to pee.*

————————ODDEST BOOK TITLE OF THE YEAR · 2006————————

The Diagram Group's *Oddest Book Title of the Year* has been contested annually since 1978. The award is administered by the *Bookseller*, and voted on by members of the book trade. The 'oddest' title of 2006, and the runners-up, are given below:

The Stray Shopping Carts of Eastern North America: A Guide to Field Identification
Julian Montague [WINNER]

Tattooed Mountain Women and Spoon Boxes of Daghestan
R. Chenciner, G. Ismailov, M. Magomedkhanov, & A. Binnie

Better Never to Have Been: The Harm of Coming into Existence
David Benatar

How Green Were the Nazis?
T. Zeller, F. Bruggemeier, & M. Cioc

D. Di Mascio's Delicious Ice Cream: D. Di Mascio of Coventry, an Ice Cream Company of Repute, with an Interesting and Varied Fleet of Ice Cream Vans – Roger De Boer

Proceedings of the Eighteenth International Seaweed Symposium
R. Anderson, J. Brodie, E. Onsoyen, & A. Critchley

————————POETS LAUREATE————————

On August 2, 2007, the Library of Congress announced that Charles Simic would become the 15th US Poet Laureate. Born in Belgrade in 1938, Simic has authored 18 books of poetry, as well as numerous essays, critical works, and translations. Frequently labeled Surrealistic, Simic's work is celebrated for its dark humor and contemporary verve. Simic won the Pulitzer Prize for Poetry in 1990, for *The World Doesn't End*, and is professor emeritus at the University of New Hampshire. At the time of writing, he was slated to give several major public readings, beginning in the fall of 2007. ❧ In September 2006, the independent Poetry Foundation named Jack Prelutsky its inaugural Children's Poet Laureate. Prelutsky, whose prodigious body of work includes the classic *Be Glad Your Nose Is on Your Face*, will advise the Foundation on projects designed to instill in the young a lifelong love of poetry.

BAD SEX IN FICTION PRIZE · 2006

Each year, the *Literary Review* awards its 'Bad Sex in Fiction' prize to a novel featuring the most 'inept, embarrassing and unnecessary' sex scene. The 2006 winner was IAIN HOLLINGSHEAD, for his funny debut novel, *Twenty Something*:

She's wearing a short, floaty skirt that's more suited to July than February. She leans forward to peck me on the cheek, which feels weird, as she's never kissed me on the cheek before. We'd kissed properly the first time we met. And that was over three years ago. But the peck on the cheek turns into a quick peck on the lips. She hugs me tight. I can feel her breasts against her chest. I cup my hands round her face and start to kiss her properly. She slides one of her slender legs in between mine. Oh Jack, she was moaning now, her curves pushed up against me, her crotch taut against my bulging trousers, her hands gripping fistfuls of my hair. She reaches for my belt. I groan too, in expectation. And then I'm inside her, and everything is pure white as we're lost in a commotion of grunts and squeaks, flashing unconnected images and explosions of a million little particles.

OTHER BOOK PRIZES OF NOTE · 2007

Bollingen Prize in American Poetry	Frank Bidart
Caldecott Medal	David Wiesner · *Flotsam*
Costa Book of the Year	Stef Penney · *The Tenderness of Wolves*
Children's prize	Linda Newbery · *Set in Stone*
Biography	Brian Thompson · *Keeping Mum*
Poetry	John Haynes · *Letter to Patience*
Novel	William Boyd · *Restless*
Edgar Allan Poe awards: novel	Jason Goodwin · *The Janissary Tree*
Guardian first book award [2006]	Yiyun Li · *A Thousand Years of Good Prayers*
Hugo Awards: novel [2006]	Robert Charles Wilson · *Spin*
Kingsley Tufts Poetry Prize	Rodney Jones · *Salvation Blues*
Man Booker Prize [2006]	Kiran Desai · *The Inheritance of Loss*
National Book Awards: Fiction [2006]	Richard Powers · *The Echo Maker*
Nonfiction	Timothy Egan · *The Worst Hard Time*
Poetry	Nathaniel Mackey · *Splay Anthem*
Young People's Literature	M.T. Anderson · *The Astonishing Life of Octavian Nothing, Traitor to the Nation, Vol. 1: The Pox Party*
National Book Critics Circle: Fiction	Kiran Desai · *The Inheritance of Loss*
Nonfiction	Simon Schama · *Rough Crossings: Britain, the Slaves and the American Revolution*
Autobiography	Daniel Mendelsohn · *The Lost: A Search for Six of Six Million*
Nebula Awards: Novel	Jack McDevitt · *Seeker*
Newbery Medal	Susan Patron & Matt Phelan [illus.] · *The Higher Power of Lucky*
Orange Prize	Chimamanda Ngozi Adichie · *Half of a Yellow Sun*
PEN/Faulkner Award	Philip Roth · *Everyman*
PEN/Saul Bellow Award for Achievement in American Fiction	Philip Roth
Truman Capote Award for Literary Criticism	William H. Gass · *A Temple of Texts*

[Awards announced during 2007 unless otherwise noted]

─────HARRY POTTER MANIA─────

The publication of the 7th (and supposedly final) installment of J.K. Rowling's Harry Potter series – *Harry Potter & the Deathly Hallows* – was accompanied by an unprecedented avalanche of media coverage. Papers around the world dedicated reams of newsprint to 'HP7', and thousands of Potter-themed websites quivered with anticipation. A late-night post on *TheLeaky-Cauldron.org* gushed, 'we're about 25 minutes away from receiving the book, here in Naperville, Ill. It's just about starting to feel real, guys ... Living through this time together has been a privilege and an honor for all of us'. However, the prelude to the strictly embargoed launch at midnight on July 21, 2007, was not without controversy. Days before the book's official release, photographs purportedly of every page of HP7 were circulated online. The *New York Times* and *Baltimore Sun* provoked reader outrage (and a denunciation from Rowling) by publishing 'embargo-busting' reviews of HP7 days before the launch. And Rowling's US publisher, Scholastic, threatened legal action against two companies for shipping copies of HP7 early. In Israel, Orthodox Jews denounced bookshops that planned to open on the Sabbath to sell HP7. In Britain, independent booksellers were squeezed as the big chains and supermarkets fought a price war that saw the £17·99 book sold at a loss, for as little as £5. (The supermarket chain Asda apologized unreservedly after accusing the UK publisher, Bloomsbury, of 'profiteering'.) In the end, as with the launch of previous HP books, such incidents and accidents served only to stoke the fires of anticipation for the moment

J.K. Rowling

of official publication. Shops in >90 countries opened their doors at 00:01 GMT (05:01 GMT in the US) to hordes of children and adults – many dressed as characters from the series. In the first 24 hours on sale, HP7 sold 8·3m copies in the US alone – a rate of *c.*96 books/second. Scholastic's president noted, 'the excitement, anticipation and just plain hysteria that came over the entire country ... was a bit like the Beatles' first visit to the US'. ❦ The HP septuary has been translated into *c.*65 languages (including Latin and Khmer), has sold >330m copies, and has inspired 5 blockbusting movies. Its royalties have catapulted Rowling from penury to a wealth estimated by *Forbes* in 2007 at *c.*$1bn. Predictably, some critics have derided Rowling's plots, prose, and profits – notably asserting that her series does little to encourage children to read beyond its pages. As Harold Bloom asked in a vitriolic *Wall Street Journal* review in 2000, 'Is it better that they read Rowling than not read at all? Will they advance from Rowling to more difficult pleasures?' To the latter question, Bloom thought not – yet a 2005 Waterstone's survey found that 84% of British teachers said HP had a positive impact on children's reading abilities, and 67% said HP helped turn nonreaders into readers. ❦ If HP7 is the last in the series (Rowling mischievously warned, 'never say never'), it remains to be seen whether the books' legacy can be as lasting as their initial impact has been spectacular. On the day *Deathly Hallows* was published, a Google search for 'Harry Potter' elicited 167m results; in comparison, a search for 'Jesus Christ' elicited just 8·4m results.

──────────── LIBRARY USAGE ────────────

American public libraries were visited 1·3bn times in 2004 (4·7 library visits per capita), according to the most recent figures from the National Center for Education Statistics. Ohioans led the nation in library visits per capita (7·2), although New York had the greatest number of public library outlets (753). Information on library usage, from a 2006 survey by the American Library Association, is given below:

Percent of US adults with a library card 63%
Age group most likely to visit the library 25–34
Age group second most likely to visit the library 35–44
Most popular reason to use the library....... educational purposes (i.e. homework)
Second most popular reason to use the library .... entertainment

The services most often used at the library in 2006, according to the ALA, were:

Taking out books .. 81% *of users did so*	Connecting to the internet 29
Consulting the librarian 54	Speakers/movies/special programs... 22
Using reference material 45	Using computer to write papers &c. 22
Taking out CDs/videos/software 38	Checking email 13
Reading newspapers & magazines... 36	Taking a class or workshop 9

──────── MOST FREQUENTLY CHALLENGED BOOKS · 2006 ────────

A 'challenge' is a formal, written complaint requesting the removal of a book from a library or school due to its 'content or appropriateness'. The American Library Association annually compiles a list of the books most often challenged by the public. Below are the top ten most frequently challenged books (or series) during 2006:

And Tango Makes Three · J. Richardson & P. Parnell   *challenged for* homosexuality, anti-family, unsuited to age group

Gossip Girl series · Cecily Von Ziegesar   homosexuality, sexual content, drugs, unsuited to age group, offensive language

Alice series · Phyllis Reynolds Naylor   sexual content, offensive language

The Earth, My Butt, & Other Big Round Things · C. Mackler   sexual content, anti-family, offensive language, unsuited to age group

The Bluest Eye · Toni Morrison   sexual content, offensive language, unsuited to age group

Scary Stories series · Alvin Schwartz   occult/satanism, unsuited to age group, violence, insensitivity

Athletic Shorts · Chris Crutcher   homosexuality and offensive language

The Perks of Being a Wallflower · Stephen Chbosky   homosexuality, sexually explicit, offensive language, unsuited to age group

Beloved · Toni Morrison   offensive language, sexual content, unsuited to age group

The Chocolate War · Robert Cormier   sexual content, offensive language, violence

Other 'repeat offenders' frequently featured on past ALA lists: *Catcher in the Rye* by J.D. Salinger, *Of Mice and Men* by John Steinbeck, and *The Adventures of Huckleberry Finn* by Mark Twain.

—CANDIDATES & BOOKS—

The favorite books of some 2008 presidential candidates [see also p.17]:

JOHN EDWARDS
I.F. Stone · *Trial of Socrates*
Jon Krakauer · *Into Thin Air*
David Shipler · *The Working Poor*
[Source: JohnEdwards.com]

MITT ROMNEY
L. Ron Hubbard · *Battlefield Earth*
The Bible
[Source: *New York Times*]

HILLARY CLINTON
Louisa May Alcott · *Little Women*
B. Kingsolver · *The Poisonwood Bible*
Alice Walker · *The Color Purple*
J.M. Auel · *The Clan of the Cave Bear*
Jung Chang · *Wild Swans*
Beryl Markham · *West with the Night*
Amy Tan · *The Joy Luck Club*
[Source: *O, the Oprah magazine*]

BARACK OBAMA
Toni Morrison · *Song of Solomon*
Herman Melville · *Moby-Dick*
Shakespeare's *Tragedies*
Taylor Branch · *Parting the Waters*
Marilynne Robinson · *Gilead*
Ralph Waldo Emerson · *Self-Reliance*
Abraham Lincoln · *Collected Writings*
The Bible
[Source: Facebook]

JOHN McCAIN
Hemingway · *For Whom the Bell Tolls*
[Source: Facebook]

RON PAUL
Frederic Bastiat · *The Law*
Chalmers Johnson · *Blowback*
Boris Pasternak · *Doctor Zhivago*
F.A. Hayek · *The Road to Serfdom*
Ludwig von Mises · *Human Action*
[Source: MySpace]

—OPRAH WINFREY—

The books featured in Oprah's Book Club during 2006 & 2007 [as of 8·01]:

Jeffrey Eugenides · *Middlesex*
Cormac McCarthy · *The Road*
Sidney Poitier · *The Measure of a Man*
Elie Wiesel · *Night*

—YANN MARTEL—

In April 2007, Booker Prize-winning Canadian writer Yann Martel started sending Canada's PM, Stephen Harper, one book every fortnight. According to the *Globe & Mail*, these books form part of a campaign to 'affirm the importance of the arts and literature in national discourse'. Martel says he chooses books that have 'been known to expand stillness', and intends to continue sending the books for as long as Harper remains in office. Each book is accompanied by a detailed letter explaining its cultural relevance. At the time of writing, Martel had sent:

Leo Tolstoy · *The Death of Ivan Ilych*
George Orwell · *Animal Farm*
Agatha Christie
The Murder of Roger Ackroyd
Elizabeth Smart
*By Grand Central Station
I Sat Down and Wept*
The Bhagavad Gita
Françoise Sagan · *Bonjour Tristesse*
Simon Armitage (Ed.) · *Short and Sweet*

Incidentally, in September 2006, Venezuelan President Hugo Chávez sent Noam Chomsky's 2003 *Hegemony or Survival* racing to No. 1 on the Amazon best-seller list after recommending it at the UN General Assembly. Chávez's recommendation came during the same speech in which he called Bush 'the devil' and complained the podium smelled like sulphur [see p.40].

——TOP 10 BOOKS EVER——

In his 2007 book *The Top Ten: Writers Pick Their Favorite Books*, J. Peder Zane asked 125 leading writers to name their ten favorite books of all time. Based on the results, Zane compiled a 'top 10 of the top 10' list of the books that scored the highest overall:

1 ....Leo Tolstoy · *Anna Karenina*
2 .. Gustave Flaubert · *Madame Bovary*
3 .... Leo Tolstoy · *War and Peace*
4 ....Vladimir Nabokov · *Lolita*
5 .... Mark Twain · *The Adventures of Huckleberry Finn*
6 ....William Shakespeare · *Hamlet*
7 .....F.S. Fitzgerald · *The Great Gatsby*
8 ....M. Proust · *In Search of Lost Time*
9 ....Anton Chekhov · *The Stories of Anton Chekhov*
10........ George Eliot · *Middlemarch*

——2006 BEST BOOKS——

The best books of 2006, as selected by the *New York Times*:

FICTION

Gary Shteyngart · *Absurdistan*
Amy Hempel · *The Collected Stories of Amy Hempel*
Claire Messud · *The Emperor's Children*
Richard Ford · *The Lay of the Land*
Marisha Pessl · *Special Topics in Calamity Physics*

NONFICTION

Danielle Trussoni · *Falling Through the Earth: A Memoir*
Lawrence Wright · *The Looming Tower: Al Qaeda and the Road to 9/11*
Nathaniel Philbrick · *Mayflower: A Story of Courage, Community, and War*
Michael Pollan · *The Omnivore's Dilemma: A Natural Hist. of 4 Meals*
Rory Stewart · *The Places in Between*

——ARTISTIC CITIES——

MOST ARTS ESTABLISHMENTS

The metro regions [pop. >1m] with the most arts establishments (both non-profit and commercial) per 1,000 pop.:

1 .... Los Angeles–Long Beach, CA
2 ....Nashville, TN
3 .... San Francisco, CA
4 .... New York, NY
5 .... Seattle/Bellevue/Everett, WA

[Source: Urban Institute, 2006]

BEST PLACES FOR ARTISTS

BusinessWeek.com's list of the 'Best Places for Artists in America', based on cost of living, population diversity, the percentage of young people, and more:

1 .... Los Angeles, CA
2 .... Santa Fe, NM
3 ....Carson City, NV
4 .... New York, NY
5 .... Kingston, NY

FIBERGLASS FAUNA &c.

Fiberglass animals have been popular public art projects since Zurich played host to a herd of dairy cows in 1989. Below is a sampling of similar projects in North America:

Cows....... Chicago [1999], NYC [2000], Denver [2006], Miami [2007], &c.
Flamingos..................Miami [2001]
Lighthouses ....Portland, ME [2003]
Orcas...........Vancouver, BC [2003–04]
Hearts...............San Francisco [2004]
Pandas .... Washington, DC [2004]
Pigs .. Cincinnati & N. Kentucky [2000], Seattle [2001 & 2007]
Horses ....Akron, OH [2005]
Globes .... Chicago [2007]

THE TURNER PRIZE · 2006

Founded in 1984, the Turner Prize is awarded each year to a British artist (defined, somewhat loosely, as an artist working in Britain or a British artist working abroad) under 50, for an outstanding exhibition or other presentation in the twelve months prior to each May. The winner receives £25,000 – and three runners-up £5,000.

On being awarded the 2006 Turner Prize, German artist Tomma Abts at once became the first woman to win since Gillian Wearing in 1997, the first painter to win since Chris Ofili in 1998, and the very first female painter ever to win the prize. The recognition of an unassuming abstract painter was regarded by many as a 'return to basics', following many years in which controversy and personality had dominated the contest. Since the Turner Prize seems to delight in stimulating fierce debate as to the meaning and merit of modern art, critics and tabloids alike seemed slightly deflated that a relatively neutral and clearly 'artistic' artist had won. ❦ Tomma Abts was born in 1967 in Kiel, Germany, but moved to London in 1994, just as the Young British Artist (YBA) movement was coalescing. Abts says she creates her abstract, angular paintings without source materials and with no sense of how a work will turn out. As if to highlight their seemingly random,

Tomma Abts

organic creation, Abts arbitrarily titles her paintings from a German dictionary of first names. After experimenting with canvas size early in her career, Abts settled on a uniform size of 48×38cm, onto which she adds layers of color, allowing geometric forms to take shape. Abts describes her works as 'a concentrate of the many paintings underneath'. ❦ The Tate commented that Abts' winning exhibitions in Basel and London 'revealed her rigorous and consistent approach to painting. Through her intimate and compelling canvases, she builds on and enriches the language of abstract painting'. ❦ A small group of artists, who call themselves Stuckists and describe themselves as 'anti the pretensions of conceptual art', protested outside the prize ceremony, calling for the resignation of the Tate's director, Nicholas Serota. The Stuckists' leader, Charles Thomson, tried to dismiss Abts' work as 'silly little meaningless diagrams that make 1950s wallpaper look profound'.

Year	previous winner				
'92	Grenville Davey	'96	Douglas Gordon	'01	Martin Creed
'93	Rachel Whiteread	'97	Gillian Wearing	'02	Keith Tyson
'94	Antony Gormley	'98	Chris Ofili	'03	Grayson Perry
'95	Damien Hirst	'99	Steve McQueen	'04	Jeremy Deller
		'00	Wolfgang Tillmans	'05	Simon Starling

2007 NOMINATIONS

It was announced in May 2007 that the following four artists are shortlisted for the 2007 Turner Prize, the winner of which will be announced on December 3:

installation artist Mark Wallinger · *photographer & filmmaker* Zarina Bhimji
installation artist Mike Nelson · *sculptor & installation artist* Nathan Coley

LE RÊVE & THE 'TERRIBLE NOISE'

In September 2006, Las Vegas casino developer Steve Wynn agreed to sell Picasso's *Le Rêve* to a hedge fund billionaire for $139m – a deal that would have made the painting the most expensive artwork in history. Disastrously, while showing the painting to friends several days later, Wynn – raising his hand to make a point – jabbed his elbow backwards and ripped the canvas. According to the writer Nora Ephron, who was present at the time, witnesses heard a 'terrible noise' and saw a silver-dollar-sized hole trailed by two 3"-sized rips. 'Thank God it was me,' Wynn reportedly said, later calling the accident 'the world's clumsiest and goofiest thing to do'. (According to the *New Yorker*, Wynn suffers from the eye disease *retinitis pigmentosa*, which damages peripheral vision.) Understandably, the sale was canceled: Wynn later decided to keep the painting following a $90,000 restoration.

FBI's TOP TEN ART CRIMES

Since 2005, the FBI has maintained a list of the 'Top Ten Art Crimes' in order to raise public awareness of the stolen property. Below is the list at August 15, 2007:

Item(s)	stolen from	in	est. $ value
7,000–10,000 Iraqi artifacts	Iraq	2003	'priceless'
12 Isabella Stewart Gardner Museum paintings	USA	1990	300m
Da Vinci · *Madonna with the Yarnwinder*	Scotland	2003	65m
2 Van Goghs	Netherlands	2002	30m
Caravaggio · *Nativity with San Lorenzo and San Francesco*	Italy	1969	20m
Cézanne · *View of Auvers-sur-Oise*	England	1999	5.9m
2 Maxfield Parrish murals	USA	2002	4m
Davidoff-Morini Stradivarius violin	USA	1995	3m
Frans Van Mieris · *A Cavalier*	Australia	2007	1m
4 artworks from the Museu Chacara do Céu	Brazil	2006	unavailable

In March 2007, the FBI announced that Norman Rockwell's *Russian Schoolroom*, stolen in 1973, had been spotted hanging in Steven Spielberg's office. The director claimed to have bought the painting from a legitimate dealer in 1989; the FBI reportedly considers him an 'absolutely innocent victim'.

STENDHAL SYNDROME

Stendhal Syndrome is a malady in which travelers are 'overcome' after viewing art of great beauty. It was first identified in the late 1970s by Italian psychiatrist Graziella Magherini. Sufferers experience disorientation, dizziness, palpitations, sweating, and a sense of alienation or paranoia; symptoms can last for two to eight days, and cures include bed rest and a return to routine. The putative illness is named after the French writer (born Marie-Henri Beyle), who (as he noted in his diary) felt such 'ecstasy' upon viewing the frescoes in Florence's Church of Santa Croce that his heart began to beat irregularly and he felt the life 'ebbing out' of him. Since 1979, Dr Magherini has treated over 100 cases of the syndrome in Florence alone.

TOP EXHIBITIONS · 2006

The *Art Newspaper*'s figures for the most popular art exhibitions in the world:

2006 exhibition	museum	daily attendance
The Price Collection: Jakuchu	Tokyo National	6,446
Leonard Foujita	Nat. Museum of Modern Art, Tokyo	6,324
Klimt, Schiele, Moser, Kokoschka	Grand Palais, Paris	6,297
Shaping Faith: Jap. Buddhist Statues	Tokyo National	6,296
Munch: The Modern Life of the Soul	Museum of Modern Art, NY	6,184
Faith & Syncretism	Tokyo National	6,039
Ingres, 1780–1867	Louvre, Paris	5,448
Tutankhamen & the Pharaohs	Museum of Art, Fort Lauderdale	5,443
Chinese & Japanese Calligraphy	Tokyo National	5,383
M. Beckmann: Watercolors & Pastels	Guggenheim Museum, Bilbao	5,278

MUSEUM SPENDING

Figures released by the UK organization Art Fund, in November 2006, show that many US museums spend lavishly compared to their poorer international counterparts. New York's Metropolitan Museum topped the chart, spending $99·2m in 2004–05 – including $50m on Duccio di Buoninsegna's *Madonna and Child*.

Museum (2004–05)	acquisitions	total income
The Met, New York†	$99·2m	$257·7m
MoMA, New York	$37·1m	$140·8m
Louvre, Paris	$32·5m	$222·4m
The Getty, California‡	c.$20m	c.$270m
Rijksmuseum, Amsterdam	$18·4m	$93m
National Gallery, London	$12·3m	$77·9m
Tate (all UK sites)	$9·4m	$173·9m

† The Met spent an unsual amount this year; in previous years it spent c.$30m–40m on acquisitions.
‡ The Getty declined to confirm its spending. Figures are approximate, do not include gifts, and are taken from newspaper reports, including the *New York Times*. Currency conversions at 1/27/2007.

THE MOST POWERFUL PEOPLE IN ART

ArtReview's 5th 'Power 100' list of the most powerful people in the art world (in 2006) saw Damien Hirst slip from first place to eleventh. The 10 most powerful were:

1 .. François Pinault.. *owner of Christie's*
2 .. Larry Gagosian...... *dealer/gallerist*
3 .. Nicholas Serota ... *museum director*
4 .. Glenn D. Lowry .. *museum director*
5 .. Sam Keller.......... *art fair director*

6 .. Eli Broad .... *collector*
7 .. Charles Saatchi.... *collector/gallerist*
8 .. M. Slotover & A. Sharp.. *publishers*
9 .. Bruce Nauman............... *artist*
10. Jeff Koons .... *artist*

─────────TOP TEN ARTISTS BY REVENUE · 2006─────────

Artprice annually publishes a ranking of artists based on sales generated by their works at auction. In 2006, Pablo Picasso ranked No. 1 for the 10th year in a row:

Rank artist ('05 rank)	2006 sales ($)
1 .... Pablo Picasso (1)	339·2m
2 .... Andy Warhol (2)	199·4m
3 .... Gustav Klimt (359)	175·1m
4 .... Willem de Kooning (7)	107·4m
5 .... Amedeo Modigliani (21)	90·7m
6 .... Marc Chagall (6)	89·0m
7 .... Egon Schiele (47)	79·1m
8 .... Paul Gauguin (67)	62·3m
9 .... Henri Matisse (13)	59·7m
10 ... Roy Lichtenstein (11)	59·7m

[Source: artprice.com]

Below are the artistic 'movements' that have posted the sharpest gains in price over the past 10 years, according to the annual *Artprice* ranking of sales at auctions:

Cologne Group · 1980s & 1990s; examples include Mike Kelley & Christopher Wool

Arte Povera · founded in 1967 in Italy, natural materials, refused to see art as products

English Pop Art · bright colors, synthetic materials, and expressive forms

Contemporary Indian Art · current stars include Tyeb Mehta & Subodh Gupta

Minimal Art · 1960s movement focused on creating new experiences of space and time

The London School · stars include Lucian Freud, Francis Bacon, and Frank Auerbach

Canada's Group of Seven · early C20th; love of landscapes and color

Chinese Avant-Garde · stars include Zhang Xiaogang, Wang Guangyi, and Yue Minjun

Posterism · branch of New Realists working with collage and street posters

Purism · 1918–27, founded by Le Corbusier and Amédée Ozenfant; outgrowth of Cubism

─────WHERE TO SEE MAJOR WORKS OF ART IN THE US─────

I and the Village	Chagall	Museum of Modern Art, NY
Persistence of Memory	Dalí	Museum of Modern Art, NY
The Blue Boy	Gainsborough	Huntington Library, CA
Single Form	Hepworth	United Nations HQ, NY
Nighthawks	Hopper	Art Institute of Chicago
Composition VIII	Kandinsky	Guggenheim, NY
Magic Garden	Klee	Guggenheim, NY
Washington Crossing the Delaware	Leutze	Metropolitan Museum of Art, NY
Broadway Boogie Woogie	Mondrian	Museum of Modern Art, NY
The Old Guitarist	Picasso	Art Institute of Chicago
Demoiselles d'Avignon	Picasso	Museum of Modern Art, NY
Lavender Mist: Number 1	Pollock	National Gallery of Art, DC
Luncheon of the Boating Party	Renoir	Phillips Collection, Washington, DC
At the Moulin Rouge	Toulouse-Lautrec	Art Institute of Chicago
Starry Night	Van Gogh	Museum of Modern Art, NY
100 Soup Cans	Warhol	Albright-Knox Gallery, Buffalo
Marilyn Monroe print	Warhol	Warhol Museum, Pittsburgh

Because of sales, restoration, loans, multiple copies, and other factors, the location of some works may vary.

---------------ART GRAND TOUR---------------

Once a decade, the cycles of four major European contemporary art events overlap – as in June 2007, when the Venice Biennale, Art Basel, the Documenta, and the Sculpture Project Münster all opened in the same week. Organizers seized the opportunity to co-promote these four events – dubbing them 'the Grand Tour'†.

VENICE BIENNALE
Venice, Italy
June 10–November 21, 2007
2007 theme: Think with the Senses
– Feel with the Mind.
Art in the Present Tense.
Participants: *c*.100 artists
from 77 countries, incl. Jenny Holzer,
Tracey Emin, Sigmar Polke, Sophie Calle,
and Félix González-Torres
Curator: Robert Storr‡
Golden Lion for Lifetime Achievement:
Malian photographer Malick Sidibé
Held: every 2 years (first in 1895)
'the world's oldest and highest-profile
international art exhibition' [BBC]

SCULPTURE PROJECT MÜNSTER
Münster, Germany
June 17–September 30, 2007
Participants: 35 artists, incl. Rosemarie Trockel,
Bruce Nauman, David Hammons,
and Jeremy Deller
Curators: Brigitte Franzen, Carina
Plath, and Kasper König
Held: every 10 years (first in 1977)
'conceptual scavenger hunt' in which
the city becomes a gallery [*New York Times*]

DOCUMENTA
Kassel, Germany
June 16–September 23, 2007
2007 theme: Is Modernity Our Antiquity?
What Is Bare Life?
What Is to Be Done?
Participants: 120 artists, incl. Ai Weiwei,
Sakarin Krue-On, Gerhard Richter
Artistic director: Roger M. Buergel
Curator: Ruth Noack
Held: every 5 years (first in 1955)
'world's largest contemporary art show' [AP]

ART BASEL
Basel, Switzerland
June 13–17, 2007
Participants: 2,000 artists
from 30 countries, including
Louise Bourgeois, Dan Flavin,
and Tadashi Kawamata
Held: yearly (first in 1970)
'the biggest European buying event' [*Guardian*]

† In the C18th, wealthy young Englishmen and women would undertake 'Grand Tours' through Europe, most notably in Italy, as a key component of their education. ‡ Storr is the Venice Biennale's first American curator.

---------------THE GISH PRIZE---------------

The Iranian-born visual artist Shirin Neshat, noted for her 'haunting' explorations of women in Islam, was awarded the 2006 Dorothy and Lillian Gish Prize on October 12, 2006. The prize is funded by the estates of Dorothy and Lillian Gish, American stage and screen actresses of the C20th. In her will, Lillian called for the creation of an annual prize '*awarded to a man or woman who has made an outstanding contribution to the beauty of the world and to mankind's enjoyment and understanding of life*' across a variety of artistic fields. The prize – currently worth $300,000 – is one of the richest in the arts. Previous recipients include Arthur Miller, Isabelle Allende, Ingmar Bergman, Merce Cunningham, Bob Dylan, and Frank Gehry.

—BROADWAY, OFF-BROADWAY, & OFF-OFF-BROADWAY—

In New York theater, the terms *Broadway*, *off-Broadway*, and *off-off-Broadway* refer primarily to the number of seats in a venue and not its location – though in practice the two often overlap. According to Actors' Equity Association contracts, *Broadway* theaters have 500 seats or more; *off-Broadway* theaters have 100–499 seats; and *off-off-Broadway* theaters have 99 seats or fewer. Currently, there are 39 Broadway theaters in New York, clustered around Manhattan's Times Square. The term *off-Broadway* was coined in the 1950s to refer to plays considered more experimental than Broadway productions and performed on the fringes of Times Square. *Off-off-Broadway* was coined in the 1960s for theater considered even more avant-garde, which tended to be performed down in Greenwich Village or on the Lower East Side.

————THE 'VILLAGE VOICE' OBIE AWARDS · 2007————

PERFORMANCE
Betsy Aidem · 'sustained excellence'†
Andre De Shields · 'sustained excellence'†
Ron Cephas Jones · 'sustained excellence'†
Donna Lynne Champlin
The Dark at the Top of the Stairs
Ain Gordon · *Stories Left to Tell*
David Greenspan · *Faust* & *Some Men*
Nina Hellman · *Trouble in Paradise*
Nancy Opel · *My Deah*
Roslyn Ruff · *Seven Guitars*
James Saito · *Durango*
Michael Stuhlbarg
The Voysey Inheritance
Nilaja Sun · *No Child*
Harris Yulin · *Frank's Home*
Ensemble · *Tale of 2 Cities*

MUSIC & CHOREOGRAPHY
Michael Friedman · 'sustained excellence'†
Bill T. Jones · *Spring Awakening*
Lin-Manuel Miranda · *In the Heights*

DESIGN
Beowulf Boritt · 'sustained excellence'†
Robert Kaplowitz · 'sustained excellence'†
Rae Smith · *Oliver Twist*

DIRECTION
Lou Bellamy · *Two Trains Running*
Anne Kauffman · *The Thugs*

Matthew Maguire · *Abandon*
Eirik Stubo · *The Wild Duck*
Chay Yew · *Durango*

PLAYWRITING
Adam Bock · *The Thugs*

SPECIAL CITATION
Daniel Beaty · *Emergence-SEE*
Tim Crouch · *An Oak Tree*
E. Hall & Propeller
Taming of the Shrew
The Living Theatre · *The Brig*

LIFETIME ACHIEVEMENT
Alvin Epstein

THE ROSS WETZSTEON MEMORIAL
AWARD · Rattlestick Theater

The Obie awards are given to 'publicly acknowledge and encourage' off- and off-off-Broadway theater. † Awards overall achievement.
[On December 4, 2006, the playwright and former Czechoslovakian President Václav Havel finally received the Obie awards he earned in 1968, 1970, and 1984. Havel was originally prevented from receiving his awards by the Soviet-controlled Czechoslovakian government, which placed him under house arrest in Prague in 1968. He is the only head of state to ever have received an Obie.]

TONY AWARDS · 2007

Tom Stoppard's *The Coast of Utopia*, an 8½-hour trilogy concerning C19th Russian intellectuals, swept the 2007 Tonys, winning more awards than any non-musical in Tony history. *Spring Awakening*, which also featured C19th characters (though this time sexually frustrated German teenagers) dominated the musical awards.

Best play	*The Coast of Utopia*
Best musical	*Spring Awakening*
Best original score	*Spring Awakening*
Best revival of a play	*Journey's End*
Best revival of a musical	*Company*
Best leading actor in a play	Frank Langella · *Frost/Nixon*
Best leading actress in a play	Julie White · *The Little Dog Laughed*
Best leading actor in a musical	David Hyde Pierce · *Curtains*
Best leading actress in a musical	Christine Ebersole · *Grey Gardens*
Best featured actor in a play	Billy Crudup · *The Coast of Utopia*
Best featured actress in a play	Jennifer Ehle · *The Coast of Utopia*
Best featured actor in a musical	John Gallagher Jr · *Spring Awakening*
Best featured actress in a musical	Mary Louise Wilson · *Grey Gardens*
Best direction of a play	Jack O'Brien · *The Coast of Utopia*
Best direction of a musical	Michael Mayer · *Spring Awakening*
Best choreography	Bill T. Jones · *Spring Awakening*
Best orchestration	Duncan Sheik · *Spring Awakening*
Regional theater Tony Award	Alliance Theater, Atlanta, GA
Best special theatrical event	*Jay Johnson: The Two and Only*

TOP-GROSSING BROADWAY SHOWS

The top-grossing 2006–07 Broadway shows, including total sales and attendance:

$ *total gross*	[Source: League of American Theaters & Producers Inc.]	*total attendance*
73,921,259	*Wicked*	750,583
59,662,998	*Jersey Boys*	511,275
57,199,973	*The Lion King*	613,626
48,030,409	*Mamma Mia!*	603,216
47,838,261	*The Color Purple*	616,492
47,039,072	*Spamalot*	557,882
44,613,357	*The Drowsy Chaperone*	552,925
38,826,096	*The Phantom of the Opera*	575,525
35,424,624	*Beauty and the Beast*	537,692
27,196,334	*Tarzan*	455,118

17 musicals and 18 plays opened during the 2006–07 Broadway season. Theatergoers purchased 12·3m tickets, a 2·6% rise from 2005–06, for a record gross of $862m. A report on the 2005–06 season issued by the League of American Theaters and Producers found that 62% of theater tickets are purchased by women (at an average total cost of $91·50), and the theatergoers' average age is 42·1.

———————— 'SATURDAY NIGHT LIVE' HOSTS ————————

Hosts and musical guests for season 32 of *Saturday Night Live* (episodes 606–625):

Date	host	musical guest
09·30·06	Dane Cook	The Killers
10·07·06	Jaime Pressly	Corinne Bailey Rae
10·21·06	John C. Reilly	My Chemical Romance
10·28·06	Hugh Laurie	Beck
11·04·06	The Best of Darrell Hammond	N/A
11·11·06	Alec Baldwin	Christina Aguilera
11·18·06	Chris 'Ludacris' Bridges	N/A
12·02·06	Matthew Fox	Tenacious D
12·09·06	Annette Bening	Gwen Stefani/Akon
12·16·06	Justin Timberlake	N/A
01·13·07	Jake Gyllenhaal	The Shins
01·20·07	Jeremy Piven	AFI
02·03·07	Drew Barrymore	Lily Allen
02·10·07	Forest Whitaker	Keith Urban
02·24·07	Rainn Wilson	Arcade Fire
03·17·07	Julia Louis-Dreyfus	Snow Patrol
03·24·07	Peyton Manning	Carrie Underwood
04·14·07	Shia LaBeouf	Avril Lavigne
04·21·07	Scarlett Johansson	Björk
05·05·07	Best of 2006–07	N/A
05·12·07	Molly Shannon	Linkin Park
05·19·07	Zach Braff	Maroon 5

——— 2006 THURBER PRIZE ———

The Thurber Prize awards the best in American humor writing. In 2006, former *Saturday Night Live* writer Alan Zweibel won for his book *The Other Shulman*, about a middle-aged man who decides to run the NYC marathon. In recognition of his achievements, Zweibel received $5,000 and a crystal plaque. Runners-up included the iconoclastic 2006 Texas gubernatorial candidate Kinky Friedman, and *Sports Illustrated* columnist Bill Scheft. Prior winners include *The Daily Show* writers for their *America (The Book): A Citizen's Guide to Democracy Inaction* in 2005, and Christopher Buckley's satire *No Way to Treat a First Lady* in 2004.

——— 2007 TWAIN PRIZE ———

In 2007, Billy Crystal was awarded the Kennedy Center's Mark Twain Prize for American Humor. The prize was created in 1998 to honor 'the brilliant minds that elbow American culture to see if it's still alive'. During the prize announcement, Crystal was praised for his 'versatile and prolific' career, which includes famous roles in *Soap*, *Saturday Night Live*, *When Harry Met Sally*, and *City Slickers*. Crystal has also hosted the Oscars 8 times (first in 1990), and his one-man play, *700 Sundays*, debuted to critical acclaim on Broadway in 2004. Previous Mark Twain winners include Steve Martin [2005], Lily Tomlin [2003], and Richard Pryor [1998].

FAVORITE BUILDINGS

In 2007, Americans were asked to choose their favorite architectural works from a list of 248 notable buildings nominated by the AIA. The most-liked buildings were:

1 . . . . Empire State Building
2 . . . . White House
3 . . . . . .Washington National Cathedral
4 . . . . .Jefferson Memorial
5 . . . . .Golden Gate Bridge
6 . . . . US Capitol
7 .Lincoln Memorial
8 . Biltmore Estate/Vanderbilt Mansion
9 . . . . Chrysler Building
10 . . . . .Vietnam Veterans Memorial

[Source: The American Institute of Architects, Harris Interactive poll]

AMERICAN INSTITUTE OF ARCHITECTS AWARDS

Edward Larrabee Barnes was awarded the AIA's 2007 GOLD MEDAL, presented to an individual whose work 'has had a lasting influence on the theory and practice of architecture'. Barnes, honored posthumously, was praised for putting an American stamp on Modernism, creating geometric buildings that 'fused Modernism with vernacular architecture'. His work includes 590 Madison and 599 Lexington in NYC, as well as the Dallas Museum of Art.

Leers Weinzapfel Associates of Boston won the 2007 AIA ARCHITECTURE FIRM AWARD, which honors a firm that has consistently produced 'distinguished architecture' for more than a decade. The firm was praised for its 'bold and refined approach' and a willingness to tackle challenging transportation, campus, and athletic projects. Some of its notable buildings include MIT's School of Architecture and Planning, and Boston's Operations Control Center.

Recently the term STARCHITECT has emerged to describe architects whose iconic buildings are sought-after as signs of prestige. 2006–07 'starchitect' openings include: Frank Gehry's IAC/InterActiveCorp building in NYC; Zaha Hadid's Maggie's Center in Kirkcaldy, Scotland; Norman Foster's Wembley Stadium in London; Steven Holl's Bloch Building at the Nelson-Atkins Museum of Art in Kansas City, MO; Jean Nouvel's 40 Mercer St in NYC; and Toyo Ito's VivoCity in Singapore.

PRITZKER ARCHITECTURE PRIZE

The international Pritzker Architecture Prize honors living architects who have created structures that contribute to the beauty and functionality of the built environment. In 2007, the Pritzker was awarded to Lord Richard Rogers, whose work includes the Pompidou Centre, Lloyd's of London, the Millennium Dome, and Heathrow's Terminal 5. The winner receives a $100,000 prize and a medallion.

Some previous Pritzker Prize winners
2004 . . . . Zaha Hadid [UK]
1999 . . . . Sir Norman Foster [UK]
1998 . . . . Renzo Piano [ITA]
1991 . . . . .Robert Venturi [USA]
1990 . . . . .Aldo Rossi [ITA]

ARTS & HUMANITIES NATIONAL MEDALS · 2006

NATIONAL MEDAL OF ARTS	NATIONAL HUMANITIES MEDAL
William Bolcom (*composer*)	Fouad Ajami
Cyd Charisse (*dancer*)	(*Middle Eastern Studies scholar*)
Roy R. DeCarava (*photographer*)	James Buchanan (*economist*)
Wilhelmina Holladay (*arts patron*)	Nickolas Davatzes (*historian*)
Interlochen Center for the Arts	Robert Fagles (*translator & classicist*)
Erich Kunzel (*conductor of*	The Hoover Institution
Cincinnati Pops Orchestra)	Mary Lefkowitz (*classicist*)
Preservation Hall Jazz Band	Bernard Lewis
Gregory Rabassa (*literary translator*)	(*Middle Eastern Studies scholar*)
Viktor Schreckengost	Mark Noll (*historian of religion*)
(*industrial designer & sculptor*)	Meryle Secrest (*biographer*)
Dr Ralph Stanley (*bluegrass musician*)	Kevin Starr (*historian*)

NIJINSKY AWARDS · 2006

The biennial Nijinsky Awards honor the best in international dance. In 2006, German Marco Goecke was honored as Emerging Choreographer, while Lifetime Achievement awards went to French dancer Gil Roman, Spanish dancer Ana Laguna, and American dancers and choreographers Trisha Brown and John Neumeier. Brown is the artistic director of the Trisha Brown Dance Company in New York, and Neumeier has been artistic director of the Hamburg Ballet since 1973. The awards were presented by Princess Caroline of Hanover at the Monte Carlo Opera House, where legendary dancer Vaslav Nijinsky (for whom the awards are named) often performed early in the last century. Honorees received trophies modeled after Rodin's 1912 bronze of Nijinsky dancing *L'Après-midi d'un faune*.

LIVING LEGENDS

The Library of Congress established its 'Living Legend' award in 2000. Noted artists, writers, activists, filmmakers, doctors, entertainers, athletes, and public servants are selected by Library of Congress curators and specialists for their 'significant contributions to America's diverse cultural, scientific and social heritage'. Below are the artists and writers who have been named 'living legends' since the award began:

Herbert Block[†] (*commentator*) · Judy Blume (*young adult author*) · Gwendolyn Brooks[†] (*poet*) · William F. Buckley (*commentator*) · Beverly Cleary (*children's author*) · Julia Child[†] (*cookbook author*) · Walter Cronkite (*newscaster*) · Al Hirschfeld[†] (*caricaturist*) · Jenette Kahn (*comics publisher*) · Ursula Le Guin (*author*) · Annie Leibovitz (*photographer*) · Alan Lomax[†] (*musicologist*) · Robert McCloskey[†] (*children's author*) · Toni Morrison (*author*) Philip Roth (*author*) · Katherine Paterson (*children's author*) · Jaroslav Pelikan[†] (*historian*) Gordon Parks[†] (*photographer &c.*) · I.M. Pei (*architect*) · Martin Scorsese (*director*) Maurice Sendak (*children's author*) · Steven Spielberg (*director*) · William Styron[†] (*author*)

† Sadly, these legends are no longer living.

─────────── THE THIN MODELS DEBATE ───────────

In late 2006 and early 2007, a debate over the use of excessively thin fashion models raged in the media. Although skinny models had been controversial for years, the fall 2006 deaths of two Latin American models, Ana Carolina Reston of Brazil and Luisel Ramos of Uruguay, from complications of anorexia, catalyzed industry anxiety and legislative action. In September 2006, Spain banned models with a Body Mass Index (BMI) <18 from the catwalks of Madrid Fashion Week, and in early 2007, Milan banned models with a BMI ≤18·5. Taking a somewhat more measured line, the British Fashion Council, which runs London Fashion Week, wrote to designers requesting that they use only 'healthy-looking girls' over the age of 16. In New York, the Council of Fashion Designers of America (CFDA) formed a health initiative to study the issue, but opposed banning models of a given BMI. Instead, the CFDA released a series of voluntary guidelines 'designed to promote wellness and a healthier work environment'. The guidelines warned against using models under 16 for runway shows, and called for 'regular breaks and rest', healthy snacks backstage, education on the warning signs of eating disorders, and professional help for those who have developed disorders. At the time of writing, the NY state legislature was considering establishing a panel to generate employment standards for young models and entertainers. However, despite these legislative efforts, it seems likely that any sustained shift towards 'fuller' or 'natural' models will ultimately depend on modeling agencies, fashion magazines, and the designers themselves.

81% of the respondents in a 2007 worldwide ACNielsen study believe that female fashion models and celebrities are 'too thin'. 87% of Americans agreed, as did 89% of those in the UK and Canada.

─────────── CFDA AWARDS · 2007 ───────────

Some winners of the 2007 Council of Fashion Designers of America Awards:

Womenswear designer.................................... [tie] Oscar de la Renta, and
Lazaro Hernandez & Jack McCollough for Proenza Schouler
Menswear designer...Ralph Lauren
Accessory designer .... Derek Lam
Emerging talent, womenswear .... Phillip Lim
Emerging talent, menswear ..... David Neville and M. Wainwright for Rag & Bone
American fashion legend award...Ralph Lauren

─── ACCESSORIES COUNCIL EXCELLENCE AWARDS · 2006 ───

The Accessories Council awards those who have raised 'awareness of the accessories industry' and had a 'positive impact on accessory consumption' over the past year.

Brand of the year................. Fendi	*Accessory brand launch*........Tom Ford
Retailer of the year . Bergdorf Goodman	*Fashion influencer* .... Rachel Zoe
Designer of the year ....Michael Kors	*ACE award* ....Jennifer Lopez

——HOUSE DESIGNERS——

Aquascutum..............Michael Hertz
Balenciaga........ Nicolas Ghesquiere
Burberry............Christopher Bailey
Chanel..................Karl Lagerfeld
Chloé......... Paolo Melim Andersson
Christian Dior...........John Galliano
Fendi....................Karl Lagerfeld
Givenchy................Riccardo Tisci
Gucci .... Frida Giannini
Lanvin.....................Alber Elbaz
Louis Vuitton .... Marc Jacobs
Marni........... Consuelo Castiglioni
Missoni .... Angela Missoni
Yves Saint Laurent........Stefano Pilati

——FASHIONABLE CITIES——

The top 2007 fashion cities, according to a Global Language Monitor algorithm that tracks media mentions:

1 ....New York
2 ....Rome
3 ....Paris
4 ....London
5 ....Milan
6 ....Tokyo
7 ....Los Angeles
8 ....Hong Kong
9 ....Las Vegas
10..........................Singapore

——FASHION MUSES——

Designer	*muse*
Marc Jacobs	Sofia Coppola
Karl Lagerfeld	Lady Amanda Harlech
John Galliano	Eva Green
Philip Treacy	Isabella Blow
Valentino	Georgina Brandolini
Roberto Cavalli	Eva Cavalli
Zac Posen	Natalie Portman

Inevitably, designers can be fickle in their choice of muse.

——FASHION WEEKS——

NEW YORK
February & September
mbfashionweek.com/newyork
Who shows: *Ralph Lauren, Vera Wang, Diane Von Furstenberg, Calvin Klein, Zac Posen, Oscar de la Renta, Michael Kors, Donna Karan*

LONDON
February & September
londonfashionweek.co.uk
Who shows: *Aquascutum, Paul Smith Women, Nicole Farhi, Marc by Marc Jacobs, Betty Jackson, Marios Schwab*

MILAN
February & September/October
cameramoda.it
Who shows: *Gucci, Armani, Prada, Dolce & Gabbana, Moschino, Versace, Roberto Cavalli, Max Mara*

PARIS
February/March & October
modeaparis.com
Who shows: *Stella McCartney, Chanel, Vivienne Westwood, Jean Paul Gaultier, John Galliano, Issey Miyake*

——CELEB FASHION LINES——

Some of the celebrity-designed fashion lines launched in 2007:

The Olsen twins... *Elizabeth and James*
Sarah Jessica Parker .... *Bitten*
J. Simpson...*Jessica Simpson Swimwear*
Victoria Beckham...........*dVb denim*
Nicky Hilton..................*Nicholai*

2007 celebrity fashion collaborations included Kate Moss for Topshop/Barneys; Madonna for H&M; and Scarlett Johansson for Reebok. ❦ The former Philippine first lady Imelda Marcos also launched her own fashion jewelry line in fall 2006 – called 'The Imelda Collection'.

———————————COLOR FORECAST · 2007–08———————————

The 'greening of America' and concerns about climate change were key factors in 2007–08 color forecasts, according to *Graphic Design USA*'s Annual Color Forecast issue. Some of the hues forecast to be 'hot' by GDUSA and other sources include:

Benjamin Moore & Co. · *'colors conveying an aged and worn surface' such as Foggy Morning and Calming Green · 'the earth's crust, tree bark, morning frost, veins of a leaf' · the 'amazing global tapestry' of Passion Blue and Adobe Dust* [2007 forecast]

Color Marketing Group · *'softer, more botanical greens' · 'blues from nature' · 'medium to dark browns'* [2007 forecast]

PantoneView Color Planner · *'dark shadows' mixed with 'blue, green, and burgundy' · colors that 'convey a feeling of reticence', such as 'brown, gold, olive, and sesame' · black, white, and silver · mid jewel tones 'as seen through the eyes of a butterfly'* [Fall/Winter 2007–08 forecast]

Pantone Fashion Color report · *'Spicy Chili Pepper and exotic Lemon Curry' · Purple Wine, Dusk, and Carafe · 'homage to nature' in the form of Shale Green, Green Moss, and Earthy Burnt Ochre* [Fall 2007 fashion forecast]

Color Association of the US · *'sage green, rose pink, chocolate brown and deep lavender' · 'strident neons ... that recall the edgy aspects of the 80s' · 'quirky hues' · 'unequivocally pretty hues'* [Spring/Summer 2008 fashion forecast]

Pantone Color Inst. Home Forecast *'tapestry blues and muted blue-greens' 'quiet violet with muted lime' 'white, ebony black, rich browns or silvery grays'* [2008 forecast]

———————————COLOR TRADEMARKS———————————

The purpose of a trademark, according to the US Patent and Trademark Office, is to 'indicate the source of the goods and to distinguish them from the goods of others'. In 1995, the Supreme Court ruled that a color may be registered as a trademark if it has developed a 'secondary meaning' in the minds of consumers, who associate it with a particular brand. The color must have been chosen arbitrarily – in the sense that it does not serve any utilitarian or functional purpose (for instance, one court ruled bright orange could not serve as a trademark on biohazard bags, since the color was deemed to alert consumers to the bag's hazardous contents). Each trademark is limited to a specific range of products, so that while Tiffany has registered its signature shade of robin's egg blue for use on boxes, bags, and various gift items, an oil paint company could likely use the color without any problems. Some color trademarks:

Company	*color*		
Tiffany	robin's egg blue	Heinz	green
UPS	chocolate brown	Dow Chemical	blue
		Mattel Inc.	'Barbie pink'

As branding becomes increasingly globalized and develops in sophistication, the legal and technical issues surrounding trademarks become more complex. Increasingly, courts are asked to give protection to a range of sensory trademarks, including gustatory [taste], tactile [touch], and olfactory [smell].

Sci, Tech, Net

Every great advance in science has issued from a new audacity of imagination.
— JOHN DEWEY (1859–1952)

―――――――――POLONIUM-210―――――――――

Alexander Litvinenko's alleged murder in London in 2006 [see p.26] gave media exposure to the little-known element Polonium (Po). Reports quickly surfaced that Litvinenko had died from radioactive poisoning and, within days, traces of the highly toxic isotope Polonium-210 had been found in more than 12 locations in London, Moscow, and Hamburg, and on 4 aircraft. Hundreds of people with elevated levels of Po-210 have since been traced. ❦ Polonium was the first element to be discovered as a consequence of its radioactivity. It was isolated in 1898 by Marie and Pierre Curie, during their analysis of the radioactive ore 'pitchblende'. Provisionally called Radium F, the element was renamed Polonium to draw attention to the political plight of Marie's homeland, Poland, which was then under the partitioned rule of Russia, Prussia, and Austria. ❦ Po is an extremely rare and highly toxic metallic element found in uranium ores at a quantity of *c.*0·1g per ton. Po has 34 isotopes (more than any other element), all of which are radioactive. The most widely used of these isotopes – Po-210 – occurs in nature at very low levels (all humans carry harmless traces). However, in sufficient quantities, Po-210 emits enough gamma particles to produce a blue glow and, according to the CDC, the alpha particles it emits

'carry high amounts of energy that can damage or destroy genetic material in cells inside the body'. By weight, Po-210 is 250bn times more toxic than cyanide; a dose smaller than a grain of salt is fatal. ❦ In the industrial world, Po-210 is used as a heat source for satellite power supplies, a trigger for nuclear weapons, and as a means of eliminating static. (It is also found in cigarettes; according to a *NYT* article by Prof. Robert Proctor, 'pack and a half smokers are dosed to the tune of about 300 chest X-rays' a year.) ❦ The British Health Protection Agency notes that 'Po-210 only represents a radiation hazard if it is taken into the body – by breathing it in, by taking it into the mouth, or if it gets into a wound. It is not a radiological hazard as long as it remains outside the body. Most traces of it can be eliminated through handwashing, or washing machine and dishwasher cycles'. ❦ Because of Po-210's rarity, toxicity, and difficulty of extraction, it became clear that Litvinenko's death was unlikely to have been accidental. As Prof. Goodhead of the UK's Medical Research Council told the BBC, 'to poison someone, much larger amounts are required and this would have to be man-made, perhaps from a particle accelerator or a nuclear reactor'. Inevitably, speculation as to the origin of the Po-210 that killed Litvinenko focused on Russia [see p.32].

84	209
	4,2,5
—	
527	**Po**
9.3	
[Xe].4f^{14}.5d^{10}.6s^2.6p^4	
Polonium	

NOBEL PRIZES IN SCIENCE · 2006

THE NOBEL PRIZE IN PHYSICS

John C. Mather,
*NASA Goddard Space Flight
Center, USA*

George F. Smoot,
University of California, Berkeley

'for their discovery of the blackbody
form and anisotropy of the cosmic
microwave background radiation'

Mather and Smoot's research confirmed fundamental predictions proposed by the Big Bang theory. Their research used detailed measurements of cosmic microwave background radiation (CMB), gleaned from NASA's COBE satellite, to reveal an 'echo' of the vast explosion, or Big Bang, said to have formed the universe. Mather demonstrated that CMB followed the 'blackbody' curve, a pattern in the energy spectrum predicted to result from the first light in the universe. Smoot noted tiny variations, or 'anisotropies', within the CMB, that represented very faint traces of the formation of the earliest structures in the expanding universe.

THE NOBEL PRIZE IN CHEMISTRY

Roger D. Kornberg,
Stanford University

'for his studies of the molecular basis
of eukaryotic transcription'

Kornberg developed a detailed picture of molecular-level transcription – a vital part of the process by which cells construct proteins from DNA. Kornberg's research focused on eukaryotes – organisms whose cells have a defined nucleus – a group that includes humans. Understanding how transcription works has great medical potential, since disturbances in the transcription process can cause diseases like cancer.

THE NOBEL PRIZE IN PHYSIOLOGY OR MEDICINE

Andrew Z. Fire, *Stanford University*

Craig C. Mello, *University of
Massachusetts Medical School*

'for their discovery of RNA
interference – gene silencing by
double-stranded RNA'

Fire and Mello identified RNA interference – a process that regulates the flow of genetic information – used by the body to defend itself against viral infections. The discovery has opened up new fields of research in the study of gene functionality which, in turn, has the potential to advance the treatment of viruses and cancers by allowing scientists to target and shut down harmful genes.

ROYAL SOCIETY PRIZE FOR SCIENCE BOOKS · 2007

Daniel Gilbert · *Stumbling on Happiness* (Knopf)

————————THE ABEL PRIZE & COPLEY MEDAL————————

The Abel Prize was created in memory of Norwegian mathematician Niels Henrik Abel (1802–29), who is justly famous for proving that the general quintic equation is unsolvable algebraically. In 2007, the Abel Prize was awarded to Srinivasa S.R. Varadhan, from New York's Courant Institute of Mathematical Sciences, for his 'fundamental contributions to probability theory and in particular for creating a unified theory of large deviations'. The Abel Prize is worth *c.*$1 million. ❦ In November 2006, Professor Stephen Hawking was awarded the Copley Medal for his outstanding contribution to theoretical cosmology. Presented by the Royal Society, the Copley is the world's oldest prize for scientific achievement. First awarded in 1731, it has previously been won by such scientific luminaries as Justus von Liebig, Charles Darwin, Michael Faraday, Albert Einstein, and Louis Pasteur.

————————————IG NOBEL PRIZE————————————

Ig Nobel prizes are awarded for scientific 'achievements that cannot or should not be reproduced'. Some of the esteemed honors presented in 2006 include:

ORNITHOLOGY · Ivan R. Schwab (University of California, Davis) and the late Philip R.A. May (University of California, LA) *for their work into why woodpeckers do not get headaches.*

LITERATURE · Daniel Oppenheimer (Princeton University) *for his timely report entitled 'Consequences of Erudite Vernacular Utilized Irrespective of Necessity: Problems with Using Long Words Needlessly'.*

PHYSICS · Basile Audoly and Sebastien Neukirch (Université Pierre et Marie Curie, Paris) *for their investigation into why, when bent, dry spaghetti often breaks into more than two pieces.*

CHEMISTRY · Antonio Mulet, José Javier Benedito, and José Bon (University of Valencia, Spain) and Carmen Rosselló (University of Illes Balears, Mallorca, Spain) *for their joint study entitled 'Ultrasonic Velocity in Cheddar Cheese as Affected by Temperature'.*

MATHEMATICS · Nic Svenson and Piers Barnes (The Australian Commonwealth Scientific and Research Organization) *for their tireless exploration into how many photographs must be taken to ensure no one in a group picture has their eyes closed.*

[Source: improb.com]

————————————DARWIN AWARDS————————————

The annual Darwin Awards *'salute the improvement of the human genome by honoring those who accidentally kill themselves in really stupid ways'.* In 2006, this posthumous accolade went to Jason Ackerman and Sara Rydman, both 21, from Lake View, South Florida. The two students managed to pull down and crawl inside a massive, helium-filled promotional balloon, which was advertising apartments. The hapless students died from oxygen starvation while attempting to get a 'buzz' from the gas.

─────────── THE EDGE ANNUAL QUESTION · 2007 ───────────

The online magazine *Edge* annually invites notable scientists and intellectuals to answer one probing question, usually with fascinating results. Below is a selection of the 160 responses to the 2007 question, 'What are you optimistic about? Why?':

It has never been a better time to have autism · Simon Baron-Cohen (psychologist)
The evaporation of the powerful mystique of religion · Daniel Dennett (philosopher)
The acceptance of the reality of global warming has shown us the greatest and widest ranging market failure ever seen · Brian Eno (artist, composer, producer)
Truth prevails. Sometimes, technology helps · Xeni Jardin (technology journalist)
Shortening sleep will prolong conscious life · Marcel Kinsbourne (psychologist)
The decline of violence · Steven Pinker (psychologist)
The tools for cultural production and distribution are in the pockets of 14-year-olds
Howard Rheingold (communications expert)

─────────── THE IMPORTANCE OF NAMES ───────────

Research by David Figlio, Professor of Economics at the University of Florida, suggested that a girl's name can dictate whether or not she will go on to study math or physics after the age of 16. The study, published in May 2007, indicated that girls with particularly feminine names (as judged by a linguistic test), such as Anna, Emma, or Isabella, were less likely to study traditionally masculine subjects than girls with less feminine names, such as Ashley, Alex, or Grace. The study, conducted on twins, also revealed that those with 'lower-status' names, or names with unusual spellings, often performed less well in tests than a more traditionally named sibling.

─────────── THE SCIENCE OF PROCRASTINATION ───────────

In January 2007, psychologist Piers Steel published the results of his 10-year analysis of procrastination. The study includes a formula designed to predict whether a person will procrastinate in a specific situation. According to Steel, the desire to finish a task (rather than procrastinate) is based on the following four factors:

$$\text{Desire to finish} = \frac{\text{(E)xpectation of success} \times \text{(V)alue of completing the task}}{\text{(I)ndividual's sensitivity to delay} \times \text{(D)eadline of the task}}$$

Steel hopes that his formula (named Temporal Motivational Theory) may be able to help model complex systems of human motivation, such as the behavior of stock markets and even nations. Sadly, TMT does not offer a solution to the problem of procrastination, which 'chronically' affects *c*.15–20% of adults. Steel notes that in light of this issue, 'continued research into procrastination should not be delayed'.

(Apropos of nothing, in April 2007, scientists at Leeds University, UK, developed a formula for the 'perfect' bacon butty. The ideal sandwich is: 2–3 rashers of back-bacon, cooked under a preheated grill for 7 mins at 240°C, which are then placed between 2 slices of farmhouse bread, 1–2cm thick.)

──── 15 GREATEST MEDICAL BREAKTHROUGHS ────

In January 2007, the *British Medical Journal* short-listed 15 contenders for the title of 'greatest medical breakthrough since 1840', the year the *BMJ* was first published:

Anesthesia......... *developed in the 1800s by John Snow, symbol of humanitarianism*
Antibiotics............*the wonder drugs first discovered in 1929 by Alexander Fleming*
Chlorpromazine...................... *unlocking psychosis for paranoid schizophrenics*
Computers ....*transcending our limits*
Discovery of DNA's structure .... *by James Watson and Francis Crick in 1953*
Evidence-based medicine.............................*increasing, not dictating, choice*
Germ theory ....*understanding of hygiene has extended life expectancy*
Imaging .... *X-rays and scans revealed the world within*
Immunology...................... *made magic bullets and organ transplants possible*
Oral rehydration therapy .... *simple solution for saving lives after diarrhea*
The pill............... *allowing women to choose when or whether to become pregnant*
Risks of smoking............. *2 landmark studies from 1950s revealed harmful effects*
Sanitation .... *greater awareness revolutionized public health*
Tissue culture ....*allows cells to be grown on industrial scale to create vaccines, &c.*
Vaccines .... *saved millions of lives and eradicated diseases like smallpox*

11,000 votes were cast in an online poll to select which breakthrough was the most valuable. The overall winner (with 1,765 votes) was 'sanitation'. Oddly, most medical professionals chose 'anesthesia', whereas the public voted for 'antibiotics'.

──── THE MOST DANGEROUS PATHOGENS ────

The most dangerous pathogens (disease-causing microorganisms) are generally those that can survive outside the body for the longest period of time. According to research by Paul Ewald and Bruno Walther, the most dangerous pathogens are:

Pathogen	deaths per 100,000	days survival outside body			
Smallpox	10,000	885	Whooping cough	100	12
Tuberculosis	5,000	244	Pneumonia	36	29
Diphtheria	200	370	Influenza	10	14
			Measles	7	4
			Mumps	5	1

[Source: P.W. Ewald & B. Walther, *Biological Reviews*, vol. 79, p.849 · *New Scientist*]

──── THE BEST SCIENCE BOOK EVER WRITTEN ────

In October 2006, the British Royal Institution debated the best scientific read. The short list included: Richard Dawkins, *The Selfish Gene* (1976); Primo Levi, *The Periodic Table* (1975); Konrad Lorenz, *King Solomon's Ring* (1952); and Tom Stoppard, *Arcadia* (1993). Primo Levi's tale of life as a Jew in Mussolini's Italy recounted through scientific metaphor was judged to be the best science book ever written.

———SOME NOTABLE SCIENTIFIC RESEARCH · 2006–07———

{OCT 2006} · Scientists from the Children's Hospital in Boston, MA, discovered that after a heart attack, a rat's heart can be stimulated to recover by injecting 2 drugs: 'p38 MAP kinase inhibitor' and 'fibroblast growth factor 1'. It is hoped that similar regrowth and repair might be replicated in humans. ❦ A report published in the *Proceedings of the National Academy of Sciences* proposed that elephants have self-awareness – a human trait previously found only in great apes and bottlenose dolphins. The elephants were observed inspecting their reflections in a large mirror placed in their enclosure at the Bronx Zoo, suggesting that they recognized their own images. {NOV} · A study into SIDS published in the *Journal of the American Medical Association* suggested that the condition might be caused by a brain abnormality, raising hopes that those at risk could be identified and treated. ❦ Researchers at the Pasteur Institute in Paris isolated 'opiorphin' – a new painkiller found in men's saliva. Results of rat trials suggested that opiorphin could be up to 6 times more powerful than morphine. {DEC} · An Australian study published in *Neuropsychology* indicated that left-handed people could think more quickly than right-handers when performing certain tasks. {JAN 2007} · American scientists reported in *Nature Biotechnology* that they had discovered a new way to harvest stem cells without using controversial lab-grown human embryos. The new technique involves extracting amniotic fluid from pregnant women and cultivating the cells in a lab. ❦ The Roslin Institute announced it had genetically modified chickens to lay eggs containing proteins that could be used to make cancer-treating drugs. {FEB} · Andrew Oswald, professor of economics at the University of Warwick, mooted that being awarded a Nobel Prize might increase one's life expectancy by up to 2 years. Oswald compared the life spans of male Nobel laureates with nominees, and suggested that a higher social status helped the winners live longer. ❦ Researchers at the Medical Research Council Prion Unit developed a therapy that restored to health mice that had shown early signs of Creutzfeldt-Jakob disease (CJD). It was hoped that a version of this therapy, which blocks production of normal prions, might be developed for humans. {MAR} · A team of researchers at London's Hammersmith Hospital discovered that the hormone kisspeptin, which triggers fertility in teenage girls, could be used to boost fertility in older women. ❦ The American company Ventria Bioscience was granted preliminary approval to grow rice that had been genetically modified to produce human proteins. The crop will be used to develop medicines for the treatment of diarrhea in children. ❦ Research published in *Biological Psychiatry* suggested that oxytocin, a hormone linked to social behavior, could aid 'emotional recognition'. A study indicated that men were significantly better at judging the 'emotion' of sets of photographed human eyes after sniffing oxytocin than before. ❦ A US-led team developed a genetically modified malaria-resistant mosquito. Since these GM mosquitos outlived their malaria-carrying cousins, it was hoped that they might flourish in the wild and help eradicate the deadly

———— NOTABLE SCIENTIFIC RESEARCH · 2006 –07 cont. ————

disease. {APR} · An international team of researchers writing in *Nature Biotechnology* revealed that they had developed a method to convert one blood-group type to another. ❦ German scientists announced they had formed immature sperm cells from human bone marrow, which might offer some hope to infertile men. ❦ Research published in *Science* indicated a genetic link to obesity. The identification of a possible 'fat gene' might explain why some can eat a healthy diet yet still struggle with their weight. ❦ American scientists published the results of a trial in which 15 young patients diagnosed with type 1 diabetes were given stem cell treatment. 13 of the volunteers were able to stop their daily insulin injections – some for more than 3 years after the experimental treatment began. {MAY} · Three separate medical teams announced that they had successfully completed scar-free abdominal surgery by entering the patient's body through the mouth. 'Natural orifice transluminal endosurgery' (NOTES) involves putting a flexible camera and surgical instruments down a patient's throat to reach the abdominal cavity. NOTES also reduces recovery time significantly. ❦ Researchers at the University of California discovered an abnormally high number of people diagnosed with lupus living in houses built on a disused oil field in New Mexico. The findings suggested that environmental triggers, like pollution, might in part be responsible for the autoimmune disease. ❦ Dutch scientists at the University of Groningen suggested that some people might simply be more accident-prone than others. Reviewing 79 studies on accidents, they concluded that 1 in 29

people are, inexplicably, 50% more likely to suffer a mishap than those in the general population. Sadly, the research did not identify any particularly clumsy 'types'. {JUN} · Research led by Professor James Surmeier, reported in *Nature* online, indicated that the drug isradipine, normally used to treat high blood pressure, could help to control Parkinson's disease. ❦ University of Sheffield research on opposite-sex twins indicated that the influence of the male's testosterone in the womb could reduce the female twin's fertility. ❦ Norwegian researchers writing in *Science* reported that eldest children tend to have higher IQs – perhaps because the eldest get more undivided parental attention at a formative age. {JUL} · Research by the University of Arizona revealed that, on average, women speak 16,215 words a day, and men speak 15,669 – fueling the debate that women are by far the more talkative sex. ❦ Scientists at King's College London suggested that those with many moles on their skin are more likely to age well. ❦ The *Proceedings of the National Academy of Sciences* reported that genetically modified goats have been bred with a drug in their milk that serves as an antidote to nerve agents like sarin and VX. ❦ US scientists reported in *Nature* that they had used deep brain stimulation to rouse a patient in a minimally conscious state. A 38-year-old man, who had suffered a serious head injury six years previously, was able to speak, chew, and swallow after electrical pulses had stimulated his brain. {AUG} · A study reported in the *BMJ* indicated that US abstinence programs did not reduce the incidence of underage or unprotected sex.

SOLVING THE FERMI PARADOX?

The Fermi Paradox has been summed up thus: 'if the age and size of the universe suggest the existence of extraterrestrials, how come we haven't had any contact with the little green men?' Or, more pithily, 'where is everybody?' The paradox is named after the Nobel Prize-winning atomic physicist Enrico Fermi (1901–54), who first posed the question (as well as giving us the *fermi*: a measure equal to 10^{-15}m). In January 2007, Rasmus Bjork, of Copenhagen's Niels Bohr Institute, suggested that the size of space might hold the answer. Bjork calculated that if 64 probes were sent into the alien-friendly 'galactic habitable zone', traveling at 1,000 times the speed of NASA's current Cassini mission, it would still take *c.*10bn years to search just 0·4% of the stars. Bjork held out some hope that radio telescopes might shorten the search, but he explained that until aliens 'can develop an exotic form of transport that gets them across the galaxy in two weeks, it's still going to take millions of years to find us'.

PLANETARY EVENTS 2008

January 3 . . . . Perihelion: Earth is at orbital position closest to Sun
February 7 . . . . .annular solar eclipse: visible from Antarctica, Australia, & NZ
February 21 . . . . .total lunar eclipse: visible from Americas, Europe, & Africa
February 24 . . . . Saturn at opposition: closest approach to Earth
March 20 . . . . .Equinox: Sun passes northward over Equator at 05:48 GMT
June 20 . . . . Solstice: Sun directly above Tropic of Cancer at 23:59 GMT
July 4 . . . . .Aphelion: Earth is at orbital position farthest from Sun
July 9 . . . . Jupiter at opposition
August 1 . . . . .total solar eclipse: visible from Canada, Russia, & China
August 16 . . .partial lunar eclipse: visible from Asia, Europe, Africa, & Australasia
September 13 . . . . .Uranus at opposition
September 22 . . . . .Equinox: Sun passes southward over Equator at 15:44 GMT
December 21 . . . . . .Solstice: Sun directly above Tropic of Capricorn at 12:04 GMT

GEIPAN & ALIEN SIGHTINGS

In February 2007, the French space agency CNES published online its archive of >6,000 eyewitness reports of possible UFO sightings. These sightings have been collected since 1977 by GEIPAN (*Groupe d'études et d'informations sur les phénomènes aérospatiaux non identifiés*), which investigates UFO reports, and attempts to provide plausible scientific explanations. GEIPAN classifies the various sightings thus:

Unidentified	unidentified due to insufficient data	probably identified	conclusively identified
28%	30%	33%	9%

GEIPAN's website includes advice on what to do if you think you see a UFO: 'firstly, ask yourself are you really observing a UFO?' If so, 'write down the details as quickly and accurately as you can', including date, time, and location of sighting; shape, size, and color of object; and any noise it makes.

——————KEY SPACE MISSIONS OF 2007——————

MARS RECONNAISSANCE ORBITER (MRO) · NASA's MRO arrived at Mars on 10 March 2006, with a mission to explore the history of water on the Red Planet, and investigate whether water has been present long enough to have sustained life. A February 2007 report, based on early findings from the most powerful telescopic camera ever sent to Mars, suggested that liquid or gas may previously have flowed through cracks in underground rocks on the planet.

CASSINI-HUYGENS · A joint ESA and NASA project to study Saturn and its moons. Previously only two of Saturn's moons – Titan and Enceladus – were thought to be geologically active. However, in June 2007, new data from Cassini suggested otherwise. Scientists noted that Tethys and Dione were expelling particles into the surrounding atmosphere, indicating that they too were geologically alive.

ROSETTA · Orbiter launched by ESA in March 2004 with the aim of reaching the comet Churyumov-Gerasimenko by 2014. During February 2007, Rosetta performed a 'swingby' of Mars, capturing stunning images of the planet and its moon, Phobos.

THEMIS · A mission composed of 5 satellites launched by NASA in February 2007. The satellites were dispersed around Earth to study the cause of auroras in the atmosphere. By examining the Northern Lights and similar phenomena, scientists hope to learn more about the functioning of Earth's magnetosphere.

STEREO · The international Solar TErrestrial RElations Observatory, launched in October 2006, uses twin satellite observatories to trace energy and matter flowing between the Sun and the Earth. In April 2007, the STEREO team released the first 3D pictures of the Sun which, it is hoped, may improve understanding of solar physics, and allow scientists to learn more about space weather forecasting.

COROT · A French-led satellite mission launched in December 2006 to search for potentially habitable planets. In May 2007, COROT's telescope identified its first new planet, a giant world similar to Jupiter but hotter and at least 1·3 times larger. The massive planet – named Corot-exo-1b – is 1,500 light-years from Earth in the constellation Monoceros.

——NASA's CENTENNIAL CHALLENGES · SPACE GLOVE——

In 2005, NASA set a series of Centennial Challenges in an attempt to encourage innovation in the design of materials for space exploration [see *Schott's Almanac 2007*]. One of the original challenges offered $250,000 to the first person who successfully created a space glove that maximized movement while maintaining protection. In May 2007, Peter Homer, an engineer from Maine, became the first person to win one of NASA's Centennial Challenges, when he was awarded $200,000 for his home-made space glove. Homer used a standard rubber glove as his base, and created the Dacron-coated design on his dining room table. (Homer sourced most of his materials from eBay.) The remaining $50,000 went unclaimed, since there were no takers for the challenge to create a 'mechanical counter-pressure glove'.

———————SOME INVENTIONS OF NOTE · 2006–07———————

{OCT 2006} · A team at Duke University, NC, performed a series of successful tests on a device that creates an 'invisibility cloak'. The gizmo, constructed from 'metamaterial', succeeded in deflecting microwaves around a small copper cylinder and restoring them on the other side – as if they had passed directly through the object. {NOV} · The Italcementi Group developed a titanium dioxide coating for buildings that can destroy smog in the surrounding atmosphere. The coating is being developed into paints, plaster, and other building materials. {DEC} · Toshiba developed plastic 'paper' that can be reused up to 500 times. The technology utilizes heat-sensitive pigments that switch from white to black at one temperature, and from black to white at another, allowing work to be printed and later erased. ❦ Brinker Technology of Aberdeen, Scotland, adapted the principle of blood clotting to develop a system to fix leaking pipes. Small polymer cube blobs are added 'upstream' of a leak, from where they travel to form a temporary fix. {JAN 2007} · Electrolux invented a pair of shoes that 'hoover' while you walk. The Dustmate shoe (or Shoover, as it is more aptly known) has a small rechargeable vacuum engine in its sole, which sucks up dust as you perambulate. {FEB} · 6 blind patients had their eyesight partially restored by a prototype 'bionic eye'. The device, developed at the Californian Doheny Eye Institute, is implanted onto the retina, from where it receives images from a tiny camera mounted onto a pair of glasses. {MAR} · Dutch inventors produced an aerodynamic windproof umbrella that will not turn inside out during gales. An asymmetric design allows the brolly to withstand winds up to gale force 10. ❦ American engineering graduate John Cornwell developed a robotic fridge that can project chilled cans of beer to thirsty drinkers waiting across the room. ❦ The US Army developed vehicles fitted with V-shaped steel undersides to deflect the blast from roadside bombs &c. Tests in Iraq proved the design to be highly effective – after 200 sorties, no soldiers had been killed. ❦ British engineers developed a gadget which could cut the energy consumption of fridges by up to 30%. The 'e-cube' overrides the fridge's thermostat to judge the temperature of the *food* and not the *air* inside a fridge. (The air temperature will temporarily rise whenever the door is opened, forcing normal sensors to activate the cooling mechanism needlessly.) {MAY} · Nokia applied for a US patent for a system that can warn cell phone users when lightning is striking nearby. {JUN} · The US Army developed a remote-controlled robot which could retrieve injured soldiers from the theater of war. The Battlefield Extraction-Assist Robot (BEAR) can lift >135kg while traversing bumpy terrain, and should be ready for field tests in 5 years' time. ❦ Italy's National Research Council developed a pill that expands in the stomach and sates the appetite. It is hoped that this pill, manufactured from hydrogel, could be used to help the obese shed those pounds. {JUL} · Scientists at Southampton University, UK, produced a tiny generator that is powered by natural vibrations alone. The generator could be used in situations where battery replacement is impossible, problematic, or awkward – such as in cardiac pacemakers.

──────────── INTERNATIONAL PATENTS ────────────

The World Intellectual Property Organization received *c.*145,300 applications for international patents in 2006, an increase of 6·4% since 2005. The Patent Cooperation Treaty (PCT) allows inventors to file just one application which provides protection for their invention in a number of countries simultaneously. The industry sectors with the most patents published in 2006 were: telecommunications (10·5%), pharmaceuticals (10·4%), and information technology (10·4%). The countries and companies applying for the most PCT patents in 2006 were:

Most international applications		Companies filing most applications		
Country	*est. 2006 applications*	*Company*	*country*	*applications*
1 .. United States	49,555	Philips Elec. .	Netherlands	2,495
2 .. Japan	26,906	Matsushita	Japan	2,344
3 .. Germany	16,929	Siemens	Germany	1,480
4 .. Republic of Korea	5,935	Nokia	Finland	1,036
5 .. France	5,902	Bosch	Germany	962
6 .. UK	5,045	3M	USA	727

Northeast Asian countries accounted for 25·3% of all PCT patent filings in 2006.

──────────── CELEBRITY PATENTS ────────────

In December 2006, Google released a Patent Search feature that allows users to sift through the *c.*7 million patents registered at the US Patent and Trademark Office, 1790–mid-2006. Fairly quickly, curious users began to search for patents registered by celebrities and, in January 2007, the blog Ironic Sans compiled a list. A selection appears below, along with information provided by the USPTO:

Jamie Lee Curtis · INFANT GARMENT · 'A disposable infant garment' which includes 'moisture-proof pockets' for 'one or more clean-up wipers'.

[Patent 4753647, filed 1987]

Edward Van Halen · MUSICAL INSTRUMENT SUPPORT · 'A supporting device for stringed musical instruments' which permits 'total freedom of the player's hands', allowing for 'new techniques and sounds previously unknown'.

[Patent 4656917, filed 1985]

Marlon Brando · DRUMHEAD TENSIONING DEVICE · Fiendishly complex design for drum tension adjuster.

[Patent 6812392, filed 2002]

Julie Newmar · PANTYHOSE SHAPING BAND FOR CHEEKY DERRIERE RELIEF · 'Pantyhose wherein a panty portion is made of a semielastic fabric'. 'An elastic shaping band is attached to the rear panty portion ... and fits between the wearer's buttocks to delineate the wearer's derriere in cheeky relief'.

[Patent 3914799, filed 1974]

Michael Jackson · METHOD & MEANS FOR CREATING ANTI-GRAVITY ILLUSION · 'A system for allowing a shoe wearer to lean forwardly beyond his center of gravity by virtue of wearing a specially designed pair of shoes' that contain 'a specially designed heel slot'.

[Patent 5255452, filed 1992]

————SCI, TECH, NET WORDS OF NOTE————

SAT TAGS · GPS satellite markers that track the whereabouts of animals (or product shipments) in the wild. *Also* GEOSLAVERY · using technology (such as GPS tracking and biometric scanning) to track the location and activity of workers (or prisoners).

NETROOTS · online grassroots support for a political candidate.

CROWDSOURCING · where companies use the expertise and resources of the online community to solve a problem.

GOOGTUBE · the entity formed by the merger of Google and YouTube.

FLOG · a 'fake blog' run by a company or marketing department posing as a real-life consumer.

FOLKSONOMY · user generated indexes to online content, created by linking descriptive TAGs to content. *Hence* TAGGING · adding descriptive tags to online content to aid searching.

UPGRAGE · 'upgrade rage' experienced by those installing *Windows Vista* &c.

EXERGAMING · the unlikely combination of computer games and exercise.

SITELET *or* MICROSITES · temporary sites dedicated to a niche subject, or set up in response to a particular event.

ZERO WASTE · [1] using sophisticated recycling to minimize or eliminate waste; [2] factoring after-use recycling into the manufacture of a product.

HAFNIUM · a metal used to make nuclear reactors that is expected to revolutionize microchip technology.

INFOMANIA · inability to concentrate on a single task because of interruptions from email, phones, IMs, &c.

GLOBISH · a simplified form of English that uses basic syntax and 1,500 words; codified by Jean-Paul Nerrière, a retired IBM VP, to facilitate communication.

DRM · Digital Rights Management – technology used to control copyrighted digital material, like songs and movies.

WILF · unlikely neologism for aimlessly surfing the net; supposedly from 'What was I Looking For?'.

DDOS · Distributed Denial of Service, where websites are overwhelmed by malicious visits that crash servers, cut bandwidth, and render sites inoperable. In May 2007, Russia was accused of launching a DDOS attack on Estonia.

GREAT FIREWALL OF CHINA · attempt by Beijing to control the internet.

LIFECASTING · web-casting all of one's activities – 24 hours a day.

CYBER-VETTING · using the web to assess the (inter)NET REP(utation) of potential employees/employers/lovers.

BUCCANERD · internet pirates whose booty is copyright films, music, or software. *Yarrrr!*

NERDCORE · a 'hardcore nerd'. *Also* NERD RAPTURE · the ecstasy of 'gadget freaks' when confronted by objects like Apple's iPhone – known as THE GOD MACHINE or THE JESUS PHONE.

MACOLYTE · one who worships at the altar of all things Apple.

SCI, TECH, NET WORDS OF NOTE cont.

PODSLURPING · illicit copying of data to a portable storage device (e.g. iPod).

HACTIVISTS · hacker activists who (ab)use the web as a weapon.

VC² · Viewer-Created Content. *Also* UGC · User-Generated Content.

ECO-ANXIETY · concern over environmental doomsday scenarios, and the damage done by one's carbon footprint.

'meh' · a dismissive online shrug.

NPs · the New Puritans who eschew hedonism, consumerism, &c., to live a simpler, greener, and more ethical life.

BLOGOLA · fees/bribes paid to bloggers.

PAY AS YOU THROW · charging by quantity for rubbish disposal.

TIME SHIFTING · using TiVo, podcasts, &c., to consume media at a time (and location) of one's choosing.

WITRICITY · wireless electricity that could be used to power a laptop over a room-sized distance.

DIGERATI · elite members of online communities and the computer industry; from DIGital litERATI.

NETWORK PROMISCUITY · tendency for users of social networking sites (Facebook, MySpace, Bebo, &c.) – and websites more generally – to spread their membership widely. *Also* FACE vs SPACE · the 'war' between Facebook and MySpace. *Also* FACEHOOKED · an addiction to Facebook. *Also* FACE-BLOCKING · where companies ban their employees access to Facebook &c.

EARCON · a branding 'audio icon'.

SNAKE-OIL SALESMEN · EasyJet's term for unscrupulous carbon-offset traders.

RED RING OF DEATH · flashing red lights on the Xbox 360 console, which indicate a major hardware failure. *Also* BRICKING · because the broken Xbox is as much use as a brick. *Also* COFFINS · the boxes used to return consoles.

MEGANICHE · based on the idea that, because of the sheer scale of the web, even a relatively rococo subject area can attract significant web traffic.

TRIPLE BOTTOM LINE · the aspiration that companies will take into account People, Planet, and Profit when judging the success of a project.

NATURE DEFICIT DISORDER · where kids are strangers to Mother Nature.

MOST HATED WEB WORDS

A June 2007 survey for the Lulu Blooker Prize asked web users the words most likely to make them 'wince, shudder or want to bang your head on the keyboard'.

1	folksonomy†	5	blook	9	cookie
2	blogosphere	6	webinar	10	wiki
3	blog	7	vlog	† Coined by Thomas Vander
4	netiquette	8	social networking	Wal in 2002. [See p.194]

THE WORLD'S WORST SOUND

Professor Trevor Cox, an acoustics expert at Salford University, spent a year researching the world's worst sounds. Cox posted clips of 34 objectionable noises online, which were rated by 1·1m visitors. The sounds voted most unpleasant were:

1 . . . . vomiting	6 . . . . badly played violin
2 . . . . microphone feedback	7 . . . . whoopee cushion
3 . . . . wailing babies	8 . . . . .an argument in a soap opera
4 . . . . train wheels scraping on tracks	9 . . . . the hum of electricity
5 . . . . a squeaky seesaw	10 . . . . a Tasmanian devil

The 2007 survey revealed that men found the sound of babies crying more repellent than women; Professor Cox suggested that – via evolution – women might have become habituated to this sound.

LONG BETS

The Long Bets Foundation, an educational nonprofit dedicated to improving long-term thinking, operates a web site that allows anyone with $50 to post a 'societally or scientifically important' prediction concerning an event at least 2 years into the future. Bets (minimum $200) can be placed on the prediction, and the winner's spoils are donated to a charity of his or her choosing. Some notable bets include:

By 2029 no computer, or 'machine intelligence', will have passed the Turing Test[†]. $20,000

The US men's soccer team will win the World Cup before the Red Sox win the World Series. $2,000

At least one human alive in the year 2000 will still be alive in 2150. $2,000

The first discovery of extraterrestrial life will be some place other than on a planet or on a satellite of a planet. $2,000

In a Google search of five keywords or phrases representing the top five news stories of 2007, weblogs will rank higher than the *New York Times* web site. $2,000

[Source: longbets.org]

† British mathematician Alan Turing devised the Turing Test in 1950 to address the question of whether machines can think. A machine will be said to pass the test when a human conversing with it via a text-only system cannot tell whether their interlocutor is another human or a machine.

ONLINE FEARS

64% of web users avoid some online activities because of security concerns, according to a 2006 Int. Telecommunications Union study. The greatest fears are:

Theft of personal information 26%	Spam 8
Viruses & worms .25	Disturbing content 4
Spyware 19	Being diverted to 'bad sites' 3
Scams & fraud 13	Other 2

—CONSOLE TIMELINE—

'72 . . . . . . .first home console, *Magnavox Odyssey*
'75 . . . . *Atari Pong* launched
'75 . . . improved *Magnavox Odyssey* 100 & 200
'76 . . . . *Atari Super Pong* released
'76 . . .*Coleco Telstar*, first to use AY-3-8500 chip
'76 . . . . .first programmable system – *Channel F*
'77 . . . .*Atari 2600* first to use plug-in cartridges
'77 . . . . .the *Telstar Alpha* launched
'77 . . . .*Odyssey 4000* released; 8 color games
'79 . . . .*Atari 400* released, first 8-bit
'80 . . . . .Mattel's *Intellivision*, first 16-bit
'80 . . . . .Namco released *Pac-Man*
'82 . . . . *Atari 5200* released
'82 . . . *ColecoVision* feat. *Donkey Kong* launched
'82 . . . . *ZX Spectrum* launched in UK
'82 . . . . PC *Commodore 64* entered market
'83 . . . . .Nintendo launched *Famicom*
(later *NES*) in Japan
'85 . . . .*Amiga 1000*, first multimedia PC
'85 . . . *Tetris* first developed to be played on PC
'85/6. Nintendo's *NES* launched in US/Europe
'86 . . . . *Atari 7800* competed with Nintendo
'86 . . . .*Sega Master System* launched
'87 . . . . . . .the first *Final Fantasy* game came out
'89 . . . .*Sega Mega Drive*, first 16-bit console
'89 . . . . .Nintendo *Gameboy*, first handheld
'89 . . . . Atari launched color handheld *Lynx*
'91 . . . . . . Nintendo released *Super NES* in USA
'93 . . . . .Atari's *Jaguar* flopped
'93 . . . . . first first-person shooter *Doom* released
'95 . . . Sega *Saturn* bt *PlayStation* to release first
'95 . . .Sony *PlayStation* launched in US/Europe
'97 . . . .*Nintendo 64* last cartridge-based console
'97 . . . . *PlayStation*'s 20 millionth unit sold
'98 . . . .*Grand Theft Auto* debut
'99 . . . .*Sega Dreamcast*, first internet enabled
'00 . . . . Sony *PlayStation 2* launched & sold out
'00 . . . . .PC game *The Sims* released
'01 . . .Nintendo *GameCube*, interactive gaming
'01 . . . . .Microsoft *XBox*, built-in hard-drive
'01 . . . . .Sega stopped making consoles
'04 . . . . . Nintendo *DS*, handheld with 2 screens
'05 . . . . portable Sony *PSP* launched
'05 . . . . . . Microsoft *Xbox 360*, online capability
'06 . . . . .Sony *PlayStation 3*, HD games
'06 . . . . Nintendo *Wii*, wireless controller

———BEST-SELLING——— VIDEO GAMES

In January 2007, the UK *Independent* compiled a list of the best-selling video game franchises of all time, confirming the market domination of Japanese developers. The top franchises are:

Title	developer	units
Mario	Nintendo	193m
Pokémon	Nintendo	155m
Final Fantasy	Square Enix	68m
Madden NFL	EA	56m
The Sims	Maxis/EA	54m
Grand Theft Auto	Rockstar	50m
Donkey Kong	Nintendo	48m
Legend of Zelda	Nintendo	47m
Sonic the Hedgehog	Sega	44m
Gran Turismo	Sony	44m

Nielsen/NetRatings stated that, in 03/07, 37% of US adults online owned a gaming console.

———VIRTUAL BAD——— DRIVERS

Frequent players of racing video games are more likely to be aggressive drivers, according to a German study published by the *Journal of Experimental Psychology* in March 2007. The research supports the theory that 'media-primers', such as video games, can affect how people react in real life [see p.139]. To win racing games, players are encouraged to break the law (driving on pavements, at high speed, crashing into other gamers, and so on) – thereby linking risk-taking with feelings of exhilaration. The study indicated that these links were particularly strong in young males, who, after playing racing games, reported taking greater risks on the road in real life. It was suggested that those who played virtual racing games less frequently were more cautious drivers.

———WEBBY AWARDS———

Awarded by the International Academy of Digital Arts and Sciences, the Webby Awards reward excellence in web design, innovation, and functionality. Below is a selection of the winners at the 11th annual awards in 2007:

Activism...........*greenpeace.org/apple*
Best homepage................*sony.com*
Best practices................ *flickr.com*
Best writing.........*howstuffworks.com*
Blog – political............ *truthdig.com*
Community..................*flickr.com*
Education ....*howstuffworks.com*
Fashion...................*zoozoom.com*
Humor ....*theonion.com*
Lifestyle .... *bp.com/carbonfootprint*
Magazine.............. *mediastorm.org*
Movies.............. *panslabyrinth.com*
Music...........................*last.fm*
News ....*bbc.co.uk/news*
Newspaper ....*guardian.co.uk*
Politics..................*opensecrets.org*
Sports..........*thereggiebushproject.com*

———NET POPULATION———

747 million people (aged >15) used the internet in January 2007 – according to comScore Networks. Below are the countries with the most internet users:

MILLION INTERNET USERS (≥15)

Country	Jan 06	Jan 07	change
USA	150·9	153·4	+2%
China	72·4	86·8	+20%
Japan	51·5	53·7	+4%
Germany	31·2	32·2	+3%
UK	29·8	30·1	+1%
S Korea	24·3	26·4	+8%
France	23·7	24·6	+4%
India	15·9	21·1	+33%
Canada	18·3	20·4	+11%
Italy	16·0	18·1	+13%
World	676·9	746·9	+10%

———DOMAIN NAMES———

By 2006, 120m Top Level Domain (TLD) names had been registered – 65m of which were .com or .net. Top Level Domain country codes (ccTLD), of which there are >240 globally, also experienced growth, especially in registrations in China (.cn). Below are the ccTLDs with the most registrations:

1	.de	Germany
2	.uk	United Kingdom
3	.eu	European Union
4	.nl	Netherlands
5	.cn	China
6	.it	Italy
7	.ar	Argentina
8	.us	United States
9	.br	Brazil
10	.ch	Switzerland

[Source: VeriSign · Zooknic, 2007]

———WEBLOG AWARDS———

The Weblogs are independent awards, nominated and voted for by the public. Some of the winners in 2007 were:

Best new blog.........*saynotocrack.com*
Group blog...............*lifehacker.com*
Writing...................*waiterrant.net*
Blog design.............*uk.gizmodo.com*
Topical .... *postsecret.blogspot.com*
Best-kept secret . *thepioneerwoman.com*
Humorous....*gofugyourself.typepad.com*
Blog of the year . *postsecret.blogspot.com*

———BLOOKER PRIZE———

The 'Blooker Prizes' reward books that started life as blogs. The top prize (£5,000) in 2007 went to former US soldier Colby Buzzell's wartime account: *My War: Killing Time in Iraq.*

—————————— WEB 2·0 &c. ——————————

'Web 2·0' refers to the perception that the net has shifted from being an information source to a 'participatory web', in which users contribute and collaborate via blogs, wikis, social networking, and other user-focused environments. ('Web 2·0' was apparently coined in 2004 by Dale Dougherty, during a brainstorming session for O'Reilly Media.) Although in some cases enabled by technological progress, Web 2·0 is not a hardware or software development so much as a 'set of principles and practices' that prioritize collective intelligence. As noted by Susannah Fox and Mary Madden in a report for the Pew Internet Project, Web 2·0 replaces 'the authoritative heft of traditional institutions with the surging wisdom of crowds'. A September 2005 essay by Tim O'Reilly attempted to map some of the axiomatic differences between Web 1·0 and Web 2·0 [see right]. ❧ While frequently derided as conceptually (and otherwise) problematic, the ubiquity of the phrase 'Web 2·0' may be taken as a sign of its usefulness. Many offshoots have developed, including: 'Travel 2·0' [traveler 'empowerment' via discussion forums &c. – *USA Today*]; 'Library 2·0' ['user-friendly' information flows at modernized libraries – *Information Today*]; and 'Gaming 3·0' [console games featuring dynamic, user-generated content – *BusinessWeek.com*]. Splendidly, a 2005 *Economist* article expressed fears of a 'Bubble 2·0', whereby an excess of hype, and a paucity of sound business models, could precipitate a second tech bubble, with stock market consequences similar to those seen in the 1990s.

O'Reilly's 'Web 1·0 *vs* Web 2·0'

Web 1·0	*Web 2·0*
Britannica Online	Wikipedia
Personal websites	blogging
Page views	cost per click
Publishing	participation
Content management systems	wikis
Directories	tagging
DoubleClick	Google AdSense
Taxonomy	folksonomy

—————————— CYBERBULLYING ——————————

One in three American teenagers admits to having been bullied while using the internet. Research by the Pew Internet and American Life Project, released in June 2007, indicated that girls were more likely to fall victim of cyberbullying than boys. Respondents were asked if they had experienced any of the following online:

Incident of cyberbullying	♂%	♀%
Someone taking a private email, IM, or text message you sent and forwarding it to someone else, or posting it online so others could see	13	17
Someone sending you a threatening or aggressive email, IM, or text message	10	15
Someone spreading a rumor about you online	9	16
Someone posting an embarrassing picture of you online without your permission	5	7

67% of teens reported that they thought bullying and harassment were more likely to occur offline.

———————————— MALWARE ————————————

MALWARE (MALicious softWARE) is that which is specifically designed to infiltrate and harm computers. The category includes TROJAN HORSES (that contain harmful programs), WORMS (self-replicating programs), VIRUSES (that distribute copies of themselves), and SPYWARE (that surreptitiously collects user data). According to IT security firm Sophos, 30% of all malware is written in China, and 14·2% in Brazil. In 2006, the top ten countries hosting malware on the web were:

Country	%				
USA	34·2	Netherlands	4·7	Germany	1·5
China	31·0	Ukraine	3·2	Hong Kong	1·0
Russia	9·5	France	1·8	Korea	0·9
		Taiwan	1·7	Others	10·5

According to the Sophos 2007 security report, the amount of image spam sent in 2006 increased from 18·5% in January to 35·1% in December. Image spam eschews text in order to escape detection by anti-spam filters. The images are often placed one on top of another to create 'noise' that further complicates the message, and makes each one unique. Despite some efforts to reduce the problem, the US was the worst nation for relaying spam in 2006. The top spamming countries were:

Country	%				
USA	22·0	France	5·4	Italy	3·2
China (inc. HK)	15·9	Spain	5·1	Germany	3·0
South Korea	7·4	Poland	4·5	UK	1·9
		Brazil	3·5	Others	28·0

Named after a section of the penal code in Nigeria where many such scams originate, '419 scams' typically offer large amounts of money in an attempt to extract either confidential information or cash. Disguises used by scammers in 2006 included a 19-year-old who claimed to have discovered a herbal cure for AIDS, and a dying KGB agent claiming to hold the secrets to the JFK assassination.

———————— TOP TEN US SEARCH PROVIDERS ————————

Nielsen tracks the most popular US search providers. The top 10 in May 2007 were:

Provider	searches (million)	% of all searches			
Google	4,033	56·3	Ask.com	142	2·0
Yahoo!	1,541	21·5	MyWeb	62	0·9
MSN/Windows	605	8·4	Comcast	35	0·5
AOL	382	5·3	Earthlink	33	0·5
			BellSouth	30	0·4
			Dogpile.com	26	0·4

Nielsen also revealed the celebrities most frequently searched for in February 2007. The late Anna Nicole Smith attracted 6·2m searches, followed by Britney Spears, with 3·6m. *American Idol* contestant Antonella Barba was the third most popular celebrity search with 2·1m. The most popular celebrity gossip site in February 2007 was reported to be AOL TMZ, with 7·9m unique visitors and 66·2m page views. [Source: Nielsen/NetRatings MegaView Search, June 2007 · Figures are rounded up.]

—————————TOP FLOPS—————————

Flops (FLoating point Operations Per Second) are a unit of computer calculations per second. Home computers generally perform at a rate of gigaflops (billions/sec), while supercomputers are capable of teraflops (trillions/sec). In November 2006, the Pentagon divided *c.*$500m amongst several companies to create a supercomputer capable of a petaflop (quadrillion/sec). By June 2007, IBM launched the world's fastest commercial supercomputer, BlueGene/P, which is capable of operating at petaflop speed. The first BlueGene/P was purchased by the US Dept of Energy. ❦ The TOP500 list ranks the world's fastest computers which, in June 2007, were:

Computer	manufacturer	country	teraflops
BlueGene/L-eServer BlueGene Solution	IBM	USA	280·60
Jaguar – Cray Xt4/XT3	Cray Inc.	USA	101·70
Red Storm – Sandia/Cray Red Storm	Cray Inc.	USA	101·40
BGW eServer BlueGene Solution	IBM	USA	91·29
New York Blue eServer BlueGene Solution	IBM	USA	82·16
ASC Purple eServer pSeries p5	IBM	USA	75·76
eServer BlueGene Solution	IBM	USA	73·03

—————————ONLINE DATING & LIES—————————

The suspicion that the internet provides the perfect forum for embellishment and reinvention was confirmed in February 2007 by research proving that most people lie on their online dating profile. Jeff Hancock at Ithaca's Cornell University took 40 male and 40 female New York singletons and diligently assessed their physiques. Hancock found that nine out of ten participants had lied at least once on their forms – most commonly about their weight. Inevitably, all the woman that lied about their weight claimed to be lighter than they were; in contrast, men were more likely to overstate their height. Fortunately, the fibs were mostly minor and unlikely to be noticed in any face-to-face meetings. The average difference between profile and reality was: 6lbs in weight, ⅓ of an inch in height, and 5 months in age.

—————————INTERNET PENETRATION · WORLDWIDE—————————

Below are the countries with the highest internet penetration rate (i.e. the percentage of a population that is online), according to the latest Internet World Stats figures:

Country	% online			
Iceland	86·3	Denmark	69·2	Only 35 countries or terri-
New Zealand	74·9	Hong Kong	68·2	tories in the world currently
Sweden	74·7	Luxembourg	68·0	have an internet penetration
Portugal	73·8	Switzerland	67·8	rate of >50%. † The Falklands
Australia	70·2	Canada	67·5	had an estimated population
USA	69·6	Norway	67·4	of 2,736 in 2007. [Source:
Falkland Islands†	69·4	Japan	67·1	Internet World Stats, mainly
		Singapore	66·3	2006 figures]

MOST POPULAR WEBSITES

ComScore revealed the most frequently visited websites in the US, in May 2007:

	Unique visitors (000)
Site	
Yahoo! sites	130,526
Time Warner.	122,659
Google sites	120,010
Microsoft sites	113,916
Fox Interactive	82,260
eBay	79,428
Amazon sites	51,567
Ask network	50,068
Wikipedia sites	48,743
NY Times	43,603
Apple Inc.	41,909
Viacom.	40,462
Weather Chnl	38,496
CNET networks.	30,954
Gorilla Nation	29,547
Adobe sites	28,458

L33T SPEAK

'Leet speak' is an internet slang language in which certain letters, usually vowels, are replaced by numbers and symbols to form a code. It was originally developed in the 1980s by hackers, but is now more commonly used in chat rooms and by online gamers. Leet speak has also been used to circumvent filters that bar certain words (e.g. porn has become pr0n). In its most simple form, just four vowels are replaced (A=4, E=3, I=1, O=0), so the word 'leet' becomes l33t. Although leet speak is based on the English language, there are many phrases and words unique to it. According to the BBC, some of the most commonly used leet speak words and phrases are:

Leet	meaning
pwnd	to have been beaten
w00t	used as a term of elation
13wt	treasure; a misspelling of 'loot'
h4x0r	hacker
n00b	newbie
f00	fool
ph33r	fear (e.g. 'Ph33r m3!')
j00	you (e.g. 'j00 d34d f00')
m3	me

Because of its flexibility, a much more sophisticated form of the language – known as 'ultra leet' – has evolved. Ultra leet uses a complete alphabet of numbers and symbols – so, for example, the word 'leet' becomes '1337'. The ultra leet alphabet is:

A	B	C	D	E	F	G	H	I	J	K	L	M	N	O	P	Q	R	S	T	U	V	W	X	Y	Z
4	|3	C	|)	3	|=	6	|-|	!	_\]	|<	1	|V|	|\\|	0	|>	Q	|2	5	7	|_|	V	\\/\\/	><	'/	Z

ECO-FRIENDLY ELECTRONICS

Greenpeace ranked the green credentials of a range of electronics manufacturers in April 2007, rating their recycling policies and the levels of toxicity of their products. Below are the company rankings, along with their scores from 10 (best) to 1 (worst):

Company	score				
Lenovo	8·0	Samsung	6·3	Toshiba	4·3
Nokia	7·3	Motorola	6·3	Sony	4·0
Sony Ericsson	7·0	Fujitsu-Siemens	6·0	LGE	3·6
Dell	7·0	Hewlett-Packard	5·6	Panasonic	3·6
		Acer	5·3	Apple	2·7

STN SIGNIFICA

Some (in)significa(nt) Sci, Tech, Net footnotes to the year. ❧ Princeton announced the closure of its ESP lab, the Princeton Engineering Anomalies Research laboratory, after 28 years. The lab claimed modest results but suffered a degree of ridicule. ❧ The history department at Middlebury College, Vermont, became one of many colleges to ban students from using Wikipedia as a reference source. ❧ The Chinese government forced online gaming companies to install anti-addiction software, limiting those under 18 to just three consecutive hours of play per day. ❧ Google banned ads for websites that provide essay, dissertation, and thesis-writing services. Google also blacklisted sites with 'unacceptable content' – such as advertising for weapons, prostitution, drugs, tobacco, and 'miracle cures'. ❧ >200 schools, across 10 states, adopted the video game *Dance Dance Revolution* as a regular element of physical education. In the game, children follow on-screen dance instructions, mimicking movements on special mats to score points. 'Physical video games' such as this are deemed to be more inclusive than skills-based team sports, and are increasingly perceived as a useful tool in the battle against childhood obesity. ❧ The Maldives became the first country to open an embassy in *Second Life*. Later, Kan Suzuki became the first Japanese politician to open an office in the virtual world. ❧ According to Screen Digest, the market value of MMOGs (Massively Multiplayer Online Games) reached $1bn outside Asia; *World of Warcraft* was the most popular subscription game, accounting for 54% of the market [see p.316]. ❧ Sony apologized to Church of England

officials after Manchester Cathedral was featured in the video game *Resistance: Fall of Man*. The offending scene used the cathedral as the site of a bloody shoot-out between a US soldier and a fright of aliens. ❧ Research by the School of Information Sciences at UC Berkeley indicated a social divide between the users of Facebook and MySpace. Members of Facebook tended to come from wealthier homes and were more likely to have attended college than those who joined MySpace. ❧ Human rights organization Privacy International published a ranking of web companies' handling of personal data. Google ranked worst for privacy, because of the large quantity of user data it compiles, and the absence of a coherent privacy policy. ❧ Research by the Pew Internet and American Life Project indicated that Wikipedia is most popular amongst the highly educated. 50% of those who consult the site were college graduates, compared to 22% who had only a high school diploma. ❧ The Electronic Sports World Cup grand final was held in Paris in July 2007. >750 gamers qualified from around the world to compete in games such as *Quake 4*, *Warcraft 3*, and *Pro Evolution Soccer 4*. The prize money totaled $200,000. ❧ Research by WebFetch revealed significant variances in results from different search engines, indicating the limitations of relying on one search engine alone. Comparing Google, Yahoo!, MSN, and Ask, WebFetch found only 0·6% of 776,435 first-page search results were the same across the 4 search engines. ❧ MySpace announced that it had discovered and deleted the online profiles of >29,000 convicted sex offenders.

———————————— SI PREFIXES ————————————

Below are the SI prefixes and symbols for the decimal multiples and submultiples of SI Units from 10^{24} to 10^{-24}.

10^{24}	yotta	Y	1 000 000 000 000 000 000 000 000
10^{21}	zetta	Z	1 000 000 000 000 000 000 000
10^{18}	exa	E	1 000 000 000 000 000 000
10^{15}	peta	P	1 000 000 000 000 000
10^{12}	tera	T	1 000 000 000 000
10^{9}	giga	G	1 000 000 000
10^{6}	mega	M	1 000 000
10^{3}	kilo	k	1 000
10^{2}	hecto	h	100
10	deca	da	10
1			1
10^{-1}	deci	d	0.1
10^{-2}	centi	c	0.01
10^{-3}	milli	m	0.001
10^{-6}	micro		0.000 001
10^{-9}	nano	n	0.000 000 001
10^{-12}	pico	p	0.000 000 000 001
10^{-15}	femto	f	0.000 000 000 000 001
10^{-18}	atto	a	0.000 000 000 000 000 001
10^{-21}	zepto	z	0.000 000 000 000 000 000 001
10^{-24}	yocto	y	0.000 000 000 000 000 000 000 001

———————— SOME USEFUL CONVERSIONS ————————

A	A to B multiply by	B to A multiply by	B
inches	25.4	0.0397	millimeters
inches	2.54	0.3937	centimeters
feet	0.3048	3.2808	meters
yards	0.9144	1.0936	meters
miles	1.6093	0.6214	kilometers
acres	0.4047	2.471	hectares
square feet	0.0929	10.76	square meters
square miles	2.5899	0.3861	square kilometers
UK pints	0.5682	1.7598	liters
UK gallons	4.546	0.2199	liters
cubic inches	16.39	0.0610	cubic centimeters
ounces	28.35	0.0353	grams
pounds	0.4536	2.2046	kilograms
stones	6.35	0.157	kilograms
miles/gallon	0.3539	2.825	kilometers/liter
miles/US gallon	0.4250	2.353	kilometers/liter
miles/hour	1.609	0.6117	kilometers/hour

—— °C – °F ——

°C	°F		
		49	120.2
100	212	48	118.4
99	210.2	47	116.6
98	208.4	46	114.8
97	206.6	45	113
96	204.8	44	111.2
95	203	43	109.4
94	201.2	42	107.6
93	199.4	41	105.8
92	197.6	40	104
91	195.8	39	102.2
90	194	38	100.4
89	192.2	37	98.6
88	190.4	36	96.8
87	188.6	35	95
86	186.8	34	93.2
85	185	33	91.4
84	183.2	32	89.6
83	181.4	31	87.8
82	179.6	30	86
81	177.8	29	84.2
80	176	28	82.4
79	174.2	27	80.6
78	172.4	26	78.8
77	170.6	25	77
76	168.8	24	75.2
75	167	23	73.4
74	165.2	22	71.6
73	163.4	21	69.8
72	161.6	20	68
71	159.8	19	66.2
70	158	18	64.4
69	156.2	17	62.6
68	154.4	16	60.8
67	152.6	15	59
66	150.8	14	57.2
65	149	13	55.4
64	147.2	12	53.6
63	145.4	11	51.8
62	143.6	10	50
61	141.8	9	48.2
60	140	8	46.4
59	138.2	7	44.6
58	136.4	6	42.8
57	134.6	5	41
56	132.8	4	39.2
55	131	3	37.4
54	129.2	2	35.6
53	127.4	1	33.8
52	125.6	0	32
51	123.8	-1	30.2
50	122	-2	28.4

Normal body temp.
= 98.6°F (37°C)
range 97.7–98.9°F
(36.1–37.2°C)

Travel & Leisure

One half of the world cannot understand the pleasures of the other.
— JANE AUSTEN (1775–1817)

PASSPORTS

In 2007, the US government made it significantly more difficult for its citizens to travel abroad without carrying a passport. On January 23, 2007, Phase 1 of the Western Hemisphere Travel Initiative [WHTI] came into force, requiring all US citizens (with certain exceptions) returning by air from anywhere in the western hemisphere to present a passport for readmission into the US. According to the State Dept, the WHTI regulations were designed to improve national security by reducing the number of different documents accepted at US borders. Yet, many Americans habituated to traveling with only their driver's license or birth certificate were caught off guard by these new rules, and a spike in passport applications led to processing times of >10 weeks, long waits in line, and growing frustration. Faced with possible mutiny by delayed summer travelers, the government announced on June 7, 2007, a temporary respite, allowing citizens without a passport to return to the US provided they could show official proof of a pending passport application. At the time of writing, this provision was set to expire September 30, 2007. By summer 2009, Phase 2 of the WHTI is set to take effect, requiring all US citizens entering the country by sea or land to have a passport. Once Phase 2 is complete, most Americans will need a passport to re-enter the country from anywhere in the world. ❦ In all, the State Dept expected to issue 17m passports in 2007 (>5m from 2006). Earlier rates of US passport issue are charted below:

The US passport itself had a makeover in 2007. By July, all passport applicants received the new 'e-Passport', featuring a computer chip embedded in the back cover. The chip stores a digital version of the passport's data and photograph, supposedly allowing for biometric comparison using face-recognition technology. The passports have also been redesigned, and are now decorated with a panoply of engraved 'American icons', such as the bald eagle [see p.256], as well as 13 'inspirational quotes'.

———————————————— CARS & DRIVING ————————————————

CARS PER HOUSEHOLD

9% *of US households own* .... 0 vehicles
33............................. 1 vehicle
38............................. 2 vehicles
20............................. ≥3 vehicles

[Source: US Census Bureau, 2005 data]

TOP CAR COLORS

*Percent of US vehicles manufactured
in 2006 in the following colors:*

Silver 19%
White.............................. 16
Gray 13
Black.............................. 13
Blue............................... 11
Red 11
Light brown 7
Green 4
White pearl......................... 3
Yellow/gold......................... 3

[Source: DuPont] Silver has been the top
color for cars around the world since 2000,
when it overtook green. According to DuPont,
some experts say silver signals optimism.

TOP CAR NICKNAMES

*The most popular car nicknames
from a 2006 AP/AOL Autos poll:*

Betsey/Old Betsy................... 8%
Blue (or any variation)............. 5
Baby (or any variation) 3
Nelly/Nellie 2
Bessie (incl. Grandma Bessie) 2
Big Red (or any Red) 2
Suzie/Susie 1
Ghost (or any variation) 1

[Source: AP/AOL Autos. 21% of Americans
admitted to giving their car a nickname.]

Max speed limit (mph)		Drivers per 1,000 pop.[†]
70	Alabama	798
65	Alaska	733
75	Arizona	664
70	Arkansas	728
70	California	634
75	Colorado	716
65	Connecticut	781
65	Delaware	724
55	DC	600
70	Florida	752
70	Georgia	655
60	Hawaii	671
75	Idaho	685
65	Illinois	617
70	Indiana	677
70	Iowa	685
70	Kansas	719
65	Kentucky	685
70	Louisiana	682
65	Maine	760
65	Maryland	662
65	Massachusetts	721
70	Michigan	702
70	Minnesota	601
70	Mississippi	673
70	Missouri	713
75	Montana	765
75	Nebraska	751
75	Nevada	661
65	New Hampshire	762
65	New Jersey	673
75	New Mexico	677
65	New York	575
70	North Carolina	717
75	North Dakota	733
65	Ohio	672
75	Oklahoma	630
65	Oregon	740
65	Pennsylvania	681
65	Rhode Island	694
70	South Carolina	702
75	South Dakota	730
70	Tennessee	730
75	Texas	641
75	Utah	648
65	Vermont	904
65	Virginia	684
70	Washington	745
70	West Virginia	731
65	Wisconsin	721
75	Wyoming	752

† Resident pop. [Source: NHTSA, 2006]

ROAD RAGE

The term 'road rage' appears to have been coined by the press in the 1980s, and gained attention as an 'epidemic' during the 1990s. The *Oxford English Dictionary* defines the phenomenon as 'violent anger attributed to the stress and frustration of driving a motor vehicle'[†]. However, the National Highway Traffic Safety Administration defines the phenomenon rather more narrowly as 'an assault with a motor vehicle or other dangerous weapon' inflicted by a driver or passenger against another driver or passenger and caused by an incident on the road. 23% of respondents in a Nationwide Mutual Insurance poll admitted to experiencing road rage, with Southerners having the highest rate (26%), followed by Northeasterners (25%), and Westerners (21%). A 2007 AutoVantage auto club survey on driver courtesy found that the following US cities displayed the most and least road rage:

Least courteous cities – most road rage	*Most courteous cities – least road rage*
Miami · New York · Boston	Portland, OR · Pittsburgh · Seattle
Los Angeles · Washington, DC	St Louis · Dallas/Ft Worth

The Texas Department of Public Safety offers these tips for dealing with road rage:

Road rage 'red flags'	*If confronted by a 'road rager'*
running stop signs and red lights · speeding, tailgating, and weaving between lanes · passing on the right of a vehicle · making inappropriate hand & facial gestures	attempt to stay out of the driver's way · do not challenge an aggressive driver · always wear your seat belt · avoid eye contact · ignore gestures & refuse to return them

† A 1998 *Atlantic Monthly* article claimed the term stems from 'roid rage': outbursts by steroid abusers.

DRIVING WHILE DISTRACTED

'Driver distraction' caused by cell phones, eating, grooming, and other activities contributes to *c.*25% of all police-reported crashes, according to National Highway Traffic Safety Administration estimates. A 2006 Nationwide Mutual Insurance survey asked adult drivers to report some of the things they do behind the wheel:

Drivers who ...	%		
Talk on cell phones	73	Fix hair, send texts[†] or IMs	19
Use drive-in services once a week	62	Drive at or below the speed limit	16
Forget driving a certain distance	38	Comfort/discipline children	14
Daydream	31	Hold a pet in their lap	8
Experience road rage	23	Drive while drunk [see p.211]	5
		Drive with open alcohol container	4

Drivers also admitted to: changing seats with passengers, reading a book, watching a movie, writing a grocery list, nursing a baby, and putting in contact lenses. [Source: Nationwide Mutual Insurance survey conducted by MarketVision Research.] † According to the *Wall Street Journal*, Arizona, Oregon, and Washington state are all considering bills against 'driving while texting' – aka DWT.

WORLDWIDE ROAD DEATHS

Road deaths/million pop.		
USA 145	Korea 132	Germany 65
Greece 145	New Zealand 99	Japan 62
Poland 143	France 88	UK 55
	Ireland 83	Netherlands 46

[Source: OECD, 2005 figures]

US TRANSPORTATION DEATHS & INJURIES

Method of transport	deaths in 2005	Method of transport	injured in 2005
Highway	43,443	Highway†	2,675,000
Recreational boating	697	Railroad	8,116
General aviation†	562	Recreational boating	3,451
Railroad	535	General aviation	270
Transit (train accidents &c.)	183	On-demand air taxi	23
Large air-carrier†	22	Large air-carrier	13
On-demand air taxi†	18		

† Preliminary data [Source: DOT, 2007]

WORST ROADS

In 2006, the transportation research group TRIP discovered that poor road surface conditions cost the average urban motorist $383 each year in additional vehicle maintenance, fuel consumption, &c. Below are the big cities with the worst roads:

City	*% of roads in poor condition*
San Jose	66
Los Angeles	65
San Francisco/Oakland	58
Kansas City	58
New Orleans	56

['Big city' was defined as pop. >500,000;
New Orleans ranking is pre-Katrina.]

SCHOOL BUS INJURIES

A 2006 *Pediatrics* study found that 17,000 children and teenagers per year were injured riding a school bus in the years 2001–03†. Below are the average annual number of injuries, and the rates per 100,000 population, for various groups:

Group	no. injured	rate/100k
♂	8,326	20·1
♀	8,707	22·1
0–4 years old	702	–‡
5–9	4,654	23·3
10–14	7,316	34·7
15–19	4,361	21·4

‡ Insufficient number of cases

Most school bus-related injuries occurred in September/October (31·5%), followed by March/April (21·4%). Most injuries were strains or sprains (33·4%), and the head was the body part most frequently injured (29·5%). † Figures represent injuries treated in hospital emergency departments.

─────────── ON COMMUTING ───────────

The average commute time in the US rose from 24.7 minutes in 2004, to 25.1 minutes in 2005, according to the latest figures from the US Census Bureau. Commuters in the Philadelphia suburb of Vineland, NJ, had the worst average commute, at 39.6 minutes, followed by commuters in New York City, who spent an average of 34.2 minutes getting to work. Further data on commuting are below:

Method of commuting	%	Average daily commute	%
Driving alone 77.0		<10 minutes	14.7
Carpooling..........................10.7		10–14	14.3
2-person carpool.................8.3		15–19	15.5
3-person carpool.................1.4		20–24	14.5
≥4-person carpool 1.0		25–29	6.1
Public transportation 4.7		30–34	13.2
Walking 2.5		35–44	6.4
Taxi, motorcycle, or other means... 1.2		45–59	7.5
Bicycling 0.4		≥60	7.9

[3.6% said they worked from home.] The word 'commute' also means 'to make less severe'. In an April 2006 *New Yorker* article, Nick Paumgarten wrote that the term 'commuter' stems from the commuted (reduced price) train tickets issued in the 1840s. Thus, 'the commuted became commuters'.

─────────── STRESS RELIEF FOR COMMUTERS ───────────

Tactics for dealing with the stresses and strains of the daily commute were explored by British researchers at Nottingham Trent University. The 2007 study revealed that the problems which most vexed commuters were: lack of space, loud music, delays, and obnoxious smells. Researchers also identified the following coping strategies:

1 .... singing or talking to yourself		6 .... listen to audio book or music	
2 .... planning the day ahead		7 ....chew gum, snack, or chat	
3 .. working on laptop, writing, reading		8 ....smoke, or drink alcohol	
4 .... emotion-focused coping†		9 ....meditate or pray	
5 ....seek counseling		† Vent anger or look at attractive commuters	

─────────── WORST DRIVERS ───────────

New Yorkers are the worst drivers in the country, according to a 2007 GMAC Insurance National Drivers Test, which asked drivers around the US to take a 20-question version of a standard DMV exam. New Yorkers scored just 71%, compared with a national average of 77%, and had the highest rate of failure, 36%. Drivers in New Jersey, Washington DC, Massachusetts, and Rhode Island also performed poorly, while those in Idaho, Arkansas, and Minnesota scored high marks. Overall, drivers had the most trouble identifying the proper following distance (2 seconds) and the correct response to a steady yellow traffic light (stop if it is safe to do so).

—————————SUBWAYS OF THE WORLD—————————

System	est. annual ridership	no. stations	single fare	single fare US$
Tokyo Subway	2·9bn	282	160–300¥	$1·30–2·5
Moscow Metro	2·6bn	172	17 rubles	65¢
NYC Subway	1·5bn	468	$2	$2
Seoul Metropolitan Subway	1·5bn	263	900 won	96¢
Mexico City Metro	1·4bn	175	2 pesos	20¢
Paris Metro	1·4bn	380	€1·40	$1·9
London Underground	976m	275	£4·00	$8
Osaka Municipal Subway	880m	123	≥200¥	≥$1·6
Hong Kong MTR	867m	53	$4–26	50¢–$3·32
St Petersburg Metro	810m	58	14 rubles	54¢

[Sources: NYC MTA, Hong Kong MTR, Transport for London, City of St Petersburg, Virgin Atlantic, &c. All currency conversions are approximate guides and current at the time of writing.]

—————————— PUBLIC TRANSPORTATION——————————

North Americans made 10·1 billion journeys on local public transportation in 2006, a 2·9% increase on 2005. Below are the number of journeys made on various modes of public transport in 2006, along with the percentage change from 2005:

Mode	est. 2006 trips	% change
Heavy rail	2·8bn	+4·1
Light rail	382m	+5·6
Commuter rail	435m	+3·2
Trolleybus	102m	−3·1
Bus	6·0bn	+2·3
Demand response	122m	+2·9
Other	116m	+1·8

Heavy rail – subways &c. · *Light rail* – streetcars & trolleys · *Demand response* – dial-a-ride systems, such as those serving the disabled · *Other* – ferries, monorail, cable cars, vanpool, &c. [Source: APTA]

—————————— MOST TRANSIT RIDERS——————————

The regions with the most transit riders, according to the Dept of Transportation:

Metro region	2004 trips	% bus	% rail	% lt rail	% cmtr rail	other
New York/Newark	3·3bn	37·8	54·1	0·3	7·0	0·8
Los Angeles	606m	86·8	5·1	5·4	1·6	1·1
Chicago	582m	56·2	30·7	0·0	12·2	0·9
Washington, DC	442m	42·2	56·6	0·0	0·8	0·4
Boston	396m	30·6	39·8	17·8	10·1	1·7
Philadelphia	350m	55·7	27·7	7·2	8·7	0·7
Miami	151m	80·1	10·3	0·0	1·9	7·7
Houston	95m	91·7	0·0	5·6	0·0	2·7
Dallas/Fort Worth	85m	76·1	0·0	19·1	2·5	2·3
Detroit	45m	95·8	0·0	0·0	0·0	4·2

———————————— DRUNK DRIVING ————————————

Alcohol was involved in 39% of fatal crashes and 7% of all crashes in 2005, according to the National Highway Traffic Safety Administration. One person died from an alcohol-related crash for every 31 minutes of 2005, and one injury occurred every 2 minutes. Below are data on the deaths from alcohol-related[†] accidents in 2005:

Car occupants killed	14,370	– in multiple-car crashes	234
– in 1-car crashes	9,016	*Bicyclists* killed	281
– in 2-car crashes	4,449	– in 1-car crashes	268
– in >2-car crashes	905	– in multiple-car crashes	14
Pedestrians killed	2,180	*Others/unknown*	54
– in 1-car crashes	1,946	Total deaths	16,885

An estimated 13% of those aged ≥12 drove under the influence of alcohol at least once in 2005, according to data from SAMSHA's *National Survey on Drug Use and Health*. Not surprisingly, the likelihood of doing so is strongly associated with age:

Age	*% driving drunk[‡]*				
16–17	8.3	30–34	17.4	55–59	8.6
18–20	19.8	35–39	16.7	60–64	4.9
21–25	27.9	40–44	16.9	≥65	2.9
26–29	22.6	45–49	13.8	‡ Drove under the influence	
		50–54	12.8	of alcohol ≥ once in 2005	

[Sources: BOT, 2006 & SAMSHA 2005] † Crashes are considered to be alcohol-related if at least one person involved is determined to have had a blood alcohol concentration of ≥0·01 grams per deciliter.

———————————— FIELD SOBRIETY TESTS ————————————

The National Highway Traffic Safety Administration recommends police administer 3 'Standardized Field Sobriety Tests' to assess whether individuals are under the influence or drugs or drink. Failure of all three tests has been shown to correlate highly with a Blood Alcohol Concentration over the limit: 0·08g/1,000 milliliters.

WALK-AND-TURN · suspect is asked to take 9 steps heel-to-toe on a line, turn on one foot, and return in the same manner. Using arms to balance, taking an incorrect number of steps, beginning before instructions are finished, &c., are considered signs of impairment.

ONE-LEG STAND · suspect is asked to stand with one foot 6 inches above the ground and count aloud in thousands. Signs of impairment include swaying, hopping, or putting one's foot down.

HORIZONTAL GAZE NYSTAGMUS · nystagmus is an involuntary jerking of the eyes that is exaggerated by alcohol. The suspect is asked to track a slowly moving object (such as a pen or flashlight) with each eye; police watch the angle at which the jerking begins, the type of jerking when the eye is as far to one side as possible, and whether the eye is able to smoothly trace the object. Displaying four signs of impairment between the two eyes is highly correlated with a BAC >0·08.

——THE VATICAN'S 10 COMMANDMENTS OF DRIVING——

In June 2007, the Vatican's Pontifical Council for the Pastoral Care of Migrants and Itinerant People released a 36-page document entitled *Guidelines for the Pastoral Care of the Road*. While the guide noted the benefits and opportunities of driving (visiting the sick, for example), it also warned against the 'psychological regression' that cars can produce, and offered the following ten 'driving commandments':

1	*you shall not kill*
2	*the road shall be a means of communion between people and not of mortal harm*
3	*courtesy, uprightness, and prudence will help you deal with unforeseen events*
4	*be charitable and help your neighbor in need, especially victims of accidents*
5	*cars shall not be an expression of power and domination, or an occasion of sin†*
6	*charitably convince the young and not so young not to drive when they are not in a fitting condition to do so*
7	*support the families of accident victims*
8	*bring guilty motorists and their victims together, at the appropriate time, so that they can undergo the liberating experience of forgiveness*
9	*on the road, protect the more vulnerable party*
10	*feel responsible toward others*

† According to Reuters, when asked at a news conference to explain how a car could become an occasion of sin, Cardinal Renato Martino replied, 'when a car is used as a place for sin'. ❦ On June 6, a German man showing 'signs of imbalance' caused a brief scare by jumping onto the 'Popemobile' during a St Peter's Square procession. The Pope was unharmed, and in fact did not appear to notice.

——————CARBON OFFSETS——————

In recent years, environmental groups have begun selling 'carbon offsets' to individuals or companies who wish to 'neutralize' their production of carbon dioxide. These groups calculate how much CO_2 a particular activity (e.g. a flight) will create, and sell credits to reduce CO_2 emissions or increase CO_2 absorption by the same amount elsewhere in the world. Generally, credits serve as contributions to environmental projects such as wind farms, solar installations, or tree-planting initiatives. By offsetting the emission of CO_2 in this way, polluting activities are said to become 'carbon neutral'. Although carbon offset programs have been criticized as inconsistent, subject to fraud, and a distraction from the real issues of climate change, the idea has an increasing number of adherents, including the Super Bowl† and the World Bank. The idea has become particularly popular in air travel. Below are sample round-trip flights, the amount of carbon they are said to produce, and the cost of their offsets, according to the Portland, OR, nonprofit Climate Trust:

Tons CO_2	Flight	cost to offset $			
0·73	Chicago–New York	8·76	1·82	Los Angeles–New York	21·84
			3·82	Los Angeles–Tokyo	45·84
			2·18	New York–London	26·16

† The Super Bowl compensated for its emissions by buying offsets and planting hundreds of trees.

AIR TRAVEL

US airlines operated 10·5m flights in 2006, carrying 744·4m passengers, according to the Bureau of Transportation Statistics. The number of domestic flights fell by 3·3% from 2005, while international flights increased by 3·1%. Passengers lodged 8,321 complaints with the airlines, most (2,162) regarding flight problems – only 75% of flights were on time. Further statistics on 2006 US airline travel:

BUSIEST AIRPORTS		AVERAGE FARES	
Airport	*million passengers†*	*Airport*	*average fare‡*
Atlanta	40·7	Atlanta	$399·8
Chicago O'Hare	34·4	Chicago O'Hare	$374·6
Dallas/Fort Worth	28·2	Dallas/Fort Worth	$421·1
Los Angeles International	23·1	Los Angeles International	$433·2
Denver	22·4	Denver	$365·5

† Passengers boarding domestic & intnl flights   ‡ 4Q 2006 domestic fares for busiest airports

MOST DELAYED		MOST LOST LUGGAGE	
Airlines with the lowest percentage of on-time flights in 2006		*Airlines with the most reports of lost luggage, as reports per 1,000 passengers*	
Atlantic Southeast	66·0% *on-time*	Atlantic Southeast Airlines	17·4
ATA Airlines	69·4%	American Eagle Airlines	14·4
American Eagle Airlines	71·5%	Comair	12·0
JetBlue Airways	72·9%	Mesa Airlines	10·6
Alaska Airlines Inc.	73·3%	Skywest Airlines	10·2

[Source for all figures: Dept of Transportation Bureau of Transportation Statistics, 2006]

AIRLINE PASSENGER BILL OF RIGHTS

On February 17, 2007, Senators Barbara Boxer of California and Olympia Snowe of Maine introduced the *Airline Passenger Bill of Rights Act of 2007*. If passed, the Bill would require airlines to allow passengers to deplane after three hours on the tarmac, and provide adequate food, water, and restroom access during delays. The Bill's introduction followed grim incidents in New York, where a Valentine's Day storm trapped hundreds of JetBlue passengers in planes for up to 11 hours, and Texas, where *c*.5,000 passengers were stranded on the tarmac for up to 8 hours. In both cities, some passengers lacked food, water, and working restrooms. In late February, JetBlue introduced its own 'Customer Bill of Rights', yet some expressed skepticism about the industry's ability to police itself. (Previous passenger rights proposals were rejected by Congress in 1999 after airlines vowed to self-regulate. Yet the industry's voluntary code requires only 'reasonable efforts' to provide food and water and includes no limit on time spent waiting in the aircraft.) At the time of writing, the 2007 Bill was under scrutiny by the Senate Commerce, Science, and Transportation Committee. [Sources: *WSJ*; *USA Today*; JetBlue.com; *MSN Travel*]

─────────────SLEEPING IN AIRPORTS─────────────

In 1996, Canadian Donna McSherry created *The Budget Traveler's Guide to Sleeping in Airports* [sleepinginairports.net], based on her experiences as a fiscally challenged young person. Since then, thousands have contributed tips, tricks, and airport reviews, providing fodder for McSherry's periodic best and worst airport awards. Below are the site's five best and worst airports in which to sleep, as of May 2007:

BEST ('Golden Pillow Award')	WORST ('Poopy Airport Award')
Singapore Changi Airport	*Jackson Airport (Papua New Guinea)*
Amsterdam Airport Schiphol	*Mumbai Airport*
Athens International Airport	*Cairo International Airport*
Auckland International Airport	*O'Hare International Airport (Chicago)*
Helsinki-Vantaa (Finland)	*Indira Gandhi Intl Airport (Delhi)*

Some of the many tips on sleepinginairports.net: always have a backup plan; bring an emergency airport survival kit including an inflatable pool raft, toilet paper, and Post-it notes (if traveling solo, write the time you need to be awake on a note and stick it to yourself); always act innocent; dress in layers; arrival lounges tend to be more comfortable than departure lounges; if someone puts out their hand asking for a bribe, thank them, smile, then shake their hand – or pretend to speak Klingon.

─────────────ON HOTELS─────────────

4,402,466 rooms were available in 47,590 'lodging properties' in the US in 2005, according to the most recent figures from the American Hotel & Lodging Association. The average occupancy rate was 63·1%, and the average room cost $90·88. Below is a breakdown of lodging properties by location, size, and cost in 2005:

Lodging location	*no. of properties*
Suburban	15,853
Small metro/town	14,613
Highway	6,761
Urban	4,595
Resort	3,835
Airport	1,933

Lodging size	*no. of properties*
<75 rooms	27,416
75–149 rooms	14,432
150–299 rooms	4,182
300–500 rooms	1,062
>500 rooms	498

Room rate	*no. of properties*
<$30	857
$30–$44.99	7,518
$45–$59.99	10,850
$60–$85	16,562
>$85	11,803

[Source: Smith Travel Research]

Men aged 35–54 account for most business hotel use, while couples aged 35–54 account for the most leisure use, according to research by DK Shifflet & Assocs. The average business traveler pays $99 a night, while the average vacationer pays $94 per night. Both business and leisure travelers usually stay only a single night, although business travelers are somewhat more likely to stay for 3 or more nights. ❦ According to *Forbes*, the most expensive hotel room in the US is the penthouse at the Setai in Miami, which costs $25,000 a night and comes with its own butler.

———————TO-FROM TOURISM FIGURES · 2006———————

US visiting	% change 2005	to or from	% change 2005	visiting US
13·0m	+4	Europe	−1·6	10·1m
5·8m	+7	Caribbean	+6	1·2m
5·7m	+1	Mexico	+6	13·4m
5·2m	+8	Asia	−1	6·2m
3·9m	−1	Canada	+8	16·0m
2·4m	+3	Central America	0	0·7m
2·3m	+6	South America	+6	1·9m
0·8m	+6	Oceania	+3	0·8m
0·5m	−14	Middle East	+5	0·6m
0·2m	−18	Africa	0	0·3m

[Source: US Dept of Commerce, International Trade Admin. Mexico data is preliminary and subject to revision. 'US visiting' data are for air traffic only, while 'visiting US' data are both air and ground.]

———————————— US TRAVELER PROFILE ————————————

Below is a snapshot of US residents who traveled outside North America in 2005:

REGION OF RESIDENCE	%
Middle Atlantic	29
Pacific	23
South Atlantic	15
East North Central	10
New England	7
West South Central	7
West North Central	2
East South Central	2
Mountain	4

PURPOSE OF TRIP	%
Leisure/recreation/holidays	57
Visiting friends/relatives	45
Business	25
Study/teaching	5
Convention/conference	3
Religion/pilgrimage	2

TRAVEL COMPANIONS	%
Traveling alone	40
Spouse	29
Family/relatives	25
Friends	12
Business associates	5
Tour group	3

ACCOMMODATION	%
Hotel/motel	64
Private home	44
Other	6

TRAVELER CHARACTERISTICS	%
Visiting 1 country	81
Visiting 2 countries	13
Visiting ≥3 countries	7
First trip ever outside US	6
Repeat visitor	94
Avg. nights outside US	16·4 *nights*
Avg. intl. trips, past year	2·7 *trips*
Avg. intl. trips, past 5 years	10·7 *trips*

TOP ACTIVITIES	%
Dining in restaurants	84
Shopping	76
Visiting historical places	53
Visiting small towns/villages	44
Sightseeing in cities	43
Touring the countryside	35

[Source: Office of Travel & Tourism Industries In-Flight Survey, 2006. Latest data available. Some questions allowed multiple answers.]

HUNTING & FISHING

More than 87m US residents 16 or older participated in wildlife-related recreation in 2006, according to the US Fish & Wildlife Service. Over the course of the year, wildlife recreation-related spending amounted to $120bn, or 1% of the US's GDP.

Hunting
National participation 5%
Number of hunters .... 12·5m
– big game......................10·7m
– small game......................4·8m
– migratory birds..................2·3m
– other animals....................1·1m
Average days spent hunting.........18
Total 2006 expenditure....... $22·7bn

Fishing
National participation 13%
Number of anglers.............. 29·9m
– freshwater ....26·4m
– saltwater.........................7·7m
Average days spent angling 17
Total 2006 expenditure....... $40·6bn
[Source: US FWS, 2006 National Survey of Fishing, Hunting, &c., preliminary findings]

MOST-VISITED NATIONAL PARKS · 2006

Great Smoky Mtns.... 9,289,215 *visits*
Grand Canyon.............. 4,279,439
Yosemite.................... 3,242,644
Yellowstone................. 2,870,295
Olympic.................... 2,749,197

Rocky Mountain............ 2,743,676
Zion 2,567,350
Cuyahoga Valley 2,468,816
Grand Teton................. 2,406,476
Acadia 2,083,588

PORTABLE LAVATORY REQUIREMENTS

Stanford's Event and Labor Services department has calculated the number of portable toilets required for events of different sizes and duration. The department does warn: 'consider other factors such as whether food and beverages are being served'.

People/duration	1hr	2hrs	3hrs	4hrs	5hrs	6hrs	7hrs	8hrs	9hrs	10hrs
0–500 *toilets*	4	4	4	6	6	6	8	8	8	8
1,000	4	6	6	6	6	8	8	8	8	12
2,000	4	8	8	8	8	12	12	12	12	16
3,000	8	8	10	10	10	12	16	16	20	20
4,000	8	8	12	12	16	16	20	24	24	28
5,000	12	12	12	16	20	30	30	30	30	34
6,000	12	12	16	16	20	30	30	36	36	40
7,000	12	12	16	20	30	32	40	40	52	52
8,000	12	12	20	24	32	32	40	44	52	54
9,000	16	16	24	28	40	40	52	52	60	64
10,000	16	16	28	40	40	52	52	60	60	72

[Splendidly, many 'porta-potty' for-hire companies seem to favor amusing business names, including: *A-Throne · A Comfort Shack · A Royal Flush Inc. · Loader-Up Inc. · Pit Stop · Johnny on the Spot · Throne Depot · Oui Oui Enterprises · Jiffy John Inc. · Heavenly Huts · Mr Cesspool* · &c.]

WORLD MONUMENT WATCH LIST

The World Monument Fund annually issues a watch list of a hundred 'endangered architectural and cultural sites around the world'. Included on the 2008 list are:

USA
Florida Southern College campus
New Orleans historic neighborhoods
Route 66
Modern civic buildings in US towns
New York State Pavilion, Queens
Salk Institute, San Diego, CA
Tutuveni Petroglyph Site, AZ

UK
Mavisbank House, Scotland
Richhill House, Armagh, NI
St Peter's College, Scotland
Wilton's Music Hall, London

OTHERS OF NOTE
Scott's Hut, Antarctica
Burrup Peninsula, Australia
Herschel Island, Yukon, Canada
Modern Shanghai, China
Wa Naa's Palace, Wa, Ghana
Kotagede Heritage District, Indonesia
Farnese Nymphaeum, Rome, Italy
Vernon Mount, Cork, Ireland
Tara Hill, Meath, Ireland
Al-Azhar Mosque, Fez, Morocco
Las Geel Rock Art, Somaliland
Kilwa Historic Sites, Tanzania
Ayaz Kala, Ellikala, Uzbekistan

MOST ENDANGERED HISTORIC PLACES

Below are the eleven most endangered historic places in America, according to the 2007 annual report produced by the US National Trust for Historic Preservation:

Brooklyn's Industrial Waterfront (NYC) – *dockyards and factories that once supported generations of immigrants, now at risk by development*

El Camino Real Historic Trail (NM) – *site of the earliest Euro-American trade route in the US, threatened by a $225m commercial spaceport*

H.H. Richardson House (Brookline, MA) – *last home and studio of the architect who created the 'Richardson Romanesque' style*

Hialeah Park Race Course (Hialeah, FL) – *1925 horse racetrack, threatened by a megamall and condo complex*

Historic Places in Transmission Line Corridors (across 7 states) – *construction of high voltage lines 'will blight historic landscapes'*

Historic Route 66 Motels (IL to CA) – *neon-clad mom-and-pop motels torn down or 'reclaimed' by nature*

Historic Structures in Mark Twain National Forest (MO) – *from C19th farmsteads to New Deal-era fire lookouts; properties are left vacant and threatened with demolition*

Minidoka Internment Camp (Hunt, ID) – *built for Japanese American citizens interned 1942–45, now threatened by limited resources and a dairy facility*

Philip Simmons' Workshop and Home (Charleston, SC) – *master blacksmith's home and studio, now struggling to find funds – and unanchored, so vulnerable to hurricanes*

Pinon Canyon (CO) – *including river valleys and the Santa Fe Trail, threatened by army expansion plans*

Stewart's Point Rancheria (Sonoma County, CA) – *tribal historic resources of the Kashia Pomo Native American tribe, plagued by crime*

─────────GUILTY PLEASURES─────────

A host of intellectuals confided their 'guilty pleasures' to *Guardian* journalist Philip Oltermann in February 2007. Below is a selection of their censurable delights:

HOMI K. BHABHA (cultural theorist)
Project Runway
'The cut-and-paste technique is as true of working with textiles as it is of writing literary criticism'

RICHARD DAWKINS (scientist)
computer programming
'It was a classic addiction: prolonged frustration, occasionally rewarded by a briefly glowing fix of achievement'

ANTHONY GIDDENS (sociologist)
American wrestling on cable TV
'The program is politically incorrect in more or less every way one could think of '

SLAVOJ ZIZEK (sociologist, theorist)
military PC games
'I can do with impunity all the horrible things I was always dreaming of '

STEVEN PINKER (psychologist)
rock lyrics
'Dylan's "God said to Abraham, kill me a son" is a perfect example of a benefactive double-object dative construction'

NAOMI WOLF (writer)
Star magazine
'Even though it is 90% escapism for me, I do tell myself it shines a light on what the id of the culture is obsessing about: why Paris Hilton, right now?'

─────────MOST WALKABLE CITIES─────────

In 2007, *Prevention* magazine released a list of the most walkable cities in the US, based on street safety, air quality, parks and scenic points per mile, and other factors:

1 . . . . Madison, WI	6 . . . . Henderson, NV
2 . . . . Austin, TX	7 . . . . San Diego
3 . . . . San Francisco	8 . . . . San Jose
4 . . . . Charlotte, NC	9 . . . . Chandler, AZ
5 . . . . Seattle	10 . . . . Virginia Beach, VA

─────────VACATION DAYS WORLDWIDE─────────

Research by Mercer Human Resource Consulting shows the minimum number of paid vacation days and public holidays legislated by countries around the world:

	vacation days	public hols	total days off				
Australia	20	11[†]	31	NZ	20	11	31
Canada	10	10[†]	20	Sweden	25	11	36
France	30	10	40	UK	20	8	28
Germany	24	10	34	US[‡]	15	10	25
India	12	19	31				
Japan	20	15	35				

[Source: Mercer/CNN Money, 2007]

† Average. ‡ Average of large firms surveyed; no federal law mandates minimum days off.

—————————— UNCLE BEN &c. ——————————

In March 2007 the Mars company announced that their spokescharacter Uncle Ben had been 'promoted' to chairman. While the new Ben drew criticism, his upgrade focused attention on the stories behind a range of fictional food characters:

Uncle Ben · Named after a (real) Houston rice farmer known for quality crops. The image was based on Frank Brown, maître d' of a Chicago restaurant where company brass dined.

[Museum of PR; *New York Times*]

Aunt Jemima · The original inspiration for the character came from a minstrel act. The first Aunt Jemima was Nancy Green, born a Kentucky slave and hired in 1890. [AuntJemima.com; various]

Betty Crocker · Created by company managers in 1921 to answer letters. The surname belonged to a retired executive, and 'Betty' was chosen because it sounded friendly. Her portrait has been updated 7 times, last in 1996.

[George Mason University; General Mills]

Quaker Oats man · Created to embody purity, not based on a historical Quaker as many believe. The first cereal mascot in the US (registered in 1877). [various]

—————————— TRANS-FATS ——————————

In December 2006, New York City became the first American city to ban all establishments serving food from using artificial trans-fats. According to the city's Board of Health, the ban was prompted by concern over the link between trans-fats and heart disease – which is the number-one killer of Americans [see p.109]. ❦ While some animal products contain a small amount of natural trans-fats, artificial trans-fats are the most pervasive and problematic. Such fats are created when hydrogen is added to vegetable oil, a process called *hydrogenation*, which hardens the oil into a product that behaves more like butter. Foods containing artificial trans-fats generally have a longer shelf life, but their consumption has been shown to raise levels of Low-Density Lipoprotein (LDL, or 'bad cholesterol'), which in turn increases the risk of heart disease. The Food & Drug Administration (FDA) estimates that

Trans-fat per serving

147g french fries	8g
1 doughnut	5g
1 tbsp. shortening	4g
1 candy bar	3g
1 tbsp. margarine	3g
Small bag potato chips	3g

[Source: FDA]

Americans consume 5·8g of trans-fat a day (2·6% of their calories), while the 2005 USDA dietary guidelines recommend that trans-fat intake be 'as little as possible'. ❦ NYC's move was the first step in a wider effort to reduce the quantity of trans-fats consumed in the US. Philadelphia banned trans-fats in February 2007, and NY's Albany County followed suit in May. At the time of writing, several states were considering bans, and a range of food chains (including Denny's, KFC, McDonald's, Starbucks, and Taco Bell) had announced plans to replace some or all of the trans-fats currently used in their offerings. In April 2007, the American Heart Association launched a public awareness 'edutainment' campaign featuring the 'Bad Fat Brothers' – a rotund 'Sat' and a greasy 'Trans', who love to 'clog arteries and break hearts', but will gladly warn you in which foods they are to be found.

—————————————ORGANIC &c. FOOD LABELS—————————————

Demand for organic food has risen in recent years, from 1·9% of total US food sales in 2003, to 2·5% in 2005. However, many consumers are still unsure about the precise meaning of the term 'organic' – a confusion exacerbated by the profusion of 'green' claims and labels such as 'natural' or 'antibiotic free'. (Only some of these claims are regulated by the government; the rest lack a standardized meaning and may be used at the discretion of the manufacturer.) Use of the term 'organic' on food in the States is regulated by the Dept of Agriculture. Organic food must be produced according to National Organic Program standards, which include:

All food has been grown and processed without the use of most conventional pesticides, synthetic fertilizers, sewage sludge, bioengineering, and ionizing radiation ❧ Meat, eggs, and dairy must come from animals allowed access to the outdoors, fed organic food, and free of antibiotics or growth hormones ❧ Farmers must emphasize 'renewable resources and the conservation of soil and water' ❧ Farms, handlers, and processors must be inspected & certified ❧ No synthetic flavors or colors may be used

The USDA further specifies that labels bearing the claim '100% ORGANIC' must contain only organic ingredients, while food labeled 'ORGANIC', or with the USDA ORGANIC seal, need only contain ≥95% organic ingredients. Food labeled 'MADE WITH ORGANIC INGREDIENTS' is required to contain ≥70% organic ingredients.

A summary of some of the other claims and labels developed by the government, consumer groups, and manufacturers:

ANTIBIOTIC FREE · use on dairy and eggs is at the discretion of the manufacturer or marketer; banned by the USDA on meat.

CERTIFIED HUMANE RAISED AND HANDLED · label created by the animal rights group Humane Farm Animal Care. Use of hormones or antibiotics is prohibited (except for sick animals); animals must be allowed 'to engage in their natural behaviors' and must be raised with 'sufficient space, shelter and gentle handling to limit stress'.

CERTIFIED VEGAN · created by the nonprofit Vegan Action. To use the label, companies producing the food have certified that the items do not contain animal products and have not been tested on animals.

DOLPHIN SAFE · regulated by the Dept of Commerce. Under litigation; under the most recent ruling, at the time of writing, 'dolphin safe' tuna must not be 'harvested using a purse seine net intentionally deployed on or to encircle dolphins'; 'no dolphins were killed or seriously injured during the sets in which the tuna were caught'.

ENVIRONMENTALLY FRIENDLY · no government standards or regulation; use of the term is at the discretion of the manufacturer.

FAIR TRADE CERTIFIED · regulated by the nonprofit TransFair USA. Standards aim for fair prices for farmers and sustainable farming methods, and 'harmful agrochemicals and GMOs are strictly prohibited', as is child labor. 'Products must be grown by small-scale producers democratically organized in either cooperatives or unions'; buyers must pay a portion upfront in some cases.

—————— ORGANIC &c. FOOD LABELS cont. ——————

FREE RANGE/FREE ROAMING · USDA regulated on poultry to mean the animal has been allowed outside. Use on beef and eggs is not regulated.

FREE FARMED · label created by the American Humane Association. 'Animals are raised humanely in cage-free environments'; animals must 'readily access fresh water and a diet that maintains full health and vigor'; animals must be able to 'express normal behaviors and live in an appropriate and comfortable environment'.

FRESH · USDA regulated only on raw poultry, where it certifies the meat's internal temperature has not been <26°F. Otherwise, no government definition.

NATURAL · no government definition, except for meat and poultry, where use is regulated by the USDA to mean that no artificial ingredients or color have been added and only minimal processing has taken place. Label must explain

the use of the term by including 'no added colorings or artificial ingredient's; 'minimally processed', &c.

NO ANIMAL BY-PRODUCTS · no established standards or government regulation of the term; use is at the discretion of the manufacturer or producer.

NO ANTIBIOTICS ADDED · USDA regulated on red meat and poultry labels. Producer has provided sufficient documentation showing that animals were raised without antibiotics.

NO HORMONES ADMINISTERED · USDA regulated on beef; producer has provided sufficient documentation showing that animals were raised without hormones.

[Sources: American Humane Association; Consumers Union; Humane Farm Animal Care; National Organic Program, TransFair USA; USDA Food Safety and Inspection]

———————— CONTAMINATED PRODUCE ————————

In 2006, the nonprofit Environmental Working Group ranked 43 types of produce according to their levels of pesticide residue, based on tests of the produce conducted by the USDA and FDA. Each type of produce was given a combined score based on the number of pesticides found, how often pesticides were detected in the sample, and other data. Below are the most and least contaminated fruits and vegetables:

MOST CONTAMINATED		LEAST CONTAMINATED	
Produce	*score*	*Produce*	*score*
Peaches	100	Onions	1
Apples	89	Avocados	1
Sweet bell peppers	86	Sweet corn (frozen)	2
Celery	85	Pineapples	7
Nectarines	84	Mangos	9
Strawberries	82	Asparagus	11
Cherries	75	Sweet peas (frozen)	11
Pears	65	Kiwi fruit	14

DINING OUT

935,000 restaurants were operating in America in 2007, generating an estimated $53 bn in sales – according to the National Restaurant Association. The average meal tab was $32·86 and the average tip was 18·9% (according to a nationwide Zagat survey in 2006), although for unknown reasons West Coast diners tip less generously than diners on the East Coast. Other facts and figures on dining out:

INTERNATIONAL DINING COSTS

New York is the costliest dining city in the US, with an average meal tab of $39·43. Some international costs:

Tokyo	$73·69 *average tab*
London	$71·19
Paris	$65·85

MOST EXPENSIVE US RESTAURANTS

Masa[1]	$446 *est. dinner price*
The French Laundry[2]	$254
Alinea[3]	$168
The Herbfarm[4]	$152
The Inn at Little Washington[5]	$141

[1] NYC [2] Yountville, CA [3] Chicago
[4] Woodinville, WA [5] Washington, VA

FREQUENT DINERS

The US cities that dine out the most:

Houston	4·2 *meals per week*
Austin & Dallas/Ft Worth	4·0
Las Vegas, LA & Miami	3·8

[Bostonians dine out the least: 2·7 times/week.]

AMERICA'S FAVORITE CUISINE

27% *said*	Italian
16%	American
12%	French
10%	Japanese, Chinese, Thai [TIE]

[Sources: Zagat 2007 America's Top
Restaurants Survey; Forbes.com, 2006]

CHEFS' HOT & NOT

In October '06 the National Restaurant Association asked 1,146 chefs whether they considered a range of foods 'hot', 'cool/passé', or a 'perennial favorite'.

Considered 'hot' by chefs	%
Bite-size desserts	85
Locally grown produce	84
Organic produce	76
Flatbread	75
Bottled water	75
Specialty sandwiches	75
Asian appetizers	73
Espresso/specialty coffees	71
Whole-grain bread	70

Considered 'passé' by chefs	%
Scandinavian cuisine	68
Starfruit	65
Organ meats/sweetbreads	65
Ethiopian cuisine	65
Kiwi	63
Edible flowers/rose petals	63
Blackened items	63
Low-carb dough	62
Soda bread	62
Fruit soups	61

Considered 'perennial favorites'	%
Strawberries	54
Raspberries	50
Asparagus	47
Marinara sauce	47
Tomatoes	46
Chicken entrées	46
Hamburgers/cheeseburgers	46
Italian cuisine	45
Rice	44

—'FOOD & WINE' MAGAZINE'S BEST NEW CHEFS · 2007—

April Bloomfield .... *The Spotted Pig* .... New York City, NY
Gabriel Bremer .... *Salts* .... Cambridge, MA
Steve Corry .... *Five Fifty-Five* .... Portland, ME
Matthew Dillon .... *Sitka & Spruce* .... Seattle, WA
Gavin Kaysen .... *El Bizcocho* .... San Diego, CA
Johnny Monis .... *Komi* .... Washington, DC
Sean O'Brien .... *Myth* .... San Francisco, CA
Gabriel Rucker .... *Le Pigeon* .... Portland, OR
Ian Schnoebelen .... *Iris* .... New Orleans, LA
Paul Virant .... *Vie* .... Western Springs, IL

—TOP US RESTAURANTS—

Gourmet magazine's top 10 in 2006:

1 .. *Alinea* .... Chicago
2 .. *Chez Panisse* .... Berkeley, CA
3 .. *The French Laundry* Yountville, CA
3 .. *Per Se* .... NYC [TIE]
4 .. *Spago* .... Beverly Hills, CA
5 .. *Joël Robuchon* .... Las Vegas
6 .. *La Rêve* .... San Antonio, TX
7 .. *Masa* .... NYC
8 .. *Alan Wong's Restaurant* ... Honolulu
9 .. *Daniel* .... NYC
10. *Le Bernardin* .... NYC

—WORLD'S TOP TABLES—

Restaurant magazine's top 10 in 2007:

1 .. *El Bulli* ..... Montjoi, Roses, Spain
2 .. *The Fat Duck* .. Bray, Berkshire, UK
3 .. *Pierre Gagnaire* .... Paris, France
4 .. *The French Laundry* Yountville, CA
5 .. *Tetsuya's* .... Sydney, Australia
6 .. *Bras* .... Laguiole, France
7 .. *Mugaritz* .... Gipuzko, Spain
8 .. *Restaurant Le Louis XV*. Monte Carlo
9 .. *Per Se* .... NYC
10. *Restaurante Arzak* ... San Sebastián,
Spain

—————2007 JAMES BEARD AWARDS—————

Below is a selection of the honors bestowed at the James Beard Awards in 2007:

Outstanding restaurateur ...... Thomas Keller, *The French Laundry* · Yountville, CA
Outstanding chef .... Michel Richard, *Michel Richard Citronelle* · Washington, DC
Outstanding restaurant .... *Frontera Grill* · Chicago
Best new restaurant .... *L'Atelier de Joël Robuchon* · NYC
Rising star chef .... David Chang, *Momofuku Noodle Bar* · NYC
Outstanding pastry chef .... Michael Laskonis, *Le Bernardin* · NYC
Outstanding wine service .... *Michel Richard Citronelle* · Washington, DC
Outstanding wine and spirits professional .... Paul Draper · *Ridge Vineyards*, CA
Outstanding service .... *Tru* · Chicago
Cookbook of the year .... Matt & Ted Lee · *The Lee Bros. Southern Cookbook*
Cookbook Hall of Fame .... Mollie Katzen · *Moosewood Cookbook*
National TV show .... *Gourmet's Diary of a Foodie*
Newspaper food section .... *San Francisco Chronicle*

———————————— GROCERY SHOPPING ————————————

The data below illustrate some of the grocery shopping patterns of US consumers:

Who does the grocery shopping?	%
Female head of household	.69
Male head of household	.19
Both	.11
Other	1

Time of day for grocery shopping	%
08:00–12:00	.39
12:00–17:00	.38
17:00–21:00	.19
21:00–08:00	4

On which day do people grocery shop?	%
Monday	.12
Tuesday	.12
Wednesday	.11
Thursday	.12
Friday	.14
Saturday	.18
Sunday	.21
Weekends	*.39*

[Source: Food Marketing Institute, 2005 data]

Below is a breakdown of how the average $100 spent on groceries is divided up:

Group	$
Perishables	50·10
Beverages	8·26
All other grocery, food	11·30
Nonfood grocery	7·94
Snack foods	4·42

	$
Main meal items	6·84
Health & beauty care	3·58
General merchandise	4·38
Pharmacy	3·18

[Source: Food Marketing Institute, 2007 data]

According to further research by the FMI, supermarket retailers apprehended nearly one shoplifter per company day in 2005 – 4·3 per store, and $29·62 per incident. The most commonly lifted items are meat, over-the-counter medicines, health and beauty products, razor blades, and baby formula.

——————— GOLDEN TICKET THEME PARK AWARDS ———————

Some of the winners of *Amusement Today* magazine's 2006 Golden Ticket Awards:

Best amusement park	*Cedar Point*, Sandusky, OH
Best waterpark	*Schlitterbahn Waterpark Resort*, New Braunfels, TX
Best children's park	*Legoland California*, Carlsbad, CA
Best marine life park	*SeaWorld Orlando*, Orlando, FL
Best wooden coaster	*Thunderhead · Dollywood*, Pigeon Forge, TN
Best steel coaster	*Superman Ride of Steel · Six Flags New England*, Agawam, MA
Best water ride	*Dudley Do-Right's Ripsaw Falls · Islands of Adventure*, Orlando, FL
Best new ride, amusement park	*The Voyage · Holiday World*, Santa Claus, IN
Best new ride, waterpark	*Bahari River · Splashin' Safari*, Santa Claus, IN
Best kids' area	*Paramount's Kings Island*, Kings Mills, OH
Cleanest park	*Holiday World & Splashin' Safari*, Santa Claus, IN
Friendliest staff	*Holiday World & Splashin' Safari*, Santa Claus, IN
Best food	*Knoebels Amusement Resort*, Elysburg, PA
Best shows	*Six Flags Fiesta Texas*, San Antonio, TX

———— TOY OF THE YEAR AWARDS ————

The Toy Industry Association's Toy of the Year Awards (the 'TOTYs') honor the best toys developed for the North American consumer. At the 7th annual TOTYs, held on February 10, 2007, in NYC, George Lucas was both honored for his contribution to the toy industry and inducted into the Toy Industry's 'Hall of Fame'.

Toy of the year . . . . TMX Elmo
Infant/preschool toy of the year . . . . TMX Elmo
Girl toy of the year . . . . FurReal Friends Butterscotch Pony
Boy toy of the year [*sic*] . . . . Spy Video Car & Disney's Pirates of the Caribbean:
 Dead Man's Chest Ultimate Black Pearl Playset [TIE]
Game of the year . . . . Cranium's Zooreka
Outdoor toy of the year . . . . Radio Flyer Folding Trike
Educational toy of the year . . . . SmartGlobe 2·0
Activity toy of the year . . . . Moon Sand
Electronic entertainment toy of the year . . . . Kid-Tough Digital Camera
Most innovative toy of the year . . . . FurReal Friends Butterscotch Pony
Specialty toy of the year . . . . Webkinz
Property of the year . . . . Pixar's Cars

The best-selling toys of Christmas 2006, according to a retailer survey by trade magazine *TDmonthly*, included the Webkinz Tree Frog [plush pet frog with a virtual online life]; Blokus Trigon [hexagonal puzzle/board game]; Apples to Apples Party Crate [card game]; RC Forklift [battery-powered forklift with bonus warehouse]; and the Flying Flingshot Monkey [furry monkey that 'screams on impact'].

———— WORST TOYS ————

A list of 'worst toys' and their potential hazards has been issued by World Against Toys Causing Harm (WATCH) annually since 1973. WATCH's worst toys of 2006:

Toy	*WATCH's alleged potential hazard/injury*
Heelys [see p.226]	blunt impact, head and spinal injuries
Z launcher: turbo water-balloon launcher	facial and choking injuries
Pram Decoration – Blossoms	strangulation and ingestion
Pyramid Stacker	blunt impact and puncture injuries
Bow & Arrow Set	eye and other severe injuries
Zip-ity Do Dolly	ingestion and choking
Lil Snoopy	strangulation and entanglement
Superman Lamp	electric shock
Sky Blaster	eye injuries
Fear Factor Candy Challenge	choking and ingestion

While WATCH is concerned with the potential perils of inadequate labeling, the Michigan-based Lawsuit Abuse Watch believes some warning labels in the US have gone too far. The group gave its 2006 'wackiest warning' award to a washing machine label that warned against putting anybody inside, while an honorable mention went to a phone book that cautioned against its use while driving.

———————————————HEELYS———————————————

According to the manufacturer, Heelys are 'sneakers with a single stealth wheel in each heel that allow "heelers" to walk, roll, and grind their way across streets, school campuses and skate parks'. The shoes are protected by a slew of patents, including one that covers the stance adopted by heelers: 'feet staggered, toes up and heels gliding'. Since 2000, Heelys have established themselves as playground favorites in >60 countries, selling >9m pairs. Despite some financial commentators warning that Heelys may be too faddy for long-term investment, in 2006 Heelys Inc. posted net sales of $188·2m (an increase of 328% on 2005) and, according to the Associated Press, the company has a market capitalization of close to $1bn. ❦ The 'shoes that roll' were the brainchild of Roger Adams, who was born in Tacoma, Washington, in 1954. Adams' parents owned the Adams-Tacoma Roller Bowl – the largest roller-skating rink in the Pacific Northwest – where as a child he worked repairing skates. However the idea for Heelys only came to Adams in his 40s – at a time when he was disillusioned with his work as a mental health supervisor, and 'burned out' by the divorce from his wife of 21 years. As Adams told *MSNBC*, 'if there was one thing that started it, it was a midlife crisis'. Adams created the first-ever pair of Heelys by eviscerating a pair of Nikes with a hot butter knife and implanting skateboard wheels. ❦ Inevitably, Heelys (and the copycats that have rolled onto their bandwagon) have attracted safety concerns. The US lobbying group World Against Toys Causing Harm declared Heelys the 'worst toy' of 2006 [see p.225]. Indeed, Heely boxes warn that 'there is no way to heel and/or grind without running the risk of serious bodily harm, including head injury, spinal injury, or even death'. A number of medical professionals have warned of the risks of wearing Heelys, and many schools and shopping centers have banned wheeled shoes for reasons of public safety. Stung by stories that blame their shoes for causing accidents, the Heelys Inc. website contains both 'safety rules of thumb' and advice on 'common courtesy' ('crowded public areas are not good places for heeling'). Indeed, in April 2007, Heelys published the results of an independent analysis of 2 million US Consumer Production Safety Commission incident reports on product-related injuries between 2001–06. This analysis rather splendidly concluded that 'wheeled footwear is safer than nearly all other popular sports with the exception of table tennis, billiards, and bowling'.

———————————BEST & WORST CELEB DOG-OWNERS———————————

According to *New York Dog* magazine, Tinseltown's best and worst dog-owners are:

BEST *owner & pet*	WORST *owner & pet*
Oprah Winfrey & 'Solomon'	Britney Spears & 'Bit Bit'
Tori Spelling & 'Mimi La Rue'	Paris Hilton & 'Tinkerbell'
Nicollette Sheridan & 'Oliver'	Serena Williams & 'Jackie'

HEALTH BENEFITS OF PET OWNERSHIP

Research published in the *British Journal of Health Psychology* in January 2007 explored the health benefits of keeping pets. Dr Deborah Wells of Queen's Univ., Belfast, reviewed a number of studies and concluded that keeping a dog brought greater benefits to health than owning a cat. In general, pet owners were healthier than average – especially dog owners, who experienced benefits like lowered blood pressure and cholesterol. It was suggested that owning a dog improves health by lowering stress, giving companionship, and encouraging constitutional 'walkies'.

WESTMINSTER DOG SHOW · 2007

The 131st Westminster Kennel Club Dog Show, held February 12–13, 2007, at Madison Square Garden, saw 2,628 dogs from 165 breeds compete in 7 groups. The best in each group advanced to Best in Show, which was won by the 6-year-old English springer spaniel Felicity's Diamond Jim ('James'), a certified therapy dog who is noted for his 'beautiful expression' and a love of chicken-and-garlic treats.

Group	winner	breed
Working	Ch.† Redwitch Reason To Believe	Akita
Terrier	Ch. Hobergays Fineus Fogg	Dandie Dinmont Terrier
Toy	Ch. Smash Jp Win A Victory	Poodle (Toy)
Nonsporting	Ch. Brighton Minimoto	Poodle (Standard)
Sporting	Ch. Felicity's Diamond Jim	Spaniel (English Springer)
Hound	Ch. Celestial CJ's Jolly Fairchild	Petits Bassets Griffons Vendeen
Herding	Ch. Ace's Indelible Mark HT	Bouviers des Flandres

† 'Champion' denotes a dog who has earned fifteen points at other American Kennel Club shows.

PET OWNERSHIP

% US households own			
Dog. . . . . 44·8	Freshwater fish . . . . 14·2	Equine. . . . . 4·3	
Cat. . . . . 38·4	Bird. . . . . 6·4	Reptile. . . . . 4·8	
	Other small animal . 6·0	Saltwater fish . . . . 0·8	

[Source: American Pet Products Manufacturers Assoc. 2007–08 survey]

PETS & FAMILY

85% of dog owners and 78% of cat owners consider their pets 'members of the family', according to a 2006 Pew Research Center study. 94% of dog owners and 84% of cat owners said they would characterize their relationships with their pets as 'close' (87% said they felt close to their mother, and 74% to their father). Perhaps not surprisingly, women, those without children, and those living in cities or suburbs were the most likely to describe their pets as members of their family.

─────────── ANIMALS IN THE NEWS · 2007 ───────────

Some of the year's more unusual animal stories. ❦ A riding school in Ireland was forced to postpone its Christmas party after Gus, a camel, went on a rampage, eating 200 mince pies and downing six cans of Guinness. ❦ The lives of two dolphins were saved by the world's tallest man, after they swallowed fragments of plastic liner from around their pool. Bao Xishun – a Mongolian herdsman who stands 2·36m (7'9") tall – used his 1·06m-long arms (41·7") to extract the plastic from the dolphins' stomachs. ❦ A 'rogue' elephant (nicknamed Osama bin Laden) was shot dead after he trampled to death 14 people in India. ❦ A German retiree was awarded a contract to supply giant rabbits to North Korea, after he bred Robert, a 23·1lb monster. The North Koreans said they wanted to improve 'meat production'. ❦ In Tallahassee, Florida, an unnamed duck managed to survive being shot in the wing and leg and being locked in a fridge for two days. The lucky duck managed also to survive two heart attacks during surgery at the Goose Creek Animal Sanctuary. ❦ A Chilean flamingo named Florence went missing after a gust of wind blew her out of her enclosure at Drusillas Park, Sussex. Her fox-ravaged remains were found two weeks later. ❦ Mozart, a male iguana at Antwerp's Aquatopia, had his penis amputated after suffering permanent tumescence for over a week. (Fortunately, male iguanas have two penises.) ❦ A sloth named Mats was banished to Duisburg Zoo after failing to cooperate in an experiment. Scientists at the University of Jena had been trying to entice Mats to the top of a pole for three years, but the sloth consistently refused to budge. ❦ Fishermen in New Zealand caught a colossal squid that weighed 450kg (992lbs); it was the largest specimen ever caught intact. ❦ For the first time in 30 years, two snowy owls were sighted together in the UK. Hopes of the birds mating on the Isle of Lewis were dashed after it was discovered that both owls were male. ❦ One lane of a highway in Taiwan was closed so that more than a million milkweed butterflies might safely cross the road during their seasonal migration. ❦ Two labradors, Lucky and Flo, proved so successful at sniffing out pirated DVDs in Malaysia that crime bosses put a price on their heads. It was thought that 50,000 Ringgit (*c.*$14,500) was offered for each dead dog. ❦ Knut, a polar bear rejected by his parents, achieved celebrity status at Berlin Zoo, after animal rights' campaigners argued that he should be euthanized because hand-rearing would domesticate him. Knut later appeared on the cover of *Vanity Fair.* ❦ A Sudanese man was forced to 'marry' a goat named Rose, with whom he had been caught acting 'improperly'. Sadly, Rose passed away sometime later, after choking on a plastic bag while scavenging. ❦ Thousands of Japanese were tricked into buying lambs disguised as poodles – Japan's latest must-have accessory. The scam was uncovered when one owner complained that her 'poodle' neither barked nor ate dog food. ❦ The belief that seahorses are monogamous was shattered by researchers who found that most are promiscuous, indiscriminate, and (in roughly 37% of encounters) homosexual. ❦ Three elderly ladies from County Durham, England, knitted 50 woollen pullovers to help penguins stricken by an oil slick in Tasmania.

Sports

I dreamed about this when I was a kid. Unfortunately, when
I dreamed about it, I was the one hitting the home run.
— MIKE BACSIK [see p.250]

───────'SPORTS ILLUSTRATED' COVERS OF NOTE───────

Date	Cover star(s)
01·08·07	Jeff Garcia, Philadelphia Eagles
01·15·07	Chris Leak, Florida Gators
01·22·07	Drew Brees, New Orleans Saints
01·29·07	Peyton Manning, Indianapolis Colts
02·05·07	Brian Urlacher, Chicago Bears
02·12·07	Peyton Manning, Indianapolis Colts
02·19·07	Kevin Durant, Texas Longhorns
02·26·07	Lou Piniella & Alfonso Soriano, Chicago Cubs
03·05·07	Ohio State University basketball fans
03·12·07	Dontrelle Willis, Florida Marlins
03·19·07	*March Madness*
03·26·07	Daisuke Matsuzaka, Boston Red Sox
04·02·07	Tiger Woods
04·09·07	Corey Brewer, Florida Gators
04·16·07	Tiger Woods
04·23·07	Steve Nash, Phoenix Suns & Dirk Nowitzki, Dallas Mavericks
04·30·07	Adrian Peterson, Oklahoma Sooners
05·07·07	Oscar De La Hoya & Floyd Mayweather Jr
05·14·07	Grady Sizemore, Cleveland Indians
05·21·07	Barry Bonds, San Francisco Giants
05·28·07	Roger Huerta
06·04·07	Tim Duncan, San Antonio Spurs
06·11·07	LeBron James, Cleveland Cavaliers
06·18·07	Omar Minaya, Orlando Hernandez, Oliver Perez, Willie Randolph, Endy Chavez, and John Maine, New York Mets
06·25·07	Manu Ginobili, Bruce Bowen, Tony Parker, Tim Duncan, and Fabricio Oberto, San Antonio Spurs
07·02·07	Hanson Brothers, stars of 1977 hockey classic *Slap Shot*
07·16·07	David Beckham, LA Galaxy [see p.251]
07·23·07	Hank Aaron, Milwaukee Braves
07·30·07	Sheldon Brown, Philadelphia Eagles; Reggie Bush, New Orleans Saints
08·06·07	Jamal Lewis, Cleveland Browns
08·13·07	Barry Bonds, San Francisco Giants
08·20·07	Emmanuel Moody, C.J. Gable, & Chauncey Washington, USC Trojans
08·27·07	Nick Saban, Alabama Crimson Tide

BATTLE OF THE SURFACES

In May 2007, a bizarre tennis match in Mallorca pitted the skills of Roger 'King of Grass' Federer against Rafael 'King of Clay' Nadal. For $c.2\frac{1}{2}$[†] hours, Federer (Wimbledon champion for 4 consecutive years, with an unbeaten run of 48 wins on grass) fought Nadal (French Open champion, with 72 straight wins on clay) on a half-grass, half-clay court specially constructed for this one-off match, at a cost of $1·63 million. Nadal eventually emerged victorious with a winning score of 7–5, 4–6, 7–6 (12–10). Previously, Federer and Nadal had faced each other ten times:

World rank		nationality	born	turned pro	handed	wins by surface[‡]		
						hard	clay	grass
1	FEDERER	Swiss	8·8·1981	1998	right	2	0	1
2	NADAL	Spanish	3·6·1986	2001	left	2	5	0

† To allow players enough time to change into footwear appropriate for the different ends, the time allowed for the changeover was extended from the usual 90 seconds to 2 minutes. ‡ As of 5/2/2007.

THE WONDERLIC TEST

Developed in the 1930s by the industrial psychologist Eldon F. Wonderlic, the Wonderlic Personnel Test is used by recruiters, employers, and the NFL to measure cognitive ability. The 12-minute, 50-question exam has been used by the league since the 1970s, and is administered to potential draftees during the annual Indianapolis Scouting Combine. According to the Wonderlic website, the test can forecast a player's ability to learn the playbook, work within a team, and adapt on the field. The average individual score is said to be 21; the average NFL score is reportedly 19 (a score of 20 correlates to an IQ of 100). Paul Zimmerman's *The New Thinking Man's Guide to Pro Football* (1984) revealed the average scores of various positions:

Offensive tackles 26	Tight ends 22	Wide receivers 17
Centers 25	Safeties 19	Fullbacks 17
Quarterbacks 24	Middle linebackers . . . 19	Halfbacks 16
Guards 23	Cornerbacks 18	[Source: ESPN]

While NFL teams do not officially release player scores, Wonderlic tests results are routinely cited by the press. Below are the reported scores of some notable players:

Troy Aikman 29	R. Cunningham . . . 15	Eli Manning 39	Pat McInally 50
Drew Bledsoe 37	John Elway 30	Peyton Manning . . 28	Tony Romo 37
David Carr 24	Brett Favre 22	Dan Marino 16	JaMarcus Russell . . 24

After several media outlets reported (apparently incorrectly) that Texas Longhorn champion Vince Young scored a 6 on his Wonderlic, test rules were changed in 2007 to reduce access to scores. Some football experts question the continued use of the test, especially after a 2005 *Sports Journal* study found no significant link between quarterback Wonderlic scores and college passing performance – or rookie salary. [Sources: CNN/*Sports Illustrated*; *Houston Chronicle*; *Milwaukee Journal Sentinel*]

FOOTBALL & CONCUSSIONS

Football-related brain damage became a topic of considerable debate during 2006–07. In November 2006, 44-year-old former Philadelphia Eagles safety Andre Waters committed suicide. According to a January *New York Times* article, a neuropathologist who studied Waters's remains concluded that multiple football-related concussions were the likely cause of Waters's suicidal depression – reporting that Waters's brain tissue resembled that of an 85-year-old with early-stage Alzheimer's. In February, former Patriots linebacker Ted Johnson told the *Times* that he suffered from severe depression, which he linked to his multiple concussions. In June, the doctor who had examined Waters's remains concluded that another deceased NFL player – the Steelers Justin Strzelczyk – had also suffered chronic brain damage caused by concussions. (Strzelczyk died in a high-speed police chase in 2004.) ❦ Several other studies fueled this debate, including a May 2007 analysis by the University of North Carolina's Center for the Study

of Retired Athletes. This study found that retired NFL players who had suffered 1 or 2 prior concussions were 1·5× more likely to be diagnosed with depression; those with ≥3 concussions were 3× more likely. ❦ Yet controversy about concussions in football and other sports (not least boxing) is nothing new. Since 1994, the NFL has maintained an independent committee on brain injury and, in May 2007, the NFL announced a comprehensive 'concussion management plan' based on this committee's recommendations. The plan calls for neuropsychological baseline testing for all NFL players (to help track any decline), and the establishment of a 'whistle-blower' hotline to report anyone who pressures concussed players to play. A major NFL conference on brain injury was held in June, and the NFL has launched its own study of the long-term effects of concussion. These ongoing efforts, along with new helmets soon to arrive on the market, are likely to help address what has become an urgent issue for all contact sports.

The University of Pittsburgh Medical Center estimated that 100,000–200,000 concussions were sustained each year in high school and college football combined. Signs to watch for include: loss of consciousness, confusion, headache, dizziness, drowsiness, nausea, slurred speech, and a vacant stare.

TOP-EARNING ATHLETES

Although the press could not get enough of the $28m contract Roger Clemens signed with the Yankees in May 2007, once his salary was pro-rated, the pitcher came only 15th in *Sports Illustrated*'s annual ranking of highest-earning US athletes. Below are the top 10 athletes, based on pay, endorsements, &c., in the most recent season:

Athlete	*2006–07 season earnings*	
Tiger Woods (golf)	$112m	LeBron James (basketball) $31m
Oscar De La Hoya[†] (boxing) $55m		Kevin Garnett (basketball) $29m
Phil Mickelson (golf) $51m		Derek Jeter (baseball) $29m
Shaquille O'Neal (basketball) $35m		Alex Rodriguez (baseball)......... $28m
Kobe Bryant (basketball)......... $34m		Dale Earnhardt Jr (auto racing).... $27m
		Candidates had to be US citizens. [† See p.247]

———————FAN SATISFACTION RANKINGS———————

ESPN surveyed 80,000 sports fans in 2007 to discover the big-league teams that offered fans the highest return on their (emotional and financial) investment. ESPN grouped fan responses into the seven categories tabulated below – and added an eighth 'Bang for the Buck' [BNG] category which divides total costs for attending games by wins in the past 3 years. The eight category scores were then averaged to determine overall rankings. The five top-ranked teams, with their coaches, were:

Team	coach	BNG	FRL	OWN	AFF	STD	PLA	CCH	TTR
Buffalo Sabres [NHL]	Lindy Ruff	1	4	13	2	25	11	4	53
San Anton. Spurs [NBA]	Gregg Popovich	10	1	1	12	14	7	6	9
Dallas Mavericks [NBA]	Avery Johnson	11	2	4	20	4	1	1	33
Indianapolis Colts [NFL]	Tony Dungy	2	3	14	28	86	2	3	11
Detroit Pistons [NBA]	Flip Saunders	3	26	6	13	11	13	73	5

Category key: FRL [Fan Relations]: ease of access to players, coaches, and management; OWN [Ownership]: honesty; loyalty to players & city; AFF [affordability]: price of tickets, parking, and concessions; STD [Stadium Experience]: friendliness of environment; quality of game-day promotions; PLA (Players): effort on the field and likability off; CCH (Coach/Manager): strong on-field leadership; TTR (Title Track): titles already won/expected soon. [Source: ESPN SportsNation]

———————THE ESPY AWARDS · 2007———————

The ESPYs were created by ESPN in 1993 to 'celebrate the best sports stories of the year'. Below are some key awards from the 2007 ceremony, which was hosted in Hollywood by comedian Jimmy Kimmel, and basketball player LeBron James:

Male athlete......LaDainian Tomlinson
Female athlete..........Taryne Mowatt
Team................ Indianapolis Colts
Coach....T. Dungy, Indianapolis Colts
Game........Boise State *vs* Oklahoma, 2007 Fiesta Bowl
Breakthrough athlete......Devin Hester

Sports movie .... *Talladega Nights*
Moment.... New Orleans Saints return home to Superdome, beat Falcons
Champ. performance....... P. Manning, Indianapolis Colts at the Super Bowl
Play ....Boise State *bt* Oklahoma, using the Statue of Liberty play

———————THE LAUREUS AWARDS · 2007———————

The Laureus World Sporting Academy encourages the 'positive and worthwhile in sport', presenting awards to athletes in all disciplines. Some 2007 winners were:

World sportsman of the year.................................. Roger Federer (tennis)
World sportswoman of the year...................... Yelena Isinbayeva (polevault)
World team of the year...................................Italian men's football team
World breakthrough of the year......................... Amélie Mauresmo (tennis)
Comeback of the year .... Serena Williams (tennis)

2006 SPORTSMAN OF THE YEAR

Miami Heat guard Dwyane Wade won the 2006 *Sports Illustrated* Sportsman of the Year award, bestowed annually upon a team or athlete who 'embodies the spirit of sportsmanship and achievement'. 24-year-old Wade led his team to an exhilarating comeback during the 2006 NBA finals, scoring more postseason points than any NBA player ever had in their first 3 seasons. Wayde was also praised for his community work, including the youth-oriented nonprofit foundation established in his name. Previous *S.I.* Sportsmen of the Year include: Tom Brady [2005], the Boston Red Sox [2004], Tim Duncan & David Robinson [2003], and Lance Armstrong [2002].

ATHLETE ENDORSEMENTS

Below are some of the many athlete appearances in ad campaigns during 2006–07:

David Beckham	*advertisements for* Adidas, ESPN, Motorola
Tom Brady	Nike, Movado, Stetson
Brett Favre	Rayovac, Sensodyne, Prilosec, Wrangler
Derek Jeter	Movado, Ford Mustang, Gatorade, XM Radio
Peyton Manning	Nerf, DirecTV, Sprint, MasterCard, Sony, Reebok, Gatorade
Danica Patrick	GoDaddy.com, Secret deodorant, Honda Civic
Maria Sharapova	Canon, Nike, Motorola, Gatorade, TAG Heuer
Tiger Woods	OnStar, Gillette, TAG Heuer, Nike

TOP-SELLING NBA JERSEYS

The National Basketball Association's list of the best-selling player jerseys in 2006:

1 ... Kobe Bryant†, Los Angeles Lakers	6 .... Steve Nash, Phoenix Suns
2 ....Dwyane Wade, Miami Heat	7 .... Vince Carter, New Jersey Nets
3 .. LeBron James, Cleveland Cavaliers	8 .... Gilbert Arenas, Wash. Wizards
4 ......Allen Iverson, Denver Nuggets	9 ....Shaquille O'Neal, Miami Heat
5 ..Carmelo Anthony, Denver Nuggets	10.......Stephon Marbury, NY Knicks

† Some in the press linked Bryant's best-seller status to his 2006 switch from number 8 to number 24.

THE 'S.I.' SWIMSUIT ISSUE

Dreamgirl Beyoncé Knowles graced the cover of *Sports Illustrated*'s 2007 swimsuit edition (clad in a yellow and pink bikini of her own design) – becoming the first non-model and non-athlete so to do. The music-themed issue featured models posing alongside Kanye West, Aerosmith, Kenny Chesney, and Gnarls Barkley, as well as photo shoots at Graceland and the Rock & Roll Hall of Fame. Models Veronica Varekova and Yamila Diaz-Rahi appeared in a 3-D photo shoot; handily, the issue was packaged with a pair of paper 3-D glasses, for 'enhanced' viewing.

———————— BASEBALL · THE 2006 WORLD SERIES ————————

ST LOUIS CARDINALS *bt* DETROIT TIGERS 4–1

After nearly missing the playoffs, and winning only 83 games in the regular season (the fewest of any World Series champion), the Cardinals found victory October 27 with help from starter Jeff Weaver and shortstop David Eckstein. It was the team's first Fall Classic title since 1982, and their 10th out of 17 attempts overall, giving the Redbirds the most World Series wins of any team, save the New York Yankees.

Nobody believed in us but we believed in ourselves.
— DAVID ECKSTEIN, Cardinals shortstop & MVP

No.	date	result	city	sang *God Bless America*
1	10·21·06	Cardinals 7, Tigers 2	Detroit	Jennifer Hudson
2	10·22·06	Tigers 3, Cardinals 1	Detroit	Josh Gracin
3	10·24·06	Cardinals 5, Tigers 0	St Louis	Jo Dee Messina
4	10·26·06	Cardinals 5, Tigers 4	St Louis	Colleen Schoendienst
5	10·27·06	Cardinals 4, Tigers 2	St Louis	Varcity

The Cardinals also won the Series in 1934 against the Tigers; the Tigers beat the Cardinals in 1968.

————————————— 2006 MLB PLAYOFFS —————————————

American League Division Series

Athletics *bt* Twins 3–0
10·03·06......Athletics............3–2
10·04·06......Athletics............5–2
10·06·06......Athletics.......... 8–3

Tigers† *bt* Yankees 3–1
10·03·06.......Yankees............8–4
10·05·06.......Tigers............4–3
10·06·06.......Tigers............6–0
10·07·06.......Tigers............8–3

American League Championship Series

Tigers *bt* Athletics 4–0
10·10·06.......Tigers............5–1
10·11·06.......Tigers............8–5
10·13·06.......Tigers............3–0
10·14·06.......Tigers............6–3

† Wild card team

National League Division Series

Cardinals *bt* Padres 3–1
10·03·06......Cardinals...........5–1
10·05·06......Cardinals...........2–0
10·07·06.......Padres............3–1
10·08·06......Cardinals...........6–2

Mets *bt* Dodgers† 3–0
10·04·06........Mets.............6–5
10·05·06........Mets.............4–1
10·07·06........Mets.............9–5

National League Championship Series

Cardinals *bt* Mets 4–3
10·12·06........Mets.............2–0
10·13·06......Cardinals...........9–6
10·14·06......Cardinals...........5–0
10·15·06........Mets........... 12–5
10·17·06......Cardinals...........4–2
10·18·06........Mets.............4–2
10·19·06......Cardinals...........3–1

─────2006 BATTING STATS & THE TRIPLE CROWN─────

American League		*National League*
Joe Mauer, Twins [·347]	*batting average*	Freddy Sanchez, Pirates [·344]
David Ortiz, Red Sox [54]	*home runs*	Ryan Howard, Phillies [58]
David Ortiz, Red Sox [137]	*runs batted in*	Ryan Howard, Phillies [149]

Only 9 in the American League, and 7 in the National League, have led in batting average, home runs, and runs batted in, thereby earning a batting Triple Crown:

American League	*National League*
Nap Lajoie, Philadelphia 1901	Paul Hines[†], Providence 1878
Ty Cobb, Detroit 1909	Hugh Duffy, Boston..............1894
Jimmie Foxx, Philadelphia.......1933	Heinie Zimmerman, Chicago....1912
Lou Gehrig, New York...........1934	Rogers Hornsby, St Louis........1922
Ted Williams, Boston.............1942	Rogers Hornsby, St Louis........1925
Ted Williams, Boston.............1947	Chuck Klein, Philadelphia 1933
Mickey Mantle, New York.......1956	Joe Medwick, St Louis...........1937
Frank Robinson, Baltimore.......1966	
Carl Yastrzemski, Boston 1967	[Source: ESPN]

† For 90 years, Abner Dalrymple was thought to have earned the top batting average of 1878. Yet a 1968 statistical recalculation based on modern game rules showed that Hines deserved the title and, having also won for home runs and runs batted in that year, was also the first Triple Crown winner.

─────SOME ANNUAL BASEBALL AWARDS OF NOTE─────

National League MVP 2006 ....Ryan Howard, Philadelphia Phillies
American League MVP 2006 ....Justin Morneau, Minnesota Twins
Cy Young National League 2006.........Brandon Webb, Arizona Diamondbacks
Cy Young American League 2006.................Johan Santana, Minnesota Twins

─────MOST VALUABLE─────

The most valuable teams in Major League Baseball, as ranked by *Forbes*:

Rank	team	$ value
1	........New York Yankees	...1,200m
2	........New York Mets	........736m
3	........Boston Red Sox	.......724m
4	........LA Dodgers	...........632m
5	........Chicago Cubs	.........592m

Value based on 2006–07 stadium deals.
[Source: *Forbes*, 2007]

─────TOP ATTENDANCE─────

The Major League Baseball teams with the highest home-game attendance:

Rank	team	2006 attendance
1	.......New York Yankees	.....4·2m[†]
2	........Los Angeles Dodgers	....3·8m
3	........New York Mets	.........3·4m
4	........St Louis Cardinals	......3·4m
5	........LA Angels	..............3·4m

† The Yankees' fourth year of top attendance
[Source: ESPN]

———————————SUPER BOWL XLI · 2007———————————

INDIANAPOLIS COLTS *bt* CHICAGO BEARS 29–17

February 4, 2007 · Field: Dolphin Stadium, FL · Weather: steady rain
National Anthem: Billy Joel · Viewers: 93·2m (second most-watched ever)

Super Bowl XLI was the first Super Bowl played in the rain, the first to feature (not just one, but two) black head coaches, and the first with a touchdown scored on the opening kickoff. The electrifying first quarter started out well for the Bears, when rookie Devin Hester ran 92 yards for a touchdown 14 seconds in. However, the Colts overcame their 14–6 first-quarter deficit by playing a steady, careful game led by quarterback Peyton Manning. Manning (who completed 25 of 38 passes for 247 yards and 1 touchdown) took MVP, and laid to rest long-held speculation about whether he could win the big game. By contrast, oft-criticized Bears quarterback Rex Grossman did little to improve his standing, and the game's outcome was clinched with less than 12 minutes left when Grossman's ineffective pass was intercepted by Kelvin Hayden, who returned it 56 yards for a touchdown. The weather produced a messy game, with 5 turnovers for the Bears and 3 for the Colts – yet the precipitation did little to mar Prince's well-received halftime show, performed on a stage shaped like his signature symbol and capped, fittingly, by *Purple Rain*.

Super Bowl XLI ads (*c*.$2·6m for 30 seconds) included: a Nationwide Mutual Insurance spot featuring Kevin 'Fed-Ex' Federline flipping burgers; modern office warfare as envisaged by CareerBuilder.com; a (literal) bank robbery from E*Trade Financial; Bud Light as the subject of an ESL class; and a memorable attempt by Anheuser-Busch to introduce face-slapping as a public display of affection. Several ads drew controversy: the Federline spot was said to be insulting actual fast-food workers, and a Snickers ad featuring two mechanics kissing (then acting repulsed) was attacked as homophobic.

———————————2007 NFL PLAYOFFS———————————

The Colts finally vanquished their old foes the Patriots in the AFC Championship game January 21, 2007. The win (thanks to Peyton Manning's 80-yard drive late in the fourth quarter) took the Colts to the Super Bowl for the first time since 1971. The Saints ended their dream season in disappointment after the Chicago defense came through; their loss took the Bears to the game for the first time since 1985.

AFC Wild Card Playoffs	*NFC Wild Card Playoffs*
01·06·07........... Colts 23 – Chiefs 8	01·06·07.. Seahawks 21 – Cowboys 20
01·07·07...........Patriots 37 – Jets 16	01·07·07.........Eagles 23 – Giants 20
AFC Divisional Playoffs	*NFC Divisional Playoffs*
01·13·07...........Colts 15 – Ravens 6	01·13·07......... Saints 27 – Eagles 24
01·14·07.....Patriots 24 – Chargers 21	01·14·07...... Bears 27 – Seahawks 24
AFC Championships	*NFC Championships*
01·21·07.........Colts 38 – Patriots 34	01·21·07......... Bears 39 – Saints 14

—————— 2007 BOWL CHAMPIONSHIP SERIES ——————

BCS CHAMPIONSHIP: FLORIDA GATORS *bt* OHIO STATE BUCKEYES 41–14

The Florida Gators triumphed over the Ohio State Buckeyes in a stunning upset January 8, 2007. The game started out favorably for Ohio when Ted Ginn Jr returned the opening kickoff for a touchdown, but Florida's defense bounced back, sacking Heisman winner Troy Smith 5 times and allowing only 8 first downs. By halftime Ohio faced a 20-point deficit from which they could not recover – thanks in large part to Florida quarterback Chris Leak, the game's offensive MVP. The win was the Gators' second national title, and gave Florida the unique honor of being the first college simultaneously to hold titles for both football and men's basketball.

ROSE BOWL	ORANGE BOWL
1·1·07 · Pasadena	1·2·07 · Miami
USC Trojans (8) *bt*	Louisville Cardinals (5) *bt* Wake Forest
Michigan Wolverines (3) 32–18	Demon Deacons (15) 24–13
FIESTA BOWL	SUGAR BOWL
1·1·07 · Glendale	1·3·07 · New Orleans
Boise State Broncos (9) *bt*	LSU Tigers (4) *bt* Notre Dame
Oklahoma Sooners (7) 43–42	Fighting Irish (11) 41–14

————————— 2006 HEISMAN TROPHY —————————

Quarterback Troy Smith of the Ohio State Buckeyes won the 2006 Heisman Trophy, awarded annually since 1935 to the most outstanding college football player. Smith received a record 86·7% of first-place votes, and his point total of 2,540 placed third in the award's history – behind only OJ Simpson [2,853 points in 1968] and Reggie Bush [2,541 in 2005]. Despite a fraught early career, and some scandal in 2004, Smith was praised as instrumental in leading the Buckeyes through their unbeaten 2006 season. He is the sixth Ohio State player to win a Heisman, although the school has won seven total; Archie Griffin won in 1974 and in 1975.

————————— 2007 NCAA WOMEN'S CHAMPIONSHIP —————————

TENNESSEE LADY VOLUNTEERS *bt* RUTGERS SCARLET KNIGHTS 59–46

Tennessee won their elusive seventh NCAA women's title nine years after their last win, and after making five appearances in the Final Four since 1998. The Rutgers team [see p.20] allowed 18 turnovers and seemed dazzled by the Vols team effort, led by Candace Parker, who scored 17 points to be named Most Outstanding Player.

	1	2	OT
Tennessee Lady Volunteers	29	30	59
Rutgers Scarlet Knights	18	28	46

------------------------------ 2007 NBA FINALS ------------------------------

SAN ANTONIO SPURS *bt* CLEVELAND CAVALIERS 4–0

The San Antonio Spurs won their fourth championship title in nine years in a 4–0 sweep of the NBA finals. The Cavaliers rallied in the third quarter of Game 4, but the Spurs retook the lead, trouncing the Cavs on their first trip to the finals. Tony Parker [see p.120] was named MVP, after taking 24 points from the Cavaliers in the first 3 quarters. Throughout the season Parker averaged 24·5 points, 5 rebounds, and 3·3 assists per game, while maintaining a 57·1% shooting average from the floor.

No.	date	result	city
1	06·07·07	Spurs 85, Cavaliers 76	San Antonio
2	06·10·07	Spurs 103, Cavaliers 92	San Antonio
3	06·12·07	Spurs 75, Cavaliers 72	Cleveland
4	06·14·07	Spurs 83, Cavaliers 82	Cleveland

------------------------------ 2007 NBA PLAYOFFS ------------------------------

Eastern Conference Quarterfinals
Pistons *bt* Magic, 4–0 [games]
Cavaliers *bt* Wizards, 4–0
Nets *bt* Raptors, 4–2
Bulls *bt* Heat, 4–0

Eastern Conference Semifinals
Pistons *bt* Bulls, 4–2
Cavaliers *bt* Nets, 4–2

Eastern Conference Finals
Cavaliers *bt* Pistons, 4–2

05·21·07	Pistons	79–76
05·24·07	Pistons	79–76
05·27·07	Cavaliers	88–82
05·29·07	Cavaliers	91–87
05·31·07	Cavaliers	109–107
06·02·07	Cavaliers	98–82

Western Conference Quarterfinals
Warriors *bt* Mavericks, 4–2 [games]
Suns *bt* Lakers, 4–1
Spurs *bt* Nuggets, 4–1
Jazz *bt* Rockets, 4–3

Western Conference Semifinals
Spurs *bt* Suns, 4–2
Jazz *bt* Warriors, 4–1

Western Conference Finals
Spurs *bt* Jazz, 4–1

05·20·07	Spurs	108–100
05·22·07	Spurs	105–96
05·26·07	Jazz	109–83
05·28·07	Spurs	91–79
06·30·07	Spurs	109–84

------------------------------ 2007 NBA ANNUAL AWARDS ------------------------------

Most Valuable Player	Dirk Nowitzki[†], Dallas Mavericks
Rookie of the Year	Brandon Roy, Portland Trail Blazers
Coach of the Year	Sam Mitchell, Toronto Raptors

† German-born Nowitzki was the first European player to win the NBA MVP Award and be presented with the Maurice Podoloff Trophy, named in honor of the first NBA commissioner (1946–63).

NCAA 'MARCH MADNESS' · 2007

2007 NCAA Division I Men's Basketball Championship

Atlanta

National Championship — April 2

FLORIDA (1) *beat* OHIO STATE (1) 84–75

East

1st Round (March 15–16)	2nd Round (March 17–18)	Sweet Sixteen (March 22–23)	Elite Eight (March 24–25)	Final Four (March 31)
UNC (1) 86 / East. KY (16) 65	UNC 81	UNC 74	UNC 84	Georgetown 60
Marquette (8) 49 / Mich St (9) 61	Michigan St 67			
USC (5) 77 / Arkansas (12) 60	USC 87	USC 64		
Texas (4) 79 / N Mex St (13) 67	Texas 68			
Vanderbilt (6) 77 / G Wash (11) 44	Vanderbilt 78	Vanderbilt 65	Georgetown 96	
Wash St (3) 70 / Oral Rob (14) 54	Wash State 74			
BC (7) 84 / Tex Tech (10) 75	Boston Col. 55	Georgetown 66		
G'town (2) 80 / Belmont (15) 55	Georgetown 62			

South

1st Round (March 15–16)	2nd Round (March 17–18)	Sweet Sixteen (March 22–23)	Elite Eight (March 24–25)	Final Four (March 31)
Ohio St (1) 78 / C Conn S (16) 57	Ohio State 78	Ohio State 85	Ohio State 92	Ohio State 67
BYU (8) 79 / Xavier (9) 79	Xavier 71			
Tennessee (5) 121 / L Beach S (12) 86	Tennessee 77	Tennessee 84		
Virginia (4) 84 / Albany (13) 57	Virginia 74			
Louisville (6) 78 / Stanford (11) 58	Louisville 69	Texas A&M 64	Memphis 76	
TX A&M (3) 68 / Penn (14) 52	Texas A&M 72			
Nevada (7) 77 / Creighton (10) 71	Nevada 62	Memphis 65		
Memphis (2) 73 / N Texas (15) 58	Memphis 78			

Midwest

1st Round (March 15–16)	2nd Round (March 17–18)	Sweet Sixteen (March 22–23)	Elite Eight (March 24–25)	Final Four (March 31)
Florida (1) 112 / Jackson St (16) 69	Florida 74	Florida 65	Florida 85	Florida 76
Arizona (8) 63 / Purdue (9) 72	Purdue 67			
Butler (5) 57 / Old Dom (12) 46	Butler 62	Butler 57		
Maryland (4) 82 / Davidson (13) 70	Maryland 59			
N. Dame (6) 64 / Winthrop (11) 74	Winthrop 61	Oregon 76	Oregon 77	
Oregon (3) 58 / Mia. OH (14) 56	Oregon 75			
UNLV (7) 67 / GA Tech (10) 63	UNLV 74	UNLV 72		
Wisconsin (2) 76 / A&M CC (15) 63	Wisconsin 68			

West

1st Round (March 15–16)	2nd Round (March 17–18)	Sweet Sixteen (March 22–23)	Elite Eight (March 24–25)	Final Four (March 31)
Kansas (1) 107 / Niagara (16) 67	Kansas 88	Kansas 61	Kansas 55	UCLA 66
Kentucky (9) 67 / Villanova (9) 58	Kentucky 76			
VA Tech (5) 54 / Illinois (12) 52	Virginia Tech 48	S Illinois 58		
S Illinois (4) 61 / H Cross (13) 51	S Illinois 63			
Duke (6) 77 / VCU (11) 79	VCU 79	Pittsburgh 55	UCLA 68	
Pittsburgh (3) 79 / Wright St (14) 58	Pittsburgh 84			
Indiana (7) 70 / Gonzaga (10) 57	Indiana 49	UCLA 64		
UCLA (2) 70 / Weber St (15) 42	UCLA 54			

{ **2007 NCAA Women's Championship** — Tennessee *beat* Rutgers 59–46 }

Play-in game (March 13) Niagara vs Florida A&M · Niagara beat Kansas in 1st Round

STANLEY CUP CHAMPIONSHIP · 2007

ANAHEIM DUCKS *bt* OTTAWA SENATORS 4–1

The Anaheim Ducks finally secured their first Stanley Cup since entering the NHL in 1992, beating the Ottawa Senators 4–1 in the best-of-seven series final. Game 5 saw a tremendous defensive performance, in which the Ducks limited the Senators to just 13 shots on goal. Ducks captain Scott Niedermayer, originally from British Columbia, was awarded the Conn Smythe Trophy (for Most Valuable Player in the playoffs) and successfully helped his side deny yet another Canadian team – no team from 'north of the border' has celebrated the Stanley Cup since Montreal in 1993.

No.	date	result	city
1	05·28·07	Ducks 3, Senators 2	Anaheim
2	05·30·07	Ducks 1, Senators 0	Anaheim
3	06·02·07	Senators 5, Ducks 3	Ottawa
4	06·04·07	Ducks 3, Senators 2	Ottawa
5	06·06·07	Ducks 6, Senators 2	Anaheim

STANLEY CUP PLAYOFFS · 2007

Western Conference Quarterfinals
Red Wings *bt* Flames, 4–2 [games]
Ducks *bt* Wild, 4–1
Canucks *bt* Stars, 4–3
Sharks *bt* Predators, 4–1

Western Conference Semifinals
Red Wings *bt* Sharks, 4–2
Ducks *bt* Canucks, 4–1

Western Conference Finals
Ducks *bt* Red Wings, 4–2

05·11·07	Red Wings	2–1
05·13·07	Ducks	4–3 (OT)
05·15·07	Red Wings	5–0
05·17·07	Ducks	5–3
05·20·07	Ducks	2–1 (OT)
05·22·07	Ducks	4–3

Eastern Conference Quarterfinals
Sabres *bt* Islanders, 4–1 [games]
Devils *bt* Lightning, 4–2
Rangers *bt* Thrashers, 4–0
Senators *bt* Penguins, 4–1

Eastern Conference Semifinals
Sabres *bt* Rangers, 4–2
Senators *bt* Devils, 4–1

Eastern Conference Finals
Senators *bt* Sabres, 4–1

05·10·07	Senators	5–2
05·12·07	Senators	4–3
05·14·07	Senators	1–0
05·16·07	Sabres	3–2
05·18·07	Senators	3–2

2007 ANNUAL NHL AWARDS

Lester B. Pearson Award, Players' MVP........Sidney Crosby, Pittsburgh Penguins
Hart Trophy, NHL MVP......................Sidney Crosby, Pittsburgh Penguins
Vezina Trophy, Top Goaltender .... Martin Brodeur, New Jersey Devils
Norris Trophy, Top Defenseman ....Nicklas Lidstrom, Detroit Red Wings

—MARATHONS OF NOTE—

Below are the results of the major
2006–07 'Big Five' marathons:

| BERLIN | *first run* 1974 |
| 2006 · Sep 24 | sunny, mild |

♂ ......H. Gebrselassie [ETH] · 2:05:56
♀.............G. Wami [ETH] · 2:21:34
Purse......................... $340,000

| CHICAGO | *first run* 1977 |
| 2006 · Oct 22 | light rain, strong wind |

♂ .....R. K. Cheruiyot [KEN] · 2:07:35
♀............. B. Adere [ETH] · 2:20:42
Purse......................... $650,000

| NEW YORK CITY | *first run* 1970 |
| 2006 · Nov 5 | partly cloudy, *c.*40°F |

♂ .... M. dos Santos [BRZ] · 2:09:58
♀.........J. Prokopcuka [LAT] · 2:25:05
Purse.........................$>700,000

| BOSTON | *first run* 1897 |
| 2007 · Apr 16 | very windy, rainy |

♂ .....R. K. Cheruiyot [KEN] · 2:14:13
♀.........L. Grigoryeva [RUS] · 2:29:18
Purse......................... $575,000

| LONDON | *first run* 1981 |
| 2007 · Apr 22 | hot, no breeze |

♂ .... M. Lel [KEN] · 2:07:41
♀........Chunxiu Zhou [CHI] · 2:20:38
Purse......................... $295,000

The inaugural World Marathon Majors, formed
in 2006, began with the 2006 Boston run and
ends in New York in 2007. As of May 2007,
Robert K. Cheruiyot was thought untouchable
as the men's champion, while Jelena Prokopcuka
had a modest lead over Gete Wami as women's
champion. ❦ In April 2007, NASA astronaut
Suni Williams ran as an official entrant in the
Boston Marathon while on a treadmill at the
International Space Station. She finished the
run in 4 hours, 23 minutes, and 46 seconds
while the Station traveled at 17,500 mph, 210
miles above Earth.

—2007 TRIPLE CROWN—

· KENTUCKY DERBY ·
Purse: $2m
Churchill Downs, Louisville, KY
May 5, 6:04pm · Distance: 1¼ miles

STREET SENSE
Calvin Borel *(j)* · Carl Nafzger *(tr)*

HARD SPUN
Mario Pino *(j)* · J. Larry Jones *(tr)*

CURLIN
Robby Albarado *(j)* · Steve Asmussen *(tr)*

· PREAKNESS ·
Purse: $1m
Pimlico Race Course, Baltimore, MD
May 19, 6:05pm · Distance: 1³⁄₁₆ miles

CURLIN
Robby Albarado *(j)* · Steve Asmussen *(tr)*

STREET SENSE
Calvin Borel *(j)* · Carl Nafzger *(tr)*

HARD SPUN
Mario Pino *(j)* · J. Larry Jones *(tr)*

· BELMONT ·
Purse: $1m
Belmont Park, Elmont, NY
June 9, 6:30pm · Distance: 1½ miles

RAGS TO RICHES[†]
John Velazquez *(j)* · Todd Pletcher *(tr)*

CURLIN
Robby Albarado *(j)* · Steve Asmussen *(tr)*

TIAGO
Mike Smith *(j)* · John Shirreffs *(tr)*

[Key: *(j)*ockey · *(tr)*ainer]
† The first filly to win Belmont in 102 years.

TOUR DE FRANCE

'DEATH NOTICE: the Tour de France died on 25 July, 2007,
at the age of 104, after a long illness ...' — *France Soir* (7/26/07)

The Tour's Grand Départ from London on July 7, and its journey across southeast England, attracted 4m cheering spectators and launched the race with optimism and verve. Yet, after 17 days, prerace favorite Alexandre Vinokourov and his Astana teammates were forced to withdraw after Vinokourov tested positive for a homologous blood transfusion. Just 24 hours later, the Cofidis team withdrew after Cristian Moreni tested positive for elevated testosterone. At this point, it seemed victory was assured for race leader Michael Rasmussen. Yet doubts about Rasmussen's credibility emerged after it was revealed he had missed drug tests and, on July 25, he was fired, leaving the competition in chaos. (All involved deny any wrongdoing.) Though some journalists and riders called for the Tour to be abandoned, pressure from advertisers and sponsors ensured the show stayed on the road. Eventually, Spaniard Alberto Contador was declared the 2007 winner – yet, for many, the entire Tour was tainted.

Although the Tour no longer considers Floyd Landis its 2006 winner, at the time of writing Landis had not been stripped of his title, and his case was being investigated. Landis denies any wrongdoing.

THE MASTERS · 2007

The 2007 Masters was won by Zach Johnson (his first major tournament victory), who finished the final day 3 under for a 1-over total of 289 – a tie for the highest winning score in Masters' history. Below are the 2007 cash prizes and final scores:

Zach Johnson	$1,305,000...+1	Stuart Appleby	$233,812...+5
Rory Sabbatini	$541,333...+3	David Toms	$210,250...+6
Retief Goosen	$541,333...+3	Paul Casey	$181,250...+7
Tiger Woods	$541,333...+3	Luke Donald	$181,250...+7
Jerry Kelly	$275,500...+4	Vaughn Taylor	$181,250...+7
Justin Rose	$275,500...+4		
Padraig Harrington	$233,812...+5	[The total purse for the event was $7,418,464.]	

GOLF MAJORS · 2007

♂	course	winner	
US OPEN	Oakmont, Pennsylvania	Angel Cabrera [ARG]	+5
BRITISH OPEN	Carnoustie, Scotland	Padraig Harrington [IRL]	−7
USPGA	Southern Hills, Oklahoma	Tiger Woods [USA]	−8
♀			
KRAFT NABISCO	Mission Hills, California	Morgan Pressel [USA]	−3
LPGA	Bulle Rock, Maryland	Suzann Pettersen [NOR]	−14
US OPEN	Pine Needles, North Carolina	Cristie Kerr [USA]	−5
BRITISH OPEN	Old Course, St Andrews	Lorena Ochoa [MEX]	−5

TRACK & FIELD RECORDS

Event		set by	when	record
♂	100m	Asafa Powell [JAM]/Justin Gatlin [USA]	2005/2006	9·77s
♀	100m	Florence Griffith-Joyner [USA]	1988	10·49s
♂	110m hurdles	Xiang Liu [CHN]	2006	12·88s
♀	100m hurdles	Yordanka Donkova [BUL]	1988	12·21s
♂	200m	Michael Johnson [USA]	1996	19·32s
♀	200m	Florence Griffith-Joyner [USA]	1988	21·34s
♂	400m	Michael Johnson [USA]	1999	43·18s
♀	400m	Marita Koch [GDR]	1985	47·60s
♂	400m hurdles	Kevin Young [USA]	1992	46·78s
♀	400m hurdles	Yuliya Pechonkina [RUS]	2003	52·34s
♂	800m	Wilson Kipketer [DEN]	1997	1:41·11
♀	800m	Jarmila Kratochvílová [TCH]	1983	1:53·28
♂	1,500m	Hicham El Guerrouj [MAR]	1998	3:26·00
♀	1,500m	Yunxia Qu [CHN]	1993	3:50·46
♂	Mile	Hicham El Guerrouj [MAR]	1999	3:43·13
♀	Mile	Svetlana Masterkova [RUS]	1996	4:12·56
♂	5,000m	Kenenisa Bekele [ETH]	2004	12:37·35
♀	5,000m	Meseret Defar [ETH]	2007	14:16·63
♂	10,000m	Kenenisa Bekele [ETH]	2005	26:17·53
♀	10,000m	Junxia Wang [CHN]	1993	29:31·78
♂	Marathon	Paul Tergat [KEN]	2003	2:04:55
♀	Marathon	Paula Radcliffe [GBR]	2003	2:15:25
♂	High jump	Javier Sotomayor [CUB]	1993	2·45m
♀	High jump	Stefka Kostadinova [BUL]	1987	2·09m
♂	Long jump	Mike Powell [USA]	1991	8·95m
♀	Long jump	Galina Chistyakova [URS]	1988	7·52m
♂	Triple jump	Jonathan Edwards [GBR]	1995	18·29m
♀	Triple jump	Inessa Kravets [UKR]	1995	15·50m
♂	Pole vault	Sergey Bubka [UKR]	1994	6·14m
♀	Pole vault	Yelena Isinbaeva [RUS]	2005	5·01m
♂	Shot put	Randy Barnes [USA]	1990	23·12m
♀	Shot put	Natalya Lisovskaya [URS]	1987	22·63m
♂	Discus	Jürgen Schult [GER]	1986	74·08m
♀	Discus	Gabriele Reinsch [GDR]	1988	76·80m
♂	Hammer	Yuriy Sedykh [URS]	1986	86·74m
♀	Hammer	Tatyana Lysenko [RUS]	2007	78·61m†
♂	Javelin	Jan Zelezný [CZE]	1996	98·48m
♀	Javelin	Osleidys Menéndez [CUB]	2005	71·70m
♂	Decathlon	Roman Šebrle [CZE]	2001	9,026pts
♀	Heptathlon	Jackie Joyner-Kersee [USA]	1988	7,291pts
♂	4×100m relay	USA	1992	37·40s
♀	4×100m relay	German Democratic Republic	1985	41·37s
♂	4×400m relay	USA	1998	2:54·20
♀	4×400m relay	USSR	1988	3:15·17

[Records correct as of 9·3·07 · † Awaiting ratification]

———————————— THE AMERICA'S CUP ————————————

The America's Cup yacht race is considered the oldest contested trophy in sports history. The first race was staged in 1851 when the *America* (owned by the New York Yacht Club) triumphed over 14 British boats (representing the Royal Yacht Squadron) in a race around the Isle of Wight†. The original trophy was donated to the New York Yacht Club‡ under a 'Deed of Gift' which stated that it must remain a 'perpetual challenge cup for friendly competition between nations'. Nowadays, the Cup (known affectionately as the 'Auld Mug') is contested by its current holder and the winner of the Louis Vuitton Cup. By tradition, each race is hosted by the Cup's previous victor. However, since the last winners, Alinghi, hailed from landlocked Switzerland, the 2007 race was held in Valencia, Spain. (This was the first race to be held in Europe since the original contest in 1851.) Team Alinghi retained their title, for the Société Nautique de Genève yacht club, by defeating Emirates Team New Zealand 5–2 in a seven-race final. Alinghi won the last race by just a second.

† Famously, when Queen Victoria inquired which yacht had been runner-up, she was told: 'Your Majesty, there is no second'. ‡ Until the Cup was won by Australia in 1983, the New York Yacht Club remained unbeaten for 25 challenges over 132 years – the longest winning streak in sports history.

——————— WORLD SWIMMING CHAMPIONSHIP · 2007 ———————

American Michael Phelps won a record seven gold medals and broke five world records at the FINA World Championships in Melbourne on March 25–April 1, 2007. Phelps's efforts helped the American team top the medal table with a total of 40 medals – the most medals for one country in the history of the championships. In total, 15 world records were broken, with 12 new records set by Americans. 16 championship records were also broken, with 8 set by Americans. Selected results:

Event		winner	record	result
♀	50m backstroke	Leila Vaziri [USA]	WR	28·16
♂	100m backstroke	Aaron Peirsol [USA]	WR	52·98
♀	100m backstroke	Natalie Coughlin [USA]	WR	59·44
♀	100m butterfly	Lisbeth Lenton [AUS]	CR	57·15
♂	200m freestyle	Michael Phelps [USA]	WR	1:43·86
♀	200m freestyle	Laure Manaudou [FRA]	WR	1:55·52
♂	200m backstroke	Ryan Lochte [USA]	WR	1:54·32
♂	200m butterfly	Michael Phelps [USA]	WR	1:52·09
♂	200m medley	Michael Phelps [USA]	WR	1:54·98
♀	200m medley	Kathryn Hoff [USA]	CR	2:10·13
♂	400m medley	Michael Phelps [USA]	WR	4:06·22
♀	400m medley	Kathryn Hoff [USA]	WR	4:32·89
♀	4×100m medley	Australia	WR	3:55·74
♂	4×200m freestyle	USA	WR	7:03·24
♀	4×200m freestyle	USA	WR	7:50·09

Key: CR – Championship Record · WR – World Record

——— WIMBLEDON · 2007 ———

All England Lawn Tennis
& Croquet Club, London, UK
June 25–July 8, 2007
Purse: £11,282,710
Attendance: 444,810

MEN'S SINGLES
Roger Federer [SUI]
bt Rafael Nadal [ESP]
7–6 (9–7), 4–6, 7–6 (7–3), 2–6, 6–2

LADIES' SINGLES
Venus Williams [USA]
bt Marion Bartoli [FRA]
6–4, 6–1

MEN'S DOUBLES
Arnaud Clement [FRA]
& Michael Llodra [FRA]
bt Bob Bryan [USA]
& Mike Bryan [USA]
6–7 (5–7), 6–3, 6–4, 6–4

LADIES' DOUBLES
Cara Black [ZIM]
& Liezel Huber [RSA]
bt Katarina Srebotnik [SLO]
& Ai Sugiyama [JPN]
3–6, 6–3, 6–2

MIXED DOUBLES
Jamie Murray [GBR]
& Jelena Jankovic [SRB]
bt Jonas Bjorkman [SWE]
& Alicia Molik [AUS]
6–4, 3–6, 6–1

Fastest serve ♂.....A. Roddick 144mph
Fastest serve ♀.... V. Williams 126mph
Most aces ♂ ..R. Federer 85 in 7 matches
Most aces ♀ ....M. Krajicek 45 in 5

For the first time in Wimbledon history, the singles prize money was equal for both men and women. The winners each received £700,000, and the runners-up £350,000.

——— US OPEN · 2006 ———

Flushing Meadows–Corona Park,
Queens, New York
August 28–September 10, 2006
Purse: >$18·5m
Attendance: *c.*640,000

MEN'S SINGLES
Roger Federer [SUI]
bt Andy Roddick [USA]
6–2, 4–6, 7–5, 6–1

WOMEN'S SINGLES
Maria Sharapova [RUS]
bt Justine Henin-Hardenne [BEL]
6–4, 6–4

MEN'S DOUBLES
Martin Damm [CZE]
& Leander Paes [IND]
bt Jonas Bjorkman [SWE]
& Max Mirnyi [BLR]
6–7 (5–7), 6–4, 6–3

WOMEN'S DOUBLES
Nathalie Dechy [FRA]
& Vera Zvonareva [RUS]
bt Dinara Safina [RUS]
& Katarina Srebotnik [SLO]
7–6 (7–5), 7–5

MIXED DOUBLES
Martina Navratilova† [USA]
& Bob Bryan [USA]
bt Kveta Peschke [CZE]
& Martin Damm [CZE]
6–2, 6–3

Andre Agassi retired after the US Open, ending an illustrious 21-year career in which he won 60 ATP titles and 8 Grand Slams. Agassi told an applauding crowd, 'I will take you and the memory of you with me for the rest of my life'. ❦ The 2006 US Open also witnessed the last match of Martina Navratilova's pro career; her career includes 18 Grand Slam singles titles, 41 Grand Slam doubles titles, and 167 singles wins.

──────── TENNIS GRAND SLAM TOURNAMENTS ────────

Event	month	surface	♂	winner ♀
Australian Open	Jan	Rebound Ace	Roger Federer	Serena Williams
French Open	May/Jun	clay	Rafael Nadal	Justine Henin
Wimbledon	Jun/Jul	grass	Roger Federer	Venus Williams
US Open [2006]	Aug/Sep	cement	Roger Federer	Maria Sharapova

[For more on Federer and Nadal's rivalry and their strengths on various surfaces, see p.230.]

──────────── THE DAVIS CUP ────────────

The Davis Cup was started in 1900 by Harvard student Dwight F. Davis; it now includes 131 countries, of which only 16 qualify to play in the World Group. (The rest fight it out in continental leagues, in an effort to gain promotion into the elite World Group.) The US has belonged to the World Group since 1989, the longest uninterrupted run in the Cup's history, and has won 31 times – though not since 1995. Russia won in 2006, and the 2007 results at the time of writing are below:

February 9–11 · 2007 WORLD GROUP 1ST ROUND
Russia *bt* Chile 3–2
France *bt* Romania 4–1
Germany *bt* Croatia 3–2
Belgium *bt* Australia 3–2
USA *bt* Czech Republic 4–1
Spain *bt* Switzerland 3–2
Sweden *bt* Belarus 3–2
Argentina *bt* Austria 4–1

April 6–8 · 2007 WORLD GROUP QUARTERFINALS
Russia *bt* France 3–2
Germany *bt* Belgium 3–2
USA *bt* Spain 4–1
Sweden *bt* Argentina 4–1

[World Group semifinals are Sep 21–23, 2007, and finals Nov 30–Dec 2, 2007. See daviscup.com.]

──────────── MLS CUP · 2006 ────────────

HOUSTON DYNAMO *bt* NEW ENGLAND REVOLUTION 1–1 (AET, 4–3 PKs)
November 12, 2006 · Field: Pizza Hut Park, Frisco, TX · Attendance: 22,427
Honda MLS Cup MVP · Brian Ching

	total shots	shots on goal	fouls	offsides	corner kicks	saves
Houston Dynamo	15	4	24	5	10	5
New England Revolution	15	6	20	1	10	3

—————MAYWEATHER vs DE LA HOYA—————

On May 5, 2007, 'Golden Boy' Oscar De La Hoya fought 'Pretty Boy' Floyd Mayweather Jr to determine the WBO Super Welterweight title. Many fans hoped the match would help resuscitate the sport of boxing itself, which in recent years has faced charges of disorganization, and competition from the stunning popularity of mixed martial art fighting. (The contest had additional drama since Mayweather's father had worked as De La Hoya's trainer – although he was replaced in January 2007 by Freddie Roach.) ❦ For many fans, and certainly for the organizers, the fight lived up to expectations and hype. The match proved to be the richest in history, with ticket revenues of $19m and pay-per-view income of

$120m. De La Hoya carried most of the action, throwing 587 punches and landing 21%; in response, Mayweather threw 481 punches, landing 43%. Mayweather eventually triumphed in a split decision – though De La Hoya walked away with the larger share of the purse, earning *c.*$45m to Mayweather's *c.*$20m. ❦ Despite the financial success of the fight (for the contestants and organizers), it remained to be seen whether the contest could boost the fortune of boxing more generally.

Mayweather		De La Hoya
2·24·77	DOB	2·4·73
5' 8"	height	5' 10½"
72	reach	73
37–0	record [at match]	38–4

———— WORLD BOXING CHAMPIONS · AS OF 8·16·2007————

Weight	WBC	WBA	IBF	WBO
Heavy	Maskaev [KAZ]	Chagaev [UZB]	Klitschko [UKR]	S Ibragimov [RUS]
Cruiser	Mormeck [FRA]	Mormeck [FRA]	Cunnningham [USA]	Maccarinelli [GBR]
Light heavy	Dawson [USA]	Drews [CRO]	Woods [GBR]	Erdei [HUN]
Super middle	Kessler [DEN]	Kessler [DEN]	Berrio [COL]	Calzaghe [GBR]
Middle	Taylor [USA]	Sturm [GER]	Abraham [AUS]	Taylor [USA]
Junior middle	*vacant*	Alcine [CAN]	Spinks [USA]	Dzinziruk [UKR]
Welter	Mayweather [USA]	Cotto [PUR]	Cintron [PUR]	Williams [USA]
Junior welter	Witter [GBR]	Rees [GBR]	Malignaggi [USA]	Torres [COL]
Light	David Diaz [USA]	Juan Diaz [USA]	Julio Diaz [MEX]	Juan Diaz [USA]
Junior light	Marquez [MEX]	Valero [PAN]	Fana [RSA]	Guzman [DOM]
Feather	Chi [KOR]	John [INA]	Guerrero [USA]	Luevano [USA]
Junior feather	R Marquez [MEX]	Caballero [PAN]	Molitor [CAN]	De Leon [MEX]
Bantam	Hasegawa [JAP]	Sidorenko [UKR]	Perez [NCA]	Peñalosa [PHI]
Junior bantam	Mijares [MEX]	Munoz [VEN]	*vacant*	Montiel [MEX]
Fly	Naito [JAP]	Sakata [JAP]	Donaire [PHI]	Narvaez [ARG]
Junior fly	Sosa [MEX]	Reveco [ARG]	Solis [MEX]	Cazares [MEX]
Straw	Kyowa [JAP]	Niida [JAP]	Condes [PHI]	Calderon [PUR]

Category	*lb*	Jr bantam....115	Jr light.......130	Jr middle 154	Cruiser.......200
Straw 105		Bantam......118	Light.........135	Middle.......160	Heavy......>200
Jr fly.........108		Jr feather.....122	Jr welter 140	Spr middle...168	*[The UK uses*
Fly...........112		Feather.......126	Welter 147	Light heavy..175	*different names.]*

49th DAYTONA 500

February 18, 2007 · Estimated crowd: 185,000
National Anthem: Big & Rich · Prize purse: $18,386,023

Kevin Harvick edged out fan favorite Mark Martin by a mere 0·02 seconds (the closest finish since the beginning of computer scoring) at the 49th running of the Daytona 500. The wreck-filled race followed a week of cheating scandals that led to the suspension of five crew chiefs; two-time Daytona 500 winner Michael Waltrip nearly withdrew after his team was discovered to have used a banned fuel additive.

Driver (start)	team	total points	earnings
Kevin Harvick (34)	Shell/Pennzoil Chevrolet	190	$1,510,469
Mark Martin (26)	US Army Chevrolet	175	$1,120,416
Jeff Burton (7)	Cingular Wireless Chevrolet	165	$819,216
Mike Wallace (22)	Miccosukee Resorts Chevrolet	160	$615,658
David Ragan (35)	AAA Ford	155	$529,350

[Sources: Daytona International Speedway; MSNBC]

2006 NEXTEL CUP CHAMPION

Jimmie Johnson won the 2006 Nextel Cup title for the first time in 2006, after 4 seasons of placing in the top 5. Below are his final stats, according to NASCAR:

Points	starts	poles	wins	top-5	top-10	winnings
6,475	36	1	5	13	24	$8,909,140

91st INDIANAPOLIS 500

May 27, 2007 · Estimated crowd: 350,000
Distance: 500 miles · Average speed: 151·774mph · Cautions: 11

Driver (start)	team	total points	earnings
Dario Franchitti (3)	Canadian Club	181	$1,645,233
Scott Dixon (4)	Target Chip Ganassi Racing	184	$719,067
Helio Castroneves (1)	Team Penske	171	$646,303
Sam Hornish Jr (5)	Team Penske	151	$360,389
Ryan Briscoe (7)	Symantec Luczo Dragon Racing	30	$302,305
Scott Sharp (12)	Patrón Sharp Rahal Letterman Racing	110	$368,305
Tomas Scheckter (10)	Vision Racing	130	$304,105
Danica Patrick (8)	Motorola	109	$298,005
Davey Hamilton (20)	HP Vision Racing	22	$268,905
Vitor Meira (19)	Delphi Panther	103	$280,305

The 2006 IndyCar Series Champion was Sam Hornish Jr – an unprecedented 3rd championship title.

———————————— SPORTS PARTICIPATION ————————————

The National Sporting Goods Association regularly polls the number of Americans (aged 7 or over) who participate in a range of sports more than once during the year. Charted below are the levels of participation during the period 1995–2005:

Sport · Millions of participants	*2005*	*2003*	*2001*	*1999*	*1997*	*1995*
Aerobic exercising	33.7	28.0	26.3	26.2	26.3	23.1
Archery (target)	6.8	3.9	4.7	4.9	4.8	4.9
Backpack/wilderness camp	13.3	15.1	14.5	15.3	12.0	10.2
Baseball	14.6	15.4	14.9	16.3	14.1	15.7
Basketball	29.9	27.9	28.1	29.6	30.7	30.1
Bicycle riding	43.1	38.3	39.0	42.4	45.1	56.3
Billiards/pool	37.3	33.0	32.7	32.1	36.0	31.1
Boating, motor/power	27.5	24.2	23.9	24.4	27.2	26.8
Bowling	45.4	41.9	41.9	41.6	44.8	41.9
Camping (vacation/overnight)	46.0	53.4	48.7	50.1	46.6	42.8
Cheerleading	3.3	–	3.7	–	–	2.9
Exercise walking	86.0	81.6	78.3	80.8	76.3	70.3
Exercising with equipment	54.2	50.2	43.9	45.2	47.9	44.3
Fishing	43.3	42.7	44.4	46.7	44.7	44.2
Football (tackle)	9.9	8.7	8.2	8.4	8.2	8.3
Golf	24.7	25.7	26.6	27.0	26.2	24.0
Hiking	29.8	26.7	26.1	28.1	28.4	25.0
Hockey (ice)	2.4	1.9	2.2	1.9	1.9	2.2
Hunting w/bow & arrow	6.6	5.0	4.7	5.8	5.3	5.3
Hunting with firearms	19.4	17.9	19.2	17.1	17.0	17.4
In-line roller skating	13.1	16.0	19.2	24.1	26.6	23.9
Kayaking/rafting	7.6	–	3.5	3.0	2.9	3.5
Mountain biking (off-road)	9.2	8.2	6.9	6.8	8.1	6.7
Muzzle loading	4.1	3.4	3.2	3.3	2.9	–
Paintball games	8.0	7.4	5.6	5.1	–	–
Running/jogging	29.2	23.9	24.5	22.4	21.7	20.6
Scooter riding	10.4	11.9	12.7	–	–	–
Skateboarding	12.0	9.0	9.6	7.0	6.3	4.5
Skiing (alpine)	6.9	6.8	7.7	7.4	8.9	9.3
Skiing (cross-country)	1.9	1.9	2.3	2.2	2.5	3.4
Snowboarding	6.0	6.3	5.3	3.3	2.8	2.8
Soccer	14.1	13.0	13.9	13.2	13.7	12.0
Softball	14.1	12.4	13.2	14.7	16.3	17.6
Swimming	58.0	52.3	54.8	57.9	59.5	61.5
Target shooting	21.9	17.9	17.3	17.7	18.5	19.4
Target shooting – airgun	6.7	3.8	2.9	3.5	3.4	4.4
Tennis	11.1	9.6	10.9	10.9	11.1	12.6
Volleyball	13.2	10.4	12.0	11.7	17.8	18.0
Water skiing	6.7	5.5	5.8	6.6	6.5	6.9
Weight lifting	35.5	25.9	23.9	–	–	–
Workout at club	34.7	29.5	26.5	24.1	21.1	22.0

———————OTHER SPORTS STORIES & RESULTS———————

· BARRY BONDS ·

At 20:51PDT on 8/7/07, Barry Bonds hit his 756th home run, thereby smashing the Major League Baseball home run record (of 755) set by Hank Aaron in 1976. Bonds, a left-handed slugger for the SF Giants, set his new benchmark in front of home fans off a pitch by Mike Bacsik of the Washington Nationals. (That Washington won the game 8–6 is likely to be a footnote in baseball history.) In a taped message broadcast to the 43,154-strong crowd, Aaron was magnanimous: 'I move over and offer my best wishes to Barry and his family … My hope today … is that the achievement of this record will inspire others to chase their own dreams'. Although few doubted that Aaron's crown would eventually be toppled by a player of the modern game, Bond's race to 756 was dogged by allegations he had taken steroids – charges he has vigorously denied. In a statement, MLB Commissioner Bud Selig hinted at the controversy: 'While the issues which have swirled around this record will continue to work themselves toward resolution, today is a day for congratulations on a truly remarkable achievement'. Speaking to reporters after his historic innings, Bonds shrugged off the rumors: 'This record is not tainted at all, at all … Period. You guys can say whatever you want'.

· NATHAN'S FAMOUS
HOT DOG EATING CONTEST ·

On 7/4/07, the highly coveted 'Mustard Belt' finally returned to America after Californian Joey Chestnut outate Japanese 6-time champion Takeru 'The Tsunami' Kobayashi at Nathan's Famous Fourth of July International Hot Dog Eating Contest. This Coney Island event, held every Independence Day since 1916, challenges the world's most dedicated gluttons to consume the most hot dogs and buns (HDBs) in a 12-minute eat-off. Despite reports of a jaw injury, Kobayashi competed with his trademark focus until the final minutes of the challenge, when he lost ground to Chestnut and suffered what race commentators delicately call a 'reversal'. In the end, Kobayashi's personal best of 63 HDBs was not enough to beat Chestnut's world-record-setting ingestion of 66 HDBs.

· NBA 'RACIAL BIAS' STUDY ·

In a 5/2/07 article, the *New York Times* reported that an academic study had found statistical evidence of racial discrimination by NBA referees. The unpublished study, by professors from the University of Pennsylvania and Cornell, found that between 1991–2004, white NBA referees were more likely to call fouls against black players than white players, and suggested that this discrimination could affect the outcomes of several games a season. After accounting for a raft of variables, the study's authors concluded that 'black players receive around $0·12$–$0·20$ more fouls per 48 minutes … when the number of white referees officiating a game increases from 0 to 3'. The authors were careful to caution that the effect was caused by unconscious 'own-race bias', rather than intentional racism. Yet, inevitably, the report raised controversy, and was dismissed by the NBA, which pointed to its own (independent) study that found no evidence of bias. Though experts called in by the *Times* and ESPN found the academics' study the more credible, at the time of writing it seemed unlikely that the report, or the surrounding debate, would have any effect on NBA practices.

—————OTHER SPORTS STORIES & RESULTS cont.—————

· PISTORIUS *vs* THE IAAF ·

At a July 2007 IAAF Golden League meeting in Rome, Italy, the paralympian double amputee Oscar Pistorius came in 2nd in the 400m, competing against able-bodied athletes. Described as the 'fastest thing on no legs', Pistorius hopes to compete at the Olympics – however, to achieve this, he must first obtain permission from the International Association of Athletics Federations (IAAF). The IAAF have questioned whether the carbon fiber blades used by Pistorius give him an unfair advantage by lengthening his stride to unnatural proportions. The technical and ethical issues surrounding this decision have proved complex, and many have questioned whether allowing Pistorius to compete would set a precedent for able-bodied athletes to use similar technologies to enhance their performance. At the time of writing, Pistorius had agreed to undergo biomechanical tests so that the IAAF could assess whether the use of such prosthetics was 'fair'.

· SWIMMING THE AMAZON ·

On 4/7/07, 52-year-old Slovenian Martin Strel became the first person to swim the entire length of the Amazon. At an average of 52 miles a day, it took Strel 66 days to swim the 3,272-mile river. He wore only a wetsuit for the perilous journey, during which he dodged piranhas, tackled crocodiles, and suffered nausea, diarrhea, and severe sunburn. A seasoned marathon swimmer, Strel had previously conquered the Mississippi in 2001 (2,348 miles), the Danube in 2002 (1,776 miles), and the Yangtze in 2004 (3,900 miles). Strel completed his Amazon swim to raise awareness of the plight of the rainforest, saying 'I hope people remember this rainforest is our friend and stop destroying it'.

· IDITAROD ·

Alaska's Iditarod dogsled race is run annually from Anchorage to Nome, across 1,150 miles of frozen rivers, forest, and tundra. 109 mushers competed in 2007, each leading a team of 12–16 dogs. The race was won by Lance Mackey – who finished in 9 days, 5 hours, 8 minutes, 41 seconds – earning himself a brand-new pickup truck and $69,000. (Curiously, Mackey's brother and father are also former Iditarod champions; all three won while racing their 6th Iditarod and wearing the No. 13 bib.) Ellen Halverson was awarded the Red Lantern, given to the last team reaching Nome.

· 'BECKS' COMES TO AMERICA ·

On 1/11/07, soccer superstar David Beckham confirmed a ($250m?) deal to leave Spanish team Real Madrid and join the MLS Los Angeles Galaxy. Though relatively unknown in the US prior to this move, Beckham captained England's national team from November 2000 to July 2006, and featured prominently in the last three soccer World Cups. His chiseled body, ever-changing hairstyle, and marriage to Victoria (aka 'Posh Spice') ensured Beckham a near permanent presence in the British tabloids. The 'Posh & Becks' move to the US was no less devoid of media froth. On July 13, Beckham was officially declared a 'Galaxian' before 2,500 fans at an LA ceremony; he made his MLS debut on July 21. (Nursing an ankle injury, Beckham played for less than 20 minutes; he redeemed himself with his first goal on August 15.) While some fans argue that Beckham is overexposed and overrated, there can be no doubt that his move increased the profile of the MLS. The long-term effect of Posh & Becks on US soccer (and the US media) remains to be seen.

——— READY RECKONER OF OTHER RESULTS · 2006–07———

AMATEUR ATHLETICS · AAU James E. Sullivan Memorial Award	Jessica Long
AUTO RACING · F1 US Grand Prix	Lewis Hamilton [GBR]
F1 World Drivers Championship [2006]	Fernando Alonso [ESP] · Renault
F1 World Constructors Championship [2006]	Renault [FRA]
Champ. Car Atlantic Championship	Franck Perera [FRA]
Champ. Car World Series Season Champion [2006]	Sébastien Bourdais [FRA]
BADMINTON · World Championship [2006]	
Singles	♂ Lin Dan [CHI] · ♀ Xie Xingfang [CHI]
Doubles	♂ Fu Haifeng/Cai Yun [CHI] · ♀ Gao Link/Huang Sui [CHI]
Mixed doubles	Nathan Robertson & Gail Emm [GBR]
BASEBALL · MLB All-Star Game	American League *bt* National League 5–4
BASKETBALL · NBA All-Star Game	Western Conf. *bt* Eastern Conf. 153–132
FIBA World Championship [2006]	Spain *bt* Greece 70–47
BOWLING · USBC Masters [2006]	Doug Kent *bt* Jack Jurek 277–230
US Open	Pete Weber *bt* Wes Malott 210–204
Denny's World Championship	Doug Kent *bt* Chris Barnes 237–216
PBA Tournament of Champions	Tommy Jones *bt* Tony Reyes 257–222
USBC Queens Tournament	Kelly Kulick *bt* Diandra Asbaty 192–143
BOXING · *Ring Mag.* Fight of the Year [2006]	S. Sithchatchawal *bt* M. Monshipour
Ring Magazine Fighter of the Year [2006]	Manny Pacquiao
CHESS · FIDE World Championship [2006]	Vladimir Kramnik
US Chess Championship	Alexander Shabalov
US Women's Chess Championship	Irina Krush
ELEPHANT POLO · World Championships	Angus Estates *bt* National Parks of Nepal
DIRECTORS' CUP · NCAA Division I	Stanford
Division II	Grand Valley State
Division III	Williams
NAIA	Azusa Pacific
DIVING · FINA Diving World Cup	China [15 medals]
DRAGON BOAT RACING · IDBF CCWC Premier Mixed 2000m	FCRCC [CAN]
FISHING · Bassmaster Classic Championship	Boyd Duckett
IGFA Inshore World Championship	Robert Collins
IGFA Offshore World Championship	Marina Rubicon Marlin Cup [ESP]
GYMNASTICS · Acrobatic Gymnastics World Cup Finals	
Mixed pairs	Revaz Gurgenidze & Tatiana Okulova [RUS] 29·052
Women's pairs	Kristina Maraziuk & Natalia Kakhntuk [BLR] 28·630
Men's pairs	Konstantin Pilipchuk & Alexei Dudchenko [RUS] 28·661
ICE HOCKEY · World Championship	Canada *bt* Finland 4–2
LACROSSE · Division I NCAA Men's Champ.	Johns Hopkins *bt* Duke 12–11
Division I NCAA Women's Champ.	Northwestern *bt* Virginia 15–13
LITTLE LEAGUE BASEBALL · World Series [2006]	Columbus, GA, Little League
LITTLE LEAGUE SOFTBALL · World Series	Morristown, TN, Little League
MOBILE PHONE THROWING · World Champ. [2006]	Lassi Etelätalo [FIN] 292'
MONSTER TRUCK RALLY · Monster Jam World Finals	
Racing	*Batman*, driven by John Seasock
Freestyle	*Captain's Curse*, driven by Pablo Huffaker

— READY RECKONER OF OTHER RESULTS 2006–07 cont. —

MOTORCYCLE RACING · US Grand Prix	Casey Stoner [AUS]
PAN AMERICAN GAMES	USA [237 medals]
PARACHUTING · FAI World Cup Formation Skydiving 8-way	France, 204pts
FAI World Cup Formation Skydiving 4-way	Belgium, 252pts
POKER · World Series	Jerry Yang
PUZZLES · US Puzzle Championship	Thomas Snyder, 350pts
POWER BOAT RACING · APBA Gold Cup	Dave Villwock
ROCK PAPER SCISSORS · USARPS World Championship	Jamie Langridge
RODEO · World Championships [2006]	Trevor Brazille
Bareback Riding Champion	Will Lowe
Steer Wrestling Champion	Dean Gorsuch
Saddle Bronc Riding Champion	Chad Ferley
Tie-down Roping Champion	Cody Ohl
Bull Riding Champion	B.J. Schumacher
SKIING · FIS Alpine World Ski Championships	AUT [9 medals]
FIS Nordic World Ski Championships	NOR [16 medals]
SNOWSHOEING · USSSA Nat. Snowshoe Champ.	♂ G. Hexum Sr; ♀ N. Kimball
SOCCER · Copa América	Brazil *bt* Argentina 3–0
Asian Cup	Iraq *bt* Saudi Arabia 1–0
SOFTBALL · ASA Men's major fast pitch	Patsy's
ASA Women's major fast pitch	Stratford Brakettes
USSSA Men's major slow pitch [2006]	Resmondo
SQUASH · Super Series Finals	Ramy Ashour [EGY] *bt* Gregory Gaultier [FRA]
World Women's tournament [2006]	England *bt* Egypt 2–0
SUDOKU · World Sudoku Championship	Thomas Snyder [USA]
SWIMMING · ConocoPhillips National Championships	
200m backstroke	♂ Michael Phelps 1:54·65; ♀ Katie Hoff 2:10·31
200m breaststroke	♂ Brendan Hansen 2:09·91; ♀ Rebecca Soni 2:23·62
50m freestyle	♂ Ben Wildman-Tobriner 21·80; ♀ Dara Torres 24·53
100m freestyle	♂ David Walters 48·96; ♀ Dara Torres 54·45
800m freestyle	♂ Erik Vendt 7:49·75; ♀ Kate Ziegler 8·22·33
TENNIS · Fed Cup [2006]	Italy *bt* Belgium 3–2
WTA Champ [2006]	Justine Henin-Hardenne *bt* Amélie Mauresmo 6–4, 6–3
TRIATHLONS · ITU Age Grp World Champ. [2006]	M. Bonnet-Eymard [USA] 2:05·31
Aquathalon World Championship [2006]	James Lock [GBR] 0:29·54
Ironman World Championship [2006]	Normann Stadler [GER] 8:11·56
WOMEN'S HOCKEY · NWHL Ch. Cup	Brampton Thunder *bt* Montreal Axiom
WRESTLING · NCAA Division I	Minnesota Golden Gophers
X GAMES 13 · Skateboarding Big Air	Bob Burnquist 95·66
Skateboard street	♂ Chris Cole 94·33; ♀ Marisa Dal Santo 86·08
Skateboard vert	♂ Shaun White; ♀ Lyn-Z Adams Hawkins
Moto X freestyle	Adam Jones 94·40
BMX vert	Jamie Bestwick 93·66
BMX park	Daniel Dhers 91·66

All events took place in 2007, unless otherwise stated.

The Nation

*America is the only nation in history which miraculously has gone directly
from barbarism to degeneration without the usual interval of civilization.*
— GEORGES CLEMENCEAU [attributed] (1841–1929)

——US GEOGRAPHIC SPECIFICATIONS & EXTREMES——

Highest point . . . . Mount McKinley, Alaska (20,320ft above sea level)
Lowest point . . . . Death Valley, California (282ft below sea level)
Mean elevation . . . . ≈2,500ft
Northernmost point . . . . Point Barrow, Alaska
Southernmost point . . . . Ka Lae (South Cape), Hawaii
Easternmost point . . . . West Quoddy Head, Maine
Westernmost point . . . . Cape Wrangell, Alaska

GEOGRAPHIC AREA
Total . . . . .3,794,083 sq mi
Land . . . . .3,537,438 sq mi
Water . . . . .256,645 sq mi
[includes only the 50 States and DC]
LAND BOUNDARIES
Total . . . . .7,478 mi
Canada . . . . .5,526 mi
[including 1,539 mi with Alaska]
Mexico . . . . .1,952 mi
Guantánamo Bay† . . . . 17 mi
Coastline . . . . 12,380 mi
MARITIME CLAIMS
Territorial sea . . . . 12 nautical miles
Contiguous zone . . . . 24 nm
Exclusive economic zone . . . . . .200 nm
Continental shelf . . . . .not specified
LAND USE (2005)
Arable land .18·01%
Permanent crops . . . . 0·21%
Other . . . . .81·78%
different calculations exist
[Sources: USGS; CIA; Dept of Interior]

US Commonwealth & Territories
American Samoa · Guam
Northern Mariana Islands
Puerto Rico · Virgin Islands

Freely Associated States
Republic of the Marshall Islands
Federated States of Micronesia
Republic of Palau (status review in 2009)

Other areas under US jurisdiction
Midway Atoll · Palmyra Atoll
Wake Atoll · Baker Island
Howland Island · Jarvis Island
Johnston Atoll · Kingman Reef
Navassa Island (claimed by Haiti)

Extremes calculated based on the geographic
center of the US, including Alaska and Hawaii.
† Since 1903, the US has leased Guantánamo
Bay from Cuba for *c.*$4,000 per year – although
as an act of protest, the Cuban government
refuses to cash the checks.

There are 663 WILDERNESS AREAS in the US covering 105,764,330 acres (an area
greater than California). The 1864 Wilderness Act gave Congress the authority to
designate and protect these unique areas 'where the earth and its community of life
are untrammeled by man, where man himself is a visitor who does not remain…'.

LARGEST US CITIES

City	state	2005 pop.	± since 2000 (%)	nickname(s)
New York	NY	8,143,197	134,919 (1·7)	*The Big Apple; Gotham City*
Los Angeles	CA	3,844,829	150,000 (4·1)	*City of Angels; La La Land*
Chicago	IL	2,842,518	−53,498 (−1·8)	*The Windy City; Big Town*
Houston	TX	2,016,582	62,951 (3·2)	*Magnolia City; Clutch City*
Philadelphia	PA	1,463,281	−54,269 (−3·6)	*City of Brotherly Love*
Phoenix	AZ	1,461,575	140,530 (10·6)	*Valley of the Sun*
San Antonio	TX	1,256,509	111,863 (9·8)	*Alamo City; Mission City*
San Diego	CA	1,255,540	32,140 (2·6)	*Plymouth of the West*
Dallas	TX	1,213,825	25,245 (2·1)	*The Big D*
San Jose	CA	912,332	17,389 (1·9)	*Capital of Silicon Valley*

[As of July 1, 2005 · Source: US Census · Some cities have additional or alternative nicknames]

AMERICAN SUPERLATIVES OF NOTE

Highest active volcano	Wrangell, Alaska	4,316m
Highest dam	Oroville Dam, California	770ft
Highest waterfall	Yosemite Falls, California	2,425ft
Biggest waterfall (volume)	Niagara Falls, New York	168,000m³/s
Deepest depression	Death Valley, California	282ft below sea level
Largest lake	Michigan-Huron, USA/Canada	45,300m²
Longest suspension bridge	Verrazano Narrows, New York	1,298m
Largest geyser	Steamboat, Yellowstone National Park	>300ft
Tallest inhabited building	Sears Tower, Chicago	110 stories, 443m
Tallest structure	KVLY TV mast, North Dakota	629m
Longest rail tunnel	New Cascade, Washington	12,537m
Longest road tunnel	Ted Williams/I-90 Extension, MA	4,200m

Unsurprisingly, a degree of uncertainty and debate surrounds some of these entries and their specifications.

SOME BELTS OF NOTE

The US is home to many belts: the Southern and Southwest states are often called the SUN BELT; the North-central and Northeast regions are the FROST BELT; parts of the South and Midwest are the BIBLE BELT; an agricultural swath of the northern Midwest is the CORN BELT (which overlaps with the GRAIN BELT); the industrial stretch from the Northeastern seaboard to the Midwest is the MANUFACTURING BELT (or RUST BELT); several warm sections of the country are called BANANA BELTS; a section of the Atlantic and Gulf coast, once known for producing cotton, is the COTTON BELT; the BLACK BELT once referred to a Southern region of dark soil fit for growing cotton, but now refers to the Southeast states known for high concentrations of African Americans; the BORSCHT BELT is a nickname for a part of the Catskills popular with Ashkenazi Jews; and the JELLO BELT refers to Utah's, and Idaho's communities of Mormons, who apparently enjoy the wobbly dessert.

─────────────── THE BALD EAGLE ───────────────

Congress adopted the bald eagle as a National Emblem in 1782, when the bird was chosen as part of the design for the Great Seal of the United States. Benjamin Franklin famously opposed the use of the bird because he disapproved of its opportunistic hunting habits; in a letter to his daughter he declared that the eagle was '*a bird of bad moral character*'. Franklin preferred the wild turkey, which '*though a little vain and silly*' was, in his estimation, '*a bird of courage*'. ❦ The Founding Fathers gave no precise justification for the inclusion of the eagle in the Great Seal, but the bird is often thought to represent strength, courage, and freedom. Other eagles have been used as symbols of power and military might by the Sumerians, Assyrians, Romans, Greeks, Austrians, Prussians, Russians, French, Germans, and others. ❦ In addition to the Great Seal and Presidential Seal, bald eagles may be found on military and government uniforms, atop the mace in the House of Representatives [see p.296], in the Library of Congress main reading room, and on the candy in Air Force One. The birds have also been a frequent motif on US money, including the $10 gold 'eagle', the $5 'half eagle', and the $2·50 'quarter eagle' (all discontinued). Notably, the crest for the Apollo space project also depicts an eagle, and the capsule that landed on the Moon in 1969 was named the *Eagle* – hence the phrase 'the Eagle has landed'. ❦ *Haliaeetus leucocephalus* is found throughout N America, along rivers, coasts, and lakes, most commonly in Alaska and Canada. It is known for its size, and can reach 14lbs in weight with a wingspan of 8'. The birds were threatened in the mid-C20th by the pesticide DDT, which rendered some eagles infertile and caused their eggs to crack. Fortunately, federal provisions have helped eagle populations recover. In 1967, the birds were declared an 'endangered' species; and in 1972, DDT was banned. In 1995, the birds' status was upgraded to 'threatened' in the lower 48 states. On June 28, 2007, the US Fish and Wildlife Service announced that the bald eagle was 'flourishing across the nation'. Consequently, the bird was removed from the endangered species list altogether.

A bald eagle nicknamed 'Old Abe' was used as a mascot by the 8th Wisconsin Infantry in the Civil War. According to legend, the bird survived 42 battles with only the loss of a few feathers. Old Abe became famous as a war hero, and has since been immortalized in the 101st Airborne Div. insignia.

─────────────── FEDERAL HOLIDAYS ───────────────

Federal law [5 U.S.C. 6103] establishes these public holidays for federal employees:

New Year's Day · Birthday of Martin Luther King Jr · Washington's Birthday
Memorial Day · Independence Day · Labor Day · Columbus Day
Veterans Day · Thanksgiving · Christmas Day

[See also the Ephemerides chapter, p.343]

—————————— TO/FROM IMMIGRATION FIGURES ——————————

1,266,264 people obtained legal permanent residence in the US in FY 2006. Below are their top countries of birth, and the top states in which they chose to settle:

Country immigrated from		*State immigrated to*	
Mexico	173,753	California	264,677
China	87,345	New York	180,165
Philippines	74,607	Florida	155,996
India	61,369	Texas	89,037
Cuba	45,614	New Jersey	65,934
Colombia	43,151	Illinois	52,459
Dominican Republic	38,069	Virginia	38,488
El Salvador	31,783	Massachusetts	35,560
Vietnam	30,695	Georgia	32,202

[Source: US Department of Homeland Security, 2006]

—————————— NEW CITIZENSHIP TEST ——————————

Those wishing to obtain US citizenship are required to pass a naturalization exam testing their ability to read, write, and speak English, and their knowledge of US history and civic values. In November 2006, the federal government announced pilot testing for a revised exam, intended to encourage 'civic learning and patriotism among prospective citizens', rather than rote learning of historical facts – as critics of the previous test charged. Below is a selection of Q&As from the revised test:

QUESTION	ANSWER
What is the supreme law of the land?	*The Constitution*
What do we call the first 10 amendments to the Constitution?	*The Bill of Rights*
What type of economic system does the US have?	*a capitalist economy*
Why do we have 3 branches of government?	*so that no branch is too powerful*
Who is in charge of the executive branch?	*the President*
How old must a President be?	*35 or over*
Who is the Commander-in-Chief of the military?	*the President*
What is self-government?	*powers come from the people*
What are 'inalienable rights'?	*individual rights that people are born with*
What is the Pledge of Allegiance?	*the promise of loyalty to the flag and the nation*
Why did the colonists fight the British?	*taxation without representation*
What group of people was taken to America and sold as slaves?	*Africans*
Who was President during WWI?	*Woodrow Wilson*
What was the main concern of the US during the Cold War?	*spread of Communism*
What is the longest river in the United States?	*the Missouri River*
What is the tallest mountain in the United States?	*Mount McKinley*

Some questions allow for the possibility of several different answers. The revised exam is being tested in 10 cities before being released nationwide in 2008. [Source: US Citizenship & Immigration Services]

THE STATUE OF LIBERTY

The Statue of Liberty (formally titled *Liberty Enlightening the World*) was a gift from France to America in 1885, intended as a symbol of the friendship the two nations developed during the American Revolution. Designed by the Alsatian Frédéric-Auguste Bartholdi, the statue depicts a woman holding a torch [enlightenment] in her right hand, and a tablet [the law] in her left; she wears a crown with 7 rays [the 7 seas and 7 continents], and stands above a broken shackle and chains [freedom from oppression].

'Keep, ancient lands, your storied pomp!' cries she, | With silent lips. 'Give me your tired, your poor, | Your huddled masses yearning to breathe free, | The wretched refuse of your teeming shore; | Send these, the homeless, tempest-tost to me, | I lift my lamp beside the golden door!'

from The New Colossus
by Emma Lazarus

Her tablet is inscribed with the date of American Independence in Roman numerals: July IV MDCCLXXVI. (The statue was originally meant to mark the centenary of the American Revolution, but was not unveiled until ten years later, in 1886). ❧ The Statue stands on Liberty Island in New York Harbor, and was for many years the first US landmark seen by new immigrants. A poem written by Emma Lazarus to raise money for the pedestal appears at the statue's base [the final stanza is inset].

THE 'RED PHONE'

During a visit to China in March 2007, Chairman of the Joint Chiefs of Staff General Peter Pace announced that Washington and Beijing were considering an emergency hotline between the leaders of the two countries. Such hotlines tend to be known as 'red phones', after the US–Russia link established in 1963, following the potentially disastrous failures of communication during the 'Cuban missile crisis'. (For example, it reportedly took the US *c*.12 hours to receive and decode Khrushchev's first settlement message, and the Soviet ambassador later disclosed that he handed messages to a bicycle courier, who in turn sent them via Western Union.) The 'red phone' was actually used for the first time in 1967, when it helped prevent the Six Day War from escalating into a global conflict. ❧ Initially, the 'red phone' consisted of a set of teleprinters connected via transatlantic cable. In the 1970s the teleprinters were replaced with actual phones and, later, satellite communication lines and facsimile transmission. Why the phone is 'red' is the subject of some speculation. Moscow apparently called their side of the connection 'the red telephone' – though whether this was because of its actual color, the urgency of its function, or a humorous allusion to political ideology, is unclear. To this day, operators reportedly continue to send a coded message every hour for maintenance purposes, and are said to enjoy testing their colleague's skills with texts such as favorite chili recipes and (from the Russians) tricky passages from Dostoevsky.

Ironically, there has never been a red phone in the Oval Office. The phone has been black (pre-Kennedy, Nixon–Ford, Bush 41–43), turquoise (Kennedy–Johnson), and white (Carter–Reagan). In April 2007, it was disclosed that China and Japan had discussed the establishment of their own 24-hour hotline to guard against 'unexpected eventualities'. [Sources: BBC; *Time*; CNN; *CDI Russia Weekly*]

────STATE DEPARTMENT & MISINFORMATION────

The website of the US Dept of State contains a section dedicated to 'Identifying Misinformation' and debunking conspiracy theories, urban legends, and the like. The site is maintained by the Department's 'counter-misinformation officer', who 'has 13 years of experience in this area'. Inevitably, a significant part of the site addresses the many conspiracy theories relating to the 9/11 attacks, including:

'The World Trade Center (WTC) twin towers were destroyed by controlled demolitions.'

'United Airlines flight 93, which crashed in Pennsylvania, was shot down by a missile.'

'No plane hit the Pentagon on 9/11. Instead, it was a missile fired by elements "from inside the American state apparatus."'

'Insider trading in the stocks of United Airlines and American Airlines just before September 11 is evidence of advance knowledge of the plot.'

'The planes that hit the WTC towers were remotely controlled.'

'4,000 Jews failed to show up for work at the WTC on September 11.'

'WTC building 7 was destroyed by a controlled demolition.'

'Al Qaeda is not responsible for the September 11 attacks.'

Each of these 'prevalent myths' is systematically addressed and rebutted by the State Dept, using published reports and eyewitness statements. Additionally, the website offers tips for identifying misinformation – much of which, it notes, is directed against the US military or intelligence community – 'a favorite villain in many conspiracy theories'. Journalists and news consumers are advised always to ask:

Does the story fit the pattern of a conspiracy theory? [*'Conspiracy theories are rarely true, even though they have great appeal and are often widely believed. In reality, events usually have much less exciting explanations'*]

Does the story contain a shocking revelation about a highly controversial issue? [*Any highly controversial issue or taboo behavior is ripe material for false rumors and urban legends'*]

Does the story fit the pattern of an 'urban legend?' [*'Is the story startlingly good, bad, amazing, horrifying, or otherwise seemingly "too good" or "too terrible" to be true? Urban legends, which often circulate by word of mouth, e-mail, or the Internet, are false claims that are widely believed because they put a common fear, hope, suspicion … into story form'*]

Is the source trustworthy? [*'Certain websites, publications, and individuals are known for spreading false stories'*]

What does further research tell you? [*'The only way to determine whether an allegation is true or false is to research it as thoroughly as possible'*]

A number of other myths are refuted by the State Dept, including: the US will invade Venezuela in an operation supposedly entitled 'Plan Balboa'; the AIDS virus was created by the US military to be used as a biological weapon; Americans kidnap children from the Third World and murder them for their body parts; and so on.

―――――――――― THE DIPLOMATIC SERVICE ――――――――――

The origins of modern diplomacy can be traced back to C13th northern Italy, where city states like Milan and Venice exchanged ambassadors to improve relations and facilitate trade. As relationships between European countries became increasingly important, major states began to post ambassadors permanently at overseas courts. In 1487, Spain sent to England the first permanent representative. The 1815 Congress of Vienna formalized the previously ad hoc system of diplomatic rank and precedence, a system that often soured international relations when one country received only low-ranking officials from another. The diplomatic hierarchy was:

Ambassador, Papal Nuncio, or High Commissioner . . . . *represents head of state*
Minister Plenipotentiary . . . . *in charge of legations rather than embassies*
Minister . . . . *lowest rank of diplomatic mission chief*
Chargé d'Affaires . . . . *temporary head of mission, in absence of more senior staff*

With the formation of the UN after WWII, it became increasingly unacceptable for countries to treat others as diplomatically inferior. As a consequence, most legations were upgraded to embassies, and most embassies were headed by ambassadors. Rules relating to the treatment and status of ambassadors and their staff were formalized by the 1961 Vienna Convention, which created diplomatic immunity[†] and exemptions from taxation. Traditionally, the credentials of ambassadors are held in a sealed letter signed by the sovereign or head of state, which grants them powers of negotiation. ❦ Because of political tensions, the United States currently enjoys diplomatic relations with four countries via intermediaries: BHUTAN, through the US Embassy in New Delhi; CUBA, through the US Interest Section in Havana; IRAN, through the Swiss Embassy in Tehran; and NORTH KOREA, through the Swedish Embassy in Pyongyang. ❦ At the time of writing, the US had 90 career Ambassadors, 53 noncareer Ambassadors, and 27 vacant Chief of Mission posts.

† To ensure independence, diplomats are exempt from the criminal, civil, and administrative jurisdiction of their host country. Consequently, diplomats cannot be arrested, have their homes searched, be called as a witness, nor prosecuted. However, in exceptional cases this immunity may be waived.

―――――――― PRESIDENTIAL VISITS ABROAD · 2006 ――――――――

2·28·06 . . . . Shannon, Ireland	7·14–17·06 . . . . St Petersburg
3·1·06 . Bagram & Kabul, Afghanistan	11·15·06 . . . . Moscow
3·1–3·06 . . . . New Delhi &	11·16–17·06 . . . . .Singapore
Hyderabad, India	11·17–20·06 . . . . .Hanoi &
3·3–4·06 . . . . Islamabad, Pakistan	Ho Chi Minh City, Vietnam
3·30–31·06 . . . Cancún & Chichén Itzá	11·20·06 . . . Jakarta & Bogor, Indonesia
6·13·06 . . . . Baghdad	11·27–28·06 . . . . Tallinn, Estonia
6·20–21·06 . . . . .Vienna	11·28–29·06 . . . . Riga, Latvia
6·21–22·06 . . . . Budapest	11·29–30·06 . . . . Amman, Jordan
7·12–14·06 . . . . Stralsund &	
Trinwillershagen, Germany	[Source: State Department]

---CULTURALLY SIGNIFICANT PROPERTIES---

Among the 3,500 properties which the State Department owns or leases worldwide, *c.*150 are deemed 'culturally significant', and are listed on the *Register of Culturally Significant Property.* Buildings are added to the register because of their association with a significant historical event, their architectural merit, their archaeological heritage, or their contribution to US 'overseas heritage'. Some highlights of the list:

Ambassador's Residence (*Tokyo*) · Seoul Old American Legation (*Seoul*)
Villa Otium (*Oslo*) · Winfield House (*London*) · Palacio Bosch (*Buenos Aires*)
Hôtel de Talleyrand (*Paris*) · New Delhi Chancery (*New Delhi*)
Palazzo Margherita & Twin Villas (*Rome*) · Schoenborn Palace (*Prague*)
Tangier Old Legation (*Tangier*) · Tirana Embassy (*Tirana, Albania*)

---SISTER CITIES---

'Sister city' programs are long-term partnerships between cities, states, and towns around the world, formed with the aim of promoting cultural understanding and aiding economic development. In 1931, Toledo, Ohio became the first US city to establish a 'sister city' – with Toledo, Spain. Several other cities established such ties under President Dwight D. Eisenhower's 'People to People' program, which encouraged citizen diplomacy as a path to peace. The programs often feature educational and business exchanges and other collaborative projects. A selection of US sister cities:

Atlanta, GA .... Ancient Olympia, Greece; Tbilisi, Georgia; Toulouse, France
Beverly Hills, CA ....Cannes, France
Berkeley, CA .... Blackfeet Nation, California; Yurok Tribe, California
Boston, MA................. Barcelona, Spain; Kyoto, Japan; Melbourne, Australia
Dallas, TX.. Kirkuk, Iraq
Denver, CO ....Chennai, India; Nairobi, Kenya; Ulaanbaatar, Mongolia
Fort Worth, TX...Budapest, Hungary
Honolulu City and County, HI.......... Hiroshima, Japan; Incheon, South Korea
Los Angeles, CA ....Athens, Greece; Berlin, Germany;
    Bordeaux, France; Eilat, Israel; Jakarta, Indonesia; Mumbai, India; Tehran, Iran
Las Vegas, NV..Phuket, Thailand
Long Beach, CA ....Calcutta, India
Miami, FL.........................Amman, Jordan; Nice, France; Santiago, Chile
Mobile, AL.............................Kosice, Slovakia; Havana, Cuba
New Orleans, LA ... Innsbruck, Austria; Pointe Noire, Congo; Caracas, Venezuela
New York, NY ....Cairo, Egypt; Tokyo, Japan; London, England;
                                           Jerusalem, Israel; Beijing, China
Richmond, VA................ Richmond upon Thames, England; Olsztyn, Poland
Salt Lake City, UT..........................Matsumoto, Japan; Tipperary, Ireland
San Francisco....Zürich, Switzerland; Cork, Ireland; Osaka, Japan; Seoul, S Korea
Seattle, WA................. Tashkent, Uzbekistan; Reykjavík, Iceland; Kobe, Japan

[Some places have additional sister cities.]

—— USA TERRITORIAL —— EXPANSION

Accession	year	sq. miles
Total..............	——..	3,540,558
United States.........	——..	3,536,288
Territory in 1790[1]...	——....	895,415
Louisiana Purchase ..	1803....	909,380
Purchase of Florida[2] .	1819......	58,666
Texas..............	1845....	388,687
Oregon Territory.....	1846....	286,541
Mexican Cession.....	1848....	529,189
Gadsden Purchase....	1853......	29,670
Alaska..............	1867....	570,374
Hawaii..............	1898.......	6,423

Other areas		
Puerto Rico[3].........	1898.......	3,427
Guam[4]..............	1898........	210
American Samoa[5]...	1899..........	77
US Virgin Islands...	1917.........	134
Palau[6]..............	1947........	179
N. Mariana Is.[7]......	1947........	177
All other..............	——..........	16

[1] Includes part of drainage basin of the Red River of the North, south of 49th parallel, often considered part of the Louisiana Purchase. [2] Also acquired 22,834 sq. mi. west of the Mississippi River but relinquished to Spain 97,150 sq. mi. [3] Ceded by Spain in 1898; ratified in 1899; became Commonwealth of Puerto Rico, July 25, 1952. [4] Acquired 1898; ratified 1899. [5] Acquired 1899; ratified 1900. [6] Remaining portion of the Trust Territory of the Pacific Islands under UN trusteeship since 1947. The Federated States of Micronesia and the Marshall Islands, also formerly part of the TTPI, became freely associated States in 1986 and are not included in this table. [7] Attained Commonwealth status in 1986, separate from the TTPI, of which it had been a part since 1947. Land areas are approximate and may not add to totals. 1 sq. mi. = 2·59 sq. km. [Sources: US Census; US Geological Survey, which see for more detailed notes.]

—— 13 COLONIES ——

The colonies that signed the Declaration of Independence in 1776:

the New England colonies
Massachusetts, Rhode Island, Connecticut, New Hampshire

the middle colonies
New York, New Jersey, Pennsylvania, Delaware

the southern colonies
Maryland, Virginia, North Carolina, South Carolina, Georgia

By 1770, the population of these 13 colonies had reached almost 2 million.

—— COUNTIES, &c. ——

3,141 counties and their equivalents presently exist in the 50 States and Washington, DC. They are categorized:

3,007 entities named 'County'
16 Boroughs in Alaska
11 Census Areas in Alaska (for areas not organized into Boroughs by the State)
64 Parishes in Louisiana
42 Independent Cities
(1 in Maryland, 1 in Missouri, 1 in Nevada, 39 in Virginia)
1 District – the Federal District, or District of Columbia

This excludes Commonwealths and territories with county equivalents:

Puerto Rico – 78 Municipios
US Virgin Islands – 2 Districts
Guam – 19 Election Districts
Northern Mariana Is. – 17 Districts
American Samoa – 5 Districts

[Sources: Dept of Interior; USGS]

US TIME ZONES

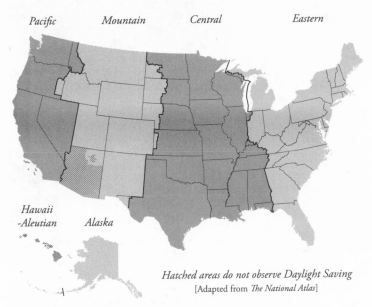

| Pacific | Mountain | Central | Eastern |

| Hawaii
-Aleutian | Alaska |

Hatched areas do not observe Daylight Saving
[Adapted from *The National Atlas*]

± hours from UTC	DST	Standard
Atlantic	−3	−4
Eastern	−4	−5
Central	−5	−6
Mountain	−6	−7
Pacific	−7	−8
Alaska	−8	−9
Hawaii-Aleutian	−9	−10
Samoa†	NA	−11
Chamorro‡	NA	+10

Coordinated Universal Time (UTC or just UT) is an international time standard essentially identical to good old-fashioned Greenwich Mean Time (GMT). † Samoa Standard Time Zone includes that part of the US that is between 169°30′W–172°30′W, but does not include any part of Hawaii or Alaska. ‡ The 9th US Time Zone was established by Congress in December 2000, for Guam and the Northern Marianas west of the International Date Line. The Chamorro Time Zone, named after the region's indigenous people, is 14 hours ahead of Eastern Standard Time.

Daylight Saving Time (DST) is not observed in Hawaii, American Samoa, Guam, Puerto Rico, the Virgin Islands, or the state of Arizona, with the exception of the Navajo Indian Reservation, which does observe DST. (Indiana adopted DST in 2006; 18 counties use Central Daylight Time, and 74 Eastern Daylight Time.) The Energy Policy Act of 2005 extended DST for one month so that, where it is observed in the United States, it will start and end on the following days:

| DST *begins*
at 2am | year
[Spring forward, Fall back] | DST *ends*
at 2am |
|---|---|---|
| Mar 9 | 2008 | Nov 2 |
| Mar 8 | 2009 | Nov 1 |
| Mar 14 | 2010 | Nov 7 |
| Mar 13 | 2011 | Nov 6 |
| Mar 11 | 2012 | Nov 4 |
| Mar 10 | 2013 | Nov 3 |
| Mar 9 | 2014 | Nov 2 |
| Mar 8 | 2015 | Nov 1 |

—————————GREATEST FOREST FIRES—————————

Below are the largest wildfires (by acreage) to have devastated the US since 1997:

Year	fire name	location	state	acres
2004	Taylor Complex	Alaska Division of Forestry	AK	1,305,592
2006	East Amarillo Complex	Texas Forest Service	TX	907,245
2004	Eagle Complex	BLM Upper Yukon Zone	AK	614,974
1997	Inowak Fire	Alaska Division of Forestry	AK	610,000
2004	Solstice Complex	BLM Upper Yukon Zone	AK	547,505
2004	Boundary	Alaska Division of Forestry	AK	537,098
2002	Biscuit	Siskiyou National Forest	OR	499,570
2002	Rodeo/Chediski	BIA Fort Apache Agency	AZ	468,638
2004	Central Complex	BLM Upper Yukon Zone	AK	451,162
1997	Simels Fire	BLM Galena District	AK	366,000

[Source: National Interagency Fire Center, 2007]

—————————GROUNDHOG DAY PREDICTIONS · 2007—————————

Although Punxsutawney Phil is America's foremost prognosticating woodchuck (his first prediction was in 1887), several other notable rodents are routinely shanghaied to foretell the arrival of Spring. According to legend, if the appointed groundhog sees his shadow, six more weeks of winter will follow; if he does not, spring will come early. Below are some forecasts from Groundhog Day† (February 2), 2007:

Groundhog	city	prediction
Balzac Billy	Alberta, Canada	saw shadow
General Beauregard Lee, PhD‡	Lilburn, Georgia	no shadow
Buckeye Chuck	Marion, Ohio	saw shadow
Charles G. Hogg	Staten Island, New York	no shadow
Dunkirk Dave	Dunkirk, New York	saw shadow
French Creek Freddie	Upshur County, W Virginia	no shadow
Jimmy	Sun Prairie, Wisconsin	saw shadow
PeeWee	Mile Square Farm, Vermont	saw shadow
Punxsutawney Phil	Punxsutawney, Pennsylvania	no shadow
Shubenacadie Sam	Shubenacadie, Nova Scotia	no shadow
Sir Walter Wally	Raleigh, North Carolina	no shadow
Wiarton Willie	Warton, Ontario, Canada	no shadow
Woody	Howell, Michigan	saw shadow

† Explanations for the origin of Groundhog Day usually cite the Christian holiday of Candlemas, about which it is said, '*If Candlemas be fair and bright, winter will have another flight. If Candlemas brings cloud and rain, winter shall not come again*'. The groundhog's role in all this is attributed to superstition that certain animals can foretell the weather. ‡ General 'Beau' Lee has received honorary doctorates from both the University of Georgia, where he is a 'Doctor of Weather Prognostication', and Georgia State University, which bestowed upon him the title 'Doctor of Southern Groundology'.

———————— WEATHER RECORDS OF NOTE ————————

Highest recorded temperature			*date*
US · Death Valley, CA	134°F	57°C	07·10·1913
World · El Azizia, Libya	136°F	58°C	09·13·1922
Lowest recorded temperature			
US · Prospect Creek, AK	–80°F	–62·2°C	01·23·1971
World · Vostok, Antarctica	–129°F	–89°C	07·21·1983
Greatest recorded rainfall (24hr)			
US · Alvin, TX	43"	109mm	07·25–26·1979
World · Foc-Foc, La Réunion	72"	182·5mm	01·07–08·1966
Minimum average yearly rainfall			
US · Death Valley, CA	1·63"	41·4mm	42-year average
World · Arica, Chile	0·03"	8mm	59-year average

[Sources: National Weather Services; National Climatic Data Center; NOAA; US Army; &c.]

———————— 2006 SEVERE WEATHER FATALITIES ————————

Heat .... 253 *died*
Flooding 76
Tornadoes 67
Lightning 47

Wind 40
Winter 28
Rip current 23
Coastal storm 7

Mud slide 3
Cold 2
Dust storm 2
Total (incl. misc.) 566

[Source: NOAA National Weather Service]

———————— 2008 HURRICANE NAMES ————————

The US National Hurricane Center began naming storms in 1953, after latitude-longitude identification proved inconvenient and time-consuming. (Female names were used until 1979, when male names were added following charges of sexism.) Six lists of names, maintained by the World Meteorological Organization, are used in rotation, meaning the 2006 list will be reused in 2012. Names given to particularly fatal or damaging storms are permanently retired (thus *Katrina* was dropped from the list after the 2005 season, and replaced with *Katia* for the 2011 season). Below are the names to be used for the 2008 Atlantic hurricane season:

Arthur	Gustav	Marco	Teddy
Bertha	Hanna	Nana	Vicky
Cristobal	Ike	Omar	Wilfred
Dolly	Josephine	Paloma	
Edouard	Kyle	Rene	[Source: National
Fay	Laura	Sally	Weather Service]

The 2006 Atlantic hurricane season was markedly less active than the 2004 and 2005 seasons. Only two hurricanes, Ernesto and Gordon, were considered major, and none made landfall in the US.

——————PRESIDENTIAL & CONGRESSIONAL AWARDS——————

The President and Congress are entitled to bestow a host of awards and medals to those they deem deserving of recognition. Below are some of the major awards:

Originally presented to military leaders (the first recipient was Washington in 1776), the *Congressional Gold Medal* is now the highest civilian award and the greatest honor Congress can bestow. No law regulates when or to whom the Gold Medal is given. From time to time, Congress selects individuals who have made a significant contribution in their field (e.g. medicine, public service, the arts, entertainment, &c.) and passes legislation authorizing the award, which must be signed by the President. The US Mint strikes a bespoke design for each award. On March 29, 2007, Congress awarded the medal to the legendary WWII Tuskegee Airmen, the first black aviators in the Army Air Corps. Nearly 300 of the surviving fighter pilots, who faced racism even while fighting for their country, accepted the award during ceremonies in Washington, DC. Notable previous recipients include Frank Sinatra (1997); Rosa Parks (1999); Charles M. Schulz (2000); and Tony Blair (2003).

The *Medal of Honor*, presented by the President in the name of Congress, is the US's highest military award, given for acts of bravery above and beyond the call of duty. Recipients are entitled to a monthly pension of $1,000 and a number of military courtesies. In 2007, Bush awarded the medal to retired Lt. Col. Bruce Crandall for his heroic efforts on November 14, 1965, in Vietnam's Ia Drang Valley, which saved the lives of *c.*70 soldiers.

The highest civilian award bestowed by the executive is the *Presidential Medal of Freedom*. It was instigated by Truman to honor those who served with merit during WWII, and reestablished by JFK in 1963 as a peacetime award for meritorious service. It is given each year to several people and, because it is the sole the gift of the President, the recipients tend to reflect the interests of the Oval Office's occupant. The 2006 recipients included 'King of the Blues' BB King, former Negro League's baseball player Buck O'Neil, commentator William Safire, and former Soviet captive Natan Sharansky.

One of the US government's oldest awards for scientific achievement, the *Enrico Fermi Award* was established in 1956 in honor of atomic pioneer Enrico Fermi [see p.190]. The prize is now awarded to scientists who have made great strides in 'the science and technology of nuclear, atomic, molecular, and particle interactions and their effects on mankind and the environment'. The 2005 award was presented in June 2006 to Arthur H. Rosenfeld, the 'founding father' of energy efficiency, who was also Fermi's last graduate student. Rosenfeld received an honorarium of $375,000, in addition to a gold medal and a citation signed by the President and Secretary of Energy.

Other honors awarded by the President include: *Presidential Citizens Medal*; *President's Award for Distinguished Federal Civilian Service*; *Presidential Award for Excellence in Mathematics and Science Teaching*; *Preserve America Presidential Awards*; *Presidential Awards for Design Excellence*; &c. [Sources: Congressional Research Service, &c.]

─────────── KEYS TO THE CITY ───────────

Many US cities honor deserving locals and visiting dignitaries by presenting them with a 'key to the city'. The practice dates from medieval times, when European towns were protected by high walls and gates, and keys were sometimes given to important merchants or diplomats. Today, the key (often an oversized ornament) is presented symbolically to honor local civic contributions, extend international goodwill, or generate publicity. Perhaps the most notable recipient of such a key was Saddam Hussein, who reportedly received the key to Detroit in 1980 after donating *c*.$250,000 to a local church. In 2006–07, keys were given to the following people:

Year	*key recipient*	*city*
2007	Boise State University football team	Boise, ID
2007	T-Rex 'Rexy' (dinosaur skeleton)	Dearborn, MI
2007	JoJo	Fayetteville, North Carolina
2007	Kay Rala Xanana Gusmão (former East Timorese Pres.)	Daphne, AL
2007	Tavis Smiley	Winston-Salem, NC
2007	Sully Erna (singer with *Godsmack*)	Lawrence, MA
2007	Rodney 'On-the-Roq' Bingenheimer (DJ)	West Hollywood, CA
2007	András Simonyi (Hungarian ambassador to the US)	Morrow, GA
2007	Rochester Knighthawks lacrosse team	Rochester, NY
2007	LaKisha Jones	Flint, MI
2007	Fidel V. Ramos (former Philippine President)	Las Vegas
2007	Vicente Fernandez	Stockton, CA
2006	Jerome Bettis	Detroit
2006	Shakira	Miami
2006	Tom Petty	Gainesville, FL
2006	Alice Cooper	Alice, ND

[This list, collated from a variety of sources, is by no means exhaustive, although perhaps exhausting.]

─────────── THE SPINGARN MEDAL ───────────

Michigan Congressman John Conyers Jr was awarded the 2007 Spingarn Medal, presented since 1915 by the National Association for the Advancement of Colored People (NAACP) for achievements in any field made by an African American during the previous year. Conyers has been reelected 20 times, serving in Congress longer than any other African American. In January 2007, he was named Chairman of the House Judiciary Committee, where his work has focused on civil liberties, voting rights, and the prevention of violence against women. He is also a founding member of the Congressional Black Caucus, formed in 1969 to help black lawmakers address the concerns of minority communities. The Spingarn Medal is intended 'to bring attention to notable merit among Americans of African descent, to reward such accomplishment, and stimulate ambition for today's youth'. It is named in honor of the former NAACP Chairman J.E. Spingarn. Some previous recipients include: Martin Luther King Jr, Rosa Parks, Duke Ellington, Alex Haley, Bill Cosby, Hank Aaron, Colin Powell, Maya Angelou, and Oprah Winfrey.

———————————— US HOMELAND SECURITY ————————————

In response to the terrorist outrages of September 11, 2001, President George W. Bush created the Department of Homeland Security to 'anticipate, pre-empt and deter' terrorist and other threats. The Department employs a five-point, color-coded Security Advisory System to indicate the perceived level of risk – the higher the 'threat condition', the greater the risk of an attack in probability and severity:

Threat	*color*	GUARDED..........Blue	HIGH...........Orange
LOW..............Green		ELEVATED ......Yellow	SEVERE............ Red

The threat condition was established at YELLOW; since then its changes have been:

Period	*shift*	cause/specific location
09·10·02–09·24·02	yellow–orange	*1st anniversary of the September 11 attacks*
02·07·03–02·27·03	yellow–orange	*the time of the Muslim Hajj*
03·17·03–04·16·03	yellow–orange	*start of allied military attacks on Iraq*
05·20·03–05·30·03	yellow–orange	*intelligence reports of potential attacks*
12·21·03–01·09·04	yellow–orange	*intelligence reports of holiday season attacks*
08·01·04–11·10·04	yellow–orange	specific *warning for East Coast financial areas*
07·07·05–08·12·05	yellow–orange	specific *mass-transit warning after London bombs*
08·10·06–	yellow–orange (& briefly red) specific *shift for the airline industry*

———— EMERGENCY COMMS & THE END OF 10-CODES ————

The 9/11 attacks revealed significant gaps in the ability of law enforcement, fire, and emergency medical services to communicate with one another during a crisis. Since 2003, $2·9bn in federal grants have been distributed to improve emergency communications. In January 2007, the Homeland Security Dept released score-cards, rating 75 urban areas by how well emergency services from multiple jurisdictions were theoretically (according to documentation) able to communicate within 1 hour of a crisis. Each region was rated EARLY, INTERMEDIATE, ESTABLISHED, or ADVANCED in three categories: governance, standard operating procedures, and equipment usage. The following cities scored at the top and bottom of the report:

ADVANCED	EARLY *or* INTERMEDIATE
Washington, DC · Columbus, OH	Chicago, IL · Cleveland, OH
Laramie County, WY · Sioux Falls, SD	Baton Rouge, LA · Mandan, ND
Minneapolis/St Paul, MN · San Diego	American Samoa

The need for standardized communication has led FEMA and the Dept of Homeland Security to press police to abandon their venerable '10-codes' in favor of plain English. Some of the earliest 10-codes, as published in a 1940 bulletin of the Associated Police Communication Officers include:

10-1 ....*receiving poorly*	10-4 ....*acknowledgment*	10-29 ...... *check for wanted*
10-2 .... *receiving well*	10-15 ....*we have prisoner*	10-31 ...*lie detector available?*
10-3 .... *stop transmitting*	10-20 .. *what is your location?*	10-32 .*drunkometer available?*

US DEFENSE PERSONNEL

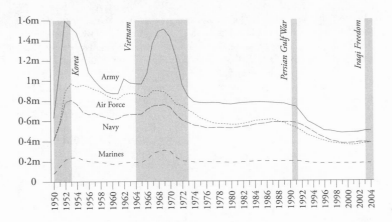

[Average military strength, man years; fiscal years · Source: DoD Washington HQ Services]

MILITARY RECRUITMENT · 2006

Force	'06 recruits	% of goal
Army	80,635	100·8
Navy	36,679	100·1
Marines	32,337	100·1
Air Force	30,889	100·5
Army Reserve	34,379	95·4
Navy Reserve	9,722	87·0
Army Nat. Guard	69,042	98·6
Air Nat. Guard	9,138	97·4
Air Force Reserve	6,989	105·8
Marines Reserve	8,056	100·4

[Source: DoD, *New York Times*]

The Army unveiled the recruiting slogan 'Army Strong' in 2006, to replace the somewhat confusing 'Army of One'. The latter slogan was used for only 5 years, replacing 'Be All You Can Be' in 2001.

DoD PRIME CONTRACT AWARDS

Ranking '06	'05	parent company [Source: Dept of Defense]	awards ($bn) '05	'06
1	1	Lockheed Martin Corporation	19·4	26·6
2	2	The Boeing Company	18·3	20·3
3	3	Northrop Grumman Corporation	13·5	16·6
4	4	General Dynamics Corporation	10·6	10·5
5	5	Raytheon Company	9·1	10·1
6	6	Halliburton Company	5·8	6·1
7	9	L-3 Communications Holdings	4·7	5·2
8	7	BAE Systems	5·6	4·7
9	8	United Technologies Corporation	5·0	4·5
10	11	Science Applications International	2·8	3·2

─────────────── US VETERANS ───────────────

*c.*25,196,000 veterans of the US uniformed services were living in the US and Puerto Rico at the end of 2000 – according to the latest (2001) National Survey of Veterans, conducted by the Dept of Veterans Affairs. The data below give a demographic, sociological, and economic snapshot of this population in 2000:

94% of vets are MALE; 6% FEMALE. (In 1992, 4% of veterans were female.)

AGE	all%	♂%	♀%
<25 years	1·1	0·8	4·7
25–29 years	2·7	2·4	7·9
30–34 years	5·3	4·9	12·6
35–39 years	5·3	4·8	13·6
40–44 years	6·7	6·1	16·4
45–49 years	8·1	7·8	13·6
50–54 years	13·4	13·8	6·5
55–59 years	11·1	11·5	3·8
60–64 years	8·6	8·9	2·8
65–69 years	10·1	10·6	2·4
70–74 years	10·7	11·2	3·4
75–79 years	9·5	9·7	6·4
≥80 years	6·8	6·9	5·5
Unknown	0·6	0·6	0·4

RACE	%
Total one race	94·7
– White	84·8
– Black or African American	8·8
– Am. Indian or Alaska Native	0·6
– Asian	0·3
– Native Hawaiian or Pacific Is.	0·2
Total two or more races	2·2
– Am. Idn, Alaska Native/White	1·4
– Race unknown	3·1

ETHNICITY	%
Spanish, Hispanic, or Latino	4·5
Not Spanish, Hispanic, or Latino	95·2
Unknown	0·3

LEVEL OF EDUCATION	%
Less than high school graduate	11·1
High school graduate or GED	29·9
Post high school school/training	35·8
Bachelor's degree or higher	23·0
Unknown	0·2

38·9% of veterans have served in a combat or war zone (40·6% of ♂; 12% of ♀). 36·4% of veterans have been exposed to the dead, dying, or wounded (37·2% of ♂; 24·4% of ♀).

PERIOD OF SERVICE	%
World War II	20·5
World War II – Korea	6·7
Korea	16·9
Korea – Vietnam era	25·6
Vietnam era	36·1
Post-Vietnam era	27·9
Gulf War	13·9

LEVEL OF FAMILY INCOME	%
≤$10,000	5·3
$10,001–20,000	12·1
$20,001–30,000	13·9
$30,001–40,000	12·5
$40,001–50,000	10·8
>$50,000	34·7
Unknown	10·7

EMPLOYMENT STATUS	%
Working (or on vacation/sick leave)	54·9
Not working, but looking	3·6
Retired	32·0
Disabled	6·9
Given up looking for work	0·2
Temporarily laid off from work	0·2
Taking care of home and family	0·8
Going to school	0·4
Other	1·0

HEALTH STATUS	%
Excellent	16·8
Very good	28·8
Good	30·1
Fair	16·3
Poor	7·9

— US MILITARY RANKS —

PAY	ARMY	NAVY & COAST GUARD†	MARINES	AIR FORCE	Number
O-11‡	General of the Army	Fleet Admiral	—	General of the Air Force	—
O-10	General	Admiral	General	General	40
O-9	Lieutenant General	Vice Admiral	Lieutenant General	Lieutenant General	130
O-8	Major General	Rear Admiral (Upper Half)	Major General	Major General	284
O-7	Brigadier General	Rear Admiral (Lower Half)	Brigadier General	Brigadier General	446
O-6	Colonel	Captain	Colonel	Colonel	11,447
O-5	Lieutenant Colonel	Commander	Lieutenant Colonel	Lieutenant Colonel	28,404
O-4	Major	Lieutenant Commander	Major	Major	45,086
O-3	Captain	Lieutenant	Captain	Captain	69,032
O-2	First Lieutenant	Lieutenant Junior Grade	First Lieutenant	First Lieutenant	26,328
O-1	Second Lieutenant	Ensign	Second Lieutenant	Second Lieutenant	22,928
W-5	Chief Warrant Officer	Chief Warrant Officer	Chief Warrant Officer		599
W-4	Chief Warrant Officer	Chief Warrant Officer	Chief Warrant Officer		2,815
W-3	Chief Warrant Officer	Chief Warrant Officer	Chief Warrant Officer		4,683
W-2	Chief Warrant Officer	Chief Warrant Officer	Chief Warrant Officer		5,572
W-1	Warrant Officer	Warrant Officer	Warrant Officer		3,461
E-9	Sgt Major of the Army	MCPO of the Navy	Sgt Major of the Marine Corps	Ch. Master Sgt of the Air Force	10,669
E-9	Command Sgt Major/Sgt Major	Fleet/Command MCPO	Sgt Major/Master Gunnery Sgt	Command Chief Master Sgt	↑
E-9	First Sgt/Master Sgt	Master Chief Petty Officer		Chief Master Sgt/First Sgt	↑
E-8	Sgt First Class/Platoon Sgt	Senior Chief Petty Officer	First Sgt/Master Sgt	Senior Master Sgt/First Sgt	27,042
E-7	Staff Sergeant	Chief Petty Officer	Gunnery Sergeant	Master Sgt/First Sgt	97,788
E-6	Sergeant	Petty Officer First Class	Staff Sergeant	Technical Sergeant	168,619
E-5	Corporal/Specialist	Petty Officer Second Class	Sergeant	Staff Sergeant	245,116
E-4	Private First Class	Petty Officer Third Class	Corporal	Senior Airman	255,821
E-3	Private	Seaman	Lance Corporal	Airman First Class	196,803
E-2	Private	Seaman Apprentice	Private First Class	Airman	82,347
E-1		Seaman Recruit	Private	Airman Basic	49,064

† The US Coast Guard is a part of the Dept of Transportation in peacetime and the Navy in times of war. Coast Guard ranks are essentially the same as Navy ranks. ‡ Reserved for wartime only. Within the O-10 rank, each service has a Chief of Staff or Commandant. · Numbers are Active Duty Military Personnel as of 04-30-2007. [Source: Department of Defense]

The States

In the United States there is more space where nobody is than where anybody is.
That is what makes America what it is. — GERTRUDE STEIN
The Geographical History of America, 1936

────────────TRADITIONAL CITY NICKNAMES────────────

A selection of (sometimes archaic) US city nicknames – current during the C19th.

Atlanta......... Gate City of the South	New Haven .... Elm City
Baltimore............Monumental City	New Orleans............ Crescent City
Bangor.................... Lumber City	New York.......Empire City; Gotham;
Boston.................Modern Athens;	Commercial Emporium;
Literary Emporium; City of Notions;	Metropolis of America
Hub of the Universe	Philadelphia... City of Brotherly Love;
Brooklyn ....City of Churches	City of Penn; Quaker City;
Buffalo............. Queen of the Lakes	Centennial City
Burlington (Iowa)........Orchard City	Pittsburgh......Iron City; Smoky City
Charleston.............. Palmetto City	Portland (Me.) ....Hill City
Chicago ....Prairie or Garden City	Providence.......Roger Williams' City;
Cincinnati......... Queen of the West;	Perry Davis' Pain Killer
Porkopolis	Raleigh .... Oak City
Cleveland.................. Forest City	Richmond (Va.)......... Cockade City
Denver .... City of the Plains	— (Ind.)..... Quaker City of the West
Detroit ....City of the Straits	Rochester.............. Aqueduct City
Hartford................ Insurance City	Salt Lake City...........Mormon City
Indianapolis.............Railroad City	San Francisco .... Golden Gate
Keokuk.......................Gate City	Savannah .....Forest City of the South
Lafayette......................Star City	Sheboygan............. Evergreen City
Leavenworth ....Cottonwood City	St Louis....................Mound City
Louisville..................... Falls City	St Paul................. North Star City
Lowell ....Spindle City	Vicksburg ....Key City
McGregor ....Pocket City	Washington .... Federal City;
Madison......................Lake City	City of Magnificent Distances
Milwaukee ....Cream City	
Nashville .... Rock City	[A number of versions of this list exist]

────────────CONFEDERATE STATES────────────

Organized in February 1861, the Confederacy consisted of eleven states that
seceded from the Union: Alabama, Arkansas, Florida, Georgia, Louisiana,
Mississippi, North Carolina, South Carolina, Tennessee, Texas, and Virginia.

THE UNITED STATES

KEY TO TABLES OVERLEAF

Overleaf are a range of tables designed to allow comparisons to be made between the various states and, where relevant, Washington, DC, and the USA as a whole. A degree of debate and dispute surrounds a number of entries, and data sources have been the most recent at the time of writing. Below is a key to some entries:

Land area	US Census Bureau
Resident population	July 2005 · US Census Bureau
Unemployment rate	% of civilian labor force · 2004 · US Bureau of Labor Statistics
Home ownership rate	% of owner households · 2004 · US Census Bureau
Persons below poverty line	2003 · US Census Bureau
Average annual pay	2004 · Bureau of Labor Statistics
Violent crime	per 100,000 population · 2004 · FBI
Racial & ethnic breakdown	2000 · US Census Bureau
Infant mortality rate	deaths of infants <1/1,000 live births · 2002 · US NCHS
Doctors	per 100,000 resident population · 2003 · American Medical Association
Traffic fatalities	per 100 million vehicle miles · 2003 · US NHSTA
Energy consumption	million BTUs per person · 2001 · US Energy Information Admin
Mobile homes	% of total housing units · 2003 · US Census Bureau
Degree	persons ≥25 with a Bachelor's degree or higher · 2004 · US Census
Highway miles	miles of functional roads (interstate–local) · 2003 · US Fed. Highway Admin
Temperatures	April 2002 · National Oceanic and Atmospheric Administration (NOAA)
Highest & lowest points & geographic center	US Geographic Survey
Morgan Quitno state rankings	morganquitno.com (with thanks)

——————— STATES · MAPS, CAPITALS, ADMISSION, &c. ———————

California · CA 155,959 sq mi *Sacramento* 31st State on 9-9-1850	Georgia · GA 57,906 sq mi *Atlanta* 4th State on 1-2-1788	Iowa · IA 55,869 sq mi *Des Moines* 29th State on 12-28-1846	Maryland · MD 9,774 sq mi *Annapolis* 7th State on 4-28-1788	Missouri · MO 68,886 sq mi *Jefferson City* 24th State on 8-10-1821
Arkansas · AR 52,068 sq mi *Little Rock* 25th State on 6-15-1836	Florida · FL 53,927 sq mi *Tallahassee* 27th State on 3-3-1845	Indiana · IN 35,867 sq mi *Indianapolis* 19th State on 12-11-1816	Maine · ME 30,862 sq mi *Augusta* 23rd State on 3-15-1820	Mississippi · MS 46,907 sq mi *Jackson* 20th State on 12-10-1817
Arizona · AZ 113,635 sq mi *Phoenix* 48th State on 2-14-1912	Delaware · DE 1,954 sq mi *Dover* 1st State on 12-7-1787	Illinois · IL 55,584 sq mi *Springfield* 21st State on 12-3-1818	Louisiana · LA 43,562 sq mi *Baton Rouge* 18th State on 4-30-1812	Minnesota · MN 79,610 sq mi *St Paul* 32nd State on 5-11-1858
Alaska · AK 571,951 sq mi *Juneau* 49th State on 1-3-1959	Connecticut · CT 4,844 sq mi *Hartford* 5th State on 1-9-1788	Idaho · ID 82,747 sq mi *Boise* 43rd State on 7-3-1890	Kentucky · KY 39,728 sq mi *Frankfort* 15th State on 6-1-1792	Michigan · MI 56,804 sq mi *Lansing* 26th State on 1-26-1837
Alabama · AL 50,744 sq mi *Montgomery* 22nd State on 12-14-1819	Colorado · CO 103,717 sq mi *Denver* 38th State on 8-1-1876	Hawaii · HI 6,423 sq mi *Honolulu* 50th State on 8-21-1959	Kansas · KS 81,815 sq mi *Topeka* 34th State on 1-29-1861	Massachusetts · MA 7,840 sq mi *Boston* 6th State on 2-6-1788

—————— STATES · MAPS, CAPITALS, ADMISSION, &c. ——————

Montana · MT 145,552 sq mi *Helena* 41st State on 11-8-1889	Nebraska · NE 76,872 sq mi *Lincoln* 37th State on 3-1-1867	New Jersey · NJ 7,417 sq mi *Trenton* 3rd State on 12-18-1787
New Mexico · NM 121,356 sq mi *Santa Fe* 47th State on 1-6-1912	Nevada · NV 109,826 sq mi *Carson City* 36th State on 10-31-1864	New Hampshire NH · 8,968 sq mi *Concord* 9th State on 6-21-1788
Oklahoma · OK 68,667 sq mi *Oklahoma City* 46th State on 11-16-1907	North Carolina · NC 48,711 sq mi *Raleigh* 12th State on 11-21-1789	North Dakota · ND 68,976 sq mi *Bismarck* 39th State on 11-2-1889
Oregon · OR 95,997 sq mi *Salem* 33rd State on 2-14-1859	Pennsylvania · PA 44,817 sq mi *Harrisburg* 2nd State on 12-12-1787	Ohio · OH 40,948 sq mi *Columbus* 17th State on 3-1-1803
South Dakota · SD 75,885 sq mi *Pierre* 40th State on 11-2-1889	Texas · TX 261,797 sq mi *Austin* 28th State on 12-29-1845	Rhode Island · RI 1,045 sq mi *Providence* 13th State on 5-29-1790
Tennessee · TN 41,217 sq mi *Nashville* 16th State on 6-1-1796	Utah · UT 82,144 sq mi *Salt Lake City* 45th State on 1-4-1896	South Carolina · SC 30,109 sq mi *Columbia* 8th State on 5-23-1788
Virginia · VA 39,594 sq mi *Richmond* 10th State on 6-25-1788	West Virginia · WV 24,077 sq mi *Charleston* 35th State on 6-20-1863	Vermont · VT 9,250 sq mi *Montpelier* 14th State on 3-4-1791
Washington · WA 66,544 sq mi *Olympia* 42nd State on 11-11-1889	Wisconsin · WI 54,310 sq mi *Madison* 30th State on 5-29-1848	Wyoming · WY 97,100 sq mi *Cheyenne* 44th State on 7-10-1890

STATES · RESIDENTS, SYMBOLS, &c.

State	Residents called	State tree	State flower	State bird	Abbreviation
Alabama	Alabamian, Alabaman	Southern Longleaf Pine	Camellia	Yellowhammer	Ala.
Alaska	Alaskan	Sitka Spruce	Forget-me-not	Willow Ptarmigan	Alaska
Arizona	Arizonan, Arizonian	Palo Verde	Blossom of the Saguaro Cactus	Cactus Wren	Ariz.
Arkansas	Arkansan	Loblolly Pine	Apple Blossom	Mockingbird	Ark.
California	Californian	California Redwood	Golden Poppy	California Valley Quail	Calif.
Colorado	Coloradan, Coloradoan	Colorado Blue Spruce	Rocky Mountain Columbine	Lark Bunting	Colo.
Connecticut	Connecticuter, Nutmegger	White Oak	Mountain Laurel	American Robin	Conn.
Delaware	Delawarean	American Holly	Peach Blossom	Blue Hen Chicken	Del.
DC	Washingtonian	Scarlet Oak	American Beauty Rose	Wood Thrush	D.C.
Florida	Floridian, Floridan	Sabal Palm	Orange Blossom	Mockingbird	Fla.
Georgia	Georgian	Live Oak	Cherokee Rose	Brown Thrasher	Ga.
Hawaii	Hawaiian	Kukui or Candlenut	Native Yellow Hibiscus	Nene or Hawaiian Goose	Hawaii
Idaho	Idahoan	Western White Pine	Syringa	Mountain Bluebird	Idaho
Illinois	Illinoisan	White Oak	Purple Violet	Cardinal	Ill.
Indiana	Indianan, Indianian, Hoosier	Tulip Tree	Peony	Cardinal	Ind.
Iowa	Iowan	Oak	Wild Rose	Eastern Goldfinch	Iowa
Kansas	Kansan	Cottonwood	Native Sunflower	Western Meadowlark	Kans.
Kentucky	Kentuckian	Tulip Poplar	Goldenrod	Cardinal	Ky.
Louisiana	Louisianan, Louisianian	Bald Cypress	Magnolia	Eastern Brown Pelican	La.
Maine	Mainer	Eastern White Pine	White Pinecone and Tassel	Chickadee	Maine
Maryland	Marylander	White Oak	Black-eyed Susan	Baltimore Oriole	Md.
Massachusetts	Bay Stater	American Elm	Mayflower	Chickadee	Mass.
Michigan	Michigander(-ian), Michiganite	Eastern White Pine	Apple Blossom	Robin	Mich.
Minnesota	Minnesotan	Red or Norway Pine	Pink & White Lady's Slipper	Common Loon	Minn.
Mississippi	Mississippian	Magnolia	Magnolia	Mockingbird	Miss.
Missouri	Missourian	Flowering Dogwood	Hawthorn	Eastern Bluebird	Mo.

STATES · RESIDENTS, SYMBOLS, &c.

State	Residents called	State tree	State flower	State bird	Abbreviation
Montana	Montanan	Ponderosa Pine	Bitterroot	Western Meadowlark	Mont.
Nebraska	Nebraskan	Cottonwood	Goldenrod	Western Meadowlark	Nebr.
Nevada	Nevadan, Nevadian	Singleleaf Pinyon & Pine	Sagebrush	Mountain Bluebird	Nev.
New Hampshire	New Hampshirite	White Birch	Purple Lilac	Purple Finch	N.H.
New Jersey	New Jerseyite, New Jerseyan	Northern Red Oak	Purple Violet	Eastern Goldfinch	N.J.
New Mexico	New Mexican	Pinyon Pine / Piñon	Yucca	Roadrunner	N.Mex.
New York	New Yorker	Sugar Maple	Rose	Eastern Bluebird	N.Y.
North Carolina	North Carolinian	Longleaf Pine	Dogwood	Cardinal	N.C.
North Dakota	North Dakotan	American Elm	Wild Prarie Rose	Western Meadowlark	N.Dak.
Ohio	Ohioan	Buckeye	Scarlet Carnation	Cardinal	Ohio
Oklahoma	Oklahoman	Redbud	Mistletoe	Scissor-tailed Flycatcher	Okla.
Oregon	Oregonian	Douglas Fir	Oregon Grape	Western Meadowlark	Oreg.
Pennsylvania	Pennsylvanian	Eastern Hemlock	Mountain Laurel	Ruffed Grouse	Pa.
Rhode Island	Rhode Islander	Red Maple	Blue Violet	Rhode Island Red Hen	R.I.
South Carolina	South Carolinian	Sabel Palm / Palmetto Tree	Yellow Jessamine	Great Carolina Wren	S.C.
South Dakota	South Dakotan	Black Hills Spruce	Pasqueflower	Ring-necked Pheasant	S.Dak.
Tennessee	Tennessean, Tennesseean	Tulip Poplar	Iris	Mockingbird	Tenn.
Texas	Texan	Pecan	Bluebonnet	Mockingbird	Tex.
Utah	Utahan, Utahn	Blue Spruce	Sego Lily	California Seagull	Utah
Vermont	Vermonter	Sugar Maple	Red Clover	Hermit Thrush	Vt.
Virginia	Virginian	Flowering Dogwood	American Dogwood	Northern Cardinal	Va.
Washington	Washingtonian	Western Hemlock	Western Rhododendron	Willow Goldfinch	Wash.
West Virginia	West Virginian	Sugar Maple	Big Rhododendron	Cardinal	W.Va.
Wisconsin	Wisconsinite	Sugar Maple	Wood Violet	Robin	Wis.
Wyoming	Wyomingite	Plains Cottonwood	Indian Paintbrush	Western Meadowlark	Wyo.

Some of the (many) theories surrounding the names of each state:

Alabama · From a Choctaw word that can be translated to mean 'thicket cleaners', or 'plant reapers'. ❧ Alaska · Derived from the Aleut word *Alyeska*, often thought to mean 'great land'. Some linguists argue the term actually means 'mainland', or more precisely, 'the object toward which the action of the sea is directed'. ❧ Arizona · Possibly from the Papago for 'little spring', although some argue it is instead derived from the Spanish *arida* for dry and *zona* for area. ❧ Arkansas · Likely the French version of the Illinois tribe's name for the Quapaw Indians. ❧ California · Often linked to the 1510 novel *Las Sergas de Esplandián* by Garci Ordóñez de Montalvo. The book describes a mythical island called California, which was populated by black Amazons and ruled by the beautiful Queen Calafia. Some believe that explorers (who initially thought they had discovered an island) were inspired by the popular novel. ❧ Colorado · Said to come from the Spanish for 'red-colored', after the ruddy waters of the Colorado river.

❧ Connecticut · From the Mohican word *Quinnehtukqut*, for 'long river' or 'beside the long tidal river'. ❧ Delaware · Named after Sir Thomas West, Lord de la Warr, first British Governor of the Colony of Virginia. ❧ District of Columbia · Named in honor of Christopher Columbus. ❧ Florida · After the Spanish Feast of the Flowers at Easter (*Pascua de Florida*), and named by Spanish explorer Ponce de León after he found the region on Easter Sunday. ❧ Georgia · For George II of England. ❧ Hawaii · The origin is unknown, although it may come from the islands' traditional discoverer Chief Hawaii Loa. ❧ Idaho · Some historians believe the name was invented by (unsuccessful) Congressional hopeful George M. Willing, who (falsely) claimed the term was of Native American origin. ❧ Illinois · After the Native American tribe the Inini, which means 'perfect and accomplished men'. ❧ Indiana · Meaning 'land of the Indians'. ❧ Iowa · The French version of the Dakota name for a tribe in the region; believed by some to mean 'sleepy heads', 'snakes', 'dusty noses', or 'this is the place'. ❧ Kansas · From a Sioux word for 'people of the south wind'. ❧ Kentucky · From the Wyandot for 'land of tomorrow'. ❧ Louisiana · After 'La Louisianne', the name given by explorer Sieur de La Salle to the area, after Louis XIV. ❧ Maine · Named either to distinguish the mainland from the nearby islands, or in tribute to Charles I's wife, Queen Henrietta Maria, feudal proprietor of the French province of Mayne. ❧ Maryland · In honor of Queen Henrietta Maria (Queen Mary). Some argue the colony's Catholic founders also approved of the association with the Virgin Mary. ❧ Massachusetts · After the Massachusetts tribe; the word allegedly means 'large hill place'. ❧ Michigan · Some attribute the name's origin to the Chippewa word for 'clearing', others to a local word meaning 'great lake' or 'swimming turtle'. ❧ Minnesota · Named for the Minnesota River, after the Dakota words for 'milky water' or 'cloudy'; some translate the term as 'water reflecting cloudy skies'. ❧ Mississippi · From local Native American words that mean 'Father of Waters'. ❧ Missouri · Named for the Missouri River, which was named after the Missouri Indians; the term is said to mean

STATES · NAME ORIGINS

those who have large canoes'. **Montana** · Possibly from the Latin word for 'mountainous'. **Nebraska** · From local words for 'flat or spreading water', in reference to the Platte and Nebraska rivers. **Nevada** · From *Sierra Nevada*, or 'snowy range' in Spanish. **New Hampshire** · Named after the English county of Hampshire. **New Jersey** · Named after the island of Jersey in the English Channel. **New Mexico** · New Mexico means 'place of Mexitli', an Aztec war god. The area was named *Nuevo Mexico* by early explorers, who hoped to discover the same bounty they'd found in Mexico. **New York** · Named in honor of the brother of Charles II, the Duke of York and Albany. **North Carolina** · First named in honor of France's Charles IX and then England's Charles I and II; 'Carolina' is the feminized form of the Latin *Carolinus*, an adjective derived from Charles. North and South Carolina were one colony until 1729. **North Dakota** · Named for the Dakota tribal grouping; also called the Sioux. In the group's own language, 'dakota' means 'allies' or 'friends'. 'Sioux' is the French version of an Ojibway term meaning 'enemy'.

Ohio · Named for the Ohio River; *oheo* is Iroquois for 'beautiful river' or 'great river'. **Oklahoma** · Allegedly suggested by Native American missionary Rev. Allen Wright, from Choctaw words meaning 'red person'. **Oregon** · Of greatly disputed origin. One theory attributes the name to the Spanish *orejon*, or 'big ear', used to describe several tribes in the region. Possibly also from the French word for 'hurricane' – Canadian fur traders may have once called Oregon's Columbia River the 'river of storms'. **Pennsylvania** · In honor of Adm. Sir William Penn, father of William Penn. *Sylvania* is Latin for 'woods', and therefore the name is thought to literally mean 'Penn's woods'. However, 'Penn' is also Welsh for 'head' or 'headland', and the name can also be translated as 'high woodlands'. **Rhode Island** · Possibly from the Dutch for 'red island', after the state's red clay shores. Also possibly for the Greek island of Rhodes. **South Carolina** · See North Carolina. **South Dakota** · See North Dakota. **Tennessee** · From the Cherokee name *Tanasi*, for a town on the Tennessee River; the meaning is unknown. **Texas** · Said by some to be the Caddo term for 'hello friend', which the Spanish used to describe friendly tribes throughout the region. Also said to be the Spanish Native Americanization of the Spanish *tejas*, or 'allies'. **Utah** · According to one theory, the name derives from the White Mountain Apache word for the Navaho, meaning 'one that is higher up'. Others say the name comes from the Ute tribe. **Vermont** · From the French for 'green mountain'. **Virginia** · In honor of Queen Elizabeth I, popularly known as the 'Virgin Queen'. **Washington** · Named in honor of George Washington. **West Virginia** · See Virginia. **Wisconsin** · Possibly from either the Chippewa word for 'grassy place' or the Ojibway word for 'gathering of the waters'. **Wyoming** · From Delaware words which may mean 'at the big flats' or 'large meadows'. *A great deal of dispute surrounds many of these entries.*

[Selected sources: State government websites (various); *Illustrated Dictionary of Place Names: US and Canada*, Keslie B. Harder, Ed.]

STATES · RACE & ETHNICITY

Race and Ethnicity 2000	White %	Black & African American %	American Indian & Alaskan Native %	Asian %	Hawaiian & Pacific Islands %	Other %	2 or more races %	(Any Race) Hispanic or Latino %	White alone, not Hispanic or Latino %	State Population 2000
Alabama	71.1	26.0	0.5	0.7	0.0	0.7	1.0	1.7	70.3	4,447,100
Alaska	69.3	3.5	15.6	4.0	0.5	1.6	5.4	4.1	67.6	626,932
Arizona	75.5	3.1	5.0	1.8	0.1	11.6	2.9	25.3	63.8	5,130,632
Arkansas	80.0	15.7	0.7	0.8	0.1	1.5	1.3	3.2	78.6	2,673,400
California	59.5	6.7	1.0	10.9	0.3	16.8	4.7	32.4	46.7	33,871,648
Colorado	82.8	3.8	1.0	2.2	0.1	7.2	2.8	17.1	74.5	4,301,261
Connecticut	81.6	9.1	0.3	2.4	0.0	4.3	2.2	9.4	77.5	3,405,565
Delaware	74.6	19.2	0.3	2.1	0.0	2.0	1.7	4.8	72.5	783,600
DC	30.8	60.0	0.3	2.7	0.1	3.8	2.4	7.9	27.8	572,059
Florida	78.0	14.6	0.3	1.7	0.1	3.0	2.4	16.8	65.4	15,982,378
Georgia	65.1	28.7	0.3	2.1	0.1	2.4	1.4	5.3	62.6	8,186,453
Hawaii	24.3	1.8	0.3	41.6	9.4	1.3	21.4	7.2	22.9	1,211,537
Idaho	91.0	0.4	1.4	0.9	0.1	4.2	2.0	7.9	88.0	1,293,953
Illinois	73.5	15.1	0.2	3.4	0.0	5.8	1.9	12.3	67.8	12,419,293
Indiana	87.5	8.4	0.3	1.0	0.0	1.6	1.2	3.5	85.8	6,080,485
Iowa	93.9	2.1	0.3	1.3	0.0	1.3	1.1	2.8	92.6	2,926,324
Kansas	86.1	5.7	0.9	1.7	0.0	3.4	2.1	7.0	83.1	2,688,418
Kentucky	90.1	7.3	0.2	0.7	0.0	0.6	1.1	1.5	89.3	4,041,769
Louisiana	63.9	32.5	0.6	1.2	0.0	0.7	1.1	2.4	62.5	4,468,976
Maine	96.9	0.5	0.6	0.7	0.0	0.2	1.0	0.7	96.5	1,274,923
Maryland	64.0	27.9	0.3	4.0	0.0	1.8	2.0	4.3	62.1	5,296,486
Massachusetts	84.5	5.4	0.2	3.8	0.0	3.7	2.3	6.8	81.9	6,349,097
Michigan	80.2	14.2	0.6	1.8	0.0	1.3	1.9	3.3	78.6	9,938,444
Minnesota	89.4	3.5	1.1	2.9	0.0	1.3	1.7	2.9	88.2	4,919,479
Mississippi	61.4	36.3	0.4	0.7	0.0	0.5	0.7	1.4	60.7	2,844,658
Missouri	84.9	11.2	0.4	1.1	0.1	0.8	1.5	2.1	83.8	5,595,211

STATES · RACE & ETHNICITY

Race and Ethnicity 2000	White %	Black & African American %	American Indian & Alaskan Native %	Asian %	Hawaiian & Pacific Islands %	Other %	2 or more races %	(Any Race) Hispanic or Latino %	White alone, not Hispanic or Latino %	State Population 2000
Montana	90.6	0.3	6.2	0.5	0.1	0.6	1.7	2.0	89.5	902,195
Nebraska	89.6	4.0	0.9	1.3	0.0	2.8	1.4	5.5	87.3	1,711,263
Nevada	75.2	6.8	1.3	4.5	0.4	8.0	3.8	19.7	65.2	1,998,257
New Hampshire	96.0	0.7	0.2	1.3	0.0	0.6	1.1	1.7	95.1	1,235,786
New Jersey	72.6	13.6	0.2	5.7	0.0	5.4	2.5	13.3	66.0	8,414,350
New Mexico	66.8	1.9	9.5	1.1	0.1	17.0	3.6	42.1	44.7	1,819,046
New York	67.9	15.9	0.4	5.5	0.0	7.1	3.1	15.1	62.0	18,976,457
North Carolina	72.1	21.6	1.2	1.4	0.0	2.3	1.3	4.7	70.2	8,049,313
North Dakota	92.4	0.6	4.9	0.6	0.0	0.4	1.2	1.2	91.7	642,200
Ohio	85.0	11.5	0.2	1.2	0.0	0.8	1.4	1.9	84.0	11,353,140
Oklahoma	76.2	7.6	7.9	1.4	0.1	2.4	4.5	5.2	74.1	3,450,654
Oregon	86.6	1.6	1.3	3.0	0.2	4.2	3.1	8.0	83.5	3,421,399
Pennsylvania	85.4	10.0	0.1	1.8	0.0	1.5	1.2	3.2	84.1	12,281,054
Rhode Island	85.0	4.5	0.5	2.3	0.1	5.0	2.7	8.7	81.9	1,048,319
South Carolina	67.2	29.5	0.3	0.9	0.0	1.0	1.0	2.4	66.1	4,012,012
South Dakota	88.7	0.6	8.3	0.6	0.0	0.5	1.3	1.4	88.0	754,844
Tennessee	80.2	16.4	0.3	1.0	0.0	1.0	1.1	2.2	79.2	5,689,283
Texas	71.0	11.5	0.6	2.7	0.1	11.7	2.5	32.0	52.4	20,851,820
Utah	89.2	0.8	1.3	1.7	0.7	4.2	2.1	9.0	85.3	2,233,169
Vermont	96.8	0.5	0.4	0.9	0.0	0.2	1.2	0.9	96.2	608,827
Virginia	72.3	19.6	0.3	3.7	0.1	2.0	2.0	4.7	70.2	7,078,515
Washington	81.8	3.2	1.6	5.5	0.4	3.9	3.6	7.5	78.9	5,894,121
West Virginia	95.0	3.2	0.2	0.5	0.0	0.2	0.9	0.7	94.6	1,808,344
Wisconsin	88.9	5.7	0.9	1.7	0.0	1.6	1.2	3.6	87.3	5,363,675
Wyoming	92.1	0.8	2.3	0.6	0.1	2.5	1.8	6.4	88.9	493,782
USA	75.1	12.3	0.9	3.6	0.1	5.5	2.4	12.5	69.1	281,421,906

STATES · SOCIAL INDICATORS

State (& rank)	Resident population		Unemployment %		Home ownership %		% of people below the poverty line		Av. annual pay $		Violent crime rate per 100,000 pop.	
Alabama	4,599,030	23rd	3.6	37th	74.2	8th	17.0	7th	34,598	31st	432	22nd
Alaska	670,053	47th	6.7	3rd	67.2	42nd	11.2	33rd	40,216	15th	632	6th
Arizona	6,166,318	16th	4.1	31st	71.6	23rd	14.2	15th	38,154	21st	513	16th
Arkansas	2,810,872	32nd	5.3	8th	70.8	29th	17.2	6th	31,266	45th	528	13th
California	36,457,549	1st	4.9	14th	60.2	48th	13.3	20th	46,211	5th	526	14th
Colorado	4,753,377	22nd	4.3	27th	70.1	34th	11.1	35th	41,601	10th	397	24th
Connecticut	3,504,809	29th	4.3	27th	71.1	27th	8.3	48th	52,954	1st	275	37th
Delaware	853,476	45th	3.6	37th	76.8	3rd	10.4	39th	44,622	6th	632	6th
DC	581,530	–	6.0	–	45.9	–	19.0	–	66,696	–	1,459	–
Florida	18,089,888	4th	3.3	42nd	72.4	18th	12.8	24th	36,800	23rd	708	3rd
Georgia	9,363,941	9th	4.6	21st	68.5	38th	14.4	13th	39,096	18th	449	20th
Hawaii	1,285,498	42nd	2.4	50th	59.9	49th	9.8	44th	36,353	25th	255	41st
Idaho	1,466,465	39th	3.4	40th	75.1	7th	13.9	17th	30,777	46th	257	40th
Illinois	12,831,970	5th	4.5	24th	70.4	31st	12.0	28th	43,744	8th	552	10th
Indiana	6,313,520	15th	5.0	11th	74.2	8th	12.2	27th	35,431	30th	324	29th
Iowa	2,982,085	30th	3.7	36th	74.0	12th	10.9	37th	33,070	38th	291	31st
Kansas	2,764,075	33rd	4.5	24th	70.0	35th	11.7	31st	33,854	34th	387	25th
Kentucky	4,206,074	26th	5.7	5th	71.7	22nd	16.8	8th	33,965	33rd	267	39th
Louisiana	4,287,768	25th	4.0	32nd	71.3	25th	19.8	2nd	33,566	35th	594	9th
Maine	1,321,574	40th	4.6	21st	75.3	6th	12.6	25th	32,701	40th	112	49th
Maryland	5,615,727	19th	3.9	35th	72.6	17th	8.2	49th	44,368	7th	703	4th
Massachusetts	6,437,193	13th	5.0	11th	65.2	46th	10.3	40th	50,095	3rd	457	19th
Michigan	10,095,643	8th	6.9	1st	77.4	2nd	13.2	22nd	41,214	11th	552	10th
Minnesota	5,167,101	21st	4.0	32nd	75.6	5th	9.2	46th	40,800	12th	297	30th
Mississippi	2,910,540	31st	6.8	2nd	76.2	4th	21.3	1st	29,763	48th	278	36th
Missouri	5,842,713	18th	4.8	17th	71.9	21st	13.3	20th	35,951	26th	525	15th

STATES · SOCIAL INDICATORS

State (& rank)	Resident population		Unemployment %		Home ownership %		% of people below the poverty line		Av. annual pay $		Violent crime rate per 100,000 pop.	
Montana	944,632	44th	3.2	43rd	69.5	36th	14.4	13th	29,150	49th	282	35th
Nebraska	1,768,331	38th	3.0	47th	67.6	41st	10.9	37th	32,422	42nd	287	32nd
Nevada	2,495,529	35th	4.2	29th	65.7	45th	11.1	35th	38,763	19th	607	8th
New Hampshire	1,314,895	41st	3.4	40th	74.2	8th	7.5	50th	40,551	14th	132	47th
New Jersey	8,724,560	11th	4.6	21st	69.0	37th	8.7	47th	49,471	4th	355	26th
New Mexico	1,954,599	36th	4.2	29th	72.0	20th	18.5	3rd	32,605	41st	702	5th
New York	19,306,183	3rd	4.5	24th	55.7	50th	13.8	18th	51,937	2nd	446	21st
North Carolina	8,856,505	10th	4.8	17th	70.2	32nd	15.1	12th	35,912	27th	468	18th
North Dakota	635,867	48th	3.2	43rd	68.3	39th	11.2	33rd	29,956	47th	98	50th
Ohio	11,478,006	7th	5.5	6th	72.1	19th	13.0	23rd	37,333	22nd	351	27th
Oklahoma	3,579,212	28th	4.0	32nd	71.6	23rd	16.5	9th	31,721	43rd	509	17th
Oregon	3,700,758	27th	5.4	7th	68.1	40th	14.1	16th	36,588	24th	287	32nd
Pennsylvania	12,440,621	6th	4.7	19th	73.2	16th	11.9	29th	39,661	17th	425	23rd
Rhode Island	1,067,610	43rd	5.1	10th	64.6	47th	12.3	26th	38,751	20th	251	42nd
South Carolina	4,321,249	24th	6.5	4th	74.2	8th	15.6	10th	32,927	39th	761	1st
South Dakota	781,919	46th	3.2	43rd	70.6	30th	13.6	19th	29,149	50th	176	46th
Tennessee	6,038,803	17th	5.2	9th	71.3	25th	15.5	11th	35,879	28th	753	2nd
Texas	23,507,783	2nd	4.9	14th	66.0	44th	17.6	5th	40,150	16th	530	12th
Utah	2,550,063	34th	2.9	49th	73.5	15th	10.2	41st	33,328	36th	227	45th
Vermont	623,908	49th	3.6	37th	74.0	12th	11.5	32nd	34,197	32nd	120	48th
Virginia	7,642,884	12th	3.0	47th	71.1	27th	10.0	43rd	42,287	9th	283	34th
Washington	6,395,798	14th	5.0	11th	66.7	43rd	11.9	29th	40,721	13th	346	28th
West Virginia	1,818,470	37th	4.9	14th	78.4	1st	18.0	4th	31,347	44th	273	38th
Wisconsin	5,556,506	20th	4.7	19th	70.2	32nd	10.2	41st	35,471	29th	242	43rd
Wyoming	515,004	50th	3.2	43rd	73.7	14th	9.5	45th	33,251	37th	230	44th
USA	299,398,484	—	4.6	—	68.8	—	13.3	—	40,677	—	469	—

STATES · SOCIAL INDICATORS

State (& rank)	Infant mortality rate		Doctors per 100,000 resident population		Traffic fatalities per 100m vehicle miles		Energy consumption million BTU/person		Mobile homes as % of all housing units		% of >25s with a BA or higher	
Alabama	8.7	5th	213	39th	1.90	11th	478	6th	14.7	5th	19.8	46th
Alaska	7.0	23rd	222	34th	1.43	26th	1,186	1st	6.9	28th	28.7	19th
Arizona	6.5	30th	208	43rd	1.97	10th	250	46th	13.3	9th	27.9	20th
Arkansas	8.7	5th	203	44th	2.03	9th	414	13th	12.8	10th	17.5	49th
California	5.2	44th	259	20th	1.31	32nd	233	48th	4.4	38th	30.4	12th
Colorado	6.1	33rd	258	21st	1.26	34th	301	38th	4.9	35th	35.4	5th
Connecticut	5.4	42nd	363	4th	0.87	49th	264	42nd	1.2	46th	36.9	1st
Delaware	9.4	2nd	248	24th	1.41	28th	368	19th	11.7	13th	25.6	26th
DC	10.5	–	798	–	1.29	–	328	–	0.1	–	46.7	–
Florida	7.5	18th	245	25th	1.76	17th	256	45th	10.4	17th	25.5	27th
Georgia	8.5	7th	220	36th	1.52	20th	352	24th	11.0	15th	26.9	23rd
Hawaii	7.5	18th	310	7th	1.39	29th	257	44th	0.2	50th	30.6	11th
Idaho	6.3	32nd	169	50th	1.85	13th	358	23rd	10.9	16th	25.9	24th
Illinois	7.7	14th	272	11th	1.26	34th	312	33rd	2.8	43rd	29.5	16th
Indiana	7.7	14th	213	39th	1.31	32nd	473	7th	6.5	29th	22.5	42nd
Iowa	5.6	39th	187	46th	1.45	24th	408	15th	4.2	40th	24.5	36th
Kansas	6.6	28th	220	36th	1.44	25th	403	16th	5.2	34th	30.4	12th
Kentucky	6.9	24th	230	31st	2.08	6th	473	7th	13.9	7th	19.0	48th
Louisiana	9.3	3rd	264	15th	2.12	5th	849	3rd	11.7	13th	19.7	47th
Maine	4.9	47th	267	13th	1.13	40th	366	20th	8.9	21st	24.2	37th
Maryland	8.2	10th	411	2nd	1.09	42nd	275	40th	2.0	45th	36.3	3rd
Massachusetts	4.8	48th	450	1st	0.80	50th	240	47th	1.0	47th	36.8	2nd
Michigan	8.5	7th	240	27th	1.09	42nd	309	34th	6.0	32nd	24.6	35th
Minnesota	4.6	49th	281	10th	0.98	47th	359	21st	3.9	42nd	34.3	7th
Mississippi	10.7	1st	181	48th	2.21	3rd	420	12th	13.8	8th	21.9	44th
Missouri	7.9	12th	239	29th	1.83	14th	322	31st	7.3	26th	24.9	34th

STATES · SOCIAL INDICATORS

State (& rank)	Infant mortality rate		Doctors per 100,000 resident population		Traffic fatalities per 100m vehicle miles		Energy consumption million BTU/person		Mobile homes as % of all housing units		% of >25s with a BA or higher	
Montana	6.8	25th	221	35th	2.26	1st	435	10th	12.8	10th	25.4	28th
Nebraska	5.4	42nd	239	29th	1.43	26th	373	18th	4.5	37th	25.1	31st
Nevada	5.7	37th	186	47th	2.06	7th	297	39th	7.9	24th	23.5	40th
New Hampshire	4.0	50th	260	19th	1.24	36th	263	43rd	6.5	29th	32.8	8th
New Jersey	5.7	37th	306	8th	1.01	46th	303	37th	0.9	49th	36.3	3rd
New Mexico	5.8	35th	240	27th	2.04	8th	359	21st	16.6	3rd	27.2	21st
New York	6.0	34th	389	3rd	1.04	45th	221	49th	2.6	44th	30.3	14th
North Carolina	8.2	10th	253	23rd	1.51	21st	318	32nd	16.8	2nd	25.4	28th
North Dakota	7.3	20th	242	26th	1.62	19th	633	4th	8.6	22nd	27.2	21st
Ohio	7.7	14th	261	17th	1.20	37th	351	25th	4.4	38th	22.9	41st
Oklahoma	7.8	13th	171	49th	1.71	18th	422	11th	9.5	20th	24.0	39th
Oregon	5.6	39th	263	16th	1.38	30th	305	36th	9.9	18th	29.1	18th
Pennsylvania	7.3	20th	294	9th	1.50	22nd	327	29th	4.6	36th	25.8	25th
Rhode Island	6.7	26th	351	6th	1.05	44th	210	50th	1.0	47th	29.2	17th
South Carolina	8.3	9th	230	31st	2.21	3rd	409	14th	18.8	1st	24.2	37th
South Dakota	6.7	26th	219	38th	2.22	2nd	342	26th	12.1	12th	25.1	31st
Tennessee	9.3	3rd	261	17th	1.79	16th	390	17th	9.9	18th	21.6	45th
Texas	6.6	28th	212	41st	1.49	23rd	532	5th	8.0	23rd	25.4	28th
Utah	5.0	45th	209	42nd	1.12	41st	306	35th	4.2	40th	29.8	15th
Vermont	5.0	45th	362	5th	0.95	48th	273	41st	7.2	27th	34.4	6th
Virginia	7.7	14th	270	12th	1.18	38th	342	26th	6.1	31st	30.7	10th
Washington	5.6	39th	265	14th	1.17	39th	323	30th	7.5	25th	30.9	9th
West Virginia	7.3	20th	229	33rd	1.82	15th	454	9th	16.0	4th	15.1	50th
Wisconsin	6.5	30th	254	22nd	1.36	31st	336	28th	6.0	32nd	25.1	31st
Wyoming	5.8	35th	188	45th	1.88	12th	899	2nd	14.5	6th	22.0	43rd
USA	6.9	–	266	–	1.45	–	342	–	7.1	–	27.6	–

—————————— STATES · CENTER & ELEVATIONS ——————————

State	Geographic center	Highest elevation	feet (′)	Lowest elevation	feet (′)	difference (′)
Alabama	12 mi SW of Clanton	Cheaha Mountain	2,407	Gulf of Mexico	0	2,407
Alaska	60 mi NW of Mount McKinley	Mount McKinley (Denali)	20,320	Pacific Ocean	0	20,320
Arizona	55 mi ESE of Prescott	Humphreys Peak	12,633	Colorado River	70	12,563
Arkansas	12 mi NW of Little Rock	Magazine Mountain	2,753	Ouachita River	55	2,698
California	38 mi E of Madera	Mount Whitney	14,494	Death Valley	-282	14,776
Colorado	30 mi NW of Pikes Peak	Mount Elbert	14,433	Arikaree River	3,315	11,118
Connecticut	East Berlin in Hartford County	Mount Frissell	2,380	Long Island Sound	0	2,380
Delaware	11 mi S of Dover	Ebright Road	448	Atlantic Ocean	0	448
Florida	12 mi NNW of Brooksville	Britton Hill	345	Atlantic Ocean	0	345
Georgia	18 mi SE of Macon	Brasstown Bald	4,784	Atlantic Ocean	0	4,784
Hawaii	20°15 N 156°20′ W, off Maui Island	Pu'u Wekiu	13,796	Pacific Ocean	0	13,796
Idaho	At Custer, SW of Challis	Borah Peak	12,662	Snake River	710	11,952
Illinois	28 mi NE of Springfield	Charles Mound	1,235	Mississippi River	279	956
Indiana	14 mi NNW of Indianapolis	Hoosier Hill	1,257	Ohio River	320	937
Iowa	5 mi NE of Ames	Hawkeye Point	1,670	Mississippi River	480	1,190
Kansas	15 mi NE of Great Bend	Mount Sunflower	4,039	Verdigris River	679	3,360
Kentucky	3 mi NNW of Lebanon	Black Mountain	4,145	Mississippi River	257	3,888
Louisiana	3 mi SE of Marksville	Driskill Mountain	535	New Orleans	-8	543
Maine	18 mi N of Dover	Mount Katahdin	5,268	Atlantic Ocean	0	5,268
Maryland	4½ mi NW of Davidsonville	Hoye Crest	3,360	Atlantic Ocean	0	3,360
Massachusetts	North part of City of Worcester	Mount Greylock	3,491	Atlantic Ocean	0	3,491
Michigan	5 mi NNW of Cadillac	Mount Arvon	1,979	Lake Erie	571	1,408
Minnesota	10 mi SW of Brainerd	Eagle Mountain	2,301	Lake Superior	601	1,700
Mississippi	9 mi WNW of Carthage	Woodall Mountain	806	Gulf of Mexico	0	806
Missouri	20 mi SW of Jefferson City	Taum Sauk Mountain	1,772	Saint Francis River	230	1,542

STATES · CENTER & ELEVATIONS

State	Geographic center	Highest elevation	feet (')	Lowest elevation	feet (')	difference (')
Montana	11 mi W of Lewistown	Granite Peak	12,799	Kootenai River	1,800	10,999
Nebraska	10 mi NW of Broken Bow	Panorama Point	5,424	Missouri River	840	4,584
Nevada	26 mi SE of Austin	Boundary Peak	13,140	Colorado River	479	12,661
New Hampshire	3 mi E of Ashland	Mount Washington	6,288	Atlantic Ocean	0	6,288
New Jersey	5 mi SE of Trenton	High Point	1,803	Atlantic Ocean	0	1,803
New Mexico	12 mi SSW of Willard	Wheeler Peak	13,161	Red Bluff Reservoir	2,842	10,319
New York	12 mi S of Oneida; 26 mi SW of Utica	Mount Marcy	5,344	Atlantic Ocean	0	5,344
North Carolina	10 mi NW of Sanford	Mount Mitchell	6,684	Atlantic Ocean	0	6,684
North Dakota	5 mi SW of McClusky	White Butte	3,506	Red River	750	2,756
Ohio	25 mi NNE of Columbus	Campbell Hill	1,550	Ohio River	455	1,095
Oklahoma	8 mi N of Oklahoma City	Black Mesa	4,973	Little River	289	4,684
Oregon	25 mi SSE of Prineville	Mount Hood	11,239	Pacific Ocean	0	11,239
Pennsylvania	2½ mi SW of Bellefonte	Mount Davis	3,213	Delaware River	0	3,213
Rhode Island	1 mile SSW of Crompton	Jerimoth Hill	812	Atlantic Ocean	0	812
South Carolina	13 mi SE of Columbia	Sassafras Mountain	3,560	Atlantic Ocean	0	3,560
South Dakota	8 mi NE of Pierre	Harney Peak	7,242	Big Stone Lake	966	6,276
Tennessee	5 mi NE of Murfreesboro	Clingmans Dome	6,643	Mississippi River	178	6,465
Texas	15 mi NE of Brady	Guadalupe Peak	8,749	Gulf of Mexico	0	8,749
Utah	3 mi N of Manti	Kings Peak	13,528	Beaver Dam Wash	2,000	11,528
Vermont	3 mi E of Roxbury	Mount Mansfield	4,393	Lake Champlain	95	4,298
Virginia	5 mi SW of Buckingham	Mount Rogers	5,729	Atlantic Ocean	0	5,729
Washington	10 mi WSW of Wenatchee	Mount Rainier	14,411	Pacific Ocean	0	14,411
West Virginia	4 mi E of Sutton	Spruce Knob	4,863	Potomac River	240	4,623
Wisconsin	9 mi SE of Marshfield	Timms Hill	1,951	Lake Michigan	579	1,372
Wyoming	58 mi ENE of Lander	Gannett Peak	13,804	Belle Fourche River	3,099	10,705

STATES · RANKINGS & TEMPERATURES

| State | 2007 Morgan Quinto State Rankings (morganquinno.com) | | | | Record State Temperatures | | | | |
	Smartest	Healthiest	Dangerous	Livable	Highest	recorded at	Lowest	recorded at	difference
Alabama	45th	40th	17th	42nd	112°F	Centerville	-27°F	New Market	139°F
Alaska	46th	36th	7th	24th	100°F	Fort Yukon	-80°F	Prospect Creek Camp	180°F
Arizona	50th	42nd	3rd	32nd	128°F	Lake Havasu City	-40°F	Hawley Lake	168°F
Arkansas	32nd	37th	13th	48th	120°F	Ozark	-29°F	Pond	149°F
California	47th	19th	9th	30th	134°F	Greenland Ranch	-45°F	Boca	179°F
Colorado	27th	28th	22nd	18th	118°F	Bennett	-61°F	Maybell	179°F
Connecticut	3rd	13th	40th	10th	106°F	Danbury	-32°F	Coventry	138°F
Delaware	28th	39th	18th	21st	110°F	Millsboro	-17°F	Millsboro	127°F
Florida	29th	46th	8th	27th	109°F	Monticello	-2°F	Tallahassee	111°F
Georgia	41st	44th	20th	41st	112°F	Greenville	-17°F	CCC Camp F-16	129°F
Hawaii	42nd	9th	28th	19th	100°F	Pahala	12°F	Mauna Kea Obs 111.2	88°F
Idaho	20th	24th	39th	14th	118°F	Orofino	-60°F	Island Park Dam	178°F
Illinois	35th	32nd	21st	26th	117°F	East St Louis	-36°F	Congerville	153°F
Indiana	24th	33rd	25th	35th	116°F	Collegeville	-36°F	New Whiteland	152°F
Iowa	9th	7th	43rd	6th	118°F	Keokuk	-47°F	Elkader	165°F
Kansas	15th	10th	27th	17th	121°F	Alton (near)	-40°F	Lebanon	161°F
Kentucky	31st	29th	34th	47th	114°F	Greensburg	-37°F	Shelbyville	151°F
Louisiana	44th	50th	10th	49th	114°F	Plain Dealing	-16°F	Minden	130°F
Maine	5th	4th	48th	16th	105°F	North Bridgton	-48°F	Van Buren	153°F
Maryland	18th	35th	4th	15th	109°F	Cumberland & Frederick	-40°F	Oakland	149°F
Massachusetts	2nd	3rd	30th	8th	107°F	New Bedford & Chester	-35°F	Chester	142°F
Michigan	39th	21st	11th	38th	112°F	Mio	-51°F	Vanderbilt	163°F
Minnesota	13th	2nd	32nd	2nd	114°F	Moorhead	-60°F	Tower	174°F
Mississippi	48th	48th	24th	50th	115°F	Holly Springs	-19°F	Corinth	134°F
Missouri	22nd	34th	19th	34th	118°F	Warsaw & Union	-40°F	Warsaw	158°F

STATES · RANKINGS & TEMPERATURES

State	2007 Morgan Quitno State Rankings (morganquitno.com)				Record State Temperatures				
	Smartest	Healthiest	Dangerous	Livable	Highest	recorded at	Lowest	recorded at	difference
Montana	7th	26th	44th	22nd	117°F	Medicine Lake	-70°F	Rogers Pass	187°F
Nebraska	11th	6th	37th	11th	118°F	Minden	-47°F	Oshkosh	165°F
Nevada	49th	47th	1st	25th	125°F	Laughlin	-50°F	San Jacinto	175°F
New Hampshire	12th	5th	47th	1st	106°F	Nashua	-47°F	Mt. Washington	153°F
New Jersey	4th	16th	33rd	5th	110°F	Runyon	-34°F	River Vale	144°F
New Mexico	43rd	49th	2nd	37th	122°F	Waste Isolation Pilot Plant	-50°F	Gavilan	172°F
New York	16th	27th	31st	29th	108°F	Troy	-52°F	Old Forge	160°F
North Carolina	23rd	31st	16th	42nd	110°F	Fayetteville	-34°F	Mt. Mitchell	144°F
North Dakota	21st	12th	50th	13th	121°F	Steele	-60°F	Parshall	181°F
Ohio	34th	20th	23rd	36th	113°F	Gallipolis (near)	-39°F	Milligan	152°F
Oklahoma	36th	41st	15th	40th	120°F	Tipton	-27°F	Watts	147°F
Oregon	40th	17th	29th	23rd	119°F	Pendleton	-54°F	Seneca	173°F
Pennsylvania	10th	23rd	26th	33rd	111°F	Phoenixville	-42°F	Smethport	153°F
Rhode Island	14th	11th	35th	28th	104°F	Providence	-25°F	Greene	129°F
South Carolina	26th	45th	6th	46th	111°F	Camden	-19°F	Caesars Head	130°F
South Dakota	17th	22nd	45th	9th	120°F	Gannvalley	-58°F	McIntosh	178°F
Tennessee	30th	38th	5th	44th	113°F	Perryville	-32°F	Mountain City	145°F
Texas	25th	43rd	12th	39th	120°F	Monahans	-23°F	Seminole	143°F
Utah	38th	8th	38th	4th	117°F	Saint George	-69°F	Peter's Sink	186°F
Vermont	1st	1st	49th	7th	105°F	Vernon	-50°F	Bloomfield	155°F
Virginia	6th	18th	36th	12th	110°F	Balcony Falls	-30°F	Mtn. Lake Bio. Stn.	140°F
Washington	33rd	14th	14th	31st	118°F	Ice Harbor Dam	-48°F	Mazama & Winthrop	166°F
West Virginia	37th	25th	41st	45th	112°F	Martinsburg	-37°F	Lewisburg	149°F
Wisconsin	8th	15th	42nd	20th	114°F	Wisconsin Dells	-55°F	Couderay	169°F
Wyoming	19th	30th	46th	3rd	115°F	Basin	-66°F	Riverside R.S.	181°F

Government

Why has government been instituted at all? Because the passions of men
will not conform to the dictates of reason and justice, without constraint.
— ALEXANDER HAMILTON, *Federalist*, No. 15, 1787–88

GEORGE WALKER BUSH · 43rd PRESIDENT

Sworn into office: January 20, 2001 & January 20, 2005 · *Affiliation*: Republican
Born: July 6, 1946, New Haven, Connecticut · *Professed religion*: Methodist
Yale University (graduated 1968) & Harvard University Business School (graduated 1975)
Served as 46th Governor of Texas 1994–2000
Marriage: November 5, 1977, to Laura Welch (born November 4, 1946, in Midland, Texas)
Children: twins Barbara (1981–), Jenna (1981–)
Pets: Barney & Miss Beazley (dogs); India 'Willie' Bush (cat); Ofelia (cow) [see p.303]

Height.....71·50 inches	Body fat......... 16·6%	Blood pressure ..117/71
Weight.........192·0 lb	Pulse (resting).. 52 bpm	Temperature..... 97·8°F
Cholesterol.. 170 mg/dl	Pulse (active)..184 bpm	[2007 annual medical checkup]

THE CABINET & CABINET RANKING MEMBERS

Vice President..Richard B. Cheney
Secretary of State.. Condoleezza Rice
Secretary of the Treasury.......................................Henry M. Paulson Jr
Secretary of Defense... Robert M. Gates
Attorney General .... Solicitor General Paul Clement [acting, see pp.27–28]
Secretary of the Interior ....Dirk Kempthorne
Secretary of Agriculture..Michael O. Johanns
Secretary of Commerce..Carlos M. Gutierrez
Secretary of Labor .... Elaine Chao
Secretary of Health & Human Services.........................Michael O. Leavitt
Secretary of Housing & Urban Development....................Alphonso Jackson
Secretary of Transportation.......................................Mary E. Peters
Secretary of Energy...Samuel W. Bodman
Secretary of Education...Margaret L. Spellings
Secretary of Veterans Affairs..............................Robert J. 'Jim' Nicholson
Secretary of Homeland Security...................................Michael Chertoff
Administrator, Environmental Protection Agency .... Stephen Johnson
Director, Office of Management and Budget........................Rob Portman
Director, Office of National Drug Control Policy ....John Walters
US Trade Representative................................ Ambassador Susan Schwab
White House Chief of Staff......................................Joshua B. Bolten

PRESIDENTS & CARTOONS

A number of American Presidents and First Ladies have lent their name to cartoon characters, or served as their inspiration. In *The Simpsons*, Bart's bespectacled friend Milhouse is named after RICHARD MILHOUS NIXON; Marge Simpson's chain-smoking mother, Jacqueline Bouvier, is named after JACQUELINE KENNEDY ONASSIS (née Bouvier); and Mayor Quimby arguably shares some characteristics with JFK – including his accent, and his wife's fondness for pillbox hats. According to one theory, WILLIAM HOWARD TAFT was the inspiration for Popeye's nemesis, Bluto/Brutus. The newspaper comic strip *Mallard Fillmore* (about a politically conservative duck) is a pun on the name of the 13th President, MILLARD FILLMORE; a Mallard Fillmore also appeared in the DC Comics series *Captain Carrot & His Amazing Zoo Crew*. Yet, while the comic strip character Garfield shares his name with the 20th President, JAMES GARFIELD, the strip's creator, Jim Davis, says the lasagna-loving tabby was named for his grandfather, James Garfield Davis.

PRESIDENTIAL CODE-NAMES

The US Secret Service bestowed the code-name *Renegade* on Senator Barack Obama, according to a June 17, 2007, report in the *Washington Post*. Other code-names are:

Hillary Clinton ....*Evergreen*	George H.W. Bush.........*Timberwolf*
John Kerry ....*Minuteman*	Ronald Reagan................*Rawhide*
Al Gore.......*Sawhorse* then *Sundance*	Dick Cheney......*Backseat* then *Angler*
George W. Bush...............*Tumbler*	(Josiah Bartlet...........*Eagle; Liberty*)
Bill Clinton ....*Eagle*	(Zoey Bartlet..................*Bookbag*)
Jimmy Carter ....*Deacon*	(Claudia Jean 'C.J.' Cregg...*Flamingo*)

Predictably, a number of people have attempted to find symbolism in these code-names – not least *Tumbler* for George W. Bush, who, in addition to alcoholism in his past, is known for a somewhat hapless style. However, the *Post* warned, 'according to a Secret Service spokesman, all code names are chosen by military officials, suggesting that they should not be examined too closely for deeper meaning'.

GIFTS TO THE PRESIDENT

President Bush reportedly receives *c*.1,000 gifts per month, most of which are stored in the National Archives pending the construction of his library [see p.304]. In 2006, according to financial disclosure forms, he received fishing equipment worth $2,600; a $915 set of golf clubs; $1,600 wooden benches carved from trees on his Texas ranch; a $658 wireless weather station; and a $400 personal trainer and cycle computer (the latter two gifts were from Vice President Cheney). Cheney himself received 3 fishing rods worth a total $2,975; $615 hunting boots; and a $7,200 sculpture of a Cheyenne warrior. In the past, Bush has received an iPod and a Bible from Bono; jars of 'various fertilizers' from Jordan's King Abdulla; a DVD of *Singin' in the Rain* from the Sultan of Brunei; and 300lbs of raw lamb meat from the President of Argentina. [Sources: Associated Press; the *Guardian*; the London *Times*]

———————————————————— US PRESIDENTS ————————————————————

president	born	star sign	birth state	age at inaug.	dates of term	political party	religion	handedness	owned slaves	facial hair	red-headed	Mt Rushmore	assassinated	served as VP	at Harvard	on a banknote	Nobel Prize	children	6ft or taller	corps	died in office	date of death	age
George Washington	02-22-1732	♓	VA‡	57	1789–1797	F	E	r	■			■				■			■	$25k		12-14-1799	67
John Adams	10-30-1735	♏	MA‡	61	1797–1801	F	U	r						■	■			5		$25k		07-04-1826	90
Thomas Jefferson	04-13-1743	♈	VA‡	57	1801–1809	DR	D	r	■		■	■		■		■		6	■	$25k		07-04-1826	83
James Madison	03-16-1751	♓	VA‡	57	1809–1817	DR	E	r	■					■	□	■				$25k		06-28-1836	85
James Monroe	04-28-1758	♉	VA‡	58	1817–1825	DR	E	r	■					■				2		$25k		07-04-1831	73
John Q. Adams	07-11-1767	♋	MA‡	57	1825–1829	DR	U	r						■	■			4		$25k		02-23-1848	80
Andrew Jackson	03-15-1767	♓	SC‡	61	1829–1837	D	P	r	■							□				$25k		06-08-1845	78
Martin Van Buren	12-05-1782	♐	NY	54	1837–1841	D	Re	r	■					■				4		$25k		07-24-1862	79
William Harrison	02-09-1773	♒	VA‡	68	1841	W	E	r	■							□		10		$25k	■	04-04-1841	68
John Tyler	03-29-1790	♈	VA	51	1841–1845	W	E	r	■					■				14		$25k		01-18-1862	71
James Knox Polk	11-02-1795	♏	NC	49	1845–1849	D	M	r	■											$25k		06-15-1849	53
Zachary Taylor	11-24-1784	♐	VA	64	1849–1850	W	E	r	■									6		$25k	■	07-09-1850	65
Millard Fillmore	01-07-1800	♑	NY	50	1850–1853	W	U	r										2		$25k		03-08-1874	74
Franklin Pierce	11-23-1804	♐	NH	48	1853–1857	D	E	r						■				3		$25k		10-08-1869	64
James Buchanan	04-23-1791	♉	PA	65	1857–1861	D	P	r												$25k		06-01-1868	77
Abraham Lincoln	02-12-1809	♒	KY	52	1861–1865	R	L	r		■		■	■			■		4	■	$25k	■	04-15-1865	56
Andrew Johnson	12-29-1808	♑	NC	56	1865–1869	D/U/R	?	r	■					■				5		$25k		07-31-1875	66
Ulysses S. Grant	04-27-1822	♉	OH	46	1869–1877	R	M	r	■	■					■	■		4	■	*$50k		07-23-1885	63
Rutherford Hayes	10-04-1822	♎	OH	54	1877–1881	R	M	r		■	□							8		$50k		01-17-1893	70
James Garfield	11-19-1831	♏	OH	49	1881	R	Di	l		■			■			■		7		$50k	■	09-19-1881	49
Chester Arthur	10-05-1829	♎	VT	50	1881–1885	R	E	r		■								3	■	$50k		11-18-1886	56
Grover Cleveland	03-18-1837	♓	NJ	47	1885–1889	D	P	r		■					□			5	■	$50k		06-24-1908	71
Benjamin Harrison	08-20-1833	♌	OH	55	1889–1893	R	P	r		■								3		$50k		03-13-1901	67
Grover Cleveland	03-18-1837	♓	NJ	55	1893–1897	D	P	r		■					□			5		$50k		06-24-1908	71

——— US PRESIDENTS cont. ———

president	born	star sign	birth state	age at inaug.	dates of term	political party	religion	handedness	owned slaves	facial hair	red-headed	assassinated	Mt Rushmore	served as VP	at Harvard	on a banknote	Nobel Prize	children	salary (½ or fuller)	died in office	date of death	age
William McKinley	01·29·1843	♒	OH	54	1897–1901	R	M	r				■				□		2	$50k	■	09·14·1901	58
Theodore Roosevelt	10·27·1858	♏	NY	42	1901–1909	R	Re	r		■		□	■	■	■		■	6	$50k		01·06·1919	60
William Taft	09·15·1857	♍	OH	51	1909–1913	R	U	r		■								3	$75k		03·08·1930	72
Woodrow Wilson	12·28·1856	♑	VA	56	1913–1921	D	P	r								□	■	3	$75k		02·03·1924	67
Warren Harding	11·02·1865	♏	OH	55	1921–1923	R	B	r										2	$75k	■	08·02·1923	57
Calvin Coolidge	07·04·1872	♋	VT	51	1923–1929	R	C	r			□			■				2	$75k		01·05·1933	60
Herbert Hoover	08·10·1874	♌	IA	54	1929–1933	R	Q	?										2	$75k		10·20·1964	90
Franklin D. Roosevelt	01·30·1882	♒	NY	51	1933–1945	D	E	l							■			6	$75k	■	04·12·1945	63
Harry S. Truman	05·08·1884	♉	MO	60	1945–1953	D	B	l				□		■				1	*$100k		12·26·1972	88
Dwight Eisenhower	10·14·1890	♎	TX	62	1953–1961	R	P	r										2	$100k		03·28·1969	78
John F. Kennedy	05·29·1917	♊	MA	43	1961–1963	D	Ro	r				■			■			3	$100k	■	11·22·1963	46
Lyndon B. Johnson	08·27·1908	♍	TX	55	1963–1969	D	Di	r						■				2	$100k		01·22·1973	64
Richard Nixon	01·09·1913	♑	CA	56	1969–1974	R	Q	l						■				2	$200k		04·22·1994	81
Gerald Ford	07·14·1913	♋	NE	61	1974–1977	R	E	l				□		■				4	$200k		12·26·2006	93
James 'Jimmy' Carter	10·01·1924	♎	GA	52	1977–1981	D	So	r									■	4	$200k			
Ronald Reagan	02·06·1911	♒	IL	69	1981–1989	R	Di	?				□						4	$200k		06·05·2004	93
George Bush	06·12·1924	♊	MA	64	1989–1993	R	E	l						■				6	$200k			
William 'Bill' Clinton	08·19·1946	♌	AR	46	1993–2001	D	B	l										1	$200k			
George W. Bush	07·06·1946	♋	CT	54	2001–	R	M	r							■			2	p.290 $400k			

NOTES: Considerable debate and dispute surround a number of these entries. ‡ = Born British. *Party*: [F]ederalist; [W]hig; [U]nion. *Religion at election*: [E]piscopalian; [C]ongregationalist; [U]nitarian; [D]eist; [P]resbyterian; [Re]formed Dutch; [M]ethodist; [L]iberal; [Di]sciples of Christ; [B]aptist; [Q]uaker; [So]uthern Baptist. A number of Presidents changed their religion. *Handedness* data are equivocal. *Slave ownership* is disputed and not necessarily while in office. *Heights* are problematic. *Red-headedness* is often subjective (e.g. JFK). *Children* includes those who died as infants; Jefferson's activity with the slave Sally Hemings is disputed; one of Reagan's sons was adopted. *Salary*: * Indicates the President also received the preceding salary. Hollow boxes indicate an assassination attempt, an obsolete banknote design, or uncertain hair color.

─────── 2007 STATE OF THE UNION ADDRESS ───────

Delivered by President George W. Bush · January 23, 2007
Start: 9:13pm EST · *Finish*: 10:02pm EST · *Duration*: 49 mins
Words: 4,839 · *Interruptions*: applause, 63; laughter, 2 [White House analysis]

Some thematic extracts

NANCY PELOSI · tonight I have the high privilege and distinct honor of my own as the first president to begin the State of the Union message with these words: Madam Speaker.

CONGRESS & THE MIDTERMS · I congratulate the Democrat majority. Congress has changed, but our responsibilities have not ... Our citizens don't much care which side of the aisle we sit on – as long as we are willing to cross that aisle when there is work to be done.

THE ECONOMY · A future of hope and opportunity begins with a growing economy, and that is what we have. We're now in the 41st month of uninterrupted job growth, a recovery that has created 7.2 million new jobs so far. Unemployment is low, inflation is low, wages are rising. This economy is on the move, and our job is to keep it that way, not with more government but with more enterprise.

EDUCATION · The No Child Left Behind Act has worked for America's children, and I ask Congress to re-authorize this good law.

HEALTH CARE · When it comes to health care, government has an obligation to care for the elderly, the disabled, and poor children. And we will meet those responsibilities. For all other Americans, private health insurance is the best way to meet their needs. But many Americans cannot afford a health insurance policy.

IMMIGRATION · We need to uphold the great tradition of the melting pot that welcomes and assimilates new arrivals. We need to resolve the status of the illegal immigrants who are already in our country without animosity and without amnesty.

GAS · Let us build on the work we have done and reduce gasoline usage in the United States by 20% in the next 10 years – when we do that, we will have cut our total imports by the equivalent of three-quarters of all the oil we now import from the Middle East.

SECURITY · It remains the policy of this government to use every lawful and proper tool of intelligence, diplomacy, law enforcement, and military action to do our duty, to find these enemies, and to protect the American people.

IRAQ · In order to make progress toward this goal, the Iraqi government must stop the sectarian violence in its capital. But the Iraqis are not yet ready to do this on their own. So we're deploying reinforcements of more than 20,000 additional soldiers and Marines to Iraq ... We went into this largely united – in our assumptions, and in our convictions. And whatever you voted for, you did not vote for failure.

FOREIGN POLICY · American foreign policy is more than a matter of war and diplomacy. Our work in the world is also based on a timeless truth: to whom much is given, much is required.

—————2007 SOTU · REACTION & ANALYSIS—————

Washington Post · The President offered the usual reassurances last night about the healthy state of the Union, but the state of his presidency has never been worse.

Miami Herald · Try as he might to deliver an upbeat message Tuesday night, President Bush could not hide the fragile state of his presidency and the troubled state of the Union.

Philadelphia Inquirer · As for the issue on most people's minds – the war in Iraq – the President seems more determined than ever to pursue a failing course.

San Jose Mercury News · The state of the Union may well be strong, as President Bush asserts, but the state of his presidency is weak and wounded.

New York Times · [the President] offered up a tepid menu of ideas that would change little ...

Globe & Mail (Canada) · a lame-duck president with two years left, quacked his State of the Union before a Congress the Democrats now control.

The Guardian (UK) · Mr Bush looks increasingly like a general who has run out of ideas, troops, and hope.

Stephen Colbert · What made it groundbreaking ... was all the new stuff we've never heard before – like a domestic agenda.

[Some alleged that (70-year-old) Rep. Sen. John McCain, appeared to be asleep during a passage where the President was discussing Iraq, though McCain was likely just reading the speech.]

WORD FREQUENCY & MICROSOFT'S AUTO SUMMARY

Afghan(istan) 5	Economy(ic) 8	Hezbollah 2	Military 4
Africa(n) 3	Enemy(ies) 14	HIV/AIDS. 2	Nuclear 3
America(n)(ns) . . . 49	Energy 3	Hope(s) 10	Palestinian 1
Baghdad. 5	Environment(ally) . 3	Immigrants(ation) . 5	Petroleum 1
Biodiesel 1	Ethanol 1	Insurance. 14	Poverty. 3
Budget 4	Extremism(ists) . . . 8	Iran. 5	Al Qaeda 10
Citizen(s). 11	Free(dom)(s) 11	Iraq(i)(is) 34	Reform(s)(ers). 9
Darfur 1	Fuel(s) 6	Islam(ist) 2	Syria(n) 2
Democracy 4	Gas(oline) 3	Israel. 1	Tax(es) 10
Determined(ation) 3	God 2	Job(s) 6	Terror(ists) &c.. . . . 22
Diplomacy(atic) . . . 5	Government(s) . . . 16	Osama bin Laden . 1	UN 3
Earmark(s). 5	Health 18	Medicaid(are) 4	Zarqawi 1

When the text of George W. Bush's speech is entered into Microsoft Word's Auto Summarize feature, and distilled down to *c.*1% of its original length, the result is:

The No Child Left Behind Act has worked for America's children – and I ask Congress to reauthorize this good law. We need to help small businesses through Association Health Plans. Extending hope and opportunity depends on a stable supply of energy that keeps America's economy running and America's environment clean.
Julie† represents the great enterprising spirit of America.
[† Julie Aigner-Clark, founder of The Baby Einstein Company]

─────────CONGRESSIONAL MISCELLANY─────────

FILIBUSTER · Based on the Dutch word for pirate (*vrijbuiter*), to filibuster generally means to obstruct the passage of a proposal by holding the Senate floor with an interminable speech. These speeches may have little to do with the measure at hand: Sen. Huey P. Long's famous 1935 filibuster included recipes for fried oysters and 'potlikkers' (seasoned broth). Former South Carolina Sen. J. Strom Thurmond holds the record for the longest individual filibuster – an impressive 24 hours and 18 minutes, against the Civil Rights Act of 1957. Thurmond reportedly prepared for his filibuster by dehydrating himself in the Senate steam room, so that he could drink water without leaving for the bathroom. Thurmond's filibuster included readings and discussions of each state's election statutes, the Declaration of Independence, the Bill of Rights, and Washington's Farewell Address. Staff concerned for his health eventually succeeded in getting him to leave the floor, but the Bill was defeated.

RULE 22 · The formal procedure for ending a filibuster. Senators present a motion to limit debate; if the motion passes, only 30 further hours of debate are allowed. The rule was first used in 1919, to end a filibuster against the Treaty of Versailles.

WHIPS · The term 'whip' derives from the British 'whipper in' – the person charged with keeping track of the foxhounds during a hunt. Use of the term in the US Congress dates back to 1897, when Speaker Thomas Reed asked Representative James A. Tawney to act as a 'whip' to help him keep track of party members. Currently, both houses have majority and minority party whips, who ensure that members of Congress are present for key votes, and urge party unity in voting on important issues.

OATH · The Constitution provides a specific oath for the President but for no other elected officials, saying only that they 'shall be bound by Oath or Affirmation to support this constitution'. Thus the first Congressional oath (in 1789) was simply: '*I do solemnly swear (or affirm) that I will support the Constitution of the United States*'. However, Civil War-era concerns about loyalty led to the creation of the current oath:

I do solemnly swear (or affirm) that I will support and defend the Constitution of the United States against all enemies, foreign and domestic; that I will bear true faith and allegiance to the same; that I take this obligation freely, without any mental reservation or purpose of evasion; and that I will well and faithfully discharge the duties of the office on which I am about to enter: So help me God.

THE MACE · One of the oldest symbols of the national government, the mace was approved by the first Speaker of the House, Frederick Muhlenburg of Pennsylvania, as a symbol of authority for the Sergeant at Arms. It consists of 13 ebony rods, representing the original colonies, bound by silver ribbons and topped with a globe and an eagle. The mace is brought to the House floor each day by the Sergeant at Arms and placed on a green marble pedestal. When the House resolves into the Committee of the Whole, the mace is moved to a lower pedestal. Allegedly based on an ancient battle weapon, the mace is also presented to unruly members of the House to restore order.

——————— CONGRESSIONAL MISCELLANY cont. ———————

SENATE SEATING & DESKS · Seating in the Senate Chamber is divided by party, with Democrats to the right of the Presiding Officer, and Republicans to the left. Independents may sit on either side of the aisle. Occasionally one party wins so many seats that it becomes necessary for majority party members to sit on the minority side. These seats are called the CHEROKEE STRIP, after a region of Oklahoma that once belonged neither to Indian Territory nor to the US. ❧ The Senate uses 48 desks built in 1819 by a New York cabinetmaker to replace those the British burned in the War of 1812; desks of the same design have been built as new states have been added to the Union. ❧ The CANDY DESK is always stocked with sweets and located on the Republican side of the aisle, near the exit. CA Sen. George Murphy is said to have begun this tradition *c.*1968 (he favored small boxes of raisins). Pennsylvania Sen. Rick Santorum occupied the desk 1995–2006, sharing treats like Hershey's Kisses and Hot Tamales. When Wyoming Sen. Craig Thomas took over the desk in January 2007, he kept it stocked with Wyoming taffy. Sadly, Sen. Thomas passed away in June 2007, and the fate of the Candy Desk was unclear at the time of writing.

BELTWAY · Coined *c.*1951 to refer to what had once been called the circumferential highway. The term 'beltway' is now most often associated with I-495 (which circumnavigates the Capitol) – as well as the state of mind found inside it.

LAME DUCK SESSIONS · A 'lame duck' member of Congress is one who has been voted out of office but whose term has yet to expire. The term originated in the London stock market to refer to those who defaulted on their debts. Sessions of Congress containing defeated members are said to be 'lame duck sessions'. Prior to 1933, these sessions were held in the December of every odd-numbered year until the following March. Concern over the unpopular results of such sessions led to the Twentieth Amendment of the Constitution, which moved the inauguration of each new Congress to January 3. Until recently, such sessions were rarely held; however, the 109th Congress was the 8th lame duck session since 1980.

PAGES · There are 72 pages in the House, and 30 in the Senate; each is a high school junior who has been appointed by a Senator or Representative to work for one semester on Capitol Hill. Primary duties include ferrying documents, fetching water, and preparing the House or Senate chambers for session. Massachusetts Sen. Daniel Webster appointed the first Senate page in 1829; the first House page was appointed in 1842. Pages live in guarded dormitories (boys and girls are separated), attend a special early-morning page school, and are paid at an annual rate of $18,817 in the House and $20,491 in the Senate. In 2007, the House voted to overhaul the board overseeing the house page program, after the 2006 scandal which revealed Florida Rep. Mark Foley had sent explicit electronic messages to several former pages.

SALARY · Congress rejected a pay increase for FY2007, freezing salaries at the 2006 rates: $165,200 annually for rank-and-file members; $183,500 for majority and minority leaders in both Houses, and $212,100 for the Speaker of the House (currently, Nancy Pelosi).

110th CONGRESS

HOUSE		SENATE	
Democrat	232 (53·3%)	Democrat	49 (%)
Republican	201 (46·2%)	Republican	48 (%)
Independent	0 (0·0%)	Independent	2 (%)
Vacancy	2 (0·5%)	Vacancy	1 (%)

Members	435	Members	100
Delegates	4	(Vice President votes in event of a tie)	
Resident Commissioner	1	Vice President	Richard B. Cheney
Female members	74 (17·0%)	Female members	16 (%)
Black members	42 (9·7%)	Black members	1 (%)
Hispanic members	26 (6·0%)	Hispanic members	3 (%)
Asian Pacific members	7 (1·6%)	Asian Pacific members	2 (%)
American Indian members	1 (0·2%)	American Indian members	0 (%)
Foreign-born members	11 (2·5%)	Foreign-born members	1 (%)
Average age	55·93 years	Average age	61·7 years
Prior military service	102 (23·4%)	Prior military service	29 (%)

CONSTITUTIONAL QUALIFICATION	CONSTITUTIONAL QUALIFICATION
Article I, Section 2	Article I, Section 3
No person shall be a Representative who shall not have attained to the Age of twenty five Years, and been seven Years a Citizen of the United States, and who shall not, when elected, be an Inhabitant of that State in which he shall be chosen.	*No Person shall be a Senator who shall not have attained to the Age of thirty Years, and been nine Years a Citizen of the United States, and who shall not, when elected, be an Inhabitant of that State for which he shall be chosen.*

Speaker	*President Pro Tempore*
Nancy Pelosi [D-CA]	Robert C. Byrd [D-WV]
Majority Leader	*Majority Leader*
Steny H. Hoyer [D-MD]	Harry M. Reid [D-NV]
Minority Leader	*Minority Leader*
John A. Boehner [R-OH]	Mitch McConnell [R-KY]

Speaker's salary	$212,100	President Pro Tempore slry	$183,500
Maj. & Min. Leaders' slry	$183,500	Maj. & Min. Leaders' slry	$183,500
Members' salary	$165,200	Senators' salary	$165,200

Chaplain	*Chaplain*
Rev. Daniel P. Coughlin	Barry C. Black
Clerk of the House	*Secretary*
Lorraine C. Miller	Nancy Erickson
Sergeant at Arms	*Sergeant at Arms*
Wilson (Bill) Livingood	Terrance Gainer

[Congressional membership data as at election · Sources: Congressional Research Service; & others]

—80th–110th CONGRESSES—

Congress	Year	Senate Rep	Senate Dem	Senate Other	Senate Total	President	House Rep	House Dem	House Other	House Total
110	'07–'09	49	49	2	100	W. Bush	202	233	0	435
109	'05–'07	55	44	1	100		232	202	1	435
108	'03–'05	51	48	1	100		229	204	2	435
107	'01–'03	50	50	0	100		221	212	2	435
106	'99–'01	55	45	0	100	Clinton	223	211	1	435
105	'97–'99	55	45	0	100		228	206	1	435
104	'95–'97	52	48	0	100		230	204	1	435
103	'93–'95	43	57	0	100	Bush	176	258	1	435
102	'91–'93	44	56	0	100		167	267	1	435
101	'89–'91	45	55	0	100		175	260	0	435
100	'87–'89	45	55	0	100	Reagan	177	258	0	435
99	'85–'87	53	47	0	100		182	253	0	435
98	'83–'85	54	46	0	100		166	269	0	435
97	'81–'83	53	46	1	100	Carter	192	242	1	435
96	'79–'81	41	58	1	100		158	277	0	435
95	'77–'79	38	61	1	100	Ford	143	292	0	435
94	'75–'77	38	60	2	100	Nixon	144	291	0	435
93	'73–'75	42	56	2	100		192	242	1	435
92	'71–'73	44	54	2	100		180	255	0	435
91	'69–'71	43	57	0	100	LBJ	192	243	0	435
90	'67–'69	36	64	0	100		187	247	1	435
89	'65–'67	32	68	0	100	JFK	140	295	0	435
88	'63–'65	34	66	0	100		176	259	0	435
87	'61–'63	36	64	0	100	Eisenhower	174	263	0	437
86	'59–'61	35	65	0	100		153	283	1	437
85	'57–'59	47	49	0	96		201	234	0	435
84	'55–'57	47	48	1	96		203	232	0	435
83	'53–'55	48	47	1	96	Truman	221	213	1	435
82	'51–'53	47	49	0	96		199	235	1	435
81	'49–'51	42	54	0	96		171	263	1	435
80	'47–'49	51	45	0	96		246	188	1	435

SENATE SEATS — HOUSE SEATS

——————————— LEGISLATIVE CALL SYSTEM ———————————

Because Senators cannot always be present in the Senate chamber, a system of electronic bells and lights was installed *c.*1891 to inform them of developments on the floor. Known as the 'legislative call system', the bells and lights are transmitted from a console in the Senate Chamber to *c.*3,000 clocks placed in the Senate wing of the Capitol Building and the three Senate offices. The system is explained below:

1 long ring..... *sounds at the hour of convening*	4 rings .... *adjournment or recess*
1 ring .... *yeas and nays*	5 rings .... *7½ minutes remain to vote*
2 rings .... *quorum call*	6 rings, lights off ... *morning business concluded*
3 rings .... *call of absentees*	6 rings, lights on .... *temporary recess*

Many of the Senate clocks also display lights, which are lit to correspond with the number of rings sounded. A red light is lit whenever the Senate is in session. Splendidly, the House employs an even more complicated legislative call system:

1 long ring, pause, 3 rings, 3 lights on left..... *notice or short quorum call in Committee of the Whole*
1 long ring, 3 lights on left extinguished .... *notice or short quorum call vacated*
2 rings, 2 lights on left .. *recorded vote, yea and nay note, or automatic roll call vote by electronic device*
2 rings, 2 lights, pause & 2 rings .. *automatic roll call vote, or yea and nay vote by roll call in the House*
2 rings, pause, 5 rings .... *1st vote under Suspension of the Rules or on clustered votes*
3 rings, 3 lights on left .... *regular quorum call by electronic device or clerks*
3 rings, pause, 3 rings...................................... *regular quorum call by call of the roll*
3 rings, pause, 5 rings..... *quorum call in Committee of the Whole, 5-minute recorded vote may follow*
4 rings, 4 lights on left .... *adjournment*
5 rings, 5 lights on left .... *any 5-minute vote*
6 rings, 6 lights.. *recess*
12 rings at 2 second intervals, 6 lights on left .... *Civil Defense Warning*
7th light.. *lit whenever the House is in session*

The legislative call system has occasionally been subject to mischief on the part of certain Senators. When tired of the legislative proceedings, Arizona Senator Barry Goldwater was known to stroll past the console that controls the system of bells and lights and press the button for an adjournment. Eventually a Plexiglas cover (the 'Goldwater Shield') was installed over the adjournment button.

——————————— FEDERAL REGISTER ———————————

The *Federal Register* is the 'daily newspaper of the federal government' published every business day by the National Archives and Records Administration and the Government Printing Office. It contains federal agency regulations, proposed rules and public notices, executive orders, proclamations, and other presidential documents. The necessity for an official record of federal regulation became urgent during the 1930s, as FDR's New Deal dramatically expanded the role, scope, and complexity of executive agencies. Established by law in 1935, the *Federal Register* was first published on March 16, 1936, when it ran to 16 pages. Today, the thousands of pages published annually are most commonly accessed online at gpoaccess.gov/fr.

———————SOME CAMPAIGN SLOGANS OF NOTE———————

I like Ike · 1952 Presidential campaign slogan for Dwight D. 'Ike' Eisenhower. During Eisenhower's reelection campaign, opponent Adlai Stevenson tried *We need Adlai badly* and *We're madly for Adlai*, but these proved less successful than *I still like Ike*, and Eisenhower was elected for a second term. ❧ Other rhyming slogans include Henry Clay's *Hooray for Clay* [1844]; William H. Taft's *Get on the raft with Taft* [1908]; Woodrow Wilson's *Row, row, Woodrow* [1912]; Calvin Coolidge's *Keep cool with Coolidge* [1924]; Lyndon B. Johnson's *All the way with LBJ* [1964]; and Ronald Reagan's somewhat unfortunate *Ron turns us on* [1980].

Fifty-four forty or fight! · from the 1844 campaign of James K. Polk. Polk's campaign platform demanded the annexation of Oregon territory up to the 54° 40 boundary, and the slogan became a popular rallying cry. ❧ Also, *We Polked you in '44, we shall Pierce you in '52* – the campaign slogan of 14th President, Franklin Pierce. ❧ And *Who is Polk?* – first asked sarcastically by Henry Clay when Polk received his party's nomination; it then became a Whig slogan.

Don't swap horses in midstream · folk wisdom popularized by Lincoln in his 1864 campaign. The phrase has since been used for the reelection campaigns of several presidents, including Franklin D. Roosevelt in 1940 and 1944. During Herbert Hoover's reelection campaign of 1932 (in the midst of the depression), some Democrats joked the Republican slogan was likely 'don't swap barrels while going over Niagara'.

Had enough? · a Republican slogan, used in the 1946 Congressional elections, asking voters if they had tired of the Democrats. Voters agreed, and Republicans took both Houses of Congress. In 2006, Democrats like Nancy Pelosi used the phrase in hopes of another about-face, after the slogan was (ironically) suggested by former House Speaker Newt Gingrich.

Two dollars a day and roast beef · a Whig slogan during the 1840 presidential election, promising prosperity during a national depression. The slogan sometimes read, *Van's policy, fifty cents a day and French soup. Our policy, two dollars a day and roast beef.* Whigs portrayed incumbent Martin Van Buren as the 'champagne' candidate, in contrast to William Henry Harrison, the 'log cabin and hard cider candidate'. ❧ Other food and drink slogans include the notorious *Rum, Romanism, and Rebellion*[†], a Republican attack on the Democrats from 1884; *Four more years of the full dinner pail*, from the 1900 reelection campaign of William McKinley; and *A chicken in every pot, a car in every garage*, a Republican campaign slogan from 1928.

It's morning again in America · the first line of a TV ad from Reagan's 1984 reelection campaign, which became an election catchphrase. Often considered one of the most effective political ads ever, the commercial featured a montage of sober Americans on their way to work, with a baritone voice-over assuring Americans that their new prosperity was a result of Reagan's policies.

---

† This phrase has since been reprised as: *Rum, Romanism, and Capitalism*; *Romanism, Roosevelt, and Rockefeller*; *Catholicism, Commercialism, and Coercion*; and *Bosses, Boodle, Buncombe, and Blarney* – 'boodle' often meaning bribery, and 'buncombe' speeches meant to gain favor with the electorate.

──AMERICAN POLITICAL NICKNAMES OF NOTE──

Some of the many colorful epithets and nicknames used in American politics:

LIMOUSINE LIBERAL · a member of the élite who affects sympathy for the poor without any genuine concern for their struggles. Reportedly coined during the 1969 NYC mayoral race. (Akin to the UK's CHAMPAGNE SOCIALISTS, said to profess egalitarian beliefs while enjoying the finer things in life.)

LOCOFOCOS · nickname for the Equal Rights Party, a faction of NY Democrats who split from the party in 1835. They were named after a type of self-igniting matches used to light their meetings.

DIXIECRATS · Originally, Southern conservatives who split from the Democrats at their 1948 convention to protest desegregation, and chose Strom Thurmond as presidential candidate.

HUNKERS · conservative, pro-slavery wing of the New York Democrats, *c.*1840; supposedly because they 'hankered' or 'hunkered' for office. Opposed to the anti-slavery BARNBURNERS, who (it was said) would 'burn' their own party to rid it of slavery, as a farmer would burn his barn to rid it of rats.

MUGWUMP · Republicans who supported Dem. Grover Cleveland instead of Rep. James G. Blaine in 1884. The term later came to mean a fence-sitter, and was defined *c.*1930 as 'a man with his mug on one side of the fence and his wump on the other'.

MACACA · in August 2006, then-Senator George Allen [VA-R] called a member of his opponent's campaign a 'macaca'. Though Allen claimed he did not know the meaning of the word, *macaca* is a genus of monkey, and the word is sometimes used as a racial slur (the targeted campaign member was of Indian descent). During the resulting furor, which may have cost him his Senate race, Allen was occasionally called 'Senator Macaca'.

KNOW-NOTHINGS · nickname for an anti-immigration party of the 1850s, officially called the American Party. The name arose because followers of the quasi-secret group were told to answer 'I know nothing' when questioned about their activities. The term is now sometimes used against those who oppose immigration.

SCALAWAGS · a derisive name for anti-slavery white Republicans in the South who participated in post-Civil War reconstruction policies. Allied with the CARPETBAGGERS, opportunistic Northerners in the South during reconstruction. The name arose from the carpetbags in which they were said to carry their possessions. It is now used to refer to politicians running in a district in which they have only recently arrived and, more generally, to any opportunistic outsider.

YELLOW DOG DEMOCRAT · complimentary term for loyal Southern Democrats. Used primarily in the early and mid-C20th, it is thought to be based on the traditional saying: 'I'd vote for a Yellow Dog, if it was a Democrat'. The phrase contributed to the origin of the term BLUE DOG DEMOCRATS – a coalition of conservative and moderate House Democrats formed during the 104th Congress. Some members explain the term (which originated as a nickname) by saying their views were 'choked blue' by their party pre-1994.

POLITICAL EPITAPHS

THOMAS JEFFERSON
1743–1826
Here was buried Thomas Jefferson,
author of the Declaration of American
Independence, of the statute of Virginia
for religious freedom, and father of the
University of Virginia.

KARL MARX
1818–83
Workers of all lands unite.
The philosophers have only interpreted
the world in various ways;
the point is to change it.

RICHARD NIXON
1913–94
The greatest honor history can
bestow is the title of peacemaker.

JOHN QUINCY ADAMS
1767–1848
This is the last of Earth! I am content!

THADDEUS STEVENS
1792–1868
I repose in this quiet and secluded spot,
not from any natural preference for
solitude, but, finding other cemeteries
limited by charter rules as to race, I have
chosen this, that I might illustrate in my
death the principles which I advocated
through a long life – Equality of Man
before his Creator.

MARTIN LUTHER KING JR
1929–68
Free at last! Free at last! Thank God
Almighty, we are free at last!

PRESIDENTIAL PETS

Although George W. Bush and his family own several pets, including a black cat named India ('Willie') and a longhorn cow called Ofelia, the most popular members of their menagerie are their Scottish terriers, Barney and Miss Beazley[†]:

Barney (the 'First Dog')	*Miss Beazley*
Birthdate .... September 30, 2000	Birthdate .... October 28, 2004
Father............................Kelly	Father..........................Clinton
Mother ....Coors	Mother .... Bethz
Hobbies ....soccer, golf, horseshoes	Hobbies ... tap-dancing, cheeseburgers

† Sadly, Bush's dog Spot died in 2004. According to the Presidential Pet Museum, most Presidents have owned pets while in office. George Washington owned dogs named Drunkard, Taster, Mopsey, Tipsy, Vulcan, Sweetlips, and Searcher, among others. Abraham Lincoln owned a pig, goats, ponies, a turkey, and rabbits; Rutherford Hayes is said to have owned the first Siamese cat in America. John Quincy Adams kept an alligator, given to him by the Marquis de Lafayette; Martin Van Buren was given two tiger cubs by the Sultan of Oman; and James Buchanan received a herd of elephants from the King of Siam. John F. Kennedy and his family owned a particularly diverse brood, including: Tom Kitten (a cat), Charlie, Pushinka, Shannon, Wolf, Clipper, Butterfly, White Tips, Blackie, & Streaker (dogs), Macaroni, Tex, and Leprechaun (ponies), Sardar (a horse), Robin (a canary), Bluebell & Marybelle (parakeets), Debbie & Billie (hamsters), and Zsa Zsa (a rabbit). Interestingly, Winston Churchill also owned an astonishing menagerie, including both white and black swans, goats, wallabies, opossums, fish, bees, lions, tigers, and white kangaroos (the latter three were housed at the London Zoo). [Sources: The Presidential Pet Museum; Churchill Museum at the Cabinet War Rooms]

PRESIDENTIAL PARDONS

The power of the President to issue pardons is enshrined in Article II, Section 2, of the Constitution. Petitions for pardon must be filed at least 5 years after conviction or release, whichever is later, and are granted only after a substantial period of 'good conduct'. The Pardon Attorney employs the following criteria to review petitions:

Post-conviction conduct, character, & reputation · Need for relief
Seriousness & relative recentness of the offense · Official recommendations & reports
Acceptance of responsibility, remorse & atonement

The granting of pardons is a year-end presidential tradition. At the close of 2006, Bush had issued 113 pardons, among the fewest of any US President since WWII:

President	pardons				
FDR	2,819	Johnson	960	Bush Sr	74
Truman	1,913	Nixon	863	Clinton	396
Eisenhower	1,110	Ford	382	Bush Jr [to date]	113
Kennedy	472	Carter	534		
		Reagan	393	[Source: US Pardon Attorney]	

PRESIDENTIAL LIBRARIES

Presidential libraries are the official repositories of papers, historical materials, and artifacts owned by former American presidents. There are 11 Presidential Libraries (as well as the Nixon Presidential Materials†), and the system is administered by the National Archives. Franklin D. Roosevelt built the first Presidential Library, using private funds and a portion of his Hyde Park estate, later donating the building to the nation. In 1950, Truman decided also to build a Presidential Library and, in 1955, Congress passed the Presidential Libraries Act, which established the Library System and encouraged other Presidents to donate their materials. Every President from Herbert Hoover through Bill Clinton now has a dedicated library. ❦ Prior to Roosevelt's library, a President's documents were considered his personal property, and were often disbursed or sold for profit at the end of his term. Roosevelt believed that a president's papers should form part of the national historical record, stating:

The dedication of a library is in itself an act of faith. To bring together the records of the past and to house them in buildings where they will be preserved for the use of men and women in the future, a Nation must believe in three things. It must believe in the past. It must believe in the future. It must, above all, believe in the capacity of its own people so to learn from the past that they can gain in judgment in creating their own future.

At the time of writing, the Presidential Library System contained over 269 million pages of text, 5 million photos, 14 million feet of film, and 78,000 hours of audio and video recordings. Roosevelt himself was known for an especially vast collection of memorabilia, which included: over a million stamps in 150 matching albums, over 200 fully rigged model ships, 1,200 naval prints and paintings, and 15,000 books. He is said to have once admitted: 'future historians will curse as well as praise me'.
† The Richard Nixon Library and Birthplace in Yorba Linda, CA, is not part of the National Archives.

2004 PRESIDENTIAL VOTES BY STATE

State	Presidential candidates		electoral college vote	State	Presidential candidates		electoral college vote	State	Presidential candidates		electoral college vote	State	Presidential candidates		electoral college vote
AL	Bush	62.5%	R-9	ID	Bush	68.4%	R-4	MO	Bush	53.3%	R-11	PA	Bush	48.4%	D-21
	Kerry	36.8%			Kerry	30.3%			Kerry	46.1%			Kerry	50.9%	
AK	Bush	61.1%	R-3	IL	Bush	44.5%	D-21	MT	Bush	59.1%	R-3	RI	Bush	38.7%	D-4
	Kerry	35.5%			Kerry	54.8%			Kerry	38.6%			Kerry	59.4%	
AZ	Bush	54.9%	R-10	IN	Bush	59.9%	R-11	NE	Bush	65.9%	R-5	SC	Bush	58.0%	R-8
	Kerry	44.4%			Kerry	39.3%			Kerry	32.7%			Kerry	40.9%	
AR	Bush	54.3%	R-6	IA	Bush	49.9%	R-7	NV	Bush	50.5%	R-5	SD	Bush	59.9%	R-3
	Kerry	44.5%			Kerry	49.2%			Kerry	47.9%			Kerry	38.4%	
CA	Bush	44.4%	D-55	KS	Bush	62.0%	R-6	NH	Bush	48.8%	D-4	TN	Bush	56.8%	R-11
	Kerry	54.3%			Kerry	36.6%			Kerry	50.2%			Kerry	42.5%	
CO	Bush	51.7%	R-9	KY	Bush	59.5%	R-8	NJ	Bush	46.2%	D-15	TX	Bush	61.1%	R-34
	Kerry	47.0%			Kerry	39.7%			Kerry	52.9%			Kerry	38.2%	
CT	Bush	43.9%	D-7	LA	Bush	56.7%	R-9	NM	Bush	49.8%	R-5	UT	Bush	71.5%	R-5
	Kerry	54.3%			Kerry	42.2%			Kerry	49.0%			Kerry	26.0%	
DE	Bush	45.8%	D-3	ME	Bush	44.6%	D-4	NY	Bush	37.7%	D-31	VT	Bush	38.8%	D-3
	Kerry	53.3%			Kerry	53.6%			Kerry	56.1%			Kerry	58.9%	
DC	Bush	9.3%	D-3	MD	Bush	43.0%	D-10	NC	Bush	56.0%	R-15	VI	Bush	53.7%	R-13
	Kerry	89.2%			Kerry	56.0%			Kerry	43.6%			Kerry	45.5%	
FL	Bush	52.1%	R-27	MA	Bush	36.6%	D-12	ND	Bush	62.9%	R-3	WA	Bush	45.6%	D-11
	Kerry	47.1%			Kerry	61.6%			Kerry	35.5%			Kerry	52.8%	
GA	Bush	58.0%	R-15	MI	Bush	47.8%	D-17	OH	Bush	50.8%	R-20	WV	Bush	56.1%	R-5
	Kerry	41.4%			Kerry	51.2%			Kerry	48.7%			Kerry	43.2%	
HI	Bush	45.3%	D-4	MN	Bush	47.6%	D-9	OK	Bush	65.6%	R-7	WI	Bush	49.3%	D-10
	Kerry	54.0%			Kerry	51.1%			Kerry	34.4%			Kerry	49.7%	
				MS	Bush	59.0%	R-6	OR	Bush	47.2%	D-7	WY	Bush	68.7%	R-3
					Kerry	40.2%			Kerry	51.3%			Kerry	29.0%	

SUPREME COURT JUSTICES

Justice	date of birth	state	law school	appointed by		term began
John G. Roberts Jr†	01·27·1955	NY	Harvard	Bush Jr	[R]	09·29·2005
John Paul Stevens	04·20·1920	IL	Northwestern	Ford	[R]	12·19·1975
Antonin Scalia	03·11·1936	NJ	Harvard	Reagan	[R]	09·26·1986
Anthony M. Kennedy	07·23·1936	CA	Harvard	Reagan	[R]	02·18·1988
David H. Souter	09·17·1939	MA	Harvard	Bush Sr	[R]	10·09·1990
Clarence Thomas	06·23·1948	GA	Yale	Bush Sr	[R]	10·23·1991
Ruth Bader Ginsburg	03·15·1933	NY	Columbia	Clinton	[D]	08·10·1993
Stephen G. Breyer	08·15·1938	CA	Harvard	Clinton	[D]	08·03·1994
Samuel A. Alito Jr	04·01·1950	NJ	Yale	Bush Jr	[R]	01·31·2006

† The 17th Chief Justice [Sources: Supreme Court; Cornell Law School]

SUPREME COURT MISCELLANY

CONFERENCE HANDSHAKE

The famous 'conference handshake' of the Supreme Court was introduced by Melville W. Fuller, who sat as Chief Justice between 1888 and 1910. To this day, as a symbolic gesture of solidarity and common purpose, each of the nine Justices shakes hands with his or her eight colleagues in private before the Court sits and before each Conference.

TERM & HOURS

The Court holds a continuous annual Term which starts on the first Monday in October and ends on the day before the first Monday in October of the following year. At the end of each Term, any cases pending on the docket are continued to the next Term. Usually, the Court sits to hear arguments from 10:00–12:00, and from 1:00–3:00.

FEDERAL JURY SERVICE

Eligibility for federal jury service depends upon being drawn at random from voter (or driver) lists, and being legally qualified to serve: QUALIFICATIONS · *United States citizen · at least 18 years of age · reside in the judicial district for 1 year · adequate proficiency in reading, writing, speaking, and understanding English · no disqualifying mental or physical condition · not currently subject to felony charges · never convicted of a felony (unless civil rights have been legally restored)* · EXEMPTIONS · *active-duty members of the armed forces · members of police and fire departments · certain public officials · others based on individual court rules (e.g. members of voluntary emergency service organizations, and people who recently have served on a jury)* · EXCUSALS · *may be granted for undue hardship or extreme inconvenience* · TIME · *trial jury service varies by court · some courts require service for one day or for the duration of one trial; others require service for a fixed term · Grand Jury service may be up to 18 months* · PAYMENT · *$40 per day (+ allowances)* · EMPLOYMENT · *By law, employers must allow employees time off (paid or unpaid) for jury service. The law prohibits employers from dismissing, intimidating, or coercing any permanent employee because of their federal jury service.*

--------------- CONSTITUTIONAL AMENDMENTS ---------------

1st ....guarantees freedom of religion, speech, press, assembly, and petition
2nd .... guarantees the right to keep and bear arms
3rd................................prevents compulsory billeting during peacetime
4th........ guarantees security of person and possessions against search and seizure
5th........... prevents double jeopardy; guarantees right against self-incrimination
6th................ guarantees fair, speedy, and public trial by jury; right to counsel
7th............................. guarantees right to trial by jury in common law suits
8th..................... prevents cruel or unusual punishments, and excessive fines
9th............................. protects rights not enumerated in the Constitution
10th .... reserves the rights of individual states
11th ....delineates judicial powers of the US in certain cases
12th .... sets procedures for electing President & Vice President
13th .... outlaws slavery
14th ....guarantees the rights of citizenship
15th ....guarantees right to vote regardless of race, color, or previous servitude
16th ....sets the powers of Congress to levy income taxes
17th ....enumerates procedure for electing Senators
18th .... introduced prohibition
19th .... guarantees the right of women to vote
20th ....sets Presidential term and succession, and terms of other offices
21st..repeals prohibition (18th Amendment)
22nd.. limits Presidents to two terms
23rd .... grants Washington, DC, residents a vote in Presidential elections
24th ....bars poll (voting) tax in federal elections
25th .... sets the order of Presidential succession
26th .... guarantees right to vote at age eighteen
27th ....postpones Representatives' pay raises until after new elections

According to the 2006 edition of *The US Constitution & Fascinating Facts About It*, more than 10,000 constitutional amendments have been proposed since 1789, including amendments to abolish the US Senate [1876], rename the US 'the United States of the Earth' [1893], outlaw marriage between races [1912]; and limit personal wealth at $1m [1933]. The 2007 book *A More Perfect Constitution*, by the founder of the Center for Politics at the Uni. of Virginia Larry J. Sabato proposes 23 new amendments, including a 6-year presidential term (with optional two year extension), a 135-member Senate, a 1,000-member House, and two years of national service for every able-bodied American.

--------------- ATTRACTIVE DEFENDANTS & JURORS ---------------

Jurors are less likely to find attractive defendants guilty, according to research presented to the British Psychological Society in March 2007. Researchers from York and Bath Spa universities gave 96 volunteers a transcript of a fictional mugging and a photograph of the defendant, and asked them for their verdict, the extent of the defendant's guilt, and the sentence that should be passed. Disturbingly, less attractive defendants were more likely to be judged guilty, and ugly black defendants were most likely to be given a harsh sentence – regardless of the ethnicity of the juror.

———————————PAPERWORK REDUCTION———————————

The 1995 Paperwork Reduction Act (PRA) is one of a number of measures designed to regulate and control the burden of official paperwork. The Act requires that the Office of Information and Regulatory Affairs (OIRA) within the Office of Management and Budget (OMB) approve all federal agency 'information collections' from ten or more people, regardless of whether such collection is voluntary. ('Information collection' encompasses a wide range of activities, from application forms and surveys to questionnaires and tax forms.) Members of the public are not obliged to provide information on a form which is subject to the PRA, unless that form displays a valid OMB 'control number'. The OMB is required to publish an audit of information collection and paperwork reduction each year. The most recent report (which ran to 142 pages) stated that, as of the end of the financial year 2005, the federal government had imposed an annual paperwork burden on the public of *c.*8·2 billion hours – an increase of 269 million hours (3·4%) from the previous year. The table below gives a breakdown of the paperwork burden imposed on the public by each relevant federal agency during the 2006 financial year:

Agency	%	hours (m)		Agency	%	hours (m)
Agriculture	1·00	84·47		Veterans Affairs	0·07	5·88
Commerce	0·18	15·22		Environ Protect Ag	1·71	143·94
Defense	0·63	52·81		Fed Aquis Reg	0·35	29·59
Education	0·49	41·53		Fed Coms Cmsn	1·72	144·68
Energy	0·04	3·13		Deposit Insure Crp	0·07	6·28
Health Hmn Services	4·37	368·14		Energy Reg Cmsn	0·07	5·75
Homeland Security	1·01	84·87		Fed Trade Cmsn	0·86	72·55
Housing Urban Dev	0·30	25·68		NASA	0·06	5·24
Interior	0·09	7·91		Nat Science Fdtn	0·07	5·8
Justice	0·16	13·12		Nuclear Reg Cmsn	0·11	9·32
Labor	1·97	166·12		Securities Exch Cmsn	2·04	171·77
State	0·42	35·57		Small Biz Admin	0·02	1·56
Transport	3·01	253·15		Soc Security Admin	0·46	38·88
Treasury · IRS	76·00	6,399·53		EGOV	0·15	12·56
Other Treasury	0·42	35·46		TOTAL		8,240·51
				TOTAL *without IRS*		1,840·98

Because of the obligation to keep tax records, the IRS is the agency that makes the greatest demands on the public, as can be seen above. The IRS Individual Income Tax Return form 1040 alone comes with 143 pages of instructions; on page 81, the average burden to complete this form is revealed to be 24·2 hours and $207 per person per year. However, from 2006, the IRS began to reassess their overall paperwork burden to reflect the fact that in 2005, <15% of tax returns were filled in by hand; >50% were filed electronically (over 4 times the number in 1993); and 60% of taxpayers employ 'tax preparers'. ✸ The OMB estimates that in 2006 the burden of paperwork will rise again – by 3·7%, or 303 million hours. However, this increase is explained by a number of new initiatives, including: new Food and Drug Administration reporting requirements on the safety of drugs for humans; the Federal Communication Commission's plans to reduce the prevalence of 'junk faxes'; and the 2007 Economic Census, to be carried out by the Dept of Commerce.

Money

My boy ... always try to rub up against money, for if you rub up
against money long enough, some of it may rub off on you.
— DAMON RUNYON (1884–1946)

MONEY · MANUFACTURE & LIFESPAN

Currency	no. produced in 2006	average lifespan	animal equivalent
$1 bill	4,512,000,000	18 months	deer mouse
$2 bill	230,400,000	9 years	fox
$5 bill	800,000,000	15 months	worker bee
$10 bill	851,200,000	18 months	deer mouse
$20 bill	889,600,000	2 years	field mouse
$50 bill	(none in 2006; 2005 = 345,600,000)	5 years	rabbit
$100 bill	950,400,000	8½ years	fox
Coins	15,517,500,000	25–30 years	hippopotamus

[Sources: US Mint; Dept Treasury · Note production for fiscal year; coin production, calendar year]

PRESIDENTS &c. ON BANK NOTES

Portrait	bill
George Washington	$1
Thomas Jefferson	$2
Abraham Lincoln	$5
Alexander Hamilton	$10
Andrew Jackson	$20
Ulysses S. Grant	$50
Benjamin Franklin	$100
†William McKinley	$500

†Grover Cleveland $1,000
†James Madison $5,000
†Salmon P. Chase $10,000
†‡Woodrow Wilson $100,000

† These notes are no longer in production.
‡ Wilson $100,000 bills were produced 1934–35, and were issued by the Treasury to Federal Banks based upon held gold bullion stocks; they were used only for official transactions.

CASH IN CIRCULATION

Year	cash ($) in circulation	cash ($) per capita
1910	3,148,700,000	34·07
1920	5,698,214,612	53·18
1930	4,521,987,962	36·74
1940	7,847,501,324	59·40
1950	27,156,290,042	179·03
1960	32,064,619,064	177·47
1970	54,350,971,661	265·39
1980	127,097,192,148	570·51
1990	266,902,367,798	1,062·86
2000	571,121,194,344	2,075·63

[Source: Federal Reserve Bank of Atlanta · Cash per capita applies to the United States]

—MISSION STATEMENTS—

A few mission statements of interest:

ANHEUSER-BUSCH · [extract] *Through all of our products, services and relationships, we will add to life's enjoyment.*

DOW CHEMICAL · *To constantly improve what is essential to human progress by mastering science and technology.*

GAP · [extract] *We create emotional connections with customers around the world through inspiring product design, unique store experiences & compelling marketing.*

IKEA · *Provide functional, well-designed furniture at prices so low that as many people as possible will be able to afford them.*

KRAFT · [extract] *Helping people around the world eat and live better.*

MICROSOFT · *We work to help people and businesses throughout the world realize their full potential. This is our mission. Everything we do reflects this mission and the values that make it possible.*

US AIR FORCE · *The mission of the United States Air Force is to deliver sovereign options for the defense of the United States of America and its global interests – to fly and fight in Air, Space, and Cyberspace.*

YAHOO! · *Yahoo!'s mission is to connect people to their passions, their communities, and the world's knowledge. To ensure this, Yahoo! offers a broad and deep array of products and services to create unique and differentiated user experiences and consumer insights by leveraging connections, data, and user participation.*

Other mission statements of interest, including Google's famed 'don't be evil', can be found in *Schott's Almanac 2007*.

—PIZZAS FOR PESOS, &c.—

Pizza Patrón, a US fast-food chain targeting the Hispanic community, caused a national uproar in January 2007 when it began accepting pesos as payment during a promotion. Although the chain's 61 locations in the West and Southwest provided an exchange rate slightly lower than official rates (*c.*60 pesos for a $4·99 15" pie), the promotion proved convenient for those who had recently traveled from Mexico. Sales increased by 18% at the chain's 3 San Antonio locations in the first week of the promotion. However, some called the decision to accept pesos unpatriotic, and accused Pizza Patrón of encouraging illegal immigration. The chain reportedly received thousands of angry complaints (including death threats), and was forced to institute extra security measures. Yet Pizza Patrón refused to abandon its promotion, and even extended it until April, past the planned deadline. Some argued that the move was just another example of globalization, noting that retailers in Mexico and Canada have long accepted US dollars, and that US shops in the North have been known to accept Canadian currency. ❦ Although US currency is defined as legal tender, there are no federal laws requiring private businesses to accept only US cash. Businesses are free to develop their own payment policies, unless a state law mandates otherwise. ❦ In November 2006, the Terra Bite Lounge opened in Kirkland, WA, describing itself an 'upscale voluntary payment cafe/deli'. Although customers are encouraged to pay the going rate, no payment is actually required. According to their website, the Terra Bite will 'cheerfully serve those who cannot pay, in a non-stigmatizing customer setting, with no political or religious message'.

———GREENBACKS———

The word 'greenback' was first used for the Demand Notes of 1861, the backs of which were printed (wait for it) in green. While the Bureau of Engraving and Printing (BOEP) explains that no 'definite explanation can be made for the original choice' of color, one theory posits that green was especially difficult for early cameras to capture and was thus chosen to outfox counterfeiters. The BOEP says green continued to be used because the pigment proved readily available and was resistant to chemical changes; the public had also developed a psychological link between green and the stability of the country's credit.

———DRUGS & MONEY———

A staggering 100% of euro notes in Ireland tested positive for cocaine, according to a January 2007 study. Greater quantities of the drug were discovered on higher denomination bills, though it was thought that only 5% of notes were likely to have been actually used for 'snorting'; the remaining 95% were suspected to have been cross-contaminated in wallets and pockets. (A 2001 US study found that 92% of the $1 bills tested showed traces of cocaine.)

———STAR NOTES———

The Bureau of Engraving and Printing inspects notes for errors made during the manufacturing process. If a note is discovered to contain an error, it is replaced with a new note that includes a 5-pointed star in place of the final letter in the serial number. The star is used to indicate the bill's status as a replacement note. Because of their rarity, star notes are highly prized by collectors.

——— FORTUNE'S TOP 10(0) ———

The best 10 companies to work for, from *Fortune*'s 2007 Top 100 survey:

1 ....Google
2 ....Genentech
3 .... Wegmans Food Markets
4 .... Container Store
5 .... Whole Foods Market
6 .... Network Appliance
7 .... S.C. Johnson & Son
8 .... Boston Consulting Group
9 ....Methodist Hospital System
10............. W.L. Gore & Associates

———WHERE'S GEORGE?———

'Where's George?' is an internet-based project that allows users to track the travels of a particular piece of US paper currency. Since 1998 (when the project was created by a Massachusetts computer consultant), 'Georgers' have written stamped '*www.wheresgeorge.com*' onto their bills before releasing them back into circulation, hoping that those who next use the bill will visit the site to log its new location[†]. Those who mark new bills receive 'hits' each time someone logs a bill they have registered. Enthusiasts compete for 'George Scores' (based on the number of bills and total hits), and play 'bingo' by attempting to register hits from every state. By February 2007, 'Where's George?' bills accounted for 0·07% of US currency in circulation. Similar sites have been launched in Germany [*Wo Ist Mein Geld* – Where's My Money?], Japan [*Osatsu* – bill], and Canada [Where's Willy?].

† 'Where's George?' says it does not encourage currency defacement, noting that the Bureau of Engraving and Printing defines illegal defacement as mutilation with the intent to render the bill unfit for reissue.

─────────────SPARE CASH─────────────

22% of Americans claimed to have no money left after paying their basic living expenses, according to an ACNielsen study in 2006. Of the 40 countries surveyed, only Portugal had a higher percentage of people who claimed to have no spare cash:

Country	*% with no spare cash*		
Portugal	23	Canada	16
United States	22	France	16
United Kingdom	17	Korea	15
		Germany	15

When they did have spare cash, Americans said they spent it in the following ways:

Activity	*Americans*	*global average*
Paying off debts	41%	32%
Contributing to savings	38%	40%
Out-of-home entertainment	28%	33%
Home improvements/decorating	27%	25%
New clothes	26%	31%
Holidays/vacations	25%	34%
New technology	17%	24%
Investing in stocks/mutual funds	14%	16%
Contributing to retirement fund	13%	11%

─────────────GREATEST TAX BURDENS─────────────

NYC has the greatest tax burden of the 9 US cities with populations over 1 million – according to a 2007 NYC Independent Budget Office analysis, $9·02 out of every $100 of business and household income go to state and local taxes in NYC.

City	*state & local taxes per $100*		
New York City	$9·02	Phoenix	6·25
Philadelphia	7·16	San Diego	6·01
Los Angeles	6·88	Chicago	5·89
San Antonio	6·73	Houston	5·53
		Dallas	5·20

─────────────FUNERAL COSTS─────────────

Below are the average funeral costs in various cities, according to planners Everest:

Most expensive	*$*	*Least expensive*	*$*
Chicago	9,990	Los Angeles	7,786
San José, CA	9,776	Mesa, AZ	7,965
Virginia Beach, VA	9,528	Miami	7,987
Nashville	9,468	Albuquerque, NM	8,021
Louisville, KY	9,408	Long Beach, CA	8,022

——— FEDERAL & STATE INCOME TAX RATES ———

Below are the basic rates of federal income tax and an indication of each State's income tax rates. For further information, seek expert advice.

2007 Federal Rate	Single Filers	Married Filing Jointly or Qualifying Widow(er)	Married Filing Separately	Head of Household	
10%	$0–$7,825	$0–$15,650	$0–$7,825	$0–$11,200	10%
15%	$7,825–$31,850	$15,650–$63,700	$7,825–$31,850	$11,200–$42,650	15%
25%	$31,850–$77,100	$63,700–$128,500	$31,850–$64,250	$42,650–$110,100	25%
28%	$77,100–$160,850	$128,500–$195,850	$64,250–$97,925	$110,100–$178,350	28%
33%	$160,850–$349,700	$195,850–$349,700	$97,925–$174,850	$178,350–$349,700	33%
35%	>$349,700	>$349,700	>$174,850	>$349,700	35%
	[Schedule X]	[Schedule Y-1]	[Schedule Y-2]	[Schedule Z]	

State	*income tax rate* (%)		
Alabama	2·0–5·0
Alaska	none
Arizona	2.59–4.57
Arkansas	1·0–7·0
California	1·0–9·3
Colorado	4·63
Connecticut	3·0–5·0
Delaware	2·2–5·95
Florida	none
Georgia	1·0–6·0
Hawaii	1·4–8·25
Idaho	1·6–7·8
Illinois	3·0
Indiana	3·4
Iowa	0·36–8·98
Kansas	3·5–6·45
Kentucky	2·0–6·0
Louisiana	2·0–6·0
Maine	2·0–8·5
Maryland	2·0–4·75
Massachusetts	5·3
Michigan	3·9
Minnesota	5·35–7·85
Mississippi	3·0–5·0
Missouri	1·5–6·0
Montana	1·0–6·9
Nebraska	2·56–6·84
Nevada	none
New Hampshire	5 (intrst & dvend)
New Jersey	1·4–8·97
New Mexico	1·7–5·3
New York	4·0–6·85
North Carolina	6·0–8·0
North Dakota	2·1–5·54
Ohio	0·649–6·555
Oklahoma	0·5–5·65
Oregon	5·0–9·0
Pennsylvania	3·07
Rhode Island	3·75–9·9
South Carolina	2·5–7·0
South Dakota	none
Tennessee	6·0 (intrst & dvend)
Texas	none
Utah	2·3–6·98
Vermont	3·6–9·5
Virginia	2·0–5·75
Washington	none
West Virginia	3·0–6·5
Wisconsin	4·6–6·75
Wyoming	none
Washington, DC	4·5–8·7

———————————— MOST COSTLY CELEB DIVORCES ————————————

In April 2007, *Forbes* magazine released a list of the most costly celebrity divorces:

Celebrity	year	cost ($m)			
Michael Jordan	2007	>150	Kevin Costner	1994	80
Neil Diamond	1994	150	Paul McCartney	2007	60
Steven Spielberg	1989	100	James Cameron	1999	50
Harrison Ford	2004	85	Michael Douglas	1998	45

[Source: *Forbes*. Clearly, some are uncertain.]

———————————————— GLASS CEILINGS, &c. ————————————————

The 'glass ceiling' is an unofficial (metaphorically invisible) barrier to promotion, usually 'hit' by women, the disabled, members of ethnic minorities, or those who for whatever reason do not match the (unspoken) requirements of an organization. In 1991, the US Department of Labor defined the glass ceiling as 'those artificial barriers based on attitudinal or organizational bias that prevent qualified individuals from advancing upward in their organization into management-level positions'. The *Oxford English Dictionary* traces the first use of the phrase to an *Adweek* article in 1984, and since then, a number of spin-off phrases have been coined:

Stained-glass ceiling.................................. *a barrier to those in the Church*
Celluloid ceiling† .... *a barrier to those in the film industry*
Marble ceiling... *a barrier to those in politics*
Paper ceiling............................ *a barrier to those in newspapers or publishing*
Grass ceiling..................................... *a barrier to those in the field of sport*
Glass elevator ...*where some are unfairly promoted over those whose careers are 'stuck'*
Pink plateau................................... *a barrier to homosexuals in any field*

† In a 2006 analysis, Dr Martha Lauzen noted that 'in 2005, women comprised 17% of all directors, executive producers, producers, writers, cinematographers, and editors working on the top 250 domestic grossing films. This is the same percentage of women employed in these roles in 1998'. ❧ Over the last five years there has been a 40% fall in the number of women holding senior management positions within the UK's 350 biggest companies, according to research by PricewaterhouseCoopers. The report, released in March 2007, suggested that women were taking themselves off the career ladder before they hit the glass ceiling, probably as a result of the high cost of child care and of increasing female entrepreneurship – which has led many women to set up their own business.

———————————————— WORLD'S RICHEST CITIES ————————————————

The richest cities in the world in 2005, ranked by Gross Domestic Product, were:

City	GDP ($)				
Tokyo	1·2tr	Chicago	460bn	Mexico City	315bn
New York	1·1tr	Paris	460bn	Philadelphia	312bn
Los Angeles	639bn	London	452bn	Washington, DC	299bn
		Osaka/Kobe	341bn	[PricewaterhouseCoopers]	

―――――――――――――― USPS BASIC RATES & FEES ――――――――――――――

First Class Mail		Priority Mail		Media Mail (Book Rate)	
Ounces	*$*	*Pounds*	*$*	*Pounds*	*$*
≤1	0·41	≤1	4·60	≤1	2·13
≤2	0·58	≤2	4·60	≤2	2·47
≤3	0·75	≤3	5·05	≤3	2·81
≤3·5	0·92	≤4	5·70	≤4	3·15
≤4	1·31	≤5	6·30	≤5	3·49
≤5	1·48	(for Zones local, 1–2)		≤6	3·83
≤6	1·65			≤7	4·17
≤7	1·82	Express Mail		≤8	4·51
≤8	1·99	*Pounds*	*$*	≤9	4·85
≤9	2·16	≤0·5	16·25	≤10	5·19
≤10	2·33	≤1	19·50		
≤11	2·50	≤2	21·40	Certificate of Mailing	
≤12	2·67	≤3	24·50	postage + $1·05	
≤13	2·84	≤4	27·60		
>13	goes Priority	≤5	30·70	Certified Mail	
Postcard rate	0·26	(from PO to addressee)		postage + $2·65	

[The above is a simplified table – for further detail on pricing, services, and restrictions see usps.com.] On April 12, 2007, the USPS began selling a 'forever stamp' for use on first-class, standard envelopes weighing one ounce or less. These stamps will always remain valid postage, although the price of purchasing new 'forever' stamps will increase. The stamp features an image of the Liberty Bell, first rung July 8, 1776, and irreparably cracked on the anniversary of George Washington's birthday in 1846.

―――――――――――――― 2007 COMMEMORATIVE STAMPS ――――――――――――――

Each year the USPS issues a line of commemorative stamps based on suggestions from the Citizens' Stamp Advisory Committee. Below are some 2007 stamps:

Oklahoma Statehood...............................sunrise over the Cimarron River
International Polar Year & *Polar Lights*....... the aurora borealis & aurora australis
Settlement of Jamestown ....3 ships carrying the first Jamestown settlers
Pacific Lighthouses.......................................5 historic Pacific lighthouses
James Stewart.....................portrait of the 'quintessential American film hero'
Marvel Superheroes.................10 classic Marvel heroes and comic book covers
Jury Duty......................................12 'representative jurors' in silhouette
Mendez vs *Westminster School District*..........celebrating the legal case that ended
                                    segregation by national origin in California schools
Holiday Knits.............. a knitted stag, snowman, evergreen tree, and teddy bear

The USPS also began selling 15 commemorative *Star Wars* stamps on May 25, 2007 (exactly 30 years after the first *Star Wars* premiered in US theaters). To celebrate, 400 mailboxes were modified to look like R2-D2 for several weeks of March and April. Fans were asked to vote for their favorite stamp: Jedi Master Yoda triumphed, and his image was issued as a single-sheet stamp in the fall of 2007.

——————————VIRTUAL CURRENCY——————————

Inside the virtual worlds of Massively Multiplayer Online Role-Playing Games (MMORPGs), players use virtual currency to buy and sell objects like houses, weapons, spells, &c. And, as MMORPGs gain subscribers and stature, increased interest (and regulatory attention) has focused on these virtual currency transactions. Although most game publishers explicitly prohibit users from trading 'game gold' for real-world money, many players have chosen to sell virtual currency online, whether through third-party brokers or via peer-to-peer exchanges. Until 2007, eBay was a primary source for trading virtual currency, but in January of that year the company announced it would no longer allow the sale of any virtual property, citing the complex legal issues surrounding the ownership of virtual goods†. In February 2007, Chinese regulators banned the exchange of 'QQ coins' (issued by the country's main provider of instant-messaging) for real money, amid concerns the coins were being used to purchase illicit services (in 2006, China's Central Bank had said the coins were so widespread they threatened to affect the value of the yuan). ❦ Below are some virtual currency exchange rates against the US dollar. Amounts listed represent the units of virtual currency purchasable for $1, as of March 28, 2007:

Game	currency unit	$1 =
Anarchy Online	credits (Atlantean – RK1)‡	3,831,417·62
City of Heroes	influence	413,564·92
Dark Age of Camelot	platinum (Galahad – Hibernia)	1·47
Dungeons & Dragons	platinum	12,515·64
EVE Online	isk	8,503,401.36
EverQuest	platinum	3,770·73
EverQuest II	gold (Befallen – Good)	43·25
Final Fantasy XI	gil (Unicorn)	24,987·50
Guild Wars	gold	12,510·42
Lineage II	adena (Devianne)	81,338·75
Second Life	Linden dollar	270
Star Wars Galaxies	credit	1,240,694·78
World of Warcraft (EU)	gold (Lothar – Horde)	21·26
World of Warcraft (US)	gold (Frostmourne – Alliance)	4·72

† Notably, 'online reality phenomenon' *Second Life* was exempt from the eBay ban. The makers of *Second Life*, Linden Labs, encourage the sale of their virtual currency for real-world money. In October 2005, *Second Life* even launched its own online currency exchange, LindeX, allowing users and the public to trade Linden dollars for US dollars. Regulatory and fraud controls are used to keep the Linden dollar stable. *Entropia Universe* also encourages the exchange of its virtual currency (the Project Entropia Dollar, PED) for real money; game currency can be withdrawn from real-world ATMs through use of a special card. In fact, virtual property may be increasingly valuable – in April 2007, the BBC reported on research by security firm Symantec suggesting that access to a *World of Warcraft* account was more valuable to criminals than a stolen credit card. ‡ In some games, currency values differ from server to server. In such cases, one server has been chosen arbitrarily and noted in brackets. The list is intended for illustrative purposes, and is not exhaustive. [Sources: IGE; *Second Life*; GameUSD.com; UMMO Letters. Linden dollar exchange rate as of December 8, 2006, via CNN.]

—INTEREST RATES · FEDERAL RESERVE PRIME RATE—

Recent rates	
Month	%
Dec '06	8·25
Jan '07	8·25
Feb '07	8·25
Mar '07	8·25
Apr '07	8·25
May '07	8·25
Jun '07	8·25
Jul '07	8·25

——NATIONAL HOUSING CHARACTERISTICS & PRICE——

Number of rooms	%	*Value ($)* [occupied]	%	*Year structure built*	%
1	0·5	<10,000	2·4	2005–09	0·8
2	1·1	10–20k	1·7	2000–04	7·4
3	8·8	20–30k	1·7	1995–99	7·1
4	18·3	30–40k	1·9	1990–94	5·6
5	23·0	40–50k	2·3	1985–89	7·1
6	20·4	50–60k	2·6	1980–84	6·0
7	12·3	60–70k	3·8	1975–79	10·2
8	7·1	70–80k	4·5	1970–74	8·6
9	3·4	80–100k	8·5	1960–69	12·2
≥10	5·0	100–120k	6·8	1950–59	10·5
Number of bedrooms	%	120–150k	9·8	1940–49	6·4
0	1·0	150–200k	13·0	1930–39	4·8
1	11·8	200–250k	8·9	1920–29	4·3
2	27·6	250–300k	6·6	1919 or earlier	7·5
3	40·9	>300,000	25·5	*Median year*	1973
≥4	18·7	*Median value* . $165,344		[American Housing Survey, 2005]	

Below are the percentage changes in house prices, ranked by Census division, for the year ending March 31, 2007. [Source: Office of Federal Housing Enterprise Oversight]

	Census division (% change)	*1 year*	*quarter*	*5 year*	*since 1980*
1	Mountain	7·47	1·11	58·61	287·06
2	West South Central	6·75	1·11	29·83	126·93
3	East South Central	6·62	0·96	30·19	189·40
4	South Atlantic	5·09	0·47	66·20	329·76
5	Middle Atlantic	4·20	0·50	63·81	439·35
6	Pacific	3·98	0·06	89·09	499·42
7	West North Central	3·51	0·68	31·83	205·41
8	East North Central	2·32	0·33	24·73	222·34
9	New England	1·11	0·03	50·56	529·67
–	United States	4·25	0·45	53·53	309·75

————————FORBES MAGAZINE RICH LIST · 2007————————

No.	billionaire	age	$ billion	activity	2006 rank
1	William Gates III	51	56·0	Microsoft	1
2	Warren Buffett	76	52·0	investing	2
3	Carlos Slim Helu	67	49·0	telecoms	3
4	Ingvar Kamprad	80	33·0	IKEA	4
5	Lakshmi Mittal	56	32·0	Mittal Steel	5
6	Sheldon Adelson	73	26·5	casinos & hotels	14
7	Bernard Arnault	58	26·0	LVMH	7
8	Amancio Ortega	71	24·0	Zara	23
9	Li Ka-shing	78	23·0	investing	10
10	David Thomson & family	49	22·0	publishing	9

————————————— MINIMUM WAGE —————————————

The federal minimum wage was introduced in 1938, at the rate of $0·25 per hour. It generally applies to employees of firms with an annual turnover >$500,000, as well as smaller enterprises engaged in interstate business. All federal, state, and local government employees are covered, as are domestic workers. That said, a host of exceptions apply, for example, to workers with disabilities, full-time students, those under 20 early in their employment, tipped employees, &c. ❧ On May 25, 2007, President Bush signed the Fair Minimum Wage Act of 2007, which set the first increase in the federal minimum wage in a decade. The Act increases the federal minimum wage to $5·85 per hour from July 24, 2007; $6·55 per hour from July 24, 2008; and $7·25 per hour from July 24, 2009. The increase was a key issue during the first session of the 110th Congress, and is estimated to affect *c.*5·6m workers, or 4% of the workforce. ❧ A number of states also have their own minimum wage, many of which are higher than the federally mandated wage. Where state and federal wages differ, employees are entitled to the higher rate. Below is a Department of Labor chart of state minimum wages, as of April 30, 2007:

AL......no law	HI...... $7·25	MA..... $7·50	NM...... $5·15	SD...... $5·15
AK...... $7·15	ID...... $5·15	MI...... $6·95	NY ...... $7·15	TN ......no law
AZ...... $6·75	IL ...... $6·50	MN..... $5·25	NC...... $6·15	TX . federal rate†
AR...... $6·25	IN...... $5·15	MS ......no law	ND...... $5·15	UT . federal rate†
CA ..... $7·50	IA ...... $6·20	MO..... $6·50	OH...... $6·85	VT ...... $7·53
CO ..... $6·85	KS...... $2·65	MT..... $6·15	OK . federal rate†	VA.. federal rate†
CT ..... $7·65	KY.. federal rate†	NE ..... $5·15	OR...... $7·80	WA...... $7·93
DE ..... $6·65	LA.......no law	NV..... $6·15	PA....... $6·25	WV...... $5·85
FL....... $6·67	ME...... $6·75	NH..... $5·15	RI ...... $7·40	WI...... $6·50
GA ..... $5·15	MD...... $6·15	NJ....... $7·15	SC.......no law	WY...... $5·15

[Sources: Dept of Labor; *New York Times*] This is a basic guide; further data are available from the Department of Labor. † States whose legislation specifies a minimum wage set at the federal level. ❧ According to figures released by the EU statistics office Eurostat, comparative hourly minimum wages as of January 1, 2007, were: Ireland, $10·96; France, $10·92; UK, $10·48; Czech Republic, $2·31.

—————————PERSONAL WEALTH OF THE RICH—————————

Official statistics on the personal wealth of the very rich are surprisingly difficult to come by – which may explain the popularity of independent data, like that collected by *Forbes* [see p.318]. The most recent source of government data comes from a 2001 paper by Barry Johnson & Brian Raub, published in the IRS's quarterly *Statistic of Income* report. In this paper, the authors employ the complex 'estate tax multiplier', which estimates the wealth of the living rich by extrapolating the wealth of the recently deceased rich. (It is assumed that the dead with individual gross estate holdings of >$675,000, for whom an estate tax Form 706 must be completed, represent a 'random sample, designated by death'.) Johnson & Raub estimate that in 2001 there were 7·4m US adults with >$675,000 in gross assets. This 3·5% of the adult population owned 32·7% of the total net worth – roughly $13·8 trillion. Of these 'top wealth holders', 54% were male and 46% female. The charts below indicate the number and concentration of millionaires by state:

States with largest number of resident millionaires			
(thousands)	*millionaires*	*adult pop.*	o|o
California	572	25,176	2·3
New York	317	14,452	2·2
Florida	249	12,566	2·0
Illinois	185	9,274	2·0
Texas	182	15,297	1·2
New Jersey	178	6,398	2·8

States with highest concentration of resident millionaires			
(thousands)	*millionaires*	*adult pop.*	o|o
Connecticut	83	2,594	3·2
New Jersey	178	6,398	2·8
DC	11	458	2·4
California	572	25,176	2·3
New York	317	14,452	2·2
Massachusetts	105	4,921	2·1

In 2001, an estimated 46,000 US adults had total assets greater than $20,000,000.

—————————WORLDWIDE PERSONAL WEALTH—————————

The *World Distribution of Household Wealth* study, released in December 2006, suggested that the richest 2% of adults owned >50% of global household wealth. The study, produced by the World Institute for Development Economics Research of the United Nations University (UNU-WIDER), included every country in the world and measured all aspects of household wealth, including: financial assets, debt, property, and land. The research highlighted the global inequality of wealth distribution, whereby just a handful of countries account for 90% of the world's household wealth. Below is a breakdown of where the world's wealthiest 1% live:

USA 37%	Italy 4%	Spain 1%
Japan 27%	Germany 4%	Switzerland 1%
UK 6%	Canada 2%	Taiwan 1%
France 5%	Netherlands 2%	*Rest of the world* 10%

To be among the 37m people in the richest 1% of the world, you require assets of >$500,000.

──────────── PRESIDENTIAL DOLLAR COINS────────────

In 2007, the US Mint issued the first in a series of $1 coins honoring every deceased US President†. The coins are to be issued in the same order the Presidents served, and each President will be featured on a single coin, except for Grover Cleveland, who will be honored with 2 coins (Cleveland is the only President to serve non-consecutive terms). The obverse of the Presidential coins depicts the President and his years of service; the reverse shows the Statue of Liberty alongside the words 'The United States of America' and the designation '$1'. Unusually, the edges of the coins are inscribed with the year, mint mark, 'In God We Trust', and 'E Pluribus Unum'‡. Coins will be issued at three-month intervals according to the following schedule:

2007........George Washington, John Adams, Thomas Jefferson, James Madison
2008 ...James Monroe, John Quincy Adams, Andrew Jackson, Martin Van Buren
2009........ William Henry Harrison, John Tyler, James K. Polk, Zachary Taylor
2010 ......Millard Fillmore, Franklin Pierce, James Buchanan, Abraham Lincoln
2011. Andrew Johnson, Ulysses S. Grant, Rutherford B. Hayes, James A. Garfield
2012....Chester Arthur, Grover Cleveland, Benjamin Harrison, Grover Cleveland
2013.... William McKinley, Theodore Roosevelt, William Taft, Woodrow Wilson
2014....................Warren Harding, Calvin Coolidge, Herbert Hoover, FDR
2015.........Harry S. Truman, Dwight D. Eisenhower, JFK, Lyndon B. Johnson
2016.. Richard M. Nixon

† Federal law decrees that only deceased Presidents may appear on US money; some argue this has historically been an attempt to separate the US from the ancient tradition of honoring kings and emperors on currency. The first President featured on a coin was Abraham Lincoln, whose 100th birthday was honored with a 1909 redesign of the penny. His depiction ended a 115-year-old tradition of producing American currency without images of a President. ‡ An unknown number (possibly *c.*50,000) of George Washington coins were released from Philadelphia on February 15, 2007, without their edge inscriptions. One such coin sold for $600 before collectors realized how many coins had the mistake; prices later settled at about $50 on eBay. ❦ In May 2007, the Mint also began issuing the 'First Spouse' series: noncirculating 24k gold coins designed to honor each former First Lady.

────────────── STATE QUARTERS──────────────

Since 1999, the US Mint has released a State quarter every 10 weeks, honoring the States in the order of their admittance into the Union. The 2007 coins were:

State	date of statehood	coin design (reverse)	inscription
Montana	11·08·1889	bison skull	Big Sky Country
Washington	11·11·1889	salmon, Mt Rainier	The Evergreen State
Idaho	07·03·1890	peregrine falcon, state outline	Esto Perpetua
Wyoming	07·10·1890	bucking horse & rider	The Equality State
Utah	01·04·1896	2 trains & 'golden spike'	Crossroads of the West

The 2008 State quarters will honor Oklahoma, New Mexico, Arizona, Alaska, & Hawaii. Designs were under evaluation at the time of writing. [Source: US Mint]

	Cent	Nickel	Dime	Quarter	Half Dollar	Dollar	Golden Dollar*
2006 Production	8,234,000,000	1,502,400,000	2,828,000,000	2,941,000,000	4,400,000		7,700,000
Composition	copper-plated Zn	cupro-nickel	cupro-nickel	cupro-nickel	cupro-nickel	cupro-nickel	manganese-brass
Weight	2·500g	5·000g	2·268g	5·670g	11·340g	8·1g	8·1g
Diameter	19·05mm	21·21mm	17·91mm	24·26mm	30·61mm	26·50mm	26·50mm
Thickness	1·55mm	1·95mm	1·35mm	1·75mm	2·15mm	2·00mm	2·00mm
Edge	plain	plain	reeded	reeded	reeded	reeded	plain
No. of Reeds†	none	none	118	119	150	133	none
Obverse	Lincoln	Jefferson	Roosevelt	Washington	Kennedy	Susan B. Anthony	Sacagawea & son
Designed by	V.D. Brenner	Felix Schlag	John R. Sinnock	John Flannagan	Gilroy Roberts	Frank Gasparro	Glenna Goodacre
Date of Issue	1909	1938	1946	1932	1964	1979,1980,1999	2000
Reverse	Lincoln Memorial	Monticello	Torch, oak, &c.	Eagle	Presidential Arms	Apollo 11 Insignia	Eagle in Flight
Designed by	Frank Gasparro	Felix Schlag	John R. Sinnock	John Flannagan	Frank Gasparro	Frank Gasparro	Thomas D. Rogers
Date of Issue	1959	1938	1946	1932‡	1964‡	1979,1980,1999	2000

[Source: US Mint] The above specifications are for US Mint legal tender coins currently in circulation. * The 'Golden' Dollar is actually 88.5% Cu; 6.0% Zn; 3.5% Mn; 2.0% Ni. † Traditionally, when coins were minted from precious metals (silver, gold, &c.), they were milled with 'reeding', or grooves, in order to foil counterfeiters and protect their edges (reeded edges show when coins have been clipped or filed for their precious metals). Although no gold coins have circulated in the US since 1934, and by the 1980s silver had also been abandoned, reeded edges remain to help the visually impaired distinguish similar size coins by touch. ‡ 1975–6 Bicentennial reverses were minted. These coins are dated 1776–1976; none was individually dated 1975 or 1976. ❦ Increasing prices of copper, nickel, and zinc (driven partly by demand from manufacturers in China) have caused the production costs of pennies and nickels to exceed their face values. In December 2006, the US Mint introduced interim legislation banning the melting, treatment, and unlicensed exportation of pennies and nickels, although individuals are permitted to take up to $5 of these coins out the country or ship up to $100 out of the country for 'legitimate coinage and numismatic purposes'. The Mint says the regulations are necessary to prevent a currency shortage caused by those who would melt coins for use as scrap metal, noting that the taxpayer cost to replace the coins would be 'enormous'. Those violating the legislation may be subject to a fine of up to $10,000 or imprisonment for up to 5 years. ❦ Despite ongoing public speculation, the Mint has (at present) no plans to withdraw the penny from circulation.

————————————————THE EURO————————————————

NOTES & COINS IN CIRCULATION

Coin	number	total value €	Note	number	total value €
€2	3,542m	7,084m	€500	423m	211,658m
€1	5,309m	5,309m	€200	152m	30,333m
50¢	4,430m	2,215m	€100	1,099m	109,852m
20¢	7,353m	1,470m	€50	3,885m	194,259m
10¢	9,250m	925m	€20	2,173m	43,460m
5¢	11,420m	571m	€10	1,753m	17,530m
2¢	13,229m	264m	€5	1,294m	6,470m
1¢	16,069m	161m	TOTAL	10,779m	613,562m
TOTAL	70,602m	17,999m			

[Source: European Central Bank, 03·07]

Coins	common side design
€2, €1	EU map before enlargement of 2004
50¢, 20¢, 10¢	individual EU countries before enlargement of 2004
5¢, 2¢, 1¢	Europe in relation to Africa and Asia

Note	color	size (mm)	architecture	Note	color	size (mm)	architecture
€5	gray	120×62	Classical	€50	orange	140×77	Renaissance
€10	red	127×67	Romanesque	€100	green	147×82	Baroque/Rococo
€20	blue	133×72	Gothic	€200	yellow	153×82	C19th iron/glass
				€500	purple	160×82	C20th modern

CURRENT CIRCULATION OF THE EURO

OFFICIAL CURRENCY
Belgium, Germany, Greece, Spain,
France, Ireland, Italy, Luxembourg,
the Netherlands, Austria, Portugal,
Finland, Slovenia
[Malta & Cyprus intend to join in 01·01·08]

DE FACTO CURRENCY
Andorra, Kosovo, Montenegro

SPECIAL ARRANGEMENTS
Monaco, the Vatican City,
San Marino

OVERSEAS TERRITORIES
Guadeloupe, French Guiana,
Martinique, Mayotte, Réunion,
Saint Pierre and Miquelon, French
Southern & Antarctic Territories

Charted below are the Euro and GB Sterling rates of exchange against the dollar:

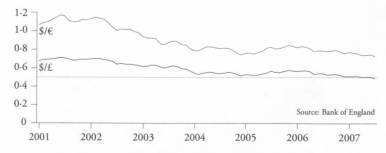

ISLAMIC FINANCE

Sharia law decrees that money is simply a medium of exchange with no intrinsic value, and that Muslims are forbidden to charge *Riba* [interest or usury] since it leads to *Zulm* [injustice]. The Koran states in verses 278–9 of Surah 2, Al-Baqara:

> *O you who believe! Fear Allah, and give up what remains of your demand for usury, if you are indeed believers · If you do it not, take notice of war from Allah and His Messenger: but if you turn back, you shall have your capital sums; deal not unjustly, and you shall not be dealt with unjustly.*

Sharia law also prohibits dealing in anything *Haram* [unlawful] (e.g. pornography, gambling, alcohol, pork, &c.) or *Bay' al-Gharar* [risky] (e.g. goods sold deceitfully). While Islamic finance existed throughout the Middle Ages, its recent popularity dates back to the first Islamic banks founded in the 1960s, with steady growth since then. And, as Islam has expanded alongside globalized capitalism, *Fuqhas* [Islamic jurists] have examined classical texts to create acceptable Islamic analogues of conventional financial products (bank accounts, loans, mortgages, &c.). Since Sharia prohibits the charging of interest, Islamic finance has developed a range of models that operate by sharing risk and reward, including:

IJARA · a form of leasing where the bank purchases an item and rents it to the customer for an agreed time and price. The bank retains ownership of the item, and reclaims it at the end of the leasing period. IJARA WA IQTINA is a similar model, except the customer is able to purchase the item at the end of the contract. A form of IJARA with diminishing MUSHARAKA allows for large investments, such as the purchase of property – for example, where the ownership of a house is gradually shifted from bank to customer with every transfer of capital over and above the rental payments.

MUSHARAKA · a joint venture where sharing of profits is agreed in advance, but losses must be in proportion to the sum invested.

MUDARABA · an investment model whereby the customer invests money and the bank invests expertise. Profits are shared and, in the event of a loss, no fees are charged.

MURABAHA · a form of credit where the bank purchases an item and re-sells it to the customer on a deferred basis, adding a mutually agreed margin of profit for the bank (reward for risk).

Estimating the popularity of *Halal* [lawful] finance is problematic, since the market is growing at such a pace. The UK Financial Services Authority reported in 2006 'assets controlled by Islamic banks at the global level are estimated to be $200–500bn and are growing at a pace of 10–15% per year'.

PRESIDENTIAL TAX RETURN

According to the White House, the President and his wife had taxable income of $642,905 in FY2006, resulting in a federal income tax bill of $186,378. The First Couple donated $78,100 (*c.*12% of their taxable income) to churches and charities.

———————————— COUNTERFEIT CURRENCY ————————————

One in 10,000 US bills is counterfeit – according to a 2006 study by the Treasury, Federal Reserve Board, and Secret Service – representing a total worldwide value of *c.*$70m. According to the Secret Service, the growth of personal computing has democratized the means of producing 'reasonably deceptive' counterfeit, with basic equipment said to cost <$300. In 2005, over half the counterfeit money circulating in the US was produced using digital methods (scanning &c.), as opposed to traditional methods like offset printing. Charted below is the rate of digitally produced counterfeit, as a percent of all the counterfeit money detected in the US:

2000.. 47% *digitally-made*	2002............... 36%	2004............... 54%
2001............... 39%	2003............... 43%	2005............... 52%

Given the advances in digital technology, the Treasury Department anticipates the need for new currency designs every 7–10 years. A new $20 bill was introduced in 2003, a new $50 in 2004, a new $10 in 2006, and a new $5 is expected in late 2007. While citizens are advised to familiarize themselves with the features of particular bills, the Secret Service offers the following general tips for detecting counterfeit:

Genuine bills		Counterfeit bills
Lifelike, distinct from background	Portrait	*lifeless and flat, dark background*
Clear and sharp points	Seals	*uneven, blunt, broken points*
Fine lines are clear and unbroken	Border	*outer margin lines blurred*
Evenly spaced, same ink as seal	Serial no.	*unevenly spaced, ink differs from seal*
Tiny red and blue fibers embedded	Paper	*red and blue fibers printed*

In consultation with the Central Bank Counterfeit Deterrence Group (CBCDG), a consortium of the world's Central Banks, the latest version of Adobe Photoshop does not allow users to scan or manipulate the latest banknotes of many major currencies. The designs of newer bank notes contain a pattern of 5 circles that is detected by the image-processing software, which then blocks user access.

———————————— COUNTERFEIT CURRENCY ABROAD ————————————

60% of US counterfeit is thought to be held abroad. Below are the top countries for US dollar counterfeiting in 2005, ranked by total value found in circulation:

Country	total value found		
Peru†	........................$2,782,200	Hong Kong	 305,910
Sri Lanka	 480,600	Philippines	 229,180
		Singapore	 208,300

† Peru's total reflects the so-called Supernotes found in the country over three months in 2005. Supernotes (also called Superbills or Superdollars) are highly deceptive $100 bills created with the same intaglio printing process used by the US government. According to the Secret Service, their production has been traced to North Korea, where the notes are 'produced and distributed with the full consent and control' of the government; not surprisingly, this is a major source of diplomatic tension between the nations. The Secret Service has seized *c.*$50m of the bills worldwide since 1989.

——HISTORICAL ECONOMIC INDICATORS OF NOTE——

Indicator · Year		2006	2005	2004	2003	2002	2001	2000	1999	1998
President		W. Bush	W. Bush	W. Bush	W. Bush	W. Bush	W. Bush	Clinton	Clinton	Clinton
Gross Domestic Product (GDP)	current $bn	13,246.6	12,455.8	11,712.5	10,960.8	10,469.6	10,128.0	9,817.0	9,268.4	8,747.0
Gross Domestic Product (GDP)	% change	6.3	6.3	6.9	4.7	3.4	3.2	5.9	6.0	5.3
Change in consumer prices (all urban consumers)	%	2.5	3.4	3.3	1.9	2.4	1.6	3.4	2.7	1.6
Unemployment rate (civilian labor force)	%	4.6	5.1	5.5	6.0	5.8	4.7	4.0	4.2	4.5
Average weekly hours worked (non-agricultural)	hours	33.9	33.8	33.7	33.7	33.9	34.0	34.3	34.3	34.5
Average gross weekly earnings (non-agricultural)	current $	567.87	544.33	529.09	518.06	506.72	493.79	481.01	463.15	448.56
Industrial output as a percentage of total capacity	%	81.7	80.2	78.1	76.1	74.8	76.1	81.7	81.9	82.8
Disposable income, per capita	current $	31,794	30,440	29,531	28,031	27,157	26,236	25,479	23,968	23,161
Personal expenditure, per capita	current $	30,926	29,450	27,932	26,455	25,494	24,723	23,869	22,491	21,291
Change in real, per capita, personal disp. income	%	1.7	0.2	2.7	1.2	2.1	0.9	3.7	1.8	4.6
Savings as % of disposable income	%	-1.0	-0.4	2.0	2.1	2.4	1.8	2.3	2.4	4.3
Consumer credit – total outstanding	$bn	2,398.0	2,295.0	2,201.8	2,087.8	1,984.1	1,871.9	1,722.4	1,532.7	1,419.4
Prime rate charged by banks	%	7.96	6.19	4.34	4.12	4.67	6.91	9.23	8.00	8.35
NYSE Composite index (Dec 2002=5,000)		8,358	7,349	6,613	5,447	5,579	6,398	6,806	6,547	5,818
Dow Jones Industrial Average		11,409	10,548	10,317	8,994	9,226	10,189	10,735	10,465	8,626
NASDAQ Composite (Feb 1971=100)		2,263	2,099	1,987	1,647	1,540	2,035	3,784	2,728	1,795
Net farm income	$bn	60.6	73.8	85.4	60.4	40.2	55.6	51.3	47.7	47.1
Total corporate profits after tax	$bn	1,336.0	1,119.4	844.2	664.8	575.8	503.8	508.2	517.2	470.0
Federal finance surplus/deficit		-248.2	-318.3	-412.7	-377.6	-157.8	128.2	236.2	125.6	69.3
US Trade, balance on current account	$m	-811,477	-754,848	-640,148	-522,101	-459,641	-384,699	-417,426	-301,630	-215,062
US Dollar/GB Pound ($/£)		1.84	1.82	1.83	1.63	1.50	1.44	1.51	1.62	1.66
US Dollar/euro ($/€) [pre-1999 estimated]		1.26	1.24	1.24	1.13	0.94	0.90	0.92	1.06	(1.12)
euro/GB Pound (€/£) [pre-1999 estimated]		1.47	1.46	1.47	1.45	1.59	1.61	1.64	1.52	(1.48)
Gold price per troy ounce	$	604	443	409	364	310	271	279	279	294

[Sources: Economic Indicators, Government Printing Office; US Annual Statistical Abstract; HM Treasury; Bank of England]

Form & Faith

Never speak disrespectfully of Society, Algernon.
Only people who can't get into it do that.
— OSCAR WILDE, *The Importance of Being Earnest,* 1895

AMERICANS & CLASS

Since 1972, the General Social Survey has asked Americans whether they thought they belonged to the lower, working, middle, or upper class. The results are below:

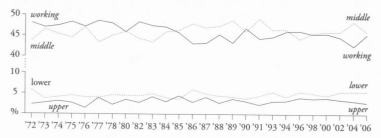

ESTATES OF THE REALM

The Estates of the Realm are those classes within the body politic with administrative powers. The original Estates of England, as represented in Parliament, were:

1st – CLERGY · 2nd – BARONS & KNIGHTS · 3rd – COMMONS

after some adjustment these became

1st – LORDS SPIRITUAL · 2nd – LORDS TEMPORAL · 3rd – COMMONS

According to the redoubtable *Oxford English Dictionary,* the Fourth Estate has been used to refer to the PRESS, since Henry Fielding wrote in 1752, 'None of our political writers ... take notice of any more than three Estates, namely, Kings†, Lords, and Commons ... passing by in silence that very large and powerful body which form the Fourth Estate in this community'. Famously, Thomas Carlyle reported that while Edmund Burke was speaking in the Parliament, he referred to the Press Gallery, declaring, 'Yonder sits the Fourth Estate, more important than them all'.

---

† Fielding erred in supposing that three Estates of the Realm were the Crown, the Lords, and the Commons. ❦ A number of institutions have been dubbed the Fifth Estate, including publicans, women, cinema, the BBC, radio, television, trades union, quangos, universities, philanthropic trusts, opinion polls, independent research centers, and most recently, 'citizen media' – notably bloggers.

FORMS OF ADDRESS

Personage	envelope	letter opening	verbal address
President	The President, The White House	Dear Mr President	Mr President
Vice President	The Vice President, Old Executive Office Building	Dear Mr Vice President	Mr Vice President
Former US President	The Honorable {A} {B}	Dear Mr {B}	Mr {B}; President {A} {B}
Attorney General	The Honorable {A} {B}	Dear Mr Attorney General	Mr Attorney General
Cabinet Members	The Honorable {A} {B}, Secretary of {department}	Dear Mr Secretary	Mr Secretary
Postmaster General	The Honorable {A} {B}, Postmaster General	Dear Mr Postmaster General	Mr Postmaster General
President of the Senate	The Honorable {A} {B}, President of the Senate	Dear Mr President	Mr President
Speaker of the House of Rep.	The Honorable {A} {B}, Speaker of the House of Rep.	Dear Mr Speaker	Mr Speaker; Speaker
US Senator	The Honorable {A} {B}, US Senate	Dear Senator {B}	Senator {B}
Congressman/woman	The Honorable {A} {B}, House of Representatives	Dear Mr/Madam {B}	Congressman/woman ({A} {B})
Secretary General of the UN	His Excellency {A} {B}, Secretary General of the UN	Dear Mr Secretary General	Mr Sec. Gen./Excellency
Ambassador of the US	The Honorable {A} {B}, American Ambassador	Dear Mr Ambassador	Mr Ambassador
Foreign Ambassador	His Excellency {A} {B}, Ambassador of {X}	Dear Mr Ambassador	Mr Ambassador
Chief Justice of the Supreme Ct	The Chief Justice, The Supreme Court of the US	Dear (Mr) Chief Justice	Mr Chief Justice ({B})
Assoc. Justice of the Supreme Ct	Mr Justice {B}, The Supreme Court of the US	Dear (Mr) Justice	Mr Justice ({B})
State Governor	The Honorable {A} {B}, The Governor of {X}	Dear Governor {B}	Governor {B}
Lieutenant Governor	The Honorable {A} {B}, Lieutenant Gov. of {X}	Dear Mr {B}	Mr {B}
Mayor	The Honorable {A} {B}, Mayor of {X}	Dear Mayor {B}	Mr Mayor
King/Queen	His/Her Majesty {name}, King/Queen of {X}	Your Majesty	Your Majesty
President of a Republic	His Excellency {A} {B}, President of the Rep. of {X}	Dear Mr President	Mr President
Prime Minister	His Excellency {A} {B}, The Prime Minister of {X}	Dear (Mr) Prime Minister	(Mr) Prime Minister
US Armed Forces	{Rank} {A} {B} {USA, USN, USAF, USMC, USCG}	Dear {Rank} {B}	{Rank} {B}

{A} = first name; {B} = last name ✿ Throughout, where appropriate, 'Madam' should be substituted for 'Mr'. ✿ For reasons of space, some titles have been abbreviated; they should not be so truncated in practice. ✿ Considerable debate and dispute surround 'correct' forms of address. The above tabulation has been compiled from a number of, often contradictory, sources. Readers in need of detailed advice, such as on the styling of US military ranks, are advised to consult the relevant organization. (The British Peerage is so complex that its customs are the subject of a series of specialist texts that detail, for example, the correct way to address the wives of younger sons of Earls.)

———————TOASTING, THE LOYAL TOAST, & POWs———————

Traditionally, a 'toast' was a lady whom guests were invited to honor in drink. The word derives from pieces of spiced bread that were floated in 'Loving Cups' of wine to improve its flavor. According to a 1709 account in the *Tatler* (No. 31), ladies were originally hailed as 'toasts' because they had the same beneficial effect on wine as did those pieces of bread. In time, as Thomas Keightley wrote in 1860, 'toast came to signify any person or thing that was to be commemorated: as "The King", "The Land we live in", etc'. By custom, a person being toasted remains sitting, while others stand. ❦ One of the curiosities of toasting in the US military relates to prisoners of war. According to the Dept of the Army's *Guide to Protocol and Etiquette for Official Entertainment*, 'when toasting prisoners of war, water should be used as the toasting beverage', presumably to symbolize hardship and sacrifice. A number of unofficial service publications detail a range of complex and symbolic rituals for commemorating prisoners of war or those missing in action, including:

At a dinner	symbolizes	Empty chair............*absent brothers*
Upturned glass....*POWs unable to toast*		Yellow candle......*a guiding light home*
Spilled salt...*the tears of those who wait*		White tablecloth....*purity of intention*
Lemon slice.....*the bitter fate of POWs*		The Bible.................*faith in God*
A rose............*the families that wait*		Round table.........*everlasting concern*

A 'Loyal Toast' is one raised to the monarch or head of state. (In some gatherings it signals that guests may smoke.) In England, the Loyal Toast is always the first toast proposed, usually as 'The Queen' – though a few areas have a modified tradition:

The Channel Islands..............................	'The Queen, Duke of Normandy'
Lancashire...	'The Queen, Duke of Lancaster'
Canada	'The Queen', or 'The Queen of Canada'
Isle of Man..	'The Queen, Lord of Man'
Australia (since 2000)......................	'The Queen and the People of Australia'

A number of British military units do not give the Loyal Toast on the grounds that their devotion to the monarch has been proven in action. For example, the 2nd Battalion KSLI were excused the toast by George IV after officers of the regiment quelled a group of rioters who had insulted him in a Brighton theater. George IV similarly exempted the Royal Welch Fusiliers (who only raise the Loyal Toast on St David's Day), since their loyalty could 'never be in doubt' after the 1797 Nore Mutiny. Members of the Royal Navy are permitted to remain seated during the Loyal Toast when on board ship – either because their loyalty is also beyond question, or because their ships are too cramped to stand safely. Under Cromwell's rule, monarchists expressed their secret allegiance by toasting the 'King of the Jews': a reworking of [I]reland, [E]ngland, [W]ales, and [S]cotland. Jacobites indicated their allegiance to the exiled James II by raising their toast over a glass of water or a fingerbowl – thereby literally and metaphorically toasting the King 'over the water'. It has been claimed that when Queen Elizabeth I visited the Royal Exchange in 1571, Sir Thomas Gresham pledged her health with a cup of wine into which he had mixed the crushed atoms of a pearl reported to be worth in excess of £15,000.

CORRESPONDENCE ETIQUETTE

CORRESPONDENCE should always include a date and address. Avoid the overuse of punctuation, especially exclamation marks. ❧ If a letter is typed or word-processed, it may be more informal to 'top and tail' the letter by hand-writing the *Dear —— and Yours sincerely*. ❧ Personal letters should ideally be handwritten; letters of condolence should always be handwritten. Letters should be written and signed in ink. ❧ EMAIL is a curiously detached form of communication best suited to business transactions. It should be avoided in all formal social situations, and rejected out of hand for the communication of any serious emotion – especially congratulations or condolences. ❧ TEXT MESSAGING and INSTANT MESSAGING are suitable only for the transmission of logistical data – and, of course, for flirtation. ❧ The formality of SIGNING OFF LETTERS has relaxed over the years. The traditional sign-off would have followed the form:

I beg (or *have the honor*) *to remain,*
Sir, Your obedient servant.

Nowadays, the formal sign-off to a letter where the addressee's name is known is *Yours sincerely*. Where the name is not known (letters that start *Dear Sir or Madam*), the sign-off is *Yours faithfully*. The formal sign-off to the Queen of England is:

I have the honor to remain, Madam,
Your Majesty's most humble
and obedient subject.

❧ Notes of INVITATION and REPLY should be good quality paper of a small size. Gentlemen should never use paper of any color other than white [though see p.356]. Invitations to very formal events may be gilt-edged, but should not be colored. ❧ Never provide less than two weeks' notice of an event, and always respond within two days of an invitation. Even when no reply is requested, it is polite to inform the host of your intentions. Do not ask to bring uninvited guests. ❧ THANK-YOU LETTERS may be brief, but should be heartfelt and prompt. It is traditional to address party thank-you letters to the hostess.

ON INTRODUCTIONS

With the exception of reigning Sovereigns (including the Pope), Presidents, and Cardinals, introductions made between strangers should abide by these four rules:

Youth is introduced to *age* – 'Strom Thurmond, may I present Doogie Howser?'

Men are introduced to *women* – 'Dame Edna, this is Count Victor Grezhinski.'

Lower ranks are introduced to *higher* – 'Colonel Sanders, this is Sergeant Bilko.'

Individuals are introduced to *groups* – 'Mickey Mouse Club, this is Britney Spears.'

Traditionally, the so-called English Rule was 'the roof is an introduction' – by which all guests 'under the roof' of a common host might feel at liberty to initiate conversation with their fellow guests without waiting for any formal introduction.

─────TRADITIONAL ETIQUETTE OF EATING─────

APPLES · should be pared, cut into small pieces, and eaten with forks.

ARTICHOKES · are eaten with the fingers, taking off leaf by leaf and dipping it into the sauce. The solid portion is broken up and eaten with a fork.

ASPARAGUS · the stalks may be taken between the finger and the thumb, if they are not too long, or the green end may be cut off and eaten with a fork, scraping off with the knife what is desired from the remaining part.

BANANAS · the skin should be cut off with a knife, peeling from the top down, while holding it in the hand. Small pieces should be cut or broken off and taken in the fingers, or they may be cut up and eaten with a fork.

BREAD · should be broken into small pieces, buttered, and transferred with the fingers to the mouth. The bread should be placed on the small plate provided for the purpose.

CAKE · is broken into pieces, the size of a mouthful, and then eaten with the fingers or a fork.

CELERY · is eaten with the hands.

CHEESE · is first cut into small bits, then placed on pieces of bread or cracker, and lifted by the fingers to the mouth.

CORN ON THE COB · is eaten with the fingers of one hand. A good plan is to cut off the kernels and eat them with the aid of a fork.

CRACKERS · should be broken into small pieces and eaten with the fingers.

EGGS (RAW) · are usually broken into a glass and eaten with a spoon.

FINGER BOWL · the fingers should be dipped in the water and gently rubbed together, then dried on a napkin.

FISH · should be eaten with a fork held in the right hand and a piece of bread held in the left hand. The bones should be removed from the mouth with the aid of a fork or the fingers. If by the latter, great delicacy should be used.

FRUIT · all raw fruit, except melons, berries, and grapefruit, are eaten with the fingers. Canned fruits are eaten with a spoon.

GRAPES & PLUMS · should be eaten one by one, and the pits allowed to fall noiselessly into the half-closed hand and then transferred to the plate.

KNIFE & FORK · The knife is always held in the right hand, and is only used for cutting the food. The fork is used not only in eating fish, meat, vegetables, and made dishes, but also ices, melons, salads, oysters, clams, lobsters, and terrapins. The knife should never be used to carry food to the mouth.

LETTUCE · leaves should not be cut, but folded up with a fork, and then lifted to the mouth. In the event of these being too large for this treatment, they should be broken into suitable pieces with the fork.

NAPKINS · when in use, are laid on the lap, and, when finished with, are not folded up unless one is a guest for a few days; on all other occasions they are left unfolded. A good plan is to follow the example of the hostess.

——TRADITIONAL ETIQUETTE OF EATING cont.——

OLIVES · are eaten with the fingers.

ORANGES · if served in divided sections, sweetened, and with the seeds removed, should be eaten with the fork. If served whole, cut into suitable portions. Remove seeds and skin.

PEACHES · should be quartered and the quarters peeled, then taken up by the fingers and eaten.

PEAS · are eaten with a fork.

SALT · is best taken up with the tip of the knife.

SALTED NUTS &c · are eaten with the fingers.

SECOND HELPINGS · at formal dinner parties, luncheons, and breakfasts, second helpings are never offered by the host or hostess, and should not be asked for by the guests. This is only permissible at a small dinner party or at the daily family meal. This does not apply to a second glass of water.

SEEDS · should be removed from the mouth with the aid of a fork, or dropped into the half-closed hand.

SPOON · The spoon should never be in the cup while drinking, but should be left in the saucer. It is used in eating grapefruit, fruit salads, small and large fruit (when served with cream), puddings, jellies, porridges, preserves, and boiled eggs.

TOOTHPICKS · should not be used in public. If necessity requires it, raise the napkin over the mouth, with the hand behind it, and use the toothpick as quickly as possible.

TABLE ETIQUETTE

It is correct to take a little of all that is offered, though one may not care for it. Bend slightly over the plate when carrying the food to the mouth, resuming upright position afterward. When drinking from a cup or glass, raise it gracefully to the mouth and sip the contents. Do not empty the vessel at one draught. Guests should not amuse themselves by handling knife or fork, crumbling bread, or leaning their arms on the table. They should sit back in their chairs and assume an easy position. A guest at a dinner should not pass a plate or any article to another guest, or serve the viands, unless asked to do so by the hostess. Upon leaving the table, push the chair back far enough to be out of the way of others.

Accidents, or anything that may be amiss at the table, should be unobserved by a guest unless he is the cause of it. In that event, some pleasant remark as to his awkwardness should be made and no more. The waiter should attend to the matter at once. If a fork or a spoon is dropped, it should not be picked up by the guest, but another used; the waiter should be asked to provide one.

Aim at bright and general conversation, avoiding all personalities and any subject that all cannot join in. This is largely determined by the character of the company. The guests should accommodate themselves to their surroundings.

Extracted from
A Dictionary of Etiquette: A Guide to Polite Usage for All Social Functions
—Walter Cox Green, 1904

——————————— DRESS CODES OF NOTE ———————————

BLACK TIE (or Tuxedo; Smoking Jacket; Dinner Jacket; DJ; *Cravate Noire*) consists of a single- or double-breasted black (or midnight blue) dinner jacket worn with matching trousers with a single row of braid down the leg, a soft white dress shirt, and a black bow tie. (Wing collars, cummerbunds, white jackets, and showy bow ties are to be avoided.) WHITE TIE consists of a black tailcoat worn with matching trousers with a double row of braid down the leg, a white stiff-fronted wing collar shirt, a white vest, and a white bow tie. MORNING DRESS consists of a morning coat, waistcoat, striped gray trousers, and (often) a top hat. Below are some of the more unusual dress codes sometimes found on formal invitations:

Bush shirt . . . . long- or short-sleeved (embroidered) shirt worn outside trousers
Evening dress . . . . white tie
Informal . . . . business suit or jacket with or without tie (not jeans)
Island casual . . . . .Hawaiian shirt and casual (usually khaki) trousers
Lounge suit . . . . business suit and tie
National dress . . . . .self-explanatory; if one has no national dress, a business suit
Planters . . . . .long-sleeved white shirt with a tie and dark trousers
Red Sea Rig; Gulf Rig . . . . .black tie (or business suit) without the jacket
Tenue de Ville . . . . business suit (sometimes national dress)
Tenue Decontractée; Tenue de Détente . . . . smart casual
Tenue de Gala . . . . .black tie
Tenue de Sport/Voyage . . . . sporting/traveling attire
Tenue de Cérémonie . . . . white tie
Windsor Uniform . . . . dark blue evening tails with scarlet at the collar and cuffs

Debate and dispute exist between different sources, and different rules apply in military, academic, and ecclesiastical settings. The above listing follows the tradition of most formal invitations in giving only the requirements for male attire, on the assumption that women have an intuitive understanding of such matters. What Ralph Waldo Emerson said of the English applies: 'they think him the best dressed man, whose dress is so fit for his use that you cannot notice or remember to describe it'.

——————————— PRESIDENTIAL WHITE TIE ———————————

On May 7, 2007, the President and Mrs Bush hosted a State Dinner in the State Dining Room on the State Floor of the White House for Her Majesty Queen Elizabeth II of Great Britain and His Royal Highness The Prince Philip Duke of Edinburgh. The dress code for the event was 'white tie'. According to the White House, this was the first white tie dinner that George W. Bush had hosted as President. Below are some of the recent white tie events held at the White House:

Japan State Dinner	1994	Spain State Dinner	2000
New Year's Eve	1999	Inaugural Balls	1981

When asked about the dinner's dress etiquette, White House social secretary Amy Zantzinger told the *New York Times*, 'I think Mrs Bush is thrilled to have a white-tie dinner, and we'll leave it at that'.

ON FLIRTING DURING DINNER

When you are seated next to a LADY,
you should be only POLITE during the *first course*;
you may be GALLANT in the *second*;
but you must not be TENDER till the *dessert*.

— *New York Mirror*, March 3, 1838

ANONYMOUS ANALYSIS OF AGES

At ten – a CHILD · At twenty – WILD · At thirty – STRONG ... *if ever*
At forty – WISE · At fifty – RICH · At sixty – GOOD ... *or never!*

MANNERS AT A DANCE

Face your partner at a distance of six or eight inches, bodies parallel, shoulders parallel.

If you are leading, place your right hand between the shoulders of your partner, keeping your right elbow well away from your body.

See that above, but not resting on this arm, is your partner's left arm, at right angles with her body, her hand just back of the curve of your shoulder.

Let your left hand, palm up, clasp your partner's right. A line from these hands to the opposite elbows should be parallel with your parallel bodies.

Remember – bobbing and wriggling are taboo. Let the spring come from the ankles and the knees. Imitate the grace of the swallow.

— Advice from
*The National Association
of Dancing Masters*, c.1921

In 1929, the US Children's Bureau (part of the Dept of Labor) commissioned Ella Gardner to explore 'the legal machinery with which communities are endeavoring to protect young people from the evils of the unregulated commercial dance hall'. Gardner's report revealed that 28 States had laws on the operation of public dances, and analyzed ordinances from 416 US cities. Most regulations controlled the licensing of dances; banned minors; prohibited the sale of alcohol; and demanded that dance halls be lit for decency. However, a TIME article from the same year noted some of the more rococo rules: Kansas allowed no unescorted woman within dance halls; Port Arthur, Tex., proscribed gyrations not approved by the *National Association of Dancing Masters*; no man was permitted to rigadoon with another in Muskegon, Wis.; at Lincoln, Neb., patrons were required to keep their bodies at least 6 inches apart at all times; and at Three Enid, Okla., censors could halt a public dance at any time.

A MAXIM OF GOOD MANNERS

In PRIVATE watch your *thoughts* · In your FAMILY watch your *temper*
In your BUSINESS watch your *avarice* · In SOCIETY watch your *tongue*

—————————————TWO-MINUTE SILENCE—————————————

At 9:45am on April 23, 2007, Virginia Tech students and staff observed a 'moment of silence'. At 9:46, 32 white balloons (one for each fatality) were released to the tolling of a bell. In observing this silence, Virginia Tech was following over a century of tradition – although the duration of commemorative silences (one minute, two, or longer) has a curious history. ❧ On May 8, 1919, the Australian journalist Edward George Honey wrote to the *London Evening News* (under the pseudonym Warren Foster) proposing a silence to mark those who had died in WWI. The letter piqued the curiosity of King George V, who, on November 7, 1919, issued this proclamation:

TO ALL MY PEOPLE

Tuesday next, November 11, is the first anniversary of the Armistice, which stayed the world-wide carnage of the four preceding years and marked the victory of Right and Freedom. I believe that my people in every part of the Empire fervently wish to perpetuate the memory of that Great Deliverance, and of those who laid down their lives to achieve it. To afford an opportunity for the universal express of this feeling it is my desire and hope that at the hour when the Armistice came into force, the eleventh hour of the eleventh day of the eleventh month, there may be, for the brief space of two minutes, a complete suspension of all our normal activities. During that time, except in the rare cases where this may be impractical, all work, all sound, and all locomotion should cease, so that, in perfect stillness, the thoughts of every one may be concentrated on reverent remembrance of the Glorious Dead. ... I believe that we shall all gladly interrupt our business and pleasure, whatever it may be, and unite in this simple service of Silence and Remembrance. GEORGE R.I.

George V's choice of a two-minute silence seems to have had no modern Western precedent – certainly there appears to be no mention of such a thing in the London *Times* or *New York Times*† prior to 1919. But this duration was not chosen at whim. Honey originally proposed five minutes' silence, and it was this duration that George V tested with Grenadier Guards at Buckingham Palace. Clearly, the sight of highly trained soldiers standing to attention for five minutes was enough to convince the King that his people needed a less daunting target. ❧ In recent years, some have looked askance at what they perceive to be an 'inflation' in silence. They argue that prolonging the duration of silence undermines its symbolism and invites unedifying comparisons of human tragedy. However, if recent commemorations are any guide, it seems that one- and two-minute silences are often now considered insufficient:

USA, 2005 · *to commemorate the 2003 death of 7 Columbia astronauts* ...... 3 mins
Worldwide, 2006 · *to commemorate the SE Asian tsunami* .... 3 mins
N. Ireland Assembly, 1998 · *1st anniversary of the Omagh bombing* .... 4 mins
Spain, 2005 · *1st anniversary of the Madrid train bombings* .... 5 mins
Spain, 2004 · *1 day after the Madrid train bombings* .... 10 mins
Iraq, 2007 · *1st anniversary of the Askariya Shrine bombing, Samarra* .... 15 mins

† On April 18, 1920, the *New York Times* reported that 24,000,000 miles of cable connecting 12,000,000 telephones were disconnected for a minute at noon, as a mark of respect for the funeral of Theodore N. Vail, chairman of the board of the American Telephone and Telegraph Company.

——————AMERICAN RELIGIOUS IDENTIFICATION——————

US religious affiliation, according to the 2006 Baylor University Religion Survey:

Religion	% of Americans		
Evangelical Protestant	33·6	Non-affiliated	10·8
Mainline Protestant	22·1	Black Protestant	5·0
Catholic	21·2	Other [Mormon, Muslim, &c.]	4·9
		Jewish	2·5

The percentage of various demographic groups that identify with these religions:

%	Black Prot	Evan. Prot	Main. Prot	Catholic	Jewish	Other	None
Male	2·8	30·0	22·1	23·8	2·5	6·0	12·8
Female	6·9	36·7	22·1	18·9	2·4	3·9	9·0
White	0·0	35·4	24·1	22·8	2·6	4·3	10·8
Black	62·5	9·5	7·7	5·0	3·7	6·0	5·7
East	5·0	13·1	26·0	35·1	4·7	4·6	11·6
South	7·2	50·3	19·3	11·5	1·9	2·7	7·1
Midwest	5·6	33·7	26·0	22·1	1·4	3·0	8·3
West	1·3	31·7	17·7	19·2	2·2	10·3	17·6

——————————THE 4 GODS——————————

A 2006 Baylor University survey polled Americans about their beliefs in God, including God's characteristics and behavior. Researchers analyzed the results to determine how engaged in the world Americans believed God to be, and whether or not they thought God was angry at humanity's sins. Researchers claimed the results showed that Americans tended to believe in 1 of the 4 following types of God:

Authoritarian · God is very involved in people's 'daily lives and world affairs'; God will punish those who are unfaithful; God is responsible for economic depressions and natural disasters.

Benevolent · God is involved in daily life but is not angry or wrathful, and is mostly a positive force.

Critical · God observes the world and is unhappy with it, but does not get involved in daily affairs; 'divine justice may not be of this world'.

Distant · God is not involved in the world and is not angry, but is rather a 'cosmic force which sets the law of nature in motion'.

The percentage of all Americans who believe in each type of God was as follows:

Authoritarian God	Benevolent God	Critical God	Distant God
31·4%	23·0%	16·0%	24·4%

The Baylor survey found that women tend to believe in an *authoritarian* or a *benevolent* God, while most men believe in a *distant* or *critical* God. Easterners were found to believe in a *critical* God, Southerners an *authoritarian* God, Midwesterners a *benevolent* God, and Westerners a *distant* God.

--------------------------- FREQUENCY OF PRAYER ---------------------------

Since 1983, the General Social Survey has asked Americans how often they pray:

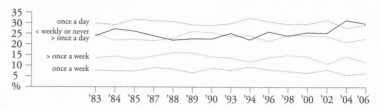

--------------------------- BENEDICT XVI & LIMBO ---------------------------

In April 2007, after a three-year study by the Vatican's International Theological Commission, Pope Benedict XVI abolished the state of limbo. The Roman Catholic concept of limbo was first introduced by medieval theologians to explain the fate of innocent infants who died unbaptized. (The word derives from the Latin *in limbo* – referring to limbo's position 'on the edge' of hell, where those who die without sin but before baptism rest.) Two forms of limbo were traditionally distinguished: *limbus patrum*, for the souls of Old Testament prophets and holy people who died before Christ's salvation; and *limbus infantium*, for babies who died before being baptized. The Theological Commission said in their report that, 'grace has priority over sin and the exclusion of innocent babies from heaven does not seem to reflect Christ's special love for the little ones'. However, the Commission warned that their conclusions did not question 'original sin', and should not be interpreted so as 'to negate the necessity of baptism or delay the conferral of the sacrament'.

--------------------------- DOCTORS & FAITH ---------------------------

91% of US doctors believe that religion and spirituality influence patient health, according to a 2007 study by University of Chicago researchers, published in the *Archives of Internal Medicine*. Only 1% of doctors said such influence was negative; 85% said it was positive (12% said it was equally good and bad; 2% said it had no effect). The study also revealed the % of US doctors who believed the following:

Doctors who believed ...   %
Religion/spirituality often/always helps patients endure illness 76
Religion/spirit. often/always gives patients a positive, hopeful state of mind..... 74
Illness often/always increases patients' focus on religion/spirituality.............. 64
Patients often/always receive support from their religious community 55
God or another supernatural being sometimes intervenes in patients' health 54
Religion/spirituality helps prevent 'hard' medical events (e.g., heart attacks) 39
Religion/spirit. sometimes causes guilt, anxiety, &c., which increases suffering.. 38
Religion/spirit. sometimes leads patients to refuse/delay/stop medical therapy .. 30
Patients sometimes use religion/spirit. to avoid responsibility for their health ...29

——————————— NEW SAINTS ———————————

A Roman Catholic saint is one who has been declared worthy of 'public veneration' throughout the Church via canonization – a lengthy and complex procedure, often spanning centuries, which depends on evidence of a candidate's exceptional sanctity, as well as proof of several miracles. (Canonization is distinct from beatification, in which the Church grants permission to venerate an individual with the titular suffix 'Blessed', but only within a particular diocese or other specified area.) Pope Benedict XVI canonized the following saints between October 2006–June 2007:

RAFAEL GUÍZAR VALENCIA
(1878–1938 · § 10·15·2006)
A Mexican priest persecuted by the revolutionary movement, he founded a religious newspaper in 1911, and was elected Bishop of Veracruz in 1919. There he helped victims of a massive earthquake, and later operated a Mexico City seminary in secret for 15 years.

FILIPPO SMALDONE
(1848–1923 · § 10·15·2006)
Known for his work among the deaf-mutes of Italy, he founded several institutes throughout the country; his Lecce institute became the basis for the Congregation of the Salesian Sisters of the Sacred Hearts. He later worked with blind children, orphans, and the abandoned.

ROSA VENERINI
(1656–1728 · § 10·15·2006)
Dedicated to the education of women as a means of cultural, spiritual, and moral improvement, she founded 'the first public school for girls in Italy', in Viterbo in 1685, and went on to found 40 more schools before her death.

THEODORE GUÉRIN
(1798–1856 · § 10·15·2006)
A French nun who led the missionary Sisters of Providence to Indiana in 1840, where she founded several schools, including Saint Mary-of-the-Woods College (now the nation's oldest Catholic college for women).

FR. ANTÔNIO DE SANT'ANA GALVÃO
(1739–1822 · § 5·11·2007)
A Franciscan monk who founded Our Lady of the Conception of Divine Providence in 1774, and the St Clare Friary in Sorocaba, São Paulo, in 1811. The Church reportedly credits him with 5,000 miracle cures.

GEORGE PRECA
(1880–1962 · § 6·3·2007)
A Maltese priest who founded the Society of Christian Doctrine (a group of evangelical laypeople), and was known for spreading the gospel throughout the Maltese Islands.

SIMON OF LIPNICA
(c.1435–82 · § 6·3·2007)
A Polish preacher who fearlessly ministered to the sick during Krakow's plague epidemic in 1482–83, before himself succumbing.

FR. CHARLES OF ST ANDREW
(1821–93 · § 6·3·2007)
A Passionist priest known as the 'Saint of Mt Argus', he worked in England and Ireland and was known both for his great virtue and his miraculous cures.

MARIE EUGENIE OF JESUS MILLERET
(1817–98 · § 6·3·2007)
Dedicated to education and social issues, she founded the Religious of the Assumption in Paris in 1839. The congregation is still active.

The death of John Paul II prompted immediate calls of '*Santo Subito*' ['saint now'] in St Peter's Square. On May 9, 2005, Benedict XVI formally waived the usual five-year waiting period so that the processes of collecting evidence supporting beatification and canonization could begin immediately. In April 2007, the Vatican announced that the beatification process for JPII was 'advancing rapidly'.

THE VEIL

Akin with many faiths, Islam requires its followers to be modest in their dress. Traditionally, Muslim men cover themselves from navel to knee. As for women, Surah 24:31 of the Koran says, '*And say to the believing women that they should lower their gaze and guard their modesty; that they should not display their beauty and ornaments except what (must ordinarily) appear thereof; that they should draw their veils over their bosoms and not display their beauty*'. However, the extent that this and other passages oblige Muslim women to wear veils is hotly debated within Islam – not least because of the gradations of modesty that different veils afford. The *Hijab* is usually a simple scarf, wrapped around the head and neck, that leaves the face exposed. The *Niqab* covers all of the head and face, leaving exposed only the eyes (though some will also wear an eye-veil). The *Burka* covers the entire head, face, and body, leaving just a fine mesh eye-veil through which the wearer can see. ❦ In late 2006 and 2007, the veils worn by Muslim women became a major flashpoint of public debate in Britain. In October 2006, Jack Straw, then Leader of the House of Commons, requested that constituents visiting his office in Blackburn (where about 25% are Muslim) remove their *Niqabs* so that he could speak to them 'face-to-face'. The ensuing controversy highlighted tensions between sections of the Islamic community and secular society, and demonstrated the complexity of public opinion in regard to religious symbols. ❦ Although the veil has yet to become a subject of major public discussion in the US, a May 2007 Pew survey found that 51% of Muslim Americans were 'very' or 'somewhat' worried that women wearing *Hijabs* were discriminated against because the garment identified them as Muslim – a finding that may augur future debate. And, the discussion is also not limited to Western countries: in May 2007 the *Economist* noted that 'in every corner of the Muslim world, female attire is stirring strong emotions' – citing poles of opinion from Iran, where women are not safe on the streets without the *Hijab*, to Turkey, where civil servants are banned from covering their hair at work. As Islam grows in popularity and the borders of the 'Muslim world' become more diffuse, the debate over the veil (and associated debates over tolerance, integration, human rights, and the rights of women) is likely to become ever more pertinent.

BELIEF IN GOD &c.

A 2007 Gallup poll asked US adults about their belief in God, and other entities:

Americans who say they believe in ...	%		
God	86	Angels	75
Heaven	81	The Devil	70
		Hell	69

Though 86% say they believe in God when given a 'yes/no' choice, only 78% believe in God when given the option to believe in 'a universal spirit or higher power' (then, 14% believe in such a being).

———THE MOTHERS' UNION TEN COMMANDMENTS———

The Mothers' Union is a Christian organization with 3·6m members worldwide. In October 2006, the Union published a booklet entitled *Fair Enough?*, which proposed ten modern 'commandments' to aid the poor and fight climate change:

[1] Turn off the television and other electrical equipment at the socket. [2] Use energy-efficient light bulbs [see p.15]. [3] Use computers less. [4] Turn down the central heating by one degree centigrade. [5] Reduce plane travel. [6] Use public transport. [7] Buy secondhand clothes and other goods. [8] Switch to ethically registered banks and investments. [9] Use local shops which stock fair-trade, vegetarian, and organic produce. [10] Reuse and recycle everything where possible.

———————THE TEN COMMANDMENTS———————

Exodus 20:1–17 ❧ And God spake all these words, saying, ❧ I am the Lord thy God, which have brought thee out of the land of Egypt, out of the house of bondage. ❧ Thou shalt have no other gods before me. ❧ Thou shalt not make unto thee any graven image, or any likeness of any thing that is in heaven above, or that is in the earth beneath, or that is in the water under the earth: ❧ Thou shalt not bow down thyself to them, nor serve them: for I the Lord thy God am a jealous God, visiting the iniquity of the fathers upon the children unto the third and fourth generations of them that hate me; ❧ And showing mercy unto thousands of them that love me, and keep my commandments. ❧ Thou shalt not take the name of the Lord thy God in vain; for the Lord will not hold him guiltless that taketh his name in vain. ❧ Remember the sabbath day, to keep it holy. ❧ Six days shalt thou labor, and do all thy work: ❧ But the seventh day is the sabbath of the Lord thy God: in it thou shalt not do any work, thou, nor thy son, nor thy daughter, thy manservant, nor thy maidservant, nor thy cattle, nor thy stranger that is within thy gates: ❧ For in six days the Lord made heaven and earth, the sea, and all that in them is, and rested the seventh day: wherefore the Lord blessed the sabbath day, and hallowed it. ❧ Honor thy father and thy mother: that thy days may be long upon the land which the Lord thy God giveth thee. ❧ Thou shalt not kill. ❧ Thou shalt not commit adultery. ❧ Thou shalt not steal. ❧ Thou shalt not bear false witness against thy neighbor. ❧ Thou shalt not covet thy neighbor's house, thou shalt not covet thy neighbor's wife, nor his manservant, nor his maidservant, nor his ox, nor his ass, nor any thing that is thy neighbor's.

———————THE WAY AHEAD GROUP———————

The British Royal family established the Way Ahead Group several years before Diana's death to safeguard the monarchy through modernization. The group, chaired by the Queen, has pioneered a range of reforms, including volunteering the Queen pay tax, and opening Buckingham Palace to the public. In April 2007, the *News of the World* reported that Prince William's (temporary?) split from girlfriend Kate Middleton was formalized at a meeting of the Way Ahead Group, at Windsor Castle.

─────────────── BELIEF IN THE PARANORMAL ───────────────

Americans who believe ...	%
Dreams can sometimes foretell the future or reveal hidden truths	52†
People on Earth are sometimes possessed by the devil	42‡
Ancient advanced civilizations, such as Atlantis, once existed	41†
In extrasensory perception (ESP)	41‡
Places can be haunted	37†
Spirits of dead people can come back in certain places/situations (ghosts)	32‡
Minds can communicate without using traditional senses (telepathy)	31‡
It is possible to influence the world through the mind alone (telekinesis)	28†
In the power of the mind to know the past/predict the future (clairvoyance)	26‡
Some UFOs are probably spaceships from other worlds	25†
The position of the stars and planets can affect people's lives (astrology)	25‡
Extra-terrestrial beings have visited Earth at some time in the past	24‡
Witches exist	21‡
It is possible to communicate with the dead	20†
In the rebirth of the soul in a new body after death (reincarnation)	20‡
Creatures such as Bigfoot and the Loch Ness Monster will one day be discovered by science	18†
Astrologers, palm readers, tarot card readers, fortune-tellers, and psychics can foresee the future	13†
A 'spirit-being' can temporarily take control of body (channeling)	9‡

[Sources: † Bayor Religion Survey, 2006; ‡ Gallup Poll, 2005]

─────────────── SURVEY OF JEWISH OPINION ───────────────

Below are selected results from the American Jewish Committee's Annual Survey of
Jewish Opinion, which was conducted in 2006 among a national sample of Jews:

Jews who identify as ...	%		
Conservative	33	Orthodox	8
Reform	31	Reconstructionist	2

[2% were not sure; 24% said 'just Jewish'.]

The following percent of Jews say they ...	%
Belong to a synagogue or temple	53
Feel being Jewish is 'very important' in their life	61 [28% 'fairly'; 10% 'not very']
Consider themselves Democrats	54 [15% Republican; 29% independent]
Think the US should have stayed out of Iraq	65
Approve of how the Israeli government handled the 2007 Hezbollah conflict	55
Favor the establishment of a Palestinian state	54
Agree 'the West and the Muslim world are engaged in a clash of civilizations'	64
Don't think a time will come when 'Israel & the Arabs will be able to settle their differences and live in peace'	56
Agree that 'caring about Israel is a very important part of my being a Jew'	74
Feel 'very close' to Israel	37 [37% 'fairly close'; 16% 'fairly distant'; 6% 'very distant']

———————COUNTRIES OF RELIGIOUS CONCERN———————

The 1998 *International Religious Freedom Act* requires that the State Department conduct an annual review of religious freedom worldwide, and enumerate any 'Countries of Particular Concern' (CPC). Such countries are those considered to engage in 'systematic, ongoing, and egregious' violations of religious freedom, based on information provided to the State Department by local NGOs, religious groups, journalists, human rights officials, academics, and others. These violations may include torture, prolonged detention without charge, the disappearance of persons, and other abuses. In November 2006, Vietnam was removed after 2 years on the list; US officials cited 'significant improvements towards advancing religious freedom', including laws prohibiting 'forced renunciations' of belief. Below, the 2006 CPCs:

Burma.........*[year designated CPC]* 1999	North Korea......................2001
China...............................1999	Saudi Arabia......................2004
Eritrea............................2004	Sudan..............................1999
Iran................................1999	Uzbekistan 2006

————————————TEMPLETON PRIZE————————————

Canadian philosopher Charles Taylor was awarded 2007's *Templeton Prize for Progress Toward Research or Discoveries About Spiritual Realities*. A professor at Northwestern University, Illinois, and professor emeritus at McGill University, Montreal, Taylor's work has focused on the need to address the spiritual dimensions of human existence, particularly when considering social problems such as bigotry and violence. 'We have somehow to break down the barriers between our contemporary culture of science and disciplined academic study ... on one hand, and the domain of spirit, on the other,' he said during the award's announcement, March 14, 2007, in New York. (The award was presented at a private Buckingham Palace ceremony on May 2, 2007.) ❦ Sir John Templeton founded his eponymous prize in 1972, 'to encourage and honor the advancement of knowledge in spiritual matters'. The prize (currently $1·5m) is said to be the richest annual monetary prize of any kind given to an individual. Templeton stipulated its value always be greater than the Nobel Prize, to 'underscore that research and advances in spiritual discoveries can be quantifiably more significant than disciplines recognized' by the Nobels.

————————————VETERANS' HEADSTONES————————————

The Dept of Veterans Affairs (VA) 'furnishes upon request, at no charge to the applicant, a government headstone or marker for the grave of any deceased eligible veteran in any cemetery around the world'. Strict regulations govern the style and wording of these headstones, including which 'emblems of belief' are acceptable. In April 2007, in settlement of a lawsuit, the VA agreed to add the Wiccan pentacle (a five-pointed star within a circle) to the list of 38 approved emblems, which includes a range of religious crosses, the Star of David, and the Muslim crescent and star.

Ephemerides

God sees their sins ... and in his Ephemerides
his Journals, he writes them downe.
— JOHN DONNE (1572–1631)

2008

Roman numerals............. MMVIII	Indian (Saka) year......1930 (Mar 21)
English Regnal year[1] .....56th (Feb 6)	Sikh year ... 340 Nanakshahi Era (Mar 14)
Dominical Letter[2]..................FE	Jewish year ....5769 (Sep 30)
Epact[3] XXII	Roman year [AUC] ......2761 (Apr 21)
Golden Number (Lunar Cycle)[4] ..XIV	Masonic year.................6008 AL[5]
Chinese New Year....Rat 4706 (Feb 7)	Knights Templar year........ 890 AO[6]
Hindu New Year.......2064 (Mar 22)	Baha'i year................165 (Mar 21)
Islamic year.............1429 (Jan 10)	Queen bee color.....................red

[1] The number of years from the accession of a monarch; traditionally, legislation was dated by the Regnal year of the reigning monarch. [2] A way of categorizing years to facilitate the calculation of Easter. If January 1 is a Sunday, the Dominical letter for the year will be A; if January 2 is a Sunday it will be B; and so on. [3] The number of days by which the solar year exceeds the lunar year. [4] The number of the year (1–19) in the 19-year Metonic cycle; it is used in the calculation of Easter, and is found by adding 1 to the remainder left after dividing the number of the year by 19. [5] Anno Lucis, the 'Year of Light' when the world was formed. [6] Anno Ordinis, the 'Year of the Order'.

ON CHARACTER & THE EYES

The long, almond-shaped eye with thick eyelids covering nearly half of the pupil, when taken in connection with the full brow, is indicative of GENIUS, and is often found in artists, literary, and scientific men. It is the eye of TALENT, or IMPRESSIBILITY. The large, open, transparent eye, of whatever color, is indicative of ELEGANCE, of TASTE, of REFINEMENT, of WIT, and of INTELLIGENCE. Weakly marked eyebrows indicate a FEEBLE CONSTITUTION and a tendency to MELANCHOLIA. Deep sunken eyes are SELFISH, while eyes in which the whole iris shows indicate ERRATICISM, if not LUNACY. Round eyes are indicative of INNOCENCE; strongly protuberant eyes of WEAKNESS of both MIND and BODY. Eyes small and close together typify CUNNING, while those far apart and open indicate FRANKNESS. The normal distance between the eyes is the width of one eye; a distance greater or less than this intensifies the character supposed to be symbolized. Sharp angles, turning down at the corners of the eyes, are seen in persons of ACUTE JUDGMENT and PENETRATION. Well-opened steady eyes belong to the SINCERE; wide staring eyes to the IMPERTINENT. [Anonymous, *c.*1830?]

——————————— FEDERAL HOLIDAYS ———————————

According to the US Office of Personnel Management, federal law (5 USC 6103) establishes the following public holidays for federal employees. Most federal employees work on a Monday-through-Friday schedule. For these employees, when a holiday falls on a nonworkday, Saturday or Sunday, the holiday is usually observed on Monday (if the holiday falls on a Sunday) or Friday (if on a Saturday).

Holiday	2008	2009	2010	2011
New Year's Day	Jan 1	Jan 1	Jan 1	Jan 1
BD Martin Luther King Jr	Jan 21	Jan 19	Jan 18	Jan 17
Washington's Birthday	Feb 18	Feb 16	Feb 15	Feb 21
Memorial Day	May 26	May 25	May 31	May 30
Independence Day	Jul 4	Jul 3	Jul 5	Jul 4
Labor Day	Sep 1	Sep 7	Sep 6	Sep 5
Columbus Day	Oct 13	Oct 12	Oct 11	Oct 10
Veterans Day	Nov 11	Nov 11	Nov 11	Nov 11
Thanksgiving Day	Nov 27	Nov 26	Nov 25	Nov 24
Christmas Day	Dec 25	Dec 25	Dec 24	Dec 26

—— TRADITIONAL WEDDING ANNIVERSARY SYMBOLS ——

1st ....Paper	10th ....Tin	35th ....Coral, Jade
2nd ....Cotton	11th ....Steel	40th ....Ruby
3rd...............Leather	12th ....Silk	45th .... Sapphire
4th..........Linen, Silk	13th ....Lace	50th .... Gold
5th...........Wood	14th ....Ivory	55th ....Emerald
6th................. Iron	15th ....Crystal	60th .... Diamond
7th...... Wool, Copper	20th ....China	70th ....Platinum
8th.............. Bronze	25th ....Silver	75th .... Diamond
9th..............Pottery	30th .... Pearl	*British symbols differ*

[Debate rages about the order of paper and cotton, and other symbols exist for certain anniversaries]

——————— KEY TO SYMBOLS USED OVERLEAF ———————

[★ FH] ....US Federal holiday	[§ *patronage*]...................Saint's day
[☉] ....Clocks change (USA)	[WA *year*]......... Wedding anniversary
[UK] .... UK Bank holiday	[Admis *year*].... Admission day [US States]
[ND]...................... National day	☺/● ....New/full moon [GMT]
[NH].................. National holiday	[☄].............Annual meteor shower
[ID *year*].............Independence day	[UN]...............United Nations day
[BD *year*]......................Birthday	[◉].............................Eclipse
[† *year*]............Anniversary of death	[£]...... Union Flag to be flown (UK)

Certain dates are subject to change, or tentative at the time of printing. Zodiac dates are approximate.

─────────── JANUARY ───────────

   Capricorn [♑]   *Birthstone* · GARNET   *Aquarius* [♒]
(Dec 22–Jan 20)   *Flower* · CARNATION   (Jan 21–Feb 19)

1★ .... New Year's Day [★ FH] · J.D. Salinger [BD1919]	Tu
2 .... Isaac Asimov [BD1920] · Georgia [Admis1788]	W
3 .... 'Lord Haw-Haw' [†1946 *executed*] · Alaska [Admis1959]	Th
4 .... Quadrantids [☄] · Utah [Admis1896]	F
5 .... Twelfth night · Catherine de Medici [†1589]	Sa
6 .... Epiphany · Theodore Roosevelt [†1919] · New Mexico [Admis1912]	Su
7 .... Nicolas Cage [BD1964]	M
8 .... ☺ · Wilkie Collins [BD1824] · François Mitterrand [†1996]	Tu
9 .... Katherine Mansfield [†1923] · Connecticut [Admis1788]	W
10 .... Islamic New Year (AH 1429)	Th
11 .... National Unity Day, Nepal [NH] · Thomas Hardy [†1928]	F
12 .... Midwinter, Norway · Pieter Willem Botha [BD1916]	Sa
13 .... Wyatt Earp [†1929]	Su
14 .... Edmond Halley [†1742] · Cecil Beaton [BD1904]	M
15 .... Edward Gibbon [†1794] · Martin Luther King Jr [BD1929]	Tu
16 .... André Michelin [BD1853] · Carole Lombard [†1942 *plane crash*]	W
17 .... St Anthony of Egypt [§ *basket-makers*] · James Earl Jones [BD1931]	Th
18 .... A.A. Milne [BD1882] · Cary Grant [BD1904]	F
19 .... St Henry of Finland [§ *Finland*] · Stefan Edberg [BD1966]	Sa
20 ...... Presidential Inauguration Day · St Sebastian [§ *archers, soldiers & athletes*]	Su
21★ .... Martin Luther King Day [★ FH] · Cecil B. DeMille [†1959]	M
22 .... ☽ · John Hurt [BD1940]	Tu
23 .... St John the Almsgiver · Rutger Hauer [BD1944]	W
24 .... Hadrian [BD AD76]	Th
25 ...... Burns' Night, Scotland · Conversion of St Paul · St Dwyn [§ *lovers*]	F
26 .... Australia Day, Australia [NH] · Michigan [Admis1837]	Sa
27 .... Holocaust Memorial Day · Giuseppe Verdi [†1901]	Su
28 .... Sir Francis Drake [†1596] · Jackson Pollock [BD1912]	M
29 ...... St Julian the Hospitaller [§ *innkeepers and boatmen*] · Kansas [Admis1861]	Tu
30 .... Franklin D. Roosevelt [BD1882]	W
31 .... Anna Pavlova [BD1881] · Norman Mailer [BD1923]	Th

French Rev. calendar ...... *Pluvôse* (rain)	Dutch month ...... *Lauwmaand* (chilly)
Angelic governor .... *Gabriel*	Saxon month .... *Wulf-monath* (wolf)
Epicurean calendar ..... *Marronglaçaire*	Talismanic stone .... *Jasper*

❦ The Latin month *Ianuarius* derives from *ianua* ('door'), since it was the opening of the year. It was also associated with *Janus* – the two-faced Roman god of doors and openings who guarded the gates of heaven. Janus could simultaneously face the year just past and the year to come. ❦ *If January Calends be summerly gay, 'Twill be winterly weather till the calends of May. Janiveer – Freeze the pot upon the fier.* ❦ *He that will live another year, Must eat a hen in Januvere.* ❦ On the stock market, the *January Effect* is the trend of stocks performing especially well that month. ❦

─────────── FEBRUARY ───────────

 Aquarius [♒]   *Birthstone* · AMETHYST   *Pisces* [♓]
(Jan 21–Feb 19)   *Flower* · PRIMROSE   (Feb 20–Mar 20)

1 .... National Freedom Day · Mary Shelley [†1851] .... F
2 .... Candlemas · Groundhog Day [see p.264] .... Sa
3 .... St Blaise [§ *sore throats*] · Felix Mendelssohn [BD1809] .... Su
4 ....Charles Lindbergh [BD1902]............................ M
5 .... Mardi Gras · Bobby Brown [BD1969].................... Tu
6 .... Ash Wednesday · Massachusetts [Admis 1788] .... W
7 .... ☺ · Chinese New Year – Rat · Sir Thomas More [BD1478] .... Th
8 ..... St Jerome Emiliani [§ *abandoned children and orphans*] · Jack Lemmon [BD1925]..... F
9 .... St Apollonia [§ *dentists*] · J.M. Coetzee [BD1940] .... Sa
10 .... St Scholastica [§ *convulsive children*] · Alexander Pushkin [†1837] .... Su
11 .... Burt Reynolds [BD1936] · Sylvia Plath [†1963 *suicide*] .... M
12 .... Abraham Lincoln [BD1809] .... Tu
13 ....St Modomnoc [§ *bee-keepers*] · Georges Simenon [BD1903] .... W
14 .... St Valentine [§ *lovers*] · Arizona [Admis1912] · Oregon [Admis1859]........ Th
15 ....Susan B. Anthony Day · Galileo Galilei [BD1564]....................F
16 ....Lithuania [ID1918] · St Benedict Joseph Labre [§ *tramps*]............. Sa
17 .... Geronimo [†1909] .... Su
18★ ..... Washington's Birthday [★ FH] · Count Alessandro Volta [BD1745]....... M
19 ....Prince Andrew [BD1960] [£] · Nicolaus Copernicus [BD1473].......... Tu
20 ....Dame Marie Rambert [BD1888]........................ W
21.... ◑ · Int. Mother Language Day [UN] · Dame Margot Fonteyn [†1991]....Th
22 .... Feast of Chair of St Peter · George Washington [BD1732] .... F
23 ....George Frideric Handel [BD1685] .... Sa
24 ....Independence Day, Estonia [NH] · HRE Charles V [BD1500].......... Su
25 ....Kuwait [ND] · Dame Myra Hess [BD1890].................... M
26 ....Buffalo Bill [BD1846] · Tex Avery [BD1908] .... Tu
27 ....Dominican Republic [ID1844] · Elizabeth Taylor [BD1932].......... W
28 ....Vincente Minnelli [BD1910] · Henry James [†1916]............... Th
29 ....Gioacchino Rossini [BD1792] · Ludwig I of Bavaria [†1868] .... F

French Rev. calendar..... *Ventôse* (wind)	Dutch month *Sprokelmaand* (vegetation)
Angelic governor...............*Barchiel*	Saxon month...........*Solmonath* (Sun)
Epicurean calendar.... *Harrengsauridor*	Talismanic stone .... *Ruby*

❦ Much mythology and folklore considers February to have the bitterest weather: *February is seldom warm.* ❦ *February, if ye be fair, The sheep will mend, and nothing mair; February, if ye be foul, The sheep will die in every pool.* ❦ *As the day lengthens, the cold strengthens.* ❦ The word 'February' derives from the Latin *februum* – which means cleansing or purification, and reflects the rituals undertaken by the Romans before Spring. ❦ Having only 28 days in non-leap years, February was known in Welsh as '*y mis bach*' – the little month. ❦ February is traditionally personified in pictures either by an old man warming himself by the fireside, or as 'a sturdy maiden, with a tinge of the red hard winter apple on her hardy cheek'. ❦

──────── MARCH ────────

Pisces [♓]   *Birthstone* · BLOODSTONE   *Aries* [♈]
(Feb 20–Mar 20)   *Flower* · JONQUIL   (Mar 21–Apr 20)

1 .... St David [§ *Wales*] · Nebraska [Admis1867] · Ohio [Admis1803] .... Sa
2 ...... Sir Thomas Bodley [BD1545] · Howard Carter [†1939 *curse of the mummy?*] ..... Su
3 .... Doll's Festival, Japan · Florida [Admis1845] .... M
4 .... John Candy [†1994] · Vermont [Admis1791] .... Tu
5 .... St Piran [§ *tin miners*] · Rex Harrison [BD1908] .... W
6 .... Ghana [ID1957] · George Formby [†1961] .... Th
7 ..... ☺ · St Felicity & St Perpetua of Carthage [§ *mothers separated from their children*] .... F
8 ..... Women's Rights & Int. Peace Day [UN] · Kenneth Grahame [BD1859] .... Sa
9 .... DST begins · Victoria 'Vita' Sackville-West [BD1892] .... Su
10 .... Prince Edward [BD1964] [£] · Zelda Fitzgerald [†1948] .... M
11 .... Thora Birch [BD1982] .... Tu
12 .... Jack Kerouac [BD1922] · Anne Frank [†1945] .... W
13 .... William H. Macy [BD1950] .... Th
14 .... St Matilda [§ *parents with many children*] · Karl Marx [†1883] .... F
15 .... Aristotle Onassis [†1975] · Maine [Admis1820] .... Sa
16 .... Palm Sunday · St Urho [§ *Finnish immigrants in America*] .... Su
17 .... St Patrick's Day [§ *Ireland*] · World Maritime Day [UN] .... M
18 .... Wilfred Owen [BD1893] · Luc Besson [BD1959] .... Tu
19 .... Dr David Livingstone [BD1813] .... W
20 .... First Day of Spring · Henrik Ibsen [BD1828] .... Th
21 .... ◗ · Good Friday · Holi (Spring Festival) .... F
22 .... World Day for Water [UN] · Sir Anthony Van Dyck [BD1599] .... Sa
23 .... Easter · World Meteorological Day [UN] .... Su
24 .... St Dunchad [§ *Irish sailors*] · William Morris [BD1834] .... M
25 .... Annunciation Day · Claude Debussy [†1918] .... Tu
26 .... Robert Frost [BD1874] · Tennessee Williams [BD1911] .... W
27 .... Burma – Army Day · Mariah Carey [BD1970] .... Th
28 .... King George I [BD1660] · Dirk Bogarde [BD1921] .... F
29 .... Jennifer Capriati [BD1976] .... Sa
30 .... Warren Beatty [BD1937] · Celine Dion [BD1968] .... Su
31 .... René Descartes [BD1596] · Al Gore [BD1948] .... M

French Rev. cal. ..... *Germinal* (budding)	Dutch month .... *Lentmaand* (spring)
Angelic governor .... *Machidiel*	Saxon month ..... *Hrèth-monath* (rough)
Epicurean calendar .... *Oeufalacoquidor*	Talismanic stone .... *Topaz*

❦ The first month of the Roman year, March is named for Mars, the god of war but also an agricultural deity. ❦ The unpredictability of March weather leads to some confusion (*March has many weathers*), though it is generally agreed that March *comes in like a lion, and goes out like a lamb*. Yet, because March is often too wet for crops to flourish, many considered *a bushel of Marche dust* [a dry March] *is worth a ransom of gold*. ❦ March hares are 'mad' with nothing more than lust, since it is their mating season. ❦ The *Mars* bar is named after its creator Frank Mars. ❦

APRIL

 Aries [♈]
(Mar 21–Apr 20)

Birthstone · DIAMOND
Flower · SWEET PEA

Taurus [♉]
(Apr 21–May 21)

1 . . . . April Fool's Day [except in Canada] · Marvin Gaye [†1984 *shot by father*] . . . . Tu
2 . . . . Hans Christian Andersen [BD1805] . . . . W
3 . . . . Washington Irving [BD1783] · Marlon Brando [BD1924] . . . . Th
4 . . . . Senegal [ID1960] · Linus Yale [BD1821] . . . . F
5 . . . . Pocahontas & John Rolfe [WA1614] · Bette Davis [BD1908] . . . . Sa
6 . . . . ☻ · Richard the Lionheart [†1199] . . . . Su
7 . . . . World Health Day [UN] · William Wordsworth [BD1770] . . . . M
8 . . . . Buddha, Siddhartha Gautama [BD563BC] · Vivienne Westwood [BD1941] . . . Tu
9 . . . . Sir Francis Bacon [†1626] · Hugh Hefner [BD1926] . . . . W
10 . . . . Joseph Pulitzer [BD1847] . . . . Th
11 . . . . St Stanislaw of Krakow [§ *Poland*] · Primo Levi [†1987 *suicide*] . . . . F
12 . . . . St Zeno [§ *Verona*] · Sugar Ray Robinson [†1989] . . . . Sa
13 . . . . Baisakhi Mela (Nanakshahi Calendar) · Catherine de Medici [BD1519] . . . . Su
14 . . . . Julie Christie [BD1940] · Julian Lloyd-Webber [BD1951] . . . . M
15 . . . . Emma Thompson [BD1959] · Greta Garbo [†1990] . . . . Tu
16 . . . . Madame Marie Tussaud [†1850] · Henry Mancini [BD1924] . . . . W
17 . . . . J.P. Morgan [BD1837] · Eddie Cochran [†1960] . . . . Th
18 . . . . Zimbabwe [ID1980] · Thor Heyerdahl [†2002] . . . . F
19 . . . . First Seder Night · Charles Darwin [†1882] . . . . Sa
20 . . . . ● · Passover (Pesach) · Joan Miró [BD1893] . . . . Su
21 . . . . . Queen Elizabeth [BD1926][£] · Charlotte Brontë [BD1816] · Lyrids [☄] . . . . M
22 . . . . Henry Fielding [BD1707] · Vladimir Nabokov [BD1899] . . . . Tu
23 . . . . St George [§ *England*] · World Book & Copyright Day [UN] . . . . W
24 . . . . Anthony Trollope [BD1815] · Wallis Simpson [†1986] . . . . Th
25 . . . . Anzac Day, Australia & New Zealand · St Mark [§ *notaries*] . . . . F
26 . . . . Rudolf Hess [BD1894] · Charles Francis Richter [BD1900] . . . . Sa
27 . . . . Sierra Leone [ID1961] · St Zita [§ *bakers*] · Socrates [†399BC *poisoned*] . . . . Su
28 . . . . Saddam Hussein [BD1937] · Maryland [Admis1788] . . . . M
29 . . . . Daniel Day Lewis [BD1957] · Alfred Hitchcock [†1980] . . . . Tu
30 . . . . Adolf Hitler [†1945 *suicide*] · Louisiana [Admis1812] . . . . W

French Rev. calendar . . . *Floréal* (blossom)	Dutch month . . . . *Grasmaand* (grass)
Angelic governor . . . . *Asmodel*	Saxon month . . . . *Easter-monath*
Epicurean calendar . . . . *Petitpoisidor*	Talismanic stone . . . . *Garnet*

❦ April, T.S. Eliot's 'cruellest month', heralds the start of Spring and is associated with new growth and sudden bursts of rain. ❦ Its etymology might derive from the Latin *aperire* ('to open') – although in Old English it was known simply as the *Eastre-monath*. ❦ *April with his hack and his bill, Plants a flower on every hill.* ❦ The custom of performing pranks and hoaxes on April Fool's Day (or *poisson d'avril* as it is known in France) is long established, although its origins are much disputed. ❦ According to weather folklore, *If it thunders on All Fools' day, it brings good crops of corn and hay.* Usually, cuckoos will first appear in the London *Times* around April 8. ❦

—MAY—

Taurus [♉]   *Birthstone* · EMERALD   *Gemini* [♊]
(Apr 21–May 21)   *Flower* · LILY OF THE VALLEY   (May 22–Jun 22)

1 .... May Day · Joseph Heller [BD1923] .... Th
2 ....Donatella Versace [BD1955] · Oliver Reed [†1999] .... F
3 ....World Press Freedom Day [UN] · James Brown [BD1933]............ Sa
4 ....Tito [†1980] .... Su
5 ....☺ · Children's Day, Japan · Karl Marx [BD1818] · Eta Aquarids [☄] ..... M
6 ....Rudolph Valentino [BD1895] · Tony Blair [BD1953]............... Tu
7 .... Gary Cooper [BD1901] · Edwin Herbert Land [BD1909] .... W
8 ....VE Day · Paul Gauguin [†1903]....................... Th
9 .... Europe Day, European Union · J.M. Barrie [BD1860] .... F
10................St Catald [§ *invoked against plagues, drought & storms*] .... Sa
11 .... Mother's Day · Whit Sunday · Minnesota [Admis1858]............. Su
12.........Dante Gabriel Rossetti [BD1828] · Burt Bacharach [BD1929]......... M
13.................Stevie Wonder [BD1950] · Chet Baker [†1988]................. Tu
14........................Paraguay [ND] · Henry John Heinz [†1919]................. W
15......... International Day of Families [UN] · Pierre Curie [BD1859]......... Th
16....................Liberace [BD1919] · Jim Henson [†1990] .... F
17....................Ascension · Dennis Hopper [BD1936]..................... Sa
18........ International Museum Day · Dame Margot Fonteyn [BD1919] .... Su
19................. Victoria Day, Canada · T.E. Lawrence [†1935]................ M
20......● · Honoré de Balzac [BD1799] · Dame Barbara Hepworth [†1975] .....Tu
21.................... Mr T [BD1952] · Sir John Gielgud [†2000].................... W
22.......Int. Day for Biological Diversity [UN] · Laurence Olivier [BD1907] ......Th
23............John D. Rockefeller [†1937] · South Carolina [Admis1788] .... F
24....................Gabriel Fahrenheit [BD1686] .... Sa
25.................... Jordan [ID1946] · Miles Davis [BD1926] .... Su
26★ ....Memorial Day [★FH] · Zola Budd [BD1966] .... M
27............... John Calvin [†1564] · Henry Kissinger [BD1923] .... Tu
28....................Ethiopia [ND] · Ian Fleming [BD1908]..................... W
29................Rhode Island [Admis1790] · Wisconsin [Admis1848]................ Th
30.........St Walstan [§ *agriculture*] · Henry VIII & Jane Seymour [WA1536] .... F
31.....The Visitation of the Blessed Virgin Mary · Clint Eastwood [BD1930] .... Sa

French Rev. cal. ....*Prairial* (meadow)	Dutch month ...... *Blowmaand* (flower)
Angelic governor...............*Ambriel*	Saxon month...... *Trimilchi* [see below]
Epicurean calendar...........*Aspergial*	Talismanic stone ....*Emerald*

❦ Named after *Maia*, the goddess of growth, May is considered a joyous month, as Milton wrote: 'Hail bounteous May that dost inspire Mirth and youth, and warm desire'. ❦ However, May has long been thought a bad month in which to marry: *who weds in May throws it all away*. ❦ Anglo-Saxons called May *thrimilce*, since in May cows could be milked three times a day. ❦ May was thought a time of danger for the sick; so to have *climbed May hill* was to have survived the month. ❦ Kittens born in May were thought weak, and were often drowned. ❦

——————————— JUNE ———————————

Gemini [♊]   *Birthstone* · PEARL   *Cancer* [♋]
(May 22–Jun 22)   *Flower* · ROSE   (Jun 23–Jul 23)

1 .... Kentucky [Admis1792] · Tennessee [Admis1796] .... Su
2 .... Coronation of Elizabeth II [1953] [£] · Thomas Hardy [BD1840] .... M
3 .... ☺ · St Kevin [§ *blackbirds*] · Josephine Baker [BD1906] .... Tu
4 .... Kaiser Wilhelm II [†1941] .... W
5 .... World Environment Day [UN] · Adam Smith [BD1723] .... Th
6 .... D Day (1944) · Captain Robert Falcon Scott [BD1868] .... F
7 .... Malta [ND] · Dean Martin [BD1917] · E.M. Forster [†1970] .... Sa
8 .... St Medard [§ *good weather, prisoners, & toothaches*] .... Su
9 .... Feast of Weeks (Shavuot) · Cole Porter [BD1891] .... M
10 .... HRH Prince Philip [BD1921] [£] · Judy Garland [BD1922] .... Tu
11 .... Paul McCartney & Heather Mills [WA2002] .... W
12 .... Russia [ID1990] · Gregory Peck [†2003] .... Th
13. St Anthony of Padua [§ *horses, mules, & donkeys*] · Harriet Beecher Stowe [BD1811] .. F
14 .... Flag Day · Jerome K. Jerome [†1927] .... Sa
15 .... Father's Day · Edvard Grieg [BD1843] · Arkansas [Admis1836] .... Su
16 .... Bloomsday (*Ulysses*) · Stan Laurel [BD1890] .... M
17 .... St Botulph [§ *agricultural workers*] · John Wesley [BD1703] .... Tu
18 .... ☽ · Seychelles [ND] · Paul McCartney [BD1942] .... W
19 .... Salman Rushdie [BD1947] .... Th
20 .... First Day of Summer · West Virginia [Admis1863] .... F
21 .... Jean-Paul Sartre [BD1905] · New Hampshire [Admis1788] .... Sa
22 .... Meryl Streep [BD1949] · Dan Brown [BD1964] .... Su
23 .... Midsummer Eve · Vespasian [†AD79] .... M
24 .... Midsummer Day · St Jean Baptiste Day, Canada .... Tu
25 .... George Orwell [BD1903] · Virginia [Admis1788] .... W
26 .... United Nations Charter Day [UN] · Pearl S. Buck [BD1892] .... Th
27 .... Vera Wang [BD1949] · Isabelle Adjani [BD1955] .... F
28 .... Mel Brooks [BD1926] .... Sa
29 .... St Paul [§ *authors*] · Fatty Arbuckle [†1933] .... Su
30 .... St Theobald [§ *bachelors*] .... M

French Rev. cal. .... *Messidor* (harvest)	Dutch month ... *Zomermaand* (Summer)
Angelic governor .... *Muriel*	Saxon month .... *Sere-monath* (dry)
Epicurean calendar .... *Concombrial*	Talismanic stone .... *Sapphire*

❦ June is probably derived from *iuvenis* ('young'), but it is also linked to the goddess *Juno*, who personifies young women. In Scots Gaelic, the month is known as *Ian t-òg-mbìos*, the 'young month'; and in Welsh, as *Mehefin*, the 'middle'. ❦ According to weather lore, *Calm weather in June, Sets corn in tune.* ❦ To 'june' a herd of animals is to drive them in a brisk or lively manner. ❦ Wilfred Gowers-Round asserts that 'June is the reality of the Poetic's claims for May'. ❦ In parts of South Africa the verb 'to june-july' is slang for shaking or shivering with fear – because these months, while summer in the north, are midwinter in the south. ❦

—— JULY ——

Cancer [♋]	*Birthstone* · RUBY	*Leo* [♌]
(Jun 23–Jul 23)	*Flower* · LARKSPUR	(Jul 24–Aug 23)

1 .Canada Day, Canada [NH] · Somalia [ND] . . . . .Tu
2 . . . . .Amelia Earhart [†1937 *disappeared over the Pacific*] . . . . W
3 . . . . . . ☺ · Tom Cruise [BD1962] · Jim Morrison [†1971] · Idaho [Admis1890] . . . . .Th
4★ . . . . .Independence Day [★FH] · Louis Armstrong [BD1901] . . . . F
5 . . . . Cape Verde [ID1975] · Sir Thomas Stamford Raffles [†1826] . . . . Sa
6 . . . . Kenneth Grahame [†1932] · Sylvester Stallone [BD1946] . . . . Su
7 . . . . Gustav Mahler [BD1860] · Marc Chagall [BD1887] . . . . M
8 . . . . John D. Rockefeller [BD1839] . . . . .Tu
9 . . . . Edward Heath [BD1916] · David Hockney [BD1937] . . . . W
10 . . . Camille Pissarro [BD1830] · Arthur Ashe [BD1943] · Wyoming [Admis1890] . . .Th
11 . . . . World Population Day [UN] · St Benedict [§ *inflammatory diseases*] . . . . F
12 .Kiribati [ID1979] · Yul Brynner [BD1915] . . . . Sa
13 . . . . St Margaret [§ *expectant mothers*] . . . . Su
14 . . . . .Bastille Day, France · Gustav Klimt [BD1862] . . . . M
15 . . . . St Swithin's Day · Rembrandt [BD1606] . . . . Tu
16 . . . . . . Feast of Our Lady of Mount Carmel · Roald Amundsen [BD1872] . . . . . . W
17 . . . . Adam Smith [†1790] · Billie Holiday [†1959] . . . . .Th
18 . . . . ☽ · Richard Branson [BD1950] · Nick Faldo [BD1957] . . . . F
19 . . . . Edgar Degas [BD1834] . . . . Sa
20 . . . . St Wilgefortis [§ *difficult marriages*] · Sir Edmund Hillary [BD1919] . . . . Su
21 . . . . .Belgium [ND] · Baron von Reuter [BD1816] . . . . M
22 . . . . .St Mary Magdalene [§ *hairdressers & repentant women*] . . . . Tu
23 . . . . .St Bridget of Sweden [§ *Sweden*] · Montgomery Clift [†1966] . . . . W
24 . . . Simon Bolivar Day, Venezuela & Ecuador · Alexandre Dumas [BD1802] . . .Th
25 . . . . St James [§ *laborers*] · Charles Macintosh [†1843] . . . . F
26 . . . . .George Bernard Shaw [BD1856] · New York [Admis1788] . . . . Sa
27 . . . . St Aurelius [§ *orphans*] . . . . Su
28 . . . . Beatrix Potter [BD1866] · Delta Aquarids (South) [☄] . . . . M
29 . . . . .St Martha [§ *cooks*] · Mama Cass Elliot [†1974] . . . . Tu
30 . . . . ☺ · Emily Brontë [BD1818] · Otto von Bismarck [†1898] . . . . W
31 . . . . St Ignatius of Loyola [§ *those on spiritual exercises*] . . . . .Th

French Rev. calendar... *Thermidor* (heat)	Dutch month . . . .*Hooymaand* (hay)
Angelic governor . . . . *Verchiel*	Saxon month . . . .*Mæd-monath* (meadow)
Epicurean calendar . . . . *Melonial*	Talismanic stone . . . . *Diamond*

❦ July was originally called *Quintilis* (from *Quintus* – meaning 'fifth'), but it was renamed by Mark Antony to honor the murdered Julius Caesar, who was born on July 12. ❦ *A swarm of bees in May is worth a load of Hay; A swarm of bees in June is worth a silver spoon; But a swarm of bees in July is not worth a fly.* ❦ *If the first of July be rainy weather, 'Twill rain mair or less for forty days together.* ❦ *Bow-wow, dandy fly – Brew no beer in July.* ❦ July used to be known as the thunder month, and some churches rang their bells in the hope of driving away thunder and lightning. ❦

---——AUGUST——---

 Leo [♌]   *Birthstone* · AGATE   *Virgo* [♍]
(Jul 24–Aug 23)   *Flower* · GLADIOLUS   (Aug 23–Sep 23)

1 .... ☻ · St Alphonsus [§ *confessors & theologians*] · Colorado [Admis 1876] .... F
2 .... Louis Bleriot [†1936] · Wes Craven [BD 1939] .... Sa
3 ....Tony Bennett [BD 1926] .... Su
4 .... Civic Holiday, Canada · Percy Bysshe Shelley [BD 1792] .... M
5 .... Richard Burton [†1984] .... Tu
6 ....Delta Aquarids (North) [☄] · Lucille Ball [BD 1911] .... W
7 ....Labor Day, Western Samoa · St Cajetan [§ *the unemployed*]............. Th
8 .... St Dominic [§ *astronomers*] .... F
9 .... International Day of the World's Indigenous People [UN]........... Sa
10 .... Herbert Hoover [BD 1874] · Missouri [Admis 1821] .... Su
11 ....Edith Wharton [†1937] · Jackson Pollock [†1956]................ M
12 .... Perseids [☄] · Pete Sampras [BD 1971] .... Tu
13 ....William Caxton [BD 1422] · H.G. Wells [†1946]................ W
14 .... Pakistan [ID 1947] · René Goscinny [BD 1926] .... Th
15 ....VJ Day (1945) · Assumption Day · Princess Anne [BD 1950] [£]......... F
16 .... ● · St Stephen the Great [§ *bricklayers*] · Bela Lugosi [†1956]........... Sa
17 ....Robert De Niro [BD 1943] · Ira Gershwin [†1983] .... Su
18 .... Robert Redford [BD 1937] .... M
19 .... Afghanistan [ID 1919] · Gabrielle 'Coco' Chanel [BD 1883] ....Tu
20 .... St Oswin [§ *the betrayed*] · Don King [BD 1931]................... W
21 ....Christopher Robin Milne [BD 1920] · Hawaii [Admis 1959]............Th
22 ....Henri Cartier-Bresson [BD 1908] .... F
23 ....Louis XVI [BD 1754] · Rudolph Valentino [†1926]................ Sa
24 ....Ukraine [ID 1991] · George Stubbs [BD 1724] .... Su
25 ....Ivan 'the Terrible' [BD 1530] · Gene Simmons [BD 1949]............. M
26 .... St Adrian of Nicomedia [§ *arms dealers, soldiers, & plagues*] ....Tu
27 ....Samuel Goldwyn [BD 1882] · Earl Mountbatten [†1979 *assassinated*]........ W
28 ....Sir John Betjeman [BD 1906]........................... Th
29 .... St John the Baptist [§ *convulsive children*] · Edmond Hoyle [†1769] .... F
30 .... ☻ · Max Factor [†1938] · Cameron Diaz [BD 1972] .... Sa
31 ....Malaysia [ND] · Caligula [BD AD 12].......................Su

French Rev. calendar... *Fructidor* (fruits)	Dutch month ...... *Oostmaand* (harvest)
Angelic governor.............*Hamaliel*	Saxon month...... *Weod-monath* (weed)
Epicurean calendar...........*Raisinose*	Talismanic stone ....*Zircon*

❧ Previously called *Sextilis* (as the sixth month of the old calendar), August was renamed in 8BC, in honor of the first Roman Emperor, Augustus, who claimed this month to be lucky, as it was the month in which he began his consulship, conquered Egypt, and had many other triumphs. ❧ *Greengrocers rise at dawn of sun, August the fifth – come haste away, To Billingsgate the thousands run, Tis Oyster Day! Tis Oyster Day!* ❧ *Dry August and warme, Dothe harvest no harme.* ❧ *Take heed of sudden cold after heat.* ❧ *Gather not garden seeds near the full moon.* ❧ *Sow herbs.* ❧

—————————————— SEPTEMBER ——————————————

🪑 *Virgo* [♍]   *Birthstone* · SAPPHIRE   *Libra* [♎]   ⚖
(Aug 23–Sep 23)   *Flower* · ASTER   (Sep 24–Oct 23)

1★.........................Labor Day [★FH] · Libya [ND].........................M
2....................Vietnam [ND] · First Day of Ramadan....................Tu
3.................Charlie Sheen [BD1965] · Ho Chi Minh [†1969].................W
4............................St Ida of Herzfeld [§ *widows*]...........................Th
5.............Rin Tin Tin [BD1918] · George Lazenby [BD1939]...............F
6......................Swaziland [ND] · King James II [†1701]....................Sa
7.............Grandparents' Day · Buddy Holly [BD1936]..................Su
8.......International Literacy Day [UN] · Nativity of Blessed Virgin Mary......M
9...........Chrysanthemum Day, Japan · California [Admis 1850].............Tu
10..........St Nicholas of Tolentino [§ *sick animals*] · Colin Firth [BD1960]..........W
11..................New Year, Ethiopia · O. Henry [BD1862]...................Th
12......................Barry White [BD1944].............................F
13.............St John Chrysostom [§ *orators*] · Tupac Shakur [†1996].............Sa
14.........Exaltation of the Holy Cross · Hicham el Guerrouj [BD1974].........Su
15................● · Battle of Britain Day · Honduras [ND].................M
16.......International Day for the Preservation of the Ozone Layer [UN].......Tu
17............................Tobias Smollett [†1771]............................W
18......................Chile [ND] · Greta Garbo [BD1905].......................Th
19.................St Januarius [§ *blood banks*] · James Garfield [†1881].................F
20..........Alexander the Great [BD356BC] · Sir James Dewar [BD1842].........Sa
21..........International Day of Peace [UN] · Larry Hagman [BD1931].........Su
22.................First Day of Autumn · Fay Weldon [BD1931]..................M
23.............Sigmund Freud [†1939] · Bruce Springsteen [BD1949].............Tu
24.................Guinea-Bissau [ID1973] · Jim Henson [BD1936].................W
25................St Cadoc of Llancarvan [§ *cramps*].........................Th
26.......St Cosmas & St Damian [§ *pharmacists & doctors*] · Béla Bartók [†1945].......F
27............................Meat Loaf [BD1947]............................Sa
28...........Brigitte Bardot [BD1934] · Arthur 'Harpo' Marx [†1964]............Su
29.................☺ · Michaelmas Day · Émile Zola [†1902]..................M
30................Jewish New Year (AM 5769) (Rosh Hashanah).................Tu

French Rev. cal. ... *Vendémiaire* (vintage) | Dutch month .... *Herstmaand* (Autumn)
Angelic governor.................*Uriel* | Saxon month......*Gerst-monath* (barley)
Epicurean calendar............*Huîtrose* | Talismanic stone.................*Agate*

❦ September is so named as it was the seventh month in the Roman calendar. ❦ *September blows soft, Till the fruit's in the loft. Forgotten, month past, Doe now at the last.* ❦ *Eat and drink less, And buy a knife at Michaelmas.* ❦ To be 'Septembered' is to be multihued in autumnal colors, as Blackmore wrote: 'His honest face was Septembered with many a vintage'. ❦ Poor Robin's Almanac (1666) states 'now *Libra* weighs the days and night in an equal balance, so that there is not an hairs breadth difference betwixt them in length; this moneth having an R in it, Oysters come again in season'. ❦ The Irish name *Meán Fómhair* means 'mid-Autumn'. ❦

──OCTOBER──

 Libra [♎]   *Birthstone* · OPAL   *Scorpio* [♏]
(Sep 24–Oct 23)   *Flower* · CALENDULA   (Oct 24–Nov 22)

1 . . . . Int. Day of Older Persons [UN] · Jimmy Carter [BD1924]. . . . . W
2 . . . . .End of Ramadan (Eid al-Fitr) · Julius 'Groucho' Marx [BD1890] . . . . . . .Th
3 . . . . Germany [ND] · Gore Vidal [BD1925]. . . . . F
4 . . . . .Lesotho [ND] · Janis Joplin [†1970] . . . . Sa
5 . . . . International Teacher's Day [UN] · Kate Winslet [BD1975]. . . . . Su
6 . . . . . . Children's Day [UN] · Elizabeth Taylor & Larry Fortensky [WA1991] . . . . . M
7 . . . . .St Sergius [§ *Syria*]. . . . . Tu
8 . . . . .Paul Hogan [BD1939] · Sigourney Weaver [BD1949]. . . . . W
9 . . . . Day of Atonement (Yom Kippur) · Brian Blessed [BD1937] . . . . .Th
10. .Taiwan [ND] · Harold Pinter [BD1930] . . . . F
11. . . . . St Gummarus [§ *glove-makers*] · Eleanor Roosevelt [BD1884]. . . . . Sa
12. . . . . .Spain [ND] · James Ramsay MacDonald [BD1866] . . . . Su
13★ . . . . .Columbus Day [★FH] · Thanksgiving, Canada. . . . . M
14. . . . . ◗ · Feast of Tabernacles (Succoth) · Errol Flynn [†1959] . . . . .Tu
15. . . . . .P.G. Wodehouse [BD1881] · Mata Hari [†1917 *executed*]. . . . . W
16. . . . . World Food Day [UN] · St Hedwig [§ *brides*]. . . . . .Th
17. . . . . Frédéric Chopin [†1849] · Evel Knievel [BD1938]. . . . . F
18. . . . . .Alaska Day · Martina Navratilova [BD1956] . . . . Sa
19. . . . . .Philip Pullman [BD1946]. . . . . Su
20. . . . . .St Acca [§ *learning*] · Elfriede Jelinek [BD1946]. . . . . M
21. . . . . .St Hilarion [§ *hermits*] · Orionids [♐] · Jack Kerouac [†1969]. . . . . .Tu
22. . . . . .Catherine Deneuve [BD1943] · Sir Kingsley Amis [†1995] . . . . W
23. . . . . St John of Capistrano [§ *jurors*] · Johnny Carson [BD1925]. . . . . .Th
24. . . . . United Nations Day [UN] · Christian Dior [†1957]. . . . . F
25. . . . . .Kazakhstan [ND] · Georges Bizet [BD1838] . . . . Sa
26. . . . . .Alfred the Great [†899] · Bob Hoskins [BD1942] . . . . Su
27. . . . . .Turkmenistan [ND] · Dylan Thomas [BD1914] . . . . M
28. . ☺ · First Day of Diwali (Festival of Lights) · St Simon the Zealot [§ *sawyers*] . Tu
29. . . . . Turkey [ND] · Joseph Goebbels [BD1897] . . . . W
30. . . . . St Marcellus the Centurion [§ *concientious objectors*] . . . . .Th
31. . . . . Halloween · Nevada [AD1864] · John Keats [BD1795] . . . . F

French Rev. cal. . . . . *Brumaire* (fog; mist)   Dutch month . . . . *Wynmaand* (wine)
Angelic governor . . . .*Barbiel*   Saxon month . . . . *Win-monath* (wine)
Epicurean calendar. . . . . *Bécassinose*   Talismanic stone . . . .*Amethyst*

❧ October was originally the eighth month of the calendar. ❧ *Dry your barley land in October, Or you'll always be sober.* ❧ October was a time for brewing, and the month gave its name to a 'heady and ripe' ale: 'five Quarters of Malt to three Hogsheads, and twenty-four Pounds of Hops'. Consequently, *often drunk and seldom sober falls like the leaves in October.* ❧ In American politics, an *October surprise* is an event thought to have been engineered to garner political support just before an election. ❧ Roman Catholics traditionally dedicated October to the devotion of the rosary. ❧

—————————————— NOVEMBER ——————————————

🦂 *Scorpio* [♏]   *Birthstone* · TOPAZ   *Sagittarius* [♐] 🏹
   (Oct 24–Nov 22)   *Flower* · CHRYSANTHEMUM   (Nov 23–Dec 21)

1...................................All Saints' Day .... Sa
2....All Souls' Day · DST ends · N. Dakota [Admis1889] · S. Dakota [Admis1889] .. Su
3................... Annie Oakley [†1926] · John Barry [BD1933] .... M
4................... Election Day · Felix Mendelssohn [†1847] ....Tu
5............ Guy Fawkes' Night · Taurids [✷] · Vivien Leigh [BD1913].......... W
6.................. St Leonard of Noblac [§ *against burglars*] ....Th
7..........................Leon Trotsky [BD1879]............................... F
8.................. Montana [Admis1889] · Bram Stoker [BD1847].................. Sa
9.............. Katharine Hepburn [BD1909] · Dylan Thomas [†1953] ....Su
10..........................St Tryphon [§ *gardeners*]............................. M
11★Veterans Day [★FH] · Remembrance Day, Canada · Washington [Admis1889] .Tu
12............ Friedrich Hoffmann [†1742] · Elizabeth Gaskell [†1865]........... W
13..... ◐ · Robert Louis Stevenson [BD1850] · Whoopi Goldberg [BD1955] .....Th
14...........Prince Charles [BD1948] [£] · Joseph McCarthy [BD1908] .... F
15........ St Albert the Great [§ *scientists*] · Sir William Herschel [BD1738]........ Sa
16........ International Day for Tolerance [UN] · Oklahoma [Admis1907]........Su
17...................Leonids [✷] · Martin Scorsese [BD1942] .... M
18...............St Odo of Cluny [§ *rain*] · Marcel Proust [†1922] ....Tu
19...............Monaco [ND] · Charles I [BD1600]....................... W
20.Queen Elizabeth II & Prince Philip [WA1947] [£] · Robert Kennedy [BD1925] Th
21..........................North Carolina [Admis1789]........................... F
22...............George Eliot [BD1819] · Mae West [†1980] .... Sa
23..........................St Felicity [§ *martyrs*]............................Su
24.................John Knox [†1572] · Billy Connolly [BD1942].................. M
25.........Andrew Carnegie [BD1835] · Yukio Mishima [†1970 *seppuku*] ....Tu
26....................... St John Berchmans [§ *altar boys & girls*] .... W
27★.............. ☺ · Thanksgiving [★FH] · Bruce Lee [BD1940] ....Th
28.................. East Timor [ND] · Manolo Blahnik [BD1942]................. F
29.............C.S. Lewis [BD1898] · Giacomo Puccini [†1924] .... Sa
30............. St Andrew [§ *Scotland & Russia*] · Mark Twain [BD1835].............Su

French Rev. calendar.... *Frimaire* (frost)	Dutch month ....*Slagtmaand* [see below]
Angelic governor............ *Advachiel*	Saxon month...... *Wind-monath* (wind)
Epicurean calendar....... *Pommedetaire*	Talismanic stone .... *Beryl*

❦ Originally, the ninth (*novem*) month, November has long been associated with slaughter, hence the Dutch *Slaghtmaand* ('slaughter month'). The Anglo Saxon was *Blotmonath* ('blood' or 'sacrifice month'). ❦ A dismal month, November has been the subject of many writers' ire, as J.B. Burges wrote: 'November leads her wintry train, And stretches o'er the firmament her veil Charg'd with foul vapours, fogs and drizzly rain'. ❦ Famously, Thomas Hood's poem *No!* contains the lines 'No warmth, no cheerfulness, no healthful ease ... No shade, no shine, no butterflies, no bees, No fruits, no flowers, no leaves, no birds —— November!' ❦

DECEMBER

 Sagittarius [♐]   *Birthstone* · TURQUOISE   *Capricorn* [♑]
(Nov 23–Dec 21)   *Flower* · NARCISSUS   (Dec 22–Jan 20)

1 .... World AIDS Day [UN] · Woody Allen [BD1935] .... M
2 .... Kyrgyzstan [ND] · Marquis de Sade [†1814] .... Tu
3 .... International Day of Disabled Persons [UN] · Illinois [Admis1818] .... W
4 .... St Ada [§ *nuns*] · John Gay [†1732] .... Th
5 .... Thailand [ND] · José Carreras [BD1946] .... F
6 .... St Nicholas [§ *bakers & pawnbrokers*] · Anthony Trollope [†1882] .... Sa
7 .... Pearl Harbor Day · Delaware [Admis1787] .... Su
8 .... The Immaculate Conception · Jim Morrison [BD1943] .... M
9 .... Kirk Douglas [BD1916] · John Malkovich [BD1953] .... Tu
10 ... Nobel Prizes awarded · Human Rights Day [UN] · Mississippi [Admis1817] .. W
11 .... St Damasus [§ *archaeologists*] · Indiana [Admis1816] .... Th
12 .... ◐ · Edvard Munch [BD1863] · Pennsylvania [Admis1787] .... F
13 .... Soot Sweeping Day, Japan · Donatello [†1466] .... Sa
14 .... Geminids [☄] · St Agnellus [§ *invoked against invaders*] · Alabama [Admis1819] .... Su
15 .... National Bill of Rights Day · Don Johnson [BD1949] .... M
16 .... Kazakhstan [ID1991] · Glenn Miller [†1944 *missing, presumed dead*] .... Tu
17 .... Sir Humphrey Davy [BD1778] .... W
18 .... Steven Spielberg [BD1946] · New Jersey [Admis1787] .... Th
19 .... Leonid Brezhnev [BD1906] .... F
20 .... St Ursucinus of Saint-Ursanne [§ *against stiff neck*] .... Sa
21 .... Shortest Day · First Day of Winter · F. Scott Fitzgerald [†1940] .... Su
22 .... First day of Chanukah .... M
23 .... Ursids [☄] · Japan [ND] .... Tu
24 .... Christmas Eve · William Makepeace Thackeray [†1863] .... W
25 ★ .... Christmas Day [★FH] · Charlie Chaplin [†1977] .... Th
26 .... Boxing Day · Kwanzaa · St Stephen [§ *stonemasons & horses*] .... F
27 .... ☺ · St John [§ *Asia Minor*] · Johannes Kepler [BD1571] .... Sa
28 .... Dame Maggie Smith [BD1934] · Iowa [Admis1846] .... Su
29 .... Islamic New Year (AH 1430) · Texas [Admis1845] .... M
30 .... Our Lady of Bethlehem · Tiger Woods [BD1975] .... Tu
31 .... New Year's Eve · Scotland – Hogmanay .... W

French Rev. calendar ...... *Nivôse* (snow)	Dutch month ... *Wiutermaand* (Winter)
Angelic governor .... Hanael	Saxon month ...... *Mid-Winter-monath*
Epicurean calendar .... *Boudinaire*	Talismanic stone .... *Onyx*

❦ *If the ice will bear a goose before Christmas, it will not bear a duck afterwards.* ❦ Originally the tenth month, December now closes the year. ❦ *If Christmas Day be bright and clear there'll be two winters in the year.* ❦ The writer Saunders warned in 1679, 'In December, Melancholy and Phlegm much increase, which are heavy, dull, and close, and therefore it behoves all that will consider their healths, to keep their heads and bodies very well from cold'. ❦ Robert Burns splendidly wrote in 1795 – 'As I am in a complete Decemberish humor, gloomy, sullen, stupid'. ❦

ANNIVERSARIES OF 2008

25th Anniversary (1983)
President Reagan dubbed the Soviet
Union an 'evil empire' ❦ The last
episode of *M*A*S*H* aired on US TV

50th Anniversary (1958)
Sir Edmund Hillary reached the South
Pole ❦ The Jim Henson Company
founded, as Muppets Inc. ❦ Capote's
Breakfast at Tiffany's published

75th Anniversary (1933)
The Blaine Act effectively ended
prohibition in the US ❦ Adolf Hitler
appointed Chancellor of Germany ❦
King Kong premiered in New York
❦ Einstein arrived in the US as a
refugee from Nazi Germany

100th Anniversary (1908)
Butch Cassidy and the Sundance
Kid supposedly killed in Bolivia ❦
Henry Ford produced the first
Ford Model T ❦ The Grand Canyon
awarded national monument status ❦
The FBI founded

150th Anniversary (1858)
The Virgin Mary allegedly appeared to
shepherdess Bernadette Soubirous at
Lourdes ❦ Fingerprints first
used to identify an individual

200th Anniversary (1808)
Beethoven conducted at the premiere
of his Fifth Symphony, in Vienna
❦ US Congress prohibited the
importation of slaves

250th Anniversary (1758)
George Washington admitted to the
Virginia House of Burgesses ❦
Halley's comet appeared for the first
time since its discovery

500th Anniversary (1508)
Michaelangelo started work on the
ceiling of the Sistine Chapel

750th Anniversary (1258)
Mongol leader Hulagu Khan,
Genghis Khan's grandson, attacked
and destroyed Baghdad

FRENCH NOTEPAPER TRADITIONS

According to the 1891 edition of *Brewer's Historic Notebook*, an attempt was made
in French Society (during the ?C18th) to create a formal etiquette concerning note-
paper. Different colored writing paper was to be used for each day of the week:

Day	notepaper color		
Sunday	delicate mauve	Wednesday (an unlucky day)...	somber gray
Monday	pale green	Thursday	blue
Tuesday	pink	Friday	white
		Saturday	straw-color

MELODY OF SINGING BIRDS

The melody of singing birds was traditionally ranked: The NIGHTINGALE first,
then the LINNET, TITLARK, SKYLARK, and WOODLARK.
The MOCKINGBIRD has the greatest powers of imitation,
the ROBIN and GOLDFINCH are superior in vigorous notes.

ST JOHN'S STAIRWAY TO HEAVEN

St John Climacus (*c.*570–649) was a Greek ascetic whose treatise on monastic virtue
– *Klimax tou paradeisou* (Ladder of Paradise) – enumerated 30 steps to Paradise:

· PARADISE ·

FAITH, HOPE, CHARITY

PEACE OF GOD

PRAYER *without ceasing*

SOLITUDE

INNER LIGHT

Death of the NATURAL MAN

SINGLE-MINDEDNESS, or ONLY ONE AFFECTION, and that FOR GOD

Abandonment of FALSE HUMILITY and DOUBT

PRIDE *utterly crushed out*

SELF-GLORIFICATION *cast out*

Conquest of FEAR

WATCHFULNESS; the ETERNAL LAMP *burning*

PSALMODY

Death of the CARNAL MIND

POVERTY, or *loss* of the LOVE OF ACCUMULATING

CHASTITY

TEMPERANCE

Conquest of INDOLENCE of MIND and BODY

Restraint of EXAGGERATION and FALSE REPRESENTATION

SILENCE

Shunning SLANDER and IDLE TALK

Forgiveness of INJURIES

EQUANIMITY

SORROW, *the seed of joy*

Constant thought of DEATH

PENITENCE

OBEDIENCE

Giving up FATHER and MOTHER

Giving up all EARTHLY GOOD and HOPE

Renouncement of THE WORLD

· THE WORLD ·

ON CHARACTER & THE FACE

Straight lips, firmly closed, RESOLUTION. Large ears denote GENEROSITY. Thick lips indicate GENIUS and CONSERVATISM. Large dilating nostrils are a sign of POETIC TEMPERAMENT & A SENSITIVE NATURE. A long forehead denotes LIBERALITY. Arched eyebrows, GOOD ANCESTRY & AMIABILITY. A bold, projecting Roman nose indicates ENTERPRISE. Delicate nose, GOOD NATURE. A large nose, STRENGTH OF WILL and CHARACTER. Lips slightly curved upward at the ends indicate a FINE SENSE OF HUMOR. Soft round cheeks denote GENTLENESS & AFFECTION; dimples in the cheeks, ROGUERY; in the chin, one who FALLS IN LOVE EASILY. A broad chin denotes FIRMNESS. An eye that looks one cheerfully and frankly in the face shows HONESTY & FAITHFULNESS. [Anon, *c.*1830?]

BEES & THE MONTHS

A swarm of bees in May
Is worth a load of hay;
A swarm of bees in June
Is worth a silver spoon;
A swarm of bees in July
Is not worth a fly.

THE CUCKOO'S YEAR

May – sings all the day;
June – changes his tune;
July – prepares to fly;
August – go he must.

A WOMAN'S CHANCE TO MARRY

'Every woman has some chance to marry. It may be one to fifty, or it may be ten to one that she will. Representing her entire chance at one hundred at certain points of her progress in time, it is found to be in the following ratio'

Woman's age	*likelihood of marriage*		
15–20 years	14½%	35–40 years	3¾%
20–25 years	52%	40–45 years	2¾%
25–30 years	18%	45–50 years	¾ of 1%
30–35 years	15½%	50–56 years	⅛ of 1%
		>60 years	⅒ of 1% (or 1 in 1,000)

[Source: *The Handy Cyclopedia of Things Worth Knowing*, Joseph Trienens, 1911]

TRADITIONAL COLOR COORDINATION

Yellow contrasts with .... purple, russet, and auburn
Red contrasts with .... green, olive, and drab
Blue contrasts with .... orange, citrine, and buff
Yellow harmonizes with .... orange, green, citrine, russet, buff, and drab
Red harmonizes with .... orange, purple, russet, citrine, auburn, and buff
Blue harmonizes with .... purple, green, olive, citrine, drab, and auburn

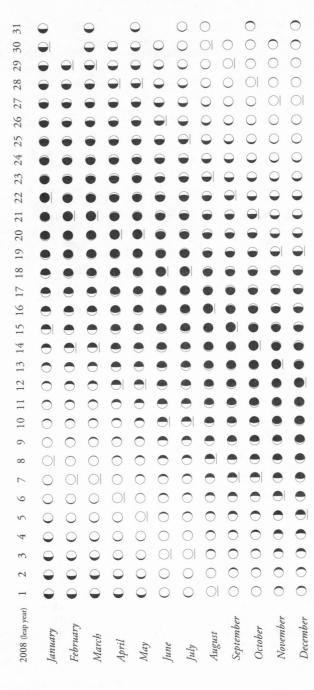

PHASES OF THE MOON · MMVIII

Key: ○ New Moon · ◐ First Quarter · ● Full Moon · ◑ Last Quarter · Dates are based on Universal Time (Greenwich Mean Time)

CHRISTMAS DAY 1684 & SOVEREIGNS

On Christmas Day 1684, the eight British sovereigns listed below were all alive:

Richard Cromwell ..10·4·1626–7·12·1712	Mary II ....4·30·1662–12·28·1694
Charles II............5·29·1630–2·6·1685	Anne...................2·6·1665–8·1·1714
James II............10·14·1633–9·16·1701	George I ....5·28·1660–6·11·1727
William III ....11·4·1650–3·19·1702	George II .... 11·10·1683–10·25·1760

FURTHER GEM SYMBOLISM

Moss agate	health, prosperity, and long life
Amethyst	prevents violent passions
Bloodstone	courage, wisdom, and firmness in affection
Chrysolite	frees from evil passions and sadness
Emerald	ensures true love, discovers false
Diamonds	innocence, faith, and virgin purity; friends
Garnet	constancy and fidelity in every engagement
Opal	sharpens the sight and faith of the possessor
Pearl	purity; gives clearness to physical and mental sight
Ruby	corrects evils resulting from mistaken friendship
Sapphire	repentance; frees from enchantment
Sardonyx	ensures conjugal felicity
Topaz	fidelity and friendship; prevents bad dreams
Turquoise	ensures prosperity in love

CANONICAL HOURS

The eight traditional Canonical hours of the Catholic Church are tabulated below:

Matins (Nocturnes) .. *midnight–daybreak*	Sexte..........*midday (6th hour of the day)*
Lauds........................*daybreak*	Nones .... *3:00am (9th hour of the day)*
Prime.........*6:00am (1st hour of the day)*	Vespers ....*sunset*
Tierce........ *9:00am (3rd hour of the day)*	Compline ....*bedtime*

JUNETEENTH

The Juneteenth holiday (sometimes called African American Independence Day) originated in Galveston, Texas, where, on June 19, 1865, Texan slaves first received word of the Emancipation Declaration. Because slaves in Texas were the last to learn of their freedom, the date is marked as the effective end of slavery in America. Juneteenth celebrations began in 1866, and spread throughout the country as Texans migrated. The holiday is now officially celebrated in 19 states, traditionally on the third Saturday of June; festivities include picnics, prayer services, rodeos, barbecues, and the drinking of traditional 'red soda water' made from strawberries.

Index

*The perfect search engine would understand exactly
what you mean and give back exactly what you want.*
— LARRY PAGE, cofounder *Google*

──────── 10-CODES – BOOKS, PRESIDENTIAL ────────

─────── BOOKS, SCIENCE – DEGREES, HONORARY ───────

————————DEPRESSION – GROCERY SHOPPING————————

— MAX CLIFFORD & FAME – PRESIDENTS, AMERICAN —

PRESIDENTS, AWARDS – SUPERNOTES

SUPREME COURT – ZIMBABWE

Bad indexers are everywhere, and
what is most singular is that
each one makes the same sort of
blunders – blunders which it
would seem impossible that
anyone could make, until we find
these same blunders over and
over again in black and white.
— HENRY B. WHEATLEY,
How to Make an Index, 1902

─────────── ERRATA, CORRIGENDA, &c. ───────────

In keeping with many newspapers and journals, *Schott's Miscellany* will publish in this section any significant corrections from the previous year. Below are some errata from *Schott's Almanac 2007* – many of which were kindly noted by readers.

[p.23 *of the 2007 edition*] The accent on Guantánamo erroneously slid onto the third *a*. [p.60] The height of La Paz was just plain wrong; it is 11,926ft, *c.*3,636m, above sea level, as corrected on p.78 – though sources differ. [p.118] Pamela Anderson and Kid Rock married in St (not San) Tropez. [p.147] The seating capacity of the Metropolitan Opera was incorrectly given as 2,065. It is, in fact, 3,800 with 95 standing-room places; an additional 35 seats can be added for ballet performances. [p.153] The designer of Rachel Weisz's dress was Narciso (not Narcisco) Rodriguez. [p.206] The number of pedestrians killed by drunk drivers in 2004 was 2,110; an extra 2 snuck in by mistake. There is some debate also about whether it should be 'drunken drivers'. [p.227] It should, of course, be Gonzaga Bulldogs, not Bullfrogs. According to one eagle-eyed reader, 'There are some folks on campus who think that changing the name to the Gonzaga Bullfrogs is a creative option, but I don't think it is really going to fly'. [p.231] France beat Brazil 1–0 in the quarterfinals of the FIFA World Cup. The table erroneously transposed the score, though France still went through to lose in the final against Italy. [p.254] There is an argument, vociferously made by a few, that the easternmost point of the US is Pochnoi Point, Semisopochnoi, Alaska. Frankly, it is complicated, and they might indeed have a point about the Point. [p.256] Questions were raised as to the correct number of commas, and their placement, in the Pledge of Allegiance. According to the US Code, the 4 commas are placed thus: 'I pledge allegiance to the Flag of the United States of America, and to the Republic for which it stands, one Nation under God, indivisible, with liberty and justice for all'. [p.265] The minimum average yearly rainfall in Arica, Chile, is 0·8mm, not 8mm. [p.353] The entry on October Surprises incorrectly stated that US hostages in Tehran were released in October 1980; in fact, they were released in January 1981. Considerable debate surrounds the political machinations of the whole episode.

─────────── ACKNOWLEDGMENTS ───────────

The author would like to thank:

Jonathan, Judith, Geoffrey, & Oscar Schott, Anette Schrag
Benjamin Adams, Richard Album, Joanna Begent, Michael Binyon,
Martin Birchall, Andrew Cock-Starkey, James Coleman, Mark Colodny,
Gordon Corera, Aster Crawshaw, Jody & Liz Davies, Peter DeGiglio,
Colin Dickerman, Will Douglas, Miles Doyle, Charlotte Druckman,
Stephanie Duncan, Jennifer Epworth, Sabrina Farber, Kathleen Farrar,
Josh Fine, Minna Fry, Alona Fryman, Panio Gianopoulos, Yelena Gitlin,
Catherine Gough, Charlotte Hawes, Mark & Sharon Hubbard, Max Jones,
Amy King, Robert Klaber, Maureen Klier, Alison Lang, Jim Ledbetter,
Annik LeFarge, John Lloyd, Ruth Logan, Josh Lovejoy, Chris Lyon,
Sam MacAuslan, Jess Manson, Michael Manson, Sarah Marcus, Sara Mercurio,
Susannah McFarlane, David Miller, Peter Miller, Polly Napper, Nigel Newton,
Sarah Norton, Elizabeth Peters, Cally Poplak, Dave Powell, Alexandra Pringle,
Karen Rinaldi, Pavia Rosati, David Shipley, Jared Van Snellenberg,
Bill Swainson, Caroline Turner, & Greg Villepique.